The First Casualty:
The Untold Story of the Falklands War

The First Casualty

The First Casualty:
The Untold Story of the Falklands War

Ricky D. Phillips

British East India Company Books

BEIC Books Ltd

2018

The First Casualty

First Printing: 2017

ISBN 978-198-05-857-94

British East India Books
(BEIC Books Ltd)
12 St. Stephen Street
Stockbridge, Edinburgh EH3 5AL

www.BEICBooks.com

The First Casualty

Dedication

Special dedication to my good friend
Robert McDonald Hardie,
who loved this book.

For Rachel
"Thanks Che"

*"It is important to me personally
that this story gets told as it happened,
since I suspect there are those
who would rather it wasn't"*

Sir Rex Masterman Hunt

Contents

Thanks and Acknowledgements

It would be both impossible and improper of me to name any one member of the outstanding men of NP8901 & Endurance before any other or without listing them all, so my eternal thanks go to all of them and their families together for their time, patience and help, and for accepting me into their family. I would, however, be remiss in not especially thanking Gareth Noott for access to the various reports and documents which have been of endless value throughout this project. I must also thank the wonderful Norman Grossman for bringing us all together and keeping us there.

Further thanks to my friends from the Falkland Islands must go to Neville Bennett and to Rachel Simons for going 'above and beyond' in making this project the success that it is and without whom it might never have been a reality. Also from the Falkland Islands I would like to thank Taff Davies, Tanya Argue, Gerald Cheek, Diane Clune, Gavin Short, Candy Blackley, Patrick Watts, and the lovely Liz Elliott from Falklands Radio, as well as Dr Alison Bleaney, now in Tasmania.

Additional thanks must also be given to Ian Whitehouse at Navy Books, to George Tosh for the outstanding cover design, to Angus Konstam for proof reading and improvements, to Paul Fraser Collard for his support and time, to Declan Power and Professor Tony Pollard for their support and for their wonderful reviews, to Mark Powell for his excellent design work on the maps, to Ben at Day Six for his outstanding design & web work, to Steve at Smash Digital for images, to all at BMH and invariably to a whole host of others from the United Kingdom, the Falkland Islands and farther afield who have given their time, knowledge and resources to this project.

From Argentina, I owe a debt of immeasurable thanks to my incomparable friends, Diego Garcia Quiroga and Hugo Jorge Santillan who have been marvellous beyond words in helping me over the last year and who have been on hand with accounts, contacts, resources, translations, advice and more whenever I needed them – which was often - as well as to Daniel Tosolini, Horacio Tello, Ernesto Urbina and many others. It would take a book longer than this to say thank you to them in any proper fashion. Thank you also to Ana Maria Santillan for allowing me to steal so much of your husband's time, especially when you were on vacation!

To all of you; abrazos.

The First Casualty

Foreword to the #1 Edition

Since the first publication of "The First Casualty", which has been widely accepted and warmly welcomed by a fascinated public in over forty countries around the world, there have been a number of developments which – almost as soon as the book began to gain notoriety – began to change the face of this history. It was always my intention (as originally stated) that this history should grow as more people, especially from the Falklands, began to come forward and add to the tale and, although I had always assumed that a second edition (and doubtless more over time) would be required, little did I know that it would happen so quickly. "The First Casualty" has, at the time at which I write, undergone numerous evolutions for a book of its age, including a first edition hardback, a second edition paperback and a second edition reprint and, realistically, this now becomes the fourth evolution of the book, as the story has grown and developed. To that end - and hoping that the story is now as complete as any historian can make it - I have determined to brand this, the most up-to-date version (and hopefully the last) as the "#1 Edition" in honour of the book having become an Amazon #1 best seller in April 2018. Therefore, if and when being referenced by future sources, it should appear obvious which edition is being spoken about. Another reason for this, I should add, is that my good friend, Argentine veteran Diego Garcia Quiroga, has also agreed to work with me on the Spanish translation of the book, to be named *"La Primera Victima"* and it is my wish that both the English and Spanish language versions of this book look much the same.

Since the first publication of "The First Casualty" in April 2017, I have been fortunate enough to have been accepted into the ranks of Naval Party 8901 as an honorary member and have had the pleasure of meeting a few of the veterans whose stories did not make it into the first edition, in particular Colin *'Tiny'* Jones, Murray Paterson and Michael *'PJ'* Berry whose stories alone change a lot of what we already understood from the first edition. Added to this have been extra quotes, comments, personal photographs and more from the men already featured in the first edition and some fascinating new background information for the historical notes and appendices at the back of the book, with added testimony on the true scale of the casualties from Dr. Alison Bleaney who tended a great number of the Argentine wounded. Therefore, whilst everything said in the original version was absolutely true, yet the evidence just kept on coming and the story has developed a richer texture than before. In particular - new accounts aside – the reader of the first edition will find more proof to the conjecture and, hopefully, questions answered which were thrown up from the first edition and even those subsequently produced. Again, whilst we cannot answer all of these, we can at the very least rule out certain rumours, myths and suggestions and focus upon that which can only be true.

It has been a work of some months to assimilate so much new information, so many new accounts and a whole raft of new evidence, check this and try it against the current history, pronounce it fit for use and then to insert it into an existing narrative without making it look lumpy and contrived. I believe that the end result is as good as can be and I hope that those who have read the original 'TFC' – as the book has become known by an army of fans – will delight to find even more from their favourite characters as well as some great new ones and a wealth of fascinating new information.

Finally, I should like to add that although 'TFC' is forming something of a 'cult status' amongst those who now find themselves confronted with an entirely new history which can only be true, yet the work of physically changing the pages of history is far from complete. The Royal Marines in particular have greeted the book with an overpowering emotion and a wholehearted support as indeed has everyone who has read it, yet the *'Defence of Stanley'* bar to their South Atlantic Medal - which was never issued - still remains so and the pages of history, both in print and on-line are still quoting the same sorry tale of a 'surrender' and but a handful of casualties. Therefore, I urge the reader, who at the conclusion of this fascinating history will understand the truth, my own passion and why this is important to the Royal Marines, to not consign this merely to a bookshelf but to tell people about the heroes of the battle of Stanley. In an age when we seem to need heroes and role models more and more, these men – true heroes though they would deny it – have still gone unrecognised by their country and their government. What happened to them was understandable and, I believe, necessary in 1982. All that is left now is their own honour. There are writers and historians, bloggers, Wikipedia and social media experts and even those who can simply tell a good tale with passion. Changing history starts with you. It is the rarest of all opportunities and I urge you to take it. This said, to both the new reader and 'TFC' fan alike, I present you their story, the original foreword to which started thus:

My own interest in the 1982 Falklands War perhaps begins with a childhood memory of the British task force coming home, of the thunderous salute of a victorious nation, of the horns of ships blasted across the Solent, of the rolling choruses of *'Land of hope and glory'* coming from the quayside and – most memorably - of my parents dancing and overjoyed and my father resplendent in a Second World War tin hat with the words *'Falklands Liberation Army'* painted across it. To me as a child, this scene was perhaps one more of confusion than of anything approaching national pride, but the memory has remained with me so far for all these years as a special one: and one which I can still recall with absolute clarity all this time later. To my parents, having just the year before sailed on 'The Great White Whale' herself, the SS *Canberra*, the moment was especially poignant.

It was probably not until 2012 that any real interest in the Falklands War was rekindled – not through any particular neglect on my part - but because other subjects and areas of interest had simply taken centre stage in my field of study, to which the Falklands War was a million miles from my intended course. Indeed, it was quite by accident that a friendly neighbour and a wrongly-addressed book landed me with a copy of Graham Bound's wonderful *'Invasion 1982 – The Falkland Islanders' Story'* which perhaps is where this journey really starts. Key to Bound's excellent book were the first-hand accounts of the Royal Marines of Naval Party 8901: the outmanned and outgunned guardians of the Falkland Islands who first faced the invasion forces of Argentina, unsupported and alone. This in itself was a fascinating insight for, although we remember the Falklands War, we in the UK do not remember it for this small and almost entirely forgotten episode; the part where Argentina invaded the Islands and a small group of Royal Marines stood, against all hope, to oppose an armada. Automatically (at least to me) things looked to be strange; us British love a 'battles against the odds' story – *'Zulu'* springs automatically to mind – yet seemingly nobody in the UK really knew about this... and that is just odd. How, I asked myself could it be forgotten? - And why?

In reading Bound's book, something else comes at once to light: that whilst the stories told to him by the Royal Marines were accounts of heroism, professionalism and that sheer bloody-mindedness characteristic of the British military in a tight spot, yet the available history on the subject did not bear this out at all. Indeed, any website or book on the subject will tell a tale of a mere 'token defence' - a few shots fired in the air to say that they were there - and of a 'walk-over' by Argentina against an outnumbered group of men who had no real chance anyway. In most books about the war, these men get barely a page to themselves (if at all) before 'the real Falklands War' seems to start some weeks later. In reading from their own histories, I soon began to realise that this was a very large and unwritten history and that worse, it was not so much a mere omission: it was as if these men had been somehow and deliberately 'blotted out' of the history books.

I have been fortunate indeed to have met with, spoken with and corresponded with so many of the men of the Royal Marines from the Naval Party 8901 who fought on that day of April 2nd 1982 and from them I have found a new history and a fantastic, wonderful, endearing, funny, loyal and engaging bunch of guys and, dare I even say, 'friends'. I have spent many hours, days, weeks and months checking every aspect of every story as told by them, of going back again to check each part and in each and every case have found them only too willing to help. They are (though they might laugh at the idea) a humble bunch of guys. Nobody wants to be portrayed as a hero and all of them speak only of what they themselves did or saw done, however one thing which is at once apparent is that all of their stories match up and what I have found is a story which has truly never been told before: a story which defies all of the established history of that short period leading up to and including April 2nd 1982. A quick check of the available history on this subject will tell the reader that an overwhelmed garrison put up a plucky defence for a few hours and then surrendered, killing but one Argentine and wounding three others. Again, the history as told by the men themselves tells a vastly different story from that which we accept to be true and indeed the evidence, which I have painstakingly gathered from the men of the Royal Marines Naval Party 8901, from the wonderful people of the Falkland Islands, from their Argentine opponents and from many other sources also shows that this history should be written anew and this time with the help of as many of the people involved as possible, so that all may look and say that this is the true and exact history of that day.

One turn of events which I did not expect, however, was the interest which this book – whilst still merely a concept - began to arouse particularly in Argentina and it came as a great surprise to me that many of the Argentine veterans of this conflict were only too eager to be included in its pages. It did not occur to me until this point that, whilst the men of the Royal Marines were eager to quash this 'token defence' story, that the Argentine veterans were also just as keen. For them, it was nothing of the sort and the general feeling is that it does nothing for the martial honour of either side to tell a tale of an 'easy victory' which was simply not the case and I should add that so many of these outstanding men have gone far above and beyond the call of duty to help to provide me with not just interviews but contacts, information, resources and inside information from the Argentine side which have never been available to readers either in the United Kingdom or in Argentina before; it is to them that this book owes so much of its accuracy.

It is quite something to write a first-person interview based narrative history (as Stephen Ambrose found out from *'Pegasus Bridge'*) and quite another to do it from two sides and indeed, if we add in the excellent testimony from the Falkland Islanders, from three sides at once, yet the people involved, from all three perspectives of this conflict, have made it a great pleasure. One thing which has become apparent whilst writing this epic tale is just *how* different the story is from that which today we accept as the truth and the reader will, I hope, be as perplexed and mesmerised by the sheer amount of new evidence presented which shows not only that this is a tale worth telling but one which should force us to look again at a great swathe of this conflict and question everything we believed to be fact. Doubtless it will add further to the wider history of the Falklands war as we begin to understand it with increasing accuracy for, as I myself have observed, the history of this fascinating conflict is anything but settled.

The First Casualty

Introduction

It was the Republican Senator Hiram Johnson who said that *"The first casualty, when war comes, is truth"* and this oft-misquoted statement, though said about the First World War, rings as true in this age as any other. It is a fact of all wars that the hardest thing to find is an actual consensus or agreement as to the turn of events devoid of bias, excuse or other interpretations which leave nearly all new suggestions to be degraded to the ranks of – at best – a hypothesis and perhaps, on a lucky day, a theory. Therefore, we should not, perhaps, be at all surprised that any in-depth look at the 1982 Falklands War should bear very much the same fruit as all wars before it and indeed after.

We accept differing opinions, natural or personal biases and omission of certain facts or evidence to slant our view in one direction or the other – this is the stuff that a fascination in history is made of - but typically after the event, these ideas or 'subjective truths' are picked through and raked over and at least, by some form of general consensus (usually on the part of the victor) something like an 'official version' can be produced. Curiously, this is something which an intimate look at the 1982 Falklands War suggests that this conflict does not entirely possess.

It has become evident that, as previously mentioned, the history of the opening day of this 74-day long conflict is as shrouded in myth and mystery as could be and I urge the reader, considering new testimony and evidence, to throw out the proverbial rule-book (or in this case history book) and view the evidence afresh. There have been narratives of soldiers, sailors, airmen and marines before but not, I believe, a narrative given from three perspectives by those still living, who have recounted their stories faithfully. I will refer, as I must, to the fact that one person can only see what they have personally seen, that there is the inevitable 'fog of war' – which certainly has its place between these pages – a lapse of memory after 35-36 years and of course, the aspect of bias. Bias is the true enemy of 'real history' – the difference between 'what actually happened' and 'what people make that mean' - and perhaps few wars in history have as much of this; personal and political as the Falklands War. It is my intention to write an unbiased history of 'what actually happened' based solely upon the evidence and testimony of the people who were there and yet it is apparent that the politics, common beliefs and misconceptions about this war are everywhere manifest, from the point of view of the man on the ground now recounting his tale to the way in which we read, weigh and judge the evidence. In this respect, I urge the reader (including those who were there) not to jump to conclusions or to try this against what they think they know, but to read the whole and judge for themselves.

Between the British, the Argentines and the Falkland Islanders I appreciate, however, that this book can and will be read three ways.

To the British reader, an untold story of heroism is a fine thing to accept despite the inevitable challenge to their own perceptions. To the Argentine reader, I accept that the challenges of bias will be different – this history does, in effect, challenge a great deal of what has become 'set in stone' Argentine history and is not to be challenged lightly except with strong evidence - whilst to the reader from the Falkland Islands this will come with a sense of sadness (as talk of the war always seems to) and yet I hope also with a strong degree of respect for the diligence and courtesy which I have shown to them. We the reader are, in effect, invading their homes – again. My main wish is to at least give justice to the people who fought in and around Stanley on April 2nd 1982; for the Royal Marines of NP8901 whose story of a gallant defence has never before been told and for the Argentine Marines and special forces whose story should not be brushed over as a mere 'parade in force' – if I can have done that then I hope that all shall be happy, whilst allowing for the fact that you truly cannot please everyone.

The biggest issue in this entire saga is of course, politics. The history of the Anglo-Argentine dispute, itself almost 200 years old, is shrouded in conjecture as are the reasons for the war, and even the actual 'cut and thrust' elements of the war itself are all still very much disputed. In short, it is impossible to write an account of the Falklands War without mentioning the politics behind it for, if it were simply avoided, it would make no sense at all, be the reader British, Argentine or from any other country apart, perhaps from the Falkland Islands themselves. With this said, I do not pretend to be a 'political historian' or indeed to write a political history, however for anyone to understand the war and the people involved, it is an essential element and must therefore be included. At the political and diplomatic level – certainly as far as this influences public thinking - this is something which must be addressed if this history is to carry any weight. I aim to separate the politics and the myth from the men who fought there themselves and their own histories and to do this, it is a fact that we will have to discuss politics.

This said, what I do not want in this book is to make any kind of political statement and I am very conscious of being accused of having done so, for then we have only added to the conjecture and the myth and done nothing to resolve it. This book is one which has not set out to resolve the bigger political issues, which are in many places deep-rooted, but simply to distil the politics from the actual story. Sadly, the politics are so interwoven even here that we must arrive at the consensus that, whatever we might believe, the 'actual story' as we understand it is as heavily tainted by 'cause', political conjecture and national pride as any other issue surrounding these Islands, if not more so; indeed, the politics seems to have a great bearing upon why this story has been deliberately blotted out in the first place. I would only add to this that where I have been brutal in my dealing with the politicians (as indeed I have) it is quite often deserved in my opinion and we should bear in mind that the actions of the British government prior to the war were quickly reversed afterwards (another good reason to cover them up) whilst in speaking of the Argentine junta at the time we should accept a past that was – not is. Many Argentines, indeed most, were very much against the junta of the day which eventually, as a result of the end of the Falklands War, was toppled by the Argentine people. Therefore, we might be deservingly harsh on a military junta without, I hope, causing offence to people today.

The Falklands War can really be split into two very unequal parts: Operation 'Rosario', the Argentine mission to capture the Falklands, and Operation 'Corporate', the British mission to retake them. If we take that old adage that 'history is written by the victors' then here we really strike the crux of the debate, for in effect 'Corporate' has become the entire war and it is a very British affair; the story of a task force ill-supplied and badly-prepared, travelling half the way around the world and fighting against the odds through to victory. We think of the Falklands war and we instinctively remember the names of many famous battles and of sunken ships however, the history of the Falklands war rapidly brushes aside the first phase of the war, Operation 'Rosario' and in so doing it conveniently forgets one of the greatest tales of arms of not just Argentine but also of British forces. This is an imbalance which I have sought to redress.

The men of both sides have had their credit largely washed away due to the overriding nature of Operation Corporate and I feel that none more so than the men of the Naval Party 8901 of the Royal Marines. These men fought against all odds and with no hope of victory and very little chance of surviving past midday. Each, as we shall see, had made their own peace with an imminent death and determined to do their duty as Marines and, as is always the case in war, for the man who stood beside him. When they returned home, having given an outstanding account of themselves, they were largely forgotten and simply fed back into the military machine to join Operation Corporate which was designed to rewrite – or more properly 'overwrite' - their part in the war so far. For Britain, Operation Corporate was destined to become, in effect, 'the Falklands war'. In this sense, we have a war of two unequal halves; Argentina has 'Rosario' and Britain has 'Corporate'. Each has written their own history of their part and with their own biases or stories, without those of the other side.

This curious effect has therefore washed away a great part of the story, of which – as we have said - the history books speak only of a 'token resistance' at best. The evidence gathered from interviews and written accounts both at the time and later suggests, however, that this was not at all the case, and this is something which this book aims to put right. It does no credit to the men on either side, and therefore I believe that their tale should be told in full. I believe that a history has been created which does not fit the actual evidence and that this evidence should (as should all evidence) be counted and weighed against the 'established history'. In writing this history of Operation Rosario from both sides therefore, we come across a very different story to that which is told in almost any other book or page of the internet.

In saying this, I wish to make it understood that I consider not one of the men I have spoken to on either side to be a liar or in any way to be 'bending the truth' and every man I have spoken to on both sides I consider to be telling the absolute truth as they saw it, understood it and, over thirty-five years later, as they understand it to be. Where we question accounts which vary – and there are many – we can only question that 'fog of war' of confusion, of nervousness and of course of the passage of time. Yet we must allow that in light of the evidence presented and uncovered, we must agree with the peerless and sadly-departed historian Richard Holmes who said of this conflict that it was; *"clear that a good deal of what has been written about the fighting (sometimes by veterans, who may be forgiven if their 'post hoc' reconstructions of a series of episodic and harrowing events are inexact) simply cannot be true."*

On this, I should add, it will be appreciated that the story here – as told by all of those involved – is entirely different to any which we were told at the time or since, and naturally, this book has come in for a good deal of controversy, as have I myself. All I can say to this is that a historian can do no more than follow the evidence, quantify or qualify statements and present it as it is and as it was. To ignore the evidence in favour of something more convenient is simply not history: it is opinion. It is my intention therefore to tell again the story of Operation Rosario from all sides of this conflict in a very new light; to compare the sequences of events and the actual impressions of the men involved at the time and now. What I hope to produce is the first full and definitive history of this operation, using first-hand accounts from all sides, that has ever been produced. Where there is conjecture – and there is a great deal – we will deal with the evidence alone and, if this is to break the narrative of a running story too much, then it will be added in a series of historical notes at the back (denoted by a numbered asterisk) or for larger subjects an Appendix at the very end for the reader to understand more of the subject and the means by which certain new evidence has been uncovered. If I can impart one piece of advice to the reader here, however, it is to use a second bookmark at the back for these, as they are quite frequent. Certainly, we shall see that the 'official version' as we understand it, is wide open to a great deal of scrutiny and questioning and that this new volume should be widely welcomed in both Great Britain and Argentina alike, as well as by military history enthusiasts around the world. I should add, of course, that in writing a first-person history – and even more so when attempted from both sides (and indeed three, for the Falkland Islanders tell their own story) - that there is going to be conjecture, confusion and a lot of 'cross-over' both in timing and sequencing of events and what was perceived at the time, therefore whilst presenting this series of interviews, stories, narratives, reports, accounts and anecdotes I am careful to remind the reader that nobody can say that this here is the 'full story' but perhaps a fuller account than we currently have in the annals of military history and one which, I hope, will grow with time, study, understanding and perhaps new contributions.

One final point I should like to make is as to the usage of terms and names. In an age of 'political correctness' we should address certain terms which today might be considered offensive whilst for a book whose aim is to be printed in both English and Spanish, certain place names will require as much attention and impartiality. Therefore, the British reader should not take offence at the term 'English' being used for what is actually 'British'. Rightly or wrongly, the Argentine term *'Ingleses'* is used interchangeably for both British and English and its natural translation is 'English'. To the Scots, the Welsh and the Northern Irish, this is a constant bug-bear and annoyance the world over. Where the interviewee has used the word 'British' it shall be stated, likewise where 'English' has been used in its stead, however incorrectly, it will be stated as meaning one and the same thing. For the Argentine reader, I should address the term which is commonly used of *'Argies'*. This should be understood to be a common term in the UK as much as 'Brits' or 'Yanks' is, without any ideas of racism. Again, it is simply a shortened or common term and no offence is intended. One omission, however, will be the word *'Kelpers'* – a common term to describe the Falkland Islanders. Although this has been used many times in the past, even by themselves, it is considered now to be derogatory and, in some cases, dehumanising and so the term 'Islanders' will be general in both languages unless specifically stated in an interview. To place names, the obvious one is the use of the words 'Falklands' and 'Malvinas'. To make this as palatable to all as possible, I have devised the simple solution; printed in English, the word 'Falklands' will be used except when directly quoting an Argentine using the term 'Malvinas' or when it is seen from an Argentine point of view. The reverse will be true in the Spanish version, therefore 'Malvinas' will be used except when quoting a British participant in the events, or when seeing events from a wholly British perspective. Hence when discussing the view from the objective of the Islanders, we will use 'Falklands' to convey their sense of identity. One other mild omission will be the term *'Puerto Argentino'* a name which the Islands' capital Stanley has never truly had. Though it was renamed so during the brief occupation (from April 21st to June 14th after several prior and discarded names were used), it has never truly held this name before or since and never in any official capacity, and it is considered to be an abhorrent term by the people of the Falkland Islands in whatever context. Therefore, unless specifically called as such by an Argentine interviewee, the name as it appears in both languages, will be *'Stanley'* – just as it appeared on the Argentine planning table prior to April 2nd 1982.

All that remains is to remind the reader that these are real events as seen by real people on both sides. As a faithful author and friend to many of these veterans (again of both sides) I should like to remind the reader that their points of view should be wholly respected. Nobody has spoken to me with any view of political gain or personal aggrandisement, indeed the opposite is universally true. My own opinions I shall attempt to keep to a minimum and, where they may be necessary, I will state them clearly so that I alone might answer for anything said. There will be conjecture which I shall deal with as and how it arises. I will omit nothing and include everything. This is the only way to be sure of producing a true and balanced history which will stand up to scrutiny and the test of time without bias or agenda.

Amongst the men who fought on the morning of April 2nd 1982 I have found some wonderful people; men who – for whatever political reasons – were thrown together by way of their professions to fight a duel in a place which most people in the world had simply never heard of. This is their story: it is not mine. We will find humour, grit, heroism and sorrow between these pages. Personal stories and personal journeys which have marked many of these men for life, for good and for bad. Personal stories which I myself have been privileged to be such a small part of. Yet it strikes me that these men of both sides (for all of them would shun the word 'hero' at any cost) have no personal animosity. They all were hoping that in the grey dawn of April 2nd 1982 they would do their duty: and all did. That is as much as anyone can ask and more than most of us could ask of ourselves. This book is here to do honour to those fighting men, regardless of uniform or nationality, for we only do justice to our ourselves by giving equal justice and credit to those 'on the other side' – men who now, if they met (and some do) those they were fighting against - find a camaraderie and a shared history devoid of all politics and all opinion. It is a lesson which many of a modern generation whose weapon of choice is the keyboard of a laptop computer would do well to learn.

Chapter 1: Guilt, Complicity and Shame

"It was the worst-kept secret since Christmas."
Ricky D Phillips - BBC Radio interview, 2017.

It is a curious misconception in the United Kingdom that prior to the Argentine invasion of the Falkland Islands, nobody had ever really heard of them. Certainly, to the layman watching television back home in the motherland when news of the Argentine invasion came, the Falklands were at best a point of trivia: a place on a map to be pointed out to demonstrate a touch of general knowledge and indeed, there were many in the United Kingdom who actually were forced to look at a map to discover where they were. Naturally in Argentina the Falklands were much harder to ignore, laying as they did some 300 miles from the southern tip of the Argentine coast.

However, the Islands have, in fact, played a major part in the history of British and international politics for many centuries ever since they were first definitely discovered by Captain John Davis in 1592 and first claimed for England by Sir John Hawkins in 1594 who gave them their first name of *'Hawkins Maiden Land'* after his patron and sovereign Queen Elizabeth the first. By 1690 Captain John Strong had become the first man recorded to have landed on the Islands and he again claimed them, though reinforcing the earlier claim of 1594. His expedition had been funded by Anthony Cary, 5th Viscount Falkland and Treasurer of the Navy and the channel between the two principal Islands he now named *'Falkland Sound'*. The name first appeared in a published map in 1700 – and a revised edition in 1702 - which now publicly declared the new territory as *'The Falkland Islands'*. Between 1701 and 1708 however, a number of French merchantmen and privateers operating out of St. Malo had begun to put in on the Islands for fresh water and shelter and the name *'Malouines'* had become common in France, from where the Spanish name for the Islands, the *'Malvinas'* takes its etymology.

The history of the Islands sways between a number of factors too lengthy and complex to discourse here – indeed it would take an entire volume (and a large one at that) to deal with the competing claims, factors and political opinions, which is outside of the stated remit of this work - however, suffice to say that, through competing claims from the British, Dutch, French, Spanish and then by the newly-established country of Argentina in 1829, the Islands had become a *de facto* British territory by 1833. The Falklands had been big news over this time, with a major war nearly being fought over them in 1770 between Britain and Spain. The

USA had also become heavily involved in them. President Andrew Jackson, Lord Cornwallis, the Duke of Wellington and even Napoleon had all given their thoughts on the Islands too, but when Britain and Argentina finally settled their outstanding differences in the Convention of Settlement between 1849-1850 it was considered that that matter, which had raged between most of the world's great powers for 250 years, was finally put to bed and the world – and certainly the British - seemingly forgot about them.*[1]

The name 'Falklands' was not really to be heard again to any great degree until 1914 with the advent of the First World War when their use as a naval station to control access to the southern seas and the passage around Cape Horn was quickly realised. In late October 1914 Stanley harbour was home to the ageing and mechanically unsound pre-dreadnought battleship HMS *Canopus* and two outdated and obsolete armoured cruisers, *Good Hope* and *Monmouth* when news came of the approach of a modern German naval squadron under command of Admiral Graf Maximilian von Spee which was currently off the Chilean coast at Coronel. On October 23rd and leaving the broken-down *Canopus* under repair, the two old cruisers set off under the command of Rear Admiral Sir Christopher Cradock to do battle with the German squadron which consisted of two modern armoured cruisers, *Scharnhorst* and *Gneisenau* and three light cruisers, *Leipzig*, *Dresden* and *Nurnberg* along with three auxiliary ships. Just nine days later, both British cruisers had been sunk along with the loss of 1,570 men. In Britain, the news was greeted with shock and horror, and soon there was a clamour to send ships to the Falkland Islands where Spee's squadron was fast approaching with a view to raiding Stanley and availing themselves of the ready supplies of coal stored in the naval fuel depot there. The race was on, and for the first time in perhaps a hundred years, the British public remembered the Falkland Islands, as the little archipelago now became once again the centre-stage for a global conflict. The British squadron consisting of the battlecruisers HMS *Invincible* and *Inflexible*, the armoured cruisers *Cornwall*, *Carnarvon* and *Kent*, the light cruisers *Glasgow* and *Bristol* and the merchant cruiser *Macedonia* raced to the Falkland Islands, reaching Stanley just one day ahead of Spee's now-outnumbered squadron. The next day, December 8th, the two sides clashed in the battle of the Falkland Islands, fought just to the north of Berkeley Sound. The battle opened with the old *Canopus* now dismasted, camouflaged and beached upon the mud-flats opening up with her 12-inch guns, sighted by spotters using a telephone from a nearby hill and, in an almost-impossible shot at 12,000 yards, one of her shells (ironically a dud practice round) hit the water, skipped, carried and crashed into the *Gneisenau*'s after-funnel. Although old, the *Canopus* was still potent and as Spee made the decision to turn about, so the rest of the British ships closed in for the kill. Now in a running fight and with great guns blazing, no less than six of the eight German ships were lost, with all except for the light cruiser *Dresden* and the auxiliary ship *Seydlitz* being sent to the bottom of the sea. The citizens of Stanley, grateful at their deliverance, paid a subscription for a plaque to commemorate Cradock and the men of the *Good Hope* and *Monmouth* and later built a galleon-topped monument to the victory on a promontory jutting into Stanley harbour.

The victory produced an effect upon the Falkland Islanders who still remembered their attachments to the mother country which had not deserted them in their hour of need and now, despite their meagre population and abilities, the Falkland Islands began to join in the war effort. Local men quickly signed up to enlist in the Royal Navy, happy at any adventure which might take them away from their small and secluded lifestyles and offer some adventure. The populace, though incredibly poor by first-world standards, donated an aircraft to the Royal Flying Corps and thousands of pounds to war-related charities and even voted 10% of their annual customs revenues to contribute to Britain's war loans. In real terms, the effort was tiny, but it was all – and perhaps more - that the Falkland Islanders could do, and history has shown them to be a people not given to half-measures when determined, when threatened and particularly where their attachment to the mother country was concerned.

Not until World War Two were the Falkland Islands to be heard from again in any great capacity, and again in one of the opening sea battles of the war; the battle of the River Plate. This time, following a savage battle with the German pocket battleship *Graf Spee* – an omen in these waters if ever there was one - the damaged cruiser HMS *Exeter* limped back towards Stanley harbour for repair, passing as she went the old heavy cruiser HMS *Cumberland* which had been refitting in Stanley and which had picked up garbled news of the action. Soon, in one of the most eagerly anticipated and widely covered incidents of the early war, the *Graf Spee* was at the bottom of the River Plate, this time scuttled by her crew when all hope of escape was lost. Again, the loyal Falkland Islanders threw their slender resources at the war effort, contributing 150 men and just over £70,000 to the British government which, amongst other things, went to pay for ten Spitfires to be flown by 92 Squadron during the battle of Britain. A further £30-40,000 was donated to war charities and a plaque in Stanley's cathedral still bears the name of Flight Lieutenant Donald Rafur, killed in action in the skies over Britain on August 8th 1940, one of 24 Falkland Islanders who gave their lives in the cause of freedom. If anyone had earned themselves the right to be called 'British' and the right to be respected and honoured by a grateful mother country, it was the Falkland Islanders. Sadly, in this they were to be woefully disappointed.

In 1941 as the war raged, Argentina was again to raise the issue of the Islands' sovereignty when it began a series of political and diplomatic campaigns to 'internationalise' the country's claim to the Islands, placing it back onto the table with Argentina's first official protest for over 90 years. This, combined with the Japanese entry into the war in the South Pacific forced Britain, already pushed for manpower, to send men to their defence with a battalion of the West Yorkshire Regiment and then, in 1944 to be replaced by a smaller contingent of Royal Scots. Although nothing of note occurred during this time (in fact, as many as 600 Argentine pilots came to Britain and voluntarily signed up for service in the Royal Air Force and 116 were killed) it was clear that Argentina was intent upon the reinvention of this old grumble by way of promoting a national cause and, finding it a popular method of distracting or appeasing the people, was determined to beat the proverbial drum until they were heard. Certain in their right and title to the Islands after so long a time, and still with the Convention of Settlement as proof of this, the British government offered on several occasions throughout the 1940's and 50's to have the matter referred to an international court of arbitration. On each occasion, Argentina's President Peron refused, not willing to risk his cause which was now growing in popularity and stating that he would not recognise the jurisdiction of such a court, having failed to convince Britain to sell him the Islands in 1953.*2

However, in 1961 the United Nations had declared a 'decolonisation committee' upon the last vestiges of an age of empires, which provided a road-map to former colonies for independence if they so wished, and Britain – pushed to the limits of her once-inexhaustible finances by two world wars - seized happily upon this opportunity to disgarnish itself of such burdens by actively encouraging participation in the scheme. Jamaica was the first country in the former British Empire to declare itself independent in 1962. However, although many of these former colonies did take advantage of the road-map to independence, yet so many (not just British but American, French and others) simply saw no need for it and to the Falkland Islanders this was simply another piece of international bureaucracy which could be happily ignored. They were content as they were, they were proudly British and they did not feel in any way like a colony or like they needed 'decolonising' – the idea that they were in any way living under some 'Imperial jackboot' was plainly ridiculous - and they knew (or they thought) that the British government would stand by them as they had always stood by the mother country. Again, the idea that this had anything to do with encouraging a claim upon them by Argentina simply did not enter into the equation. Independent or not, they were British.*3

In 1964 the issue of the Islands was now placed firmly in front of the United Nations who, ignoring Britain's protests at the Argentine claims, urged the two nations to resolve their dispute amicably. Quite what this meant was, of course, very subjective and despite various political wranglings in the halls of power of both London and Buenos Aires, in the quiet, peaceful and carefree Falkland Islands the issue went largely unnoticed. As governments argued, life in the Falkland Islands continued as normal, good trade links were established between the Islands and Uruguay which was universally friendly to them, children from the Islands attended further education at the British School in Montevideo, the critically ill were taken for treatment at the British Hospital in the Uruguayan capital, steam ships came every month from Montevideo to Stanley and back carrying exported wool and other produce and the occasional tourist, relative or colonial administrator came from there on the Royal Mail ships on their way from Southampton. To any Falkland Islander, anything Argentina might say in the United Nations was a world away from their tranquil reality of everyday life and besides, Argentina had played such a tiny and remote part in the history of the Islands, and that such a long time ago, that most Islanders remained convinced that nothing could ever change.*4

It was not until September 26th 1966 that anything was to alter the view of the Falkland Islanders and convince them that Argentina really intended to follow up on its claims, for on that day the four-engined roar of a Douglas DC-4 aircraft bearing the colours of the Aerolinias Argentinas was audible over Stanley. The curious sound – and then sight - attracted the attention of the people who were used to a remote, routine and uninterrupted lifestyle, and soon Islanders were pouring out onto the streets to observe the aircraft which seemed to be circling over the capital and gradually losing height. The aircraft – by far the biggest that had ever been seen over the Falklands - had been travelling from Bahia Blanca in Patagonia to Rio Gallegos when eighteen of the passengers produced handguns and ordered the plane to divert to the Islands. These 'air pirates' (as they were later to be termed, for this was truly the first hijacking of an aircraft) now announced themselves as members of the paramilitary 'Condor' group and stated their intention to 'reclaim las Malvinas' for Argentina. Their plan, however, was to come apart almost immediately due to a failure to realise that Stanley did not actually have an airport.

The DC-4 was now low on fuel and needed to put down on the Islands, and the pilot now sighted the racecourse towards which he gradually descended to the gasps of the onlooking crowd. It was a great landing: the pilot managed to avoid the fences and grandstands and put down gently on the grass with the landing gear ploughing through the soft turf and eventually bringing the aircraft to a juddering halt. Ever hospitable, the Islanders at once jumped into their Land Rovers (a vehicle forever associated with the Falkland Islands) and sped towards the racecourse eager to give assistance and instead found themselves facing a bunch of gun-toting hijackers for which their pastoral lifestyles simply did not equip them.

Now many, including police officer Terry Peck, were herded aboard the aircraft as hostages as meanwhile the hijackers unveiled an Argentine flag and began to distribute leaflets to state their aims which included the suggestion that they had arrived to *'liberate the Islanders from the British colonial jackboot'* – something which drew blank looks and the odd laugh from the bemused Islanders. Once here, however, the hijackers seemed not quite sure as to what to do next, although they were not alone in this. Telephoning back to London for advice, the Islands' Financial Secretary - and at that time senior civil servant - Les Gleadell and his secretary Nap Bound were unhelpfully told to manage the situation as they saw best. Finally, the professionals of the Falkland Islands' Royal Marines contingent came to the fore to support the unarmed local police and the armed but wholly inexperienced members of the local FIDF or 'Falkland Islands Defence Force.' Royal Marines they might have been, however there were only six of them; all that had been provided by an unconcerned British government who considered that nothing of any importance was ever going to happen in the Falkland Islands.

The farcical situation continued at stalemate until the Falkland Islanders unveiled a plan determined to break the very will of determined and hardened terrorists, and found their salvation in the music of Russ Conway and Jimmy Shand. With the hijackers surrounded, loudspeakers and a DJ were sent for and soon the full force of a series of Scottish jigs and lively piano tunes was unleashed at full volume. At first the hijackers considered this unorthodox tactic as merely annoying but gradually as the hours went on, they began to go mad with it and worse, the Falkland Islanders with their limited supply of music provided by the wonderfully-named FIBS (Falkland Islands Broadcasting Service) radio station, seemed immune to its effects. By evening the hijackers were in dire straits; the music blared on unabated, the toilets on the aircraft had backed up, it was freezing cold and the water on the aircraft had reduced to nothing. The local Anglican priest had been allowed onto the aircraft to negotiate and Terry Peck, the police officer, somehow comically smuggled himself out beneath the priest's robes, with the pair making an ambling and lurching escape back towards the FIDF lines somehow unnoticed by the hijackers. Now the DJ upped the ante and unleashed his collection of Beatles singles throughout the night to keep them awake and by morning the hijackers sent for the priest again to signal back their unconditional surrender just as *'Yesterday'* played again for the umpteenth time. They were disarmed and searched, and amongst them was a stunning blonde lady who seemed to be their second-in-command. A search of her bag produced no more weapons but a great stash of condoms, which news was treated with shock and derision by the womenfolk of the town and guffaws of crude humour from the men, as might have been expected from a small, insular island community."[5]

Though comical and indeed farcical in the extreme, this event showed – or should have – the fact that the Falklands were woefully unprepared for defence. London had provided absolutely no guidance, the Royal Marines were at a loss as to how to deal with a situation which had simply never been considered or trained for, and the victory was owed chiefly to a plucky disc-jockey and his meagre collection of records. The entire incident was simply treated as a curious talking-point in the Islands whose inhabitants – their natural tendency to be friendly and open to strangers now removed – had little knowledge of how to deal with their new prisoners. They were held in an outbuilding of the local Catholic church (typically of the Falkland Islanders, this was considered more amenable to their visitors than the Anglican church) and when a few days later an Argentine steam ship *Bahia Buen Suceso* made port in the Islands, they were sent on board to be repatriated. In Argentina – now ruled by a new military junta after a revolution in June 1966 - the returned hijackers were hailed as heroes far beyond anything which their endeavour deserved. The military government tried them on the most minor charges, suspended sentences prevailed and even the leaders, including the condom-toting blonde, were free in just a few years. If the Condor hijack was the most famous incident to have beset the Falklands since the war, then another incident that same year – almost unnoticed - was to take on a more sinister tone when the Argentine submarine ARA *Santiago del Estero* arrived in the Islands just 40km from Stanley and made a covert landing with a 12-man special forces team under the command of a man named Juan Jose Lombardo. The special forces were not detected in time or met with force and silently slipped back to Argentina, but it was now apparent that the defences of the Islands were being tested with a view towards invasion and that the British government was still inclined to do absolutely nothing about it.

By 1968 the Falkland Islands, being a simple matter of cost and the Islanders showing no interest in the decolonisation scheme, presented a major problem to the Foreign & Commonwealth Office, who now seemed determined to rid itself the brave and loyal Falkland Islanders and strike another name off the decolonisation list if it could find a way. The Argentine government now provided the solution and eagerly offered to exercise sovereignty over the Islands and thus it was that in this year the first in a series of shameful steps was taken to rid Britain of the inconvenient problem when Michael Stewart, the Foreign Secretary under the current Labour government now shocked parliament by admitting that he had instigated talks with the Argentine junta over the sovereignty of the Islands. Key to the signed 'Memorandum of understanding' was the line that when it would be in the 'best interests' of the Islanders, that '*The Government of the United Kingdom as part of such a final settlement, will recognise Argentina's sovereignty over the*

Islands from a date to be agreed' and to ensure that Argentina took the deal, he even threw in the Islands of South Georgia, the South Shetland, South Sandwich and the South Orkney Islands to sweeten the pot.

This act of outright betrayal did not go unmissed by the Falkland Islanders who were horrified to learn that, after 135 years of inhabiting and building their home, they were to be given no say in the matter at all. However, if history should have taught the British government one thing, it was not to underestimate the Falkland Islanders. Stating their intention to resist the Foreign Office at all costs, the Islanders now mobilised and first contacted a number of influential friends in Britain, including several members of parliament, into what became known as the 'Emergency Committee', a body which proactively and skilfully began to counter every argument which could be used to ride rough-shod over the Islanders, and which raised awareness of their rights to determine their future as set out by the United Nations Charter. Stewart, trying to defend his position, was summarily mauled by parliament who now determined that British policy would dictate not the *'best interests'* of the Falkland Islanders, but absolutely their *'wishes'*. That same year the British government increased the Royal Marines detachment on the Islands from six men to a detachment of forty-four, classifying these men as 'Naval Party 8901' and housing them in the old (and almost derelict) wireless transmission station at Moody Brook just to the west of Stanley. Argentine ministers now began to grow angry at the new change of heart, which they had considered a 'done deal' and they hated the intercession of the Emergency Committee who seemed to road-block their every attempt at negotiation over the heads of the Islanders.

These proceedings should have settled the matter but the Foreign & Commonwealth Office, instead of accepting that they had been caught flagrantly selling the Islanders out, now determined to force them to submit to its demands by effective blockade. If they could not be forced into accepting Argentine sovereignty and 'like it or not' then they would be cut off from Britain and forced to accept reliance upon Argentina until an integration would be accepted as the only choice, therefore their 'wishes' – however enforced - could be shown as being respected. In 1971 they entered into the 'Communications Agreement' with Argentina, which was dressed up as a 'joint commitment' to support the Falkland Islanders, and to begin a process which historian and author Hugh Bicheno*[6] rightly termed *'intellectually dishonest and ethically indefensible'*. At first, they removed the subsidised shipping link to and from Montevideo, to be replaced with a temporary airstrip to be built on the Islands and operated by Lineas Aereas del Estado – or LADE for short - Argentina's military-controlled state airline. LADE would build and run an office in Stanley and even the mail was now to be sent by way of Argentina where it would be double-stamped in English and Spanish before travelling to its final destination. Additionally, Argentina undertook to provide medical treatment and educational scholarships for Falkland Islanders, now that they were cut off from Montevideo, and Argentine teachers would be sent to the Islands to teach the children Spanish. Meanwhile, YPF the Argentine state oil company, was awarded the contract to supply all petrol and diesel in the Islands and the state gas company tried to encourage the Islanders to accept its own supplies to heat their homes rather than the unlimited supplies of peat which the Islanders had always enjoyed. Finally came the Immigration Act of 1971 which effectively removed the right of abode in the UK to the Islanders. Unless they were born in the UK – which most Island parents-to-be could not afford to travel there to do - the Falkland Islanders were not even to be issued with a British passport. The Falkland Islanders could smell the wind of change but were powerless to prevent the new stealth-tactic even when told that, as they would now be routed through Argentina for any outbound or incoming flights, they would be issued with a white 'provisional card' or 'tarjeta provisiorio' or effectively their Argentine passport which bore their details underneath an Argentine coat of arms. They were now no longer even allowed to be British; they were foreigners from a foreign country, with a foreign passport. Helpfully, Argentina suggested that it would accept the Islanders as Argentine citizens, however it would not expect Falklands men to enlist for national military service. The offer did not have a helpful effect.*[7]

The Foreign Office had attempted to sugar-coat this deal by promising the Islanders their own permanent British airstrip and also the provision of a passenger cargo ship. Few were surprised when the promised ship was cancelled and a small airstrip eventually laid out, too short by far to accommodate aircraft from Britain. The Islanders now fought to wriggle free of the trap which was closing around them and saw their way out in a financial opportunity which would grant them a measure of fiscal independence. Although by now they produced more in tax revenues to the British government in most years than they cost to run, they considered that, if they could generate some real and substantive income, they might at best force the government to consider them again as a worthwhile cause or, at worst, could wield the financial power to more tangibly determine their own future. They appealed to Britain to extend their territorial waters so that they might grant fishing licenses over thousands of square miles of abundant ocean but, of course, nobody in the Foreign & Commonwealth Office heeded their calls. The people of the Falkland Islands had no choice but to accept their fate with growing anger and not a little confusion.

Fortunately for the people of the Falklands, the Argentines sent to the Islands some excellent and friendly ambassadors. Seemingly devoid of politics and eager to ingratiate themselves with a sometimes suspicious and alien culture which their government had done little to make friends with, the Argentine representatives to the Falkland Islands were found, by and large, to be friendly, cheerful people whose natural demeanour fitted in nicely with the Islanders. Whilst not simple in any way, the Islanders were content and trusting people, as is common in such a place where everybody knows everybody and there is virtually no such thing as crime. There was a little distrust at first but gradually the Argentines were accepted into Island life so long as politics was never mentioned. One of the more popular men amongst the new arrivals was Vice Comodoro Carlos Bloomer Reeve, the head of the LADE airline who, of part-Scottish descent, speaking fluent English and being something of an Anglophile, was a welcome ambassador for Argentina. Cheerful, always smiling and appreciating the slower pace of life, Bloomer Reeve and his wife Mora fitted in well. Their children attended the local school and the Vice Comodoro and his wife were regular and popular guests at the cocktail parties hosted at Government House by the Islands' Governor Rex Hunt and his wife Mavis. Many other Argentines who came to the Islands likewise found the atmosphere friendly and there were even a few marriages between local girls and members of the YPF and Gas del Estado companies. In all, many began to consider, perhaps, despite the British government's own lack of moral integrity, maybe the Argentines were not as bad as they had feared.

Then in Argentina began a dark period which was to terrify the Islanders, for in 1976 came another coup and the new junta began what was known as the 'Dirty War', at first consisting of executions and disappearances of 'subversives' and suspected Communists and Marxists but later a full scale civil war against armed resistance groups in which there were stories of murder, abduction and the disposing of undesirables by throwing them from helicopters over the Atlantic, often bound and drugged, with numbers of 'disappeared' people stretching into the many thousands. Naturally this systematic eradication of opposition became an institution of which the Falkland Islanders absolutely refused to be a part, although island life with the Argentines in the Falklands continued as relatively normal, albeit with a growing suspicion.

Argentina now began to slowly ratchet-up its aggressive foreign policy towards the Falklands, with the new junta eager for a galvanising victory and exasperated by the seemingly sluggish efforts of the Foreign Office to produce a result. Argentine officials called for progress and now began to issue thinly-veiled threats; the Islanders had had to accept their hated 'white cards' and a level of dependency but were no more Argentine now than before and to some in Argentina, it was apparent that a stronger political line was needed. Now Argentine warships and aircraft aggressively harassed Falkland Islands' fishing boats, Britain was denounced by Argentina as an *'international pirate'* for daring to set up a 'colony' in the Falklands and a survey vessel, the *John Biscoe*, was even fired upon by an Argentine destroyer the ARA *Almirante Storni*. In 1977 the very first hints of military action and of an aggressive step-up in Argentine policy towards the Islands occurred when Admiral Anaya – fresh from a two-year stint as Argentina's Naval Attaché to London in which he had been fawned at for military contracts from British ministers - now installed a military base at Southern Thule in the South Sandwich Islands, the easternmost of the Falkland Islands' outlying dependencies. James Callaghan – now Prime Minister and urged to make a response - sent an attack submarine to the Islands but with the ridiculous orders to stay out of sight and submerged. In all, Callaghan's response was as inadequate as it was limp-wristed and timid and, had the Argentines even known of it (which they did not until after the war), it doubtless would have prompted even greater disdain. Instead of standing up for itself, the British government instead now embarked upon a policy of appeasement without resolution. Rightly, as Churchill had said, appeasement was the idea of feeding a crocodile in the hope that it will eat you last, and if anything, it worked to encourage the junta's demands rather than placate them.*[8]

In 1979 Britain, after years of internal 'appeasement politics' to trade unions which also led more to encouraging of demands, seemed ready for change and the country's first female Prime Minister, the Conservative Margaret Thatcher came to power. At once, she adopted a more American style of hard-line 'new right' politics which sought to counter the years of post-war self-deprecation and, as far as went the issue of the Falkland Islands, she determined to resolve the issue quickly. In 1980 came Nicholas Ridley, a junior Foreign Office minister who found at his desk a bulky file marked 'Falklands' and he at once set off for Buenos Aires to catch the LADE flight to Stanley. His arrival had not been announced and Ridley was met by a hastily-assembled and irritated group of Argentine officials who told him that he could indeed travel on to Stanley to meet with the Islanders, but that he must return to the next round of talks with some proposals which would end the dispute over the sovereignty of the Islands in favour of Argentina. Already, tensions were high and Argentina was now very unsubtle in suggesting that, if its demands were not met, military action would likely follow. This was not helped along by a report in the Buenos Aires Herald of June of that year in which retired Admiral Jorge Fraga opined that *"An armed invasion of the Malvinas Islands would not be too much of a problem,"* although he hastened to add that it would not be the right way to resolve the issue.

Ridley came to Stanley under a cloud of growing tension and suspicion; *"What is he here for?"* the Islands' local newspaper the 'Penguin News' has asked rhetorically, and he seemed, according the Governor Rex Hunt, to be spending an inordinate amount of time in the Islands devoting himself to fishing and sketching rather than coming down to business. When he did meet with Hunt, he explained the idea of 'leaseback' – the concept that Britain would effectively give the sovereignty of the Islands to Argentina and then, at the same time, would lease them back for a decent period of time: perhaps 99 years. This would effectively placate Argentina and, at the same time, would guarantee the rights of the Islanders then living, presenting the issue to the next generation. It seemed like a useful temporary solution but one which, as Rex Hunt knew, was not likely to appeal to the Falkland Islanders who had been born there, had lived there and would be buried there also. Not one of them wished for a foreign flag to fly over their graves even when long gone, or to present the same situation to their children or grandchildren. Nevertheless, as far as the Islanders' concerns went, Ridley seemed convinced that he could persuade them by himself and, as Rex Hunt later said, Ridley's message to the Falkland Islanders was that the 'dead hand' of the sovereignty dispute was the very basis of the economic stranglehold on the Islands, to which Hunt had replied that it was the more a case of the dead hand of the Foreign Office in not allowing the declaration of a fishing zone. Ridley however, seemed determined to try, and met with the Islanders in a public meeting at the Town Hall which was so widely attended that Islanders were queueing out of the door. He proposed to them three solutions, two of which were obviously unworkable; the first was the 'freeze' idea, whereby both Britain and Argentina would agree not to discuss the matter for a specified time, to leave things as they were for another year. The second was the 'condominium' – the idea of joint sovereignty which of course would require both languages, both flags, two police forces and two governors – again the Islanders grew restless. The third option, of course, was 'leaseback' and Ridley forced a smile and suggested that a period of 99 years more of being British would be sufficient to come to terms with the inevitable. Suddenly the Town Hall which had been quiet in order to hear every word was a cacophony of noise. The Falkland Islanders were livid; they were being converted, assimilated, sold into extinction and not one of those gathered was going to accept that fact. They were looking for an option which would simply allow them to stay as they were. They were not Argentine. They did not want Argentina. They did not need Argentina. Why could the British government not see things as they really were and simply make the whole thing go away? Rex Hunt, in silent agreement with the Islanders despite his official position, did little to discourage them as he stood alongside Ridley. The minister tried to reply but was shouted down by a people now fighting for their right to exist. At this, Ridley grew angry and shouted back at the crowd that, if they did not accept one of the solutions, ideally the leaseback proposal then Argentina would most likely invade, adding that; *"They cannot be strung along much longer!"* - After this the meeting broke down.

In the next few days of his visit, Ridley was toured around the Islands but met with general disdain and sullen faces. He had come as the Islands' last hope and was now leaving having tried to convince them to shoot themselves in the foot. The people of Green Patch issued a statement upon his visit that they wanted nothing to do with either of the three proposals and a local song, penned by musician Des Peck, was sung inviting the Minister to *'hang down your head Nicholas Ridley, hang down your head in shame...'* the Minister left the Islands to the jeers of a crowd from Stanley and the honking of Land Rover horns from a people determined not to be sacrificed upon the altar of convenience. Almost laughably, Ridley's report to London upon his return stated that there was some objection but that the majority were a little undecided with a few favourable to the leaseback idea. It was an extremely hopeful – and unhelpful - suggestion on his part. By January 1981 the Islanders were pressed for a response to Ridley's three proposals and, although the other options had been added in to make the 'leaseback' proposal look more attractive, the Islanders instead voted for the 'freeze' option. This was one which had never truly been considered as a tangible solution either for Britain or for Argentina and indeed it would constitute for both governments a nasty 'running sore' which those in office at either end of the Atlantic did not want or foresee.*9

British diplomats tried to work with the Argentine Foreign Office to smooth things over, but they were not to be placated and by February 24th the Argentine Foreign Office had issued a statement that the opinions of the Islanders were not important: they would only deal directly with Britain and the 'freeze' option was ruled out completely. Conversely, however, the Argentine delegation to talks held that February in New York had offered the Islanders a life-line. If the Islanders were to submit to some telling gesture of acceptance of Argentine sovereignty – largely anything which symbolically would have the effect of allowing the Argentine government to show its people that *'Las Malvinas'* were now Argentine - then they should be given largely anything else that they demanded. The Falklands representatives, however, had no mandate whatsoever to make such a concession and seemed set against it anyway. They left with an absolute promise ringing in their ears; if no solution could be found then Argentina would provide one by military means. When Rex Hunt returned to England on leave, he met with Ridley in person where he was informed that the Foreign Office was still confident that some accommodation could be made to appease Argentina. However, though Argentine diplomats were reasonably calm about the situation, yet their military men – those truly in charge of affairs - were losing patience at the dogged determination of the Islanders and at the inability of the British Foreign & Commonwealth Office to simply force them to some decision.

Thus, it was that a new direction was now urged; instead of trying to 'sell' the idea of Argentine rule to the Islanders, they should be more actively threatened with the idea that their resistance to change would be costly. 'Leaseback' was the only acceptable option. For those who did not like the idea, perhaps a resettlement package in the UK could be made more attractive to them? Rex Hunt listened with incredulity at an idea which he recalled as *"far removed from the realities of the situation in the Falklands"* and to his credit, he fought the Islanders' corner to the point whereby the only option was to play for time and keep talking. Perhaps Argentina would give up or the Islanders would give in? In Argentina, a failure to understand the slow – and sometimes glacial - pace of politics of this nature was beginning to grate, and it wasn't long before Argentine Foreign Minister Nicanor Costa Mendez penned a letter to the British Ambassador stating that; *"The time has come for these negotiations to be effective. It is not possible to postpone without territorial integrity and national dignity being affected."* - More than anything else, this statement really summed up the mood in Argentina. The junta had promised the people *'Las Malvinas'* and now that the issue seemed to be dragging its heels, they were in grave danger of looking politically impotent unless something could be done. Meanwhile, tensions with Chile were rising over the Beagle Channel and Peru indicated that it would be ready join in an attack from the north if Argentina would lead the way from the east. The junta needed a victory and the easiest of these would, of course, be the Falklands.

As the year 1981 went on, there were many more alarming and disturbing signals from Argentina that an armed invasion would follow in the wake of any stagnation of talks, and this did not come only from Mendez's office or the Argentine government as a whole. By now, a possible invasion was being spoken about by many people in the South Atlantic region, with reports from British Intelligence operatives, leaks – almost blatant ones - from within Argentina and also from Chile who looked with growing concern at a joint Argentine-Peruvian invasion of its territory. A date for the end of March came up frequently for a suggested invasion and even a senior British officer, Colonel Sidwell had visited Argentina and been shown their new American-bought LVTP-7 'Amtrack' amphibious assault vehicles at which his Argentine hosts had proudly boasted that these were what they were going to use when they invaded the 'Malvinas'. Surely someone in Britain had to know?[*10]

By a curious mixture of what Hugh Bicheno termed *'guilt, complicity and shame'* both Britain and Argentina had now set the wheels in motion for war. At the turn of the 20th century, both had vied with the United States as amongst the richest countries in the world and now both, severely financially stretched – Britain by a crushing war debt and the demands of the trade unions and Argentina by a wasting of its assets and with rocketing inflation - had entered into a pact-of-sorts to resolve their issues over the heads of the Falkland Islanders; Britain by disgarnishing itself of a costly and embarrassing colonial throwback and Argentina by the announcement of a victory to distract the population from a civil war and economic meltdown, galvanising them back into a nation with a cause. Finally, after years of Britain's hinting, of trying and of virtually promising Argentina the Falkland Islands in everything but actual title, Margaret Thatcher was to slam the door in the faces of the Argentine diplomats, but by now it was too late. The wheels were in motion, Argentine national pride and the credibility of the junta were at stake and the erring, swaying appeasement of successive British governments and the Foreign Office had mismanaged the situation entirely. The cost of this mismanagement was to be a tug-of-war over some islands which the world had largely forgotten and a people whose voices were lost in the tirade in a case of what could best be described, as it was by the Argentine novelist Jorge Luis Borges, as *"Like two bald men fighting over a comb."*

Chapter 2: Azul

"Lord, I ask of you only two things; the victory and the return.
But if it must be only one, let it be the victory."
Motto of the Buzo Tactico.

Although Argentine plans for the invasion of the Falklands dated back as far as some early draft proposals in 1976, yet nothing had truly been considered in any real depth before December 1981. The new junta was a 'triumvirate' representative of all three branches of the Argentine military with the President, General Leopoldo Galtieri the head of the Army, Brigadier General Arturu Dozo the head of the Air Force and Admiral Jorge Isaac Anaya the head of the Navy. Of these three, Anaya was the most fervent in his cause for the Islands and many consider that he had made this a condition of his support for Galtieri. As the President and leader of this 'three-way-junta' Galtieri had his hands full already, imposing new financial regimes designed to halt the spiralling inflation and enjoying reciprocal visits to and from the USA with President Ronald Reagan who, impressed by Galtieri's strong anti-communist stance and eager to depart him from friendly relations with Russia, seemed inclined to be on friendly terms. This left Admiral Anaya with an almost free hand in dealing with the Falklands issue as an almost entirely naval operation.

It was Tuesday December 15th 1981 when Anaya flew from Buenos Aires 280 miles to the south-west to the main Argentine naval base at Puerto Belgrano, ostensibly to officially install Vice-Admiral Juan Lombardo, the commander of the submarine force, as his new Chief of Naval Operations. After the ceremony, however, Anaya took Lombardo to one side and now asked him to prepare a plan to take the Falkland Islands, to which he had led his covert landing in 1966 and this time to *'take them but not necessarily to keep them'* as Lombardo recalled. The meeting was brief, after which Anaya flew back to Buenos Aires leaving Lombardo perhaps with more questions than answers. There had been plans to invade the Islands, of course, but these had mostly been academic exercises to be used in the War College and Lombardo soon flew to Buenos Aires armed with a list of three questions for Anaya which were delivered and answered as follows:

Q: *"Is the operation to be purely naval, or joint with the other services?*
A: *"It will be a joint operation, but no one else has yet been informed."*
Q: *"Is the intention to take and keep the Islands, or take them and then hand them over to someone else and, if so, would this be an Argentine force or a world force – the United Nations?"*

A: *"You are to plan a takeover, but not to prepare the defence of the Islands afterwards."*

Q: *"Can you guarantee that the secret nature of the planning be maintained?"*

A: *"You will only be working with three other Admirals – Allara, Busser of the Marines and Garcia Bol of the Naval Air Arm."*

Anaya was noted for being a solitary character, severe and self-disciplined and perhaps a little taciturn; *"quite unlike the normal naval officer"* as many of his peers noted. His answers were still not clear, Lombardo thought but, being what they were, he returned to Puerto Belgrano and at once began to speak with the three men he would be working with; Allara, Busser and Garcia Bol but these came back to him with the very same questions. Again, Lombardo was forced to return to Buenos Aires to seek further clarification, particularly as to concerns which all of these naval men had as to the joint nature of the planned operations. Anaya replied that he had in mind one man – General Osvaldo Garcia of the army – who might yet be included, but that he had not yet spoken with him; *"He repeated that it was a Navy task to take over the Malvinas,"* Lombardo recalled, *"what followed was for the junta to decide. They did not think that there would be a military reaction by the British."*

Returning to Puerto Belgrano, Lombardo presented his answers again before his assembled senior commanders and soon a plan began to take shape, codenamed *'Azul'* or 'Blue' after the robes of the Virgin Mary. Secrecy was the supreme key as, although it was known the British had scrapped ships due to defence cuts and were about to sell the ageing aircraft carrier HMS *Hermes* still they maintained an effective nuclear-powered submarine fleet which could quickly create havoc in any naval operation. In secret offices, the plan for the invasion began to take place throughout January 1982. General Garcia, commander of the V Corps of the infantry was brought on board, as was Brigadier General Plessl of the air force, although their roles seemed less defined and more inclined to promote harmony amongst the members of the junta than to produce any tangible results for what was essentially a naval operation.[*1]

One of the first ideas to be scrapped was the concept of taking the Islands but not preparing to defend them, as it was seen that, if the Islands were to be integrated into Argentina failing any major diplomatic fall-out, a period of sustained garrisoning would be required to oversee the process and to keep the population at bay. As to dates for the invasion, all were in general agreement for the date of September 15th which would leave time for a new round of negotiations with Britain and a diplomatic offensive by Galtieri to ensure that the world powers looked favourably upon the occupation. By this date, of course, the worst of the winter weather would also be over and the conscripts would be trained ready for the operation. Then there was welcome news that the Royal Navy ice ship *Endurance* which maintained patrol around the Falklands, was to be withdrawn at the end of her 1982 tour and not replaced, whilst *Hermes* would be sold on to India by then, and the new assault-carrier *Invincible* to Australia, which would deny Britain a considerable air advantage. Finally, by September the full complement of fourteen Super Etenard fighter jets and fifteen Exocet anti-ship missiles would have arrived from France.[*2]

On January 29th Rear-Admiral Carlos Busser of the Marines received his orders and by February 2nd had set up a five-man-strong 'Landing Force Cell' in a small office at the naval base at Puerto Belgrano as Lombardo, with just two other naval officers, produced the ship-support plan. The two 'cells' were to be kept in communication by a naval intelligence officer. Busser first selected the unit for the task and opted for the 2nd Marine Infantry Battalion (BIM2) - the self-styled *'Black Panthers'* - who were to begin practicing for their landing along a stretch of coast on the Valdes Peninsula in Patagonia where a perfect location was found, with a beach resembling that on the coast by Stanley and even a network of small roads and tracks from the beach to the nearby town which closely followed the line of route which was to be taken upon landing on the Falklands. After a discussion with Anaya, Busser was authorised to now incorporate Commander Alfredo Weinstabl – the BIM2's new commanding officer - into the planning, adding (from his own memoirs) that; *"I estimated that the appointment of the Commander of BIM2 could give us the advantage that in this way, and in a framework of absolute discretion, the training of the battalion could orient toward implementing what we were planning."* Weinstabl had only joined the BIM2 on January 26th fresh from an administrative role in Buenos Aires but had a sound reputation as a planner and a leader. Now Busser hoped Anaya might approve his inclusion into the plan and was happy when Anaya told him cheerfully; *"Add all you want, as long as you know that they remain at risk of dying if planning transcends!"*

It was January 29th – just three days after his appointment - that Weinstabl received the order to visit Busser in his office and, as he remembered, the journey filled him with trepidation; *"While driving the short trip to headquarters, I began to worry about what could be the reason for the call. Surely something had gone wrong or had been done wrong. Maybe some administrative failure of the unit... Or maybe some fight or riot from someone from the unit who had been excessive in drink in some bar of the nearby city of Punta Alta, or some other impropriety of that sort."* He was shortly shown into Busser's office where he met the Admiral - a man whom he had known as a raw cadet and whom he knew by reputation as; *"A mild-mannered man, but tough, demanding and very strict in the service. The Prototype of the Marine."* - Busser welcomed him to the area and to the BIM2 with

Weinstabl chiding himself upon not having come to introduce himself first, and then, as he continues; *"After a few minutes of formal conversation, he made me sit in front of him on the other side of the desk and, with serious gesture and without a word he handed me a sheet of paper hand-written by himself which I read. When I quickly read over the first two paragraphs, I was already mentally telling myself, 'Exercises of this magnitude are usually prepared in the second part of the year. He must know I wanted to start the year with full steam. I can't believe my bad luck! He wants me to prepare an exercise of this nature three days after having reached the battalion and in full time of recess!' - The Admiral, noticing the perplexity, amazement and probably annoyance on my face, said to me sternly: 'No Weinstabl, it's not what you think. This is not a drill. It's a real operation.' - I should start with the planning immediately in order to be completed as soon as possible. The probable date of the operation was not certain, but it wouldn't be before the 15th of May."*

Weinstabl at once went to work, visiting the planning office and the Chief of Intelligence, Guillermo Botto, whom he found exhausted, having worked for twenty days solid, alone in his office, poring over maps. Even now, Weinstabl checked with him that Busser's orders had not been some kind of a joke on his newly-appointed battalion commander. Botto's face gave him his answer quickly. The BIM2 was in its annual recess – a period lasting from mid-December until mid-March - during which the recruits were trained and equipment repaired and, as a top priority, Weinstabl was ordered to oversee the repair of the LVTP-7 Amtracks which would be used in the operation. Busser, having found that twelve of the twenty-one vehicles were 'operationally restricted' and in need of repairs and spare parts, now also looked to matters personally to oversee the work and, having visited the battalion every three or four days – which was noted as very unusual - Weinstabl had taken him to one side and now asked him if he was feeling okay; *"He wanted to find out how I was, and basically wanted to know if I was kinda crazy."* Busser remembered fondly.

Although the Marines now trained and practiced several landings between February and March, yet only three officers, amongst them Commander Weinstabl and Lieutenant Commander Hugo Santillan – the XO or Executive Officer of the battalion - were to know the real purpose of the training. For the rest, the natural assumption was that this was a practice-run for a landing in Chile, which with growing tensions over the Beagle Channel, most expected to be forthcoming. Indeed, the BIM2 were largely all that would be available along with a portion of one army brigade of the V Corps, with the rest of the forces preparing to engage Chile offensively or defensively as circumstances dictated. During the practice landings, Hugo Santillan remembered being particularly impressed by Weinstabl; a man with 'movie star' looks as he recalled, considered by the whole battalion to be a 'mister cool' with a 'poser' image and with something of a reputation. However, now that he knew that 'the real thing' was coming, he stepped up and immediately impressed everybody; *"He really became a true leader"* Santillan recalled.[3]

Hugo Santillan, now brought into the planning and soon running most of it in Weinstabl's stead, also remembered Admiral Busser fondly as a friendly and humane man, a true gentleman and popular with the rank and file for his habit of referring even to the lowest rating as *'Senor'* as opposed to just his rank or surname, (conversely he was known jovially by the navy as *'Old Busser'*) however if he disagreed – privately at least - with Busser, it was in the Admiral's belief that, so long as the Argentine forces came in enough strength, the British detachment of around forty Royal Marines there would not fight, but would simply surrender to an overwhelming force. Hugo Santillan knew the Royal Marines perhaps better than his superior; as a marine himself, he – like many and perhaps most of the Argentine Marines - had a deep-rooted respect for them, coloured even perhaps with a hint of awe. Santillan had trained only a few months before with the United States Marines in Patagonia, particularly with new equipment such as the American-made LVPT-7 Amtrack amphibious assault vehicles and recounted that; *"We considered the US Marines to be the best in the world, but we considered the Royal Marines to be the finest."* - One thing was apparent to him; the British did not and would not just give up, however few of them, *"They will need to give us a bloody nose first,"* he said, *"give them a chance to fight back, then – hopefully they will surrender."* One thing he did know was that they were not to be underestimated: Nobody wanted another 'Rorke's Drift.' Busser, however, was quietly confident that they would lay down their arms once they saw what he was bringing to the Islands, yet others were not so sure. One famous anecdote during the planning stage, which was witnessed by many, occurred when a highly respected retired Admiral was brought in to give his own opinions on the plans then being discussed. When they were presented to him, he read through them and then asked to see the plans for attacking London. Every head in the room turned sharply and quizzical faces stared incredulously at the Admiral as one of the senior planners finally asked; *"London! With all due respect, Sir, are you out of your wits?"* Turning to him, the Admiral now replied; *"If you are planning to make war on the Brits and do not have plans to attack London, then the mad one is not me!"* - After an awkward silence, the planning continued as before, albeit more ominously than before.[4]

Although the navy was quite sure that the final plan would fall to them, yet several plans were put forward which at least considered the inclusion of the air force and which would begin to test the relations of the three arms of the Argentine forces. The air force put forward a seemingly impressive plan for an all-airborne assault using C130 Hercules transports which began to attract some attention. However, the navy was adamant that they could carry off an amphibious operation and, perhaps seeing more of a role for themselves, the army now backed them. The air force was now relegated to a role which would involve little more than initial covert photo-reconnaissance and then the bringing up of supplies after the invasion, whilst the navy considered that, as far as went the army, some concessions would need to be made to accommodate them into the plans for the invasion.[*5] By March 9th the basic landing plan was presented to the junta and, being approved, was forwarded to Admiral Suarez del Cerro – Chief of the Joint Armed Forces Headquarters - who now began to tie this into the 'national plan' of obtaining the Islands by whichever means; *"We were told to be prepared to continue the planning right up to the last three months of the year,"* Busser stated, *"I have to stress that it was truly a national plan, not just a military one, with the main emphasis always on recovering the Islands by negotiations."*

From hushed conversations in small offices in the naval base at Puerto Belgrano, Operation Azul was expanded to incorporate a larger planning team and the inclusion of the senior officers who were to lead the invasion, and next on the list was the Commanding Officer of the elite *Buzos Tacticos* – Lieutenant Commander Alfredo Raul Cufre - who was to lead the Tactical Frogmen (the Argentine equivalent of the British SBS or US Navy Seals) and who was to be the first man to set foot on the Islands.[*6] Cufre was an experienced man, not long returned to duty after three years spent with his left leg in plaster. In August 1977 he had received several shots from a .38 revolver during the 'dirty war' and still had some shrapnel in his leg. *"I first heard the word 'Malvinas' on March 18th,"* he later recalled, *"but in December 1981 they were preparing my unit, about 150 men to 'do something important'. This order came from Commander Otero who received his direct orders from the Commander of Naval Operations, Admiral Lombardo... The Commander of the Submarine force came to my house in Mar del Plata late one evening and told me I had to go to Puerto Belgrano for an urgent mission. There, the Commander of the Fleet told us that we were the first to know that they were doing something, and here we first heard the name 'Malvinas'. Five minutes later, we met with the commanders of all units of the sea fleet, and then I returned immediately to Mar del Plata."*

Now the plans were well advanced and yet still the actual date, at least for many, seemed so far off. The senior officers of the landing force – all Commanders or Lieutenant Commanders - were now notified at least; amongst them Alfredo Cufre, Alfredo Weinstabl and Hugo Santillan who were to command the amphibious invasion with the Amtracks, Guillermo Sanchez Sabarots who was to lead the team to neutralise the Royal Marines on the Islands and finally Pedro

Giachino who was to lead a special 'snatch squad' to seize the Governor Rex Hunt and to escort him to the local radio station and there force him to order the Islands to surrender.[*7] Of these four men, perhaps few stood out as much as Giachino, the Lieutenant Commander of BIM1. Described by his peers as *'hot headed'* with rugged good looks and a natural camaraderie went a great athleticism which was the pride of the navy's rugby team where he played always as Number 8 – a position disposed to those with an innate sense of position, of knowing where their comrades were and of being part of a 'specialist group of marauding forwards' – strong, tough, able to take the ball through the opposition or to defend it in the thick of things - Pedro Giachino was, according to his friend Hugo Santillan, the ideal man for either job.

As the amphibious planning of Operation Azul progressed, so now there was a change of name as Hugo Santillan recalled; *"...some Admiral changed it to 'Operation Carlos' because 'Carlos' was the name of the Landing Force Commander, the Naval Air Commander and the Amphibious Task Force Commander..."* from here on the operation was to be referred to by this name, now almost forgotten in the wake of what was to come. By late March, political tensions were rising and not just over the Falklands. By now there were tensions also over South Georgia where an Argentine expedition had aroused the suspicions of the British and Falklands governments and the Argentine press was reporting that the Islands would be in Argentine possession by *'no later than January 3rd 1983'* – the 150th anniversary of Britain's reassertion of sovereignty over them.

Meanwhile tensions between the respective branches of the Argentine forces were further frayed, with the air force having sent several missions to the Islands, seemingly intent upon pursuing its own plan. The first had occurred on March 7th and consisted of a Hercules transport aircraft which had radioed in a spurious report of needing an emergency landing due to a fuel leak. The aircraft had landed full of air force officers – who were seen and who LADE's chief officer Gilobert packed into a Landrover and took on a tour of the Islands - and which then went through an awful sham of pretending to refuel as the local firemen and even the Royal Marines had peered inside of the aircraft to find that it was full of heavy equipment and not the postal drops which had been claimed as the reason for the mission. It being a very windy day, the air force had taken the opportunity of scouting the Islands and the pilot was, in reality, demonstrating a landing at the airport in the all-too-likely conditions to his crew of less experienced pilots, whilst looking out for places of strategic interest. Next had come the monstrous charade of March 19th in which a C130 Lear Jet supposedly bearing LADE's new chief Vice Comodoro Gamin had set off for the Falklands, circled over and then returned to Rio Gallegos without landing or without excuse. It had returned a second time, again circling and claiming undercarriage problems before returning home once more and then trying a third time. This time it had landed at 16.29 exactly, offloading Gamin but instead of greeting the duty customs officer, as was standard practice, the pilot had slammed the door, taxied around and then yanked back the throttle to make his nervous escape just minutes later. The aircraft had been conspicuous with the addition of a camera pod on its fuselage, from which it had taken numerous photographs of the area around Stanley, and the pilot's actions were altogether blatant in arousing suspicion.

Back in Puerto Belgrano the navy officers, including Hugo Santillan, were angry at this obviously ludicrous facade which could only have the result of compromising the security of the operation, *"The Navy was furious!"* Santillan remembered, *"Secrecy was compromised. The pilot had declared an emergency, so everyone had rushed to the airfield and they were all there to see it! We assumed that tactical surprise was now compromised."* - The air force, not content with what was at best a tertiary role in this operation, had tried to intervene - the 'help' was not received as being very welcome; *"Jealousy and suspicion between the forces is a known fact."* Busser was given to write, *"In all countries of the world between the different services of the armed forces, jealousy, suspicion, differences, animosities and many other variations in their relations, which must be cordial and cooperative, are in practice. The armed forces of our country were not an exception."*

With chances of security having been compromised, and unconfirmed reports of two British nuclear-powered submarines having been deployed towards the South Atlantic from Gibraltar, it was now determined to step the operation up. It was mid-morning on March 25th when Admiral Busser burst into the operations room where his officers were in a meeting and at once announced; *"Bullshit! You can throw all of that rubbish away; we are going into serious business. We must be ready to sail in seventy-two hours!"* This decision shocked the planning teams who had been working at leisure to draw up a plan designed for September. Almost nothing was ready and, as was said later; *"He told us that the junta's decision was not necessarily to land, but to sail to the target area alongside the diplomatic moves in progress. We in the planning team didn't sleep in that period. The outline plan was ready but not the logistics, and we had to do everything in a way that would make the men in the units concerned think that it was a routine training operation. Then there was the communications plan, the boarding plan and the last touches to the landing plan. It was all done in one room still, but we had to increase the planning group to twenty officers. We got it all done in the end. As marine officers, we were very proud to be a force 'in readiness'. There might have been a little more expertise if we had had until the original September deadline, but only minimal."*[8]

Now Operation 'Carlos' stepped into top gear as a flurry of orders went out. The more senior officers and those entrusted with the most important tasks were allowed to go home for one more night to spend with their wives and families before setting off the next morning although each was sworn to silence, as meanwhile the rank and file and line officers were assembled and all navy leave was cancelled. Those more junior officers who had important tasks in the mission to come were also allowed home – those who knew that something big was about to happen, but still did not know the mission to be achieved. One of these was twenty-eight-year-old Lieutenant Diego Garcia Quiroga of the *Buzo Tactico* who at the time was duty officer at the Mar del Plata naval base, some 400km north of Puerto Belgrano, where both the *Buzos Tacticos* and the *Commandos Anfibios* had their Headquarters.

Quiroga's XO was Lieutenant Carlos Robbio, a dear friend of his for fifteen years, three years his senior and a former classmate from the Naval High School; *"I had just talked to Carlos Robbio on the phone"* Diego Quiroga remembered, *"he and his wife had arranged to join me and my (then) wife for dinner. Instead, Carlos showed up by himself right after reveille and told me that I was going to be relieved of my shift and had to report to the unit ASAP. As I entered the unit I found Carlos engaged in a conversation with the CO (Cufre) in the latter's office. Cufre waved me in and told me that the unit was to deploy on a real mission. I immediately thought about Chile, but said nothing. I was then instructed to select six experienced divers whom I would feel comfortable to lead on a combat mission in a populated area. He also advised me to select senior NCO's. I knew the men well and quickly made my choice, which both Cufre and Carlos approved. Then we went into the details; clothing and weapons to take, length of the mission, etc. I soon realised that both were discussing another mission, 'their' mission, and noticing this, Cufre told me to go over to the Commandos Anfibios in order to get the particulars of my own, for my group was going to be working with them... I then went to the classroom of the Commandos Anfibios which was now converted into an operations room where on a blackboard, Lieutenant Bardi was filling out an equipment entry for an operation of which I yet knew nothing... I met Sanchez Sabarots, with whom I had had very little contact so far. He was friendly and adroit. He told me that my men and I were going to join a mixed group of Commandos and Buzos led by Giachino, who was waiting for us in Puerto Belgrano 400km further south. Buses to get there would be leaving that very night. We should take with us warm clothing, dry suits and hand or shoulder weapons suited for short range combat."*

For Diego Quioroga there was now great excitement and anticipation. Here was the real thing, and now he was to be working with Pedro Giachino, a man whose name was legend in the Argentine Navy; *"The first impression I had of Giachino was back when I was still a sophomore cadet in the Naval Academy."* he recalled, *"He and his mates (all 1st Lieutenants at that time) were visiting officers taking a course. We often saw them during breaks, but we would never have dreamed of addressing such senior officers without being asked for. I remember thinking that the guy looked like a real athlete. We never exchanged a word, and the next time I saw him was during a parachuting exercise. By then he was already CO for the Commandos Anfibios and I had just arrived in my unit, the Buzos Tacticos."* - now Diego Quiroga was going to work with the man, and he was determined to be ready.

"I returned to the Buzos," he continued, *"Carlos was at the armoury, choosing weapons with the men. I had wanted to take one of the new .222 Steyr AUG rifles that had recently arrived in the unit, but Carlos advised me to take a slightly lighter and less complicated weapon. I chose a Falcon 9mm submachine gun of Argentine make, typically used by the police. In addition, I had my favourite Browning 9mm pistol, a present from my father. Others took as their respective 'brides' the popular FAL. After I had seen that my group was ready and equipped, I returned to the Commandos Anfibios and asked Sanchez Sabarots how much time we had to wait for the buses, for I really wanted to see my wife whom I had not talked to since the day before. We had been married only three months. He said we could take five hours; the buses were to be leaving at 02:00. One of his officers, Junior Lieutenant Bernardo Schweizer was precisely about to go home to say goodbye to his family. Bernardo was a year my junior, but our fathers had been classmates at the military high school and I knew him well."*

Bernardo Schweizer – only 24 years old - had just been recalled from honeymoon in Rio de Janeiro where he had spent the first half of his two-week vacation before being recalled. He had been married on March 12th and had been in his hotel on March 20th when he received a call ordering him back *"into the drive to participate in a real operation, without further details"* and he had set off to return to Argentina the next day. Now at Mar del Plata, three officers – Diego Quiroga, Bernardo Schweizer and Carlos Robbio - climbed into Robbio's car. All three lived at the same naval housing apartment building in town and made the short journey to the apartment. On the way, Quiroga told the newly-arrived Schweizer that this was, as he understood, to be a risky mission, and to be careful. Finally arriving at the apartment, the three officers parted, having first made their arrangements to meet later to board the bus for the long journey down to Puerto Belgrano.

Arriving home, Diego Quiroga recalled that *"I had a brief dinner and went to bed sort of right away. Alejandra, my wife at that time, had been listening to the news and probably hearing the gossip in the building's hallways – 'I think you'll be going to the Malvinas or something like that' – she said, not alarmed. I had come* back from manoeuvres just a week before and we were sort of used to not getting surprised by shifting routines. In any case, it was the first I had heard about anything in connection with the Islands and I don't remember it having made an impression. Anyway, I was as tired as a dog and slept like a baby for a good three hours. At 01:30 and already dressed in combat fatigues, Bernardo Schweizer knocked at our door. I kissed my wife goodbye, promised her I'd come back soon and left for the base using Bernardo's car."

Travelling back to the base, the officers found the buses waiting to take them on the 400km drive through the night. Diego Quiroga recalled that he slept all through the journey and arrived in Puerto Belgrano at dawn, waking up as the bus entered the naval base. As the bus carried on to the 2nd Marine Battalion headquarters, he could see a great deal of activity along the piers, where ships and supplies were being prepared in earnest. Offloaded, the men found some breakfast waiting for them. The officers were then called into the Officers Mess – a place to which Quiroga recalled he had never yet been; *"There were combat-dressed officers all over the place and most of them were senior to me."* he said, remembering that he felt somewhat out of place being there, *"However, the reigning camaraderie increased, perhaps because we knew that we were on the eve of great events. I spotted Giachino and went to meet him. He came forward as he saw me, shook my hand and said loudly, 'Now we are all here!' - He then introduced me to the other officers in the group: 1st Lieutenant Alvarez and 1st Lieutenant Lugo. Both were Commandos Anfibios and I knew them well from the Naval Academy, having been cadets together. They were excited, though we did not yet know any details about the mission."* Giachino explained briefly that they were all there as part of a patrol for a special task of the highest importance. One man asked if, by chance, it would be to the Malvinas, to which Giachino replied *"That much I can't say."* When the meeting broke up, the junior officers and men went to make ready as the senior commanders went off to meet with Admiral Busser for a higher-level planning meeting. There Giachino met his friend Hugo Santillan who asked how his night had been; *"Hugo I have a heavy heart,"* said Giachino, who had gone home the night before and opened bottle of champagne to share with his wife Cristina, *"I said goodbye to my wife. She was very angry because she said I was the same old stupid man again, that I volunteered all the time for exercises and always went away... and I couldn't tell her! This was the real thing! I was so happy, I was so enthusiastic because I was going to the Malvinas... and I couldn't tell her!"*

Now the officers assembled into the meeting room with Busser to receive their instructions as the plan was confirmed. The operation was to involve almost everything the navy had to hand and all was to be thrown jointly at the Falkland Islands on April 1st and at South Georgia on April 2nd. It would involve the submarine ARA *Santa Fe* which would lead the way and land the tactical divers under Alfredo Cufre, the American-designed tank-landing ship ARA *Cabo San Antonio* which would carry the LVPT-7 Amtracks and Delta, Echo and Fox companies BIM2 under Weinstabl and Santillan, as well as a platoon of army soldiers of the 25th Infantry Regiment. Hugo Santillan recalls this section of the meeting as he now unfurled his plan; *"We gathered and unfolded the map, explaining the situation... Although we were all certain that the operation was going to be done, at that moment it felt like a rare sensation. We had never done a real amphibious operation. It was a mixture of anxiety, worry, great excitement and enthusiasm. Imagine, we had the destiny to be those who were going to see the dream of the Republic to recover the Malvinas. We were well prepared and we felt empowered to do so. They were at most 90 men, we more than 1000. There was no possibility that the operation would go wrong. At that time, we were at the peak of the historical operational capacity of the Argentine Navy... I remember Seineldin looked over and told me: 'Look Santillán, I know that I am senior you, but this is an operation of the Marine Corps and is very well done, so without inconvenience, I'll act as your subordinate...'*

In addition to the plan, both Type-42 destroyers - the *Hercules* made for Argentina by Britain (for which Argentina still owed Britain £3.4 million) and the other one ARA *Santisma Trinidad* manufactured in Argentina under license - which would carry Giachino and Sanchez Sabarots to their goals, the ex-Royal Navy aircraft carrier ARA *Veinticinco de Mayo*, which would carry no less than 1,500 soldiers by helicopter for the second wave, and a vast number of other ships to include ARA *Comodoro Py*, *Hipolito Bouchard*, *Segui* and *Piedro Buena* – all ex-American destroyers built at the end of the war - an armed ice-breaker ARA *Almirante Irizar* which would also carry helicopter-borne troops and three smaller Corvettes, the ARA *Drummond*, *Granville* and *Guerrico* which were to provide support and naval gunfire as needed. In short, the operation to capture the Falklands and South Georgia would be an absolute case of 'overkill' with only one possible result. Quite an armada with which to take on a detachment of Royal Marines on one island, and an Antarctic Survey team on the other.

Arriving in the Falklands, the landing to the east of Stanley would be spearheaded by Alfredo Cufre and the tactical frogmen who would come ashore at the main landing beach, secure the beach-head and signal in the main amphibious force under Weinstabl and Santillan. Meanwhile, two groups would land simultaneously to the south of the Island's capital and make their way north and west, behind the British force; the first under Sanchez Sabarots to neutralise the Royal Marines' barracks at Moody Brook and the second under Pedro Giachino to pounce upon Government House, just to the west of Stanley, and from there to carry away the Governor Rex Hunt and convey him to the radio station to announce the surrender. Here was where Lieutenant Diego Quiroga would come in useful: he spoke perfect English. On the way, they should meet the amphibious force coming up the airport road in their armoured vehicles, the helicopters would land the second wave and, attacked simultaneously from all sides, the Islands would then be in Argentine hands. The key to this plan, however, would be the parts played by Sanchez Sabarots and Giachino respectively, in a move which would 'decapitate' the small British command there; taking out the Royal Marines and the Governor in one fell swoop and overwhelming the defenders, and Busser had reason to believe that it could be done without a single casualty on either side. Again, Hugo Santillan gave his opinion; *"The British will not surrender, not even if they are overwhelmed."* he reaffirmed, *"They will fight. They have to leave your face bleeding and then, if there is no other way but suicide, they will surrender."*[9]

Hardly anything was ready, but Busser intended to hit the small British detachment with overwhelming numbers in terms of manpower, armour, artillery, warships and aircraft; there were only to be around forty of them: surely, they would present no obstacle and just surrender? Each man was to be provided with eight days' worth of rations and ammunition. By then – long before then - the bulk of the Argentine forces would have come up and the matter would be a foregone conclusion. Busser impressed upon his men that there were four conditions to the operation; that it should be conducted with speed, secrecy, surprise and above all without bloodshed. Nobody wanted a protracted incident which would provide Britain with a reason to respond. British casualties would certainly do this, whilst Argentine casualties – well, hopefully there would be none - but the British did like a famous 'last stand' story. On the whole, both were to be avoided, but they were so small; just forty of them. Forty Royal Marines to face this avalanche. It was no competition.

That night, the men slept on the base, ready to depart in the early morning. There was excitement as well as tension. Diego Quiroga recalled that he slept almost completely dressed, and that it was not an easy sleep. The next morning, March 28th, he was sent with the rest of the party to the ARA *Santisma Trinidad* for embarkation; *"I remember thinking briefly to myself that if we were to be using a destroyer to get there, that probably ruled out Chile as a possible destination,"* he recalled. Once aboard, he helped load the equipment, most of which was to be stored in the hangar, checked the accommodation, took possession of his bunk and then with the others, began to make a space in the cabin to place maps, photographs and other data for the target to be announced. There he also placed two books given to him by his wife for the trip; *'On War'* by Clausewitz and *'American short stories'*.

The ship sailed, and immediately Quiroga and several other men went to the stern of the ship to check on the boats to be used in the landing. There were twenty-one of them, rubber in construction and powered by outboard motors, with two kayaks stowed alongside them for a silent vanguard, all strapped to the side of the ship towards the stern; *"I was discussing with the men the best way to lower the rubber boats from the deck to the water,"* he remembered, *"There was a Commander present there, also a Buzo Tactico. I knew who he was, but we had never met before. It was hot, and I was wearing only a tee-shirt over my fatigues, with no rank insignia on. As this officer heard me discussing with the NCO's (he knew them all well, for he had commanded the unit some years before), he said to me 'Listen kid, it's great that you try to help, but why don't we better leave the experienced guys to decide on the matter?' - There was an awkward silence before I answered, 'Excuse me sir, but I am the officer in charge of this party."* - Luckily enough, he took it very well, so we all had a good laugh."

By now, the men were talking amongst themselves and, at least for the officers, the word *'Malvinas'* was being mentioned as the invasion fleet moved ever eastwards. The officers and men who were to be involved in the initial landing were soon called to the hangar of the ship where four men carried a huge roll of paper which they unfurled on the floor, filling the room. The roll was a mosaic of photographs which had been taken by LADE aircraft showing beaches and a town and now it was explained that the target shown was indeed the Falkland Islands, and that the landing would take place on April 1st. Quiroga remembered that he did not feel *'any particular elation'* either in himself or amongst those who were gathered in the hangar, but more rather a tense excitement, the likes of which Shakespeare had managed to capture and apply to Henry V's speech before the battle of Agincourt, he thought; *"Although there was nothing that one would label 'patriotic' in my attitude, I was as sceptical as ever about the soundness of the decision, and cannot recall many of us having intense feelings about the Islands. Speaking only for myself, the whole idea of fighting was a personal challenge."*

It was a long night in which Quiroga and others spent their time trying to read, digest and remember every facet of their well-planned operations which, now that the whole was laid out before them, they could see was a massive undertaking. *"We were to spearhead an operation directed against an enemy I had learned to admire,"* he later wrote, *"As a young man, my concepts of courage and duty were shaped on a mixture of Argentina's own war-waging tradition and many of Rudyard Kipling's characters, probably because I had been educated at an English school in Buenos Aires. Combat was the perfect arena to find out the type of stuff I was made of. And there I was, going in with a group of men who were as brave as, or possibly braver than, myself. We were perfectly honed for the mission, fit as fiddles, and happy as partygoers. I trusted all and everyone, as I had not trusted anyone before."*

The 'snatch squad' to be led by Giachino then met to go through their final plans and to look through a series of plans and photographs of Government House which had been obtained by a deception and delivered to the navy by a Captain Gaffoglio when he was running the *Transportes Navales* in the Islands, however it transpired that Gaffoglio had transferred ship to the ice-breaker and designated hospital vessel *Almirante Irizar* and had taken his plans and his photographs with him; *"However, Captain Giachino had managed to get as much data as possible,"* Quiroga recalled, *"and the general feeling was that there was going to be a heavy guard in the house."* The fifteen men who were to form the snatch squad were now increased to sixteen with the addition of Corporal Ernesto Urbina, a medic who was also commando-trained.[*10]

That day a storm hit the fleet which was the worst that many of them could remember. The ships were tossed about on the sea, lurching wildly to each side, pitching and rolling and throwing the men aboard in every direction as those packed in the cramped quarters below deck were sent sprawling into each other, adding to the discomfort as many men began to get violently sea-sick and on deck, two drums of fuel broke loose and smashed one of the two kayaks, sending both them and it sprawling into the churning black sea. On the tank-landing-ship *Cabo San Antonio*, the men of Delta and Fox companies of Alfredo Weinstabl's 2nd Battalion Marine Infantry were suffering the worst of the storm, huddled amongst a mass of equipment and the giant LVTP-7 Amtrack amphibious armoured personnel carriers as well as other LARC-V support vehicles, which their crews battled to keep fastened down; *"The strong storm got more and more violent,"* remembered Weinstabl, *"and the majority of the battalion – at all levels – was practically out of service for sickness and dizziness. The famous 'cruel sea' caused havoc and often gave no time to throw-up over the side of the vessel, which is the why the corridors, holds, communal areas and bathrooms were covered in vomit. In this situation, without a doubt, the battalion was in no way fit for the fight... The situation was so critical that, in that condition, all combat capacity had practically been lost...This was so much so that we began considering changing our landing day and the Marines started saying that God was English."*

Daniel Tosolini, a young man of Delta company BIM2 was also suffering badly from the effects but he was excited, having gone through months of amphibious training by day and night, and was sure that they were being sent upon a real combat mission. Nobody knew for sure, although there were excited rumours that the target – if there was to be one - was to be the Malvinas. Certainly, he had noted, the ship, which had been part of the training exercises for some time, had been loaded with more men, vehicles and equipment than before – she was designed for a complement of 450 men - she now carried 880. Now the *Cabo San Antonio* – being flat-bottomed and without a keel - was hurled about violently and

Daniel Tosolini, like so many others, was vomiting constantly, being thrown one way and then another into a press of men who stumbled as the ship rolled as far as 44 degrees and back again. Glancing out of the window, he saw the sea churning violently and terribly, with waves at least ten metres high. The men felt awful; they had been on board since the 26th, had few basic facilities such as toilets and had gone the whole time with barely any food, and many now hoped and prayed that the order would soon come to return home and relieve them from their miserable condition.

Up on the top decks, where the senior officers were gathered, there was also trepidation; would the operation be called off at the last minute? Hugo Santillan remembers that; *"At the last moment, there were calls from Reagan to Galtieri and demands from Foreign Secretary Haig to stop the operation. It was on April 1 at 18.00 when the ship received the order from the Presidency of the Nation ordering: 'Execute the amphibious operation'..."* – They were now going, and the operation would not be called off. Then the ship's loudspeakers crackled into life as Admiral Busser, no doubt seeking to lift the men's spirits, delivered the men the news they had all been waiting for: *"I am the Commander of the landing force, composed of the members of the Marine Corps and the Argentine Army embarked on this ship, some others aboard the Destroyer Santisma Trinidad and the icebreaker Almirante Irizar and tactical divers embarked on Submarine Santa Fe. Our mission is to land on the Malvinas and evict the military and the British authorities who are in them. And that's what we will do! As fate would have it, we are responsible for repairing the almost 150 years of usurpation. In these Islands, we will find a population to whom we must give special treatment. They are inhabitants of Argentine territory and therefore should be treated as are all living in Argentina. You must strictly respect private property and integrity of all people. You will not enter any private residence if it is not necessary for reasons of combat. You will respect women, children, the elderly and men. You will be tough with the enemy, but courteous, respectful and kind to the population of our territory, which we must protect. If someone incurs rape, theft or looting, they will incur immediately the maximum penalty. And now, with the permission of the Commander of the Group of Transport, I trust that the success the landing force will result from the brilliant work that members of that group have already made. Thanks for bringing us this far, and thanks for putting us tomorrow on the beach. No doubt the courage, honour and training of all of you will give us victory. For a long time, we have been training our muscles and preparing our minds and hearts to the supreme moment of facing the enemy. That time has arrived! Tomorrow you will be the victors. Tomorrow we will show the world a courageous victory generous in Argentina and mighty in the war. May God protect you! Viva la Patria!"*

Men now began to cheer wildly with as much energy as they could muster, with Hugo Santillan again recalling the scene; *"When Busser finished speaking the conscripts began to jump and shout: 'Long live the Fatherland! Fuck! If my old lady were here! She would not believe me!' They hugged, it was a blast!! It was a difficult feeling to describe. Unrepeatable. We embraced everyone..."* With his own men cheering and celebrating below decks, Weinstabl now decided to add a finishing touch of his own; *"I went down to the deck where I found the conscripts of the battalion between nervous and excited, commenting on what they had just heard over the loudspeakers,"* he remembered, *"I didn't see fear or dread or anything like that. On the contrary: eager and expectant. After a few words with a group which had approached me, I delivered my own pep-talk, in much less scholarly terms than the Admiral. All present – several hundred voices – responded with a strong and manly 'Viva la Patria!' It was the exteriorisation of patriotism, vocalised with that roar of the 'Black Panthers' as they called themselves, making reference to the distinctive panther motif of the battalion. They definitely weren't 'Los Chicos de la Guerra'... they were the 'Black Panthers' of the BIM2."* Finally, when the excited cheering died down and the realisation of the task before them kicked in, the men looked to their company officers and Daniel Tosolini remembered one officer calming their nerves, telling his men that this was the same as they had been practicing for years and especially for the last few months, only this time the enemy would be real and, he added - perhaps not helpfully - the bullets too.

The storm still raged, the ship rolled and lurched and, despite the news which had now heartened every man, the dread of the crashing, battering waves was beginning to creep back in. Up top and in a planning session, the senior officers, including Hugo Santillan, were also feeling the effects of the storm as Santillan recalled; *"We sustained very heavy weather during the navigation from our naval base to the target. In the middle of a planning session aboard, the Commanding Officer of the 25th Army Infantry Regiment Lieutenant Colonel Mohamed Ali Seineldin (who was suffering with sea sickness as were 90% of the men on board) said 'If we call this Operation 'Rosario' instead of 'Carlos', our Holy Virgin Mary will calm the wind and the waves and will point us to a safe course...' - his proposal was instantly accepted."* - Seineldin's reasoning harkened back to a similar incident in 1807 when, just as now, the storm had gripped the Argentine navy, and the adoption of that name had calmed the seas and brought victory. *"What Seineldin ignored is that this phrase '... our Holy Virgin Mary will calm the wind and the waves and will point us to a safe course...' is a verse from the prayer of Stella Maris, the Patron Virgin of our Navy,"* Hugo Santillan recalled afterwards, *"he simply said a sentence we navy men recite every time we pray our Holy Mother of God! That was a delicious episode!"* The gale blew and the sea rolled throughout the night, but by the morning of April 1st, Seineldin's prayer had been answered; *"The sea was like a swimming pool,"* Hugo Santillan remembered, *"one of maybe 10 days out of 365 when you can expect almost perfect weather in the South Atlantic!"*

The operation, now adopted by all as *'Rosario'* due to the miracle of the storm, would have to be delayed for a day. The ships and men were battered and behind schedule. Men could now eat at last and there were repairs that had to be made and equipment to be checked. Back on the *Santisma Trinidad*, the destruction of the kayak and the loss of two drums of fuel for the motor boats was discovered, and it was found that, with the fuel they had left, they might manage at best half a tank each for the 21 vessels. It would be enough. Now the armada was approaching the Falklands as the sun began to drop in the sky and the reality of the task at hand began to dawn on each man. Chief Petty Officer Pedro Lopez – one of the *Buzos* who was to go with Giachino's party to Government House – remembered that; *"I remember it was about seven in the evening of April 1st when I went out on deck and caught sight of the Islands on the horizon. A chill ran through my body, doubts assailed me… would we do it or would we cancel everything at the last moment?"*

With the Islands in sight, men now began to make themselves ready, checking weapons and kit, going back over the same plan endlessly in their minds; *"We were doing tests, repeating instructions, preparing and testing the communications, updating orders and intelligence,"* Lieutenant Bernardo Schweizer recalled, *"Some officers, according to their personalities, quietly focused, surely thinking of the importance of the historic event that they were about to live through… some prayed intimately, putting their faith in God's hands and asking for his support and in my case, I regretted not having left offspring…"* he reflected that he should still have been on honeymoon in Rio right now, yet now he was part of the force that was going to take out the Royal Marines in their barracks at Moody Brook under Lieutenant Commander Sanchez Sabarots. Understandably, he was nervous yet excited and then he received some welcome encouragement as he recalled; *"Captain Giachino approached me in a moment and this is what he told me verbatim: 'Go quietly, asshole, and take care of your people. Be successful.' It was a very breathy, important voice that gave me confidence and focused more on my team than on thinking of my own luck."*

Corporal Ernesto Urbina – the Commando-trained medic who was to accompany Giachino's snatch-squad - remembered a strange sensation that night as a young man now going into combat; *"There were any things I thought which you cannot define with a single word."* He recounted, *"Upon receiving the novelty of what we had to do, I felt first, surprise, then nervousness: the uncertainty of being able to do things well, the fear of the unknown element of real combat. After* we received Giachino's instructions of what to do and how, it became a sensation like living a movie, because once you are in a real situation of war, you do not feel yourself – you are another – with all of the fear, but with the conviction to carry out your orders and to copy your older and more experienced colleagues."

Corporal Carlos Cequiera, another member of Sanchez Sabarots' party was also making his preparations as he later recalled; "There was an uncertainty, a fear and we were all afraid for our survival," remembered the twenty-seven-year-old, "Who says that he was not afraid is either lying or insane. The fear exists. It is real. I wrote a letter to my wife, we had a son and she was pregnant with our second child. I gave it to an NCO who knew my brother, saying; 'If you hear for certain that I have not survived, deliver this to my family'." Cequiera and Schweizer had been tasked to be the first people to set foot on the Islands to the south of Stanley.

As darkness began to fall, Giachino called his own party to dinner and all sat around the table although Diego Quiroga recalls that he ate lightly, and Giachino was annoyed that nobody had thought to bring a camera to document their being together, and someone made a nervous joke about 'the last supper.' After dinner, they began to get ready; they would land before midnight to the south of Stanley and then make their way overland towards the target. Donning black uniforms and bullet proof vests, black woollen hats and squeezing into dry suits, Giachino's and Sanchez Sabarots' parties now began to stain their faces with black camouflage cream; "It is not necessary for some faces!" joked Lieutenant Bardi, referring to the Creole complexion of some in the group.

"The mood was high," Quiroga recalled, as his section readied themselves under the dim red night-lights of the Santisma Trinidad's helicopter hangar. Each man was checking and re-checking his weapons for the hundredth time and Quiroga was armed with his Falcon, his Browning pistol and, as a last thought, had attached a Swiss army knife to his belt just left of the buckle. Others were armed with an assortment of grenades, pistols, British-made Sterling 9mm submachine guns and the ever-popular FAL (Fusil Automatico Liviano) or light automatic rifle; a 7.62mm weapon with a hollow folding stock which made it light and compact and which was a favourite with paratroopers. "Open your eyes," said Giachino suddenly, "because for those who return, this will be the first time we will be in actual combat, and that experience, it will be necessary to tell of."

At a signal, the men began to file out of the helo-hangar, their eyes adjusted to the darkness by the red night-lights as they stood and waited to be called to the side to disembark and the boats were lowered by specially constructed davits; "The night was black; dark like few others, 'Ideal for an attack' I thought," Quiroga said, recalling his impressions, "Hands that guided us, pressed us firm, whispers of 'luck' and 'hope'... At one moment, the ship's First Lieutenant waved my group to come out to the side. As I went by him, he caught my hand and put a candy in it.

'God be with you,' he said, 'good luck.' I was not to meet him again before many years later. By then he was already an Admiral and my boss in the Naval Education Department."

Silently, the twenty-one rubber boats slipped into the water at 21:15 on April 1st 1982 taking their crews towards the target; some Islands shrouded in myth, mystery and national legend, and somewhere on those Islands would be the men of the Royal Marines: the finest fighting men in the world. But there were so few of them - maybe forty at most? Still less than half of the force now packed into the small rubber boats which motored their way towards a distant shore which none could see. Would they fight? Did they know what was coming? Maybe if they saw the strength of the force coming to oppose them, they just might surrender. By morning the full force of the Argentine invasion would be upon them with heavy weapons, artillery, armoured vehicles, aircraft, naval gunfire and hundreds more men. So much to fight against so few. Every man back on the ships now hoped, feared and prayed together, as the twenty-one boats disappeared into the darkness.

Chapter 3: Three Little Birds

"Young men, cheap booze, bad combination!"
Andy Macdonald.

In September 1981, Royal Navy 1st Lieutenant and hydrographic surveyor Chris Todhunter travelled to Chatham Naval Dockyard in Kent to meet his new assignment, the ice-breaker and patrol vessel HMS *Endurance*. True to her name, she was an old ship, built in Denmark in 1956 and sold to the Royal Navy eleven years later, since when she had supported the British Antarctic Survey teams in the South Atlantic and had maintained her patrol around the Falkland Islands, taking the annual draft of NP8901 detachments down to the Islands from Montevideo for their year of deployment. She was not a warship as such; her entire armament consisted of just two 20mm Oerlikon guns and she was more suited to surveys and the odd rescue mission than to anything like combat. Due to her bright red hull – a curious feature of ice ships to aid her visibility to other vessels - she was known fondly as *'The Red Plum'* but this was to be her last voyage. A Ministry of Defence 'White Paper' earlier that year had proposed defence cuts and one of these was to be the *Endurance* – she was to complete her last mission and then return home with her decommissioning date set for April 15th 1982: she was not to be replaced.

A clergyman's son from Cumberland, Todhunter had grown up in Australia and then moved back to London where he had been a part of the St Paul's Cathedral choir as a child and had joined the Royal Navy in 1975 specialising as a hydrographic surveyor after studying history at Durham University - a subject which had enthralled him since childhood; *"I'd been brought up on Scott, Shackleton, Marco Polo; and this idea of going to remote places – exploring them, collecting scientific data – all that was my childhood come true."* he fondly recalled. His service had indeed taken him far and wide, from West Africa to Barbados, Venezuela and Brazil but Todhunter had a burning desire to walk in the footsteps of the great Antarctic explorers on the *Endurance's* last voyage. He joined his new crew under Captain Nick Barker and *Endurance* set sail for Antarctica that October. It was to be a memorable and fulfilling six months for Todhunter, *"an absolutely fabulous time,"* as he recalled, as the ship put in at the island of Madeira where at a cocktail party he first met a young lady named Rosemary who was staying there with her mother who had moved to the island for health reasons. The pair at once hit it off and parted with Todhunter promising to write and call at every stop on the journey, which he did. By stages, *Endurance* then travelled south and west, stopping briefly in Stanley in December and then on to the Antarctic Survey research station situated some 600 miles from the Chilean coast. There, Todhunter enjoyed his time carrying out surveys amongst the icebergs; *"The aim would be to go back to the exact positions where great explorers had made readings 70 or 80 years earlier and record the change."* he remembered, *"It was like a sort of hallowed activity, standing where Otto Nordenskjöld took his observations: romance, drama and fun all rolled up in one!"*

Finally, with the surveys complete, *Endurance* was turned around and headed for the long journey home, where she would be decommissioned, sold on and cut up for scrap. It was a sad ending to a great ship which, at least, had had a fitting last voyage. However, there was to be at least one last stop in the Falkland Islands before heading for Montevideo, bringing the new Falklands detachment to Stanley and then heading for home. *Endurance* put into Stanley where, as a frequent visitor, she was always welcomed with joy, only this time the joy was coloured with a hint of sadness for the old ship which had always served to remind the Falkland Islanders that their mother country was not always so far away, for after she left, they knew they would never see her again. Times were changing; to the Islanders, each maternal cord to their identities seemed to be being cut, slowly but surely and replaced with a new, ominous and alien culture from their neighbours in Argentina.

Meanwhile, on the Falls Road in Belfast, Northern Ireland, the demarcation line between the Unionist north and the Republican south, Royal Marine Danny Betts sat and waited in an observation post; two tall white buildings which dominated the skyline and which were inhabited by nurses from the local hospital. The Marines humorously termed them 'Tampax Towers'.

Danny Betts was a part of Royal Marines 45 Commando Group. He had just turned 20 that February and had been a Royal Marine ever since he left school but now he found himself going through what he termed as *'an angry young man stage'*. Everything about the Royal Marines, Northern Ireland, the future and life in general seemed dismal and foreboding - but then service in Northern Ireland could do that to a man. He wanted to get away, to be a better Royal Marine and to see some action. He had completed Arctic Warfare training in Norway before and liked it and, whilst in Northern Ireland, he had even taken a motorbike and a horse-riding course, but Danny Betts had different dreams.

For a young Royal Marine, he had more money than most. Northern Ireland wasn't the kind of place where an off-duty Royal could just go to get his hair cut or spend time at the pub, and so living had been very cheap and, for extra money, he had entered into a competition to determine the best man in the unit for cutting hair. The winner would then have the job of being the official 'barber' for the men and would be paid for it. Danny had won, and with more money than he could spend came the nickname of 'Vidal' – as in Sassoon - for his hair-cutting skills. Now he had saved his wages and his new-found earnings and had a plan to get out: He had put in to be considered for the NP8901 detachment to the Falklands where he planned to get his sniper's cross-hairs and also his driving license and then, saving up the money from the year on the Falklands and adding it to his impressive stash, he dreamed about owning an MGB-GT sports car: that was the plan at least. Of course - for many reasons – the NP8901 detachment list was always full of names of hopeful candidates and so it really was a lottery. The odds of getting in were slim and each man would have to wait until eventually, most likely, being told that he had been rejected, and so Danny Betts sat in 'Tampax Towers' and waited until one day, a fellow Royal ran up the stairs and gave him the news; *"Vidal! You've got the Falklands!"* Danny remembered his joy at his plans coming to fruition and his way out of Northern Ireland being laid out before him; *"I was like a kid at Christmas!"* he said.

the NP8901 detachment was being formed in Poole on the English south coast and soon Danny was on his way to meet his new detachment and the men with whom he would live for the next year. They were mostly all from 42 or 45 Commando and nearly all of them were strangers but then Danny received his second piece of luck which made him think that this next year in the Falklands was going to be a great time; he saw two friendly and familiar faces, and Mark Coombs and George Brown welcomed him with disbelief as they saw him. All three had met in commando training and had been friends but hadn't seen each other probably since 1978. Now they were going to spend a year together in the Falklands. George Brown wasn't actually called *'George'* of course; being a Royal Marine, each man went by a name given to him by his mates and George (whose real name was Stephen) was from Newcastle and hence what the British term a 'Geordie' – in the Royal Marines, all Geordies were automatically re-Christened 'George'. These names had been handed down often for centuries of Royal Marine tradition and almost every man had a pet-name and often did not even know the real name of the man next to him. Scots were instantly called *'Jock'*, Welshmen *'Taff'*, Red-heads were *'Ginge'*, Liverpudlians *'Scouse'* and Geordies were *'George'* – sometimes the names were quite inventive. Other times they were not, but everyone had one.[*1]

From assembling in Poole, the new detachment of Naval Party 8901 made their way to Gatwick Airport to fly first to Montevideo and then to travel on by ship to the Falklands. At the airport they were allowed a few minutes for phone calls home. It had all happened so fast; from selection to travel to Poole, debriefing and then straight to the airport so that most men had not had time to even say their farewells to their families. Danny Betts called home and spoke to his Mum; *"Mum* it's brilliant, I'm going to the Falklands!" he told her excitedly, "Oh that's lovely, I'm so happy for you, duck!" his Mum replied, "I've always wanted to visit Scotland!"

Two other men who knew each other in this detachment had perhaps colder relations; Corporal Stefan 'Yorkie' York and Major Mike Norman. Major Norman – a towering and imposing man at six feet two inches tall and stockily built - had quite a name for himself. At 38 years old, he had seen combat before in a number of places and had been in the Royal Marines since he was 19, starting in the ranks and working his way up to an officer's commission. He was known as a hard man, someone who, as fellow officers recalled, "reinforces his arguments" and who "doesn't like being messed about," and he had a reputation as a brawler for several fights he had allegedly gotten himself into over the years, which led to him being given the nickname of 'Punchy'. Norman and York had crossed paths before, lastly some time ago back in England where Norman had given York a severe reprimand for being drunk. The two men did not like each other, and it had taken the intercession of several other officers pleading York's good qualities as a Marine to have Norman accept him into the detachment. Another of the newcomers was Corporal David 'Lou' Armour who was looking forward to his year-long deployment as he recalled; "I went out there with positive thoughts, mainly because I was a weapons instructor and I was told that there was a big opportunity for a lot of field-firing. That was the sort of thing I was interested in. We were looking forward to what was going to be a fairly quiet year." - To which he later added simply; "Wrong." [2]

Mike Norman now briefed the men alongside his Colour Sergeant Major Bill Muir, a stocky Scotsman who looked every inch a Sergeant Major. Dick Overall, another of the new detachment recounted a stern lecture from Norman, reinforced by sterner looks from Muir. There had been rumours back from the Falklands that the detachment currently out there had 'gone native' and a report circulated to say that the Royal Marines were seen with long hair, drooping moustaches, a fondness for beer and – worst of all - earrings. Norman was determined that his men would not fall into the same disrepair; "You will not get into the Falklands way of life!" Norman had barked at them, "If you do, you will get a boot up your arse! You are Royal Marines!"

One of the Royal Marines, Gary 'Bungy' Williams, was going for his second tour in the Falklands, having already spent a year there as part of the 79/80 detachment and knew what it was like. It was inevitable in the end. He was personally looking forward to going back, although his initial experiences should have told him that this was not going to be an easy tour; "As we left RM Poole to Gatwick airport to catch the flight to Montevideo strange things started to happen," he remembered, "the coach we were travelling on had the windscreen *break due to a stone chip and we went on to Gatwick without a windscreen. We got to Gatwick and were told that we would be staying for 24 hours in Montevideo. No one had any foreign currency."* Now the plane left for Montevideo bearing what would henceforth be called the 82/83 Detachment NP8901. The men travelled, due to security and safety concerns, in plain civilian clothes and unarmed. There were uniforms on the Islands and enough weapons for the one detachment, which would be handed over by those who would soon be going home. For now, the joking, laughing bunch of forty-one Royal Marines would have looked more like holiday-makers than highly-trained specialists, at least to the casual onlooker.

In the Falkland Islands, the 81/82 detachment NP8901 were looking forward to going home. A year in the Falklands could be a long time; the southern hemisphere winters between May and September could be bitter and the summer was never exactly tropical: many days looked the same. The Royal Marines were based at the barracks at Moody Brook: the old wireless station which had been falling down when they had inherited it; even now it wasn't much, indeed a recent naval study had deemed it 'uninhabitable' but it was home – at least for the year. There had been a plan to replace the old wood and corrugated iron building with a modern complex in 1981 and design blueprints had even been produced, but like everything these days in the Falklands, the idea had been scrapped. Often, the Royals bunked down in the houses of the Falkland Islanders, which at least made their leave time feel somewhat homely; they were welcome to find 'alternative accommodation' if they could, and often found families to stay with. Every year several Island girls would get married to Royal Marines. Sometimes the girls would go back with them to the UK, a few times the Royals would stay in the Islands and some had children between them too. It was not like Northern Ireland in this sense; the Falkland Islanders were, on the whole, a very welcoming and friendly people who worked to make their home feel just a little more homely to the Royal Marines. Privately there was always fun-poking, of course, which is a great British tradition. The Islanders called the Royal Marines *'Booties'* - the Royals in turn called them *'Hobbits.'*[*3]

The Falklands was a quiet, friendly and tranquil place for the Royals, although for young men in the 1980's it was more like living in the 1940's at times; most houses did not have a television set and contact with the outside world was kept via radio. The most popular channel was the FIBS, followed by the BBC World Service. Other than that, only long-distance Argentine channels could be picked up, which were no use to the Islanders, most of whom did not speak Spanish. The quick way of getting a message to the other side of the Islands was simply to telephone the local FIBS radio station, as everyone was usually listening. Two Marines, Corporals Nick Williams and Neil *'Figgy'* Duff even had a 'slot' on the FIBS of their own, *'The Nick and Fig Show'* in which they would play popular music. Two of their most requested songs were that curious alternative national anthem of the British, *'Always look on the bright side of life'* from Monty Python and *'Three little birds'* by Bob Marley with the famous lines; *"Don't worry about a thing, 'cause every little thing is gonna be alright."* - both of which probably summed up the mood of the Falkland Islanders entirely.

Nick Williams was anticipating the end of his year-long tour with mixed emotions although he was looking forward to getting home to the UK to see his wife and children; *"A year is a long time to be away from home without any leave or regular contact."* he remembered, *"There was one flight a week that came from Argentina (the only link with the outside world) - our mail came on the flight, and that only happened when the Argentines felt like loading the BFPO mail sacks onto the aircraft. We went weeks without any mail, I think the longest was six weeks without our mail being put on the aircraft... we were very isolated."* Nevertheless, what with regular drill, good mates, nights at one of the several local pubs and his radio show with Figgy Duff, Nick Williams had a happy enough stay in the Falklands as he recalled; *"The Falklands were a wonderful place if you liked the outdoor life, wilderness and wildlife. The Kelpers were a very friendly bunch of people and would welcome you into their homes in Stanley. In camp, because of the isolation (at that time there were no roads), most times when you visited a settlement you were assured of a friendly welcome. If you took advantage of the hospitality and showed an interest into the way of life in the Islands during your deployment, you would take home some mementoes of your stay and some lifelong friendships."*

With a love of wildlife, nature and of photography, Nick Williams had been in his element in the Falklands. It was this which had drawn him to volunteer for service in the Islands and he was able to escape the months of inaction by indulging his passion. He volunteered often for duty in 'camp' – that being the term for largely anywhere outside of Stanley itself - and swapped shifts with others whenever he could. Camp life was friendly, the little settlements welcomed the Royals and there was a great sense of freedom. In this, Nick was joined by two others; Dave Gerrard known as *'Ginge'* for his red hair and Mick Sellen and together *'The three Amigos'* as they sometimes jokingly termed themselves, had a better time than most. When a section of men was asked for to travel to some of the outlying Islands and check for anywhere which might be usable as a landing zone for Argentine aircraft, they all volunteered at once and took the Falkland's patrol boat *Forrest* – little more than a tug - on a tour. This was a magical time for the small group of friends who remembered being buffeted in the sea by dolphins and even visiting the Jason Islands, being the first people to have set foot on them for three years. Here was a great colony of black-browed Albatrosses and also of King Penguins and, having no fear of humans, the Royals were able to get up close to the animals and even pose for photographs. In short, the Royal Marines of the 81/82 detachment NP8901 were looking forward to home but they were going to miss the Falklands and the Falkland Islanders immensely.

The 81/82 detachment was led by Major Gareth Noott, known as *'Gary'* for short, although he didn't much like it. Noott had been a Royal Marine since the age of nineteen – he was now thirty-seven - and had seen action in various places around the world including Aden and Borneo and he was not a complete stranger to Stanley before his deployment either, having commanded a platoon of Royal Marines on board HMS *Endurance* in 1969 which had put in frequently upon the Islands. He had been promoted just prior to his deployment in March 1981 and the briefing at the time was that the posting should be a quiet but watchful one and, in case of any invasion – not that it was considered in any way likely - he well-knew that his small force was to constitute what was known in military circles as a 'tripwire': a minimal commitment of men and resources which was effectively expendable, but whose being attacked would trigger a full-scale response.

The worry for Gary Noott, of course, was that Britain seemed to be both under-equipped and disinclined to actually react to any attack on his small command, and the constantly more aggressive stance from Argentina had been a natural concern. However, before he had departed from the UK almost exactly a year ago, intelligence reports suggested that the Falklands would remain safe, at least until Argentina had resolved its Beagle Channel dispute with Chile and as he recalled; *"My briefing suggested that there might be a lot of shouting, but nothing would happen."* Regular updates from London during the last year had only ever said the same thing.

Noott's biggest enemy on the Islands was, in reality, boredom. He had at his command forty young, energetic and often mischievous Royals and in the last year, he had found the challenge of commanding a group who, typically for young Marines in an isolated place, were prone to drinking away their year. Many had been warned before they had ventured out that the Falklands was a remote posting; that there was no night life, no disco's and none of the amenities and enjoyments of modern life to which the Royals had been accustomed to, indeed the national sport was darts which seemed to provide the only great enjoyment other than drinking or chasing girls, however some seemed to disregard the warning and many soon found themselves quite dispirited; *"The first three months were usually the hardest until the guys got to know the place and get used to no TV, no mail often for up to six weeks and the likes."* Royal Marine Andy Macdonald recalled, *"We usually just got pissed a lot."*

Andy's good friend and fellow Royal Marine Colin *'Tiny'* Jones remembered a great time being had in the Falklands and recalled the camaraderie in the detachment, where the men lived in close quarters, drinking, laughing and fighting, as fit - and often bored - young Marines often did; *"My best memories of the Falklands were that I was in great shape all the time and we really did have some of the best piss-ups of all time too,"* he remembered, *"it really is something to see a load of drunken bootnecks re-enacting the movie 'Grease', 'Airplane' or going around the town with only a sheet on, to a toga party. My room-mates over there were Jock Wilcox and Benny Bennett and our 'Grot' was called 'The Ghetto'. Everything was painted black and white – I mean everything – and we actually won the prize of a couple of cases of beer from the commander of HMS Endurance for 'Best Grot' which was never paid. Jock still complains about it to this day. Harry Dorey kept plants in his Grot – he would talk to them and all that jazz – I salt-watered them daily for him. 'Torchy' George Carr - great guy – called 'Torchy' because he showed us this great trick one night where he covered his hands in lighter fluid: you can guess the rest. Jock Milne – also known as 'The Ninja' – get him drunk and tell him some guy was looking at him and 'The Ninja' would always get his arse kicked! Of course, it wasn't a hundred per-cent 'love and kisses' detachment; you can't have that many guys living on top of each other without realising it and, to be honest, there were a few who, locked in a room with a porn-mag and the best wankers in the world, would still come out with a trophy."*

When not drinking, the Royal Marines – those not inclined to wildlife and nature - often attempted to make fun for themselves by tormenting their outnumbered senior officer and, when Noott had determined to make a kite to fly out at the water's edge, the Marines, seeking some devilment, had gathered and waited for something to go wrong; *"He used fishing line as the string,"* Marine Ray Bloye recalled, *"and duly sent the kite up into the sky. I have to say, it did look impressive and we were very surprised that he had made such a good job of it. The kite was getting higher and higher and I think Noott was getting quite excited by it. However, he had also lost concentration and all of a sudden, the kite started to tumble and fly very erratically. He had forgotten to tie off the end of the fishing line and the kite was now lost. We laughed (although out of his earshot) and thought it was hilarious. Sometime later, Noott appeared again with Kite mark 2. We gathered again (only a few of us) and thought 'this should be good'. In fairness, his previous kite was very good and we thought this one should be even better. Noott sent up the kite and once again it was doing really well and looked very impressive. It was getting higher and higher and we were thinking about his previous effort where he hadn't tied the fishing line on. We all believed he must have done that this time. When we thought the kite was about the same height as previously, we started to make comments about searching for the new kite again. I don't to this day know how we didn't die laughing but 'all of a sudden the kite started to tumble* and fly very erratically' and yes, you've guessed it, Noott hadn't tied the fishing line off again."

This kind of behaviour was, of course, something which all British officers were accustomed to. The class-distinction between officers and enlisted men had always created a 'them and us' situation which was tolerated by the officers. Noott ignored it often; it was good for morale. Sometimes when a man stepped over the line and was caught, his officer would put him on a charge. Most times, in any unit in the world, this made the enlisted men even more keen to get their own back. Curiously it worked, as it had always done, because it made the men think, communicate, bond and work together. It made them a team. A good officer learned that quickly; they could go so far, but if they were caught, they would be punished: that's how the game was played. Gary Noott knew this and accepted it and tried to give his small command as much gainful employment as he could in order to curb their ways which, if the inevitable boredom set in, could be troublesome; *"The main thing was to stop the Marines from going mad through boredom or inactivity."* he later said, *"There was always something to do though, not just limited to the football and rugger matches against the local Stanley team. When I took command, the situation was very different and the old plans really needed modifying, as did much of the equipment and our own knowledge of the area. I devised a simple system of breaking the detachment down into three sections – one would be on maintenance duty, the second would be training and the third would be patrolling out in camp - all on a weekly rotation. I saw the patrols in camp as paramount: it helped build up our very inadequate knowledge of the Falklands and its people and let them know that they were being protected. They needed to see us out and about on the farms and settlements and were always very welcoming to the Marines. It was all about information, preparation, prevention and cooperation. I saw the patrols, in particular, as a great opportunity for individual leadership in testing conditions for the Patrol Commanders."*

The training plan for the year was an essential part of the duties of an officer in the Falklands. It kept the men busy, kept them sharp and allowed them a good chance to gain some experience and due to the vast amount of open space there was no better place for live-firing exercises, which the Marines set to with enthusiasm. Noott was, at least, seconded by some good non-commissioned officers including Colour Sergeant Major John Noone – a Royal Marine of 27 years' service - including Malaya, Aden and Northern Ireland. Described as; *"both an excellent bloke and Sergeant Major – two positions which don't usually exist together"* Noone had been recommended for the Meritorious Service Medal and was looking forward to receiving it upon his return to the UK. Of other NCO's, Noott also had a raft of good, dependable sergeants and corporals, one of whom was Corporal Barry *'Geordie'* Gill – a qualified sniper who had married a local girl on a previous Falklands tour - and was happy to be back in his adopted home amongst friends and family. Geordie was what would be known in Britain as a true 'character' – a well-liked professional Royal Marine, a natural leader amongst the group and very popular among the people of the Islands, being described by his friend Nick Williams as *"Quiet but forceful, a bit of a legend in the corps."* He now came to Gary Noott and suggested that the Royals practice hostage rescue situations with live ammunition and hand grenades, and Noott was more than happy to let him run the exercises; *"Under Geordie's excellent management – which is to say that nobody actually got killed – each of the sections were trained to carry out live firing and hostage rescue in a timber and canvas simulated building,"* he recalled, *"It was basically the art of bursting in, firing a few shots and chucking grenades about the place. Obviously, there were no real live hostages, but there was a natural scope for fuck-ups if it went wrong! I declined on more than one occasion the offer to go along and watch – if anyone in the UK heard about it, I'm sure I would have been court martialled on the spot, so all I asked was for him to observe the blue book rules and such likes, and to come back at the end of each day to report no fatalities. I suppose it was a risk, but in the Falklands, you had the latitude to do that kind of thing and, if the men got something out of it, then I considered that it was of benefit."*

As well as the training plan and keeping the men busy, a part of Noott's duties as commander of NP8901 was to develop the annual 'defence plan' for the Islands. In truth, it was a paper-exercise; the small detachment could do very little to defend itself if attacked and most of the scenarios were based around events such as the 'Condor' raid of 1966 or the landing in the same year of Lombardo's twelve-man squad. Twice previously, a lone man from Argentina had come to the Islands in a light aircraft to cause more of a political embarrassment than anything else. In 1964 he had landed on the race course, handed a bemused Islander a note claiming the Islands for Argentina and had then taken off again. Four years later, the Argentine press had backed him to do the same again accompanied by one of the original Condor hijackers; this time he had failed to take account of the obstacles which were now placed on the racecourse to deter such landings, and this time he crash landed instead. These types of scenario were all considered in the defence plan. There was a plan, however useless, to attempt to retard a full-scale invasion if it came, but it was seen as something which would only come with good prior warning and, as the year went on, definitely not on Noott's watch. Still, he revised the defence plan to take account of the rising political tensions, drawing his forces closer to Stanley as his quarterly report from July 1981 stated; *"The original operational plan, which has been in being for some time, envisaged the detachment deploying to widely dispersed locations initially. This left the rifle* sections relatively isolated and liable to neutralisation or being bypassed. The revised plan reduces this possibility and allows for the closer defence of Stanley and ultimately the actual seat of Government. The other advantage of the revised deployment is that it will allow the detachment to react more flexibly to differing situations." - On the whole, it was expected that Argentina might make yet another ridiculous political stunt or statement, might land some people somewhere – perhaps by submarine - to fly a flag or distribute leaflets or something equally annoying, and there was a fear that some form of settlement might be landed on one of the outlying Islands (hence the tour of the *Forrest* to check for potential landing zones), but this was it and, if it happened, at least the Royal Marines were ready for it. The Royals trained some weekends with the men of the FIDF whose weapons, at least, had improved somewhat since the days of the Condor raid, but in total it was an ineffective force for anything other than a political charade, the likes of which, at least, they vaguely suspected might occur at some point, although Noott felt uneasy enough to make sure he would have all of his men to hand should the need arise, even repeating his request, in vain, for a mortar platoon, heavy support weapons and night sights, which he saw as woefully lacking should anything stronger than a diversion or raid come his way.

Still, despite Gary Noott's best endeavours to keep them occupied, when off duty, the Royals would mostly turn back to drinking to pass the time. Stanley had a few rough and ready pubs and it was a case of what Marine Andy Macdonald called *"Young men, cheap booze, bad combination"* - typically after closing-time, trucks would be sent into the town with duty drivers to pick up the Marines and take them back to Moody Brook barracks where they could be kept under control, and to where the bar – not restricted by licensing hours - was open much later. Freed from the 'spit and polish' of regular duty under watchful eyes, the Royal Marines in the Falklands grew their hair longer than was acceptable in the forces, and moustaches became fashionable as well as earrings, which the local men typically wore. These had to come off and hair be cut whenever the Royals were required to parade in front of the Governor alongside the members of the FIDF, but these were rare occasions, and even Gary Noott had his hair long. Certainly the appearance of the NP8901 detachment was a shock to those who – used to the more regulated ways of the British armed forces - saw them after a year's deployment in the Falklands. Nick Williams remembered that when he had first arrived in March 1981 he had seen the outgoing detachment who appeared to him and the rest of the newcomers to look scruffy and to be drinking a great deal too much; *"We thought to ourselves; 'I'm not going to end up like these piss-heads' but of course, by and large, we did."* - Once, back in December as the *Endurance* had pulled in to Stanley harbour on her way to the Antarctic Survey, Captain Nick Barker had inspected NP8901 and a report had found its way back to London about the long hair and earrings. Noott had, of course heard of it, but was determined not to lose much sleep over it. So long as the Marines got something of value out of their time in the Falklands, he could let such things pass. Out in the most far flung military outpost Britain had, 'spit and polish' had to take a back seat to comfort and practicality. Noott, sensibly, ignored it, although others did not.[*4]

By late March therefore, the Royal Marines were, for the most part, looking forward to going home. They had served their year and were happy to be returning to their families. Many of them were leaving behind many great friends and sometimes family and promised in many cases to put in again for NP8901 service before too long with one Royal, Dave Morris, successfully applying to serve in the next detachment for another year to stay with his wife Alana and their children. A few, with their bank accounts nicely full after a year of subsidised living, could not wait to get back to the UK and the modern life of the 1980's and as March drew on, they were looking forward to the final visit of the *Endurance* and welcoming the new NP8901 detachment to the Islands, which would involve a good final drink-up to greet the new arrivals, followed by a handing over of weapons and equipment before leaving for home. Gradually the Royals began to pack up their belongings, some paid last visits to local girls and families in Stanley and others, such as *'The three Amigos'* – Nick Williams, Dave Gerrard and Mick Sellen - took some last visits out to 'camp' at Green Patch to say goodbye to the people who had welcomed them so warmly throughout their year, which was now almost at a close.

The *Endurance* arrived on Saturday 20th March, bringing Nick Barker, Chris Todhunter, a small platoon of twelve Royal Marines under Lieutenant Keith Mills and several other sailors and hydrographers with her. She would berth in Stanley for a few days and then travel to Montevideo to pick up the new NP8901 detachment, drop them off in the Falklands and then head for home on her last voyage. During her brief stay, there would be the usual inspections and formal visits with the Governor Rex Hunt and a drinks party was proposed by Iain Stewart, the manager of the local Cable & Wireless Office for the officers, whilst the crew mingled with the Royals of NP8901 and went out on the town or drank in the Moody Brook bar where newcomers were always invited to scrawl their names and other slogans on the 'graffiti wall'. It was during the Cable & Wireless party that Chris Todhunter first heard some alarming news; *"A signal came in that the Argies had landed on South Georgia."* he recalled, *"The Governor, Rex Hunt, and our Captain and the Royal Marine Major and two or three of our other officers all went into a huddle in the kitchen about what should be done. That was fine, except all the booze was in the kitchen! And so, our hostess went in and said, 'Excuse me' and picked up the booze and came out again, leaving us all in there."*

South Georgia had been a small bone of contention for some time between the Falklands and Argentina and now it looked likely to be a 'tripwire' of its own, set to spark a confrontation. South Georgia was classified as a Falkland Islands Dependency and license had been granted in Scotland by Christian Salvesen for an Argentine firm under businessman Constantino Davidoff to scrap the old abandoned whaling station and factories on the Island. Davidoff's men had first caused ruffled feathers when they refused to present themselves to the British Antarctic Survey team at Grytviken which constituted the only British authority on the island, and next when they raised the Argentine flag in defiance of international law. This had met with protests both from the Falkland Islands Governor and also from London, and the situation had been tense for a couple of weeks. Finally, the Argentine flag was hauled down but reports of gunfire were heard by the British team there (which transpired to be Argentine crew hunting seals) and upon investigation, a detachment of Argentine Marines were soon discovered to have landed with the party. Codenamed Operation 'Alpha' it transpired that the Argentine Navy had effectively hijacked Davidoff's business enterprise to bring a small force ashore on the fleet transport ship *Bahia Buen Suceso* and to seize the Islands.

Now in Stanley, it was determined to respond. Already for the last two weeks, the Royal Marines had been in a heightened state of alert, what with the growing tensions over South Georgia and a number of other strange events and it was determined to send *Endurance* on to South Georgia the next day to defuse the situation. The ship would carry her party of Royal Marines (reinforced by nine men offered by Gary Noott to bring them up to a strength of 22) to strengthen the position although it was hoped that they would not be needed; Captain Nick Barker knew Captain Briatore of the *Bahia Buen Suceso* well from a time when they had been neighbours in Sunderland where their ships had been undergoing maintenance in the shipyard there and it was hoped that the two old friends might be able to sort the mess out between themselves. At about midnight, as the crew of the *Endurance* socialised in one of the local pubs with the Royal Marines of NP8901 and Lieutenant Mills' detachment, the music was suddenly stopped, and the DJ announced that the sailors and Royal Marine detachment from *Endurance* were to report to the ship immediately. The next day, Sunday 21st March, the sailors and Royals of the *Endurance*, some with sore heads from the night before, departed for South Georgia, leaving their eleven-strong survey team behind in Stanley; *"The ship sailed away and never came back!"* Chris Todhunter recalled. Now the survey team, stuck on the Falklands, determined to at least be productive with their time and, being lent a room in Government House for their purposes, began to make charts of the surrounding ocean using the raw data they had collected. In *Endurance*'s absence, a message was sent to the survey and supply ship RRS *John Biscoe* which was in the area, to make for Montevideo and to bring the new NP8901 detachment to the Falklands.*[5]

Peter Short, a fifth-generation Falkland Islander descended from one of the original Chelsea pensioners who had formed the first garrison and settlement in the Islands, was working privately at the time, providing Cape Pembroke lighthouse with supplies and visitors with trips to visit the penguin colonies. He had noticed curious flights and irregular happenings for a few weeks now, but on the day of the announcement of the South Georgia incident, he himself witnessed yet another sign that things were happening already which could only mean one thing; *"I was taking a bunch of Argentines to see the penguins at Kidney Cove, Murrell Farm,"* he remembered, *"When I went to Sparrow Hawk House to pick them up, the owner John Smith whispered to me that something had happened at South Georgia. On arriving at the Murrell Farm, I needed to tell the farmer, but because my passengers were Argentine, it was difficult. Eventually I got the owner on his own and told him what we thought, then left for the penguins. On arrival, my passengers had no interest in what they had paid money to see, and on returning to Stanley I mentioned to several people what I had experienced and was soon made aware as to what happened on South Georgia. Whilst at the penguins, an Argentine ship passed and sailed into Stanley – we now know with supplies for the invasion."* - The ship in question had been the *Yehuin* an Argentine oiling ship. When asked her business, the captain had stated that he was merely sheltering from bad weather: a curious statement considering that the weather was actually very calm. The men he had taken to the penguins this day were supposed to be LADE officers but nobody had seen them before. He noted that they paid extreme attention to the beaches instead. Something was definitely brewing, and he was not alone in his suspicions.

The next few days were more tense as Gary Noott's detachment was now reduced by nine men and military action was becoming increasingly more likely, with the fear that the recent flag-raising incident on South Georgia was potentially to be repeated in the Falklands. On the night of Saturday 20th – the night that the call had come to alert the Falklands to the situation in South Georgia - a small bunch of local youths, no doubt emboldened by alcohol and angered at the news, had broken into Vice Comodoro Gamin's office in the LADE building, draped a British Union Flag over the Argentine one and written *'tit for tat, you buggers'* across the desk. It was a small gesture of defiance, backed up two nights later by the spray-painting of *'UK OK'* on the outside wall of the building. In fairness it was justified, but unwise, for the newspapers in Argentina were soon inflating the story into an attack by an armed mob which had assaulted the Argentine workers in Stanley and torn down the Argentine flag from the flagpole outside of the building where it had been burned. There had, of course, been no mob, not one attack upon any Argentine and the flagpole so vividly described did not even exist, but the Argentine press lapped up the story and Rex Hunt, eager not to give any excuse for an escalation, went onto the FIBS radio to appeal for calm. Now Gamin was worried and more so in that one of LADE's Fokker aircraft had developed a fault and had to be left on the tarmac where it might present a tempting target to vandals. He now insisted that Gary Noott send a section to the airport to guard it overnight and Noott happily agreed: ever since events had begun to look increasingly suspicious, he had been keeping a section under cover at the airport already in case of incursions, with a support section ready and armed at Moody Brook should they be needed. Gamin's request now simply rubber-stamped his actions. The residents of Stanley, however, had heeded the Governor's words and there were no more incidents. The nights passed quietly but with the Royal Marines in a more heightened state of readiness than before.

Finally, on Monday 29th March, the survey and supply ship RRS *John Biscoe* came into port from Montevideo bearing the 41 men of the new 82/83 NP8901 detachment under Major Mike Norman. On deck, the new arrivals now had their first glimpse of Stanley and, as with all new arrivals, they goggled at the tiny stature of the place. Stanley was a small picturesque town built on a gentle slope running down to the harbour, dotted with multi-coloured houses made mostly of wood and with a few old Victorian and Edwardian brick-built houses – the kind one might see in London - which on the whole made the rest stand out as even more quaint and unusual. There was a great deal of greenery, hedges, bushes, flower gardens and white picket fences and the colour scheme was almost entirely white, with orange, red, blue and green dotted around typically on the rooftops as suited the owner. It looked tiny and delicate – a 'picture postcard village' almost - as the *John Biscoe* pulled in and Gary Williams remembered the scene; *"If I remember right it was around noon, a fine day and everybody was on deck waiting to dock at the government jetty at the rear of the town hall. There were lots of the Islanders, then I heard, 'Where's Bungy Williams?' - it was Nidge Bucket who I knew from the year I had spent on NP8901 in 79/80. We were all then taken to Moody Brook which was around a mile outside of Stanley, a journey I'd made lots of times before. We were then allocated our rooms and started to settle in, nothing much had changed at the Brook. We had a proper meal of roast mutton, the first we had really had in around five days, we then relaxed for the rest of the day."* - Mutton and potatoes, the staple diet of the Falklands which the Marines termed '365' for its regularity, was yet another thing that the newcomers would have to learn to get used to.

The two senior officers Mike Norman and Gary Noott knew each other from their earliest days in training and soon sought each other out. After friendly handshakes and the usual exchange of pleasantries, they met to discuss the hand-over of the command as the Royals under their command settled down to eat and socialise, updating each other on the situation which was brewing between Britain and Argentina and, being old friends, they sat down that night with a bottle of strong spirit to go through things. *"So what's the briefing from the FCO?"* Noott asked. *"Same as you had,"* Norman shrugged, *"they won't do anything until the Beagle Channel dispute is resolved. I'm told they're going to get stroppy, the LADE flights will probably be withdrawn and we'll see in eight months."*

Noott told Norman that all seemed, *prima facie* to be quiet in the Islands, however that the situation was becoming increasingly more suspicious. There had been reports from locals of strange aircraft noises overhead at night, of strange ships off the coast and of lights seen out at sea since December, and they were increasing in their regularity. The LADE flights were also becoming alarmingly erratic; in December the *Endurance* had been circled by an aircraft off its usual flight path which Vice Comodoro Hector Gilobert, the friendly and popular head of LADE had failed to be able to explain, later calling back to Argentina and being told that it was an unscheduled 'calibration flight' to test the beacon near the airport, an explanation which even he thought was weak in the extreme. Then there was the recent 'emergency' incident with the Argentine Hercules which had certainly not looked like it had come from a mail-drop to an Antarctic base when the Royal Marines had looked inside and even taken a photograph. It had complained of a fuel-leak yet the fire crew in attendance had seen no evidence of it, and also one of the technicians had afterwards rather worriedly informed the Governor's Chief Secretary Dick Baker that there had been no evidence whatsoever of a fuel leak as far as he had seen. This had been followed by Gamin's strange landing and claims of undercarriage problems in an aircraft carrying a very-obvious camera pod which had not made the routine stop by customs, and just recently there had been the incident with the Argentine officers at the penguin colony, who had seemed far too interested in the beaches for comfort.

On top of this rather blatant evidence there were still more indicators that the Islands were being spied out, including unscheduled nocturnal flights, two of which had dropped flares over Stanley, no doubt checking their accuracy in homing in on the LADE beacon at the airport, which would be reported back to them. Other reports told of a submarine which several people claim to have seen off the coast and evidence of people having come ashore as well, including farm gates being left open, damaged fences, military-style boot-prints and most recently, it was believed, a group of shadowy figures seen moving in the twilight with a military precision. There were even a number of supposed *'tourists'* and other strange faces which had been seen in Stanley, some taking photographs of local landmarks, buildings and even the Islanders themselves, which the locals had found at least quite odd. In short, something curious and ominous was happening; the Islands were being infiltrated, staked out and spied upon. Gary Noott knew only too well of the situation and had reported such things regularly back to Government House from where these reports were sent duly back to London, where the Foreign & Commonwealth Office seemed to whole-heartedly ignore them. There was, of course, always local gossip in the Falklands, but could everybody be wrong?[*6]

For his part, Mike Norman told Gary Noott what he knew; the *John Biscoe* had certainly been repeatedly 'buzzed' by an Argentine Hercules on the four-day journey from Montevideo to Stanley. The few Falkland Islanders on the vessel had been instantly enraged by the stunt, indeed the Hercules flew so close that it nearly touched the ship and the Islanders had to be restrained from turning the ship's fire-hoses on it. Not until this moment had Mike Norman realised the intensity of the feeling among the Falkland Islanders to the Argentines. Nobody in Britain had experienced the daily bullying and harassment, or even knew about it.[*7]

Before he departed, Major Norman had received several debriefings and intelligence reports on the situation which were less than comforting. He was told, as he had said, the same as Noott had been told when he took over the command; that Argentina would do nothing more than shout, make a noise, make life unpleasant and try to provoke a reaction, that they could, of course, always take the military route but that this was considered unlikely, however - an intelligence officer had told him - the Argentines were a very unpredictable race, so who knew what they might do? These words were greeted ominously by Norman and did not fill him with confidence although the general feeling was that Argentina might tighten the economic screw, blockade the Islands, cut off the fuel and withdraw the LADE flights. A sort of political strangle-hold would be placed upon them, but this was probably all, he was told. His next briefing was with members of the SAS and Norman, not feeling encouraged by the easy confidence of the intelligence staff, had asked how reinforcements were to be sent to the Islands in case of attack. He was told with a straight face and a large dose of irony that they would be parachuted in by Concorde. The message was certainly clear; if anything happened, he was on his own.

However, the tensions arising in South Georgia had certainly changed the situation and, at least until anything further was known, London ordered that Noott's detachment was to stay on the Islands until the *Endurance* and the nine men lent for the expedition came back safely. Until then, the men of Gary Noott's detachment would have to make way for the newcomers. They were allowed a quick two-minute phone call home to tell their loved-ones (the first call they had been allowed for twelve months) and then they piled arms in the armoury to be handed over to the new detachment and were found emergency lodgings in the houses of the Islanders who, with the rising tensions and that typical 'blitz spirit' of the British, welcomed them and did everything to make them feel at home. Two of *'The three Amigos'* Nick Williams and Mick Sellen were billeted together at the home of Trevor and Marjorie Bernsten, whilst Dave Gerrard, the third, billeted with another family, the Reids; *"I found it quite amazing that the people put us up and looked after us for that short period of time"* he later recalled. At least for a time there would be two detachments on the Falklands, although only with arms for half that number.

The men of the new detachment, meanwhile, were first installed in Moody Brook where they dropped their gear and then were inducted into the makeshift bar there which could accommodate the men of both detachments who now got to know each other. Typically during 'handover week' the bar would be kept open almost constantly to allow the outgoing detachment to unwind and the newcomers to get a feel for their surroundings, which would also keep them away from the town until they knew the basic 'do's and don'ts' of Falklands life and the little idiosyncrasies such as not swearing in the town; *"We had just moved into our accommodation at Moody Brook and were finding out where we were going to sleep,"* Lou Armour recalled, *"meeting the lads who were already there, whom we were going to replace. We were 'sussing out' what we were going to do for a year, which didn't seem like very much. I hadn't a chance to see all the Island, but my first impression was that it was pretty barren."*

That night, the old detachment welcomed in the new with a few drinks in the Moody Brook bar, *'The Frog and Nightgown'* as it had long since been known, although the reason for this name had long ago been lost to memory. Danny Betts recalled a room with two barrels in the centre of the floor, each adorned with a pyramid of beer cans. One stack was of green cans, the other of red; they both tasted the same. Each time a beer was removed, it seemed to be magically replaced moments later. It was, as Andy Macdonald remembered, *"a mega piss-up – if the Argies invaded then, they could have taken us with a wet lettuce as everybody was legless – I was comatose on the floor."*[*7]

As Gary Noott and Mike Norman caught up on the strange and ominous goings-on, so the men of the two NP8901 detachments drank and chatted long into the night, unaware that somewhere out at sea, riding the waves in a furious black tempest, an armada of men and ships were coming ever-closer to the Falkland Islands.

Chapter 4: April Fools

"I really don't find this particularly fucking funny!"
Dave 'Ginge' Gerrard – April 1st 1982.

The next morning, Tuesday 30th March, the Falklands seemed different. The outgoing detachment was now staying – at least for a time - and everybody was waiting to hear the news from South Georgia as fears grew that something similar, perhaps even bigger, was intended for the Falklands; *"By this time we were on full alert as it was clear that something was going on,"* remembered one of 'The three Amigos' Dave Gerrard, *"Normally when the new detachment arrived, there was lots of socialising going on, both between the two detachments and the locals in town. Clearly this was not going to happen this time."* - Now the men began to check their kit and prepare for whatever might come, although as Nick Williams recalled; *"We didn't have a clue what was going on."*

Gary Noott and Mike Norman both went to Government House that day to talk with Rex Hunt. The Falklands' seat of government was a large Victorian manor house just to the west of Stanley and separated from the town by the local hospital, a small brook which ran into Stanley Harbour, then a football pitch and surrounding grounds and gardens. The original building had been made with bricks and tough Falklands stonework and extensions and out-houses had been built in wood with a large glass-fronted area at the back overlooking the gardens where Mavis Hunt, the Governor's wife, kept a beautiful vegetable garden and rose bushes. Out on the front lawn, a flagpole stood, upon which fluttered the Union Jack, the very symbol of British sovereignty over the Islands.

Rex Hunt himself was an experienced diplomat. Now 55 years old, he had joined the RAF in 1944 after several years as a cadet and had flown Spitfires both during and after the war. He had left in 1948 and had spent his years in the Colonial Service, finishing in Uganda in 1963. From then, he had seen the world in a number of diplomatic postings, from Sarawak and Sabah through to Indonesia, Brunei, Malaysia and then, at perhaps the most demanding point of his career, he had served at the British embassy in Vietnam during both the Tet Offensive and at the fall of Saigon in 1975 which had been a terrifying ordeal. In January 1980 he had been posted to the Falkland Islands with a remit from the Foreign & Commonwealth Office to persuade the Islanders that Argentine rule was in their best interests. From his first day to the present, however, he had never believed this and had fought to represent their rights. A polished, though blunt-speaking Yorkshireman, the Falkland Islanders loved him and the FCO complained regularly that he too had *'gone native'*. The three senior men now looked over Gary Noott's defence plan which he had revised in the previous winter upon taking over the detachment and which, in the light of growing tensions and aggressive behaviour from Argentina, he had recently revised again, the current plan only having been approved a few weeks before by the Governor. The plan to counter a full-scale invasion was one which nobody had ever envisaged might be required, but which now the three men studied at length. There were three key points to it; firstly, that there should be no fighting in Stanley itself, which would spare the populace the ravages of war, secondly that the Governor should be protected at all costs and thirdly that there should be an initial stand of extreme, violent and bloody opposition which would delay the invading force and, essentially, which would rack up casualties so that Argentina could not go on to claim a 'peaceful annexation' to the world. Politically they would have to appear as the aggressor, not some phoney-liberator, and the stand made would allow for at least one section of Marines to spirit Rex Hunt away into 'camp' where there were a number of prepared dumps complete with preserved food, clothing and shelter. This, it was hoped, would give the United Kingdom time to react or the United Nations time to intervene.

However, Hunt now declared that he would not flee into 'camp' and had only agreed to the idea of laying dumps so that the Royal Marines, if attacked, might find sanctuary if the worst was to happen. He was not about to go with them and live like a hermit in exile; if an invasion came, he would meet it as a senior British diplomat and Governor and spare himself the ignominy of being captured in a cave half-way up a hill and paraded like some escaped convict. The news from London did not seem to offer any reassurance as to the political situation being resolved and although the defence plan was a simple yet effective one, Mike Norman decided that he was, in his own words *"sufficiently worried"* enough that he now asked Gary Noott to walk him through it as he had had no time to even become familiar with the town, the beaches or the best places for defence.

Together the two old friends left Government House and began to look over the town, heading towards the beaches and the airport when they bumped into Vice Comodoro Hector Gilobert, the former chief of LADE until he had been replaced by Gamin, who was supposed to be back in Argentina. Gilobert told them that he had returned to help sort out the LADE accounts, and Gary Noott quipped that he could come and help them with the accounts at Moody Brook when he had finished, as these were in a mess, and the three men had laughed and moved on. Having walked through the basics of the defence plan, surveyed the beaches and the airport and the one road which led from the airport to town, the two officers began to discuss scenarios and assess any modifications which the plan might require, especially as they now had a few more Marines than the original plan had envisaged. On the way back to Moody Brook, they met a trio of UK journalists outside the Upland Goose Hotel who were seemingly led by Simon Winchester of the *Times* who asked them what was going on. Mike Norman replied that they had better come to Moody Brook for tea and tell him and Noott what was going on as they hadn't a clue, although the arrival of the three journalists set him ill at ease and he asked if their presence meant he should start to worry.

The mood in Stanley was now a strange one. On the surface it all seemed quiet; there was no activity, no news from London and no news from South Georgia either, indeed everything seemed to be perfectly normal, yet there was *something* – undetectable, silent and ominous - a foreboding or a feeling perhaps? A calm before the storm which made the men more tense and alert. Perhaps it was instinct. Stanley seemed its usual quiet self. The people talked about the threat from Argentina, of course, but it was not pressing on their minds. People spoke of South Georgia and eyed their Argentine visitors suspiciously, speaking in hushed tones whenever they went past, but this was normal to a degree and life seemed to pass by as ever it did in that 'Keep calm and carry on' way. Mike Norman remembered that still, with military action and invasion at least highly likely, he was required to attend a drinks reception, dinner party or buffet every night that week. The idea of an invasion was simply impossible to comprehend. Okay, many thought, they *could* but nobody ever thought for a moment that they actually *would*. Invasions – at least for the British - were something for the history books. Surely nobody would actually invade the peace and tranquillity of the Falklands? Yet despite the still-relaxed attitude of many of the Falkland Islanders, Majors Noott and Norman began to view the situation with a growing uneasiness.

The next day, both Noott and Norman were called up to Government House where there was fresh news from London which now altered the situation dramatically; US Intelligence had intercepted a partially complete radio signal which had been telexed in via 'signit' - the secure communications line from the FCO. The message went something like *"...recce party due to land tonight at* (garbled) *south of Stanley..."* it wasn't quite clear how fresh the intelligence was – it might have already happened or else still be about to - *"Just look at a map of the coastline 'South of Stanley' and it is obvious that, given the limited manpower and surveillance equipment there was no practical way of covering that distance."* said Gary Noott, *"I turned to Rex and said; 'We can look for them but the chance of finding them... what's the point?'"* - Rather than send much-needed men off searching for what might or might not be there, it was safer to have all of the men close to hand and under orders. Rex Hunt was sure that the intelligence was fresh and told Noott and Norman that it was likely that an Argentine submarine might carry out a 'surfaced overt' mission in the next day or so. Mike Norman, turning to

Gary Noott, questioned it. Would anyone honestly carry out a reconnaissance in a surfaced submarine in Port William or Stanley Harbour where everyone could see it? It seemed unlikely. Nevertheless, they had to take the threat seriously and now began to study a large map of the area and identify the best points for defence. The men would be put on standby, the rapid reaction force was to be reinstated at Moody Brook and it was decided to send a small section to Cape Pembroke lighthouse and another to Sapper Hill to the south-west of Stanley which would have a good commanding view of the beaches. The orders were that the sections were to look out for a submarine and observe and, if any Argentine forces did come ashore, to 'arrest them peacefully.'

Gary Noott and Mike Norman headed back for Moody Brook and called the Royal Marines to a briefing as Nick Williams remembered; *"A briefing was held in the dining hall. We were given an update on South Georgia and what was thought might happen on the Falklands. It was assessed that the Argentines may try to land a party of men from a submarine close to Stanley and raise the Argentine flag. I was briefed to take three Marines to Cape Pembroke lighthouse and keep watch for the submarine and any landing party. I was ordered to take a radio, binoculars and an IWS (1st generation night-vision goggle) to aid me. In a functioning lighthouse, the IWS was a complete waste of time; every time the light went round, it blanked out. There was no mention of weapons, so I questioned Major Noott about it and he said no weapons were to be taken as we didn't want to alarm the lighthouse keeper. I told him that I wanted some weapons for self-defence; if we did see a landing party, what were we supposed to do? Cape Pembroke is about 40 minutes from Moody Brook and any reinforcements. There was a bit of a stalemate. In the end, Sergeant Shepherd who was stood behind Major Noott signalled me to be quiet and winked at me. When the briefing was finished, Sergeant Shepherd told me to get a holdall and go to the armoury where he gave me an SMG (submachine gun) and some ammunition for each man. He told me to keep the weapons out of sight. My observation party was driven to the lighthouse and dropped off. When we arrived, I told the keeper there was nothing to worry about and we made ourselves comfortable. I set up a watch routine and we kept the weapons hidden."*
Along with Nick Williams were his fellow DJ Figgy Duff, Michael *'PJ'* Berry and also Ray Bloye, the Royal who had so humorously described Gary Noott's kite incident; *"I don't know if I should feel privileged or sad that Nick and I were the last ones (besides the lighthouse keeper) to see the lighthouse lit."* he remembered, *"From that time to today, the light has never been back on. And so our long watch commenced... I know that in this period I had about five hours' sleep in three days."*

For Gary Noott and Mike Norman, the situation seemed tense, but under control. At last they had some intelligence and it was only what they had feared - a submarine and a landing - perhaps a flag being raised for political bluster but nothing more. Arresting the Argentines, if they came, might be difficult, but it was clear that the situation – if and when it came – should be dealt with gently. An arrest would certainly be a lot less embarrassing than an actual shooting-match or casualties which could spark a confrontation. Certainly some more intelligence was needed though. There were British agents in Buenos Aires who, although well-known to the authorities and certainly not 'secret agents' might have picked up some more information. This being the day that the usual run to Buenos Aires with the 'diplomatic bag' for the Consulate was due to happen, it was decided to keep up the routine and see if anything could be found out. The mission was always accompanied by at least one Royal Marine for protection and Dave Morris was sent for the task. It was a hard decision, as he was leaving his wife Alana and their children in Stanley, and it would leave the Royal Marine detachment yet another man short if any attack came. The LADE flight took off from the airport bound for Buenos Aires. Almost instantly, Dave Morris noticed a curious problem; the aircraft was circling in a strange pattern for some time before heading in a different direction – he later realised that it was to ensure that he did not see the Argentine task force at sea.

One thing which did have to be addressed was the lack of weapons for the men. Normally, each new detachment simply inherited the weapons of the outgoing detachment, but now this was obviously impossible. Luckily, the FIDF had an armoury which contained modern weapons and several Marines were sent off with a truck to gather up some of the SMG's and the faithful SLR Self-Loading Rifles which were the mainstay of the British military. It was a long-barrelled high-velocity single-shot weapon which fired a 7.62mm bullet from a 20-round box magazine. The range and accuracy were impressive, the stopping power absolute and the damage caused almost always lethal. The British had long-since Christened it *the elephant gun*. Now these were taken out to the firing range where their new owners tested them and adjusted the sights to perfection.[1] That night, the Royal Marines waited. Some were at Cape Pembroke lighthouse, some at Moody Brook and some out on the heights south of Stanley. The rest slept uneasily. Was something actually coming? Was it all just some latest charade which would blow over? Was there really a submarine out there in the darkness? It all seemed so fanciful.[2]

Out in the dark, masked by the wind and the waves, something stirred beyond Cape Pembroke lighthouse where Nick Williams, Ray Bloye, PJ Berry and Figgy Duff stood watch. It was small and undetectable as it drew closer, careful to stay out of the revolving beam projected from the lighthouse: a snorkel of a submarine. Through the periscope, Lieutenant Commander Alfredo Cufre of the *Buzo Tactico* now began to scan the area. It was marked on his plans as *'Red Beach'*

– the area where he was to land, create a bridgehead and then lead his team to secure both the airport and the lighthouse itself. Scanning his periscope over Stanley, he saw the twinkling lights of the houses, the glow of stoves showing through windows and the beams of car headlamps as civilians drove home for the night; *"Everything was normal,"* he remembered, *"a small town running."* Yet there was nobody to begin the invasion. It was 23:00 on March 31st and according to the plans, the invasion should be starting now but the fleet, rocked, buffeted and delayed by the tempestuous weather was still out at sea. The invasion would have to be delayed. His study of the area complete, Cufre collapsed his periscope and the ARA *Santa Fe* slipped back into the darkness of the South Atlantic.

April 1st 1982 dawned bright and sunny in the Falkland Islands. The night had passed peacefully. The section in the lighthouse had seen nothing whilst those who had camped out on the Murray Heights stamped the life back into their legs and waited to be relieved so that they could return to Moody Brook and have some hot food. Gary Noott and Mike Norman checked in the sections and any reports of activity; there had been none - no submarine, no flag being raised - it might all come to nothing, but it was best to be on guard. The morning passed uneventfully. The new detachment, most of whom had been busy making Moody Brook homely and eating and drinking at the barracks bar, were allowed to venture into the town. They had been in Stanley long enough to let their exuberance wear off and, with no knowledge of the island or even of Stanley, they had been largely kept away from everything. If anything did happen, they might well simply get lost and so it had been deemed appropriate to simply keep them away from the town and the people and to let the experienced guys pull 'submarine-watch' duty.

Noott and Norman were still on edge and did a tour once again of the area, surveying the beaches around Yorke Bay, the airport and then visiting the lighthouse where Nick Williams' small section was awaiting relief. It was 15:00 as they stood scanning the coast that the radio now crackled into life; it was from Moody Brook on behalf of Rex Hunt. He had received an encrypted 'secret/flash' telegram from London and now needed them back at Government House immediately. They at once left the lighthouse, leaving Nick William's' section to sit and await the relief section which they had hoped and assumed were coming and raced back to Government House. The journey from the lighthouse to 'GH' as it was known, took them 45 minutes. At Government House, Rex Hunt now met the two officers with an embarrassing piece of protocol; the 'signit' or signals intelligence could only be shared with the Officer Commanding NP8901 and, as Mike Norman was now officially the OC, Rex Hunt had to ask Gary Noott to leave the room. Now alone with Mike Norman, Rex Hunt fixed him with a grave look; *"We've got another signit."* he said resignedly, *"I'll read it to you: 'We have apparently reliable evidence that an Argentine task force will gather off Cape Pembroke early tomorrow morning, 2nd April. You will wish to make your dispositions accordingly'."*

For a moment, there was silence and then Norman cursed and let out a short, sharp rant. For twenty-five years the British had been calling Argentina's bluff and now, on his tour and only a few days into his new command, he was going to catch the full force of the invasion. Rex Hunt stared at him calmly and then pronounced simply; *"It sounds like the buggers mean it."* Mike Norman thought for just a second, composed himself and then told Hunt he would prepare. There would be a lot to do in a short time and he would come back and update Hunt when he was ready, and with that he left the room to find Gary Noott pacing up and down anxiously outside the door. Hurriedly Mike Norman gave him the whole story and the two decided that it was time to get moving – and quickly. The first thing he did was to visit the naval hydrographers whose charts of the area would now come in very handy; *"Look, the Argentine fleet appears to be at sea and getting closer,"* he told Chris Todhunter, *"we've got to prepare for an invasion. Where do you guys think the most likely landing areas are?"* Now Todhunter and his colleagues pulled out their maps and charts and gave him a few ideas. If the Argentines were coming, the Yorke Bay beaches would be a prime location. Norman now asked him if his Navy men could take up arms and support the Marines if an attack came as 'additional rifles pointing outwards'; *"I said 'Yes, of course, but you've got to bear in mind that my guys are only sailors, engineers, cooks, stewards, mapmakers... and you'll have to remind them which is the sharp end of the rifle!'"* Todhunter recalled.

With an idea of which direction the attack would come from and a small, if unprepared, force of Navy men, the first thing to do would now be to gather in the Royal Marines and get them ready for action. Many of them were out in Stanley; some were in the pub or out to lunch, many of the new detachment had gone into town to buy stationary for writing home and warm clothes for the winter which would soon be upon them. Even the ten hydrographers (the 11th man, Leading Seaman Brook, had been left at Green Patch to maintain tidal records) were cleared out of GH and ordered to assemble at Moody Brook; combat was not their thing, but they were serving Royal Navy men, and everybody was needed. Quickly, trucks drove off into Stanley to find the men and bring them back to the Brook where Mike Norman and Gary Noott waited to brief them and, although nothing had been said, many of the men could already guess what it was about. Danny Betts and the men of the new detachment were just finding their way around their new surroundings as he recalled; *"We had literally just arrived and were in town when Andy Timms drove up with a message from Sergeant-Major Muir; 'We want you back now' he said, 'apparently they're coming.' But it was April 1st – April Fool's*

Day, so we all just laughed! 'Yeah right I said! Fucking April Fools, right? Aye, fucking good one!' - I swear, we all thought it was a joke, just keeping up morale! But Andy looked at me seriously and said again, 'Mate... they're coming. He wants you back now.'"[3]

Geordie Gill was an easy man to find; having been back and forth to the Falklands since 1967 he was now on his fourth NP8901 tour and, having children, family and a great many friends in the Islands, had his lodging above the *Globe* bar which was owned by a relative by marriage. The duty driver found him in his room after a few drinks as he was preparing for lunch as he remembered; *"I was staying at the Globe when the duty driver from the new detachment came and told me I had to go with him and show him where our lads were staying with friends in town and pick them up and get them back to Moody Brook. When we arrived and as the lads were getting off the truck, I went to see Gary Noott to see what was going on as the lads wouldn't be happy if it was just another drill. He said, 'It's not. I'll tell you but don't tell the others until I can brief them.' He then told me to close the bar. Not a popular move with sixty-plus Marines wanting a few beers with their mates! The new detachment was already in there. I told the barman quietly to close up and he looked at me and said, 'Is it THAT serious?' - 'Put it this way,' I said, 'you don't want the lads drunk.'"*

Now the Royals, grumbling as they went, assembled in the bar area, some grabbing seats with others sitting on the floor as latecomers arrived and a murmur of *'April Fools'* amongst them. Despite the seriousness of the situation, George Brown was still waiting for the joke to be revealed; *"I thought, 'Is this some kind of initiation? Every April the first, the new section gets told the Argentines are going to invade?' - I was convinced they would start laughing any second. They didn't."* - Soon the reality became apparent, as Ray Bloye, fresh from Cape Pembroke lighthouse recalled, *"If we hadn't been on standby for so long, I would have thought the day – April Fool's Day – was living up to its reputation. As it was, it was fairly serious. Having spent most of my time up at the lighthouse since Mike Norman's detachment arrived, I really hadn't got to know any of the new guys other than two of them I knew from when I was in 40 Commando. This briefing was the first time we'd all been together since they arrived."*

Finally, the room grew silent and Mike Norman took the floor; *"Now this isn't an April Fool's joke,"* he started, as the Marines remembered, *"those of you who thought you were going home, we've got new plans for you. It looks like the silly buggers are heading towards the Islands. They will be here tomorrow and it is very likely they will invade. We will now start getting the defence plan ready. Tomorrow is the day you'll really earn your pay."* The mood amongst the Royal Marines was, remembered Geordie Gill, calm. Men who had waited for the punchline of *'April*

Fools' somehow knew already that it was not coming, and Mike Norman's stern face told them that this was no joke. It was what they were there for, Geordie Gill remembered afterwards; what they had trained for, and now everybody wanted to prove themselves. Corporal Lou Armour had been sat in the bar when Geordie Gill had been ordered to close it, and now he too faced the reality; *"We thought the Argentines would land and then say: 'We can land here if we want.' We didn't really believe there was going to be a full-scale invasion... We didn't know where they were going to come from and we didn't have the equipment to defend the Islands."*

Now Mike Norman now set out the plan: The two detachments were going to break into small sections to be harder to detect. It was likely – according to intelligence - that the Argentine force would come ashore off of Yorke Bay, capture the airport and then move inland, up the narrow isthmus and onto the airport road, heading towards Stanley, Government House and lastly Moody Brook. The plan would be for a 'rolling defence' to meet them head on at the beaches first and then for each section to 'pepper-pot' back under cover of the supporting sections. Each stand would, it was hoped, cause damage and casualties and force the Argentines to stop and deploy. When they came again, the sections would pull back again and repeat the process. This would buy time, time which would be needed for London or Washington or the United Nations to intervene. If they could retard the advance, cause maximum casualties and stack the Argentines up, they might think again and perhaps someone, somewhere, would start negotiating. Finally, there was to be a last stand at Government House, and then God only knew what. As Gary Noott later recounted; *"The basic fact of our situation was that, from the minimal information we had, it was obvious that the opposition could, and would, come with sufficiently large forces to preclude prolonged, organised resistance – in other words, the thought of winning was impractical; it was merely a question of how long we could resist before being overwhelmed. Quite how long that would be remained variable, but the outcome was in little doubt."* There was a hope that, if resistance was strong and the Argentine force weak, they might simply pull back, but privately Mike Norman thought he knew what kind of force must be coming. He had been asked by one of his Marines prior to embarkation what the best thing was that they could do if the Argentines did come, and how many men they would send. Thinking about it, Norman had replied that he would not attack with much less than a brigade if it were him, and if that was the case, the best thing the Marines could do would be to go fishing for the day!

Two Scots – Roderick *'Jock'* Wilcox and Les *'Ninja'* Milne - were to be at the sharp end of the beach assault. They would have a GPMG and be emplaced in a 'shell-scrape' behind barbed wire. When the Argentines came up the beach in landing boats, they were to fire a belt's worth of ammunition – 200 rounds – into them and then run for it to where two canoes were on the shore. From here they would paddle across a short stretch of water to where two motorbikes would be waiting for them to head back towards Stanley and link up with the first section they came across. Their crime had been to admit that they could both ride a motorbike, yet Ray Bloye remembered feeling that he wished he could have been one of them. Nick Williams remembered differently; *"I will never forget the looks on their faces,"* he said of it, *"It was a death sentence."*[*4]

Gradually each section was allocated their tasks, with Ray Bloye and Nick Williams ordered to go back to the lighthouse to give advanced warning and then take up a position on the Murray Heights to the south of Stanley, which overlooked the beaches and coves to that side and which was also a potential landing site for a helicopter. All other sections were to take up positions between the isthmus (known as the 'Canache') and Stanley, one more would be posted on the far side of the harbour opposite the narrows to Yorke Bay in case of a direct seaborne attack upon GH and any others were to assemble at GH itself and prepare for the defence of the place. Trucks would be on standby there to take men and ammunition up to the front of they were needed, or to take casualties back. Finally, Mike Norman asked if there were any questions; the only ones asked were as to ammunition counts and if they could have more. Norman told them that all quotas were a minimum; so long as they could carry it, they could take what they liked.

Now the Royal Marines went to work. Trucks were sent to clear out the remaining stores of extra weapons from the FIDF headquarters as the men were led to the armoury and ammunition dump: great metal shipment containers which contained all of the armaments for the detachment. Each man was issued with an SLR and five magazines – a hundred rounds a man - and then the doors to the containers were thrown open and the men were invited to help themselves; *"We didn't need to be asked twice,"* remembered Gary Williams. Only now did the reality of the situation seem to hit home. There was none of the usual paperwork or officiousness which went with taking anything out of the armoury. Now the men were simply let off the leash to take whatever they wanted and whatever they thought might keep them alive. Nick Williams remembered that; *"We could take as much as we could carry. There was going to be no resupply. Once the shooting started, we were on our own. I think all of our thoughts were 'no this is really not happening, not to me'... even Mike must have had those thoughts."*

For once ignoring what they termed the 'Gucci' stuff – which included leather gloves and the much-coveted watches - the men now stocked up, trying to cover every eventuality as they went; *"As I had never fired my new SLR before, I didn't know if the sights were okay for me or way out,"* recalled Ray Bloye, *"I therefore* grabbed 40 rounds of tracer so my first mag was solid tracer. I then mixed up my other mags with tracer, about 1 in 4 or 5: I was determined to know where I was shooting. I then grabbed a further 300 rounds in bandoliers, two 66mm LAW anti-tank rockets, two high explosive grenades and two white-phos grenades. We were all also given a tray of GPMG ammo (200 rounds per tray) but I took an extra one so had 400 rounds of gun ammo. We were given rations for a couple of days and a spare battery for the radio."

Danny Betts was elated at the offer to disgarnish the armoury of anything and everything to be used at once; *"It was great,"* he recalled, *"for once we didn't have to fill out any of the stores paperwork three times over and we could just take what we wanted. There were lads literally carrying out boxes of stuff."*- He and George Brown now helped themselves to one of the two Carl Gustav 84mm rocket launchers and a few twin-packs of rockets, which were the heaviest weapons on the Islands and George Brown produced a brand new Berghaus Bergen which he had bought just prior to leaving for the Falklands into which he now crammed extra magazines, belts of link, grenades and then crammed a stack of 84mm on top of that just to be sure. *"It was so weird to grab-and-go-dash and pack however you wanted to,"* remembered Tiny Jones, *"in the RM it was always so strict, signing out shit, weapon numbers, ammo and the like. Me personally, I heard the words, 'We will probably end up fucking off into the hills', so I grabbed my SLR and as much 7.62 as I thought I could run with after a skirmish, and I was good with that. I would have liked a 9mm also, but by now there were no more available."*

Whilst some packed light, so as to be able to fire and manoeuvre at speed, many others armed up with as much as they could physically carry; *"I knew we were in the shit,"* Andy Macdonald remembered, *"it was 'Open House'. I took 12 mags and about 8 bandoliers and was issued one white phos and a 66mm."* Others did the same; *"It was like little kids in a sweet shop,"* remembered Gary Williams, *"I picked up a pack of mini flares thinking if it came down to the fact that I ran out of ammo, then I had something I could fire at the enemy, along with my boning and filleting knives just in case of a bit of hand-to-hand, or for taking to the hills for slaughtering purposes – always being practical minded!"* Geordie Gill, as a trained sniper, reached at once for his faithful L42 sniper rifle and, as he recalled; *"My first thoughts when the stores were opened was that this time it was really serious, I had an SMG and 5 bags with extra 9mm ammo, as an L42 is not ideal for close quarter fighting which I guessed it would come down to at the end!"* Marine Marc Branch, at 19 the youngest man in the detachment, had the same idea; *"I think I walked out looking like a squirrel with its nut allotment for the '82 winter deployment,"* he said, *"bulging from every pocket with every grenade I could get my hands on, a 66mm rocket launcher, 7.62 rounds, my survival knives and I may even have had my Sony Walkman handy!"*

Lou Armour, heading Section One, recalled that; *"Because of where we were being deployed – covering the isthmus – I asked if my section could have two GPMG's but it was agreed that a shortage of guns meant I could take only one. We loaded up with link, grenades and 66's and I told my guys to grab their small ear defenders as I wanted everybody to be able to hear me should it get noisy."* Meanwhile, Wilcox and Milne – the two Scotsmen who were to meet the beach assault head-on - took not 200 but 800 rounds for their GPMG. They looked for a spare barrel as, after 500 rounds, the barrel would expand, and the gun would jam and be useless - there were no spares. They took the ammunition anyway.*5

The men of the Naval hydrography department were also to be armed and they were given SMG's to cries of laughter and *"Matelots with guns! We're in trouble! Show them which bloody end to use!"* Nick Williams felt sorry for them and tried to give them *"lessons one-to-six in how to use them all in about five minutes"* as Dave Gerrard joined him and demonstrated over and over; *"You put the magazine in the side, you pull back the lever and you pull the trigger. When it stops firing, you pull the mag out, check to make sure there's no bullets in there in case you have a jam, then you put the next mag in, pull the lever back and away you go again...."* after which, the men from *Endurance* were handed over to the experienced watch of Colour-Sergeant Noone. Meanwhile, the Royal Marines packed away ammunition and both fragmentation and phosphorous grenades into every pocket, hung bandoliers of bullets across their shoulders, grabbed sniper rifles, GPMG's, 9mm pistols and SMG's and seized hold of the 66mm LAW – Light Anti-Tank Weapon – an American-made one-shot disposable rocket launcher, of which there were at least several boxes full and Lance Corporal Michael *'Burt'* Reynolds backed a Land Rover up which the men packed full of weapons and ammunition of every sort. Gary Noott checked the detachment's only mortar: it was cracked. He swore to himself. He had put in for two replacement 81mm mortars some time ago to replace the lone and rather feeble 60mm but then, so had his predecessor and still they had been forgotten.

Of the SLR's liberated from the FIDF headquarters, it was found that there were some slight differences with the Marines' own weapons as PJ Berry remembered; *"There was a problem with them where our magazines wouldn't fit unless the gun was cocked, and we never had time to fire them before we were give them, so the new detachment had our weapons and the blokes from our detachment had the defence force weapons."* Worse still, many of the FIDF rifles were still packed and had to be thoroughly cleaned as Andy Macdonald recalled; *"I was issued with a manky FIDF weapon that was still in grease, and I had to clean this off... my weapon would only fire four rounds at a time, then would have to be unblocked... I was trying to swap the manky FIDF SLR with some of the new blokes*

– and was promptly told to 'Fuck off' - I was dejected and nearly in tears sitting there removing years of grease." If anyone in the detachment knew that they were coming, it was Andy Macdonald; *"I was in Argentina in January '82 and we knew something was up then."* he remembered, *"I was even warned by a Chilean Marine SNCO."* - it was not a comforting thought that the 8901 detachment was so woefully under-manned and equipped when everyone, apparently, barring the British government, seemed to know that it was coming.*[6]

To defend the beach, a few Claymore mines were made up and men were sent to gather old oil drums to fill with rocks and munitions to see if they could make makeshift mines or mortars out of them but this plan was later abandoned. In the stores, just two rolls of somewhat rusty double-dannert barbed wire – fifty yards in total were found - barely enough for one beach. This would pose a problem; in Yorke Bay there were two likely beaches and so the Royals would have to hope to heaven that they chose the right one. Mike Norman decided to mount more men on motorbikes to create a mobile patrol who might be able to plug the gap and asked if any man here could ride a motorbike; Danny Betts raised his hand; *"Betts, get as much ammo as you can in the side panniers,"* Major Norman ordered him, *"put a GPMG over your shoulder and go up and down"* - this Danny Betts did and then returned, *"Now get somebody else on the back with as much and do the same again to see how you can handle the weight."* - Again Danny Betts did as he was ordered, repeating the comical process, with the motorbike groaning and lurching under the weight of two men, both fully loaded, *"The idea was for us to be able to ride along the cliff-tops."* he remembered. Gary Williams was watching on and described the scene as like *"something out of the book of Fred Karno's army manual"* - in the end, the idea was abandoned also and the bikes were to be sent up front to help as many men get back from the beaches as possible when the time came, ready to form the next line of resistance.

As the men of NP8901 busied themselves, frantically searching for any idea which might lend them an advantage, so PJ Berry realised that in the rush, something had been missed; *"The one point that Mike Norman didn't address was that of comms."* He remembered, *"During the year, as part of the training and in readiness for anything that may happen if they decided to invade, we hatched our own little plan to defend the Islands. The basic plan was to defend from the shore and then retreat into the hills behind Stanley and live in the caves, to attack them from somewhere more defensible. We had probably practiced this about three times over the course of the year and we all knew where we had to go; some to the airport, some to the jetty and the others around GH. The points that we had to defend were right, but the problem was that we couldn't contact each other – I don't know if Gary Noott forgot to say or was just overlooked – but they had no one on Sapper Hill and we needed someone there to keep all the Sections in contact with each other so they could come through there if they couldn't get through themselves. I was originally placed in Figgy Duff's Section, but I went to see Majors Noott and Norman and explained that they needed someone up on the hill, and they both agreed that because I knew it, that I should go up there... The reality of what I just said started to sink in. I was going to be up there, all alone in the dark with nobody to talk to."* Gary Noott and Mike Norman sent PJ off to see if there was a spare motorbike to take him out of Stanley and up the long hill; *"I went down to the garage and met the vehicle mechanic, a new guy named Van Heerden,"* he remembered, *"he said there was a bike, but it was in bits, with no battery and the lights not working. It couldn't be fixed in time, but if I came back in a bit, he could bodge it to get me where I needed to go."*

As Gary Noott headed back to GH to prepare the HQ, so Mike Norman now set out with a section in a four-ton truck loaded with men, the two rolls of barbed wire and the Claymore mines to survey the beaches and prepare one of them for defence. Dave Gerrard was a part of the section that went with him; they had tried to give him an SMG but he had grabbed an SLR because, if and when the time came, he wanted some stopping-power. Major Norman had seen the beaches before but now he had to make a choice as to which one would be defended. There were two in Yorke Bay, separated by a rocky promontory, codenamed *'Orange'* and *'Purple'* beach respectively. He would have to choose the right one to defend – a case, Gary Noott had told him of, *"Either bingo or bollocks."*

Thinking of landing craft – the LCVP or *'Higgins boat'* as it was sometimes known, of which Argentina had a good few - Mike Norman decided that the eastern beach would be the most likely place for a landing. The west beach, *'Orange'* was gently sloping, which would mean that a landing boat would have to deploy much farther out, whilst the east beach, *'Purple'* was free of rocks and kelp – the tangling inch-thick seaweed which was the bane of boats in the Falklands - and which also had a much steeper shelf and would be perfect for a landing. Being a Marine, Mike Norman knew about such things and made his dispositions accordingly to defend *'Purple Beach'* – this was to be a catastrophic failure of intelligence, for news of Argentina's Amtrack amphibious assault vehicles had not been passed on and, had Mike Norman known, he would naturally have selected the other beach for defence. Meanwhile Wilcox and Milne had been waiting to make their dispositions at the selected beach and had been looking over the two canoes in which they were to make their escape; one had a leak, the other was missing a rudder. The plan was changed; they would have to run for it once they had fired off their ammo and then get to the bikes before being killed; *"I was scared shitless,"* Les Milne remembered, *"I couldn't see how we were going to get out of there."* This was mirrored by *'Jock'* Wilcox who, realising the futility of the situation remembered that; *"We had resigned ourselves to the fact that we were going to die."*

Now the barbed wire was unfurled and staked out along the beach under the watchful eye of Geordie Gill who had just received a promotion – due to his experience and local knowledge - to the temporary rank of Sergeant. Ray Bloye – part of the wiring party - remembered feeling a pang of sympathy now for the two men who were to sit out here on their own and face the first wave of the invasion unsupported and ensured that as many of the Claymore mines as they had were there to give them a fighting chance. Untangling and spreading out the wire, Marc Branch remembers suddenly thinking; *"What if the penguins get tangled in this shit?"*

Out on Cape Pembroke lighthouse, Nick Williams – who had returned to his post - had been alerted to the presence of one of the four-tonne trucks on the beach and now watched the work through his binoculars; *"We were not sure what they were doing but they looked like they were a wiring party."* he remembered, *"The lighthouse keeper joined us with his bino's and asked what was going on. All I could think of saying was that we had told the new detachment not to take a truck on the beach and that they must have got bogged in; whether he believed my excuse, I have no idea."* - The wiring party was to work until sundown preparing the beach when a moment came which every man there was to remember; *"It was coming up to dusk as we were putting the barbed wire out,"* Geordie Gill remembered, *"and it was one of those absolutely amazing Falklands sunsets. The sky was blood red and everybody stopped what they were doing on the beach and turned to look at it. I've talked to a couple of the guys since, and we were all thinking the same thing; if this is going to be the last one that we see, then at least it's a good 'un."*

With the beach being prepared for defence and Wilcox and Milne digging in, Mike Norman now turned his attention to the airport. It was obvious that at some point the Argentine forces would land aircraft on the runway – they had been secretly practicing for months, so Noott had told him and had even listed the Entebbe operation of 1976 as an example of what he feared might happen here. Norman's first thought was to crater the runway, but he lacked the explosives to do it and the island's Clerk of Works, hurrying to meet him from GH, suggested that it could be done but might take a week, so he had to make do with driving the airport fire truck along with tractors and other heavy vehicles onto the asphalt to impede any landing. It wasn't perfect but now time was running short. The airport was almost directly behind *'Purple'* beach and was an obvious target and here Mike Norman hoped to rack up more casualties as he placed the next supporting section of six men under Figgy Duff. Canopus Hill – named after the old warship which had defended Stanley in 1914 and from where indirect fire had been telephoned in by

Royal Navy spotters - lay just beside the airport and would make a decent position from which to dominate the beach or engage any aircraft which lingered, unable to land on the blocked runway. It was crowned by two rusty old naval six-inch guns which had been placed there for the Islands' defence back in the 1930's – it was a shame that they were not operable now - their sole defiance coming from some local graffiti scratched into the flaky paintwork stating simply; *"Fuck the Argentines."* Now the men began to dig trenches in the position with mounting nervousness as Dave Gerrard recalls; *"We split into two three-man teams and dug our shell scrapes. While digging, Marine Brian Hobbs asked me to tell them a joke as I was a bit of a comedian. I looked at him and replied that I really didn't find this particularly fucking funny! At which we all cracked up laughing."*

Now the plan was for Wilcox and Milne (5A) to hit the invasion force with everything they had and then retire, for Duff's section (5) to take up the fight to cover them and then to pepper-pot back to the Canache where Lou Armour's section (1) awaited to contest the narrow isthmus from Hooker's Point, Chris Bryan's section (2) would then take up the fight with Steve Johnson's section (3) after that on the airport road just outside of Stanley and so on back to Dave Carr's section (6) and finally to GH where there was the HQ section. Each time, the Argentine invaders would walk into a hail of fire, would stop to deploy and then come again with the section racing back to reinforce the next before the brunt of the assault could fall upon it. Mike Norman would command in the field with his radio operator, Marine Robin Farnworth and one of Gary Noott's detachment, Murray Paterson (who knew the area well) in the Land Rover, and Troop HQ would be there to lend support in the field, consisting of Lieutenant Bill Trollope, Sergeant Shepherd and Marine Armourer Mark Gibbs. The Royal Marines were going to be outnumbered more than twenty-to-one but they would not go down easily; they would meet each attack with as much violence as they could, for as long as they could, cause delay and casualties and finally there would be a last stand around GH. Though Rex Hunt had refused to flee to the 'camp' yet there was a hope that Gary Noott could still persuade him and maybe, just maybe, a stand at Government House might buy that time for Hunt, Noott and at least a section of Marines to 'go covert' and escape into the hills.

Gary Noott was now back at GH working on organising the last line of defence for the Islands. His job would be to keep up communications with the people in the Islands and also with London, to organise the defence of GH, to advise Rex Hunt as to the best deployments for the FIDF, to prepare the Islanders who, although ignorant of the armada which was descending upon them, were growing suspicious and finally, if he could, to escape to 'camp' and keep up the resistance of the Falklands as long as possible. This last element was, despite Rex Hunt's wishes, an important one; if the Falklands fell then a resistance story might persuade London to act. The Governor – the living symbol of British sovereignty in the Islands - would be still *in situ* and politically – with that shifting collage of events which surrounded the Falkland Islands and its history and politics, this would be a vital element. Government House was, as everyone seemed to say on the day and afterwards, *"not exactly the Alamo"* - built mainly of wood around the original stone core with large windows, a glass-fronted conservatory running almost along the entire rear of the building and the southern approach covered by a belt of trees and a broad ridge covered in boulders, which would make a perfect position from which to engage the defenders. The only defensible part was the ante-room to the Governor's office and a stone wall running around one side of the building. It was, in Rex Hunt's own words; *"A ridiculous place to try to defend."*

Hunt did, however, have certain powers and certain duties to perform which were a good mixture of common sense and protocol; he had not survived the Tet Offensive and the fall of Saigon without being resourceful. He was due to meet the three press-men who, seemingly still led by Simon Winchester, had wanted a story from him on the ongoing tension but now he had a use for them and called Simon Winchester asking for all three press-men to come for a meeting at GH at 16:30 - *"You will know what for"* he said ominously. If Argentina truly was going to invade, then Rex Hunt wanted the story told around the world. Argentina had a history of making people 'disappear' and he was determined that whatever befell, the truth would come out. Next he put a call out to all of the Islands' heads of department to meet with him in his office, amongst them the Chief of Police – Ronnie Lamb, the Senior Medical Officer – Daniel Haines, Acting Matron of KEMH the King Edward VII Memorial Hospital - Valerie Bennett, Head of Civil Aviation – Gerald Cheek, Superintendent of Education – John Fowler, Treasurer – Harold Rowlands, Harbour Master – Les Halliday, Acting Director of Public Works – Harry Bonner and to the head of the FIDF Major Phil Summers.

The senior government officials were soon crowding into his office and being told the news; the diplomatic efforts had finally failed, Argentina was coming to invade and they would have some last duties to perform before they were, in all likelihood, overrun. The police should all be notified and special constables called out to help keep the peace: nobody wanted a panic or Islanders arming themselves with shotguns and Molotov cocktails or anything and making themselves a target. The Public Works Department should attend the airport where Mike Norman would require heavy vehicles to use to block the runway. The hospital staff were told that they would have to prepare for the worst, which was not helpful as Matron Valerie Bennett pointed out that none of her staff were trained in the treatment of gunshot wounds or bomb blasts, and there were several ladies in the town in advanced stages of pregnancy for whom the stress and excitement could be harmful. Gerald Cheek was told to bring over the Government-owned *Islander* aircraft from its hangar on the runway to the racecourse where it might be used for reconnaissance or at least to block the racecourse from any landings, and was then to report for duty with the FIDF where he held the rank of Sergeant. The *Forrest* was to be deployed with her radar to give advanced warnings of any approaching force. Brian Summers was to hand over his duties as head of the Stanley Fire Service to his deputy, Neville Bennet (Valerie Bennett's husband) and then to report to the FIDF and from there to Cable & Wireless. All of them were to be discrete and were not to cause alarm and Rex Hunt would make his announcement to the Islanders in a few hours' time. The mood was sombre but, Dick Baker – Hunt's private secretary recalled, there was no panic, just a stony-faced mixture of anger and a resigned determination. So, it had come at last. For years they had threatened, always had they bullied and cajoled and although nobody ever mentioned what had become known as *"the 'I' word"* everyone had known that at some point an invasion was possible, if not actually likely. John Fowler asked after the FIDF; they were just civilians who trained and paraded more for ceremonial duties than for actual combat – could something be done to ensure they were not exterminated, he asked? Rex Hunt – overall Commander in Chief of the Islands forces, said that he would see to it that they were not.

Finally, all of the assembled heads of department were sent on their way except for two; Harold Bennett the senior legal officer in the Islands was asked to stay so that he might advise upon the legal procedure for declaring a state of emergency. It had never been done in anyone's memory and now he had to go off and consult a dusty old tome to find the correct way about it.*[7] The other man was Dick Baker the Chief Secretary, for whom Rex Hunt had an altogether more difficult task. A second message from London had arrived stating that they had *"reason to suspect there may be an inside element to this invasion"* and now he would be tasked with putting together a team of men; police officers backed by the men of the hydrographic survey team, who were to round up and arrest the Argentine workers in Stanley. The Argentines already in the Islands had been joined just a few days before by seventeen men purportedly from *Gas del Estado*, here to install some new oil-storage cylinders, but who looked, unlike their other co-workers, to be particularly young and muscular. Mike Norman had spotted them the day before and swore that they had *'soldier'* written all over them – military men instinctively know their own.*[8] These arrests of Argentine workers in Stanley would include the LADE staff; Vice Comodoros Gamin and Gilobert and any others who had come with the hated 'Communications Agreement' of 1971. There were also several 'tourists' from Argentina who had arrived in the last few days, notably one Rafael Wollmann, a journalist who seemed very active with his camera and seemed to be following the British press-men everywhere. Was it right to arrest tourists if they were suspected of being more than they appeared? Rex Hunt had sought advice from London on the issue and had been told to be ready but to delay any such arrests *'until the last possible moment'* for fear of giving a further excuse to Argentina to invade. A 'liberation' story was not exactly the kind of propaganda which London wanted to give to Argentina at this stage.

That afternoon, Stanley residents went about their business, still unaware of what was headed to the Falkland Islands or the danger they were now in. Dr Alison Bleaney, a native of Skye in Scotland who had served in medical postings in the Arctic, Antarctic and most recently in the Falklands, was at home with her six-month-old baby Emma. Nine months previously, she had taken maternity leave from the local hospital and now, after several years, considered the Falkland Islands as her home. That afternoon, her telephone rang, and she was happy to hear the familiar voices of some friends who currently living in the United States. Their call, however, was not a social one; *"We just wanted to make sure you're okay?"* her friend asked earnestly, *"We heard on the news that you're going to be invaded by Argentina in the morning."* Alison Bleaney laughed; *"Where did you get that from?"* she asked, *"No, everything is fine here! We're not getting invaded!"* and she left the conversation feeling somewhat confused. If Argentina was going to invade the Falklands, well, *someone* in the Falklands or the UK would have known about it before the American news channels, surely?

At the same time, Stanley resident Neville Bennett was in his kitchen, helping to prepare the evening meal for his family when he first saw signs of activity which soon told him of what was coming; *"I heard the sound of aircraft engines,"* he recorded, *"that's odd, I thought, a bit late in the day for a medical flight. I nipped into the front room and looked out of the window and there was the Islander Aircraft of the Falkland Islands Government Air Service flying low from the east. Stanley Airport and the Islander hangar were at the east end of the harbour. The plane swung round and landed at the race course, west of Government House. Why was that then? It's a bit late for a medical flight. FIGAS was created primarily as a 'Flying Doctor' service."* For some time, Neville Bennett had had a feeling that something strange was going on; he had, in his capacity with the Stanley Fire Service, attended both recent emergency landings from LADE aircraft and had found them both to be suspicious. The Hercules which had complained of a fuel leak had been one, and he had even checked and seen that the aircraft contained not postal drops, as had been claimed, but parachutes and other military equipment – one of the Royal Marines had even taken a cheeky photograph of it, he remembered. As to the idea of a fuel-leak, he hadn't smelt any fuel or seen any and, when he had checked the control panels by the refuelling drogues on the aircraft, he had noted that all of the needles were hard-over to the right indicating a full fuel-load. It had been a very windy day, he had recalled, as the Hercules had taken off again; *"Was this a genuine cry for help or a familiarisation flight to demonstrate to various air-crews how to land a heavily-laden aircraft at Stanley in adverse conditions?"* he asked himself. He had certainly been suspicious for a while with all the odd behaviour from the Argentines and, being a keen diarist, he noted down everything such as exact times, names places and what was said, seen or felt at the time, in case one day it might be useful. *"There seemed to have been some tension in the air for a while in the Falklands,"* he recalled, *"the sort of feeling that, if you stop and think, the hairs on your neck tend to stand up."*

At 19:20 there was a frantic knocking at the door and Brian Summers – chief of the Fire Service was there looking flushed and shoving a bunch of keys into Neville's hand; *"You've got full responsibility for the Fire Service until further notice."* he told him, *"I'm going to be rather busy for a while with a Morse key and one hand and an SLR rifle in the other."* - It didn't make much sense at the time, but what with the tensions in South Georgia, maybe the FIDF was going on exercise? Summers had certainly looked in a hurry, thought Neville, as he returned to his kitchen. As ever, the radio was on. It was a Thursday and so there would be the usual news, 'Special Requests' (known as 'music for the ill and elderly'), the 'For Sale and Wanted' messages, 'Sing Something Simple' and then tonight's broadcast of *'The Nick and Fig show'* from FIBS. Then at 19:30 at night came a special announcement from His Excellency the Governor which interrupted the schedule and Neville Bennett – as did all the people in the Islands, stopped to listen;

"I have an important announcement to make about the state of affairs between the British and Argentine Governments over the Falkland Islands dispute." Rex Hunt began, *"We have now sought an immediate emergency meeting of the Security Council on the grounds that there could be a situation which threatens international peace and security. I don't yet know whether it has been possible to arrange a meeting today, but our spokesman has been asked to make the following specific points. The Secretary General has today summoned the British and Argentine Permanent representatives to express his deep concern over the situation in the South Atlantic and has urged restraint on both sides. It is right that the Security Council should endorse and back up his approach. We, for our part, have continued to make every possible effort to resolve the current problems by diplomatic means. The British Ambassador in Buenos Aires yesterday delivered a further message to the Argentine government urging a negotiated settlement to current problems, and offering to send a senior emissary to Buenos Aires. The Argentine Foreign Minister had today responded to this approach in negative terms. He had declined to discuss further the problems occasioned by the illegal presence of Argentine nationals on South Georgia, and he had specifically stated*

that he no longer wished to use diplomatic channels to discuss the situation in South Georgia. In addition to the Foreign Minister's unwillingness to pursue diplomatic exchanges, there is mounting evidence that the Argentine armed forces are preparing to invade the Falkland Islands. In these circumstances, it is essential that the Security Council urge that there should be no resort to armed force and that diplomatic negotiations should be resumed. In these circumstances, I think it is necessary to take certain precautionary measures here in Stanley. I have alerted the Royal Marines and now I ask for all serving members or active members of the Falkland Islands Defence Force to report to the Drill Hall as soon as possible. They will be on guard tonight at key points in the town. Schools will be closed tomorrow. The radio station will stay open until further notice. If the Security Council's urging to keep the peace is not heeded by the Argentine Government, I expect to have to declare a state of emergency, perhaps before dawn tomorrow. I shall come on the air again as soon as I have anything to report. But in the meantime, I would urge you all to remain calm and to keep off the streets. In particular, do not go along the Airport Road. Stay indoors and please do not add to the troubles of the security services by making demonstrations or damaging Argentine property. This would play into their hands and simply provide them with the excuse they need to invade us. So please, do not take the law into your own hands. Let us show our visitors that we are responsible, law-abiding and resolute citizens. I shall let you know as soon as I have anything further to report."

In the silence that followed, there was a deathly calm in every household in Stanley. Finally, after all this time, they were coming. They had been in the Islands for years, spying most people said, taking over slowly, but now that taboo – the *'I-word'* which was never spoken - had been said: *'Invasion'*. People sat down shocked, breathed hard, reached for cigarettes, a stiff drink or that most British of panaceas – a cup of tea. *"I began to think what we were up against,"* Neville Bennett recorded, *"a town of some 1,200 people who mainly lived in wooden buildings..."* now they were going to face an invasion with only the boys of the Royal Marines there to stop them. He thought of the Argentine fuel depot just to the east of Stanley which contained fifty thousand or more gallons of jet fuel and petrol and the enormous containers to the south-west which housed diesel oil for electricity generation; *"I didn't know how much fuel they had in stock,"* Neville thought, *"a bit late in the day to start asking those sorts of questions. If that lot got hit by a mortar bomb or any incendiary device, we might as well write the lot off and any houses for quite a way around...fingers crossed and keep a loo-roll handy."*

At home in Stanley, baking bread was Jim Fairfield, a Stanley resident and former Royal Marine of NP8901 with several tours under his belt. Just one of many men who had married local girls and settled down in the Islands. Jim had been a Corporal and trained Assault Engineer who first came to the Falklands in 1974 almost by accident; a friend of his was up for 8901 duty when he got married and had been desperate to exchange drafts. Jim had been a single man looking for a posting that was exciting and demanding and so the swap was made. That year he met his wife: indeed the 74/75 detachment was quite infamous for no less than nine marriages which had caused an emergency meeting in the Falklands Council as so many of the girls wanted to follow their men back to the UK, which Jim's wife did. They returned with the 78/79 detachment and Jim had managed to stay an extra year with the 79/80 detachment too and finally had retired from the Corps in September 1981 and stayed in the Falklands.

Jim had been on edge ever since the Davidoff incident on South Georgia and had promised his wife that, if it came to it, he would have to go and give the lads a hand; *"We have a saying in the Corps, 'once a Marine, always a Marine' and I was certainly not going to let my mates down"* Jim remembered. He now grabbed the phone and called Moody Brook to offer his services and within twenty minutes a Land Rover was outside his front door waiting for him. Jim was ready, back in his old uniform with his green beret and after a fond goodbye to his wife and children, he jumped in and set off for the barracks; *"While I really didn't expect anything to happen, I had to face the fact that it might,"* he recalled, *"and that we would no doubt be heavily outnumbered. I knew what that would mean... but there was no conscious thought of not going and 'doing my bit' – only a feeling of inevitability, fatalistic reality and 'what will be will be'. Something was about to happen that could threaten my family. I was sure that the best way I could protect them was to join forces with the Marines... not to do so was not in my make-up; not an option. Even though I knew the odds were heavily stacked against me coming out alive. If the invasion happened, I would fight alongside my mates no matter what, for my family, for duty, for the Islanders and finally for me."*

Jim arrived back at Moody Brook to the greetings and usual jeers from his mates, but they were happy to see him and quickly brought him back into the family; *"When I arrived at Moody Brook the place was buzzing, there was not a weapon or any ammunition left anywhere, after the usual ribald greetings the lads soon had me fixed up, self-loading rifle, four full mags, two primed grenades and a smoke grenade. There was a quiet purpose in everything that was happening, and, as was a Royal Marines wont, humour - black and blue - was being thrown back and forth while Marines carried on their own preparations for war. I soon reverted to mode, it was just like I had never left, all those hundreds probably thousands of hours of training meant we all just knew what to do and when to do it; we were like the famous well-oiled machine. Looking at these lads so far from home, sure to be outnumbered and out gunned but ready to fight none the less, I knew I had made the right decision; I was where I should be."*

As evening wore on and the shadows of the autumn sun lengthened, and the realisation of the impending invasion dawned on the civilians and Marines alike, the work of trying to make the Islands defensible became more frantic. In the sand dunes and along the Canache by the airport, the men dug deeper into their 'shell-scrapes' for protection. On a patch of ground near the Airport Road, Danny Betts, George Brown and the other men of Chris Bryan's section heaved rocks, earth, planks and old sleepers into position to form a makeshift defence just south of the road – they were going to be the anti-tank team if anything came, armed with their Carl Gustav and a stock of several LAW rocket launchers as well as a GPMG and their SLR's – it wouldn't be much to stop a tank if it came, but it was all that they had. On the beach, Ray Bloye, Andy Macdonald, Marc Branch, Dick Overall and Geordie Gill were still staking out the barbed wire and hoping it would buy time for their mates who were now condemned to a suicide mission if their legs or notoriously unreliable Can-am bikes failed them. The bikes were known for the terrible electrics and the Marines had even taken the precaution of strapping additional lamps to the handlebars in case the lights failed, which was likely. On Canopus Hill, Figgy Duff and Dave Gerrard were also digging in above the airport and wondering what would be coming at them in the night. Across the narrows of Stanley Harbour at a place called Navy Point, Corporal Stefan York and his section wondered if they would catch anything coming through to attack Stanley from the seaward side, where numerous fishing vessels bobbed in the calm water. Just before the Governor's broadcast had been issued, Nick Williams had received the call to leave Cape Pembroke lighthouse with his section and make his way back to the airport, there to link up with Figgy Duff's section and then to make their way back to Moody Brook for a final briefing. He had borrowed Basil Biggs the lighthouse keeper's transistor radio and had heard the announcement as his men walked back along the dunes through the darkness; *"I thought the shit was about to hit the fan,"* he remembered, *"I briefed the men. It was a very nervous yomp back to the airport. When we got there, we linked up with the other section, they had been digging a slit-trench and they told us it looked like we were going to be invaded in the morning... It was not a good feeling."*

It was April Fool's Day 1982 and someone, somewhere had most certainly been fooled. Now the Royal Marines of NP8901 were going to pay the price for that. Someone 'up there', they reflected, must have a twisted sense of humour.

Chapter 5: No Need for Medals

"You are the Green Berets... The Royals.
And that means you're going to knock seven shades of shit out of
the bastards before you go down!"
Major Mike Norman – April 2nd 1982.

As the Royal Marines of NP8901 made themselves ready, so too did the men
of the FIDF. Major Phil Summers had called up his volunteers to the Drill Hall as
ordered, although not every one of the one-hundred or so men on the rolls had
answered the call. The local men were dressed in military uniforms, but it was
evident that they were not soldiers. Some quite young, some middle-aged and
with their portly commander, they were known affectionately by the Royal
Marines and the Islanders as *'Dad's Army'* and Summers was the perfect caricature
for the name of *'Captain Mainwaring'* – yet still they came, eager to do anything to
defend their homes from invasion. Now Summers briefed them and told them of
their jobs, which would be local patrol and the guarding of the key facilities of
Stanley such as the racecourse, the football field, the YPF fuel depot, the power
station and the telephone exchange. Mike Norman had been grateful for any
assistance which might tie the Argentine force down longer, yet he was amazed to
find that he could not take the FIDF men under his command, having instead to
observe protocol and merely *suggest* orders to the Governor who was their
Commander in Chief. He had wanted to place them on the rocky ridge to the south
of Government House where they might have cover and, perhaps as importantly,
where they would be out of the way of friendly fire. His warnings had gone
unheeded however, as Rex Hunt was determined not to sacrifice them, if it came
to it, in the open field against what would obviously be experienced Argentine
Commandos, not the conscripts of the regular army who, at any rate, were still
going to be better trained and equipped than the FIDF men if it came to a stand-up
fight.

The Marines were going for a final 'scran' before a long night and possibly a
longer day tomorrow, and then a briefing from Mike Norman, and so the FIDF
would make ready and patrol in the meantime to give any warning and would keep
up their patrols throughout the night. On this night, the FIDF were to gain one
more recruit – indeed the only man amongst them who had seen any action before
- Anthony Davies, known by everyone as *'Taff'*. Taff Davies was not a native
Falkland Islander but a former Royal Marine of the NP8901 detachment from

78/79 who had met his wife Jackie whilst in the Islands, had left the corps and who now called Stanley home. With his home and his former colleagues now in danger, Taff had felt that he had to do something more than just sit and wait, and now strode into the Drill Hall asking for a uniform and a weapon. His help and experience were a major boost to many of the nervous part-timers.

Finally, with the men briefed as to their roles that night, the armoury was thrown open, but it was now found that the Marines had already got there first as Taff Davies recalled; *"What happened was this; the Royal Marines were informed of the Argies' intentions long before the FIDF. Consequently they 'raided' the FIDF's armoury and removed most of the modern weapons, to be used by them. What was left was 12 SLR's and, if I remember correctly, not enough magazines to even provide one per SLR."* Somewhere at the back of the armoury, however, was the old store, which the former Governor Sir Neville French (who had served in the Islands from 1975-1977) had managed to retire in favour of modern weapons. Now the men of the FIDF were forced to look through these unfamiliar old pieces and see if anything was serviceable. Taff Davies, with his experienced eyes led the way; *"The FIDF was left with these,"* he recalled, *"SMLE's – Number 4's and a couple of other variants - several .303 Bren Guns all with their barrels shot out, a couple of old Vickers Guns, a couple of even older Lewis Guns, a few Stens and that was about it... Those weapons were museum pieces and the FIDF had no training on them. They were simply relics from the past."* The FIDF men had to be armed up as best they could, and mainly with the SMLE or 'Short Magazine Lee Enfield' Rifle – it had been a wonder-weapon in its day; a ten-round, single-shot, bolt-action rifle which in experienced hands could be fired rapidly and could kill at a mile, but that was seventy years ago, and these were not experienced hands now holding them and working the awkward and unfamiliar bolt mechanisms, wondering how in the hell they were going to face machine guns and assault rifles with such antiques. These had been the weapons which their fathers had used during the 'Condor' raid sixteen years previously and whilst most were of a more modern 1950's pattern, they were probably going to prove useless. Taff Davies gave the men a sharp lesson in using them anyway.[*1]

FIDF Private Fraser Wallace was, apart from Taff Davies, the unit's newest recruit, having signed up only a few weeks before. There had been no training barring a bit of marching and he had never even fired a rifle before, so now he was put to loading the SLR magazines with bullets. When he was done, he asked what he was to do with his gun if he actually saw an Argentine soldier, and Summers had replied simply that, if he saw an Argentine, he should shoot him, pointing out rather obviously which bit was the magazine and which was the trigger. Wallace remembered later that he hadn't got a clue what he was supposed to do. About as much knowledge as he had was which end the bullets came out of. It would have to be enough. As the men of the FIDF rummaged, a stash of hand-grenades was found which might at least prove useful, but now Phil Summers – perhaps remembering his daytime role in the Treasury, uttered the words which have become local legend to this day; *"You can't use those, they're far too expensive!"*

In all, if the FIDF were going to meet highly trained Argentine Commandos in the night, then it wasn't going to last long. Hand-grenades were probably only going to get other civilians killed, not the Argentines. Taff Davies remembered that, despite the obvious nerves, the men were reasonably calm. They had come to defend their homes and they would use the tools to hand, if they had to. Gerald Cheek, now in his role as a sergeant in the FIDF recalled that; *"I, together with a section was sent to the racecourse principally to guard the Islander aircraft and to prevent if at all possible, Argentine helicopters from landing there, i.e. shoot them down if necessary. That was also the reason for the positioning of the machine gun posts. Prior to leaving our HQ we were all issued with 100 rounds of ammunition, I think the machine gunners carried 300 rounds. Obviously, we were all, to say at the least, somewhat apprehensive if indeed not quite worried as to just what our fate was going to be. Although we had all been trained in basic military field crafts, weapon handling etc, mostly by the Royal Marines just for what we were about to do - defend our Islands against an invasion - I don`t think that any one of us ever imagined that this was likely to happen."*

As the men of the FIDF went out on patrol, so the Royal Marines of NP8901 now returned to Moody Brook for a last hot meal and a final briefing before the firing began; *"When we arrived back at the Brook, all hell was breaking loose,"* Nick Williams remembered, *"the blokes were rushing all over the place and I thought, 'this is for real', I was extremely scared. We were told there was hot food on the go and to get something to eat. I couldn't eat anything; my stomach was doing handstands."* PJ Berry, who had arrived back with him felt the same, remembering that; *"I filled my face with whatever I could eat but it was not a lot... I remember having that feeling in my stomach that makes you want to chuck up when you're scared..."* The men of the FIDF were on patrol and the *Forrest* was keeping radar watch for any Argentine task force which might appear – so in all, the Marines were safe in taking a last break which might easily also be their last meal. Some remembered eating to the point of bursting whilst others, like Nick Williams, could barely manage a mouthful. They ate with weapons piled, just in case. When they had finished, the Royals were then ordered to gather in the bar area for a final briefing. It was 23:00 as they assembled in the disco area of the bar, pulling up chairs or just finding a seat on the floor; *"It's hard to say what the mood was like,"* remembered Nick Williams, *"I think there was some bravado and a bit of banter, however most of us were deep in thought, wondering what was going to happen."*

Now, officially, Mike Norman was in command as of 09.00 that morning, a day later than the planned hand-over of command had been scheduled for. Just a few days into his new command and with limited knowledge of the ground and surrounding area, Mike Norman would now have to lead the men of both detachments to battle and was grateful for Gary Noott's being on hand to advise him. They were old friends and nobody was going to be offended either way. Mike Norman had been worrying for some time about what he was going to say to the men. What could he say? *"You're all going to die tonight or tomorrow, but give it your best"* was about the sum of it, he knew, but it wasn't what the men were wanting to hear. First there were some formalities to get out of the way; there had been a message sent from the Argentine task force telling the Islands to surrender and intelligence as to the size of force they were bringing which now had to be read out so that the men knew what they were up against. This was the most difficult part - the position no military leader ever wished to be in – that of giving convincing orders to men who had no chance of winning and every chance of dying. The Royal Marines watching him and listening, gobsmacked, were mostly in their twenties yet all had seen combat and they were not fools. They knew what was coming and that they would surely die.

As the men all gathered round, he began and, as Nick Williams remembered; *"When Mike Norman started his orders, you could have heard a pin drop. He gave a comprehensive set of orders, the enemy forces paragraph lasted for what seemed like an age."* The Royal Marines sat in silence as they heard the sheer size of what was now coming at them; an aircraft carrier, destroyers, corvettes, armour, artillery, aircraft and thousands upon thousands of men. Looking around the room, the group of Royal Marines and Royal Navy hydrographers numbered in total just seventy men. It was a terrifying thought. Mike Norman had read the entire list of enemy forces in page after never-ending page. The men listened intently, some shaking their heads, some sighing and a few actually smiling.

The 'friendly forces' list was barely a few paragraphs, consisting of what the men already knew and ending with; *"there may be two 'grey funnel lines' in the area, but that's just rumour... so, it's just us."* - The 'grey funnel line' was slang for Royal Navy warships and by these he meant submarines - if there were any about, now would be a great time for them to put in an appearance. Finally, the orders from CINCFLEET ending with the ominous words; *'You will fight until overrun'.*

Nick Williams could not believe how much information Major Norman had about the force now coming towards them; *"It seemed to me that the British government knew what was going to happen in advance,"* he remembered, *"but chose not to inform us until it was too late for us to put together a good defence. Mike told us that there were three choices; one was to surrender the Islands now, before they landed, two was to take the Governor into the mountains and conduct a 'hit and run' campaign until reinforcements landed, or three, meet them head-on, give them a bloody nose and then take the Governor and head for the mountains. Mike told us that we couldn't do option one or two – the people of Stanley wanted and expected us to defend them - and that therefore we would meet them head-on."* This, of course, was the only logical choice, but it didn't inspire the Royal Marines with confidence as to their chance of coming out of this alive; *"I don't think any of us could believe it,"* Nick Williams continued, *"I don't think believe Mike Norman could believe it. He then asked, 'Any questions?' and Jim Fairfield asked if we should blow up Moody Brook to save the Argentines from having it. Mike replied that, what if we blow up Moody Brook and they don't invade? - Where are we going to live? - We were actually talking about blowing up Moody Brook – it was surreal."*

One other Marine who had served in Northern Ireland asked if, like there, they should issue a verbal warning before opening fire. Mike Norman told them no. Yes, Jones? *"Can we make sure nobody drinks all the fresh milk, Sir? Just there'll be fuck-all left for tea when we come back tomorrow?"* - Any more serious questions? - Yes; *"I don't suppose, sir, there's any chance of settling this with a game of football, is there?"* - This at least got a laugh from the men and Mike Norman let them joke; they were in high spirits and trying to play it all off the cuff but he knew they were ready for it, even if it meant dying. With the questions over with, Mike Norman now summoned himself to give the speech of his life and he went for it, he recalled, in an upbeat fashion, joking as he went and appealing to the Marines' own bawdy sense of humour which seemed to be working tonight. He told the men that they were Royal Marines – the elite, the best of the best - and that the poor sods coming against them were a bunch of dagoes; a 'hobo army' of conscripts and national servicemen whose only experience was in bullying natives and civilians. Who the hell – the men remembered him asking – did they think they were, coming and expecting to run over the Royal Marines? Did they know who they were up against? Norman left the men confident, laughing – albeit nervously - and promised that, if the Argentines came, they would get a very bloody nose. So far, so good, now for the practical part. With a stern face, he addressed them as once again, all of the men listened intently. He hadn't bullshitted them about the odds, he told them, which meant that they would fight on until either the Governor threw in the towel or they were overrun... and that probably meant death. He let the word linger before continuing, telling the men to swallow that word down, accept it and to forget it when the firing started; *"You are the Green Berets."* the men now heard him announce, *"The Royals. And that means you're going to knock seven shades of shit out of the bastards before you go down!"* He told them that the Argentines would be arrogant, would expect a walk-over and that wasn't what the Royal Marines were going to give them and finally reminded them, as the men recalled, that; *"Tomorrow you are fighting for yourself. We are going to be totally outnumbered, and each of you will be fighting for your own life."*[2]

"When he finished, the room was deathly silent with all of us in a state of disbelief," Dave Gerrard remembered, *"then came the Monty Python song, 'Always look on the bright side of life' and we went on our way whistling."* Mike Norman stood by the door, saying a few words to each section as they filed out of Moody Brook, covered from head to toe in weapons and ammunition and heading for the Land Rovers and four-tonners which were to take them to their positions. He remembered feeling in awe of them as they departed, yelling *"Let's get 'em! We're off!"* to each other for mutual encouragement. They were being let off the leash, released to do what they had signed on to do if necessary, and what they had trained for, for all of their careers: to be tougher, faster, harder to hit and to hit back harder than anybody else ever could. Mike Norman saw them all off with the same words, calling after them as they headed out into the darkness; *"Do your jobs well – nothing stupid, mind. There's no need for medals."*

The Royal Marines were on their way to meet the enemy, laughing, encouraging each other and joking. Those poor Argie bastards were going to face the Royal Marines tomorrow, they told each other and themselves, but inside each man knew that he was walking out into the darkness and would probably never return; *"I realised that we didn't stand a chance and that we were all going to die in the morning,"* remembered Nick Williams, *"there was going to be no other outcome. We could have walked away but it was what we had all signed on for if it came so now it was a case of, 'now go out there and wait for it' – That's what courage is all about."*

Most of the Royal Marine sections were going back to their original positions with one reinforced section being sent to the Murray Heights to the south and slightly west of Stanley, which dominated the skyline and the southern approaches across the common into town; *"It was assessed that if it was a helicopter-borne invasion, this would be the most likely landing zone."* said Nick Williams, *"If they did attempt a landing here, our mission was to open rapid fire for as long as we could, take out as many men and choppers as we could, then withdraw to Government House."*

Nick was made second-in-command of Corporal Dave 'Scouse' Carr's section and found himself with Ray Bloye, Marcus 'Benny' Bennett, Terry 'Tel' George and George 'Torchy' Carr; just six men to hold the flank, with PJ Berry, all on his own, stationed out to their right to keep a look out on Sapper Hill and coordinate between the sections; *"I said my final goodbyes and wished everyone luck and had a word with Jock Wilcox, who was still walking around in disbelief at what they'd asked him and Les to do.*" remembered Berry, as he waved goodbye and headed back for the garage to collect his motorbike. The men of Section Six now also shambled off towards their truck which would take them to the heights, laden down with weapons and ammunition; *"Benny had the GMPG,"* Nick remembered, *"I had an SLR and the SMG I had brought back from the lighthouse – it was tucked in the bergen with some ammunition as backup. Myself and Benny carried as much 'link' as we could, and I had SLR ammunition and an L2 grenade. We also passed belts of link to all the other section members to carry. The GPMG was the most effective weapon we had, and it was imperative that we had enough ammunition to keep it firing for as long as we could. Ray Bloye was carrying 66mm anti-tank rockets as well, I'm not sure who else had them. We were all carrying a huge amount of kit and ammunition, because there was going to be no resupply; what we stood up in and carried, that was it. At the given time, our section loaded ourselves and our kit onto a four-tonner with at least one other section. We were driven to the top of the town, where our section disembarked. When I jumped off of the back of the four-tonner, I nearly fell over. I had stuffed the front of my windproof jacket with belts of 50-link – as many as I could get in – the weight of which unbalanced me.*" Now at the foot of the heights, Dave Carr carried out a recce and, finding the heights deserted, called the rest of the section up to prepare their position.

Back at Moody Brook, Andy Macdonald was in the communications-centre, little more than a cubby-hole where the link to London was maintained and trying to get intelligence and news of any support; *"I was present in the Detachment Comcen – a small pokey two-man room - and typed (one finger level) a message to CINCFLEET, Northwood, appraising them of our status and a sitrep and requesting Service support - the answer back was 'No support available' and 'Good Luck'. I believe we repeated the request again and requested it be made direct to CINCFLEET, the reply was 'This is CINCFLEET!' My feelings at this time were, 'Oh fuck... we've been abandoned!'*"

With Moody Brook now emptying out, at 02.00 Gary Noott did a last check and then set off with Geordie Gill to set up the HQ section at Government House. He turned the lights out as he left but forgot the one in his office; if the next 24 hours worked out as he suspected, then it would not be Her Majesty's Government who would be picking up the electricity bill anyway. Geordie Gill was not best pleased that his new temporary promotion to HQ Sergeant would take him away from the fighting – as a qualified sniper who knew every inch of ground perfectly, he had wanted to be up front where the fighting was - but his experience and knowledge were also invaluable to an HQ commander. Now he sat and watched as the sections were transported off into the night towards who knew what; *"People*

– many of whom I had known for years - were driving off into the darkness and I knew I might never see them again," he recalled, *"the Argies were coming with warships, overwhelming force, artillery, air and armour and we were on our own. We'd had a signal from UK saying, 'you will fight till overrun', not even a 'good luck', (I did think Nelson did it better), and I always knew, from every other conflict I had been in, that there was a chance you could get killed or injured. This time though, it wasn't chance. We knew it was going to be us."* He thought of his daughters, Tanya and Alicia, just a few hundred metres away on Pioneer Row. Now there was nothing he could do to help them as their father but to stay here and do his duty as a Royal Marine. The Falkland Islanders had taken him in, had made him one of their own; *"It was something worth fighting for,"* he said later, *"we were fighting for each other and the other 7,000 Royal Marines wearing the green beret in the UK, but the fact that we were fighting for OUR Islands, OUR people and OUR flag was a bonus. But for me it was personal. I was fighting for my country and for my kids."*[*3]

As the sections set off into the dark, so PJ Berry entered the garage to see what Van Heerden, the mechanic, had managed to make of the broken motorbike; *"He said it would go, but there were no lights and we'd have to bump the bike down the hill to get it started."* He remembered, *"If it stalled, he told me I would never get it going again. If memory serves me right, I think he taped a big torch onto the handlebars to give me a bit of light. I left Moody Brook, carrying my SLR, boxes of tracer rounds and a few white-phos grenades as well as the radio - it was one of those really old A41 types that carried the world's largest battery and weighed about a ton - and rode into Stanley and up the back road to an off-road track, then started to make my way up Sapper Hill. It was quite a clear night and I remember getting about half way to where I wanted to get to when the bike stalled and I had to leave it half-way up the hill. I also remember thinking it was very quiet and it took me about twenty yards to realise that I still had the crash helmet on, which I took off and threw down the hill after the bike. I walked up the remaining part of the track, which narrowed and just below the summit, the rocks formed a little hollow that gave me shelter from the wind. When I got there, it seemed that I was in the loneliest place on earth. Reality kicked in and I started to set up the radio. It was big and cumbersome with an aerial of about four feet and when I was ready, I started doing radio checks so that I could contact each section."*

Meanwhile, back at GH, the work had been going on for some time to prepare the Islands for defence with the men aware that with each passing minute, the full force of a nation in arms was going to descend upon them. Rex Hunt was calm, almost serene, and this gave even the Royal Marines hope. He was, however, determined to arm and defend himself and went looking for his twelve-bore shotgun which he kept in one of the rooms with his fishing tackle and golf clubs, but which he now found to be missing. It had been already swiped by his chauffeur / major-domo Don Bonner who was found stood with it by the window overlooking the flagpole to the front of the house; *"Don, you've bagged my twelve-bore!"* Hunt said in a friendly, chiding way. Don Bonner explained that he was guarding the flag which this night had not been lowered at sundown as per usual, and that he was going to *"shoot the first Argie bastard who tries to take it down."* Hunt smiled, announcing *"That's the spirit!"* and then went to ask Mike Norman for a weapon instead. He was given a 9mm pistol. Hunt had been an excellent shot with a pistol back in his day, but they were revolvers and he had to be given a quick lesson in how to load and cock the semi-automatic weapon, which he never really got the hang of anyway. Mike Norman now also gave him a permanent bodyguard, Royal Marine Harry Dorey who was ordered not, under any circumstances, to leave the Governor's side.[*4]

It was going to be a long night; certain things were being packed up and sent into safety with the GH staff including a portrait of the Queen, which Hunt was most determined should be hidden in a house somewhere and not open to defacement. Meanwhile government papers, ciphers, codes and other important documents were gathered for burning, to save them from falling into the wrong hands. The intelligence was still that 'they' were coming and Rex Hunt was determined that there should be nothing of value if and when 'they' arrived.

In his house in Stanley, Neville Bennett received an emergency call about a fire from the direction of Government House. He had been listening intently to the 'box' – that being the name for the crude local devices which made-do as radio receivers in the Islands; *"Our two daughters, aged 10 and 13 were in bed,"* he recalled, *"we had told them there might be something unusual happening and there could be a bit of noise during the night, if they heard any shooting, they were to keep down as low as possible. At 9.45 the phone rang; my immediate reaction was that disaster had happened.* Pat McPhee (his colleague at the Stanley Fire Service) *had had a call from the telephone exchange to say that report had come in of smoke and visible flames at the rear of Government House; he would call for me in the Fire-fly which was kept on Callaghan Road just behind his home. We approached GH quietly along Ross Road using the rotating light only in case the siren caused a bit of panic. We entered the courtyard behind the main building and saw two 40-gallon petrol drums, which is the standard rubbish bin, well alight, a very large man, I had never seen him before, in a white sweater, was feeding papers into the flames. I asked him what he was doing. 'Have a beer mate' he replied, 'we're burning classified documents from the communications centre in the Governor's office,' he thrust a couple of cans of Brown Ale into our hands. I explained that the usual procedure was to ring the exchange and tell the operator before lighting a bonfire after dark, and it may have been prudent to do so at this time. 'Bugger off mate; we've got other things on our mind tonight.' I then noticed a pair of self-loading rifles leaning up against the fence as well as other military bits. Things were tending to get serious after all."*

It looked like being a busy night for the Royals. Neville and Valerie had taken in Andy Macdonald when Mike Norman's men had arrived and now as he got home, Andy called him and apologised that he would not be home that night, *'as they were expecting a bit of a party'* – Neville wished him luck, told him he would see him later and that he would put the cheese omelette he had prepared for him in the fridge. 'A bit of a party'? - He hoped that was all it was; *"I didn't sleep very much that night,"* he remembered, *"I don't think Valerie did either. We had both gone to bed half undressed in case the call came. FIBS could be heard quietly coming from the kitchen through the open doors. The night dragged on. The waiting was as nerve-wracking as sitting in the dentist's waiting room with your ears tuned in to hear the footsteps in the surgery, then the doorknob turns and the voice says, 'come in' – that's when the toothache stops. I thought our trauma would last longer than that."*

Andy Macdonald's 'party' now began with a patrol around the grounds as he recalled; *"One of my duties at Government House was to provide a wandering patrol around the perimeter. I was given a Matelot from the Hydrogophers branch, HMS Endurance. He had been issued with an SMG he had only been taught to use hours before. I took up point-man with 'Jack' trailing behind. He kept catching up to me and kept asking what to do if an Argie pops up. I told him 'Keep your spacing from me and just point the SMG and keep firing!' On the last occasion, I noticed he had his safety off and was on full auto all the while he had been on patrol. So, after escaping a near-death experience I managed to convince 'Jack' that it might be better if he took point, then I could watch his back. He was most pleased with this - and commented 'You're a great bloke, Royal!'"* [*5]

Chief Secretary Dick Baker arrived at GH just before midnight to find Rex and Mavis Hunt sitting down to dinner in the formal dining room.[*6] Dorey, stood guarding the doorway, had thrust his rifle dutifully towards Baker and had to be told to stand down and let the Chief Secretary past. The Governor was dressed formally for dinner, just himself and his wife eating quietly together, contemplating the obvious: it had seemed like Saigon all over again. That time, he had sent Mavis reluctantly away to safety – something for which she never quite forgave him - and was determined not to do again. This time, she would face the invasion at his side, she said determinedly, although he was still trying to persuade her to take herself and their son Tony off to the Baker's house for safety. She was still annoyed at Rex for even allowing Tony to try to volunteer for the FIDF as a dispatch rider, although it was not really annoyance at him but frustration at what was coming. The problem was obvious; they were coming for Rex. The Royal Marines were in the way and the Islanders needed protection, but it would only end with him. They both knew it and now ate together more for formality than anything else.

Whilst there, Hunt had cursed himself for a fool, recounting how, some months before, a supposed 'tourist' from Argentina had come to the Islands with an interest in Victorian Colonial Architecture. Rex Hunt had even given him a tour of the house and sent him away happily with a set of plans for the building. It dawned upon him now that Argentina had been staking out the Falkland Islands for months. Now the Governor had a somewhat forlorn look about him as he realised his error and Dick Baker recalled the sight of his esteemed boss, sitting there trying to summon up an appetite – quiet, depressed and stony. The truth was that the responsibility was his alone, however many people were around him. He was the seat of government. The Argentines would have to fight through the Royal Marines to get to him, but in the end, they were coming for him.

Seeing his friend's concern, Hunt offered him a seat and something to eat and drink but Dick Baker refused politely, stating that he was on business and might have a useful plan which could serve well in the defence of the Islands. Rex Hunt instantly brightened. Enter Bill Curtis, a Canadian resident of Stanley and former air traffic controller and electronics buff who had, ironically, moved his family to the Falkland Islands in the late 1970's to escape the likely outcome of a nuclear holocaust should the USA and Russia 'push the button' as had seemed likely on a few occasions. Now he found himself in a war zone but was determined to help where he could and suggested two key pieces of local sabotage which might serve the defence of the Islands well. The first plan was to readjust the LADE beacon on the ridge near the airport: if the Argentine pilots had grown used to trusting it then a redirection of the signal could, at worst, send them off course and delay them and at best might send a Hercules or other aircraft tumbling into the sea if it were dark enough. The second was more obvious; to turn off or smash the light in Cape Pembroke lighthouse which for years had warned mariners of the perilous rocks around Stanley. There was a brief discussion over the technicalities of damaging the LADE beacon – after all, it was Argentine government property - but it was quickly decided to dispense with the formalities and soon Mike Norman was racing off in the dark in his Land Rover with Bill Curtis towards the beacon as others went out to disable the lighthouse.

The Land Rover hurtled through the darkened streets, drawing the attention of a few late-night strollers as they broke the strict 20mph speed limit. They passed the telephone exchange, where the FIDF men were on duty, waved at them and drove on, with Bill Cutis commenting that it was probably going to be a nice day tomorrow at least; *"Yeah, a great day to die."* Norman laughed dryly. Arriving at the LADE beacon, Mike Norman and Bill Curtis managed to force the door open and soon found themselves staring at a wall full of wires and boxes which Curtis could make no sense of. The idea of misdirecting the beacon was now quickly given up and Norman opted instead for the less subtle act of destroying as much kit as he could, until the beacon was rendered inoperable. It would have to do in the circumstances.

Back at GH the Royal Marines were ready, the HQ had been set up and the men were now waiting and trying to keep their spirits up; *"You made jokes,"* Geordie Gill remembered, *"but deep down you didn't want to let your mates know you were scared. It was the waiting; it's always the waiting that is the worst thing. I could see a lot of the lads looking at me because I was thirty-five and I'd been in the Marines a pretty long time. I thought 'If I show them that I'm scared - which I was, I've never been so scared in my life - it's going to make it worse.' So I was putting an act on. I remembered an old three-badge Marine telling me something just before my first battle in Borneo and so I was saying, just as he had said to me; 'If you're scared, think how scared they are. We've only got to take on them buggers, but they know they've got to fight the Royal Marine Commandos, which is enough to scare anybody!' - It was when I was on my own and had time to reflect that the reality of it came crashing back down... I knew I was going to die."*

Rex Hunt was doing his best to show that he also was not scared and making sure that the young Royal Marines were encouraged but even he was looking for reassurance and soon sought out Geordie; *"I was at the east end of Government House with two of the others,"* he remembered, *"We were all in darkness and waiting when suddenly I felt this tug on my sleeve. I looked round and there was Rex in his suit, shirt and tie, whispering, 'Everything alright Corporal Gill?' I thought, 'Oh yeah! We're just about to be attacked by about 2,000 enemy soldiers and there are about sixty of us. I couldn't be bloody better!' - But he was a good man. I always had a lot of respect for him."* Dick Baker was meanwhile doing his best to convince Jim Fairfield to go home while he had the chance; *"But soon gave up,"* Jim remembered, *"when I told him – not unkindly – to get lost."*

Just before midnight, the *Forrest* slipped her moorings and headed off into the dark and foreboding sea beyond Port William. The ship's captain, Jack Sollis, was joined by two of the naval hydrographers, Lieutenant Ball and Lieutenant Todhunter as she set out to scan the horizon for Argentine ships. She was 80 feet long and unpopular with the Royals due to her tendency to roll, but she was equipped with radar and would provide some useful warning. Of course, if she could see the Argentine navy then they could see her. She was unarmed and not kitted out for war. One missile or well-aimed shot would do for her, but she was at least fairly small and nimble, and this would have to do. At around 02:00 Sollis radioed in to Mike Norman that he had detected one very large contact – too large to be anything other than a warship and perhaps even an aircraft carrier - about five miles from Mengeary Point and coming in fast. The three men on board the *Forrest* scanned the horizon with their binoculars in the direction of the contact but could see nothing. If they were coming, they were coming in 'dark' and without navigation lights. Quickly the *Forrest* retraced her steps and was back at her moorings by 03:00.

The invasion was certainly coming – of this each man had no doubt - although there was always a chance that, as many thought, the task force might pull up in Stanley Harbour and simply sit there until somebody started negotiating. Nevertheless, if they did come, even with his tiny force, Mike Norman was determined to be ready. He radioed once more to the *Forrest* asking Jack Sollis to take her out again and Sollis now replied that he did not think it a wise idea as he could now see the lights of an aircraft carrier from beyond the Canache out towards Surf Bay to the south. Back at GH, Mike Norman now contacted Lou Armour's Section One who were at Hooker's Point overlooking the Canache – could they confirm an aircraft carrier? Lou Armour replied that no, he could not see one, although the wreck of the ship *Lady Elizabeth* was visible and with the lights of the oil refinery on her, she might well have passed for a more distant and larger vessel. Norman now radioed back and told Sollis that he might well be seeing things as all men were on high alert and starting at every shadow or noise. Grudgingly, Jack Sollis put to sea again, this time taking a longer route and weaving through the fishing vessels in the outer harbour – with luck, if anyone was picking this up on radar, he might just pass for a fishing vessel.

In GH, the situation was tense. At 03.30 Rex Hunt now received more news from London; US President Ronald Reagan had finally managed to reach Galtieri (who had refused to answer several prior calls) and had told him to halt his invasion. Galtieri had flatly refused stating that now he could not call it off even if he wanted to. Now Hunt telephoned Dick Baker – the 'last possible moment' had arrived - and it was time to round up the Argentine workers in town including the LADE staff, Gamin and Gilobert, the Gas del Estado men and several others. If there was a 'fifth column' in Stanley, it would be wise to keep them under observation. Now Baker set off with a force of two Royal Marines and the armed Royal Navy men to make the arrests. The newly-arrived team from the gas company had seemed the most dangerous and had also been showing a more than curious interest in Stanley's dock facilities too. Luckily, they were staying at the *Upland Goose Hotel* and Dick Baker could potentially round them up quickly. He was unsure of what to expect or even do, but remembering the old movies, he positioned an armed man out of sight on either side of the first door and knocked.

Alison King, the hotel owner's daughter, spoke Spanish and translated as Baker apologised that the men would have to be taken into custody. The Gas del Estado men had all been asleep and were groggy still, expressing a mixture of amazement and disbelief and one even asked if he should settle his bill before leaving. Dick Baker told him pleasantly that they could probably worry about that later. He noted that none of the men even seemed angry or upset by waking up to be told they were under arrest and must be placed under guard until the present situation was resolved. It was a simple affair and quite standard although the Argentine junta was to make much of it afterwards and level charges of 'hostage taking' for the act.

As Dick Baker had set out to make his arrests, so Rex Hunt now took to the airwaves once more. FIBS typically broadcast only until 22.30 each night and then closed down with the national anthem. Tonight, the radio's DJ Patrick Watts had declared that he would be broadcasting all night and had gone to Government House to install a microphone and transmitter there to keep up contact. The residents of Stanley, most of whom – with the rumour-mill running rife - were staying up during the night, were still listening to his collection of records and regular updates, and Watts was about to give the world's first example of an interactive 'invasion radio phone-in show' with everyone invited to join in and telephone in whatever they saw or heard.

First, the Governor called in to the switchboard, the operator of which had agreed to work through the night for the purpose, and apologising that he could not remember the number for the radio station, asked to be put through, and Studio Manager Patrick Watts now made an announcement that His Excellency the Governor was about to speak. Hunt first reiterated the latest news; Galtieri had refused President Reagan's calls for peace, stating that unless Britain recognised Argentine sovereignty then the action he was taking would be all that was left to him; *"I have no alternative other than to declare a State of Emergency with immediate effect under the Emergency Powers Ordinance of 1939,"* Hunt continued, *"Under these emergency powers, I can detain any person, authorise entry to any premises, acquire any property and issue such orders as I see fit. I must again warn people in Stanley to stay indoors. Anyone seen wandering on the streets will be arrested by the security forces. I have no further news about the Argentine Navy task force, but may I just say that the morale of the Royal Marines and the Defence Force is terrific, and it makes me proud to be their Commander in Chief."*

Neville Bennett, listening to the radio as he lay in bed, too edgy to sleep, heard the broadcast followed by the resumption of the cheerful radio show; *"Patrick and Dave, the two men on duty in the studio were playing any records they could pick off the shelves,"* he remembered, *"Strangers in the Night came to the top of the pile quite often. I made a cup of tea. The kitchen was quite cool, as I had turned off the oil-fired cooker, just in case, and back to bed for more sleeplessness. I wonder what the Marines are up to? Something nasty, no doubt."*

In fact, the men of the Royal Marines were not having too bad a time of it and for the curious reason that, with the obvious about to come, they had all made their own peace with death. If it came, they were determined, it would only go one way, so it was time to get rid of the fear. Accept the inevitable and go down fighting, don't let your mates down, don't let the Royal Marines down and stand and fight until the end comes – hopefully quickly. There was no way out anyway. The rest was all that they had been trained for. In the dark, cold night, some checked the SLR's again for the umpteenth time. It was a big rifle, a single-shot killing weapon, powerful and accurate. If anyone did come, well – they would have to get past 'the elephant gun' first - it was a comforting thought. In Government House, the men were staking out the ground, checking their range and their sights and clearing fields of fire. Jim Fairfield and another Marine of the new detachment were patrolling outside when some figures appeared in the darkness, walking straight down the drive of the building. It was the journalists, all the worse for drink and approaching, *'without a care in the world'*. Due to the Governor's declared state of emergency, which they seemed to have missed, Jim arrested them and shut them in the Bonner's cottage in the grounds of GH.[*7]

Now as he remembered, the Governess, Mavis Hunt, *"appeared carrying the largest box of posh chocs I'd ever seen. Every single Marine and Matelot had a dip in that box, Mavis would not take no for an answer and though she tried to hide it she was obviously distressed that 'her' Marines were to be put in danger, as she made her way from man to man I could hear her saying over and over, 'Oh my lovely Marines, have some chocolate.' Later while taking a brew by the front door Mavis appeared, she stood and looked around and started to call, 'Fifi, Fifi where are you?' - as I knew they did not own a dog I and a few of the lads assumed she was calling for a cat so joined in the search, all calling for Fifi, while looking in bushes and shrubs, it was several minutes before Don Bonner arrived to ask me what the bloody hell was going on, I explained we were helping Mavis find her cat, Fifi. Don burst out laughing and so infectious was it that soon we were all doubled over in laughter while not having a clue why. Don eventually composed himself to tell us that Fifi was in fact Mavis's little car that he had just put in the garage. It transpired that Mavis, armed with several bottles of brandy (and perhaps just a dash on the inside) had at last been convinced by Rex to go to the safety of the Baker's home and had come out to find her car, she in turn was wondering just what 'her Marines' were up to and thought we were taking the rise out of her! Talk about the fog of war, it was a wonderful moment that broke the building tension in no uncertain terms. Don took me back to his hideout and offered me a tot of rum, Don was, and still is teetotal but he had a few bottles stashed away and nearly everyone got a generous tot from him that night. Another young marine was also having a tot and I remember him asking me with tears in his eyes if I thought they (Argies) would really come, in the most fatherly manner I could muster (I was only 28 myself) and really feeling for the guy I told him that I was sure they would, but not to worry as we'll all do our job and that's all that was important, he looked straight at me and said something like 'I know you're right, I'll keep an eye on you' and walked off, I was later to remember his comments, and his bravery. I also robbed the Governor's fridge that night and made sure everyone, including himself got a nice cold beer."*

With 'Fifi' safe, the next job was to convince Mavis and the Hunt's son Tony to leave which, as Tiny Jones remembered, was not nearly as easy; *"She was nearly screaming at Rex and it was nearly a fireman's lift to get that great lady out of there,"* he recalled, noting that she refused to leave her husband's side, come what may, *"their son Tony had – I think – found some 'fire-water' somewhere and was going to go and 'Meet the fuckers on the beach'. It was kind of amusing. I remember myself and Andy Mac having a 'young guy' conversation with him about his father being under immense pressure as it was, and if his son's life was in his hands, he might make the wrong decision which could affect us all. It was true. Luckily, he made the big-man decision and did what his Dad said. I have to say, Rex Hunt was truly remarkable and I mean that; this short, softly-spoken man was immense. No matter when he spoke to you – on parade, in the barracks or on this night – he was always the same; a gentleman with a genuine interest in all. He used to call me 'Tony' – fuck knows why, but I guess he mistook 'Tiny' from the other guys - I never corrected him. When we were wandering in and out of his office that night, we heard every word he said on the phone or to our two bosses. It was as if he had made the decision to keep no one in the dark. That was Rex Hunt. Truly remarkable."*

Now the Royal Marines continued in their preparations. Most of these were psychological; overcoming the fear of death. Weapons and ammo were checked a hundred times, camo-cream applied and topped up regularly just in case and fields of fire cleared or checked; *"We went into all-round defence. As best as twenty Marines could..."* remembered Jim Fairfield, *"As the night progressed we were given our 'stand to' positions (positions we would man during any attack) about six of us were spaced along the wall and hedge line stretching from GH to the front road and the sea. Once again, my luck fled me as I was to be on my own on the far-right flank, right alongside a gate painted the most brilliant white you have ever seen, the stone wall finished several yards away where my nearest oppo (Marine speak for any other marine or mate) was stationed, the wall was then replaced* with a decorative neatly clipped non-bullet-proof hedgerow! I was facing east towards the barracks at Moody Brook and had a good view of the approach road and the ridgeline to my left, all in my arc of fire but only fully visible when I stood up! After the Sergeant Major declined my offer to give him my shilling back, he told me that as I knew the ground so well I was to be the 'trigger' if any Argies tried to flank us or land by the beach. I felt much better after that - not. I considered my position carefully, there were perhaps two areas, one each side of the gate where I could see all or most of my arc through the hedgerow and from where I could put down fire with any reasonable chance of hitting my target without being seen by the enemy. I would also have to be several feet back from the hedgerow and move positions every few seconds. I knew if I was in the attacking force the white gate would be a focus for my attention because of the view it offered and I'd be sure to keep my eye on it and any movement around it. I tested many different fire positions both back from and close up to the hedge. I also considered that if the situation required I could lay down accurate and heavy fire over the gate for at least three seconds, but could do that only once. I also noted that if I moved back too far I would be visible from the ridgeline to my left until I reached the cover afforded by Government House. I'd been in some stickier situations before I'm sure, but at the time I could not remember when or where!"

The Royal Marines at Government House now all took up their positions and did the same, as Tiny Jones remembered; "The night passed in a blur. We had all done out own recce outside, to check the ground, any cover and our arcs of fire and when I came back, I was told I would have the rear-left-hand corner backing onto the football field with a small fence in between, as I remember. We were also told that on top of the hill at that corner, the FIDF had been requested to take up position, so all good. I remember myself and a few others were standing off to the side of the house, it was now starting to get on in time and Sergeant-Major Johnny Noone was with us. We all felt nervous as fuck – anyone who says different is full of shit – you think to yourself, 'There is this huge fucking gang from the hood about to come into our patch and really fuck us up, the authorities who put you here don't really give a fuck and you are on your own' – it's a changer - when asked what he thought would happen, Johnny Noone said he thought there would probably be a bit of a skirmish on the beach, then there would be a fighting withdrawal to GH, a stand-off and then it would be in the hands of the government. I remember getting the hump with him at this point and thinking my best mate, Jock 'old man' Wilcox was one of the poor fuckers elected to be down there at the front, so I was pissed off about that. Then I shrugged and said, 'It doesn't matter, the old cunt always smells of death anyway,' which we had a chuckle at. Jock was a little older than me and I never missed the opportunity to remind him."

Now the men of the Royal Marines waited. All they could hear was a gentle breeze, the 'hiss' of the sea rolling in and back again with every ear and eye strained for what might come. Somewhere out there was an Argentine task force. Between GH and them were several detachments out there on the hills to the south, by the airport, across the Canache, on the Airport Road and across the Harbour. At GH, some men were thankful for a wall to hide behind whilst others considered that 'out there' they could at least move and fire if they had to and, perhaps, dodge the blow that was coming. In the dark, those outside of GH were preparing their positions, digging in, checking their arcs of fire and trying to come up with plans of their own to survive the onslaught which would soon be heading their way; *"We dug shell scrapes at our position,"* recalled Lou Armour whose section would meet the enemy coming down the Canache, *"mine was in the centre and slightly to the rear of the forward left and right positions, for command and control purposes. I was acutely aware that I was going to be directing the type of fire required when we made contact. However, I recall deciding that this was less a defensive position and more of an ambush scenario, so I placed myself with the gun team of Jonny Alden and Gaz Clifton. At Troop and Section level, an ambush is usually initiated by GPMG and/or Claymore fire. We didn't have any Claymores, so my plan, if the enemy approached with armour, was to give Jonny a tap to fire at the lead vehicle or any troops in the open, which would be the signal for the others to let loose with their 66's. We would then run like fuck to what we hoped would be the other Bootneck positions 300-500 metres behind us! It seems funny to say it now but, as we lay waiting in the dark, I recall seeing a train, which of course was impossible... just fear I guess..."*

Out on the Murray heights, the Marines of Dave *'Scouse'* Carr's section were spread out in case of a naval bombardment and expecting the inevitable; *"Myself and Benny located ourselves on a flat rock platform overlooking the common,"* remembered Nick Williams, *"we had a good field of fire. We then built a defensive wall around ourselves with rocks that were laying around. When we were satisfied, we got back into position but realised that our field of fire had been greatly reduced due to our defences, so we knocked down our defensive wall; no matter what direction the attack came from, we could engage the enemy. We laid out the ammunition for the GPMG, I was on the left of Benny and I had loads of belts of link laid on the rock platform, ready to feed the gun. I had my SLR to one side with the magazines laid ready for action. Between me and Benny I had the SMG and ammunition ready to go in case the gun failed, and finally the L2 grenade. It was a dark night with little wind. With every noise we heard or imagined we heard, we thought, 'This is it'. Myself and Dave had decided that if the attack came our way, we would respond with maximum fire for as long as possible until we reached a point where we were in danger of being overrun. At this point, myself and Benny would cover the riflemen back up the hill about 150 metres towards town and cover. We were confident we could keep the enemy's heads down with the firepower we had and enable the rest of the section to reach safe ground, the plan then called for the riflemen to cover us back to join the rest of the section. It was a hell of a distance uphill over a bare-arsed feature with the weight of the gun and ammunition to carry. Myself and Benny settled down to wait. We were lucky that we were together and could talk. The rest of the guys were on their own; it must have been dreadful for them... We talked very deeply, we both thought we would die and we came to terms with whatever was going to happen. After a while I said to Benny that I had to have a smoke to settle my nerves. I unrolled the sleeping bag, crawled head-first into it and lit up, this was so we didn't show any light... When I surfaced, Benny asked me if it made me feel any better and I said yes, it calmed me down a bit, he then said, 'Have you got a spare ciggy?' (He did not smoke) After Benny had finished his cigarette we talked some more about what was going to happen. We came to the conclusion that we would be able to cover the rest of the section back when it was time to withdraw but they didn't stand a chance of covering us and that we would die if we tried to make it to safety. We decided that when the time came for us to withdraw, we would stay where we were and take out as many Argentines as we could before they killed us. We made a death pact. If one of us was wounded and we were being overrun, the other would detonate the L2 grenade to kill us both. Thinking back after all these years it sounds surreal but it was the truth, we were 8,000 miles from home, on our own and we were going to die. It is a hard pill to swallow."*

Somewhere in the dark on the same piece of rocky ground, Ray Bloye was straining his ears when suddenly; *"In the still of the night, I heard the sound of helicopters. As we didn't have any on the Falklands it meant only one thing. At least it solved one question as to whether the Argies would actually invade or sit off the coast. It was difficult to gauge where the sound was coming from but I did think it was north of our position. After the sound of the choppers, it was once again silent. Was it more so or did it just seem that way? Having heard the choppers, we were now waiting for the next move but we didn't hear anything from HQ. The radios we had in the Falklands were brilliant for transmitting back to the UK but crap at getting someone a couple of miles away."* Nick Williams heard the noises too but remembered that; *"They were faint in the wind, and we were not sure whether the noises came from boats or choppers. This made us very jumpy."*[8]

It was not just Ray Bloye or Nick Williams who could hear the noises. The night was still and calm and every sense was heightened. The acoustic shadow of the noise allowed some farther away to hear it as well, if not better than those closer to it. Mike Norman was on Lookout Rocks just to the south and east of

Stanley and the Airport Road, scanning the horizon, when his ears also picked up the sound which he thought to be coming from the direction of Mullet Creek some two miles to the south; *"I don't like the sound of that..."* he said to his driver, Murray Paterson. He now radioed PJ Berry, alone on Sapper Hill more to the west and much closer to Mullet Creek, but with the constant howling of the wind and the crackle of the radio, Berry reported back that he could not hear anything. At 'Purple' beach, Royal Marines Wilcox and Milne were quite sure they could hear something which sounded like helicopters. They made to call it in on the radio but found that, for some reason, it would not transmit. Mike Norman quickly called back to Gary Noott in GH to ask his opinion. If the Argentines were landing to the south then this would put the entire defence plan in ruins – there were just seven men guarding the right flank however and it was possible that the noise was a trick of the wind. Dare they send men out there to look for anyone? It would pull apart the layered defence and could lead to some very obvious friendly fire incidents. In the end, the two Majors agreed to leave things as they were and hope. They were too thinly stretched with what they had anyway, to send men running around in the dark on a wild goose chase with some itchy trigger fingers.

It was still an annoyance to Mike Norman that the FIDF men were not under his command. He had 'suggested' that men might be sent to the rocky heights above the racecourse, but Rex Hunt had seemed half-hearted about the idea and Norman did not even know if they were there. He was worried about 'friendly fire' incidents in the extreme, which could happen easily and indeed had almost happened already. He had been on patrol in his Land Rover just to the east of Stanley when the first of several incidents that night occurred; the four FIDF members sent to the Wireless Station were patrolling back through the town and approached the cattle grid by 'White City' at the entrance to Davis Street, not knowing that Mike Norman was parked in his Land Rover just off the road and talking with Murray Paterson. Suddenly Mike Norman saw movement in his peripheral vision, hissed to Paterson that somebody was coming up the road and both jumped out of the vehicle and were trying to wrestle their rifles from behind the seats and flip the safety catches off when Paterson recognised one of the men and called out to him. It had been a tense moment and could have been serious. They had been ordered back to the Drill Hall for first light, they said. Mike Norman sent them on their way with a sigh of relief. It was a close call, but it would not be the last one. The FIDF men had been on duty all night but their task was not an envious one; *"The Royal Marines had taken all the communications equipment,"* Taff Davies recalled, *"so the FIDF went out patrolling with what they had and to contact base was a case of knocking on a householder's door and asking to use the telephone. Consequently, as you can imagine, there were a number of 'nearly' blue-on-blue incidents – thankfully all resolved before anybody got injured or killed."*

It was a shame, perhaps, that in the early hours of April 2nd the order came that the FIDF men should begin to make their way back to the Drill Hall for first-light and were under no circumstances to engage the enemy but to offer no resistance and lay down their arms when ordered. Most had been itching for a fight if someone came to take their homes from them. Some now begrudgingly began to shift position, although not all, for some - including Pat Peck and Gerald Cheek's section - were going to maintain their position whatever the case; *"We had positioned ourselves along the southern perimeter of the racecourse which had the better view and defensive positions,"* Gerald Cheek remembered, *"it was quite a mild night with little wind and not particularly cold temperatures. About every hour we received a telephone call from our Headquarters to update us regarding the situation. In the early hours, we were informed that the BBC reported that the US President Reagan had personally requested Galtieri not to proceed with the invasion of the Falklands but Galtieri said unless the British Government agreed to 'return the Islands to their rightful owners' the invasion would go ahead. This was obviously not going to happen. We then realised that this was it, would we be able to continue living on our Islands as British citizens or were we about to lose our lives?"*

The night passed by. Every noise and every shadow seemed to presage disaster or the impending inevitability of invasion which now was coming inexorably closer to the Falkland Islands. PJ Berry, alone on Sapper Hill, was listening to the faint noises of the radio and wishing he had brought the night scope which he and the section at the lighthouse had left behind, intending to return to it later; *"Then something happened which made me crap myself."* He remembered, *"About twenty yards from me, I observed 4-6 figures walking to the hills behind Government House. I radioed in and told the boss that the FIDF were well out of position. His reply was that they were not out. I grabbed my radio, bent the aerial down and laid on top of it to keep it quiet as there was a lot of mush coming over the air. I then started swearing to myself and asking why the Hell I volunteered for this gig!"*

Tense moments passed in GH and Berry now radioed in that he had heard more men moving around his position just to the west of Stanley and reckoned it could be anything up to a hundred of them; *"What shall I do?"* he asked in a tense whisper. Mike Norman considered his options; he had requested that FIDF men take post on the hill by the racecourse, could this be them returning, or a section which had its own ideas? He radioed back to Berry that all might be well, but just in case, to; *"Keep your ruddy head down!"*

At 05.15 Jack Sollis on board the *Forrest* made another report. He had detected two further contacts just off Mongeary Point and the Argentine ships had closed in on the *Forrest* from the east, coming on fast. Mike Norman now ordered him back quickly, but on the way, Sollis reported two more contacts off Charles Point and approaching the Yorke Bay beaches. This was confirmed by Basil Biggs who was watching from the blacked-out lighthouse and who could see ships in the dark. Ten minutes later, Sollis radioed in again that he could actually see smaller vessels – landing craft perhaps - heading for Yorke Bay. The *Forrest* now raced back to the narrows before she was fired upon or seized, but now she came under the guns and rocket launchers of Corporal Stefan York's position at Navy Point. York's men had been listening to the radio traffic and knew what was coming. They had checked their kit one last time, had their Carl Gustav rocket launcher ready and had flicked off the safety catches of their weapons and GPMG, eager to catch anyone coming through the narrows towards Stanley. As the *Forrest* approached in the dark, York now had the thought to radio back his contact and request permission to engage and Mike Norman, quickly thinking, barked back to hold fire. York's section relaxed the pressure on the triggers of their weapons and were glad to have done so when the boat's lights suddenly came on and the familiar silhouette of *Forrest* drifted past them into Stanley Harbour.

At 'Purple' beach Royal Marines Wilcox and Milne had been listening to the radio traffic, unable to respond, when all doubt of an invasion was to be removed at once. As they nestled in their shell-scrape on the beach above the barbed wire and small cluster of Claymore mines they suddenly saw the looming figure of the *Cabo San Antonio* as she rumbled into view on the horizon – a great black leviathan on the waves which came past their beach. The suspense was over: they were here.

The two Royals now considered opening fire with their GPMG. It wouldn't do much damage at this range but it would tell the Argentines that they were willing to make a fight of it. It might stop them but then again it might bring down all hell against their position. In the end, the matter was decided for them; in their haste to carry ammunition for the gun and in the hunt for a spare barrel they had forgotten the tripod. Without that, it was going to be a very ineffective and inaccurate barrage. Instead they waited and watched as the *Cabo San Antonio* sailed straight past them and on towards 'Orange' beach where they heard the engines stop. The Argentine task force was heading straight for the undefended beach: they were in the wrong place. Realising that they were in danger of being completely outflanked and cut off the second the Argentines hit the beach to their left, they now began to gather up their weapons and ammunition. They ran through the darkness, stumbling on sand dunes as they dragged the weight of the kit with them and headed for where they had stowed their bikes. The rest of the section under Figgy Duff was up on Canopus Hill and now they determined to reach them before the hammer fell.

On the radio, Rex Hunt was broadcasting that the Argentine fleet had just been seen. He ended with the words; *"Good luck. Good luck."* Overlooking the Canache, Lou Armour was listening to the radio and heard the broadcast; *"Actually I laughed at that message because it was ironic,"* he remembered, *"'Good luck. Good luck' – wow thanks! We looked at each other in the dark and suddenly all pissed ourselves laughing. We were desperately trying not to make a noise but it was like being caught laughing at school. It was infectious and we couldn't stop! Eventually we did stop and I sent the guys who were with me back to let the others know what had been said. I don't think they thought it was at all funny when they heard it! That's when I reached into my bergen. One of the things I had in there was two cans of beer and I remember crawling around with them and giving each guy in my section a swig of them. I wanted to reassure my guys and this seemed one way to do it. After that, we dug our shell scrapes a bit faster. I told the lads in my section not to do anything stupid and to play it off the cuff. It might have been a bit easier for me because I had them to worry about. It was a bit worse for the lads because they were just thinking about themselves."*

At GH, the men moved about, seeking encouragement and saying last words to each other and Tiny Jones remembered that; *"It was really surreal, we just wandered around talking with everyone and anyone who would listen..."* Every man now waited and watched; their eyes peeled, ears straining, safeties off, hands patting in the darkness for spare ammunition and clips. It was going to be quick, bloody and violent. It was what they had signed on for after all: if only the odds weren't so bad. Well, that was the luck of it. Now it had come. There was no fear of death now, the men recalled. They had dealt with it and swallowed it down. All that was left was the fear of letting their mates down, themselves down, the Marines down, the people of Stanley down and the people back home down. The world would know that they stood and fought; that they did their jobs. Now that the fear was gone though, it seemed easy. It was five minutes past six, the sun was nearly up. Now let them come......

BANG! BOOM! RATATATATAT! BOOM!

Every head in the British force turned around as the cacophony struck their eardrums. Explosions, rapid fire, flashes in the night and tracer bullets were screaming through the night air behind the Royal Marines' positions as each man realised that something had gone badly wrong. The noises and the flashes told them that it was Moody Brook which was now under a ferocious assault of explosives and gunfire. They were being attacked from behind! *"Oh Christ, they've taken out the Brook!"* yelled Colour-Sergeant Noone as he ran from the house, up the gravel drive and now stood in the road listening and staring to where the Marines' barracks was now under assault. *"Before the action started, a feeling of* suspended animation had descended, brought about mainly by our loss of contact with the outside world, and the waiting," Gary Noott remembered, "now with the sound of the first explosions and firing from our recently-vacated barracks, reality was restored within the immediate vicinity... The penny had dropped."

The mood now, however, was not fear. That time had passed. The waiting was over and it was time to go to work. The Marines described the flashes from the west as a fantastic sight and something which automatically triggered their instincts as professionals who had all seen combat before. Now the waiting was over and they could do their jobs. Fear was not part of that job.

The explosions and rattle of grenades and machine gun bullets and the flashes of blasts and tracer fire filled the night air for several minutes as each man stared expectantly to the west; "The night sky lit up with tracer rounds and phosphorous grenades, as well as small arms fire," Jim Fairfield recalled, watching from his vantage point to the west of GH and wishing now that he had been allowed to rig the barracks with explosives, "I could make out the chatter of machine guns and a big 0.5 calibre as well. It only went on for about 10 minutes but seemed much longer and focused everyone's minds, this was the real deal and it was obvious they wanted us as dead as we now wanted them. The game, as they say, was afoot." - Striding out of the Drill Hall onto John Street, FIDF Major Phil Summers tried to look calm and composed in front of the members of the defence force who were now gazing in shock over to where Moody Brook was lit up as if by a firework display; "Right lads," he said calmly, "it's started."

Chapter 6: Strangers in the Night

"I remember thinking to myself; These guys are trying to kill us...
I think we've upset them..."
Mark 'Gibbo' Gibbs – BBC Radio Interview 2017.

"On April 1st at 21:00 we looked through the periscope," Lieutenant Commander Alfredo Cufre recalled, *"there was nothing. Not a car that moved or a light. The surprise was over but we had to disembark as per orders. I had to go. We decided to do it on the other side of the island with rubber boats. There were fourteen of us. We went around the back, against what the English expected."*

The invasion of the Malvinas had now been confirmed and Cufre's men made themselves ready, emerged from the *Santa Fe* and came into shore around Yorke Bay by boat. There was no resistance; no sign of anybody. He would secure a beach-head and space out landing beacons on the beach for the fleet to follow – dim red lamps which could be seen from the sea, but which would give no glow to the landward side. This was an important time for Cufre – the man who had spent three years with his left leg in plaster and who even now had shrapnel stuck there for life - now set foot onto the Islands at midnight; *"The left foot"* he remembered fondly.[*1]

Somewhere out on the dark sea, twenty-one rubber boats came towards the shore bearing the two teams which were to lead the attack upon the rear or the Royal Marines, but now the Falkland Islands themselves seemed to offer their own natural form of resistance; *"As we were slowly motoring in the dark towards the coast, the outboards muffled by thick wet blankets we had thrown on top of them, the column formation we tried to keep was completely messed up because of the propellers catching on the kelp."* Diego Quiroga recalled, *"As my boat went by one of the boats that was so delayed, I caught sight of two dark silhouettes of the occupants as they tried to lift the leg of the engine out of the water to free the weed. They were talking in hushes and I heard one ask, 'Hey man, do you think they will pay 'Zone'?' - 'That's the spirit!' - I thought to myself. The question was referring to the chance of whether the pay supplement for tasks carried out in the 'Austral zone' would apply to this mission."*

The organised formation was coming apart in the kelp. Men were using their hands and knives to clear it as it clogged the outboards, lifting the engine legs into the air, some swearing, some resorting to paddling. The reconnaissance was to be led by the kayak parties – now reduced to one kayak and two men - Lieutenant

Bernardo Schweizer and Corporal Carlos Cequeiera; *"We first became entangled and we lost patience and got into the kayak and started paddling,"* Cequeira remembered. They had launched when some 500 metres from the beach, leaving the others to battle against the thick, clinging kelp as they made their way forward to scout the area and mark the landing beach around Mullet Creek. Schweizer carried a night-vision scope in the front of the kayak and Cequeira a compass in the back to keep them on track; *"As we approached the beach, I had been observing with night-vision goggles but the moonlight was in front and caused me no little discomfort in sight."* Schweizer recalled as he paddled in silently, staring ahead, squinting past the high crescent moon and trying to get a fix on the right location. *"Schweizer told me that he saw a light on the coast and warned me,"* Cequeira recounted, *"I borrowed the viewfinder to look, and saw that there was someone on the coast and assumed they were English."*[2]

Schweizer now decided to select a slightly different beach. The setbacks and delays caused by the kelp, through which the others were still struggling, were a concern. If there were people on the beach, then sailing slowly towards them was not going to be a good idea, particularly if they were armed. Now Schweizer paddled farther east to a beach marked *'Green Beach'* on his map, which was closer and would allow the men to disembark sooner, but which would leave them with another kilometre to walk. *"The sea was calm,"* remembered Cequeira, *"there was only one breaking line and the moon that dazzled us, but when we got to the beach, the moon had set."* - Bernardo Schweizer became the first Argentine to set foot on the Falkland Islands. It was 22.45 on Thursday April 1st 1982 and the invasion of the Falklands had begun.

Now ashore, Schweizer and Cequeira had a lot to do. The landing party was already delayed, they now had farther to walk and if they were caught at sunrise they would be easy prey for the Royal Marines and those dreaded long rifles of theirs. The two men now flashed a light back and slowly the rubber boats began to come in. All order was lost; they came in any old how with some boats towing others and some men even rowing, their outboards having given up altogether. Diego Quiroga remembered that; *"We arrived at the beach in some disarray. My group and Lieutenant Alvarez were responsible for providing security whilst others removed their dry-suits and we rotated positions."* As each man came ashore, he peeled off his dry-suit, helped drag the boat ashore and unpacked his weapon from the protective waterproof bag. Many of the men carried the British-made Sterling submachine gun – a perfect fit for such operations. Still the men were coming in slowly, some were missing or terribly late. Schweizer waited and then ordered one man – Corporal Pereya - back in a boat to round up the stragglers and make sure they came to the new beach. Somehow, Pereya passed by all of the boats unnoticed in the dark and ended up back at the *Santisma Trinidad* where now, despite his extreme protests, he was ordered to stay. Finally, after what seemed like an age, the men were ashore, their equipment ready, their boats ashore and still they had managed to do so undetected. It had cost them time - it was now 23.45 – it had been an hour since Schweizer and Cequeira had first landed.

The two groups now split up; Sanchez Sabarots leading his larger party off towards Moody Brook and Pedro Giachino leading his own force off towards Government House. It was pitch dark and now, having landed at 'Green Beach' the men were late and out of position, with the ground around Mullet Creek to navigate and still a kilometre farther to walk in the unfamiliar ground; *"We had to walk between two lagoons and were worried at the time that that land was waterlogged but it was not."* recalled Bernardo Schweizer, *"The hasty choice of Green Beach was very lucky because subsequently found in the Mullet Creek positions were four Royal Marines with a heavy machine gun. We made preparations for the mission with the indication that we would have the element of surprise, but in reality, the British were waiting for us."* - Corporal Jacinto Batista, leading the way with a night-scope, now questioned whether a section should be sent around to take out the position on Mullet Creek from behind as he remembered; *"A very short distance from the beach was a Jeep with four men and a machine gun, waiting. We passed very close to them and I asked permission to seize them, but it was denied: first, because there had to be no casualties and secondly because they did not want the operation to be unveiled."* - This was not part of the mission and there was no point giving their position away for an outpost. The men would continue on towards their objective and hope to remain undetected.[*3]

The two parties first walked parallel to Mullet Creek and then split up. Sanchez Sabarots' team headed more to the west to reach Moody Brook, skirting around Mount William and then crossing the creek, followed shortly after by Giachino's party; *"All sight of the marching column of Commandos Anfibios towards Moody Brook disappeared, swallowed up by the darkness, and we set off."* Diego Quiroga recalled. Giachino's team now took its own route and found it hard going. They groped their way forward in the darkness over boggy peat, rocks, boulders and pot-holes, using Sapper Hill, silhouetted against the night sky as their guide; *"The road was difficult,"* remembered Quiroga, *"and worse because I could not see anything... During the march, I stumbled to my knees, hitting them on a fairly large rocky ledge, which made Captain Giachino have to send out explorers at the head of the patrol. We would stop every fifty steps or less until we heard the two whistles of the explorers indicating that the way was clear. As we approached the target and the reflection of the light allowed us to see better, these distances of fifty steps were growing larger, making the explorers be absent for periods of up to twenty minutes."*

Lieutenant Commander Sanchez Sabarots' party pushed on with six miles to cover to Moody Brook; *"It was a nice night, with a moon, but the cloud covered the moon for most of the time,"* Sanchez Sabarots later recalled, *"We were only a few minutes late but we had farther to go now. We didn't take a direct route; there would have been no landmarks that way. We went along the coast to Mullet Creek and set out from there, following a fence line which was shown as running due north on the map. We were very surprised at the difficulty of the ground. What the reconnaissance photos showed as 'grass' we found to be great hummocks. It was very hard going with our heavy loads; it was hot work. We eventually became split up into three groups. We had only one night-sight; the lead man, Lieutenant Arias had it. One of the groups became separated when a vehicle came along the track which we had to cross. We thought it was a military patrol. Another group just lost contact, and the third separation was caused by someone going too fast. This caused my second-in-command Lieutenant Bardi, to fall. He suffered a hairline fracture of the ankle and had to be left behind with a man to help him. But, except for Lieutenant Bardi and his helper, we all got there by various means; I think we had a certain amount of luck. We were at Moody Brook by 05.30, just on the limits of the time planned, but with no time for the one hour's reconnaissance for which we had hoped."*

In all, the six-mile march had taken six hours and already one man was out of action and another left to help him. As they had approached, Captain Robles of Sanchez Sabarots' command remembered an incident; *"When we reached Mount William we stopped and took a break. I went ahead with Lieutenant Arias, nicknamed Negro, to a position beyond the cusp of heights. From where we were, with our backs supported by a rock, we could see Port Stanley to the right and almost opposite we guessed were the barracks, our objective. We had this short dialogue: 'Negro, what do you think about everything?' He said that it seemed to him impossible that all that was happening, that it was reality and that we were going to capture the Royal Marines in the Falkland Islands. 'Arias,' I told him, 'unless someone calls us on the radio and give us a counter-order, that is precisely what we are going to do...'"*

Slowly the teams gathered around Moody Brook and reported no sentries. There was a light shining from the office there; probably the only light that shone in the Islands at this time. Now they split into seven groups to surround Moody Brook from all sides with machine guns and assault rifles as others prepared to charge at the barracks with stun and gas grenades; *"It was still completely dark,"* Sanchez Sabarots continued, *"We were going to use tear-gas to force the British out of the buildings and capture them. Our orders were not to cause casualties if possible. That was the most difficult mission of my career. All our training as Commandos was to fight aggressively and inflict maximum casualties on an enemy. We surrounded the barracks with machine gun teams, leaving only one escape route along the peninsula north of Stanley Harbour, so that anyone who did get away would not be able to reach the town and reinforce the British there..."* They checked the time, it was five minutes past six. The attacks were supposed to be coordinated but there was no noise from Government House or indeed from anywhere barring the occasional call of an animal in the darkness. Giachino's party was not answering their radio. It was time to launch the attack and Sanchez Sabarots now gave the order; *"Then we threw the tear-gas grenades into each building..."* he recounted. Ten men armed with grenades had approached the entrance to the barracks, *"Who threw, threw and threw for ten minutes,"* as Carlos Cequeira remembered. The idea was to shock and overawe the Marines into surrender with a cacophony of noise and smoke, soon machine guns and rifles opened up as others joined in; *"warning shots were made"* Schweizer recalled, *"and at a given moment, we ceased fire."* Cequeira continues. *"There was no reaction,"* Sanchez Sabarots ended his account of the action, *"the barracks were empty."*

Cautiously the men moved into Moody Brook. It was abandoned. The room with the light on; Gary Noott's former office, was vacant too. Those outside waited to get clarification that the barracks were cleared and were then ordered to form a cordon in case the Royal Marines came to investigate the firing. They waited but nobody came. From the direction of Government House, they could now hear the sounds of gunfire and grenades. Sanchez Sabarots sent some men to the east to reinforce Giachino but told the rest to hold their position a while longer in case anybody retreated that way. He would wait until dawn. Some of his men even amused themselves by playing pool in the Moody Brook bar as they awaited the order to advance. At 07.15 Sanchez Sabarots' men hauled down the Union Jack that hung above Moody Brook and replaced it with their own flag. The sounds of fighting at Government House had increased and now he ordered the bulk of his command to march to join the fight that was raging two miles to the east.

The moment that Moody Brook barracks had been hit, the Royal Marine parties which were strung out from the airport to the Canache, along the airport road and to the south at the Murray Heights had all turned to realise that the attack was coming from the rear, yet now also the main amphibious landing was coming in towards the beaches at pace. The men thought frantically; should they hold their positions and meet the attack or dash back to the defence of Government House? Then the radios crackled into life as Mike Norman put out the word; Moody Brook had been hit. *"When they mortared Moody Brook, we could* see the flashes and hear the guns." Lou Armour remembered, "We watched tracer bounce into the night sky and the flashes from the explosions mixed with the rattle of rifle, grenade and GPMG fire. My immediate thought was, 'This is it' before realising that we had to pay attention to our front and flanks and I remember hoping that the lads would realise this too. The urge to shout an order or do something reassuring was very strong but I knew we had to remain silent and hidden as best we could, lest we give our position away to anybody recce-ing the route from the direction of the airport. We heard a lot of chat over the radio. We stayed where we were, because we were told not to move until we were either called or actually engaged with somebody. Eventually we were told to head back to Stanley and try to get to Government House. I thought, 'Fuck me, that's miles, and we've got a ton of ammo!' I quickly rounded everybody up, told them what was happening, and we packed up the kit and set off running bent-backed along the road to Stanley."

Figgy Duff's section on Canopus Hill above the airport had also joined the withdrawal back to Stanley as Dave Gerrard recalled; "We got the word to go straight back to Government House. Looking down, we had the 66's laid out ready. Scooping them up, we tossed them on the floor of the Rover, jumped in and headed for GH. On the way, we had two cattle grids to go over. Travelling at speed, we hit both of them, with us and the rockets bouncing all over the place in the back of the Rover."[*4]

Running back from 'Purple Beach' Wilcox and Milne had mounted up on their motorbikes and made for Figgy Duff's position on Canopus Hill but now found the hill deserted. The lights on one of the bikes didn't work and so now they raced back in tandem towards Stanley, hoping to link up with the other sections. Meanwhile on the Murray Heights, Corporals Dave Carr and Nick Williams had also heard the attack; "We heard a series of explosions and small arms fire coming from Moody Brook," recounted Nick Williams, "it was lighting up the sky in the distance. This was it, it was starting. Shortly after that, the guys at Government House reported that they had come under attack. We had been wrong-footed, the Argentines had come in behind us. We could hear a lot of gunfire coming from GH, the situation over the radio became confusing. After a while we were ordered to make our way to GH to reinforce it. Dave told us to get ready to move, it took me and Benny a while to pack up all the kit and ammo we had laid out."

Now the men of the section were running back towards Stanley dragging their immense haul of weapons and ammunition with them; "We left our positions and started to make our way back into town," Ray Bloye remembered, "En-route, I took my green beret off and stuck it inside my windproof as I didn't want to lose it. We were making fast progress but I found I was somewhat encumbered with all the ammo and kit I was carrying. If we came under fire, I would not be in a good *position to fire back. I had the bandoliers of extra ammo across my chest and was carrying one of the gun ammo trays in my left hand, leaving my SLR in my right. Despite what Hollywood depicts, firing an SLR single-handed is not good and it would be a miracle to hit anything. With that thought in my mind, I threw the tray of ammo over a hedge and immediately felt better. I still had another tray stowed in my kit for when needed. I took a 'proper' hold of my SLR and felt ready if anything should happen."*

Now all of the sections barring Lieutenant Bill Trollope's team on the airport road were pouring back to into Stanley. They alone would have to face whatever came up that road. To help the other sections get back to where they were now needed, Burt Reynolds was sent in the Land Rover to try to round them up and soon came across Section One who – new to Stanley and now in the pitch dark - had lost their way; *"After what seemed like miles of running and stumbling, a vehicle with no lights appeared, heading towards us from Stanley,"* remembered Lou Armour, *"We took cover initially but the vehicle began to crawl along slowly and we realised it was a Rover. I flagged it down to find it was being driven by Burt Reynolds and he seemed to be wearing a sleeveless jacket of the kind mountain men might wear in a Western movie. We piled in and dashed back through Stanley with me hanging halfway out the back, towards the sound of gunfire in the streets."*

Out in Yorke Bay at 'Orange Beach' the bow doors of the *Cabo San Antonio* opened up. The men of BIM2 and the 25th Infantry Regiment had been ordered into their Amtrack vehicles at 05.45 and now made ready; *"I went down the stairs of the Cabo San Antonio to get to the hold,"* remembered Daniel Tosolini of the BIM2, *"all the vehicles were formed ready to disembark. There was great excitement and nervousness. My head of company Di Paola gave the instructions of the assigned vehicle, I do not remember the number, but I know that our section of Delta company was of twenty-five men."* - Indeed, as confirmed by Hugo Santillan, each of the vehicles was going to exceed maximum capacity. Each Amtrack usually carried a crew of three and a compliment of twenty, today they were going to be packed, each one full of twenty-five men plus the crew.*[5]

Hugo Santillan, now about to lead the amphibious assault up the beach, had not slept well; *"The fear arose and it was hard for me to sleep,"* he remembered, *"I had a wife and three children... I had promised Stella Maris a million things and had asked for a million more... at 04.30 in the morning, before breakfast, I went up to the bridge and I was surprised to see the lights of Stanley turned on as if I was looking at Corrientes back home... Although we were all certain that the operation was going ahead, at that moment it was a rare sensation. We had never done a real amphibious operation. It was a mixture of anxiety, worry, great excitement* and enthusiasm. *Imagine, we had the destiny to be those who were going to see the dream of the Republic to recover the Falkland Islands. We were well prepared and we felt empowered to do so. The British were - at most - ninety men, we more than a thousand. There was no possibility that the operation would go wrong. At that time, we were at the peak of the historical operational capacity of the Argentine Navy... Finally, at 05.40 we all went and climbed into the amphibious vehicles in the hold... the lights went out, the compartments of the vehicles were closed, the red light was turned on and the engines were started..."* Finally, the target beach was signalled, the green light came on and the bow doors opened. There was a roar of engines as the vehicles revved up and five minutes later radio silence was declared as Lieutenant Commander Hugo Santillan led his vehicle first into the water. It dropped, bobbed, came back up and now began to swim towards the distant shore. There was a gap perhaps of thirty seconds between each vehicle to ensure that one did not land on top of another and sink it, and then each one would veer alternately to the left or right to leave room for the one behind.

Slowly the Amtracks crawled their way through the darkness towards the dim red glow of the target beach which Cufre and his men had marked for them. The two-mile journey to the shore would take ten minutes. Whilst in the water, they would be vulnerable, but were afforded cover by the Corvette *Drummond* which hovered just off to their right. The men travelled in silence; *"Nobody said a word,"* Daniel Tosolini recalled, *"some prayed. I think I laughed about what would happen, but said nothing to cause panic amongst the men."* Another of the Amtrack commanders, Lieutenant Mario Forbice was very proud of his men. He had worked hard to get them trained for this mission and recounted that; *"Everyone was very emotional. We were going into a real action for the first time; an action to recover the Malvinas. It was a particularly proud moment for the Marines, because every man had trained for action and this was our first opportunity. We were recovering something that belonged to us and had been taken from us."*

The amphibious attack broke into three groups; Hugo Santillan was to lead the vanguard of four vehicles, then Weinstabl was to lead the second wave of fourteen vehicles, one of which contained Admiral Busser himself and finally the last two vehicles would come in escorting the load carrying LARC's which carried the artillery and other equipment. Hugo Santillan came in with his first four Amtracks in a diamond formation with his own vehicle No.05 in the lead, No.07 fifty metres to his right and rear under Sergeant Quiroga, No.19 to fifty metres to his left and rear under Lieutenant Schweizer and finally No.10 one hundred metres to the rear which contained the platoon of the 25th Infantry Regiment under their commander Lieutenant Colonel Seineldin. If Hugo Santillan hit resistance or struggled on the beach, he would radio and the other three would swing off to the left and attempt the beach on that side instead.

He had six orders;

1 - Clear the beaches of any anti-tank weapons.

2 - Overrun any enemy infantry which might jeopardise ship-to-shore movement.

3 – Make sure there are no mines in the area.

4 – Produce early combat intelligence.

5 – Provide time and space to subsequent assault waves.

6 – Detach the LVTP-7 which carried the army platoon to secure the airfield.

This last order was a last-minute change of plans. In the initial planning stage, due to the army's support for the navy's plan against that of the air force, it had been decided that the army was to be given a leading and honourable role and that it was to capture Government House whilst Giachino's party secured the government buildings such as the radio station and the power station. However better counsels had prevailed; the infantry battalions were conscripts and each battalion was drawn up in five sections over the year. Therefore, whilst one fifth of each battalion was completely green, another fifth would be fully trained. Those in the middle had, of course, various degrees of experience. The men now in vehicle No.10 were now perhaps only three months into their training and were not going to be sent against the Royal Marines. Hugo Santillan did not want to risk them and Admiral Busser had agreed and made the changes.[*5]

H-Hour, D-Day had come. It was supposed to have been 06.00 but Busser had moved it to 06.30 – still half an hour before dawn; *"It all went as though we were on an exercise in Patagonia,"* Hugo Santillan remembered, *"My call-sign was 'Alborada' – 'Dawn' - very poetic! My group of four Amtracks approached the beach in a diamond formation. If I got ashore safely, the others would form a column and follow me in, but if I bogged down in mud or something, the others could swing left and lead the battalion on to Purple Beach and be prepared to fight their way in there. When I felt the Amtrack 'touch bottom' I radioed 'Touch-down'; it was 06.30 exactly – a credit to the people on the Cabo who guided us in by radio - then, ten or fifteen seconds later, the driver engaged the tracks and I radioed that the ground was firm, that the tracks were running well and that there was no enemy in sight. I gave the order; 'Everyone up!' The three forward hatches were opened – one for me, one for the driver and one for the gunner – and the two long hatches at the sides were opened for the marines to man their weapons... again, the soldiers now started to scream like the night before and I had to shout to make them shut up! ... All went well. The beach was incredibly white, to my surprise, with a steep slope ten metres from the waterline and a few rocks; there was no cover for my huge*

Amtrack and I thought I was a sitting duck coming up that slope – but the place was deserted."

Now the battalion commander Alfredo Weinstabl led the rest of the force in to make the landing. There had been a slight delay; Admiral Busser's own vehicle 'Charlie One' had suffered a break in the deflector plates behind one of the propellers which ruined the forward steering. The vehicle could only go around in circles when in forward gear and now the commander of the force – who had flustered over putting his vehicles into full working order for so many months - had to come in backwards due to a broken part. There on the beach, Hugo Santillan waited for Busser and Weinstabl to come up; *"When I was up on the slope, Commander Weinstabl came on the radio and said that he could see me in his night-sight and was following me in,"* he recounted, *"I drove on to the south, over open ground, through a narrow valley 200 metres wide with my other three Amtracks following in column. It was rocky, and we could not go fast. I thought the Royal Marines were being very clever, that they were allowing me to come off the beach and had prepared a killing zone in that valley; I thought I was a sitting duck again. I reached the track and could see details of the ground now because it was getting light. It was going to be a beautiful day; no wind, very mild. I hit the track and turned east towards my first objective, the airport. I could see that the main group were following us."*

Now the Amtracks were landing across 'Orange Beach' and moving on to the airport where they found that Cufre's squad had already cleared the area and were holding it. Hugo Santillan stopped, covering the landing as Amtracks #04, #08, #09, #11 and #15 containing Echo company under Lieutenant Carlos Arruani took the lead and moved ahead to secure the isthmus. At the airport – still nervous as to the lack of resistance - the platoon of the 25th Infantry Regiment under Lieutenant Colonel Mohamed Ali Seineldin disembarked and along with some of the men of Echo company, began to clear the runway, which was clogged with a fire truck, tractors, concrete blocks, a bus and other heavy vehicles – 23 in total - to allow the rest of the battalion to land later in the day. Commander Weinstabl now detached three of his Amtracks to help push the obstacles away and soon became aware that; *"There were shots being fired at the other end of the town... However, something must have happened, since on the radio, someone was calling repeatedly and urgently for a doctor to come to the area..."* The airport and runway were quickly cleared, Amtracks were headed for the Canache, marked as *'objective Zulu'* in the plans and on a nearby hill, crowned with two rusting old cannon, trenches were found abandoned. Despite a few shots which could be heard through the darkness far out to the west, all was deathly silent. So far it had been too easy; *"Watch out! Locate the enemy!"* Admiral Busser had scrawled in his personal notes at 05.25, now at 06.45 he was scribbling in frustration; *"Where is the enemy??"*

Already the people of the Islands were phoning in to the FIBS to report what they had seen and heard and giving a running commentary on the invasion as it happened. The second the explosions and gunfire at Moody Brook had been heard, every light in the town had seemingly been switched on at once. Nobody had truly been asleep and now people were up and eager to witness the invasion for themselves, calling in to the radio station with anything which might be of use or of value to the Marines and the defence force. Quickly the lights went out again as people now peered from their windows and turned the radio up to see and hear anything that could threaten their homes and families. Now Rex Hunt came on the radio and every family in Stanley stopped to listen; *"This is the Governor speaking. This is just to let you know that the first Argentine ships have been sighted in Port William and one landing craft approaching the narrows. Everything is under control, we are keeping them under surveillance. That is all for now. There have been one or two bangs at Moody Brook but we consider that this is a diversion. And, if we go off the air, the radio station will carry on. That's all for now."*

Rex Hunt had sounded calm, measured and wholly unflustered. The radio went on to play an ominous piece of classical music – 'Fingal's Cave' - which was interrupted moments later by a fresh update again from Rex Hunt; *"This is the Governor speaking,"* he opened again, *"those of you who are living in Stanley will have heard some shots... some confused shooting... we do not know yet what that's all about but we have had sightings of an aircraft carrier and a destroyer in addition to the three other vessels that I mentioned earlier. It appears that the first vessel is attempting to come through the narrows into the harbour and is probably heading for, or trying to get to Government House. We'll keep on and keep you up to date for as long as we can here, and if we go off the air, the radio station will carry on. That's all for now."* With ships and a landing craft now coming towards the narrows, Mike Norman radioed Corporal York, heading Section Four at Navy Point to get a clearer view. York reported back that three potential targets were in sight and asked which should he engage first. *"What are the targets?"* Norman asked him, *"Target number one is an aircraft carrier,"* York replied, *"target number two is a cruiser..."* at which the line went dead.

Neville Bennett was at home in Stanley in his house overlooking the narrows. He had his diary in hand, ready to record anything which might be of use or interest and now, with the Governor's words about a landing craft coming through the narrows, he raced to the kitchen and the back window to get a view of it and peered out across the water. His words are recorded here exactly as he wrote them; *"**WHAT THE HELL WAS THAT?** - His Excellency the Governor had said that a* boat had come in through the narrows and was firing on Government House... no it wasn't... something had blown up in the narrows. Anyway, it was a big explosion, or magnified by the stillness of the night and the psychological effect. The studio went on to play 'Strangers in the Night.' Back to bed as I couldn't see anything from the front windows." - The landing boat, which Neville Bennett later described as '" Exactly like they used on Iwo Jima" - an LCVP or 'Higgins boat' as they had first been termed, had erupted in flames in the narrows, turned over and sunk. Someone had blown it up with an 84mm Carl Gustav rocket: he was quite clear on this part. The complement of those boats was supposed to be forty men, but they could handle more at a push and the US Marines, with whom they had trained, did so often. Whatever it was, it had rolled over almost instantly and vanished beneath the surface with whomever was in it. Nobody got out.[*6]

With Sections One, Five and Six having pulled back towards Stanley and GH, only Sections Two and Three now held the Airport Road against any advance from Yorke Bay. Section Three was in place near the LADE Beacon and just south of the road; six men in total, Corporal Steve Johnson commanding and five others including a GPMG team of which the youngest Marine in the Islands, Marc Branch, was number two, as he recalled; "It seemed like we were really exposed in the middle of very flat but grassy peat fields. We'd taken position the previous night only half taking the notion that the attack was going to happen seriously. At around 06.00 we heard explosions and gunfire. Someone informed us that they were expelling excess ammunition at Moody Brook which seemed odd to me as I thought there was no one there. It seemed everything escalated very quickly. It was broad daylight in short order and from the radio chatter and the reverberation of gunfire and explosions it was apparent we were under attack. It seemed like there was gunfire and explosions in several directions. We were all laid to ground waiting for 'something' to happen or to receive orders."

The radio now sprang into life, with Mike Norman ordering Section Three back towards the Power Station but Steve Johnson, not knowing the area, said that he couldn't find it and Norman ordered him instead back towards GH via the rear entrance. The section set off, skirting around Stanley and mounting the shoulder of Sapper Hill when all of a sudden, as Marc Branch remembered; "We suddenly came under fire and could hear the rounds passing overhead and hit something behind us (I think a telegraph pole). It wasn't automatic bursts and was determined to be from long range and possibly a sniper. Problem was we couldn't see where it was coming from exactly. It appeared to be coming from the east or south-east. Murdo Macleod saw what he thought was a muzzle flash coming from what appeared to be a barn attached to a farmhouse around 1/2 mile away. Somewhere during that process Steve Johnson and Steve Black had either got a brief from Government House or lost radio contact and determined for themselves that we were fighting an overwhelming force and GH was either taken or surrounded. The decision was made to head out to a settlement or seek refuge in the mountains and regroup and possibly assess a strategy to do some kind of counter-attack. Steve Black was a Royal Marine sniper and by all accounts a damn good one! He'd been on the Falklands tour before and was married to an Islander and knew the lay of the land. The plan was to follow the coastline around, I think behind Sapper Hill, and had a good chance of remaining undetected in the long grass. First, we had to get out of the position we were in. There was a road or track about 100 metres behind us with a dyke running alongside it. Eggman (Steve Dronfield) and I were to remain in position and put down covering fire for the section and once they made it we would follow and they would cover us. The lads took off and suddenly Eggman and I felt very alone! We determined that it would be dangerous to just randomly pelt the barn with GPMG fire especially with the spread of the rounds over that distance and specifically into a farmhouse where civilians obviously lived (good choice by a sniper probably knowing this). The rest of the section were in position in the dyke by the road and we were called to move. All I recall is thinking, 'I'm carrying tons of GPMG ammo, my rifle and all of its ammo and the rest of my gear. If I don't get picked off it would be a miracle.' - With that we took off, zig-zagging along the way going as fast as our legs would carry us. I'm sure we jumped the last 10 feet and came crashing into the dyke! That's where things turned strange for a moment. Apparently something, no one was sure what, landed several yards away in the peat field. Nobody could tell if it was a round, a mortar shell or a kamikaze carrier pigeon, but I was oblivious to it. When we finally stood up after catching our breath it seemed everyone was looking at us. Then someone said, 'Come on lads get moving, they're bringing in the hardware!'"*7

Meanwhile the Amtracks of Weinstabl's command had all come ashore and finally the LARC's carrying the artillery radioed in that they too were now on the beaches and deployed as Hugo Santillan recounted a humorous moment; *"Our field artillery battery commander had 'Aconcagua' for his call sign. Aconcagua is the name of a huge mountain in the Andes range. When he landed his howitzers, he made a mistake with his call sign and radioed, 'This is Tupungato and I´m ready for fire requests' - Tupungato is another high Andes mountain… but also the brand of a well-known red wine of Argentina. He then had to suffer all kind of jokes related to his wine preferences!"* Now Hugo Santillan led them across the Canache or 'the Neck' as it had been termed in the Argentine plans. It was a killing ground had it been chosen for defence but Santillan led the advance and somehow made it across unmolested and then veered right on to the airport road heading for Stanley. He was stood up in his cupola, scanning the dark horizon with his binoculars, with a rifleman in each corner of the vehicle peering out to locate and engage the enemy; *"It was quiet,"* he remembered, *"too quiet, and I was looking for a trap because it felt like nobody was there and they must be waiting for me to get in close."* As the vanguard of the armoured column passed the Canache, the Falkland Islands again seemed to offer their own natural form of resistance. Hugo Santillan recalled the incident; *"When we left the isthmus behind, my third LVTP-7 under Lieutenant Carlos Schweizer got stuck in a patch of damp peat. I have to admit that this was the first time in ten years that one of our Amtracks ever 'bogged' – down to the extent of getting immobilised! I radioed Schweizer to 'Get out of the bunker!' (we both played golf together) and to catch up as soon as possible. As the vanguard, I couldn't wait for him, so I pressed on. Some five minutes later, he signalled that he was on the move again and he regained his station on my left."*

Now the Amtracks were coming down onto the position of Section Two, hurriedly joined by Lieutenant Bill Trollope and his men, who were waiting by their low barricade of rocks, sleepers and other hastily-assembled debris. The plan had been for each section to cover the next one back, yet obviously this was not going to happen now; *"The tension was unbearable... the waiting,"* Mark Gibbs recalled, *"and then when I saw these Amtracks coming over the Canache and on to the airport road towards us, I actually started laughing crazily... The tension had finally broken."*

"This position's shite against armour, let's get out of here!" Gibbs remembered Trollope saying, *"Right, everyone back into the Land Rover apart from the anti-tank team!"* Released from having to sit in the open and await the attack, the rest of the section piled into the Land Rover and headed back towards Stanley to make a new position, leaving Danny Betts and George Brown alone behind the barricade. Quickly the section unloaded a stack of 66's around the two, wishing them good luck and then climbed aboard and headed off with a call of *"Right lads, we'll see ya!"* as they raced off to the west leaving the two friends alone to face the onslaught with nothing but a Carl Gustav and a stack of disposable 66's; *"Danny and I just looked at each other and then it dawned on us,"* George Brown recalled, *"and we both just said the same thing – 'Fuck'!"*

Together in the grey dawn Danny and George waited. They could hear the noises of the engines and the clanking of the vast leviathans as they came closer; *"I can hear them George."* said Danny, then after a while, *"I can see them George.... George they're coming.... George they're here.... they're here George..."* later he laughed that; *"I just kept saying 'George' with everything!"* - Yet they were coming; *"And we were going to take as many out as we could."* he said later. George Brown watched the giant Amtracks coming along the road and through the tussock grass to either side in formation. He had seen them in the United States only the year before and knew what they were capable of; *"Oh shit they've got Amtracks,"* he said to himself, *"they're going to bypass everything!"* Suddenly from behind came a screech of brakes as their mutual friend Mark Coombs dashed back in the Land Rover to fetch them. So transfixed were Brown and Betts by the oncoming Amtracks that they had not even heard the vehicle approach and now they gasped, startled at the sudden noise from behind with George Brown remembering that; *"I literally nearly shit myself."*

The rest of the section were back and in position on the outskirts of Stanley behind a slight fold in the ground and just beside a small cluster of white houses known locally as 'White City' which stood like the gateway into town along the road. White City was known as an *'Expat'* in Falklands terms; like 'Little Italy', 'German Camp' and several others, it had been built beyond the old town to house expats from an empire a century ago who had come, many said; *'expecting servants, gin and tonic, circuits and the like'* – naturally in the Falklands this mistake had been quickly rectified by harsh reality - now it would become the scene of a clash between British and Argentine Marines.

Having provided 'point-section' to cover the withdrawal, Brown and Betts now bundled their collection of rocket launchers and other kit into the back of the Land Rover, snatching glances nervously over their shoulders to where the great black shapes of the Amtracks were visibly approaching through the murky dawn. Finally aboard, the Land Rover sped off along the road with George Brown realising that he had forgotten his brand new Berghaus bergen in the rush, complete with ammunition and spare rockets. The vehicle raced and bounced along the rough road, throwing the Marines everywhere and sending armed LAW rocket launchers rolling and bouncing around, something which George Brown later described as; *"one of the bumpiest rides I've ever had in my life!"*

The Land Rover pulled up in dead ground to let them out and the two hastily decamped, dragging their stash of 66's with them along with the Carl Gustav for which they still had two twin-packs of rockets which Danny Betts had taken with him. They were ordered to take up a position and prepare to fire – the problem was where. There was no cover at all except for the long, yellow tussock grass. The ground was totally flat. The rest of the section were formed some fifty feet to their right, with a GPMG, a sniper rifle, their SLR's and a small clutch of 66's ready to offer flanking fire. Now the Amtracks were getting closer and Danny Betts and George Brown threw themselves down flat in the tussock grass and hoped it would conceal them enough to get a good shot in. George Brown had the Carl Gustav ready as Danny Betts loaded the first round. His job would be what was termed as 'load and cuddle' – to hold his friend firm to save him from the worst of the thunderous back-blast - and then to load the next round as quickly as possible. George Brown was now aware of how roughly they had bore-sighted the weapon;

with all the rushing, they had had time only to do a quick job to correct the sights and he wished it had been more thorough. He would have to let them get dangerously close if he were to hit the lead vehicle, and then all hell would break loose. Each one would be packed full of soldiers and was armed with a 30mm cannon which could spray bullets as large as a beer bottle at a rapid rate of fire: if they opened with those and deployed their men, then the Marines were dead men. A hit, however, would mean only one thing – a 'brew-up' as the Marines called it - even a '66 could tear through an Amtrack's armour with ease. The 'Charlie-G' would make mincemeat of it. It was all a case of who hit first.

Now the Amtracks pushed on up the road towards White City, with Hugo Santillan in the lead in vehicle No.05 on the main road, with the other vehicles spaced around him – No.07 to his rear and right and No.19 to his rear and left, he recalled. Here, however, the tale becomes quite distorted and we must momentarily break from our narrative to present it. There are here two accounts – both entirely incongruous and indeed they appear as two entirely different actions with very little relevance to each other. Whilst there are anomalies and the inevitable 'fog of war' which can be covered and made into a generally accepted version, yet these still do not bear out the core elements of both stories and, whilst the more in-depth elements of this are discussed in the relevant Appendix, yet they are so incongruous that it is necessary to tell both stories, as agreed to by the men on both sides, firstly through their official reports and secondly through the words of the men themselves.[*8]

Hugo Santillan's official report states that: *"We were on the last straight stretch of road into Stanley. I saw a yellow road repair machine which appeared to be broken down on a bend in the road and partially blocking it. We were running very fast by then and I told my men to be careful; perhaps the road was mined or the machine was booby-trapped. I never really finished the message. A machine gun fired from one of the three white houses about 500 metres away and hit the right-hand Amtrack (No.07). The fire was very accurate. Then there were some explosions from a rocket launcher, but they were inaccurate, falling a long way from us. We followed our standard operating procedure and took evasive action. The Amtrack on the right answered the fire and took cover in a little depression. Once he was out of danger, I told all three vehicles to disembark their men. I needed to evaluate the situation. I ordered my subordinate leaders to report what they could see. I radioed to the battalion commander and he told me to stop and wait for him to come forward. He soon arrived. He told me to organise a fire-base from my position, so that the other two companies could deploy to the south and swing round into the town. The same group of Royal Marines opened fire on my position again, fortunately ineffectively, and no one was hit. Commander Weinstabl and I decided it was time to force the British to withdraw. I ordered the crew with* the recoilless rifle to fire one round of hollow charge at the ridge of the roof of the house where the machine gun was, to cause a bang but not an explosion. We were still following our orders not to inflict casualties. The first round was about a hundred metres short, but the second hit the roof. The British troops then threw a purple smoke grenade; I thought it was their signal to withdraw. They had stopped firing, so Commander Weinstabl started the movement of the two companies around the position. Some riflemen in one of those other houses started firing then; that was quite uncomfortable. I couldn't pinpoint their location, but one of my other Amtracks could and asked permission to open up with a mortar which he had. I authorised this, but only with three rounds and only at the roofs of the houses. Two rounds were short, but the third hit right in the centre of the roof; that was incredible. The British ceased fire then."

Now Lieutenant Bill Trollope's own report which stated that; "Six Armoured Personnel Carriers began advancing at speed down the Airport Road. The first APC was engaged at a range of about 200 to 250 metres. The first three missiles, two 84mm and one 66mm, missed. Subsequently one 66mm fired by Marine Gibbs, hit the passenger compartment and one 84mm (Marines Brown and Betts) hit the front. Both rounds exploded and no fire was received from that vehicle. The remaining five APCs which were about 600 to 700 metres away deployed their troops and opened fire. We engaged them with GPMG, SLR and sniper rifle (Sergeant Shepherd) for about a minute before we threw a white phosphorus smoke grenade and leap-frogged back to the cover of gardens. Incoming fire at that stage was fairly heavy, but mostly inaccurate."

These two reports are, quite evidently at odds. Did George Brown, Danny Betts and Mark Gibbs blow up the leading vehicle, or did they not? This we will discuss in the appropriate Appendix to the book, which should answer many of the questions which disagree as to the range, the number of vehicles, the amount of rockets fired, the effect and even the colour of the smoke used upon withdrawal, however this subject remains in contention to this day. If this vehicle was hit then between 23 to 28 men would have been in it when it 'brewed up' – even the 66mm LAW had an armour penetration of almost five times the thickness of the Amtrack's armour and the Carl Gustav anywhere between five and ten times that, depending on the range - the Royal Marines seem in no doubt about the result. Hugo Santillan certainly disputes this and again we shall discuss in the appropriate place. However, let us now come back to the story, not from reports but from the men who were there as our narrative continues:

George Brown and Danny Betts lay waiting in the tussock grass as the formation of Amtracks came down the road and through the rough ground to either side. This was the moment they had been trained for; all of the men, on both sides. The giant vehicles clanked along at speed as the road straightened out – they could see sixteen of them now tailing all the way back to the Canache - but the advance guard was descending swiftly upon them; *"When the first Amtrack came towards us, I saw blokes shaking hands,"* Danny Betts remembered, *"I think we all thought at that time 'this is it' – maybe I feel ashamed or maybe guilty to say, but I resigned myself to the fact that in the next ninety seconds I was going to die - as they came towards us – and I'm not a religious man – I remember looking up and saying, 'If there's anybody up there, for fuck's sake, do something now!'"*

With the lead vehicle now comfortably within range and still seemingly unaware of their position, it was time to unleash what they had against it as Danny Betts continues; *"One was quite far in front of all the others and it was coming down the road straight towards me and George. We had about as much cover as Wembley bloody stadium: The ground was completely flat. As I looked to my right, Sergeant Shepherd looked back and said with a nod, 'Right, when you're ready lads.'"* - To which George Brown added; *"My one thought was 'This is it... okay let's go for it!"*

Firing from a prone position so as not to give away his location, Brown squeezed the trigger and he and Danny Betts at once felt the screeching rush as the shockwave hit them and the rocket screamed out towards the lead vehicle – and missed. *"The first shot fell very short,"* Danny Betts recalled, *"then fifty feet to the right the 66 fired..."* that round fell short also, *"...we got the next round in."* Now there was no time to stop, to think, to consider but just to keep loading and firing, beginning that mechanical process which had been trained into each man since the first day; *"A tap on the head and we go again,"* recalled George Brown, yet this round also fell short and cartwheeled wildly into the grass beyond, *"Then the boys opened up with a bit of small-arms fire,"* Betts added, *"and now it turned slightly to its right, off the road but then it just sort of stopped..."* - Brown now continues; *"It stopped and turned a bit – it gave me a good side-on view - we said 'Let's get it!' so this time I knelt up – I exposed our position but I was sure of getting it - I focused...that was the whole job..."*

Now in the ditch to the right, the rest of the section was opening up, throwing everything they had at the lead vehicle. Burt Reynolds, having rejoined Section Two and now in command of the GPMG with Sean Egan as gunner remembered hearing first the sound and finally seeing the giant mechanical monsters climbing up a bank into full view; *"Wait until it's within two hundred metres!"* Sergeant Shepherd had hissed in a low voice and Reynolds rolled to one side and picked up a 66mm LAW, rolling onto his back to extend the launcher tube and pull the sights up and then rolling back again to aim the weapon across his shoulder. To his left, Mark Gibbs also primed a 66mm and now there were three rocket launchers all aiming at the lead vehicle which, as Gibbs recalled, was out a distance ahead of the others and was about to receive the full attention of the Royal Marines. At Shepherd's order, Brown and Betts had fired at the lead vehicle, their rocket landing short, and now Reynolds too opened up, with his round also going wide. He swore as he threw the now-useless launcher away and rolled to grab a second one, repeating the process to arm the weapon and taking his time as he primed it ready. Meanwhile Mark Gibbs now fired his LAW only to see the round catch on a single-wire electric cattle fence to his front and career into the grass away from the target. Rolling back with his freshly-primed weapon, Burt Reynolds just saw the round ricochet from the fence and cursed to himself; *"What are they fucking doing!?"* thinking it had been an 84mm round upon which the destruction of the Amtrack would rely. Now the section opened up with small arms as Brown and Betts primed their third rocket and the Amtrack began to turn to its right, away from them, revealing a tempting side profile as it stopped, seeming to run its tracks back and fore as if stuck on the bank or in the ditch beside the road. Burt Reynolds fired. The rocket screamed from the launcher as Reynolds and the others followed it in, watching the smoke trail and finally a flash and then smoke from the crew compartment; *"Yes! Got it!"* Reynolds yelled, as Mark Gibbs now fired his own weapon; *"And I saw it go and it definitely hit,"* he remembered, *"it was hit about three-quarters of the way up and along. It rocked on its suspension and blew a huge great cloud of black smoke then died."* ... *"Then I fired,"* George Brown continues, *"and I hit it – I know exactly where I hit it - just behind the commander's cupola just a moment after the other guys hit it with the '66's – there was a flash then a moment later the smoke started to come out as she brewed up."*[*9]

"After that we didn't see much," Danny Betts remembered, *"just flames and thick black smoke. By now we'd given our position away and the other Amtracks were opening up with their 30mm cannon. There were clumps of grass a foot square flying over us. If you've ever felt your life fall out through your arsehole – that's what it's like being fired at by one of those – the speed and size of the rounds was overpowering."* Following this, the rest of the section poured in fire with their GPMG, SLR's and Sergeant Shepherd with his sniper rifle, trying to bounce rounds back into the crew compartment of the smoking vehicle as the rear door opened or perhaps just burst. One or two men were seen to try to exit the vehicle but were either hit or forced back and nobody was seen to come out. The fire soon switched to a new target as the other vehicles came up, passing the smoking wreck and then veering left across the open ground in front of the Marines' position. They singled out the next vehicle and peppered it with what Burt Reynolds, now furiously working the GPMG remembered as; *"everything we possibly had... literally everything, it was impossible to miss..."* and as the bullets hammered and clanged

across the hull and it tried to turn to deploy, they again attempted to bounce rounds off the rear ramp back into the crew compartment as it came down, whilst Gibbs, remembering a useful trick he had been taught, let off two rounds at the gunner's periscope and was impressed to see it smashed and the vehicle's gun blinded. By now the 30mm cannon from the other Amtracks were blazing, Argentine Marines were deploying and returning fire, a recoilless rifle and then a mortar were tearing into the houses and government buildings around them and the order was shouted for the Royal Marines to withdraw, with Reynolds and Egan giving covering fire on the GPMG and peppering the deploying Amtrack with a torrent of fire. Gibbs threw a white smoke grenade to cover them and Reynolds a white phosphorous before he and Egan stood up and ran; *"We tried to pick up a box of 800-link but we couldn't carry it,"* he remembered, *"so we just ditched it. We hung what we could over our necks, ran and dived into the nearest gardens, trying to zig-zag under fire."*

Now, almost thirty-five years after his report had been written, let us go back to Hugo Santillan and tell this curious episode from his own side from the start of the action as vehicle No.07 under Sergeant Quiroga passed by the yellow earth-moving vehicle; *"I was constantly on the radio checking if anyone had seen anything,"* he recalled, *"it was still so quiet. Then I saw this Caterpillar and I thought it must be booby-trapped. 'Move away from the Caterpillar – over!' I said. When I said 'over' the first rocket hit. It landed quite far in front and to the left, then another landed even farther to the left. Then I shouted on the radio 'Hull defilade, hull defilade!'... in a high-pitched voice - much like a young lady in distress!"* By now vehicle No.07 was taking a vast amount of small arms fire as it turned to find a patch of lower ground; *"... on the radio, Quiroga was yelling,"* Santillan continues, *"he had his hands against the inside of the vehicle and could feel the bullets smashing into it; 'It's getting hot!' he was yelling. I was shouting orders back and a few minutes later, I ordered Quiroga to neutralise the enemy machine gun with his 81mm mortar. As time passed and the mortar was not firing, I asked on the radio; '¡Negro!¡ La puta madre! ¿Cuando carajo empieza el reglaje?'* (A liberal translation could be; 'Black!¡ (Quiroga's call sign) Whore mother! When the fuck are you going to start adjusting?' - Three comments: I never curse; I never use foul language upon my subordinates... except that day at that time!"*

Hugo Santillan remembered that he still could see nobody. It was, he remembered, like being on exercise; lots of action and fire but no enemy. Although he could see the bullets ricocheting from vehicle #07 to his right, yet he could see nobody and was yelling down the intercom for anyone to acquire a target as the vehicles opened up with their cannon and started to deploy the men who returned fire as they skirted around to the south and west to take the position in reverse. In one of the Amtracks, Daniel Tosolini of Delta Company was given the order to prepare; *"The long-awaited order to remove safety catches, the section commander gives the last harangue – we were entering a real combat zone with the English forces in just a second. I closed my eyes and all my family went through my mind; my parents, sisters, uncles, cousins, my godmother, my fellow high-school friends... I did not know if I would see them again but I just thought they would feel proud of me for defending my country. Now we were given the order to exit and leaving, we heard a strong fire of guns and missiles of the enemy. Advancing, the first five minutes were hard; the fire of the enemy was intense..."* - Now as Delta company deployed and skirted around to the south and west to flank the position, the Royal Marines deployed white phosphorous and, watching through his binoculars, Hugo Santillan saw two men stand up and run – it was George Brown and Danny Betts – someone else now came onto the intercom to say that the Royal Marines were in the houses to either side of the road and that their GPMG was firing from there, and he ordered the recoilless rifle to fire upon that position from which it was assumed that the GPMG was firing. Finally, and after much swearing and cursing, the 81mm mortar came into play which, combined with the fire from the cannon and the recoilless rifle, seemed to put an end to the action as the Royal Marines disappeared through the smoke.

Now on foot, Hugo Santillan gathered his men about him, *"News?"* he asked urgently, *"Sir, I got hit."* - Horacio Tello, a fire team leader from vehicle No.07 was kneeling to Santillan's left and now held up his hand where a star-shaped, bloody and gaping wound went through the middle. *"Then I asked the silliest question ever,"* Hugo Santillan remembered, *"'Does it hurt?' - He just looked and then said 'No' - Tello had been riding in the troop compartment; he was standing chest-high on the left of the hull, just behind the troop leader's hatch; he was holding his FAL. One of the shots hit Tello's FAL in the handguard, destroying both halves of the handguard, the gas cylinder, the gas piston, the gas regulator and the gas piston spring. Splinters and fractions of those parts were expelled in all directions; some lodged in Tello's left hand, which started to bleed. A piece of the gas piston spring stuck in his face, but Tello managed to retrieve it. As blood dripped down, a fellow Marine dragged Tello inside the hull. Tello sat down in the safety of the armoured hull of the Amtrack showing some pain. That's as I understand it. Tello was the first Argentinian wounded in the Malvinas."* - Inside the Amtrack, Horacio Tello was given first-aid by Marine Medical Corpsman Gustavo Moreno who urged him to leave his post and seek medical attention; *"No!"* roared Tello, *"Not even farting drunk am I missing this!"* Unable to make him depart, he was bandaged and taken along to continue the fight.

With the Royal Marines gone for a time, Hugo Santillan now called a halt to let the rest of the column catch up. Remembering his camera, he quickly took a picture of the site of the action, including the yellow Caterpillar-type vehicle he had remembered so well. He also looked at the damage to vehicle No.07 which, along with a smashed scope had no less then ninety-seven bullet marks in it by his own count. It was serviceable but its capacity would be somewhat reduced, mainly by the damaged scope. By now, Delta company were working their way around White City to cut off or encircle the Royal Marines and, shortly afterwards, he ordered the next company around to follow them and led his vehicles around with them, going along Callaghan road.

The action at White City had been captured first-hand by the people of the houses who were calling in to FIBS Radio as it was happening. First Alistair Grieves – a government laboratory technician - called in and Patrick Watts put him on the air; *"Alistair, I understand you've seen some of the vehicles, have you?"* he asked. *"No, we haven't sighted vehicles, Pat,"* Grieves replied, *"but there have been some really heavy bangs. The whole place is shaking, it's a bit nerve-racking to say the least. There's a lot of machine-gun fire and small-arms fire as well. I had a quick look out through the curtains and all I could see was smoke, so I honestly haven't a clue what's happening, but every time something big goes bang, it shakes up here!"* - *"And where are you giving this report from, Ally?"* Watts asked him, *"Are you standing up, sitting down, what are you doing?"* - *"I'm lying on the floor, boy!"* - came the answer, with a nervous chuckle. *"And can you see if any of our chaps are defending at all?"* Watts asked, *"Are they returning any fire or anything like that? Can you see?"* - *"I can't see, but it was all happening,"* Ally Grieves replied, *"they were lying on the opposite side of the road in amongst the white grass and stuff there, but I can see nothing but smoke now, whether it's from their arms or from stuff that's being returned, I haven't a clue!"* - Patrick Watts told him to keep down and to call in when he had more news and Ally Grieves was not to be remiss in doing so.

The moment that the order to withdraw had been given and the white-phos deployed, Trollope's Section Two pulled out. The Argentine fire was; *"heavy but mostly inaccurate"* Danny Betts remembered as he and George Brown pulled back, grabbing as much of their kit as they could but abandoning many of the 66's. The mortar shells were landing with explosive force but no shrapnel came their way, indeed the shells and bombs seemed to be landing amongst the houses of White City and George Brown felt a pang of anger that the houses, still full of people, were now bearing the brunt of the Argentine fire. *"We doubled back through the gardens of White City, moving and firing the whole time,"* Danny Betts recalled as the Argentine men of Delta Company closed in. George Brown was lagging seriously behind, dragging his heavy Carl Gustav; *"Right leave it! Leave it!"* Sergeant Shepherd barked, and Brown tossed it away and continued after his comrades as they laid down fire to cover him.[*10]

The Argentines had been clever and, as Weinstabl's column came up and deployed to the left of Santillan's advance-guard, so they had set up a barrage of blocking-fire to the south, to funnel the Marines back into the town and along the main road. As the Royal Marines sprinted for cover across the road, a heavy machine gun now opened up, with a torrent of rounds punching the air around them and kicking up dirt and stones from the road; *"They started targeting the digger,"* Mark Gibbs recalled, *"and as I was running past it, a big fifty-calibre opened up on it. The shots were hitting the cast steel back-hoe arm and as they hit it, there was a big 'splash' and the rounds carried straight on through... they didn't stop. The windows in the digger were shattering and glass was flying everywhere... I thought, 'Shit, these people are really trying to kill us!'"* - As the rounds came down, Gibbs pulled up short and stumbled; *"And I'll never forget the look on Mark Coombs' face as I slipped and he thought I was done for..."* he remembered, as he scrambled across the road and dived for cover into a nearby garden after the others, with the Argentine marines of the BIM2 now hard on their heels.

Crashing through the gardens, through and over fences and low walls, the men of Section Two now piled back along the rear of the houses on Davis Street to get back towards Government House, firing blindly behind themselves as they went in a mad steeplechase until the Argentine Marines who had been after them seemed to have been shaken off. In one garden, Burt Reynolds remembered looking up to see a family peering out of the kitchen window at him and he frantically waved them down, yelling at them to take cover only to see them smile and wave back! Sprinting on, Section Two vaulted fences and walls as they raced back but now, on the western fringes of Stanley, they had run out of cover and ducked into an alleyway between the houses, with Alistair Grieves reporting back to FIBS that he had just seen six or seven of them racing away, abandoning some heavy weapons; *"...some bazookas and things... but now there's no sign of the lads, they must have all got away."*

Now safe for a moment in the alleyway, behind a wall, the men of Section Two did a quick check on casualties and ammo. Nobody was hurt; *"I was amazed everyone was still intact,"* remembered Danny Betts, *"and now I just started stripping off layers of clothes. It had been a cold night so I had more layers on than an onion and I was boiling hot from all the running. Suddenly from one of the houses, a window opened. Every rifle went up but there we saw staring back at us a little old man – 'Are you us... or are you them?' - he asked. 'We're us!' I shouted back, 'Now go and lay down and someone will come and fetch you when it's all over!' - I couldn't believe it. About three to five minutes later, the door opened. All the rifles went up again and out came the man and his wife with a tray, five or six cups of coffee, a jug of milk, a bowl of sugar and a little saucer of shortbread* biscuits - 'Would you like a cup of coffee?' she asked nicely. I still get emotional thinking about that. They were helpless and it was all that they could do. At the time though, I actually swore and said, 'For fuck's sake, get down!'" - Still the men of the Royal Marines were ignored and quickly set to drinking their coffee and taking a shortbread biscuit each. George Brown later recalled that his endearing memory of that day was being sat in a hedgerow drinking coffee – somehow for all the lads, it made them proud of what they were fighting for.[*11]

The Argentine Marines of Delta and Fox companies had not captured their prey but now moved along, descending into Stanley from the south; *"After the first five minutes it got a little easier,"* Daniel Tosolini recalled, *"I do not remember the distance until we saw the town in the dawn. Our first target was the weather station, we had to cross barbed wire – it was electrified. As I and an officer crossed the rise, my comrade Jose Luis Denti entered the building and found all of the communications equipment broken..."* Now the men of Delta and Foxtrot companies moved on into town and towards Government House; *"My first impression was of a ghost-town,"* Tosolini remembered, *"we only heard the wind until someone alleged to have heard the enemy. We all dived prone into combat positions... I stayed very nervous. The words of 'Old Busser' passed through my mind, that we should not shoot. Then we moved on through the town. It was all very calm and we saw no inhabitants. We the Marines entered into a very large warehouse painted with white letters saying, 'We do not want to be Argentine, we are British'... The head of the company, Captain Di Paola, told us to pay attention to the roof as there could be English there. I looked up and then started looking for where I could take cover in case I had to shoot. I was very nervous as I was an easy target and had to pay attention to two fronts..."* - Finding nothing, the Argentine Marine companies moved on towards Government House.[*12]

Still stuck in an alleyway between and behind the houses at the end of Davis Street, the men of Section Two now decided to try to move. They had kept low and had gone undetected, listening to the firing which seemed to come from the direction of Government House and trying to gauge what was happening. Bill Trollope asked George Brown if he could check to see if there was a way out – perhaps the enemy had gone around them and there might yet be a way to break out to camp; *"As I stuck my head out, a couple of shots fired out just over my head,"* he remembered, *"We can't get out, Sir,"* he reported back, *"We're well covered."* - The men lay ready to defend themselves or to act as circumstances dictated when gradually the firing died down and all seemed quiet. Perhaps it was over or perhaps it was a ceasefire? They waited with ears pinned back as the minutes ticked by. Suddenly the firing started up again, a few shots at first and then rising to a crescendo. Everyone knew what that might mean. Danny Betts now remembered Sergeant Shepherd turning to them and saying grimly; *"That's it lads, we're here till the end! - It's the Alamo!"*[*14]

Chapter 7: The Battle for Stanley

"I never knew our Marines could fight so hard...
They were fighting like lions to protect us."
Rachel Simons – Stanley Resident - Personal Account 2017.

Pedro Giachino's group crawled their way towards Government House from the south, using Sapper Hill as their landmark in the darkness of the night. Just before ascending the shoulder of the hill, they first heard the sound of a vehicle coming and then the lights of a Land Rover which roared through the darkness along the road which ran along the base of the hill towards them, forcing the men to double towards the top for concealment. There, breathless, they waited. They had not been seen. Pushing on towards a low, rocky hill which overlooked Government House from the south, the group stopped; two men were missing. Giachino called for Lieutenant Alvarez – there was no answer. He and one other seemed to have been left behind; *"We decided to press on, hoping they would catch up,"* Diego Quiroga recalled, *"and they eventually did."*[*1]

The group advanced another thousand metres towards the low, rocky ridge and there saw below them the white and green structure of Government House. There were a few lights but not many, with the glow of an old oil drum which was still burning its contents inside the grounds; *"From that point we had a perfect view of both Government House, Stanley, the football pitch and the waterfront..."* continued Diego Quiroga, *"...it must have been about five thirty, local time. Giachino's instructions were to try to make contact with Admiral Busser in order to confirm whether the attack was a 'go' for as you can realise, war had not been declared between our countries and everything could – up to that very moment – be aborted. We had our portable radios and promptly found out that they wouldn't work. Probably the batteries, already weak, had not survived the cold night."*

The attacks upon Government House and Moody Brook were supposed to have been coordinated but now this could not happen. For a moment the group waited – should they press on? Who should move first? It was decided to go with the plan as ordered. Giachino scanned the area with his binoculars... all seemed quiet; *"Then he whispered orders,"* Diego Quiroga recalled, *"Lieutenant Lugo with Orange group would move toward the house and around it on the left flank in order to position his men between the house and the water. Lieutenant Alvarez was to cover the left flank proper and Giachino would lead Green group – including myself – in person around to the right flank, which we thought was the front of the house. I was to remain put until Giachino called me down to come and meet him.*

'Come with me' he whispered to the others... everybody went rushing down the slope in an almost shoulder-to-shoulder fashion."

Diego Quiroga was left on the rise with two men; Cardillo and Urbina - the medic - to await the call from Giachino. The minutes ticked by then; "I began to hear many shots from the direction of Moody Brook. Captain Sanchez Sabarots was attacking." He waited as per his orders, watching the flashes and explosions to the west and noticing that all at once, every light in the town came on, illuminating the area. After ten minutes, the noise of firing and explosions died down and then suddenly from the left came the sound of automatic weapons fire – it was Lieutenant Alvarez who had just opened the attack against Government House; "Almost immediately we could see vehicles moving from the town and two trucks, one full of Marines, were speeding down the coastal road. They stopped right in front of the house where I assumed Lieutenant Lugo's position was (in fact it effectively blocked Lugo's view of the house for a while as I learned later). One of my men aimed his rifle at the truck and shouted that there were men coming down from it and that he was ready to shoot. I ordered him not to do it, for I did not want to disclose the direction of our attack, but my order came too late. I then heard Giachino call my name and started down the slope towards the front of the house followed by my two men. On the way down, I trampled on rose bushes, an incivility Mavis Hunt was to jokingly remind me of many years later." - Quiroga clambered down the rocky slope, angling to his right, crashing through the rose beds. The sounds of firing off to the left grew and was now added to by the explosions of stun grenades as he found Giachino in the darkness and from there, their leader led them forward, ordering them to fan out as they approached to within shouting distance of the house to where he was now - as the only English-speaking member of the group - supposed to call out and encourage the Governor Rex Hunt to surrender. He had his doubts that it world work; "Talk!" - Giachino growled at him, and Diego Quiroga cupped his hands to his mouth and shouted....

Chief Secretary Dick Baker heard the opening shots of the attack on Moody Brook as he and his party of sailors and Marines were still mid-way through making their arrests of the Argentine workers in the town. There were a few still to round up including the two senior LADE men, Gilobert and Gamin. Now, with the invasion upon them, he turned his truck and headed back towards Government House to check the situation and ask Rex Hunt what he should do and now sped along Ross Road and pulled up at GH, entering the house and making straight for Rex Hunt's HQ. There he found Hunt a little perplexed by the firing and sounds of explosions coming from the direction of Moody Brook but the Governor ordered him to continue with the arrests and then to make his way home to his wife Connie and their daughters to keep them safe. It was 06.15 as he exited GH by the west door and walked into a storm of automatic gunfire which soon had him reeling and stumbling back inside for cover. Running to Rex Hunt's office, Baker told him breathlessly; *"I can't get out! They're firing on us! And I still haven't got Gamin and Gilobert! What should I do?"* Luckily Sergeant Al Short came quickly to the rescue with some sound advice, telling him; *"Sit in that corner, Sir, with your arse against the wall and keep out of the fucking way. That's the best thing you can do!"*

Mike Norman at once realised the situation as soon as Moody Brook was hit. He had been at Lookout Rocks, just to the east of the town when he realised that the attack was coming from behind. Quickly on the radio, he ordered Section One – Lou Armour at the Canache - back to GH, Section Five – Figgy Duff on Canopus Hill - back to take up positions around the Cable & Wireless building just to the west of GH and Section Six – Dave Carr - back from the Murray Heights to the south. All sections were now to converge upon GH with the exception of Section Four – Stefan York at Navy Point - and Section Two – Chris Bryan, now joined by Bill Trollope's small group - who was to hold the airport road as long as possible. Norman and his own command would race back to GH ahead of them. The 'collapsible defence' both Mike Norman and Gary Noott had envisaged had just collapsed of its own accord. Now Mike Norman and his own small command dashed back towards GH. The journey took just six or seven minutes, with Murray Paterson driving at full speed with the lights of the vehicle turned off so as not to attract attention. Before the vehicle had even stopped, Mike Norman jumped out and sprinted for the entrance to GH and, as Paterson hit the brakes, the brake lights came on and a barrage of machine gun fire now came hammering down on the driveway; *"The rounds missed us, but hit the truck next to us,"* Paterson recalled, *"we vacated and legged it across the driveway for the cover of a small cannon by the doorway and I remember Farnworth, the radio operator, still had his headset attached and nearly strangled himself as he ran…"* As Mike Norman entered the building, he heard the fusillade of shots ring out by the west entrance behind him and doubled back instinctively, calling out to the men; *"Who fired those guns? What are you firing at?"* in a split second, he realised that the fire, now added to by torrent of thunderous explosions, was incoming. Gary Noott ran up now; *"Mike, what are they firing?"* he yelled, to which Norman replied, *"It sounds like bloody artillery to me… Or mortars."*

Royal Marine Gary *'Bungy'* Williams had just returned in the four-tonner from where he, George Duncan and the sailors had been rounding up the Argentines in town when a rifle shot cracked over the top of the vehicle, fired from the heights to the south, quickly joined by a flurry of shots from several directions at once; *"…and as I was in mid-air getting off the four-tonner all hell broke loose,"* he remembered, *"George and me managed to make it to the field in front of the house that Don Bonner was living in, shortly afterwards the firing started and we* realised that we were about five yards too far forward as there were rounds going over our heads. We were in the open, so we inched our way back to the hedgerow. I laughed as George told me that he'd got a tree stump between his legs and couldn't get any farther back, funny as it seems we both tried to use our bodies to dig a hole so we were lower down!" - To the west end of GH, Royal Marine Graham Evans was amongst the first to see the fire coming from the Argentines to the west and from the hill to the south; *"I was at Government House as part of the HQ group,"* he recounted, *"I was on standby to supply more ammunition as required by the outlying sections in a four-tonner. Suddenly the truck started taking hits! All I saw were the tracer rounds going into the back of the truck. I think I counted to three about ten times before finally making a dash for cover, thinking, 'I hope my number's not showing here' – lucky that time and no clean keks required as I made a dash across the yard to take up a firing position."*

Jim Fairfield was also now in the firing line as he recalled; *"Although I was waiting for it I remember it came as quite a shock when the first rounds rattled into Government House and our four-ton truck which had been left sitting in the driveway. The Argies seemed to be tempting us at first, just a few shots here and there but all the time I and everyone else were noting the muzzle flashes and positions of the enemy. After a few moments of this I noticed that the enemy were starting down the slope using very basic and uncoordinated fire and movement tactics, the words 'turkey shoot' flashed through my mind. I was obviously not the only one to notice this movement but everyone held their fire, we were the defenders, in cover but short on ammo, we could pick our moment. They could not."* Colour Sergeant Noone remembered the same feeling which, after 27 years and combat in three continents, now came naturally and, he remembered, almost calmly; *"When I took up my firing position, my mouth went a bit dry, the old tongue was rasping, that familiar burning sensation and what have you... I got into a comfortable position in cover, flicked up my sights and just sat there, happy to bide my time..."* The old hands were now watching, waiting and ready to meet the attack; *"Positions, guys,"* he said softly and then, looking over to Tiny Jones and remembering his guess that the enemy would come first up the beach, he flashed him a smile; *"Told you not to listen to me."*

Out on the west porch, Gary Noott was shouting orders as Mike Norman ran out with Chris Todhunter next to him, clutching his SMG; *"All I had was two magazines of ammunition,"* Todhunter remembered, *"of course, the professional Marines had whole bandoliers hanging round their necks, but I in my innocence had grabbed only 20 rounds. I found cover just outside and waited for them to pour over."* Norman ducked behind an ancient and rusting Norwegian harpoon gun which had found a new life as a garden ornament. On the other side of the harpoon gun, Chris Todhunter also hugged the ground beside him, the pair having been forced to duck by the incoming fire; *"Suddenly I became very aware of my very delicate, soft, pink body..."* Todhunter recalled, as the tracer rounds began to fly and make what he described as; *"one hell of a mess of the wooden wall of the Government House office immediately behind me. I have to confess that I was confronted by my own inadequacy: my own fear and knowledge that I actually wasn't a terribly brave person after all..."* Around them, stun grenades started to land and Mike Norman began to grow worried; if the Argentines were throwing grenades in, they must be very close indeed, he thought. The stun grenades were working; their deep, percussive bang knocking the senses from the Marines in an instant, pounding concussion so that some, stunned and bewildered, actually got to their feet and had to be dragged back down by their comrades. Clinging to the old harpoon gun for cover from the barrage, Todhunter looked earnestly at Mike Norman and remembered Norman saying to him; *"Don't worry about it; the blast normally goes straight up... well, except if you get hit by the base plate."* It was not a comforting thought.

Bullets were now tearing into Government House and glass and wooden splinters were flying everywhere as the men ducked for cover and the explosions of the stun grenades and now rifle grenades pounded the air all around them; *"I couldn't believe how much fire was coming into GH,"* Geordie Gill recalled, *"It absolutely wrecked upstairs which was mainly wooden, but downstairs was mostly built of brick and good old Falkland stone - good enough protection - but glass and splinters were flying everywhere and most of the windows were shot out in minutes."*

In the gardens facing the rocky ridge from which the fire seemed to be coming down upon them, the Royal Marines half-ran, half-crawled towards a stone wall which would provide them with some cover. There were Argentines within feet of them on the other side. Beside his harpoon gun, with Chris Todhunter on the other side, Mike Norman recalled almost going to pieces before snapping himself back into his training; *"I was laying there, shaking from head to foot like a piece of jelly!"* he remembered, *"I suspect all the others were the same. In those situations, you have to give yourself a talking to. I said to myself, 'You knew it was going to come to this. You told the lads it was going to come to this. Now get a grip, because if anybody climbs over that wall now, you are not going to be able to hit the wall, let alone the target.' I shouted to the Sergeant-Major, 'You okay Sarn't Major?' - He said he was fine and asked how I was. Suddenly everybody started talking. In that strange time when it was all quiet, the Marines were saying goodbye to each other; 'It's been good to know you,' that sort of thing."* Beside him, Chris Todhunter huddled for cover and remembered Norman suddenly looking at him and asking; *"Are you married?"* - Perhaps thinking of the girl he would probably never see again, Todhunter replied sadly; *"No... it's much easier for me."*

Suddenly; *"Telescopic sight! Suspect sniper! Permission to fire?"* Gary Williams had shouted the warning as a long sight now protruded from an upstairs window of the Bonner's cottage; *"Half a dozen rifles and a couple of LAW's instantly went up and aimed at the point just below the window, ready to flatten the place,"* Williams recalled, *"and Mike Norman suddenly shouted, 'No! Hold fire! It's the Governor's son!' - and right enough it was - Tony Hunt was sticking a telephoto lens out the window and trying to get a picture of the Argies! 'Get the fuck down! Get away from the fucking window!' we all shouted... he didn't know how close he'd come."* Now the Royals threw themselves flat again as tracer ripped into everything and Government House rocked with the explosions of grenades; *"...and not just stun grenades..."* Andy Macdonald recalled, *"...they were using a little knee-type two-inch mortar too. They were literally using the only bushy-topped tree around to disguise their smoke signature. I could see the rounds land but, being mostly paddock, they exploded in the wet ground around us and didn't do too much damage..."*

Racing back towards Government House along Ross Road, the men of Figgy Duff's Section Five had just managed to get back to GH as the firing began; *"We deployed along the bushes at the road going from the driveway towards the houses,"* remembered Dave Gerrard, *"I tried to blend with concrete and grass as the rounds flew past. Every time I called to Brian Hobbs to get a sit-rep from him, Brian from the Cable and Wireless building kept poking his head out the door and I kept telling him to get back and stay in. Whilst lying there, I remembered what the Chaplain had said to us in training; 'Whether we believe or not, there comes a time in our life when we will call to God for help' and this was that time."* - It was not just Brian Summers whom Dave's calling nearly got killed, as Andy Macdonald remembered; *"I was running across the paddock beside GH and Brian opened the door at Cable and Wireless to see what was going on. This lit me up like a Christmas tree and it attracted a lot of Argie fire onto me. I hit the deck, laid in a muddy wheel-rut and crawled back to cover – very fast as well – calling upon God, Jehovah, Allah, Krishna, Buddha and anyone else I could think of as the bullets cracked overhead and tore up the ground around me."*

The automatic fire was now tearing through Government House, sending glass, fragments of stone and wood and now water – as the pipes in the kitchen were shot through - cascading onto the floor and onto the Royal Marines. In the operations room, Rex Hunt had dived beneath the desk, clutching his pistol which he kept trained on the door to shoot the first person who came in, and worried in case he did fire and hit one of his own men. Now Brian Wells, Hunt's cypher clerk also dived beneath the desk almost on top of him, having failed to hide beneath a sofa. The bullets tore up the room above them, ricocheting from the walls as the percussive blast of grenades seemed to rock the building and Rex Hunt began to contemplate that, if he was to die, at least Mavis wouldn't have to suffer him dragging her around the world any more. Calmly, resignedly, he accepted that his fate, if it were to come, was not altogether a bad thing. Now amidst the fire he suddenly reached for the telephone and asked the operator, calmly, to put him through to FIBS to give the people an update and Brian Wells remembered the bizarre sight of Hunt chatting happily and politely as if it were just another day in the office despite the bullets which were flying in through the smashed windows and ricocheting around the room.

Suddenly the firing ceased and every man waited, poised and ready when a voice came through the still night air towards them; *"Mister Hunt! We are Argentine Marines. The Island is taken, amphibious vehicles have landed and we have cut your phone lines. Please leave the house alone, unarmed and with your hands on your head, to prevent further mishaps. I assure you that your rank and dignity as well as your entire family, will be duly respected."* Each man heard the caller – he spoke good English - but the Royal Marines said nothing. Eyes and ears were searching the darkness for targets, the men keeping their heads down and not yet giving away their position. Diego Quiroga had shouted his scripted message and now felt awkward at the silence; *"Even then, right in front of the house where I called to Rex Hunt to come out with his arms upheld, something told me that the whole display was perhaps a bit excessive,"* he remembered later, *"I was convinced that nobody in his position could afford to answer to threats without putting up resistance, and I have always wondered whether we could simply have carried out the mission by talking and presenting Hunt with the obvious facts of force supremacy, given that this was hardly Rorke's Drift... At a signal from Giachino, I repeated my message. Again, there was no answer. 'Throw in a grenade' said Giachino and so we threw a grenade which exploded in the corner of the garden as it faced towards the sea. Then a voice said, 'Mister Hunt is going to come out...' we waited and hoped for what must have been two minutes. Giachino grew impatient; 'Make them hurry, for fuck's sake!' - I repeated my message again..."*

In Government House, the Royal Marines still waited silently. Someone had shouted; *"Don't go, Mister Hunt!"* but then they had fallen silent again to see what the Argentines would do. After several minutes of silence, the voice came again; *"Mister Hunt. We know you are a sensible man. You are surrounded. There is no escape. Come out with your hands up."* - There was a pause, then came the reply; *"Fuck off, you spic bastards!"* – it was Colour Sergeant-Major Bill Muir who broke the silence - at which the air was filled with a torrent of return fire as the Royal Marines, having found their targets, now blazed away into the night.

"The gunfire grew in intensity and the shooting was widespread," Diego Quiroga recalled, "we were all crouching low. Giachino was on my left side and a little forward, to my right was my Sergeant, Cardillo. I suddenly saw Cardillo and my comrades Flores, Alegre and Ledesma bathed by a beautiful orange light and for a moment I thought that it was a pity that the sun was shining so prettily on such a disturbed scene, until I realised I was looking at the orange wake of tracer bullets that were being fired at us from the corner of town, over the football pitch..." - the fire of the Royal Marines was now intense and coming from both sides, and Giachino's squad threw themselves flat to avoid the cross-fire; "Boss, either we move or they'll fry us!" shouted Quiroga, "Yes," replied Giachino, "yes, we must go."*[2]

Now the 'snatch squad' started to crawl forward towards the house, making short dashes from cover to cover, unaware that at least one man had spotted them; "I was aiming at a gap between a corrugated iron hut in front of me and the garden fence on the right," Murray Paterson recalled, "I was paying particular attention to that gap because this would be the path the enemy would use if coming down from the ridge above us... suddenly, I saw a figure appear in the gap and flit past and I whispered over to Mick Sellen, 'Mick, they're here...' the guy I had just seen moved behind the hut towards the back door by the maids' building when a second figure appeared... I counted up to six figures and had my rifle trained on the gap, so when the seventh figure appeared, I fired. The guy dropped. I don't know if I hit him but I never saw him again and I saw the eighth guy, who had just started to appear behind him, jerk back out of sight and go scrabbling back up towards the ridge..."*[3]

The rest of the snatch-squad had made it to the cover of a low stone wall when, as Diego Quiroga recalled; "Giachino rose and went right over the stone wall that separated us from the house. Flores followed, then Cardillo, Ledesma and I... We at once came to a door of an out-building. Quickly, we kicked it in and entered a hallway that showed no exit save for a side door, just beside the entrance. We tried the door handle but the door was locked. Cardillo tried to kick the door in but only succeeded in hurting his foot and getting a sore ankle for his efforts. Then Giachino smashed one of the glass panes with a hand grenade, stuck his arm through the gap and turned the key. The door opened into what seemed to be an empty room with a semi-destroyed corner that I thought to be due to the effect of the hand grenade I had thrown into the garden. There were no other doors but the other three men; Cardillo, Ledesma and Flores discovered a staircase in one corner of the room which led upwards. Bullets were now coming into the hallway at an angle, piercing the wall. I remember thinking that they were still coming from across the field. Giachino then said, 'Let's not stick around here, we have to go *around' and he left, still with the grenade in his hand. I left behind him, almost stuck to him. We exited the hallway and immediately turned right in order to get around the house, this put us right into the back yard... From this moment on, I remember everything as if it were a slow-motion movie..."*

The snatch-squad had entered via the maid's quarters and found no way through. Now the five of them were moving at pace around the house to find another way into the building; a route which took them straight towards four Royal Marines; Mick Sellen, Tiny Jones, Murray Paterson and Andy Macdonald who remembered that; *"I heard chickens being disturbed behind the up-righted corrugated metal fencing that surrounded gardens at the rear. I thought it may have been FIDF but was informed they not there, so I decided to throw a grenade over the fence. Unfortunately, I only had a white phos, so I then decided to prime my 66mm LAW. A young Marine I was with tried to do the same - but his hands were shaking so much he could not prime it - so I did. He was terrified... and I was not too far behind. I was about to throw the phos grenade but thought I could set GH on fire - and be known forever as 'the Royal who burned down Government House' – right, alternative plan; I will use my 66mm - hang on, I thought - the back-blast may blow down Government House. So I asked anyone if they had an HE grenade the answer was no. As the activity and noise on the other side of the wall was becoming more pronounced I told the lads I was going to get a grenade and inform Detachment HQ, which was in the house, of our situation. I got up on my feet and started to contour back against the walls of Government house. My tactical position was not helped by the glow of the fire from the 45-gallon drum that we had used earlier to burn the classified documents. I was the only prick standing up, well, hugging GH's walls now ...All hell let loose - as they started shooting at me - they must have thought, 'Who is this nobber presenting himself as well-lit target?' – Fortunately, they were firing on full auto - rounds going over my head..."*

In the dark, the Royal Marines now crouched and waited; *"I saw some shapes coming down the hedgerow,"* remembered Tiny Jones, *"FIDF, I thought. I was on one knee with no silhouette behind me because of the fence. I remember the password for that night was 'Fourteen' but now, like a cunt, I called out 'Seven!' They stopped, it seemed the front two half-turned to go back but the third and fourth opened up with small-calibre auto..."* Meanwhile, Andy Macdonald had contoured around the building and now he found himself staring straight at the snatch-squad with Pedro Giachino in the lead and Diego Quiroga stuck close behind him, Giachino fired, his rounds went high; *"... I fired low..."* remembered Andy, as three SLR's and an SMG now all erupted simultaneously.... *"Next thing I know is I'm changing mags having deployed twenty hot-and-ready 7.62's in their direction,"* remembered Tiny Jones, *"I think my larger calibre and the swiftness of it* *all had completely drowned what they were throwing back. I never saw or knew an SLR could fire so fast.* *4

As Diego Quiroga rounded the bend with the rest of the party behind him, Giachino was to his right; *"Suddenly he turned around and shouted, 'Oh Cristina they got me!' and fell to the ground. At that moment, I felt a tear in my right arm; it was like an axe, then I felt an enormous blow, as if a mule had kicked me right on the chest, and I fell on my back. I was immediately stunned, but nevertheless remained conscious. There was a fire in my abdomen. I thought about talking. I know I called my wife's name and fell against a small shed in which the bullets were embedded. I saw the sky. I thought I was dying and I thought to myself, 'Is this it?' - The shooting continued. Beside me, Giachino was moaning slowly. I wondered if he would die. I unzipped my parka, I did not feel my wounded arm, only a sharp overriding pain. I wanted to move. I shouted. I screamed because it hurt a lot and I wanted to hear that I was still alive. I realised that Giachino was calling the medic and I also started calling him loudly. Giachino was speaking to me in an urgent and obviously very painful way..."* *5

Now, as the bullets stung the air overhead, Giachino began to shout for medical treatment; *"I was exchanging fire with the enemy when I heard someone calling a medic,"* Ernesto Urbina recounted, *"he was calling me by name: it was Captain Giachino. He was badly hit, and I made the decision to go."* Urbina had been behind the wall with Chief Petty Officer Pedro Lopez when the call came. Now he grabbed his medical bag and ran forward towards the wall; *"When I went to jump that wall, I remember Alegre yelled at me not to do it as in that place there was no cover,"* he remembered, *"I moved farther down towards the house, through a gap and on my right, there was a place where the wall was missing. I crouched down and went to the gap, calling out to my partner to ask where Giachino was, and he called back that he was on my left..."* Urbina now ran towards the back garden, startling the Governor's geese which reared up as he came, stopping him in his tracks. In the darkness, the waiting Royal Marines could not see his insignia as a medic and they fired again in a ripple of shots; *"Those geese saved me from the first shots as they made me change direction,"* Urbina recalled, as he dived toward a mound of earth, *"then two shots fired from in front of me which filled my face with dirt. That made me change direction again and I ran to my right, seeing that a few metres away, there was a wooden shed about two or three metres wide, and I ran for it. I'm not sure, but I'm sure I heard a shot pass behind me. I ran three or four steps and suddenly felt a blow to the waist on the lower left side that lifted me into the air and I fell back."* Watching on, Pedro Lopez recalled seeing Urbina lifted 'clean into the air' and thrown back several metres and now seeing that the situation was becoming critical, he determined that it was time to summon some help; *"Covering myself as best I could, I went for reinforcements."* he recounted, *"The Amtracks of the main landing group were now near the Governor's house. The wounded were bleeding badly, and time was worth gold..."* Lopez now sprinted off to summon support, leaving the three men groaning in the garden.

"I heard Urbina's cry of frustration when he was hit." Diego Quiroga recalled, *"He called over weakly to say that he could not help as he had also been shot. I remember hearing him say 'Jefe, me dieron,' - 'Boss, they got me' – Maybe I didn't even hear that. It was a beautiful morning. I waited, conscious of a growing pain in my back. I felt something move behind me, over my head, and I could see a group of the Governor's geese, which increased my anxiety by imagining the possibility of a peck on my wounds as they walked clumsily around us, oblivious of the bullets..."* he lay there bleeding with his arm shattered, a bullet in his liver and a wound to the left of his groin, where his hastily secured Swiss Army knife had taken the brunt of the last blow. Now all three men; Giachino, Quiroga and Urbina lay in the garden moaning and calling out the names of their loved ones by turns; *"I must have murmured something in English,"* Quiroga remembered, *"and one of the Royal Marines shouted to call for a cease-fire and they would send a doctor. I said I did not have enough breath to scream. I was becoming delirious... then Giachino said, 'Kid, if I faint, I have this grenade primed.' - 'Drop it, by God!' - I murmured back, but he said that he could not."* [6]

Andy Macdonald found that his SLR had jammed again after just four shots. Now with his rifle requiring attention and three wounded men in the yard, he and the others were facing a barrage of fresh fire. If the Argentines had been firing to miss or to intimidate then, as he recalled; *"Giachino's screaming like a banshee probably put that thought out of the window. He was now screaming - 'Madre! Madre!' - and the others seemed to go mad with it. The fire coming down on us was now heavy and accurate... I decided probably through a combination of terror and concern to run to Detachment HQ to get some help and, for some reason, a grenade. I ran around to the side entrance of Government House to look for help. At this time, I must have been moving very fast, as I ran past the side entrance and ended up near a small stone wall which bordered the front lawn. I noticed a Marine staggering about near this wall - 'Fuck me he's pissed' – I thought! Apparently, he had been hit by a stun grenade. I helped him and made sure he was okay, he thanked me then proceeded to puke - which splattered over my denims and boots - fuck me, this night is just getting better, I thought! I then ran back to the side entrance of Government House and I found our Detachment Sergeant-Major Noone standing there; he was as cool as a cucumber, rounds were going over our heads, coming from the high ground above GH – and he was chuntering, 'Twenty-seven years in the Corps and the wankers do this to me!' - Or words to that effect."*

Government House was now under a barrage of fire with glass and wood splinters flying everywhere and the Royals forced to duck for cover or hug the ground as closely as they could. In the back garden, Murray Paterson dived for cover as a heavy machine gun from the ridge above was used to pepper the building, ricocheting rounds into the lawn where the wounded Argentines now lay helpless; *"I called for the medic, Alec Pickthall,"* Paterson remembered, *"I said, 'We've got to help these two poor bastards or they'll die out there!' but the fire was coming down so heavy that he couldn't, 'I'll probably get killed or badly wounded and then I'm no use to anyone!' he told me, 'My first job is to look after all of you!' Meanwhile, their Captain was still waving a grenade around and I called out to the second man, who was sat against the shed, as he seemed to speak some English, 'Tell your friend to throw his grenade to the left or to the right...' I said, indicating which was which, 'if he throws it at me, I will shoot him.' The guy muttered something in Spanish and the Captain seemed to stop what he was doing..."*

With the fire now coming down hard from the ridge above, Mike Norman now got on the radio, realising that he had a man directly behind the Argentine lines, and put in a call to PJ Berry; *"I got a call over the radio that they were getting pinned down and could I go and find them and take them out!"* Berry remembered, *"I don't know what was going through my mind after that, but something along the lines of, 'You're kidding me!' I crawled to where I had seen them pass me earlier and checked as best I could, but it was still dark. They must have been well hunkered down by then, so I crawled back to the radio and said I couldn't see them, although I could hear the battle as it raged around Government House..."*

Back in Stanley, the men of Section Six under Dave Carr and Nick Williams were racing back into town from the Murray Heights, as Nick Williams remembered; *"We made our way back to the top of town and then down Philomel Hill towards Ross Road. We were on foot and carrying all our kit but we were moving as quickly as we could. When we got close to the town hall, we heard motorbikes coming from the direction of the airport. It turned out to be Les Milne and Jock Wilcox. They came flying down the road towards us. When they got to us, they dumped the bikes and joined us. They had their GPMG with them so now we had eight men and two GPMG's."* - The section now pushed on along Ross Road by the sea front towards the hospital and began to hear first a flurry of shooting from GH and then the screams of wounded men, with each man praying that it was not their own side making the blood-curdling noise. They hurried towards the sound, dragging GPMG's, belts of link, 66's and all manner of kit with them as they made their way into the open ground beyond the town where then they would have to make a mad dash across 200 yards of flat ground and the football pitch to get to the tree-line at GH. Now as they emerged into the open, they came under heavy fire from the rocky hill to the south of GH including from a heavy machine gun and numerous smaller automatic weapons; *"I know it sounds daft,"* remembered Ray Bloye, *"but having taken my beret off earlier, I now quickly took it out from my jacket and put it back on... I returned fire but couldn't actually pick out individuals; it was more covering fire to make them get their heads down while we backed away."*

Quickly back down Ross Road, the Royal Marines retreated past the hospital towards the town hall to regroup. All hell was breaking loose at GH and it seemed that they would have to find another way around. After a quick discussion amongst themselves, Dave Carr decided to lead them up Barrack Street from where they might be able to come in around the flank and rear of the Argentine position. By now it was becoming light. The sounds of explosions and automatic fire came from all sides. The screaming continued from the direction of Government House and Nick Williams remembered thinking; *"Fucking hell, that's our guys! - My natural assumption was that everyone else was getting slaughtered."*

As Barrack Street ran into St Mary's Walk, the section once again came under fire from the Argentine forces on the hill and now some coming into the town from the west; *"Benny was putting rounds down, giving us covering fire, and once in cover, we did the same for him and Nick,"* Ray Bloye recalled, *"We managed to get the Argies' heads down with the firepower we were putting down and so we started moving down St Mary's Walk again using cover and fire tactics."* - The section was moving towards the Argentines, engaging them with both GPMG's and their SLR's, taking cover behind cars, fences and hedgerows as they moved. From the direction of the hospital they now came under fire from a new contact as Nick Williams recounted; *"We saw an Argentine in the grounds of the hospital behind a corrugated iron fence. He was using a classic American trick of firing his rifle blindly around the corner at us. I pointed to Benny with the GPMG – 'Target, fifty yards, behind the fence!' - and Benny opened up with a full burst and took him out. The GPMG made a wreck of the fence and we saw the gun drop."*[7]

As they came closer, so the Argentine fire increased as Ray Bloye continues; *"I saw rounds coming my way as I could see the splash marks in the road – and they were getting closer - at this point I had nowhere to take cover... I looked across the road where there was a small children's park surrounded by a wooden fence and saw that the fence opposite me had two or three wooden slats missing... This left a very small gap and although the fence wasn't particularly high, it was beyond hurdling due to everything I was carrying. I also thought the gap would be rather tight! I had nowhere else to go though, so I ran for the fence. I could see in my mind's eye what I would do, which was to dive through the gap doing a roll, as I landed on the other side and came up into a firing position... I went for it. I dived through the gap and rolled just as I had seen myself doing, came up into a firing* *position and started putting rounds down, giving covering fire for the other lads. More than thirty years later, I recounted this story to Tel George who told me, 'You didn't get through that fence. You took the whole bloody thing down!' - All those years, I had wondered how I got through that small gap!"* *8

Now the Marines began to sprint for the playground with Nick Williams, Wilcox, Milne and Benny Bennett on the GPMG's; *"It was fire and movement the whole time,"* Nick Williams recalled, *"My gun teams covered the riflemen across the playground, then the riflemen covered us across. I was loaded down with ammunition for the guns and when I got to the wooden fence around the playground I couldn't get over it because of the weight; I had belts of 50-link down the front of my windproof, belts of 200 draped around my neck and hanging close by my ankles and I had three liners of 200's and my SLR which I was carrying by the handle – and I was also carrying a Bergen. When I got to the fence, I couldn't physically get over it with all the gear and then I came under fire. I shouted to the rest of the section, 'Someone come and get this fucking ammo off of me!' - I wasn't going to ditch it as it was all we had..."* - Under fire, some of his oppo's ran forward, grabbed armfuls of link and dragged him over the fence into cover just as the rounds cracked into the road where he had been standing a moment before.

The Royal Marines now ran to the junction of Allardyce Street and King Street, opposite Neville Bennett's house as the Stanley fireman peered out of the window to see the fighting; *"I could hear footsteps on the hill alongside the house and some voices,"* he recorded, *"so I went quickly and quietly upstairs to look out of the west window. I could make out the forms of six or seven Marines in the early morning light, crouching down at the corner, using my uncle's house and the pillar box as cover. They were firing continuously at the trees at the back of Government House – or where the trees would be if there was enough light to see them by. There was one tall 'Bootie' with a general-purpose machine gun, blazing away to the westwards and getting some answering fire, complaining that he had put so many rounds into the 'bastard' but the '?*?' idiot didn't know when to give in."*

Safe for a moment behind the houses, the section took a minute to regroup before Dave Carr ordered them to push on up Allardyce Street; *"We went around the corner and before we had gone five yards, the Argies opened up on us again,"* remembered Ray Bloye, *"and all I could do was hit the deck. Beside me on my right was a corrugated iron fence and suddenly a row of holes appeared in it just above my head. It felt like they were only inches away and I tried to melt into the deck. As soon as there was a break in the shooting, I retreated back to King Street after some choice words from all of us – especially Nick!"*

Now the section pushed on higher into the town, up King Street where they met the men of Lou Armour's Section One in the Land Rover and quickly flagged them down; *"I was half in and half hanging out of the Land Rover and Dave told me that GH was being attacked by the Argentines."* Armour recalled, *"A lot of tracer started flying down the road and we just scattered. We jumped out of the Rover and dived into the gardens, trying to figure out what the hell was going on."* Under cover, the two section commanders had a discussion as to what to do between them as the men rested for a moment; *"We took a five-minute break,"* Nick Williams remembered, *"trying to decide what our next plan was going to be. We were laid in a ditch. We all needed a breather and to gather our thoughts. Physically it had been a very demanding time. I lit up a cigarette and relaxed. We had little radio traffic from GH and I could still hear people screaming in agony between the shooting – it was horrible and I thought it had to be our boys, as we were losing. I could also hear explosions coming from the direction of the Airport Road – it sounded like mortar fire and we knew that there were sections in that area and that they also must be taking casualties. Things were not looking good. I then realised that our section had been fighting for an hour or so and hadn't taken any casualties – I then thought, 'Maybe there is a way out of this. Maybe I might survive' – then I got scared again..."*

Lou Armour decided to push on down the road for GH as Dave Carr decided to go back down into town; two sections together would be too big a target and perhaps one section at least might make it. It was decided to split up and try again, with each section acting as a supporting 'brick' to the other as they went. By now, the town seemed to be full of Argentine soldiers and the Royal Marines shook hands, said 'good luck' and ran, with Lou Armour's section filling the air with bullets as Dave Carr's section ran back down the hill towards the sea-front and took up position to cover Section One in turn; *"It was all a bit chaotic,"* remembered Lou Armour, as the Argentine fire came down again, *"Dave Carr began returning the fire and there was fire being exchanged down the road I had to go along... One Section pepper-potted down the road towards the wood where we knew Government House to be... we skirmished our way along the road, firing at gun flashes from five or six concealed men... Movement was slow as we had to crawl and monkey-run, fire-and-manoeuvre across roads and garden-hop until we reached the hospital. It was at this point that I thought Richie Parker had been hit and I ran over to him but luckily, he had just taken a fall. It was now daylight. From there, the section fired and manoeuvred behind the nurses' home... We got to the hospital wall and then we had no choice: we had to leap across the football field... We were still under fire from the Argentine attackers and in serious danger of being fired at by the defenders inside the house. And then we were! I took off my beret and placed it on top of the barrel of my rifle, calling out, 'We're Marines! We're Marines!' Richie was also shouting the same thing behind me. We were eventually heard by Corporal Terry Pares and I heard someone shout, 'Cease fire! They're* ours!' - I replied, 'It's Lou, we're trying to get in!' - and I heard this voice from inside the House suddenly shouting, 'It's Lou's section!' then I was told to hang on... I signalled for the section to stay low and to close up. I told the guys that when I said 'move', we'd go for it in one big rush, so as not to present multiple regular targets for snipers, a classic FIBUA tactic for crossing streets known to be covered by the enemy..." Across the field at GH, Geordie Gill could hear Lou Armour calling out the orders in a textbook fashion as Section One prepared to advance at the run; "I heard someone say, 'What about the machine gun, Corp'?' and Armour said, 'Don't worry, there isn't one.' – I mumbled to myself, 'Yes there fucking is....'

At a signal, a wall of fire went up from the defenders of GH and Lou Armour gave the order; "Move! Follow me! And we ran... The next few seconds were a cacophony of noise and flashing images, of gunfire, rounds striking and then a body..." Out in the open, Section One were at once singled out by heavy machine gun fire from the ridge, and watching on as the rounds came down, both Rod Wilcox and Geordie Gill heard one man yell out; "You bastard, Armour! What have you got us into now?"

Now Section One charged pell-mell across the pitch with Argentine bullets tearing up the turf around their feet and cracking the air around their heads as they raced for the cover of a hedgerow; "I informed Richie Parker to keep calling out 'Royal Marines!' as we approached the house," Lou Armour continues, "and we ran forward like crazy shouting, 'Marines, Marines, Marines!' - We didn't want to get killed by our own guys at that stage - I remember flying through the door and collapsing in a heap with my section right behind me. My most vivid memory then is looking to see if we were all inside and then reaching for my water bottle. My thirst was overpowering and I could barely talk... fear, I suppose. I got into the kitchen and the first thing that struck me was that there was water everywhere from burst pipes that had been shot away. My boss, Major Norman, said, 'Well done,' and told me to put some of the lads upstairs. I was relieved to be among the crowd..."*9

Now Section Six was left in the town with the Argentines closing in on all sides, coming into town from the south and east and they had to battle their way back with enemy soldiers springing up from everywhere and seemingly all around them; "I could see numerous figures and took on a number of targets," Ray Bloye recalled, "I had used my first mag of tracer rounds and knew my sights were fairly 'well on'. I can't say that I hit any Argies but I do know that when I fired at some of them, they went down... I didn't think of it as shooting people, they were merely targets like on a range. I saw a target, fired at it and it went down or away. I will never know if I hit anyone, but I believe I did." - Nick Williams continues; "I think the Argentines got a real shock. Every one of us thought we were dead and thought, 'If I'm going to go, I'm going to take a few of them with me.' So now there was no firing from cover or the usual precautions: it was more John Wayne or Audie Murphy style, blasting away from the hip at close range and I think that really shocked them."

Section Six was putting up an epic fight in the streets of Stanley against what were becoming overwhelming odds, as they pulled back towards Ross Road fighting the whole way; "At every junction we came to, we put down heavy fire before venturing down the road." Ray Bloye continues, "Benny had the GPMG going for what seemed to be all the time. Every time I looked his way, he always seemed to have a full belt of ammo on the gun and that was purely down to Nick Williams. I still had my spare tray of gun ammo ready to pass over but somehow, Nick always seemed to magic up a new belt out of nowhere. During a slight pause in the firefight, I was reloading my mags when the front door of the house opposite me was thrown open. I swung around, pointing my SLR only to see the lady resident of the house standing in the doorway. Before any of us could say anything, she calmly asked, 'Is my Land Rover in the way?' - I think we all shouted at the same time, 'Get back inside and stay away from the windows!' - Her Land Rover was, in fact, in the way, and almost to highlight the fact, a burst of Argie fire hit it." [*10]

Now the section, having held off the Argentine forces for as long as possible, doubled back down towards Ross Road to the edge of the harbour; "It was becoming clear that we couldn't get around behind the Argies from where we were, so we decided to head back down to the front," recounted Ray Bloye, "We'd been fighting for some time now and thankfully nobody had been hit on our side whilst we knew for a fact that several Argies had been taken out – and I, for one, was very grateful for this – we made our way back down to Ross Road, avoiding the areas where we had been fired upon. En-route down, I was passing a large bush when a rifle barrel came out from underneath it. I swung around with my SLR and almost squeezed the trigger when I realised it was a member of the FIDF; 'Don't shoot!' he shouted, and I responded with; 'What the hell are you doing down there!?' he told me he had got separated from his section and didn't know what to do. I told him to go home and hopefully, he did...."

Emerging onto Ross Road between Barrack Street and Villiers Street, the men of Section Six quickly realised that they were not going to get near to Government House and crossed the road to the Police Station from where they hoped to get some better information as to what was happening; "What the fuck is going on?" was the discourteous question. Quickly the policemen gave them some answers, gleaned mostly from the running commentary on FIBS and from a pair of binoculars they had with them, which kept them abreast of the action. Firstly, the Marines were pointed to the east, to where an armoured column could be seen making its way down Philomel Street towards Ross Road, then up to the south where a second column was clanking down Callaghan Road and deploying scores of steel-helmeted Marines into the town and finally towards GH in the west where the heavy firing from both sides was still evident. Penned in against the sea and with the Argentine forces closing in on all sides, Section Six knew that they were surrounded.

Ray Bloye now primed a 66mm LAW and moved into position should the Amtracks come his way; *"I was going to fire on the first APC that turned into Ross Road from Philomel Street,"* he remembered, *"extreme range for a 66 but it would be worth a go."* Now, however, he began to think about the wooden houses in Stanley, still packed full of people and the idea of a missed or ricocheting rocket made him think twice. With difficulty, he collapsed the weapon again, still loaded – something he had never actually had to do before – and slung the weapon over his shoulder, hoping he would get another chance to use it, then ran and joined the rest of the section on Victory Green; *"Just then, another thing happened which will stay with me for life,"* he continues, *"a local Falkland Islander – Henry Halliday – came walking along Ross Road from the Philomel Street end, clutching his lunchbox under his arm. We shouted, 'Get off the street! Don't you know we're being invaded?' and he replied, 'It's alright for you lot, some of us have got to get to work!' I next saw PC Anton Livermore run out of the police station and drag him inside..."*

Comical it may have been however, things were now becoming desperate for the men of Section Six with the Argentine invaders closing in on all sides; *"We had very little time before the armour would be in town,"* Nick Williams recalled, *"we only had small-arms and a limited supply of 66mm's and no defensive positions. If we stayed where we were, we would be slaughtered. What to do? I suddenly had a thought, I asked the policeman if Jack Sollis and the crew were still on the Forrest, alongside Government Jetty behind the town hall. He said they were still on board..."* - Nick Williams now suggested a plan for the section to take the *Forrest* out through the narrows and to drop them on a nearby beach. His knowledge of the Islands, of the camp, of the food and ammunition dumps and safe places and of course of all the people, would mean that the section could stay secure for some time and perhaps continue resistance. Quickly, every man in the section agreed and they raced off towards Government Jetty.

Almost the instant they approached Government Jetty, the section came under fire again from the hills above GH and from the streets which rose ever higher to the south: the jetty was fifty yards long and completely exposed to the Argentine troops in the town above them; *"The options were either to go individually, using covering fire or en-masse in the hope of the Argies not looking that way,"* remembered Ray Bloye, *"in the end, we did a bit of both."*

Quickly, both GPMG's were set up and were soon hammering fire back along the ridge line as the men of Section Six ran for the *Forrest* as Ray Bloye continues; *"That fifty yards felt like a mile and reminded me of those dreams where you are running in quicksand and not getting anywhere... The Argies spotted us and opened up, but the GPMG's started up on them which stopped their fire as we reached the safety of the ship. We then put up covering fire and the gunners ran for it in turn... We all made it."* Safely on board, the men now found a bemused Jack Sollis and his crew; *"I told Jack that I wanted him to take us out through the narrows,"* Nick Williams remembered, *"he refused point-blank, even when I threatened to shoot him. He knew I would never do it anyway but at this point the situation was getting desperate and we had to do something."* - Jack Sollis had made a wise decision; the *Forrest* was bright red and it was now daylight. The chances of making it past the aircraft carrier and several other warships now in Port William were, of course, zero. *"Look, we've killed a lot of fucking Argies and I don't think they're going to be in the mood to talk about it!"* Dave Carr yelled, and now Sollis instead suggested they take his inflatable Gemini boat as Nick Williams continues; *"As there were eight of us and the outboard wasn't very powerful, we decided that we would just take our weapons and ammunition and leave the bergens behind. If we did manage to get away, I was going to head to the North Camp, Long Island, Green Patch, Port Louis and eventually Seal Bay. I thought we could hide out in that area for ages and I knew and trusted all the farmers in that area, so knew this was the safest place to hide. We quickly lowered the Gemini into the water, Benny climbed down into the boat and prepared to start the engine as the rest of us started to pass the equipment down, but no matter what he tried, it refused to start..."*

In desperation, the others tried everything they could think of to make the outboard work as Ray Bloye continues; *"We tried another engine with the same result... To this day, I still think someone must have sabotaged them... We were determined to escape, so now decided to try and paddle our way across. The bay was probably 700-800 yards wide at this point and we started to get into the boat. There were not enough paddles for all of us, so those without would have to use their rifle butts. We'd got four or five of us in the boat when we heard the sound of aircraft screaming overhead: the Argies had got two of their Pucaras up and over us. In hindsight, they probably saved our lives as we were about to try to paddle across open water, exposed to enemy fire. Even with an engine, I doubt we would have made it, so with paddles only, we definitely wouldn't. The aircraft made the decision for us and we weren't prepared to commit suicide..."*

By now, Jack Sollis was shouting down from the wheelhouse that the Argentine armour was in the town and coming down Ross Road, that the firing had stopped and that it looked like it might all be over. With nowhere else to go, the men of Section Six now crowded below deck onto the *Forrest* to hide and await their fate. What did 'might be over' mean? - They all feared the worst. Perhaps, many thought, they were now the last ones left alive. With the order on the radio to 'stop fighting', Nick Williams suggested that the men pile their arms on the deck to show that they were offering no resistance. Below deck, the men were worried. These men, whose average age was perhaps twenty-one, now began to grow fearful; *"We knew we had given the Argies more than just a bloody nose,"* Ray Bloye remembered, *"between us we knew that we had hit several Argies and with all of the shooting going on, we knew that more of them had probably been killed or wounded and we had all heard the stories of people who had 'gone missing' in Argentina. We all knew that this was what could await us, if they didn't just put a bullet in the back of our heads first."*

Nick Williams now made a list of every man's name, rank and serial number and gave it to Jack Sollis so that, if the men of Section Six were made to 'disappear' he could attest to their murder. He then asked Jack to arrest them or call the police to come and get them when it all seemed quiet. They waited for an hour or two; *"During that time, there were some tears,"* he recalled, *"we really did think they would kill us. We were also thinking of the other guys and how many had been killed or wounded. I kept telling the guys it was a 50/50 situation; either we would be killed or we wouldn't and to try to focus on the positives. A lot of cigarettes were smoked..."* *[11]

Chapter 8: The Battle for Government House

"This is British territory. You are not invited here. We don't want you here. I want you to go and to take all of your men with you now."
Rex Masterman Hunt – Government House, April 2nd 1982.

At Government House, the firing had been intense once the three Argentines – Giachino, Quiroga and Urbina - had been shot and now the bullets seemed to come with more accuracy than before, as if the Argentines on the hill to the south and in the grounds around were now determined upon taking their revenge; *"Their rate of fire seemed brutal and sustained most of the time,"* Graham Evans recalled, *"it was a hell of a firefight. The usual thing; see movement, take your shots. It was constant from the start. Ammo wasn't a problem. We kept up a fast rate of fire to try to keep their heads down so that they couldn't advance with speed."* Still the Argentines were coming, rushing in in small groups, shoulder to shoulder and covered by their comrades; *"They appeared to be using SWAT hostage style tactics,"* recalled Andy Macdonald, *"and I fired about thirty rounds at targets from 10 metres to 80 metres. They just kept advancing and going down like bags of shite and I know I took down two or three more at least. One guy was very close and running at me when I got him, and he went down head first into a bush and stayed there with his legs sticking up in the air. Of course, every fourth shot, the bloody gun jammed again, so I was taking good aim and swearing a lot."*[1]

"I made every shot count." remembered Jim Fairfield, *"Most of us had only got 4 mags and I, like my oppo's intended to make the most of them. I was amazed at how calm I was. I think I went into autopilot; quick, aimed fire and movement followed, sight the enemy, two rounds, change position, acquire new target, incoming rounds, hold fire, sight enemy, two, three rounds, move, keep to my arcs and support my flank man, counting out rounds expended, shouting out enemy positions to nearest oppo and so it went on. A great weight of fire went down in a short space of time and I know the enemy took several casualties, on the whole their fieldcraft and fire positions were of a very amateur standard, but I remember thinking that it might just be a ruse to get us to become over-confident, luckily our high standard of training, common sense and self-preservation prevented this happening. I had an empty mag and had gone to ground to the right of that dreaded white gate to fit a full one when I had my first close call. I had just fitted the new mag and was about to cock my weapon, to do this I rolled slightly to my right just as two rounds burst over the top of the gate into the ground just about where I thought my head might have been a few seconds earlier. Several things,*

some of them really weird all happened in a split second, although at the time they seemed to happen in slow motion and are forever etched in my memory. First, I smelt the rounds as they hit the wet, soft lawn, a peculiar smell that anyone who has ever been in action knows immediately as a near miss, then I felt the wind from the rounds as they hit, and then the ground seemed to shake like a mini earthquake and dirt hit my eyes and face, somewhere mixed in with it all was the sound, a cross between a bang, whoosh and thud, you only hear those that miss... So I'm told."

Somewhere, an Argentine sniper was picking his shots and, as Geordie Gill remembered; *"I tried to find a window upstairs to attempt to engage him with my L42, however there was no suitable vantage point, so I ran back downstairs to find a good position..."* Scanning the ridge and suddenly seeing the sniper, Mike Norman now ordered his radio operator Robin Farnworth to shoot him. Farnworth took aim and let off three rounds, rapid fire, so close to Mike Norman's head that he momentarily deafened him; *"Stop it Farnworth, let him live!"* Norman shouted, as he held a hand to his ringing ear and then another loud bang erupted. *"If you fire that weapon again I'll wrap it round your neck!"* Norman growled – but Farnworth instead was pointing to where a bullet was sat, smoking away in the woodwork just an inch from Mike Norman's head. The firing was coming down heavily and it was amazing that there were no hits although by now, the near misses were, all the men agree, becoming alarming.[*2]

Down by the white gate, Jim Fairfield was also now aware that; *"...some Argie up there was not an amateur and had at last targeted the gate and had been taking his time to acquire me as my target. 'Sniper' was the one word going through my mind. I crawled, at light speed, to the left of the gate and into the cover of the hedgerow which I knew might hide me and looked out to see if he would try again. I spotted movement and muzzle flashes but none of the rounds seemed to be coming close to me. It was about this time that the Sergeant Major Bill Muir (behind the bullet proof wall) shouted for a sit-rep as he had obviously seen something he was concerned about. I shouted back something like, 'Pants full of shit, 3 mags, 2 grenades, suspect sniper, ok!' - (I've always thought it strange that you give the ammo report before reporting on whether you're wounded or not) his next words were 'Well get back to that fucking gate then!' - I replied, politely, that I would sooner eat the contents of my pants but did edge closer so I could see all my arcs of fire. The conversation might have gone on but the Argies were on the move again, some back up the slope this time while others came down and targets were available, we took targets of opportunity... there were a lot of targets... and I'm a good shot."*

The firefight around GH continued sporadically, a burst of shots, return fire, the men calling out sit-reps and the movements of the enemy to their flank man but finally, by 08.00 an undeclared ceasefire seemed to be in effect. The Argentines had been stung. They had taken casualties including the three men who now lay, groaning, yelling and screaming by turns in the garden. Mike Norman, Gary Noott and Rex Hunt had already been informed on the radio some fifty minutes before of their situation by Marine Berry, still ensconced on Sapper Hill behind the Argentine position who now radioed in that Argentine Marines were making their way to GH from Moody Brook and that there had been a battle on the Airport Road with an armoured column which was now making its way toward town. This, Mike Norman supposed, was why the Argentines were now taking their time. They didn't need to throw themselves at the house repeatedly; they just had to sit and wait for the armour and artillery to come up and then it would be no contest. In the Operations Room of Government House, Rex Hunt emerged from beneath the table he had been using as cover and went with Mike Norman to check on the men when, approaching the kitchen; *"I heard this moaning and I said to Mike: 'We had better get our wounded in.' He said: 'We haven't got any wounded... it's them...'"*

Now in the quiet period, men were calling out sit-reps. By a miracle there were no casualties although the men had fired a vast amount of ammunition already. Tiny Jones received a call; *"The OC wants to see you round by the door."* Andy Macdonald took his place now as Jones crawled around the house to the main door beside which was a small set of downward steps leading to a locked wooden door and a basement beyond, where he found Gary Noott and Robin Farnworth. Giving Noott an update on the condition of the Argentine wounded, he was then directed to shelter in the staircase with Farnworth although there was barely enough room to hide the pair of them; *"I spoke to Noott about what had gone on, then I got down the small couple of steps to where Farnworth was,"* remembered Jones, *"as the gap was not good cover, looking back up the hill with the light now coming, I decided to kick the door in to give us more cover. I started to kick it repeatedly and it was making a lot of noise. Major Noott couldn't see what I was doing and suddenly I heard this shout, 'Whatever you're doing, stop it!' my reply was, 'Fuck off, Sir!' and as the door gave way, Farnworth and I sat there in the basement, giggling like school-girls at having pissed off both Majors, me by telling Noott to fuck off, and him by deafening Mike Norman."*

Meanwhile, in the garden, Geordie Gill now decided to venture out during the ceasefire to help the three wounded men who lay groaning and screaming by turns, Giachino, Quiroga and Urbina; *"Ever since the first assault, there had been moans and screams from the three Argentinians hit in the engagement."* He remembered, *"They were just poor bastards like we were, doing a lousy job for their government, so I thought I'd get out and see if I could pull them in or perhaps give them some first aid. Corporal Pares and myself moved out into the gardens at the east side of the house to attempt to find and, if possible, bring them back inside. Pares covered me while I went to the lawn at the top of the drive and from there I saw one of them about thirty metres south of the main building, but to get to him we would have had to climb two fences and our faith in the ceasefire was not that good. While in the garden, we saw a section of Argentines on the ridge pepper-potting forward to better positions – I thought, 'Hold on! You're not allowed to improve your positions during a truce!' I looked at the wounded guys and realised that what with their mates on the move and me having to clamber over two fences in the open, I had little chance to get to them. I thought, 'sorry'... I shouted to Major Norman about the Argentines improving their position and two heads appeared in the window of Government House. They were Majors Noott and Norman. I shouted, 'They're up there and moving. They're getting closer and if they move again, I'm going to take them out.' I got told, 'You can't, it's a ceasefire. Don't shoot!' I thought to myself, 'Nah! This isn't a way to run a war.' Just then, someone from up the hill fired a shot at me, so I hit the deck. Next thing, they both appeared at the window again and one yelled, 'Corporal Gill, if you fire again, you'll be on a charge!' I thought, 'Hang on! I'm going to be dead by dinner but they're threatening to put me on a charge.' I pointed out – not very politely – that it wasn't me who had fired. They both looked at each other and one of them asked, 'Can you still see them?' - I said, 'Yeah', and the reply was, 'Well take 'em out!' - I thought to myself, 'Oh yes... This is Christmas.'"*[3]

Geordie was an excellent marksman who, armed with an L42 sniper rifle and within easy range of his targets, was now in his element. The uneasy truce had allowed one advantage to the Royal Marines; now that the sun was rising, the Argentines were silhouetted against the high ground and their black clothes now made them discernible against the yellow-green grass and undergrowth as he singled out a section commander and a rifleman next to him, firing from behind a rock; *"I engaged the section commander on the ridge with my L42,"* he remembered, *"my first two shots must have gone low, so I racked the sights up and on my third shot I saw the guy go down; he dropped his weapon, jerked upright and slid over the rock he was using as cover, falling in full view where he remained unmoving. His mate stuck his head out to see what had happened and I got him too, he jerked and slumped behind the rock, leaving his rifle on top of the rock. No further movement from that position. I was firing through a hole in the hedge, up on one knee over about 500 yards and then Terry Pares shouted that he could see the radio operator and, as he could see him and I couldn't, he asked if he should take him out. I said 'Yeah!' so he opened up with ten rounds rapid from his SLR and shouted, 'I think I got him! I think I got him!' – He did - I looked through my scope and saw his body fall down in my arc of view and lay writhing on its back until he went still, 'Oh yes...' I said to Terry with a smile, '...yes, I think you did.'"*[4]

With three more of their number killed or wounded, the Argentines, with a heavy machine gun from the ridge and joined by the rest of their steadily-growing force, now poured rounds back into GH which tore through the flimsy building and the grounds around; *"It's amazing just how small you can make yourself when you have to!"* Jim Fairfield remembered, *"We were soon on the lookout for its position and the Sergeant Major was going blue shouting out the query, 'Any fucker see it!?' - It was to be very unfortunate for me that nobody did! - The machine gun team had taken their time with their position and their short well-aimed bursts of fire were textbook stuff. When all other methods of finding the enemy fail, a last resort is to offer them a tempting target in the hope that they will let loose a long burst of fire, the resulting smoke and muzzle flash giving away their position. One look from the Sergeant Major and I knew that the tempting target was to be me. I was well out on the right flank, the last man, any fire would be from the high left, across the front of our position giving the lads a good opportunity to spot the source. I would actually only be in their sights for about ten or so yards before the body of Government House blocked out the whole ridgeline. I was banking on them having a position on the high ground which would offer them the best view and not lower down where they could track me for considerably more than ten yards. Thinking like the enemy had kept me going so far but I was beginning to feel like a cat counting out its lives."*

Now all eyes were peeled as Geordie Gill and Terry Pares waited for a target, as Jim Fairfield continues; *"I carefully drew back from the hedgerow keeping my eyes on the enemy positions and, with my head still facing them, I rose to a commando crouch and ran for the other side of the lawn and the cover of the house. I soon decided that I could run faster if I straightened up, no sooner had I done so than the machine gun opened up and I was watching the neatly cut lawn being stitched up just to my rear and left. I thought up to that point that I had been running as fast as I could go, it was not so, and I would have given any gold medal sprinter a good race. I soon reached the cover of the house but such was my speed that I did not stop until I reached the wall at the other side of the lawn. I'm sure I heard a cheer and someone clapping their hands, bastards that they were. At this time, I was also aware of another section of Marines coming back in to Government House from the direction of town. I guessed these were the guys who had been stationed on the beach - this small group all made it back safely. I could not hear any fire going down from the lads and had feared the worst. Once I got my breath back I asked if the gun had been spotted, a chorus of 'No's' sounded from the wall followed by, 'You'd best get back and try again!' followed by several titters and one loud laugh. I set my eyes on that bloody white gate, shouted, 'Okay!'*

and legged it back. As soon as I came out from the cover of the house that gun opened up to my front and right this time, so the gunner wasn't as good as he thought after all. I also remember smiling as a great wall of fire was returned from the lads and I thought, 'Bastards had him all the time!' It was just as these thoughts were leaving my head that I literally fell over my own feet and crashed to the ground severely winding myself. Before I could start dragging myself into cover, I felt a huge weight land on my back which didn't help me to get my breath back at all. I was being dragged back towards cover and could hear a voice repeatedly asking me where was I hit. I just could not get my breath to reply until I had been dragged all the way back to cover when I managed to croak out that I was just winded. I looked up to see who had put himself in the kill zone to pull me out, it was the young Marine who had said he would look out for me earlier, I never did get a chance to thank him properly while he called me all the sons of bitches for not being shot!"*

Now, however, Geordie Gill had found his machine-gunner and here they had what Geordie later described as, *"an interesting little time,"* with the others watching on as the two traded shots; *"After my 3rd or 4th round there was no more return fire coming in,"* remembered Gill, *"and when I very cautiously got up on one knee and looked through the scope I saw the bi-pod legs of the weapon on its side by the rock he had been using as cover."* The prone man's leg was now seen to thrash and twitch and then then finally he ceased moving. No more fire came from him after that.

With the sun up and with the arrival of Pedro Lopez from GH, the Commandos Anfibios of Lieutenant Commander Sanchez Sabarots' command moved on towards Government House to reinforce the position there; *"but before reaching the Governor's house, someone appeared in civilian clothes who was an Argentine of the Civil Aviation who had not been captured the night before,"* Corporal Carlos Cequiera recalled, *"and he told us that some 400 metres behind the Governor's house were about twenty English... We moved cautiously and narrowed the gap..."* now Government House was surrounded on all sides as Sanchez Sabarots' men closed in from the west and the men of BIM2 closed in from the east, with the firefight now intensifying again. Meanwhile, helicopters were landing more troops – the first at 07.34 exactly - and now with the runway cleared, a Hercules flew in the remainder of the 25th Infantry Regiment who closed in towards the scene of the fighting.

On FIBS, Rex Hunt took again to the radio to update Patrick Watts and the residents of the Islands on the situation; *"They infiltrated a party behind us,"* he told Watts, *"once, they got very close to us, but they've now withdrawn. It's only a matter of time before they regroup and come again. They have five armoured personnel vehicles on the way from the Canache that landed in Yorke Bay. It's just a matter of time until they overrun us, but we'll see how long we can hold on anyway."*

"Sir, are you going to try and hang on and keep them back for as long as possible, or are you going to surrender?" asked Watts. *"We are not surrendering, we are resisting."* Hunt replied, *"If someone is prepared to come in and talk to me, I'll have them in but I'm not going out to talk to them or to surrender to them. We're staying put here, but we are pinned down. We can't move."*

"They're obviously trying to just get Government House, are they?" Watts asked. *"They are not doing any damage, I hope, to the rest of the town,"* Hunt replied again, *"but obviously when the armoured personnel vehicles come, we'll have to give in because they can flatten the place... They must have 200 around us now. They've been throwing rifle grenades at us; I think there may be mortars, I don't know. They came along very quickly and very close, and then they retreated. Maybe they are waiting until the APC's come along as they think they'll lose less casualties that way. But I'm waiting for them to send somebody in to see me. It's getting light and they have a much more commanding position. We can't move from here without being shot at because they are up above us and behind. So I'm afraid it's just a matter of time, but... well, we'll do what we can."*[5]

The situation was becoming bleak. The men of the Royal Marines were mostly down to their last magazines of ammunition by now and were working to make their shots count. The Argentines were keeping low and out of the way until armoured support arrived but Geordie Gill and Terry Pares were still picking them off, stirring up a fire-fight as they went, and they had developed a good system for taking out the enemy, Gill with his L42 sniper rifle and Pares with his SLR, as Major Mike Norman's report went on to say; *"Corporals Pares and Gill were doing an excellent job. Gill would look through his sniper scope and tell Pares where the enemy were and Pares would fire ten rounds rapid, and as soon as that got them on the move, Gill would take them out with the sniper rifle."* Gill and Pares were now encouraging the others, giving a running commentary on their success; *"At one stage we were in the 11-5 club,"* Graham Evans remembered, *"eleven wounded, five dead as we were hitting them hard up on the hill behind GH."*

The Argentine forces had been hit hard and the Royal Marines were still fighting despite the growing odds. Still, despite some awfully near misses, there was not one man killed or wounded, yet what were they to do when the Amtracks arrived? Stanley residents – Alistair Grieves included - had seen five coming into town and several others behind them, with 30mm cannon which could simply flatten GH. The Marines had bought time, had made the world sit up and take notice and had not given in. Still, there was more, they hoped, that they could do until the inevitable came. The men were moving and firing, picking their targets and dodging the bullets but now the firing was sporadic as the Argentines waited for the support which they knew would soon be coming. By now, their ranks were already swelling with men coming from Moody Brook and now 2nd platoon Echo Company BIM2 under Marine Midshipman Sanchez was on the way from the town as meanwhile Delta Company were coming from the east to close the net.[*6]

By this time, it was obvious that GH was being surrounded and that, whatever damage the Royal Marines might yet do, the outcome could only go one way, as hordes of Argentine Marines and special forces now converged upon GH from all sides; *"I was starting to panic by then,"* PJ Berry recalled, *"as they were still getting nearer and, knowing that we had killed some of them, what would they do if they found a lone Marine on a hill with no one else around? Probably what we would have done and said he fired first. I got on the radio and explained to the boss that they were now only about 300 metres away and he gave me permission to leg it. I scrambled the radio frequency and started to leg it across the scree – running – not knowing what I wanted to do but all that was in my head was to get as far away as possible from the Argies. The scree-run went on for ever, but I don't think anyone in the world at that moment in time would have kept up with me... I decided to head towards the caves in the next hill along, that were supposed to have had stores stashed inside them. As I was running near them, I came across a gap in some rocks, which I climbed down into and found a perfect cave. I lay there for about 15 minutes, knowing I was safe as no one could have found it, and I closed my eyes, hoping to wake up and it would all be a dream. I was so tired, as I had had no sleep from the previous day at the lighthouse, then suddenly I could hear dogs barking, which made me realise that I was not safe, and I started to leg it again. I could see the road to Fitzroy down below, and decided to stay high but follow the road, as I wanted to be with people rather than be on my own. By then I had ditched everything that was heavy except for basic fighting order..."*

Meanwhile, in the garden of Government House, the three Argentine casualties were still in a bad way. Urbina had managed to inject morphine into his leg to stem the pain and had crawled away, *"guts dragging on earth"* as he recalled, and then; *"I took out my backpack, grabbed the ampoules of Demarol and injected it into my right leg, not even feeling the sting. I took another blister and now injected my left leg and after that, I went through my clothes and searched with my hands for the area of the wound, on which I put a dressing. I took my backpack and put it under my head and told myself: whatever God wills..."* Urbina was now laying back, smoking a cigarette and waiting for help as meanwhile Diego Quiroga, not too far away, lapsed in an out of consciousness; *"I could not move and had lost the grip on my weapon,"* he recalled, *"the sun was quickly coming up and I could still hear the voices and bullets, but was sinking away very fast. I heard the rotating blades of a chopper, but could not see it. The sky was blue and I remember thinking that it was not bad to die on such a beautiful morning, amongst friends and lying on the grass..."*

Now Rex Hunt went again onto FIBS as Patrick Watts asked him; *"How much longer do you think you can hold out, sir?"* - *"Oh, they've got 30mm cannons on these armoured personnel carriers,"* Hunt replied, *"so one or two shots from them and we'd be finished, I'm afraid. But I'm hopeful that they'll send somebody in to talk."* - Hunt was being clever, now hoping that someone on the Argentine side was listening in. It was evident that the contest would soon become unwinnable. *"And you'll talk to them, will you sir?"* Watts asked. *"I'll talk to them,"* Hunt answered, *"but I'm not walking out. I'm not surrendering to the bloody Argies, Patrick. Certainly not!"* - *"Fantastic!"* Watts sounded proud, *"Well done sir!"* then as the line went dead he spoke directly to the listeners; *"Well, you heard the Governor. I never thought they'd do a thing like this, I can tell you. I told everyone they wouldn't. Anyway, the problem is that they are here."*

With the Argentine forces closing in, Major Mike Norman went to talk with Rex Hunt, determined to try to convince him to escape while there was still time. Entering the Operations room, he found Hunt ensconced beneath a huge oak table covered with a green baize cloth, his telephone in one hand and pistol in the other. It was time to make a decision. Norman now gave him a sit-rep and three options; they could, while there was still time, break out towards Ross Road, crawl along the shoreline to Moody Brook and make a break for camp to set up an alternate seat of government until help arrived. Hunt looked up at Gary Noott who muttered something about *"bloody suicide..."* and Rex Hunt repeated that he would not entertain the thought anyway. Or, Norman continued, they could fight until overrun. He promised that the defence would be strong, violent, determined and unrelenting, but short-lived at best, but that he was quite willing to take that option if that was what Hunt wanted him to do. Finally, he gave the third option, to hold out as long as possible until the armour arrived and then to negotiate a truce; *"I knew I would have to give in some time,"* Hunt recalled, *"I knew that Mike wouldn't want to give in... My big anxiety was, have we done enough to get the majority of the Great British people to support us and the Islanders?"*

Rex Hunt was now determined: he was not going to run away and would face what was coming, but he would not ask the Royal Marines to sacrifice themselves needlessly. He would try to get someone in to talk. The Royal Marines had done their jobs. So far, by some miracle, not a man of them was so much as wounded whilst the Argentines had taken a good score or more of casualties by the count of the snipers and others who were fighting alongside them. Now was the time to stop the madness before things became serious. Abandoning the Islanders and the people of Stanley was not an option. Fortunately for him, the Argentines had indeed been listening in to his conversation with Patrick Watts and now it seemed that they were willing to respond as he had hoped. They began to broadcast on a frequency which the Islanders commonly used and soon Patrick Watts was playing it directly to the people of Stanley through the radio. The message was full of static and feedback, with high-pitched whistles which blocked out some of the words, but the message was clear enough and very scripted; *"This is a call to the British Colonial Government of the Islas Malvinas,"* it began, *"In order to fulfil orders from the Argentine Government, we are here with a (unintelligible) task force (unintelligible) remaining faithful to our (unintelligible) principles. For the purpose of avoiding bloodshed and property damage among the population, we hope that you will act prudently. Our concern is for the welfare and safety of the people of the Malvinas."*

In every home, the words put a chill up the spine of the people. These were not the 'Malvinas' they were the Falkland Islands. In Government House, Rex Hunt and Dick Baker commented that the voice sounded very much like Colonel Belcarce, an Argentine officer who had visited the Islands many times. A second message followed which now suggested that further resistance would endanger the population, and this was not helped by the fact that several Islanders were now talking on FIBS about damage to their property, especially Tom Davies in White City whose roof had a metre-square hole in it from Sergeant Quiroga's mortar round, which had blown up his water tank and landed in his wardrobe. He was fine, he said, but he and his wife were slopping about in water and the house was probably a write-off. Property was getting damaged and people were now at serious risk. The new message, therefore, seemed to contain a more sinister meaning, and ended with the warning that Argentine armoured vehicles were now in the town. Rex Hunt looked at Noott and Norman and asked them what he thought it all meant; *"It means we're stuffed, Sir."* Norman replied. It was a dilemma for Mike Norman and the Governor. Would the Argentinian forces act correctly, or would they simply shoot everyone and hammer the town if the Royal Marines didn't lay down their arms? The message seemed to imply that if they surrendered no one in the town would get hurt and in this, there was seemingly a veiled threat to the opposite. By this time messages from the other end of town were reporting shells and bullets going through houses. Nobody had been hurt, but the damage was alarming. If the people of Stanley were being put in danger then there could be only one course of action, and Rex Hunt announced that he was prepared to negotiate if the Argentines would, but that he would not, under any circumstances, surrender.

The Argentines were broadcasting but, without knowing their frequency, Rex Hunt was powerless to reply. Someone then suggested that surely Gamin or

Gilobert would know at least the most common frequencies and Rex Hunt now put in a call to LADE House where Hector Gilobert answered the phone. Gilobert, long considered a friend to the Islanders, sounded practically in tears as Hunt asked him to put him through to the Argentine commander, explaining that he didn't know who that could be. At first, Hunt had difficulty in believing him, remaining sure that Gilobert must have been in on the plan, but Gilobert protested emotionally that he was always a friend to the Islanders, that it was nothing to do with him and that it was the most terrible thing. If he was acting, Hunt recalled later, it was worthy of Olivier. Gilobert had not known and Hunt told him he believed him. Gilobert asked what he could do to help and Hunt replied that he might like to take an Argentine flag and go to see who was in command of the Argentine landing force so that they might arrange a truce to get their wounded to hospital. Sadly, Gilobert didn't have an Argentine flag; the nearest was in his office and right now that was the scene of a war zone. Finally, exasperated, Hunt asked him to come to Government House with a white flag and see if he could try some frequencies from which to contact the Argentine commander. There was a pause and finally Gilobert replied that he could be there in ten minutes. When the phone went down, the farcical nature of the conversation, which had been heard by all, gave rise to a moment of respite as the men in the Operations room all fell about laughing. Ten minutes later, Gilobert, as good as his word, approached GH carrying a white flag when suddenly, as he walked up the driveway, a burst of firing rang out and bullets began to kick up the gravel around his feet. With the Argentine Commandos firing on him, Gilobert sprinted the last few yards and fell in the door looking whiter than the flag he was carrying, to the cheers and congratulations of the Royals.

Again, a silence dropped over GH as the men of both sides kept their heads down and Geordie Gill and Terry Pares watched to see if anyone else fancied improving their positions a second time. This time, nobody did. Inside GH, Gilobert suggested a few common frequencies and now Rex Hunt had an idea as he turned to Dick Baker; *"Rex was looking at me,"* Baker recalled, *"and saying, 'Someone... 'Someone' has to go out there and stop those tanks. It has to be someone who can talk to the commanding officers.' I knew it had to be me, because if Rex went out, it would be construed as surrender, which was what he did not want."* - Now Hunt tried every frequency Gilobert had suggested, from which he broadcast that two men, Baker and Gilobert, would leave GH under a white flag and make their way to the town hall on Ross Road where they were prepared to meet the Argentine commanders. They waited a few minutes to see if anything happened. There was no response. Baker and Gilobert would just have to hope that there were not any itchy trigger fingers out there. It was 08.45 when they were ready to set off and someone realised that they didn't have a white flag. Tearing down a white lace curtain, Rex Hunt now tied it to his umbrella and handed it to Baker, uttering the famous words; *"Don't lose my umbrella, Dick, I paid the earth for it from Briggs in Piccadilly."* Now Baker and Gilobert exited gingerly through the east door, waving their makeshift flag as a flurry of shots punched the air and kicked up the gravel around them but, as Baker recalled; *"they were either trying to put the wind up us, or else they were bloody bad shots."*[7]

As they set off up the road, during what Dick Baker later remembered as the longest walk of his life, Rex Hunt looked on through the open door as Geordie Gill covered the pair; *"Does this mean I can't shoot at the bastards anymore?"* he asked Hunt with a look of disappointment, *"Not at all, Geordie!"* Hunt answered back brightly, *"If they shoot at you, you shoot back. And if they try to move, you shoot!"* Geordie Gill now beamed back at Hunt; *"Ah, thank you Sir. You see there's one of them just up there, behind that rock and he'll have to move some time."* Hunt smiled and passed on, thinking to himself that he did not rate highly the chances of survival of the Argentine behind the rock.

Back in the Ops room, Mike Norman had one last card to play; all of his sections were now either engaged or in hiding somewhere in the town except for one; Section Four under Stefan York out at Navy Point. They were the last men still able to move, and he intended to make full use of them. Royal Marine Dick Overall who was with Section Four remembered a feeling of helplessness as his section were forced to watch the invasion unfold from the other side of the harbour. As it had become light, they had watched the Amtracks crawling up the Canache and along the road towards Stanley, had seen the smoke from the firefight with Bill Trollope's Section Two, had watched Dave Carr's Section Six battling through the streets and had observed the battle which had raged all morning around Government House; *"When we saw the heads of those Amtracks coming up the airport road I remember thinking, 'Oh shit, this is the shit hitting the fan!'"* he recalled, *"And then we saw the firefight in and around Stanley and that was the hardest bit because we couldn't do anything."* Later, Wilf 'Smudger' Smith recounted to Ray Bloye how the men of Section Four had been amazed at the sheer amount of shooting going on in and around Stanley. All they could see was tracer flying around town everywhere which, with tracer being on average one in every five rounds, showed the sheer intensity of the fighting. Now Mike Norman was on the radio and ordering York to 'thin out' – to escape in the small Gemini boat they had with them and to carry on a small-scale guerrilla war as best they could - to keep up resistance; *"Right boss,"* York replied and, remembering Norman's earlier joke, added, *"We're going fishing."*

Quickly, the men packed up what they could take with them. The Carl Gustav was too heavy, so the men primed two white-phosphorous grenades and crammed them down the barrel as a nasty surprise for anyone who picked it up. The second they came rolling out of the barrel, it wouldn't be pretty. *"Right lads, let's fuck off!"* said Corporal York as the men jumped into the Gemini, got it going after several attempts and in broad daylight tried to make their escape across Port William. Now the ARA *Drummond* one of the Argentine Corvettes, was descending upon them at pace, and the men were weaving in and around the various vessels in the port trying to find sanctuary. Of these, the largest in port was a Polish factory ship and now the men made for it watched by the Polish fishermen who stood on the deck; *"We were shouting, 'Can you help us?'"* Dick Overall remembered, *"And they were waving their arms as if to say, 'Go away, we're not interested.'"* Luckily, as the *Drummond* went to one side of the factory ship, York's section slipped out the other and made their way to land beyond Port William where they quickly moved off to the relative safety of the camp. Someone, at least, had escaped.*[8]

Now in Government House, the tension seemed to be easing. If Baker and Gilobert could fulfil their mission, then someone might come to talk. Nobody yet was talking about the word 'surrender' but it was clear that the Royal Marines had done their job. They were a tripwire; a small force designed to trigger a reaction. They had fought – and hard - they had given the Argentines a very bloody nose, now they could not win but they could protect Stanley and, if they were lucky, they could survive. In the relative calm, Major Gary Noott walked through GH to check the building's defences and see to the men when, as he recalls; *"I arrived in the dining room where Marine Dorey, my detachment armourer was. He told me he had been down the covered walkway which connected that end of GH to the old maids' quarters and he thought he had heard voices, so off we went to investigate. The walkway was wood or brick to waist height, topped with clear glass windows and because we would have been in view we crouched and crawled our way along to the maids' quarters. Where the walkway entered the quarters was a largish, squarish hall. We stopped and listened and heard muted voices. I signalled to Dorey that I was going to do the old 'house clearing bit' of putting a burst of SMG through the ceiling to liven / deaden the buggers above up, maybe damage them a bit and make them less keen to play. Sadly, my rusty weapon handling let us down because I moved the safety catch to single shot rather than automatic. The result was, as they say, 'written on the tin' - one bang - rapidly followed by the thought 'Oh shit!' and the expectation of all hell descending through the ceiling onto Dorey and myself! However, all that happened was a lot of somewhat louder Spanish emanating from above us!"*

Luckily, at the other end of the room, Geordie Gill - now also carrying an SMG - arrived and he put a full burst through the ceiling above him. The men upstairs were Cardillo, Flores and Ledesma – one of them a Commando Anfibio and the other two Buzo Tactico - who had found their way upstairs from the maid's quarters and had been hiding in the upstairs store room. Now as the shots tore through the floor, two men jumped into a bathtub and another vaulted over a sofa and landed in a 200-litre water tank, as Gary Noott continues; *"At this stage, still feeling somewhat vulnerable, I decided on the 'bullshit baffles brains' approach to our predicament, namely using the little pidgin Spanish I could come up with to shout authoritatively, 'Arriba los manos!' - 'Put your hands up' (I think) - There was more chat from upstairs so I repeated it a couple more times, joined in this by Corporal Gill and the reply was 'OK, OK!' - As 'shit and derision' was not being visited on us, Dorey proceeded up the stairs and 'invited' our guests to come down, which they did without fuss."*

As Cardillo, Flores and Ledesma came tumbling down the stairs *"very warily"* as Geordie Gill remembered, so he, Gary Noott, Harry Dorey and now Mick Sellen, just arrived, covered them with their SMG's. Later, Geordie Gill was to recount the struggle with his own feelings as he saw them; men who had invaded his home and that of his children, men who (as he then thought) had taken out at least one of the sections of Royal Marines, and he admitted that he had never been closer to murder in his life. The moment lasted only a second and he was later glad that he had not given in to it. Now the three Argentines stood there in the hall, scared and shaking as Geordie covered them with a look of hatred in his eyes. They were dressed all in black, with blackened faces and black woollen hats. Gary Noott felt a little elation at the capture of three prisoners of war, but remembered that it would be short-lived and that soon, doubtless, the Royal Marines would be their prisoners in turn. He reflected later with a note of satisfaction that if these were Argentina's crack troops, he was not very much impressed; he had expected them to come charging down the stairs firing and hurling grenades. It was a victory of sorts, albeit a hollow one. Gill, Dorey and Sellen now marched them away as Gary Noott went to inform Mike Norman and Rex Hunt of his new captives; *"Not scared, English!"* one of the captives was heard to say as he was led away, *"I have bullet-proof vest!"* – *"Oh, really?"* Geordie was heard to retort, *"You got a bullet-proof mouth as well?"*

Down on Ross Road, Dick Baker and Hector Gilobert walked towards the police station where they entered and called FIBS where Patrick Watts patched him through to the channel which had received the Argentine broadcasts. Live on air, Hector Gilobert delivered his message; *"Soy el Vice Comodoro Gilobert. Quiero hablar con el comandante de las fuerzas... I am with the Deputy Governor at the Police Station. We both want to speak to the commander of the forces. If you are listening, I propose that we meet in front of the town hall, in front of the Catholic Church. He should come with one man and a white flag. There is absolute guarantee of mutual respect."*

A few minutes went by as Gilobert repeated his message and then translated it for the listeners in Stanley, when the reply came back in broken English; *"We are accepting your requirement, the officer commanding the force of disembarkment is coming up now to the Catholic Church, to the square near the Catholic Church to meet the people that you have suggest."*

Admiral Carlos Busser was already in Stanley when the call came through; *"We were ready for this,"* he recalled, *"and I had ordered a white flag to be packed. But when I told the officer concerned to get it out, the flag wasn't there! He had thought the order was a joke and had not packed it! We had to take a white waste-disposal bag from one of the Amtracks. I walked several streets to reach the meeting place..."* now Dick Baker saw him approach and remembered seeing 'this John Wayne type' striding down the road with his helmet on and goggles strapped to it – General Garcia, with the tall, beak-nosed figure of Admiral Busser beside him - and several others in attendance under a white flag. Busser stepped forward, offering Baker his hand who, without thinking, took it, hearing Busser utter some banality about being a brave man and then; *"Are you going to take me to meet Mister Hunt?"* - Busser remembered his own disappointment at not meeting with Hunt personally as he had hoped, and had even for a second considered refusing to talk to anyone but Hunt himself, but then; *"Gilobert told me about our wounded men outside Government House and we all went back there."* he recalled. As the party walked along Ross Road towards GH, several Argentines started to fire on them, but Busser, cool and collected, made a megaphone of his hands and yelled out; *"If you can hear what I am saying, raise your right arms!"* - Slowly an arm went up from the surrounding rocks and hedgerows followed by many others. They had recognised their commander and now all fell silent again. Turning to Dick Baker, Busser suddenly laughed; *"And they call this the age of electronic communications!"* - Baker, somewhat perturbed, considered that at least the Argentine commander was a man with a sense of humour. Now as they walked along Ross Road, ever close to GH, Dick Baker could first hear and see men standing up and a curious, low chant which he later realised was, *"Ar-gen-tina"* recited over and over. [9]

In the grounds around GH, Corporal Figgy Duff watched Gilobert leading the party towards the house with the Amtracks now coming up in his wake. Behind hedges and a bank of earth, his section had been safe from most of the action and had had to endure the tracer fire coming over their heads – almost from behind - for most of the morning. Now he looked around to get a good view of the approaching Argentine forces and remembered a feeling of fatalistic resignation; *"I realised to myself that there wasn't any point in fighting on any more,"* he recalled, *"I didn't see the point in just dying. By now I wasn't going to die for the Islanders – though I would have – but by now it wasn't about dying to defend them. If we* carried on now, we were just going to die, and if we went much further, we would have just put the whole population of Stanley at risk."

Now Busser came up the drive, joined by several more of his men from around the grounds as Tiny Jones remembered; *"There were one or two guys skipping along, trying to catch up with him and it just reminded me of that 'Life of Brian' scene from Monty Python, so I called out that, 'Penny for an ex-leper!' line, which brought giggles from our guys, followed by, 'Shackle for an ex-leper!' being thrown back from somewhere across the gravel drive. We were all laughing as they turned up for this momentous moment!"* Now Geordie Gill met Busser and his entourage at the door; *"He had five or six of these special forces guys as an escort. Me and a couple of other guys went out to say Busser could come in, but they couldn't. One of the guys leaned over and tried to take the magazine off my SMG, which nearly got him a face full of nine-mil – bad move. From behind us, all you could hear were the clicks of the safety catches coming off the rifles of our guys who were hidden among the trees lining the drive. His special forces guys were looking at each other in a panic and suddenly realising they were in the middle of a killing zone. To tell the truth I was almost hoping they would try something; we were really psyched up and ready to fight to the end, but they backed down. Busser came in on his own and the special forces guys just stayed there and waited for him to come out. They were under quite a few weapons by that time."*[*10]

Having told his men to stand down, Admiral Busser now entered the wreck of Government House alone and was shown to Rex Hunt's office; *"I thought that in the next few moments I would be either a prisoner or the victor,"* he remembered later, *"I thought it was advisable to act coolly..."* He now entered Rex Hunt's office where the Governor had taken a few minutes to brush down his pinstriped suit, smarten his hair and adjust his tie. The two men; Rear-Admiral Carlos Busser and Governor Rex Masterman Hunt locked eyes at 09.15 exactly. Busser made to speak but Rex Hunt stood up and addressed him loudly and clearly and in a tone of the most noble defiance which silenced him at once; *"This is British territory. You are not invited here. We don't want you here. I want you to go, and to take all of your men with you now."*

In the moment's silence that followed, Mike Norman recalled that; *"I looked across at Gary and cocked an eyebrow thinking, 'Well we've tried everything else, perhaps this one is going to work.'"* Busser stopped for a moment and then smiled. He recognised Gary Noott from intelligence photographs and offered his hand first, then to Mike Norman and finally to Rex Hunt himself, who refused it. Busser now replied; *"I've got 800 men ashore, another 2,000 on the way. I have a crushing superiority. You have your job to do and I have mine. Your job is to prevent my men killing all of your men. My job is to prevent British soldiers killing some of mine. We don't want to kill any of these Marines. We thought that if we came in such numbers, they would not fight, but they have fought with bravery and skill. I want you to stop the action now before Marines are killed and civilians of Stanley are killed."* There was a pause; *"The Governor asked the two Royal Marine officers what they thought,"* Busser recounted later, *"I think they answered more with their eyes than anything else."*

It was clear that the end had come. Rex Hunt had done all that a Governor could do. He had not fled or run. He had kept up the morale of the people of Stanley and had stood with them throughout the invasion. Somehow, not one of his Royal Marines had been killed or wounded so far as he knew, whilst the reports that had come in testified to a dogged and heroic defence in the face of overwhelming odds. Glancing up, he was surprised to see the journalist Simon Winchester hastily scribbling notes in the corner; now the world would know what was done and what was said, just as he had planned. He had done his job. His job would now be to look after the safety and the welfare of his people – and that meant stopping the fighting. He now looked at Busser and finally said; *"In that case, you don't give me any option,"* and turning to Gary Noott and Mike Norman, said simply, *"Tell your men to stop fighting and to lay down their arms."*[11]

It was 09.25 on Friday, April 2nd 1982 and the battle for Government House was over.

The Falkland Islands had fallen.

Chapter 9: Counting the Cost

"For life is quite absurd, and death's the final word, you must always face the curtain with a bow. Forget about your sin, give the audience a grin, enjoy it, it's your last chance anyhow."
From 'Always look on the bright side of life' – Monty Python.

The order went around that the fighting was over. Every man was to file out of GH with his arms up and to lay his weapons on the ground; *"I was actually quite pleased we were stopping,"* remembered Lou Armour, *"I make no bones about it. I didn't fancy getting shot to bits. I was just glad it was finished. There were two APC's of theirs hit; they must have lost guys in them. There were three casualties laying in the garden of Government House. You think: What sort of mood are they going to be in when their oppo's are shot up?"* Now, relieved but nervous, he led the way out, with his SLR raised in his right hand and several others behind him covered by a black-clad Argentine with a sterling submachine gun. Already, some Argentines were taking photographs and a few recognised Rafael Wollmann – the supposed 'tourist' who had arrived a few days before - now mingling with the Argentine Special Forces and taking pictures. He was now, whether on purpose or not, Argentina's official war photographer and his pictures would soon become world-famous.[*1]

Jim Fairfield had still, to the last minute, been considering his escape routes when, as he recalled; *"The Governor then came out and said, 'Well done lads but the game's up, it's time to stop fighting.' There were lots of moans and mumbles. I went up to him and in my best voice said, 'Fuck off, Sir' - Rex smiled, put his hand on my arm and said, 'Sorry Jim but we can't win this one.' I turned around looking at the lads, their faces etched with strain, if Rex had told us to 'go for it' then we, to a man, would have but here we were, all alive and passed a life-belt that we would have been foolish to pass up. I unloaded my weapon and threw it muzzle-first into the lawn. I saw many of the lads do likewise. I made my way into Government House as did a few of the lads. I went straight to Rex's beer fridge, broke the lock with my bayonet and started dishing out the beer to the lads, believe me, beer never tasted so good."*

Upon hearing the order to cease fire, Colour Sergeant John Noone remembered feeling resentful; *"We thought, 'Christ, it's daylight, now we could have them all!'"* he remembered, *"If it hadn't have been for those Amtracks, they could have had 600 guys up there and we could have kept bringing them down like flies all day long."* Now slowly, almost obstinately, the Royal Marines began to file out and lay down their weapons. Some remembered being scared, as the Argentines had a reputation for making people 'disappear' but others had a surlier attitude. They had done their jobs well and had not lost a single man. The Argentines had outnumbered them and had been stung badly by their response. They had lost, but they were defiant; *"We came second,"* as Mike Norman was heard to say later, *"but at least we won the body count."*

In the back garden, Pedro Giachino, Diego Quiroga and Ernesto Urbina were now seen to as the Argentines rushed to the scene and the British moved in to help, with the men of both countries coming out with blankets and bandages, first to Giachino who seemed to be in the worst condition, with a shot through the chest, his stomach torn open and blood thick on the floor around him from a gunshot to the leg which was bleeding profusely. Gently they prised the grenade from his hand and put the pin back in and then slid a blanket beneath him to carry him to the hospital; *"I was lifting one side of the blanket, but Giachino was a very big man and very heavy"* Admiral Busser recalled, *"and suddenly two hands appeared at my side, helping me to lift. It was Major Norman. I have a very good feeling towards him; his attitude is something I shall never forget."* Giachino was pale. He had lost a lot of blood from a severed femoral artery in his leg and looked to be dying. Quickly, he was bundled into the back of a Land Rover, with the Royal Marines kicking down the fence to the back garden to allow it through and was driven to the hospital. Diego Quiroga watched the scene; *"I recall witnessing what appeared to be his death when he was being lifted onto something that resembled a stretcher. I was somehow confused and felt weird rushes of pain from my injured back. My injured arm hurt terribly. However, by and large, I appeared to be alright even though feeling very light headed after an injection of morphine given to me by a quick-thinking Royal Marine Commando... The marine who gave me the morphine snapped me out of my reverie. I could not speak or move, and my vision was already tunnelling. I nevertheless could interpret he was not one of us and, for one endless moment, was convinced that he had come to finish me off with his combat knife. After being given the morphine, I clearly remember my desperation at feeling unable to draw enough air into my lungs... Using my blood as makeshift ink, he daubed the letter 'M' on my forehead to indicate that morphine had already been injected. Another morphine injection by error could have fatal consequences. I was extremely cold...."* He remembered now hearing the blades of a helicopter as it came, bringing help, as Urbina picks up the tale; *"I think I was wounded at approximately 06.30 and the fight lasted until 09.30... that's approximate, since I didn't have a watch. They came to help us, and a companion had to scare away the geese who were pecking at me. They lifted me off of the floor and took me to the* hospital, where they operated on me, with surgeons Rosas and Gatica and the British nurses, and finally took me away by helicopter at midday..."

Meanwhile Diego Quiroga was also bundled off to the nearby King Edward VII Memorial Hospital where, as he remembers; *"My injuries were inspected by a team of doctors. I clearly remember a female doctor providing me with a confusing diagnosis. 'You're through, baby,' she said. I wondered for a long time whether this meant that I was alive or already dead."*

Quickly the Argentine killed and wounded were carried or driven to the hospital and a field hospital was set up outside of GH for others less seriously injured. Rex Hunt now surveyed the wreckage of Government House and passing by the front door, was shocked to see two body-bags being carried by Argentine troops, who slipped and stumbled across Mavis' rockery with their heavy loads. Making for the kitchen, he later described the scene as if a hurricane had struck it; the entire room was wrecked and the freezer had been blown apart, with splinters of grenades visible everywhere. He quickly switched off and unplugged everything in the kitchen as water was now cascading everywhere from the burst pipes and then went to find the stop-cock to cut the flow of water.

Meanwhile the men of the Royal Marines filed out of GH and were now made to suffer the indignation of being forced, at gunpoint, to lay down face first on the ground as the Argentines searched them, prodded them and even posed for photographs beside them as Jim Fairfield remembered; *"The Argies herded us towards the main road with lots of shouting and the odd jab in the back from a rifle for those who were a bit slow; needless to say, we all had bruises after that. We were then told to lay on the road with our hands on our heads and our heads towards the kerbstone and were then none-too-tenderly searched. During this process, Argie Amtrack vehicles moved up from the town towards Moody Brook, there could not have been many inches between their tracks and our toes but at the time it seemed a minor point!"*

Now that the fighting was over, Lieutenant Bill Trollope ordered his section, still under cover in a garden at the end of Davis Street, to prepare to give themselves up; *"First we stripped our weapons down and threw the bits all over the place,"* George Brown recalled. Firing pins, barrels, anything that could be removed was taken out and buried in the ground or bits of kit bent and smashed so that they would be of no use to the Argentines. Mark Gibbs remembered looking up to see the old man who had brought them some coffee now watering his plants through his glass conservatory, *"without a care in the world"* and decided to light a cigarette. Realising that he had lent his lighter to Mike Norman to burn documents with, he asked the man for a light; *"He gave me a box of matches,"* Gibbs remembered, *"but how I got it lit, I don't know... my hands were shaking so much...*" Finally, the order was given for the men to march out and they came up actually behind a platoon of Argentine soldiers who *"got the fright of their lives as we walked down the road with our hands in the air"* as George Brown remembered. Danny Betts now recalled feeling that he had drawn the short straw when; *"They marched us off to be with the rest of the lads at GH but first they made me and Burt Reynolds walk back through the positions we had occupied in case anywhere had been booby-trapped or trip wired. I knew I hadn't but couldn't be sure about anyone else. I just kept thinking, 'I hope nobody has tried to be a hero, because I'm going to be the poor bastard to walk right through it' – but nobody had. Thank fuck."*

As Section Two marched into view, there was an ironic cheer from the guys still laying face-down on the floor who had thought their mates to have been killed when they heard the explosions and firing on the airport road. Now they were told to lay down with the others as the Argentines prodded and searched them and the press men came in, including all three British journalists who had spent the entire morning cowering in Don Bonner's cottage; *"Smile please, gentlemen, they'll see this at home!"* said one of them, *"And he was met with an angry grumble and told to go away in no uncertain terms!"* George Brown remembered. Finally, as Lou Armour recalls, the situation improved when Busser himself saw what was happening; *"When we were actually laying down I felt a bit humiliated, but I also felt apprehensive about what was going to happen next. One of the Argentine officers came along and actually struck one of the guards and told us to stand up. We stood up and he shook my hand and a few other guys' hands and said that we shouldn't lay down, that we should be proud of what we'd done. I liked him."* Murray Paterson remembered a similar incident; *"As we were laying down along Ross Road, some conscript soldier started to search me,"* he recalled, *"he pulled my jacket and pointed to the Royal Marine Commando flash on my jersey: 'Commando!' he said with a sneer and spat in my face. On the earth embankment near where we were, some of the Argentine special forces guys were sat there eating something... I remember they looked as knackered as we were. Suddenly, one of them got up – it was obvious he was very angry – and he punched the soldier who had spat at me and shouted something in Argentinian then went and sat back down, watching. The soldier picked himself up off the floor, approached me and in good English, said, 'I have been ordered to apologise to you', which he then did..."*

Now the Royal Marines were corralled into the paddock beside GH where they were told to sit on the grass under guard and wait as more of the Royals and a few FIDF men were searched for and rounded up; *"We assembled on GH lawn and were quietly handed round some papers that we didn't want the Argies to get,"* remembered Dave Gerrard, *"we tore them into little pieces and buried them in the* grass." Men now started to light cigarettes, to talk amongst themselves, to laugh and even to sing. They went through every patriotic song they could think of, several times over; *'Rule Britannia'* came out often, *'There'll always be an England'* and then some bright spark began to sing *'Always look on the bright side of life'* and the Royal Marines laughed and whistled along as the Argentines stood there bemused and began to grow annoyed at their merry-making, which had the effect of making them sing and whistle even louder; *"By now people were coming down from their high and as always with Marines, bawdy banter took over,"* Jim Fairfield recounted, *"and much to the Argies' consternation we were all soon laughing our heads off and giving them a hard verbal time of it. For some I'm sure it was a cover for nervous tension and some no doubt had started to feel fearful of what would happen next, I certainly was. Judging by the Argies' faces, a lot of them understood what we were saying but didn't really appreciate it too much and there was quite a bit of Argie posturing and shouting, which only made us goad them more, it may have been foolhardy but it helped to ease the tension and confusion that was written in everyone's face... The ex-wife of one of the Marines, Geordie Gill, later turned up at the fence line and was told by Geordie to bugger off home and let everyone know we were all okay, she didn't want to leave but soon got the message that she had been given an important job to do, we all thought it was important that the locals' morale should be boosted by knowing we had all survived, not to mention the nerves of our wives and girlfriends. The area around Government House was now crawling with Argies, mostly officers who all came to gloat and have their pictures taken, every time one tried to get us in the background a shout would go up from us followed by two fingers, just the way the great man Churchill did it, they didn't like that much but what the hell!"*

As the Royal Marines talked amongst themselves, they began to piece together the action as Gary Williams remembered; *"It was a warm sunny day with hardly any wind. Whilst we were on the lawn was when we learnt that Yorkie's section had taken to the hills to carry on the fight, meanwhile, medical helicopters were constantly flying over Stanley picking up wounded or dead Argentinians and stories started to emerge of deeds that the lads had got up to; Geordie Gill and Terry Pares taking out three guys from a machine gun nest, the lads up on the airport road getting an Amtrack with a Charlie Gustav, it seems they got three goes before they hit it, Lou Armour doing a fire and manoeuvre over the football pitch by GH with no casualties, unbelievably we had no dead and no injuries by some miracle."*[2]

The men of the FIDF were now slowly rounded up. Most were found and made captive in the Drill Hall where they had piled arms at one end and were sat at the other, ordered to passively await their arrest. Taff Davies remembered feeling very sore about the fact that the men of the Defence Force had not been allowed to fight for their homes. Most of them, supplementing the household food by hunting, were excellent shots, but Rex Hunt had decided not to throw them into the path of well-armed, highly-trained Argentine Marines and they had to accept ultimately that it was the right decision; *"We had 2,000 screaming Argies breathing down our necks,"* remembered Taff, *"We got off very lightly that night, but the decision didn't make sense to us at the time and we all felt we could – and should - have been allowed to do more."* Some others from Pat Peck and Gerald Cheek's section were found on the racecourse not far from GH. Seeing the Argentine special forces coming from the direction of Moody Brook, they could have opened up with their GPMG's and .303 rifles but chose to follow orders and lay down their arms, waving to attract the Argentine Commandos' attention; *"I remember when we went across the field to meet up with the Argentine section after being shouted at by them to do so,"* recounted Gerald Cheek, *"and as we got close to them they all went down to the ground cocking their weapons as they did so, although we weren`t carrying our weapons, having left them in the racecourse buildings. Their commanding officer then came forward and asked if we were Royal Marines. I told him no, we were FIDF. He then instructed one of their soldiers to return with me to collect our weapons."* Now disarmed, the FIDF men were marched down to Ross Road and lined up against the wall of Sullivan House with weapons pointed at them. Most thought they were about to be shot but they were instead offered cigarettes and were soon escorted to the Drill Hall with their comrades and finally sent home. The section which had guarded the football field had joined up with the section guarding the power station and were there likewise disarmed and sent home whilst a few others, found in and around Stanley, were corralled with the Marines in the paddocks.[*3]

At the airport, Lieutenant Commander Alfredo Cufre waited for news and was soon met by Cardillo, Flores and Ledesma, the three men who until recently had been prisoners of war in Government House; *"They told me they had been unable to fulfil their mission of taking the Governor's House,"* he recalled later, *"when one of them came over and pulled his beret off, some of his hair dropped out. I ran a hand over his hair and pulled some more to show him. I realised then what extreme stress can do."* The three men told him of the failure of their mission and of the casualties. From a window, they had covered Giachino, Quiroga and Urbina with their weapons in case the British had tried to finish them off, but they had been left alone and so they had not given away their position. Cufre believed that they had stayed in hiding the whole time until the fall of Government House.[*4] Now from the airport which they had been guarding, the men of the platoon of the 25th Infantry Regiment swept across now towards Cape Pembroke lighthouse where they found Basil Biggs still at his post. The Argentines hung a flag off the top rail of the lighthouse and ordered that it was not to be touched; *"It's okay, it's only temporary,"* Biggs replied, *"the British will soon sort this lot out."* - *"No, no,"* replied the Argentine officer Roberto Reyes, *"this is for ever."*[*5]

Finally, the Argentine forces entered FIBS where Patrick Watts was still announcing their entry. The listeners could hear orders shouted loudly and Watts saying that he refused to do or say anything with a gun in his back. Then they were treated to his humorous observation that the three men who had entered had now left the room and were audibly arguing and shouting at each other. Listening at home to the Argentines shouting, Neville Bennett humorously observed that; *"I suppose the Argies were, in their usual fashion 'quietly' organising things and arguing who was going to be in charge."* Patrick Watts found a man who spoke English and asked him; *"Who are you?"* - *"We are the armed forces of the Glorious Argentine Republic"* came the answer. *"Why have you invaded our home?"* - *"All people must stay inside."* - *"The people have things they must attend to, hens to feed and animals and pets."* - *"Much more safe they stay inside."* He was now handed a tape to play which, after a brief announcement, went on to play a scratchy copy of the Argentine National Anthem at the wrong speed, followed by a number of communiques and edicts greeting the people of the 'Malvinas' as fellow Argentines and telling them to stay indoors and offer no offence to the Argentine forces, to which it illustrated a number of infringements to that order, finally exhorting the people to continue with their normal lives, with the support of the Argentine government who had now liberated them from British Colonial Imperialism; *"Blimey,"* wrote Neville Bennett, *"We were quite happy as we had been."*

Out on the *Forrest* the men of Section Six waited anxiously to be picked up and wondered what mood the Argentines might be in. Eventually the Commandos Anfibios from Sanchez Sabarots' detachment came down to take them in and Ray Bloye remembered seeing them and saying; *"I didn't realise that Argies were black?"* - He didn't realise until they got closer that it was black camo-cream which was smeared across their faces, *"They looked like the Black & White Minstrels and we even started laughing about them,"* indeed as the Argentines ordered them out, they found the men stifling giggles which baffled them; *"However I was not stupid enough to laugh too long or let them realise what we were laughing at."* he remembered. The Argentines saw the piled weapons but gave them a thorough search; *"There was a little manhandling but nothing brutal,"* Nick Williams said, *"I was happy with that."* Now the men of Section Six were told to march off under guard along Ross Road towards Government House; *"The guys fell in double file,"* said Nick Williams, *"myself and Dave were at the back as we set off down the jetty. It was the walk of defeated men, shuffling along with drooping shoulders. I got really annoyed at this and shouted, 'Come on you bastards, you're Royal Marines! March like Royal Marines! Show these spics who we are!' and started calling time. The shoulders went back, heads up and we marched towards GH - like Royal Marines."*

Outside GH the section was stopped in front of the flagpole and there forced to watch the Union Jack being run down and the Argentine flag being hoisted in front of GH. There were Argentine cameramen waiting beyond the flagpole, eager to get a shot of the Marines being forced at gunpoint to salute the Argentine flag but despite having the cannon of a nearby Amtrack pointed at them, the Marines refused and even turned their backs on it. The Argentine flag was enormous and, as the wind caught it, the halyard broke and sent it tumbling to the ground instead. The Royal Marines gave a great laugh and a great cheer which got them all a solid rifle-butt in the back but, as they knew, it was worth it and the omen was not lost on the Argentines.[*6]

Quickly a man was sent scurrying up the pole to fix it, incurring more laughter until the flag was fixed and finally raised with much difficulty. As he made his way towards Government House, Daniel Tosolini of the BIM2 now remembered hearing a growing cheer amongst the men as the flag was raised, as he recalled; *"My officers and sub-officers were shouting 'Viva la Patria! The Malvinas are ours!!!' I felt very proud to have been a part of history. In the distance, I could see our flag hoisted and the pride zoomed in me... I was thinking about my parents and what they would think if they knew I was here..."* With the flag now flying, the cameramen on the lawn tried to get the Marines of Section Six in the shot a second time, but by now they were too much of a nuisance and were being marched around to the paddock. They still believed that they must surely be the last ones left alive, but as Nick Williams recalled; *"When we came into view of that field, a big cheer went up from a load of Marines. There was total disbelief on my part. I thought loads would have been killed but they hadn't and here they were cheering us in."* It was incredible – every single man was safe - and now the Marines were singing loudly again; *"Someone started to whistle 'Always look on the bright side of life',"* Ray Bloye remembered, *"this was taken up by everyone but I don't think the Argies 'got it'. The reason the cheer went up was that, like us, the other sections didn't know how many casualties we had. It turned out we were the last section to be brought in and so it was now apparent that we had got away with no casualties at all. It had already got around that one section had managed to escape into the hills but they were from the new detachment."[*7]*

Geordie Gill remembered a sudden feeling of pride as he looked around the men who now assembled in the paddocks as he recalled; *"It's totally different going into a battle you know you'll most likely win, than it is going into a battle you know you won't win! I've always been proud to be a Royal Marine, but I've never been prouder than I was on that day. It was an honour to serve with those lads, even though I didn't know half their names then, it was a privilege to be part of it."*

The men of the Royal Marines had indeed come through as if by a miracle, but not so the Argentines as KEMH's senior medical officer Dr Daniel Haines recalled, as he was called upon by shouts and gestures to attend to two severely wounded Argentines who had been found at the back of the hospital along St. Mary's Walk. Donning his white coat and with red adhesive tape affixed front and back in a red cross to show his purpose, Haines ventured out where he found the men; *"horribly wounded"* as he recalled from his own memoirs, behind the wreckage of a corrugated iron fence. Quickly, Haines signalled for the men's comrades to lift them onto stretchers where they were carried inside the hospital. Both had multiple gunshot wounds; one through the chest and lungs, he recalled, the other through the abdomen and liver. Carrying them into the operating theatre he described the scene as like 'a mad blood-bath' as the two men were laid on the operating tables, soon joined by a third Argentine whose leg had been shattered by a high velocity round, followed by another whose femoral artery had been severed by a shot to the leg and who was bleeding out fast. Haines' operating theatre was now full to capacity and, as he, a nurse and two Argentine army doctors performed emergency surgery on the men, he bade them take away the man whose bleeding would cost him his life, so that he could be operated on by his own people. The bleeding man being flown out post-haste, Haines returned to his business only to have the room invaded by Argentine soldiers, one with a heavy machine gun, who roared at Haines and their own doctors to work more quickly as there were other seriously wounded men who urgently needed treatment, even going so far as to try to turn up the oxygen concentration and anaesthetic machines of the current patients to maximum in a fruitless effort to speed things up.

With order finally restored, Haines, his staff and the Argentine medics returned to their gory business. The man with the chest and lung wounds was most seriously injured and, recounted Haines, he died soon after being anaesthetised; *"with good grace"* Haines remembered, although the man's death prompted another invasion of the operating theatre from enraged Argentines, festooned with weapons and grenades and bawling that Haines must have intentionally killed the man. With the Argentine medics assuring them that this was not the case, the angry men were again ushered out and the medical staff set to treating the man with abdominal and liver wounds. Haines identified multiple wounds to the liver as well as to both small and large intestine, but the Argentine medic would not let him help or suggest appropriate treatment as he sewed the man up with speed, effectively condemning him to death. A first-year surgical trainee could have done the obvious, Haines thought, and removed the dead tissue and bowel contents which now sat inside the sealed cavity, therefore saving the man's life. It was, he remembered, not to be the case. Finally, the man with the shattered leg was seen to and Haines, recalling the Argentine medic as more of a taxidermist than a surgeon, watched incredulously as the man worked at a fevered pace to replace every piece of shattered bone and tissue – living and dead – back inside the wound like a jigsaw puzzle and sewed him up before allowing him to be taken away. Haines was left feeling that in the very best case the man would lose his leg although more than likely, his life.

King Edward Memorial Hospital was now packed to overflowing and calls went out for all off-duty staff to come in urgently as nurse Diane Stewart – then just 19 years old - remembered; *"At around 10am I cautiously walked from Fitzroy Road to the hospital escorted by my boyfriend at the time,"* she recalled, *"this was terrifying as there were shots being fired at anything that moved! So, walking briskly whilst waving my white flag, we got to the hospital without incident. Arriving at the hospital was something else, as everyone was in shock. The wards had only a couple of locals in the beds, whilst the majority of the beds were filled with injured – and very drunk - Argentine servicemen. We were not allowed near them as they had their own medical team, but it was fair to say that they had bottles of Gordon's Gin and Johnnie Walker Whisky bottles empty by their beds. When I eventually got my act together, I went to do my normal nursing duties, however the hospital was swarming with Argie personnel, which made me very nervous. I was instructed to clean up the sluice rooms and get rid of all of their paraphernalia, this being flak jackets and clothing. There was a morgue full of their deceased, there were three at the time and the other nurses said there were still more but they had already been taken away, including two who were pronounced dead during surgery and a lot more seriously wounded."* She checked over the three dead men then there in the morgue. They were, as she later recalled; *"Very dead."*

Meanwhile, in town, Dr Alison Bleaney, hearing the call, decided that she too would return to the hospital and help where she could, as she also recalled; *"It was a hectic running street battle that day. I assumed with all the street battles in Stanley and the fight around GH – we could hear it – that people had to have been killed or wounded. I came in the back entrance and passed one of their big, tracked amphibious vehicles. The ramp at the back was open and there were bodies just stacked up on top of each other in there. I could see at least six, but the way they were just crammed in all together, it was obvious that it was full and that there were a lot more behind them. They were very obviously dead. The bodies in that vehicle made a very deep impression on me… I assumed then, I still do now, that they were picked up from the streets where they fell fighting. I was in a hurry to get* to work, because if there were that many dead, there would be many more wounded, and the Argentine soldiers were all around me, looking very nervous and unsettled. As soon as I got in, the hospital was already chaos; wounded Argies laying everywhere, and a lot of walking wounded too. The place was packed, there must have been thirty, forty, fifty wounded easily – and that was just in the bit I was in, but they were everywhere – and that's not counting the dead: I just left them to others and concentrated on the wounded men. I got straight to work and must have operated on easily ten or more people. I remember an annoying priest with an eye wound who kept walking around and shouting, and one poor guy with a nasty gunshot wound to the groin, but he was taken away by the Argie soldiers: they took a lot of them away from the hospital even before they were properly treated. There were a handful of seriously wounded – what I'd call critical – who I wanted to get to, but the Argies carried them off too. They seemed to be in a hurry to clear the place. You'd be operating on someone, turn around to get something and they would be gone. They were racing to drag them out of there. There were so many, it was chaotic and Argie officers were revved up and shouting, trying to get their men treated before others... we did everything we could, but nobody had had any war experience. Nobody had ever treated a gunshot wound... and there were so many. We kept going all through that day into the next, just trying to save lives. How no one on our side, RM or FIDF was killed or injured is a complete mystery to me. When I heard later that Argentina claimed an almost bloodless takeover with one man killed and a couple wounded, I was gobsmacked.... It was incomprehensible."*8

In the Bennett household, the phone rang at 11.00 - "Would Matron Bennett please get over to the hospital as soon as she could? There's a bit of an emergency." Neville Bennett called FIBS who were still broadcasting, and asked if Patrick Watts could put a call out to tell the invaders what route she would take. They replied that she must carry a white flag. Her daughter Rachel remembered watching her mother in uniform with a white pillowcase tied to a broom handle, walking across the playing field and out of sight; "Two armed men fell in a few yards behind her with rifles at the ready, an escort, I presumed," recorded Neville, "I thought they were pretty quick off the mark, rounding up an escort that fast. When speaking of this some years later, Valerie said she hadn't been aware of these men and if she had seen them, she might have had a 'nasty' there and then. I also found out that they weren't an escort but a couple of soldiers having a look round and probably 'souveniring'. It did look a bit worrying though, the acting matron of the Hospital with a white flag over her shoulder, followed by two armed men."

At the hospital, two Argentine soldiers presented her with the Royal Marine, who asked her to treat him. He had cut his leg whilst jumping over a metal fence. He was 'fairly messy' and Valerie wanted him to be bathed so that she could clean him up. The Argentines in the hospital refused and just wanted him treated and sent out again. Valerie Bennett stitched the wound and gave him a tetanus injection. She then gave a tetanus injection into the backsides of all of the Argentine wounded too, just for good measure. Many of these now-paralytic wounded men were being shipped out including – by actual count - eleven more with gunshot wounds and one man who, whilst still critical, was quickly spirited away despite the protests of the staff that he would not live if he were moved. Valerie was, she remembered, very impressed by the Argentine military's body bags. They were strong and even had zips down the front. She found it interesting that they came prepared to use them and so she did. Soon the last three dead men in the mortuary were shipped out too by helicopter. By now, Argentine Marines and Commandos were gathering around the hospital, waiting for news on their killed and wounded and in particular Giachino, who was a man considered a true hero by all. When news of his death was announced, many were inconsolable as Carlos Cequeira recalled; *"Colonel Seineldin went in and out to give condolences to all. It was very hard, because Giachino was a leader appreciated by all people, NCO's and officers... We did not have to kill or hurt the English...and we did so at the expense of our own dead. Captain Giachino was our first casualty."*

Diego Quiroga was flown out the hospital ship *Almirante Irizar* and recalled that; *"The sailors were having difficulties in getting my stretcher through the narrow passages on board. There was blood pouring from it and, as this was tilted at every door entrance, a mess was made on the deck. All the faces I saw were talking to me – but I could not hear them. Once again, one question came to my mind: Was I still alive? A classmate recognised my face under the camouflage and grasped my wounded arm passionately. It hurt like hell, but I could not tell him to let go. I could not speak at all. Members of my APBT unit were standing on the tarmac as I was being lifted inside the aircraft. My Commanding Officer was there with them. As the stretcher went by, I saw them looking at me, their faces grey with exhaustion and eyes lowered. Nobody spoke. Nobody reached to touch me. I was certain that death had incurred. It did not feel too bad. The interior of the aircraft had been stripped bare of all seats and, throughout the flight to Comodoro Rivadavia, a soldier kept slapping me on the face to prevent me from losing consciousness. I would not have survived without him. I was angry with myself for being unable to get back to the front in the Islands. The war was certain to end soon and I felt the opportunity of experiencing it had been missed by me being shot on its very first day."* - For Diego Garcia Quiroga, the war was over – but he had survived.

Now the Royal Marines were being rounded up and men were despatched along with Gary Noott to bring in the men of Section Three who had 'gone covert' in the region south of Sapper Hill as Marc Branch again recalled; *"We made it down to the coast and were in formation in single file. Someone had obviously made contact with Government House which at this point had laid down arms. We were being ordered to surrender arms also. We were to give our position and an HG Truck along with an RM Officer and an Argentine Officer were going to come along and pick us up from the road that was about 1/4 to 1/2 mile north of us. We discussed the possibility that whoever made the radio call was in fact either genuine or being forced to make the call and it was a trap. We determined to prepare either way. As I'd already said, Steve Black was a sniper and so the plan was for him to take up a hidden position and when they approached us we'd keep in formation until it was determined it was a genuine proposition, bearing in mind we had no idea if any of our fellow Marine brothers were even alive! If something, anything, were out of whack, Steve would start picking off the enemy and we would go to ground and fight our way out of it. I'm not sure how long it took but sure enough an HG Truck came trundling along and pulled up. Major Noott and an Argentine Officer jumped out. Steve Black was in position and unseen. We fanned out and moved toward the vehicle. Just as we were about to move toward the vehicle Murdo Macleod (who was a man of few words but they were always gems) said in his broad Scottish accent, 'There's got to be an easier fucking way to make a living Branchy!' - This cracked me up and actually eased my tension slightly. Eggman and I went to the right flank and went to ground to train the GPMG on them. THAT apparently freaked out the Argentine Officer as he ran behind the vehicle yelling at Noott to tell us not to shoot! This was conveyed to us but we stayed in position until it looked as genuine as it could get under the circumstances. As the rest of the section got closer Eggman and I moved towards the vehicle. We were just a few metres away when suddenly a group of the Argentine Special Forces jumped out the vehicle training their SMG's on us. Things seemed like they were about to kick off! There was some yelling about staying calm and everything was okay. The Argies laid capes on the floor for us to disarm. The looks on their faces were priceless as we started to empty our pockets; grenades, 66's, ammo etc. We all stood with our hands behind our heads and they frisked each one of us. The guy who searched me seemed rather nervous and didn't do a good job. As he went onto the next man I pulled out my survival knife I had in my top left pocket which was also attached to a lanyard and said to him, 'Here, aren't you missing something?' I threw it on the cape to make a point. At some point during the disarming the Argie Officer enquired, 'Where's the 6th man?' This caught us by surprise and later initiated the discussion as to where they got their intel from! I'm not sure if someone yelled or waved to Steve Black but we couldn't see him either. He could have taken out every one of them and they knew it. They looked at each other almost in disgust at their negligence as he approached and gave up arms. We were transported to GH and the rest is well photographed and documented. I recall being shocked at how nice the Argies were being. Trying to shake our hands and congratulating us for putting up such a good fight. It was if they'd just played us in the World Cup. I think we were the last section to arrive at GH other than Yorkie's section who remained on the Islands. Everyone was sitting on the grass exchanging their accounts of what happened. It quickly became apparent the Argies had sustained a large amount of casualties."*

The Argentines soon made a list of names and realised that still six – indeed they thought seven - Marines were missing. On-air they kept broadcasting the names of all six and the seventh name *'Swaffam'* which in fact was a call sign of the new NP8901 detachment, which caused some amusement and confusion in equal measures. Hugo Santillan was already pushing that way with his Amtracks; exiting Callaghan Road and circling around the power station to the south, another vehicle had become stuck in the peat and required the men inside to disembark and push the 29-ton vehicle free, much to the amusement of Patrick Watts who, announcing it on the radio, pronounced that there was 'always something happening in the Falklands.' The Amtrack being finally freed, Hugo Santillan's next order was to round the harbour onto the Camber Peninsula and Wireless Ridge and to capture the small naval facility at Fairy Cove; *"I assumed the task of becoming the moving force to link up with the Commandos Anfibios that would be found at Moody Brook neutralising the Royal Marines,"* he recounted, *"I made the journey with my three LVTPs. I found the Commandos Anfibios some 200 metres to the west of the residence; they kept walking to the east and I rode to Moody Brook. As my task to link with the Commandos Anfibios was over, I went on to my next task: to secure the naval facility across the harbour on the Camber Peninsula. After bypassing Moody Brook (I knew it was abandoned), I turned east to secure the naval facility. As we reached Fairy Cove, one of my LVTP's lost a track; at the same time, I was ordered to stop: there was a Royal Marine patrol who were not aware that the Governor had already surrendered, hence, Major Noott and Argentine Marines Lieutenant Commander Roscoe flew aboard a Lynx helicopter searching for the British patrol in order to have them under control. I was not to move forward until the missing patrol had been found. As the Royal Marines were not found, I was ordered to continue to the East. Because the situation of that patrol was unclear, I ordered Lieutenant Schweizer to move his Rifle Platoon plus two machine guns and two rocket-launchers on foot to secure the naval facility; I would be prepared to provide on-call fire support (.50 machine guns, 75mm recoilless rifles and 81mm mortars). When Lieutenant Schweizer was some 200 metres short (West) of the facility, I loaded my heavy weapons on my two remaining Amtracks and approached Schweizer's position in order to establish a new fire base. The road took me to a point just to the north and above of the facility; the LVTPs, mortars and recoilless rifles assumed fire support positions. When ready, I ordered Lieutenant Schweizer to move and secure the facility from the East. Schweizer's Platoon reached his objective without opposition and, as there was no enemy in sight, I moved on foot down the slope to join Schweizer. When I was some 100 metres short (North) of the first buildings, two or three rifle shots were heard. As the fire teams took cover, my party dashed down the slope – it was crazy, these two or three shots and then the whole platoon just charged down the slope yelling and shooting and going mad! I went with them and my foot got stuck in a crevice on the rocky floor; I fell down hitting the ground with violence; my runner shouted, 'Are you hit, Sir?'. I was in pain as my ankle started to swell almost instantly. Tello (my runner) and someone else simply lifted me and ran for cover to the buildings. Lieutenant Schweizer joined me on the spot and informed that the objective was secure. A new radio message ordered me to halt and wait. Shortly after, I was cleared to carry on my last task: to secure Navy Point in order to protect Argentine Navy transports that were to dock in Stanley Harbour. I order Lieutenant Schweizer to consolidate the naval facility with his rifle platoon, LVTP, two machines guns and two anti-tank teams. Then I ordered that mortar and recoilless rifles crews would be armed only with rifles and move on foot forward (East) to secure Navy Point, followed by my LVTP to provide radio and fire support. As I was unable to walk, my men lifted me to my Amtrack (the most expensive and comfortable crutch in the world!). The riflemen reached the Point unopposed; they found on the ground ammo, military gear and weapons (later we learned that these items were discarded by the RM patrol when evacuated the area to the North in a boat). My last task was over; I received orders to wait for Admiral Busser at the naval facility. He came on a jeep and pulled a joke on me: 'Mr. Santillán, you are so rookie that the English don´t need to shoot; you become a casualty just by yourself!'"*[9]

Curiously, whether Giachino, Horatio Tello or whomever was the true 'first casualty' of April 2nd 1982, Hugo Santillan was certainly the last. He was taken back to King Edward Memorial Hospital where his ankle, not broken but with an acute sprain, was set in plaster and he was given a cane to walk about on. To this day neither he, Lieutenant Schweizer, Jorge Tello his runner or Sergeant di Filippo his 75mm recoilless rifle squad leader, all of whom had good positions, knows who fired those shots; *"Even more: now no-one sustains to have seen that mysterious Royal Marine dashing out of a building and firing his rifle at Schweizer´s riflemen and – of course - there was no RM taken prisoner on the site! The only thing that we agree is that two (or three) shots were heard when my guys were in immediate proximity of the first buildings."* he recalls.

At the time, his men had said that they saw a man fire the shots then coolly put down his rifle. Now nobody seems to recall too much about the mysterious man who shot at them or how he got away. Across the harbour, Neville Bennett was watching the spectacle and recorded that; *"Some of the armoured personnel carriers were seen to be moving down the other side of the harbour. One appeared to be in some sort of difficulty – I think it had shed a track. One of the helicopters goes over to look at it, all fixed and they move off again towards the Naval Fuel Depot with its tanks of diesel and other stores. They went up the hill towards the caretakers' house and the sound of machine gun fire came over the water. What were they doing? Were there some 'booties' hanging around there or were Hector and Millie inside? No one came out and no bodies were carried out. Just pure bloody-mindedness. Vandalism!"*

Hugo Santillan was taken to Stanley's Town Hall to recuperate, where he met Horacio Tello and several others; *"Any news?"* he asked, *"Sir, I broke my rifle."* said Tello. With his hand in bandages he held up the two ends of his broken rifle which a GPMG bullet had cut in two: he had been carrying both halves together, unaware that it was shot through until this moment.

Out on the grass outside of Government House, the Royal Marines were growing hungry. The Argentines had taken their rations from them and swapped with their own; *"I received a tin of something,"* said Ray Bloye, *"it turned out to be tripe and onions. I'd never had tripe before but I was so hungry I ate it all. It hasn't made me crave for tripe since then though."* Nick Williams was also annoyed not just at the food but at the Argentines having taken his cigarettes and swapped with their own; *"the food was inedible, and the cigarettes were pretty dreadful as well"* he remembered, whilst Dave Gerrard remembered being given 'Mondongo' – tripe in tomato sauce - *"and basically dog biscuits,"* he said, *"I was hungry but only managed half the can."* The Royals were still talking amongst themselves and working out who was missing. They realised that Berry was still up on Sapper Hill and that Section Four had managed to get away. Some of the Argentines told them that they were going to take South Georgia the next day, where 22 men of the NP8901 detachment and Endurance platoon had been sent: the Argentines seemed to know about Lieutenant Mills' force but not that it had been reinforced; *"and we were not going to tell them."* recalled Nick Williams. The men were discussing the South Georgia detachment quietly amongst themselves and realised that constant head-counting was baffling the Argentines; *"They had been told there were only 44 men in the detachment and it was confusing them."* remembered Ray Bloye, *"Needless to say, nothing was said and the guys down south would take the Argies there by surprise come the following day."*

Eventually the Argentine head of intelligence, Major Dowling, rose to the challenge and now called up the Royal Marines, making them approach one at a time to give their name, rank and serial number so that he could count them and check them all off, as Murray Paterson recalled; *"Some bright spark had the idea of re-joining the queue and going around again and soon we were all doing it. As each guy gave his name, rank and number, he went and mixed in amongst the others and came out again with a different set of information. When he realised he had a lot more names that he had people, the Argentine officer went crazy! He truly was a horrible man although his English was excellent and he started screaming, 'There must be more of you! There's got to be more of you! How many do you say...? Sixty? Seventy? No chance! It's got to be more, to fight like this! Who are they? Where are they!?'"* Happy to have confused him still further, the Royal Marines now gave no further information and sat back down in the paddocks, chuckling to themselves as Major Dowling fumed and ranted.

Patrols were sent out looking for the escaped Marines and several attempts were made to hail them by radio. Admiral Busser had tried to corner Rex Hunt on who the men were who had gotten away but Hunt, guessing his man well, made a haughty shrug of; *"I only know the officers"* which he seemed to accept. Busser then took Gary Noott to one side and made him scribble out on a map where the other sections were or had gone to, and though he placed Berry out on Sapper Hill, knowing he had already gotten out, Noott drew in big arrows on the map where Section Four were concerned, telling Busser that they had escaped by way of Mount Longdon to the west. Trucks with armed special forces at once assembled to head after them, with Royal Marines who knew the area made to drive them. Noott's deception might at least have given the fugitives a head-start. He quickly turned Busser's attention to the amount of forces he now had and Busser, feeling no reason to mask them, told Noott plainly that he had thought about fifty Royal Marines had been in the Falklands and that it was suggested that the figure to take with him would be three times that number; *"I told them I wanted five thousand!"* he told Noott with a laugh.

Out in the rocky, grassy wilderness to the south-west of Stanley, PJ Berry had still been running towards Fitzroy when suddenly; *"I heard the noise of a truck and could see it was a four-toner, one of ours. I thought that the blokes had got out and were heading for Fitzroy, so I ran down the hill, which was quite grassy, and hid in some rocks nearby. As the truck was approaching, I recognised that it was Murray Paterson driving. I ran out and shouted for him to stop. Big mistake. Murray stopped and out jumped four Argies, weapons pointing at me, and told me to surrender. They searched me and stuck me in the back of the four-tonner with their guns trained on me the whole way back. I was even more scared than I had been at the start. Murray drove back to Government House and they took me out and put me with the rest of the lads, who by then had all been captured or laid down their weapons with orders from above. I couldn't believe that I would ever see Jock Wilcox again – I thought that his had been a suicide mission - but there he was, which was a massive relief."*

It was now a lovely sunny day and, despite having been invaded, attacked and corralled, the men of the Royal Marines were on a high. They had survived. They had proved themselves. It was the same for the Argentines who were mainly gripped with a euphoria. Many were seen joy-riding around the streets of Stanley in the Moody Brook Land Rovers with the doors off, yelling and laughing in the sunshine. Figgy Duff thought that the Argentine special forces who had carried out the invasion were incredibly professional; *"but by mid-late morning the people who were looking after us changed to being young kids – conscripts - they were more nervous than we were and they didn't like our singing particularly and some of them tried to take stuff off of us..."* Mark Gibbs remembered the same; *"They were terrified of us as we sat there – unarmed – in the paddocks, I was busting for a piss and in the end, I got up and went to the hedge-row to pee and they were all pointing guns, shouting and getting nervous!"*

Although the Royal Marines were now held captive, yet they still managed to play tricks on their guards to amuse themselves. It was the same old game they had always played against each other and their officers, but now amongst young, nervous conscripts, the devilment of Marine humour was rife; *"During the afternoon, Ginge Gerrard pulled something out of his combat jacket pocket,"* Ray Bloye recalled, as the Argentines were now asking if anyone had any weapons on them or anything else to hand in, *"It turned out to be a phos-grenade safety lever. He said in a conspiratorial voice, 'Watch this!' - and with that he approached one of our guards and presented the lever to him. It was hilarious as he immediately went into panic mode and was squawking at Ginge in Spanish and this spread to a lot of his compatriots. Only when an English-speaking Argie arrived did he explain that he had had just the lever in his jacket. They searched Ginge again, thinking he still had the grenade – we couldn't believe this as without the lever it would have gone off. The handle was left over from where he had thrown a white-phos grenade earlier. Entertainment over, we settled down to await whatever was going to happen."*[10]

Although to the Argentines, the Royal Marines seemed to be taking the whole thing as a massive joke, each man in the paddock was secretly fearing the worst and laughing to get himself through it. The junta had, as everyone knew, an atrocious record for human rights and each man feared being executed or made to 'disappear' which, at least to them, seemed a high probability, however, as Gary Noott soon realised; *"Our treatment was mild – so mild that we quickly realised that they had no intention of ill-treating us. Consequently, we – if anything, became indignant, turning as time went on, to outright stroppiness! We were subjected to inefficient searches ranging from nil to poor and our initial concern for our future was replaced by an attitude of professional contempt for our captors. The result of this was to make it easier for us to slowly take charge of the situation – and this was particularly so for myself and the other officers. By reverting to the tried and trusted 'British Raj' method of talking slowly, authoritatively, in English, implying thereby that any fool should be able to understand, as well as throwing Admiral Busser's name in occasionally, one was able to coerce, certainly, the private soldiers into acquiescence. With the Argentine officers, an appeal to old traditions of officer class honour and exploiting inter-service rivalries, had a similarly beneficial effect."*

The traditions of impish humour, of teamwork and of that 'them and us' divide were now beginning to pay dividends as the Royal Marines began to attempt to bemuse their captors; *"It was about this time that I started to wonder how I might get myself out of yet another mess I had managed to get myself into,"* Jim Fairfield recounted, *"I knew my only hope of escaping home would come whenever the Argies decided to move us and I began to speculate as to when and where this would happen and how I might be able to take advantage of it. I obviously was not thinking straight, there were by now hundreds of the buggers all over the place and by the sound of things every other one had their own Amtrack! It didn't stop me plotting though and several stupid 'James Bond' type scenarios were played out in my obviously malfunctioning mind. This wasn't helped by several of the lads making equally daft suggestions and offering to 'make a scene' as a diversion, I could then, being invisible of course, crawl to the hedgerow and hide out till the heat was off! Luckily for us salvation came marching down the road in the form of a contingent of FIDF lads led by their O.C Pat Peck and guarded by several Argies. They were halted on the road by GH and Pat and an Argie officer started heading our way, it didn't take long for my muddled brain to figure out that they just might be coming to collect the FIDF lad that had been put with us earlier, with his brown beret on he stood out in a forest of green ones, the chance was not lost on some of the lads either and there were several whispers of 'here's your main chance coming Jim' - and right enough they walked over to us and started motioning for the FIDF lad to follow them. Several things then happened all at once, there were shouts from the lads of 'don't forget Jim!' and the like, I remember the TQ, Bill Aspinall talking directly to Pat saying, 'Jim's one of yours too, don't forget him' and Pat replied quick as a flash something like, 'Come on Jim, don't sit there let's get you home!' - I stood up as did some of the lads, causing quite a commotion amongst our guards but no one really gave a shit. I had a couple of very odd thoughts in my head at that moment, I really did want to get home to my family and make sure they were okay but at the same time I was looking at people I* had just fought a battle with and we had all survived and I felt we should stay together somehow and was totally undecided as to what I should do. The guards were getting very jumpy by now and most of the lads had sat back down, I truly believe I was about to do the same when someone said, 'Get yourself home for fucks sake!' – So, amid cheers and shouts of 'Lucky bastard', 'Good luck', 'Thanks mate' and other little ditty's I walked slowly over to the waiting FIDF lads, never turning my back on my mates until I tripped over the cattle grid, that of course was the signal for some very rapid and targeted piss taking, some exit!"

Finally, it seemed that the Argentines had got themselves in order and now it was decided that the men of the Royal Marines should be sent to Moody Brook to collect their belongings. The men of the new detachment all went as too did some of the older detachment, just to see what had happened to the place; *"All my stuff was at Nidge and Ron Bucket's"* remembered Figgy Duff, *"I just went there to be nosey. We got into the back of a four-tonner and the truck turned right, then right again, heading towards the rifle range. We thought we were all going to get shot but fortunately it was a map reading error and the driver soon took us off to Moody Brook."* Mark Gibbs remembers the journey; *"As the Argentines were taking us back to the Brook, I sort of felt like the kid who's been kicked out the playground by the school bully,"* he recalled, *"and my thought was that now I was going to go home, get my big brother and sort the bully out. I said to the driver, 'There were sixty of us today, when we come back we're bringing all of us... there'll be six thousand of us then...' he was terrified... absolutely terrified. He started praying and all sorts. That was a good feeling, knowing I had started the mind games early..."*

When the Royal Marines reached Moody Brook, they were allowed in groups of ten at a time to collect their belongings. The scene which presented itself to them is worth recording from several points of view; *"There wasn't a room that was complete,"* Figgy Duff recounted, *"there was water everywhere from burst pipes, electrical cables hanging out, every room was devastated, grenaded, bullet holes through everything and shrapnel everywhere. Thank God we weren't there when it was hit or we all would have died."* Mike Norman described the barracks as being 'riddled with machine gun fire' declared the scene like a 'classic house-clearing operation' – thorough and brutal - and found that his civilian clothes had been shot through with bullets and were in tatters. Lou Armour found his passport with a giant bullet or shrapnel hole through it and wondered if it might be enough to get him home and Nick Williams found later that they had rifled through his belongings and someone had taken his Northern Ireland Service Medal amongst other things. *"It was shot to ribbons,"* Mark Gibbs remembered, *"the place absolutely reeked of CS gas and you could see where the grenades had gone off. They weren't just stun grenades either... these were fragmentation grenades. There* were shrapnel holes, bullet holes... they knew exactly where the beds were in each room and they'd nailed every single one of them... every single one, hoping to kill us all." Andy Macdonald remembers the same, and he managed to take advantage of the confusion; "There were bullet holes through everything, they shot up the detachment HQ the most – Major Noott's office - meanwhile, the Argies were stealing stuff, so while nobody was looking, I nicked the Brook's VCR machine and fucked off with it." Waiting outside, Danny Betts remembered "...this big fucking Argentine Marine. He put his hand out to me and said, 'Marine' and then to himself, 'Marine. Five minutes.' I respected him for that. But when I got inside, the place was shot to pieces. It was bullet holes just everywhere.'"*[11]

"When it was my turn, I was taken into the accommodation to see the devastation that had taken place when they had attacked the Brook," Gary Williams recalled, "If there had been anyone there they would not have survived. There were bullet holes everywhere. I got to my room and found a bag to pack some things into, at this point I spotted a case of Tennents lager and saw the opportunity to get some free beer, the Argie that was with me as my guard was not for letting me take it, but he must have taken pity on me by the look on my face as it was packed in my baggage for a souvenir afterwards." - Every man of the Royal Marines repeats the same thing; Moody Brook had been destroyed and not a man of them would have survived. The grenades used were not, they all say, stun grenades. There was HE grenade shrapnel everywhere and a mass of bullet holes in everything. Gary Noott's office, where the light had been left on, was destroyed. Not a man of them, the Royal Marines insisted, would have walked out alive had they been in their bunks as they would have been.

All the men were taken back to GH clutching their bullet-riddled bags and clothing and soon told the others what they had seen. There were low grumbles of disapproval as the men settled back down in the paddocks, lit up more cigarettes and began chatting and singing amongst themselves. If they had been allowed to collect their personal things, most reasoned, then perhaps they were not going to be executed. Some wondered if they dared to hope they would make it out alive and see their families again. "Later in the afternoon they told us we were going to be flown out of the Islands and to Argentina." Nick Williams recalled, "They then realised that one or two of the men were married to Falkland Islanders and put an announcement over the radio that the Marines' wives could join them to be flown out as well. I then remembered that the only man married to a local on our detachment was Dave Morris and that he was in Buenos Aires on the diplomatic bag run. His wife Alana and their children were in Stanley. I spoke to our Sergeant Major about it and he asked me if I knew where they lived. I replied that I did. He said if the Argentines would allow it, would I go and pick them up? I agreed. I was taken in one of our Land Rovers. I had an Argentine driver, one of their officers as vehicle commander and a conscript in the back with me. He was armed with an FN and kept it pointed at me the whole time. I don't know what he thought I was going to do! When I got to Alana's house, I hopped out the back of the vehicle and made my way down the garden path and the conscript followed me. I wasn't sure what to do. If Alana saw the conscript, she would break down – this was the Islanders' worst nightmare coming true. Once I got to the front door, I walked straight in and slammed the door in the conscript's face. He was outside and didn't know what to do, I knew that I had only a few minutes before he got brave and walked in. Alana and the boys were in the house with one of her friends, I told her all was well and that she and the boys were to come with me and that she had two minutes to pack some stuff. She was in pieces. I told her to hurry, as I was aware of the conscript outside the door, so speed was of the essence. After a couple of minutes, we left the house and all climbed in to the back of the Rover. I suddenly had a thought and asked the officer if we could make one more quick stop. He agreed so I directed the driver to Marjorie and Trevor Bernsten's house as Mick Sellen and I were staying with them. Again, I hopped out of the Rover, up the path with the conscript in tow, walked in the door and shut it in his face. All the family were in the kitchen, they were all very upset and scared. There were a lot of tears. Marjorie asked how many Marines were killed – I told her not to worry, that we were all safe. She gave me phone numbers for family in the UK and made me promise to call them, to tell them that the family in the Falklands were all okay. I grabbed a bottle of rum, stuffed it down the front of my jacket and went back to the Rover."

Back in Government House, Rex Hunt was given only a short time to settle his affairs before he and his family were to be deported, first to Argentina and then to the UK. He and his small staff had been working to rescue anything else of value from the house, and he had a few last duties to attend to before he left his post by way of forced eviction. Patrick Watts called him from FIBS – now officially renamed 'LRA Islas Malvinas Broadcasting Station' - first turning down the in-studio speakers so that his Argentine captors could not hear him. Live on air, Hunt, sounding tired and emotional told the people of the Falkland Islands that Government House had fallen and that it was all over. He paid tribute to the bravery of Dick Baker and Hector Gilobert and told the listeners that he had ordered Admiral Busser to withdraw immediately, but had been ignored. Watts asked if he should keep broadcasting under the new administration; *"Yes please,"* replied Hunt, *"for the sake of the Islands it is necessary for you to keep up the Falkland Islands Broadcasting Service. I don't know how many hours you've been on the air, but I think you've done a tremendous job. I think you've reported everything well and keep it up, even with a gun in your back."* Finally, he ended with a note of hope for the Falkland Islanders; *"That's all I've got to say. I'm sorry it has happened this way. It's probably the last message I'll be able to give you. But I wish you all the best of luck and, rest assured... the British will be back."*

Hunt was determined upon wearing his full ceremonial uniform upon leaving Government House but found that his belongings had already been rifled through and his medals were missing. He folded a more practical travelling suit neatly at the top of his luggage as a burgundy red London Taxi pulled up on the drive and he and his family got in and drove off. Diane Stewart, the young nurse at KEMH looked up to see him go as she was pulling three bullets out of an Argentine flak jacket, and he waved at her as he went past. That was Rex Hunt. He knew everyone in Stanley and they loved him. When he got to the airport, he was herded towards the waiting aircraft but now made the Argentines wait as he ducked into the LADE office and appeared several minutes later in his travelling suit, much to the annoyance of the Argentine officer, Major Dowling, who seemed intent upon making Hunt's departure as uncomfortable as possible. Hunt had been cunningly foiling Dowling's attempts to open the safe and cypher room for some time, even though both were now empty and, when Dowling had gone to fetch a Land Rover to take Hunt back to the airport, he had cunningly slipped out in full uniform and boarded his London Taxi with Union Flag pennant flying as he was driven to the airport. Even then, an enraged Dowling, arriving red-faced and angry, had snatched the pennant from the Taxi and searched Hunt's luggage thoroughly, looking for codes, ciphers and reports. Tony Hunt, the Governor's son, managed to sneak Simon Winchester's press report out in his shoe, something which - Hunt observed - showed that Dowling was not as professional or efficient as he pretended to be.

Despite enjoying his cat-and-mouse game of baffling Major Dowling, Rex Hunt had still managed to be efficient in his own duties and, as he was now being escorted out of the Islands, had convinced the Argentines to let a few of the government administrators to stay on at their posts to oversee the running of the civil departments until Argentina's own people could come in. He was surprised that they agreed. It was 16.30 in the afternoon when one of them noticed the telex machine suddenly jump into life;

'HELLO WHAT ARE ALL THESE RUMOURS WE HEAR, THIS IS LONDON'
'WE HAVE LOTS OF NEW FRIENDS' came the reply.
'WHAT ABOUT INVASION RUMOURS?'
'THOSE ARE THE FRIENDS I WAS MEANING'
'THEY HAVE LANDED?'
'ABSOLUTELY'
'ARE YOU OPEN FOR TRAFFIC I.E. NORMAL TELEX SERVICE?'

'NO ORDERS ON THAT YET. ONE MUST OBEY ORDERS'
'WHOSE ORDERS?'
'THE NEW GOVERNOR'S'
'ARGENTINA?'
'YES'
'ARE THE ARGENTINIANS IN CONTROL?'
'YES YOU CANT ARGUE WITH THOUSANDS OF TROOPS PLUS ENORMOUS
NAVY SUPPORT WHEN YOU ARE ONLY 1800 STRONG. STAND BY.'

The Royal Marines were now loaded up into the back of Hugo Santillan's Amtracks, covered four-tonners and LARC amphibious vehicles; *"It feels like ENDEX!"* Gary Noott heard one of the new detachment say out loud, *"You know, waiting for the transport to turn up to take us back to camp for a shower and a shave, then a run ashore this evening!"* Noott pondered to himself the difference in experiences between the old detachment and the new – most of whom seemed to be somewhere between incredulous and bewildered - whilst his own men of the old detachment seemed to take the situation with more reality; *"I would have been bloody pissed off to have spent a year in this lousy place only to have missed this if we'd gone home earlier!"* he heard one of his own men say with a laugh. The Royal Marines were now driven back along St Mary's Walk and up Philomel Street towards the airport and there, as Dave Gerrard recalled; *"we passed a group of their special forces and Marine Murray Paterson shouted out that we would be back. They didn't look too pleased!"* Neville Bennett watched the Marines go along St Mary's Walk and out of Stanley, recalling a feeling of worry for the boys who had fought so hard to defend them and what might happen to them now; *"Where they were going, we didn't know,"* he recorded in his diary, *"but we hoped they would be treated fairly even though they had tried to take out the whole of the Argentine forces. Still, that's what wearing the Green Beret is all about..."*

Passing through White City gate, Danny Betts and George Brown recognised the scene of their earlier action against the Amtracks and Brown distinctly remembered looking down and seeing his brand new Berghaus bergen which he had left behind in the rush. He cursed to himself that some Argentine soldier or Marine would soon be the new owner of it. Murray Paterson, driving a four-tonner with a gun in his back, now recalled looking over the scene of the action fought by Section Two and seeing the wreckage of the battle; *"We passed by the Amtrack that the boys had knocked out with their rocket launchers,"* he remembered, *"slewed across the left-hand side of the road as we passed, about thirty degrees to the right, the nose up and the right-hand side down in the ditch, smoking away. The back doors were open and I stole a quick glance inside as we passed by... it was a bloody mess. I remember seeing the mess – bodies, blood and body parts - and thinking to myself, 'Well, nobody got out of that!' then we drove on to the airport, leaving it behind...'*[12]

Nick Williams soon joined the rest of the men at the airport, having been driven directly there in the Land Rover with Alana and the boys as he remembered; *"When I took Dave's family to the airport, we had government officials and wives in one plane and bootnecks in the other. They had a jet plane and we had a military Hercules. I remember looking around and seeing an awful lot of blood-stained stretchers laying around in the airport and thought to myself, 'Well, they're not ours.' Alana and the boys went one way and I went and re-joined my comrades waiting to board the Hercules. We were searched before we got on board and I lost my bottle of rum."* At the airport, there were many Argentines there, taking pictures, celebrating and some taunting or goading the Marines who all shouted; *"Don't get too comfortable, we'll be back!"* and similar words of defiance. Seeing their reaction to this, Geordie Gill remembered that; *"It was strange how they totally misjudged the situation. They were convinced it was a done deal – that the Falklands were theirs for good – and they couldn't believe it when we told them that we – and a lot more of us – would be back. You'd have thought someone would have got the message that when you pick a fight with the British, you have a big problem! These guys knew we'd hurt them, and telling them we'd be back now gave them food for thought about what they were in for when the task force arrived."*

Seeing that it was having an effect, the Royal Marines were doing it all the more, telling the Argentines that they would be back and that they would see them again soon. Hearing this, one English-speaking Argentine Major now approached Mike Norman and told him; *"We have provided a solution that your government and Mrs Thatcher are desperately looking for. I don't think there will be any reaction."* Mike Norman told him prophetically by reply that; *"You have completely misjudged the British people. They will not stand for this. We will be back."*

As the aircraft took off from Stanley, heading for Argentina, the people of the Falkland Islands were left alone, defenceless and scared. They were now under military rule, under a flag which was not their own and a language which most of them did not speak. The Argentine soldiers entered houses one by one, looking for weapons and anyone else who might be in hiding, but found nobody. Patrick Watts reported that they were being respectful and that people should not fight them or be afraid, but let them in to do their jobs. It was noted that many of these – the newly-arrived conscripts of the 25th Infantry Regiment - seemingly had little idea of where they were. One was heard to ask why there were so many English people here in Southern Chile and several others asked where all of the Argentine people were whom they had come to liberate from colonial oppression? - It was all so alien; *"So ended quite a traumatic day,"* reported Neville Bennett in his diary, *"having one's home invaded and the established representative of the Head of State being deported and being confined to one's own home by the people who said they had come to liberate us from British oppression. I think that they had wanted us to have been down on the beach waving banners and shouting 'Viva!'... what a silly idea. We don't even get excited about a church bazaar."*[*13]

Chapter 10: Dawns and Departures

"There go our boys..."
Neville Bennett - April 2nd 1982.

The men of the Royal Marines crammed into the Hercules, overseen by Lieutenant Commander Alfredo Cufre whose only orders were to look after them but not to allow them to talk to each other on the flight. There were not enough seats on the aircraft and some men had to sit on the floor where, as Ray Bloye recalled; *"One of the first things I noticed was the RAF markings on the bulkheads. This was painful, to think we had supplied this aircraft to them and we were now being taken to Argentine in one of 'our' planes."*

In the cover of tussock grass and rocks, now on the far side of Port William, Corporal York's section saw an Argentine Hercules taxi across the runway and then take off, circling to gain height and coming straight over the top of them. Unaware of the cargo, York's section now prepared their rocket launcher to take it out of the sky. As the plane came closer, York suddenly countermanded the order to fire as he didn't want to give his position away. The Hercules flew over the men as they ducked for cover and then made their escape towards camp. It was a close call. The men in the Hercules only found this out when Wilf *'Smudger'* Smith told Ray Bloye at a reunion, some thirty years later, just how close Section Four had been to killing all of them. The Hercules now gained height and headed on a course over the South Atlantic towards Argentina. Some of the Royals, having heard stories from the so-called 'Dirty War' were now somewhat concerned that the depths of the South Atlantic might be their last resting place and the nervous behaviour of some of the Argentine conscripts was making them edgy as Gary Williams recalled; *"Whilst we were in flight the young Argentinian in the back of the plane with us was constantly playing with the safety catch on his weapon. I think everybody was quite nervous and thoughts started to go through my mind. More than a few of us thought the rear ramp would open and we would be thrown out of the plane in mid-air. The whisper started to go around the lads, 'Right, the second that fucking ramp moves an inch we'll just fucking rush them.' It was a nervous flight..."*

Spotting some packed parachutes, Lou Armour now began to consider his options should it come to it; *"I think those of us who were Para-trained were intensely focused on the three jump exits; the tailgate and the port and starboard doors,"* he remembered, *"The guards were not our worry, it was what the back-end crew were up to that concentrated our minds..."* However, as the journey went on and their captors made no sudden moves, the men began to relax and at last hope that they might reach home again; *"This was the first time I'd been in a Hercules,"* continued Ray Bloye, *"and it was not long into the flight that I felt my backside getting rather hot. I asked someone if the floor always got hot but nobody knew. It got hotter and hotter and I had to take my combat jacket off to sit on. I half expected the plane to blow up but eventually we arrived in Comodoro Rivadavia which was their naval and air base."* - they had landed safely and Alfredo Cufre remembered one of the Marines thanking him and exchanging berets as a sign of respect.

The Marines now walked off into Argentine territory and were processed through Comodoro Rivadavia air base, as Ray Bloye continues; *"Then came the scariest thing that happened to me that day. We were led off of the plane and herded along a corridor of what can only be described as the Argie version of 'Dad's Army.' There were old blokes and some very young guys in varying degrees of uniform, from full combats to some with combat jackets and jeans and some with combat trousers and civvy jackets. Their weaponry was something out of the Ark. Some had shotguns, some had rifles and one even had a blunderbuss! They looked terrified and I had the impression that if one of us had said 'Boo!' they'd have opened on us. They were that jittery that I would never have believed it. Thinking about it now, they were probably just workers / dockers given a gun and told to do what they did, as all their forces were either in the Falklands or on their way to it."*

The Royal Marines were now funnelled through another cordon of armed men and onto another aircraft bound, they were told, for Buenos Aires where, they later found out, they were to have been paraded through the streets but somewhere along the way this idea changed – perhaps making a trophy out of them was not in the junta's interests – and the aircraft now changed course; *"I slept through the landing,"* remembered Mark Gibbs, *"and this young Argentine scrote from the back of the plane smashed me in the face with a rifle butt to wake me up..."* Now the Royal Marines, exhausted, starving and edgy, were pushed towards the exit of the plane, expecting to see Buenos Aires. Stepping out into the darkness, Stephen 'George' Brown looked around him and suddenly thought; *"I've been here before..."* but it wasn't until their passports were stamped at immigration – still in full combat gear and cam-cream – that the men of the Royal Marines truly knew where they were: Montevideo, Uruguay. It was neutral territory, they knew, and this meant only one thing - they were safe; *"To say I was elated is an understatement..."* remembered Ray Bloye, *"it meant we would not be seeing Argentina any time soon."*

A coach now took the men through the darkness, *"speeding through town with police bikes and cars leading the way"* as Dave Gerrard remembered, to a hotel in the city centre, the Carrasco, where they seemed to be met by a million flashes of cameras from the world's press, come to see them. Geordie Gill, who had slept most of the way and been half-asleep passing through immigration remembered thinking that he had arrived in Buenos Aires; *"And as the cameras went off, I gave two fingers from both hands and was yelling, 'Yeah! Fuck off!'* he remembered, *'Then someone said, 'No! We're in Uruguay, they love us and they hate the Argies!' and I quickly changed to waving and saying 'Hi!' with a smile!"*

Although it was now 03.00 the men were told that they should go and get themselves something to eat. Ambling into the foyer, the men of the Royal Marines did not look the type of guests typically seen at the Carrasco in their camouflaged clothes, but the hotel had been emptied of all guests and now it was just them; *"We were led straight into the restaurant and food was very soon delivered to my table,"* remembered Ray Bloye, *"there was a giant T-Bone steak that filled the plate placed before me with a bowl of chips on the side. A drinks trolley was brought round with a lot of soft drinks on the top tray and half a dozen beers on the second tray..."*

"We told the waiter not to bring any more soft drinks and just bring beer and wine," Gary Williams remembered, *"we were then given rooms and people went and got a shower and a bit of rest. My phone went in my room so I answered it and I was told by the person on the other end that he was from the Daily Mail and could I give him a story? My reply was, 'How did you get this number?' - and a polite 'Fuck off' - followed by the phone being put down."*[*1]

The Royals had barely eaten nor slept and many were unable to sleep despite being desperately tired. They were still buzzing and now more so with the idea that they had survived and were going to live. After a few hours, there was a knock on each man's door and they were asked to come downstairs for a briefing; *"Mike Norman and Gary Noott were there and briefly went over the 'do's and dont's',"* recalled Ray Bloye, *"We were in Uruguay under diplomatic immunity and were restricted to the inside of the hotel. We could buy what we wanted from the bar and could do so by giving our name and room numbers for every order and we would eventually receive a bill on return to the UK. There were no immediate details of how long we would be there but the RAF would be sending a plane for us at some point. Until then, our time was our own, but only within the hotel."* Gary Noott recalled perhaps the most famous incident of the 'do's and dont's' speech; *"...on completion of which, the Sergeant Major gave out some admin detail, finishing with the usual 'Any questions?' - 'Yes, Sergeant Major' - a hand went up at the back of the room - "What is it, Jones?" - 'Sir... can we fuck the maids?'"* The meeting descended into uproarious humour as the men, chuckling to themselves, were dismissed; *"I and some others went to have a look outside the hotel via the windows at the front,"* remembered Ray Bloye, *"I was amazed to see a large crowd of people there and, on seeing us, they started cheering! I found out that the Uruguayans didn't like the Argentines and thought we were great. This happened whenever any of us went to the windows and I have to say, we did milk it a bit!"*

The men had to first get processed and were met by a British Embassy official – a Scotsman as they recall - whose initial reaction to Mike Norman and Gary Noott's brief appraisal of their battle against the odds and subsequent removal from the Falkland Islands was, incredibly, a startled gasp of; *"Do you mean to say that there was... you know... some 'shooting' before you left?"* - Almost stunned by the man's reaction, Noott and Norman looked at each other blankly and then back to the embassy man. Devoid of anything more useful to say, they simply said yes and, having been processed, passed the embassy man on to the men where, as Dave Gerrard remembered; *"He came floating by with papers and saying, 'It's okay for you lot, I've been up all night sorting this mess out!' - I thought he was going to get decked!"*

Once processed, the Royal Marines now decided to order drinks. They had been through an ordeal and decided that the best way to breakfast was with beer. Dutifully giving their names and room numbers, the Marines now began to unwind with, as Gary Williams recalled; *"lots of stories being told and everybody in great spirits, laughing and joking."* Mike Norman in particular took some funny criticism of his clothes, for he had nothing that wasn't riddled with bullet holes and looked like a hobo. After a few rounds, the Royals seemed to realise that the staff didn't seem to mind whose name or room number was given; *"Someone went to the bar and gave the name FW Woolworth and a room number that probably didn't exist,"* remembered Ray Bloye, *"when this was accepted, we started coming up with all sorts of different names like 'DMS Boot', 'DPM Smock' and 'WH Smiths' to mention a few..."* and after a few more drinks, the men became a little bolder and began to add *'Gary Noott'* to the drinks list amongst a sea of other names as the drinking and merriment continued; *"I don't think the waiters were too impressed to be told that people were called Maggie Thatcher, Ronald Reagan and Mickey Mouse,"* remembered Gary Williams, *"let alone that their room numbers were in the high 500's when they only had around 200 rooms in the place. Rumour has it we drank the entire hotel dry three times whilst we were there."*[2]

Now they heard from the newspapers the story of what had transpired in South Georgia on April 3rd and a cheer went up around the hotel with more merry-making. It transpired that the Argentine forces had run into Lieutenant Keith Mills' detachment and this force, just 22 men strong, had learned of the Argentine invasion of the Falklands and had dug in at King Edward Point near the Antarctic Survey Station at Grytviken, spread barbed wire across the beach and built a makeshift mine on the jetty for when the Argentines came. The messages from London, wired to the *Endurance* had ordered Mills' force to *'Fire only in self-*

defence after a warning,' later reinforced by *'Do not resist beyond the point where lives might be lost to no avail.'* In short, they were being ordered to offer only a token resistance to which Mills' reply has now become Marine Corps legend; *"Sod that, I'll make their eyes water."*

The Argentine forces were landing via helicopter from the ship *Bahia Paraiso* and were closing in on Mills' position with fifteen men and two more waves to go. When Mills' men spotted the Argentine Puma helicopter returning with the second wave, they now opened up with small arms and GPMG fire, hammering 500 rounds into it, which sent it spiralling to the ground where it crash-landed, with several fatalities and many men wounded. The Argentine forces already on the ground now moved in against Mills' position and the Royal Marines returned fire, pinning them down until they called upon the Corvette *Guerrico* for support. Now the warship steamed in and opened fire, but Mills' men blazed away at her with everything they had, spraying the bridge with small arms and GPMG fire to keep the crew's heads down and firing first a 66mm LAW which wrecked the main gun's elevation mechanism and then as she passed, firing their Carl Gustav 84mm with the rocket skipping once from the waves and then crashing into the side of the ship, holing it. The *Guerrico* passed by into the bay, a listing and smoking wreck, with her 100mm gun having been knocked out of action after just one round, her 40mm secondary armament knocked out and even her 20mm guns jammed, with electrical cables shot to pieces.

Now in the bay and hidden from view by the buildings of the British Antarctic Survey Station, the *Guerrico* would have to turn and make the dash back to the open sea. Colour Sergeant Pete Leach, a 19-year veteran of Borneo, Northern Ireland and Cyprus and a qualified sniper, now ran to Shackleton House, broke in and set up with his L42 sniper rifle, ready for the *Guerrico* as she passed again and on she came, running the gauntlet, with Leach putting out all of the windows in the bridge by turn and then switching his fire to the port side as she passed. Emerging past the station, the ship now came under another barrage of fire and Dave Combes managed to fire another 84mm round which screeched across the bay and slammed into the ship's Exocet launcher. By the time she was out of range, there were no less than 1,200 bullet scores and holes in the vessel and one seaman was killed and five others wounded as the crippled ship limped back out of the bay. By now, more Argentine troops had landed from the *Bahia Paraiso's* second helicopter and were moving in on Mills' position from behind. The two sides had exchanged fire and one of the Marines, Nigel Peters, was hit in the arm as he stood up to fire a LAW at them. The Argentines behind them were pinned down under heavy fire, the second helicopter, an Alouette, was also hit by small arms, wounding the pilot in the leg, and only after the *Guerrico* got her 100mm gun working again and opened fire did Mills decide that the contest was unfair. Waving a white coat, he left his position and told the Argentines that he could happily go on all day unless they agreed to stop fighting: and they did. In a battle which lasted almost three hours, the men who would forever be known as 'Mills' Marauders' had destroyed a helicopter, damaged another, severely crippled a Corvette, killed three of the enemy and wounded nine others. Although it was the Argentines who had agreed to stop fighting, the Royal Marines were now taken prisoner. It had been an excellent complement to the heroic defence of Stanley and the men in the hotel eagerly drank to their comrades' gallant stand.[*3]

The Royal Marines stayed in Montevideo for three days. They spent much of it drinking, laughing, feeling happy to be alive, swapping stories, swimming in the pool, bathing in the adulation of the crowd outside the hotel who grew daily and also in reflecting during the quiet moments; *"It was a very reflective time,"* remembered Danny Betts, *"the general sense was that we had given a fucking good account of ourselves. It had been a personal test and we didn't fail. All the training had paid off and we felt good. We had all come through it, with each other, for each other. We were on a total high. I felt good that I had faced up and not bottled and that I had served with such a great group of guys. We were a band of brothers, and I was proud that my 'brothers' had done the same. Every man did his job. We could always be proud of that."* Others, later thinking over their experience, came to the same conclusion; *"It was that whole Royal Marine ethos that worked for us, because we didn't expect to get out at the other end."* recalled Graham Evans, *"Still I reckon that it was a lot more than just good luck that we made it to fight another day."*

As some laughed and joked and drank, others sought solace to reflect upon what they had just been through, although the memories usually drove them back to the bar and their mates quite quickly as Colin 'Tiny' Jones remembered; *"To be honest, I personally didn't have a good time when I was sober and on my own,"* he recalled, *"and I'll leave it at that. I do remember the funnier parts though; a couple of weeks before the shit had kicked off, a motorbike had been 'borrowed' from Stanley and found in a ditch by the base. There had been a lot of shit about it which, under the circumstances, was forgotten. Then in the hotel in Montevideo, Jock 'Ninja' Milne came up to a table where we were getting merrily pissed; 'Do you remember that motorbike?' he said, as he threw the keys on the table. What a guy! Why would he still have the keys? Ask the Ninja!"*

After three days, the Royal Marines were told that the RAF had sent a plane for them and they were to be going home. Every man was overjoyed. The crowds of Uruguayans now gathered to see them off, as Ray Bloye remembered; *"It seemed like thousands of them had turned out to cheer us off and this made me feel that we were at least appreciated by Uruguay."* Now the men climbed into the

RAF DC10 where they were reunited with Rex Hunt and their wives and families in an emotional moment. Hunt told them all how proud he was of them and what an excellent job they had done and most of the men began to wonder at the fantastic reception they would surely receive when they returned home. As the DC10 took off into the air, the Royals began to talk with the men of the RAF and naturally asked what reception their gallant defence had met with in the UK. Were they heroes? Did everyone know what they had done? Many, remembering that the British and American press had been present, assumed that the story would be well known in the UK by now. The men from the RAF met them instead with blank, quizzical looks of disbelief and a question as to whether they had actually read the news which, of course, having been under press blackout for three days, they had not. Now, a copy of the Daily Mail was passed around and suddenly the headline struck them all dumb:

'SHAMED' was emblazoned across the top of the page, beneath which the men of NP8901 saw the images of themselves spread face-first down on Ross Road with the Argentines standing over them and then below that, the most damning headline of all; 'ROYAL MARINES SURRENDER... WITH BARELY A SHOT FIRED'.

It had come from an Argentine press release which had been given out, which was then spread across the United States, then the UK and was now being recited the world over; *"You can imagine how that made us feel, knowing what we'd just been through."* remembered Ray Bloye, *"If we felt bad, Rex Hunt seemed to feel it more, if that were possible. He got up in front of us and stated that he would call a press conference when we came back and if the person who had written that report was there, he would punch them on the nose for all of us. I believed him, having got to know him, as did everyone else. It suddenly felt that not only had the UK Government abandoned us, but they had let this disgusting paper print such lies about us. The sooner we could get back, the better."*

Now many of the men slept as Mike Norman and Gary Noott put together the various reports from the section leaders and came up with a post-action report which would be required when they returned home; especially in light of the erroneous press reports. As to casualties suffered by the enemy, they were told be very conservative and to state only those which they were sure of, killed at 100% certainty, wounded at 80% or more; *"We were very conservative with what we said,"* remembered Nick Williams, *"I think Dave Carr only put down the one guy by the hospital that Benny got with the GPMG, and we didn't see if he was dead, much as we know we got him, so he went down as wounded if we added him in at all. Of course, had we been Paratroopers we'd have probably have claimed to kill about forty thousand of them! So we kept it conservative, more than the Argentines claimed, certainly, but definitely nowhere near as many as we thought we got."*

The final figures from ammo counts and on all of the reports showed that no less than 6,462 rounds of ammunition and twelve rockets had been spent, with enemy losses of five men killed, 17 wounded, three prisoners and one enemy Amtrack destroyed with one more damaged and all for no loss; *"It was initially estimated that we had killed five and wounded seventeen,"* Sergeant Major Bill Muir said later, *"but we only counted the bodies that we saw drop in front of us."* It was, all the men agree, conservative and indeed the generic figure they all come up with individually is 60 killed and wounded with only one guess as low as 30 and another as high as 100 and these figures were only taken from the area around Government House itself. When the report was finished, Bill Muir decided to put a final flourish to the report and added that; *"At no time during the conflict were earrings worn by any member of the Royal Marines."*[4]

Now on the return home, Rex Hunt was serving whisky from a huge coffee pot, ignoring the crew who insisted that all RAF flights were 'dry' and encouraging the men and, despite the knock-down blow from the British press, he promised to put it right and had already penned recommendations for no less than five Military Medals and twelve Mentions in Despatches for the brave men, to include Mike Norman, Geordie Gill, the anti-tank teams on the airport road, PJ Berry and several others, all of whom had more than earned them. They would put this right, Hunt, Norman and Noott told their men. Nobody would believe that they had simply surrendered without a shot being fired, and Rex Hunt reminded them that nobody had surrendered at all; his order had been to 'Stop fighting' – nobody had said the word 'surrender'.[5]

The plane landed at Ascension Island for fuel and the Royals were allowed to stretch their legs and get some food on the base, as Murray Paterson remembered; *"I was walking beside Rex Hunt and Major Noott as a Chief Petty Officer was showing us the way to get some food. There was a hangar there with the door open and inside it was absolutely crammed with stores and munitions, 'Look at that!' I said to them, pointing, 'Those stores couldn't get here in time to stop an invasion. This is a build-up! Someone knew they were coming!' The Petty Officer ran for the hangar doors and pulled them shut behind him and we walked off to the canteen, feeling as if someone had known a lot more than we did right now. We were discussing it between us in the canteen and I said to Rex Hunt, 'Before I left Poole in '81 they gave us the briefing and told us that there was always a submarine in the area twenty-four hours a day... where the hell was it? We were told it would be there!' Rex and Major Noott both said the same thing: 'That's the first question I'm going to ask when I get back...' I don't think they got their answers but I do know we were using those stores at Ascension a few weeks later..."*

With the plane refuelled, the Royal Marines took off on the final leg of their journey to RAF Brize Norton in Oxfordshire, not far outside of London. During the flight, the men grumbled and stirred, with most of them anxious to get home and put their story straight. Burt Reynolds remembered feeling like the government knew exactly what story they wanted to tell when the comm-system on the plane suddenly came to life; *"Margaret Thatcher had a message played to us in which she basically told us to keep our mouths shut! No 'Thank you' or 'Well done' even!"* later, the men were to receive written instructions to the same. The Royal Marines landed by night. It was dark but, as Ray Bloye remembered; *"I was disappointed not to see any kind of welcome committee. We were ushered inside the terminal building and had to go through Customs and Immigration which I thought was a bit pointless. I couldn't believe the crassness of the Customs Officer who asked us if we had anything to declare. I think he was told to go away by a senior RAF officer as we couldn't believe we had just been asked that. I was standing with all my worldly goods and was lucky to even be here. Having 'cleared' customs, we were held in a hall and asked a few questions such as how many rounds did I fire? Did I hit any Argies? Was there anything else I could say? Someone else asked if we wanted to go back, as by now Maggie Thatcher had ordered the task force to retake the Islands. All bar a couple (two who were due to get married) said yes and I certainly wanted to."*

Then, as Gary Williams remembers, the men were given a debrief; *"We were told we were not allowed to talk to the press and if they did try, to ring the police who would then deal with them. In another of the rooms everything had been set up for us, did we need clothes? Did we need money? Did we need to contact anybody? - Highly efficient, even for the RAF!"* After the debrief, the men were organised into groups of those who lived fairly close to each other from all across the country and then led outside, where Gary Williams remembered that; *"there was a big line of vehicles to take us home; staff cars, hire cars, mini buses, I suppose I drew a short straw, I got a mini bus that went from Brize over towards the east coast and eventually home, it was only then that I found out that Frank Sugden from the outgoing detachment lived about half a mile from me. The driver asked if there was anything we wanted and the reply was the nearest off-licence for some beer. The driver duly obliged and the nearest one found, if I remember we didn't have enough money and he bought it for us. I eventually got home to Heywood for last orders at about 22.45 at the Seven Stars, when I got in the bar my family was waiting for us, a few beers later and off to bed."*

Each man now set off on his own journey. Figgy Duff remembered being driven out in the back of a Transit van, given a warrant and stuck on a train back to Finchley where he remembered that the feeling from the British government to the man in the street was simply; *"Nobody knows, nobody cares."* Stephen 'George' Brown remembered sharing a General's staff car back to Newcastle with Geordie Gill, Ray Bloye went home to Kent, many to the south coast and Danny Betts climbed aboard a coach going north which would take him eventually to Chesterfield. On the coach, he remembered, the guys were happy, joking and laughing until they made their first stop and saw one of the Marines' mothers running alongside the coach to embrace her son; *"Then after that you could have heard a pin drop."* he remembered. As word of the boys coming home spread, small crowds gathered from their local communities, *"I just want to kiss one of them!"* was a call heard quite often and the people seemed a little in awe of them. Burt Reynolds recalled that; *"I travelled back home in a minibus with four or five other guys and we stopped off along the way at a pub which had a TV. As we were ordering our drinks, the news came on and showed us all. We all started cheering and the Landlord waived our bill as a thank you..."* For some, the idea was still there that they would not be forgotten. That the record would be put straight.

The men were given a weeks' leave to recuperate. Mike Norman's detachment, having already signed up for NP8901 duty, were going back. Gary Noott's detachment, by the Geneva Convention could not be made to but most volunteered anyway. Many had friends or family in the Islands, their mates were going back anyway and they had a score to settle. Majors Noott and Norman had no such luxury as a break and were soon *"summoned to Northwood, CinCFleet's HQ with Admiral Fieldhouse,"* Gary Noott remembered, *"I recall little of the meeting except that I was made to feel that the failures of the FCO, MI6, MOD, DIS and our immediate boss in not being able to see the real and present threat was somehow our transgression. It ended – and I paraphrase – with the idiotic statement, 'Go and get it back!' (The Islands, that is) and I thought two things to myself at that time – A: What a prat to issue such a ridiculous order. B: I wonder what General Julian Thompson would say if I pitched up and said that CinCFleet had just said that I'm in charge!"*

Still on the Falkland Islands, the men of Stefan York's Section Four had finally handed themselves in. Their epic escape had kept the Argentines guessing and kept up morale, from where a score of small mishaps were attributed to them fighting a covert war against the invaders and laying booby-traps. Hard on their case came Major Patricio Dowling of the Argentine Military Police Intelligence, the same man who had plagued Rex Hunt's last hours in Stanley and a man described as both sinister and dangerous. He described himself as an Irish-Argentine, although Rex Hunt had considered his demeanour more of a classic Prussian officer from bygone days. Tall and slim with red hair and blue eyes, Dowling took every opportunity to goad the British and the Falkland Islanders about his sympathies with the IRA. He was a sadist, many said a fascist who would not have been out of place amongst the ranks of the SS, and the Argentines hated him every inch as much as the Falkland Islanders. He swaggered around town in a grey woollen sweater and khaki combat trousers, brandishing a captured British SLR and always with two or three henchmen in tow, he systematically bullied everyone, evicting the Police Chief Ronnie Lamb from his office and commandeering half of the Upland Goose Hotel on threat of taking the whole if not given up immediately. He beat up, threatened and evicted Islanders whom he considered subversive and did it with pleasure and was even overheard discussing a 'Final solution to the problem of the Malvinas' – which he explained as 'getting rid of the Islanders'.*6

The men of Section Four had escaped to the north. As the Gemini boat touched the shore on the other side of Port William, the men had jumped out, thrown the boat on the beach and quickly yomped into the hills. Tired, hungry and exhausted, they found a secluded place, went to ground, climbed into their sleeping bags and tried to sleep out the rest of the day, determined to move by night; *"When we were lying up during the day, we looked over towards Stanley,"* Dick Overall remembered, *"and all we could see were Hercules transports flying into the Islands, one after another. We quickly realised what we were up against."* When night fell, the six men moved off in the pouring rain; *"I've never known so much rain in all my life,"* Dick Overall continued, *"and we were soaked through and miserable, but it gave us cover."* Looking at the map, the men of Section Four pushed on, travelling for two days over rough ground in heavy weather until they arrived at the home of Neil and Glenda Watson at the remote Long Island Farm on April 4th. Knocking at the door, the six exhausted, soaking and hungry men, smeared with mud, camo cream and adorned with weapons made a frightening sight to the Watsons, who soon realised who they were and took them in readily; *"I think Glenda Watson was a bit concerned that the Argies would be hard on our heels,"* said Dick Overall, *"but at that point we were just happy to be fed, warm and dry, even just for a few hours."*

Regaining their strength and the feeling in their frozen limbs, the men set to talking and exchanging what news they had with the Watsons and working out their next course of action. Half of the six-man section, including Dick Overall, were for procuring food and going back out to the hills to fight a campaign against the Argentines, hidden by the people of the north camp. The others were not so sure, and worried in case it might bring down the wrath of the Argentines upon every family who helped them. Together, the Royal Marines and the Watson family listened to the BBC World Service for news. It said that Margaret Thatcher had despatched a task force to take back the Falkland Islands but that it would not be in the area for at least a month; *"So then Jeff Urand - an old three-badge Marine - said, 'Look! We can't live out here for a whole month!'"* remembered Dick Overall,

"The Argies will have helicopters, they'll have dogs and mobile patrols...we don't know what's out there. We'd never get away with it. We're going to have to turn ourselves in.'"

Collectively the men voted on their plan: to go back out to the hills and fight on, or to wrap it in. By four votes to two, they agreed, for the safety of the Islanders, to turn themselves in and Neil Watson agreed to telephone the Argentines, calling upon Hector Gilobert whose first question was after their health and who then asked Neil Watson if he could keep them safe until the morning. Sadly, Dowling quickly heard the news and set out after them, and Gilobert put in a call to advise them that the forces were coming now; *"We dashed outside, taking our weapons and ammo with us towards the beach,"* remembered Dick Overall, *"and we buried everything – rifles, grenades, ammo and some 66's - then sprinted back just in time. We were all sat in the house and then these two Pucara ground attack planes buzzed over at low level and we thought that was our time to go. We walked out, hands on our heads as this Lynx helicopter landed, followed by two more, and out stepped this guy who I would later know as Major Dowling..."* Out in the farmyard Dick Overall remembered the men now being tied up and made to lay down face first with Dowling pushing a .45 calibre automatic pistol hard into the back of his head and screaming at him; *"I shoot you now!"* - Dick was 21 years old and wondering if he would ever see home again; *"It was at that point that I thought I was going to die,"* he recalled, *"we were physically manhandled and tied up with plasti-cuffs, causing our hands to go blue, this was very painful and seemed like torture to me. Some of the guys complained, but Dowling treated us with the utmost disrespect, saying that he didn't care about the Geneva Convention, boasting to us about being a third-generation Irish Argentinian and being fully supportive of the IRA."*

As Argentine soldiers posed for photos over their prone bodies, Dowling interrogated them all and asked where their weapons were amongst other things; *"And the truth was, we didn't really know,"* said Dick Overall, *"so we just lied and said we had dropped some of them and thrown most of them into the sea. He seemed to accept that. They then bundled us into the helicopter and we were all giving the Argies stares and saying, 'We'll be back' and that sort of thing..."* Manhandled into a helicopter, the Royal Marines were taken away as Dowling now entered the farmhouse and began to threaten the Watsons with his pistol, telling them to line up against the wall when Lisa Watson, the family's twelve-year-old daughter, let out a defiant *"No!"* and obstinately stuck her thumb in her mouth. Dowling went crazy, pointing his gun in her face and screaming that he would shoot her unless she did as he ordered, but each time he was met with a defiant, *"No!"* and in the end, was forced to give up and departed after a few more boasts about his Irish roots. As his helicopter took off into the sky, he suddenly looked down to see Neil Watson brandishing a rifle and waving at them; Dowling had managed to leave his weapon behind on the sofa and now he was embarrassingly forced to go back and retrieve it, which did not add to his humour.

The six remaining Royal Marines of NP8901 were taken to Stanley's prison, held by a Captain Bruno, and Jeff Urand, known as a funny man, tried to keep up their spirits by continually poking fun at the guards, much to their annoyance. After a few days, they were deported to Comodoro Rivadavia where Dick Overall remembered being heavily shoved by an Argentine conscript; *"You think you're fucking hard, mate?"* he said, only for the Argentine to snap back, *"I speak good English!"* - eventually the six were kept in confinement and looked after by two conscripts, Eduardo and Claudio whom all the men liked very much and who looked after them well. Eventually they were taken to Buenos Aires and finally to Montevideo where the British Naval Attaché informed them not - under any circumstances - to speak to the press, who were offering them vast amounts of money for their stories. Finally, along with Keith Mills' men, all of the heroic defenders of the Falkland Islands and South Georgia returned home.[*7]

Epilogue

"I start feeling that we are all – the men of both sides who fought that day - somehow dinosaurs today, and we belong in a certain tribe that crosses over normal human boundaries. But boy, did we have fun!"
Diego Garcia Quiroga – Personal email to the author.

So ends the story of brave men of both sides who fought in the cause of their governments – whatever they may have been, for right, for wrong, for better or for worse - and whose history has been buried, hidden or simply not told for thirty-five years. It is evident that in the telling of this story, none of it (or certainly very little of it) as told by the men who were there matches the history which we understand today and if we combine those stories, along with the accounts of the Falkland Islanders and put them all together then we can begin to see that the story as we have been led to understand it is, quite simply, untrue. The initial reports stated that the Royal Marines had surrendered without a shot being fired. Plainly this was untrue although sometimes this ridiculous statement does get repeated even today. For Argentina it was, perhaps, a political necessity to make the entire invasion look more like a peaceful annexation, but for the British press to repeat this line was, in the estimation of myself and all of the men of the Royal Marines NP8901 detachment, simply criminal. Just as criminal, perhaps, is the assertion made by a certain Mr. Carlisle that the Argentines were firing blanks throughout the invasion. This story even made it into at least the local English press as recently as 2012 and was refuted by several of the Royal Marines including Nick Williams and Mike Norman. I have spoken with several of the Argentine veterans about this too, and they find the entire suggestion absolutely laughable. Gary Noott had also met with the person in question and told him straight, even asking him if he had ever himself been fired at or in a combat situation: I am informed that he left rather shamefaced and admitted he had not. Still the rumour persists, despite all of the evidence, and there are some, it seems, only too ready to believe it.[1]

Sadly, this is just one of many indignities the Royal Marines of the NP8901 Falklands detachment have had to put up with for so many years. It is a story which has gone on too long and one which, I hope, their own words and those of the men they fought against will now put right. It says much that many of these men – and I especially state Nick Williams although there are many others - felt too ashamed to return to the Falkland Islands. The men felt that, with the history now taken as 'fact', it might be thought that they had not done their jobs. What, they asked, if people now came to believe it? Happily all have since found out that the people of the Falkland Islands, and in particular of Stanley, have long-since held them as heroes; *"We were there and we know what they did that day,"* is the most common statement, *"they fought like lions to protect us"* and it is perhaps most telling that, now as then, the Falkland Islanders still refer to the defence of Stanley as their very own 'Rorke's Drift'.

The question remains, therefore, as to why this story has simply been ignored for thirty-five years and supplemented – perhaps even supplanted – with a new history. Certainly this history – or I should say the history as we have grown to understand it - is little short of a politically convenient farce for both the UK and Argentina and does not in any way reflect the truth, as told by the men of both sides who fought there on April 2nd 1982. The UK simply ignored its veterans (something which the Argentines who surrendered at the end of the war know only too well about) whilst the Argentine junta created a story which fitted the result it wanted and, it is fair to say, denied an awful lot of losses. The Argentine reports first admitted to three men killed (although more were seen) then their press release said none and not even a shot fired and finally it was settled upon one man; Pedro Giachino – the 'Superman' of the Argentine Navy - a man undeniable, a suitable martyr for the cause and for many, known as 'The first casualty' of the Falklands war. The outstanding Diego Garcia Quiroga is, of course, accepted as one of the wounded as is Ernesto Urbina and I hasten to remind many Argentine sources who forget Horacio Tello as well, a man whom Hugo Santillan refers to as the actual 'first casualty of the Malvinas'. As the story has shown, perhaps it could be neither of them. However, this is to get ahead of ourselves and any more specific points are dealt with in the appendices. Either way, we should do honour to these incredibly brave men, of whatever nationality and not declare their shared history 'a walk-over' – which it was certainly anything but.

It is the feeling of the Royal Marines of Naval Party 8901 that they have been forgotten on purpose and covered up as an embarrassment, their story papered over by the success of Operation Corporate and simply left with no need to talk about it. They were, they insist to a man, left there to die and indeed, most attest, they believe that they were sent there to die as well, perhaps as a cause for war or perhaps there is another reason to which we are simply not privy. Most believe that simply by not dying and by each and every man surviving the battle unscathed, they caused the greatest embarrassment of all. Again, we may only speculate. One thing which should not be in doubt, however, is that their outstanding defence of the Falklands and South Georgia was, by the accounts written and recorded here, one of the utmost bravery, of skill, determination and selfless courage as can be seen perhaps anywhere in history. Yet this story is found nowhere else. Pick up a book about the Falklands War and these men might warrant perhaps a page and, on a rare day, two, typically with the phrase 'token defence' or 'nominal defence' to describe their actions of April 2nd 1982 – I would now ask the reader if it is worth revisiting our entire understanding of this history.

One other salient point, of course, is that so many of the Argentine veterans of April 2nd also feel that this story of a mere token or nominal defence does them no justice either. This was an operation for which the men had trained their whole lives and a story of a 'walk over' – that the Argentine Marines, Commandos Anfibios and Buzos Tacticos simply arrived and forced the men of the Royal Marines to give up without barely a shot – does them no justice whatsoever. Indeed, it can be read in hundreds of articles how the Argentine forces numbered just 16 men or sometimes stated at just 84, which entirely scrubs the BIM2, Alpha Company BIM1 and many others from the history. It is a curious anomaly that, in a great fight of Marines versus Marines – truly the first special forces versus special forces battle in history - both sides should be as forgotten as they are. All of them were brave men, highly trained, highly skilled, at the peak of their physical fitness and ready to do the job for which they had been trained; a job which, according to the history books, none of them – British or Argentine – did. If we can find our common ground at all, it surely must be here. It is evident that this history should be told anew and that questions should be asked as to why our understanding is so different to what we now feel we know at the end of these pages having read the accounts of the men themselves. We began this epic tale with a chapter named 'Guilt, Complicity and Shame' and perhaps, we might conjecture, we are still seeing much of the same when we speak of this battle – and of course, as before, from both sides. That's governments for you. I will go on record to say this, in defence of every man whose name appears between these pages: There was no 'token defence' – and not one of the men on either side has suggested the same. Yet someone has and I believe, as do the men of NP8901, that we should begin to ask why.

The British diplomats and senior military staff promised that they would fix it – they did not. Rex Hunt and Major Mike Norman put in for five Military Medals and twelve Mentions in Despatches – not one was given. When the Falkland Islanders proposed, after the war, their own medals for the brave boys of NP8901 this idea was, I am told, also blocked and indeed 'stamped upon' by the UK government. It is time to ask why. These men don't want to be heroes and I believe that not one of them would describe himself as one, yet they deserve their justice. They deserve their story. They deserve their truth and their nation's thanks and recognition for standing and doing their jobs when for three and a half decades they have been remembered as 'the guys who surrendered without a shot being fired' – it is a tough pill to swallow.

For the Argentine side, we should also ask some serious and searching questions, and I hope that people in Argentina will do so. So much of what is 'accepted' history over this day has already been shown to be false and primarily, I should like to address the sheer number of men seen and engaged in Stanley itself. The Argentine accounts say that there was no fighting in Stanley whatsoever and indeed, that was a crucial element in the orders, so that there were no civilian casualties. Yet the damage in Stanley (which is still there today) the individual section reports from Sections One and Six (who alone fire off over half of the rounds ascribed to the entire battle in Stanley) the contacts seen and the casualties incurred – and confirmed – suggest otherwise. A large part of this history has been scrubbed clean which would suggest that something is amiss and, much as the men of the Royal Marines have had their honour stolen from them, so too has that of these Argentine servicemen. My good friends in Argentina, in particular Hugo Santillan and Diego Quiroga, saw nothing out of the ordinary but then, they wouldn't have from their locations and positions and it is clear that there was very much a 'second battle' on the periphery of the one which we think we know. In truth, it almost sounds as if the story accepted as fact today was contrived before the battle was fought, and I would not be too surprised if it were the case. General Galtieri could certainly not have gone to the people and announced the capture / recovery of the Islands whilst admitting such severe losses. Instead, it would seem, he- or someone close to him - 'wrote down a victory' to borrow a term from the Duke of Wellington.

The body count is, I suppose irrelevant, although it is certainly an indicator of the toughness of the fighting and I should add that Hugh Bicheno, working as an MI6 agent in Buenos Aires, picked up reports immediately after the invasion of 'dozens of dead' which he has told me himself. He also wrote this in his book 'The Razor's Edge' although, for reasons unknown, it did not appear in the final cut. It was, however, repeated in a limited-run Spanish translation, which he tells me is almost impossible to obtain a copy of now. Speaking of books, one more has come to light which demands some study, and this is the testimony of the nurses in Argentina who were mobilised immediately after the invasion to deal with an unprecedented amount of wounded. They recount their stories faithfully without, one would suppose, any thought to whatever the junta might have said. In all, I think that anyone would agree that the history of April 2nd 1982 is not the one which we, the British or Argentine people, deserve, and whilst the UK government should be asked some very pressing questions about why its heroes have been ignored, I believe that in Argentina, people should start to ask too. I believe, the nurses of the KEMH believe, the people of Stanley believe and the veterans of the Royal Marines believe that more Argentinian men died on that day – and potentially an awful lot more – than are recorded. Personally, I would like to wonder who those men were who died in the course of their duties and in the cause of their country and why they, like the Royal Marines of the NP8901 detachment, are simply erased. These things are not accidents and it is time that all of the men who fought there on that day should be honoured correctly and appropriately. I have stated before and I will do so again, that not one man whom I have interviewed, spoken to, spent time with and corresponded with is a liar and yet their reports have either been muted, hushed or ignored. In Argentina I accept that certain evidence presented here might, at first, be unacceptable and might even cause anger – I hope that it will not. One of the key points of history is to accept all of the evidence against our own bias, what we are told or what we wish to be true. When the only other option to the facts presented are *everyone else is lying* then they become evident. Nobody on either side is lying, and there have been over 300 contributors to this book. Therefore, the truth must remain and, if the junta did cover up losses on April 2nd as everything seems to indicate that they did, it is only right to find out who these men were and to do them justice too. I hope that people in Argentina now begin to ask the difficult questions of their government as the people in the UK should of their own.

Naturally, due to proximity and language barriers, this book slants more towards the British side than the Argentine - this is not intentional - and the book here presented was initially to be from one side until I was fortunate enough to meet with so many of the fascinating Argentine veterans who have made this story what it is. Naturally I would have liked to have spoken with many more of them - time, space and language barriers permitting - however the true injustice is certainly that done to the martial honour of the fighting men of both sides and none more so than the men of the Royal Marines and unashamedly I have to say that ultimately this is 'their story' first and foremost.

In 2017 the campaign began to attempt to gain the men of NP8901 and Endurance their recognition, by way of a simple bar to their South Atlantic Medals stating 'Defence of Stanley' or 'Defence of Grytviken' as appropriate. Operation Corporate was not to be launched for three days after the Falklands invasion and two days after that of South Georgia, which thereby comprise entirely separate actions outside of what we now term 'The Falklands War'. The story was picked up by the Portsmouth News and even by BBC News where Nick Williams represented the Royal Marines in this appeal. It was felt – and hoped – that without admitting to anything, the UK government would want to grant their case a review, in light of new evidence, as was the case with their 'brothers in arms' who fought at Jadotville in such similar circumstances. The reply from the RN as given by Admiral

Parry was that the Royal Marines were lucky to get away with their lives and should be grateful at that; *"We won the match, what does it matter now who scored the goals?"* was the unbelievable answer which these brave men received. Their campaign and petition can still be signed, if the reader would like to Google 'Royal Marines NP8901 Medal Petition' and I hope that they shall feel these brave men worthy of such an award after so long in the shadows. Meanwhile, in Argentina, the Argentine navy has appointed its own Admiral to oversee things since the publication of this book, and I am told that nothing more must be said by anyone unless it is cleared by him first. We, the people of the UK and Argentina, are being hoodwinked on our heroes. It is time that we both begin to ask why. There are some – especially in Argentina – who might treat this story with anything from derision to at least an understandable caution, for April 2nd is of course Veterans Day in Argentina and it may feel that I am somehow taking something away from them. The best I can say is that I have spoken to hundreds of people from three countries, that I continue to do so even today in search of the answers, that nobody here is lying or has cause to, and that, as unpopular as it may be – at least to some – in Argentina, I hope that I am giving a nation back its heroes, as I am also doing in the UK.

One final point I should like to make is just how much of a true privilege it has been to work on this project with these amazing men who fought there that day: both British and Argentine. They are all Marines of one type or another, all experts and professionals doing their jobs, all fantastic people to speak to and work with and now they share a history and – I hope – a new story of which the men themselves can be proud. Not a story of a walk-over, or of a token or nominal defence, but a story of real men at war whose respect for each other has, by and large, grown over the years. I believe that these men deserve their story and that this is merely the first chapter and not the final word, in what they are due. In truth, I believe that all of the men I have met and worked with over these many months deserve that sobriquet first given by my good friend Hugo Santillan to the men of the Royal Marines; *"The finest Marines in the world."*

END

Post War

THE BRITISH

Sir Rex Masterman Hunt was restored to his position as Governor of the Falkland Islands in June 1982 and received several awards in recognition of his brave defence of the Falklands. In 1980 he was created a Companion of the Order of St. Michael and St. George, in 1981 he was made a Freeman of the City of London followed by a knighthood in 1982 and Freeman of Stanley in 1985 when he retired as Governor. In 1987 he was made an Honorary Air Commodore by the RAF and in 1992 he published his memoir 'My Falklands Days'. In 2004 Sir Rex retired as Chairman of the Falkland Islands Association and moved to Elton, County Durham. He died in November 2012 and his funeral was attended by most, if not all, of his veterans. He is still remembered as the most beloved Governor in Falkland Islands history

Mike Norman returned to the Falklands heading J Company 42 Commando (most of his old NP8901 command) as part of Operation Corporate, where he fought in the actions of Mount Kent and Mount Harriet, receiving a mention in dispatches for his skill in leading the assault and finally being accorded the honour of raising the flag once again above Government House which he had defended so valiantly 74 days before. Upon return to the UK he found that none of the men he put forward for decoration for heroic defence of the Falklands was accepted. He wrote a strong letter to Admiral Fieldhouse, offering to hand back his decoration if none of the men he had fought alongside could be accepted for theirs. Ten years after the war, Norman acted as advisor in the television film 'An Ungentlemanly Act' which depicted the story of the defence of the Falklands and in which he also played a cameo role as a member of the FIDF. Mike Norman is lionised by the men of NP8901 and by the Falkland Islanders to this day, all of whom remember his gallant leadership of the defence of the Falkland Islands. In April 2017, Major Mike Norman asked me to lead in the top table at the NP8901 reunion at 42 Commando barracks, Bickleigh. It was, I believe, the highest honour I could receive, to lead these brave men anywhere.

Gareth Noott returned briefly to the Falkland Islands with Operation Corporate before returning to the UK where he sold his house in Devon, did a tour in the RNC Greenwich and relocated to Pembrokeshire in 1984. There he enjoyed village life plus shooting and trout fishing as well as sailing and catching lobsters, crabs and sea fish. For two and a half years (1985-1987) he toured on 'loan service' to the Barbados Defence Force - a much better island, he said, especially for a Jamaican like him (his mother's side of the family was based in Antigua). He retired in December 1992 still a Major and, after retraining, ended up running the finances for an agricultural co-operative near St Davids in Pembrokeshire. He and his wife moved to the Isle of Wight in 2003 where he is now retired.

Geordie Gill returned to the Falklands as part of Recce Troop 40 Commando, utilising his local knowledge and skills as a sniper, including at the battle of Mount Kent. After the war, he completed tours in Northern Ireland, completing a total of ten tours, served in Cyprus as part of the UN Peacekeeping Force and as a UN Observer in Cambodia. Later he joined HMS Protector as part of the South Atlantic Patrol Fleet and finally served in the Gulf War and Operation Haven in Kurdistan. He retired after an incredible 40 years served mostly with 40 Commando and now works for her Majesty's Prison Service. He is, rightly, remembered as one of the great heroes of the battle of Stanley on April 2nd 1982 and, as was said of him, a legend in the Royal Marines.

Nick Williams was asked whether he wanted to go back to the Falklands with the task force. He posed the question to his wife at the time, who threatened to break both his legs if he said yes. Discretion being the better part of valour he stayed at home. He re-joined 45 Commando on their return from the Falklands and resumed his role as a carpenter. He had various postings over the next few years but found it very difficult to settle back into his former life. After a couple of years, he attempted to give up his carpenter's role in the Corps and return to a General Duties role. About two years later, a number of interviews and him being a nuisance, his request was granted. Nick was then employed from 1990 until the end of 1994 in a voluntary operational role in military intelligence. June 1995 Nick retired from the Corps after a full career service having reached the rank of Colour Sergeant. He settled into civilian life, ran his own small carpentry business and became a retained firefighter with the local fire brigade. In 2004 adventure called and he went to Iraq as an armed private security contractor, a role that he enjoyed. Early in 2007 he had a serious motorcycle accident that nearly killed him, it left him partially disabled and unable to work for three years. In 2010 he was offered a job with a small maritime security company as a security trainer and consultant. He was employed training seafarers and port security staff around the world in how to protect themselves from acts of piracy and terrorist attack. The company ceased trading in 2014 due to the downturn in international oil prices. Over the years, he has been involved with many military charities. He has now moved back to his hometown of Bournemouth, lives with his partner Sandy and currently works for the NHS as the manager of the Porter's Department at the Royal Bournemouth Hospital.

Ray Bloye remained on standby during the rest of the Falklands War, waiting for a call which never came. To this day, he cannot understand why he was not called upon to serve alongside his comrades, most of whom had joined J Company 42 Commando. He left the Royal Marines on Christmas Day 1987 after nine and a half years' service. He later joined the Police Force and served in the Hampshire, Kent and Metropolitan Constabularies including as a firearms officer and later moved to St. Helena with his wife Sharan, joining the Constabulary there as a Training and Development Sergeant. Now returned to the UK, he works seasonally as an Immigration Officer for the Channel Tunnel. In 2015, he and Figgy Duff returned to the Falklands where they scattered the ashes of the late Mick Sellen (who sadly passed in 2013) and performed a small private ceremony on the Jason Islands; a place Mick loved so much from his time in the Falklands, when he had toured with his friends, just before the invasion.

Neil 'Figgy' Duff did not return to the Falklands as he was due to be married upon his return from the NP8901 tour. Instead, he and his wife-to-be took their honeymoon as a holiday and went to South Africa, marrying in August 1983. Before he left, he was quizzed extensively by the British senior commanders as he was one of very few (the others being Mick Sellen and Harry Dorey) to have 'yomped' from San Carlos to Stanley during his tours of 'camp' and was able to provide excellent intelligence which was later to aid in the recovery of the Falklands. Returning from South Africa, he became a platoon weapons instructor and finally left the Royal Marines as an SNCO in 1988, serving another 21 years in the police force. In 2015 he returned to the Falklands with Ray Bloye and their families for the aforementioned ceremony to pay his respects to Mick Sellen. He is still remembered in the Falkland Islands as one half of the 'Nick and Fig Show' and also as 'Old Blue Eyes' and, although he denies it strongly, I am assured from several sources that he was the poster-boy of the 81/82 detachment NP8901.

Andy Macdonald returned to the Falklands with 40 Commando, working with Joint Intelligence aboard the SS Canberra and returned with that unit to serve in Northern Ireland after the war. In 1984 he bumped into Neville Bennett outside of a supermarket in Plymouth and Neville apologised that he had had to throw the omelette away that he had made on the night of April 1st. Andy replied that it was okay and that it had probably gone off by now. He still stays in touch with the family. He joined the Police in 1984 and served as a firearms officer, being medically retired in 2003 and moving to Florida where he ran a property management business before returning to the UK in 2008 and working as a bailiff. He has since passed a degree in Biochemistry and is still attending university at the time of writing. Diagnosed with severe PTSD from the events of April 2nd 1982 he maintains he would do it all again. He is still a regular visitor to Stanley where he often gives guided tours around the grounds of Government House and describes the battle on April 2nd. He also never gave up and did eventually find out what happened to his friend Alan Addis – the reason for which he went to Stanley in the first place – although that is quite a different story.

Dave 'Ginge' Gerrard continued in the Royal Marines with a Vehicle Mechanics Class I course and Senior Command Course, being promoted to Sergeant in April of 1984. He then served as Beach Armoured Recovery Vehicle (BARV) Commander for 4th Assault Squadron on HMS Fearless. During a visit to Mayport Naval Base, Florida, he met his future wife, Marsha, whom he married in July 1986. His last draft before leaving the Corps in May 1987 was for the Inspectorate of Motor Transportation, RMR (Royal Marine Reserves) based out of RM Poole. He emigrated to Florida in May 1987 where he now owns 'The English Garage', a British vehicle repair shop, which he has run for the last 22 years. The ginger hair has now, sadly, gone, but Dave still enjoys his role as the 'joker in the pack' of NP8901 to this day and has since challenged Figgy Duff's role as 'Official NP8901 pin-up' recounting how, in the last week of duty in the Falklands, he was asked to present the award to the best-looking girl in Stanley. When he pulled the cord to unveil the photograph of NP8901 81/81' official pin-up, he was confronted with a picture of himself, passed out drunk and entirely naked. Ginge is thereby the 'official' official pin-up of NP8901 81/82 to this day.

Marc Branch returned to the Falklands with J Company 42 Commando and was amongst the first men of 42 Commando to enter Stanley alongside Lt. Bill Trollope and others from the 82/83 NP8901 detachment. Famously – although sadly – he served as a pall bearer for one of the three Falkland Islanders killed in Stanley on the night of April 12-13 by naval shelling. He finally left the Royal Marines as Marine 1st Class in July 1983 after which he spent a brief nine-month spell in the 21st SAS Reserve Regiment. He emigrated to the USA in 1990. Graduating with a degree in Aeronautical Science from Emery Aviation College, Colorado, he has lived for the last 25 years in Michigan and is one of the owner / operators of Universal Aviation and is Type-Rated in multiple jet aircraft. He also co-owns a multimedia business with his photographer wife Yamile. In April 2017 Marc flew all the way from Michigan to Portsmouth for the launch of 'The First Casualty' which is an honour and a credit both to himself and the corps.

Gary 'Bungy' Williams returned to the Falklands where he not only fought through the many battles to Stanley, but also struck up a relationship with a pen-pal whom he would write to from the conflict. Upon his return, he was stationed at RM Poole until September 1985 during which time he married the lady to whom he would write from the war. He was promoted Corporal and joined 42 Commando and was posted to Seaton Barracks in early 1989 for his final six months with the Royal Marines. He later worked for the Boston Consulting Group in Mayfair, London for eleven and a half years before returning to his native

Manchester where he now works for the Prison Service. He has returned to the Falkland Islands several times and has developed a keen interest in wildlife photography.

Graham Evans returned to the Falklands with J Company 42 Commando and finally left the Royal Marines in 1998 as Commandants Driver at CTCRM. He spent ten years with the United States Military Sea-Lift Command as a Security Supervisor and now works as a Barge Master. Graham returns to the Falkland Islands every year to visit family and friends and to pay his respects to the fallen. He is heavily involved in charity work for wounded Royal Marines who require ongoing support and left a detailed diary of his time in the Falklands war.

Danny Betts returned to the Falklands with J Company 42 Commando and fought through to the end of the Falklands War. He later joined a free-fall parachuting display team and an unarmed combat team for the Marines Recruitment branch, finally discharging from the Royal Marines in 1989 and working in several roles (initially wanting to be a deep-sea diver). He now works in HGV Class-1 haulage. He never did get his MGB GT.

Stephen 'George' Brown Returned to the Falklands as part of J Company 42 Commando and headed a mortar team to support 2nd stage operations at Goose Green before fighting his way to Stanley. He went on to have a distinguished career in the Marines, ending as Colour-Sergeant. He later joined the Police Force and now lives in Northern Ireland where he has finally, after decades, re-established contact with Danny Betts as a result of this book.

Michael 'Burt' Reynolds returned to the Falklands with J Company 42 Commando. On Mount Kent, he was flown out due to a recurring injury and narrowly avoided being on the Sir Galahad. He was on board HMS Hydra when the war ended. He later served in the Royal Marines' unarmed combat team and also its free-fall team, which broke world records and won both the British and European championships. Upon leaving the Royal Marines, he worked as a stuntman on such films as Tumbledown, Queen and Country and Air America and later returned to college, set up a security company working with high profile clients and now runs a property portfolio.

David 'Lou' Armour returned to the Falklands as part of J Company 42 Commando, reinforced the 2nd stage attack at Goose Green and fought through Mount Kent and Mount Harriet to the end of the war. He was discharged from the Royal Marines in November 1986 with the rank of Sergeant. His discharge carried with it the words 'exemplary' and 'a cheerful, energetic man who will be missed' – all true words. His photograph, with SLR aloft being escorted by a black-clad Argentine with a sub machinegun has become one of the most iconic pictures of April 2nd 1982 and he has given a number of talks about his experiences on that day. He now works with people with autism and additional support needs and has a doctorate in the subject, and currently also stars in a popular dramatic production 'Minefield' – a tale of reconciliation about the Falklands war - alongside Argentine veterans, which recently finished touring in Argentina with the cast, where the play was a major success. He remains to this day one of the most popular veterans of the Falklands war on either side.

Jim Fairfield returned home to his family in Stanley and was active in espionage during the remainder of the Falklands War, after which he was – as a civilian – awarded the British Empire Medal for his actions: the only man of the Royal Marines force to be decorated for bravery. When Rex Hunt presented the award, Jim said that he hoped the other NP8901 members would in time receive their own medals as per Mike Norman's recommendations; *"They bloody should do."* Hunt whispered quietly: Jim got the message. He later returned to the UK where, at his wife Michelle's encouragement in dealing with PTSD, wrote a fantastic personal memoir which I have been fortunate enough to have been able to use in recounting his tale. Jim recorded his experiences on YouTube in 2017 under 'My Falklands War Story' which is a goldmine of information covering everything from life in the Falklands through to the invasion, occupation and liberation, which is well recommended. He now works as an Enforcement Officer in the Environmental Directorate and has a passion for foreign travel and vegetable gardening. In April 2017, at the cajoling of myself and his wonderful wife Michelle, Jim attended his first NP8901 reunion. He swears he will never miss another.

Richard 'Dick' Overall spent a brief spell as a prisoner of war in Argentina along with the other men of Section Four before being repatriated back to the UK. After a brief period of leave, he joined Mike Norman's J Company 42 Commando and returned to the Falklands, fighting at the battle of Mount Harriet through to the liberation of Stanley. After several more years' service with the Royal Marines, he joined West Midlands Police dealing with serious assaults and later relocated to Avon and Somerset Constabulary, where he retired having been awarded three commendations. He now lives in West Somerset and enjoys sea fishing and trail biking.

Chris Todhunter managed to slip away immediately after the fall of GH, taking off his combat jacket and acting as a civilian. He destroyed many of the surveys made by his hydrographic team before they fell into Argentine hands (until caught by Major Dowling) and was later repatriated with the Marines and civilian staff. Upon his return, he contacted Rosemary, the lady he had met in Madeira. He told her he was safe. She asked if there was any reason he shouldn't be. It transpired she had not even heard of the battle in the Falkland Islands and had not been aware of his part in the defence. Todhunter returned as part of Operation Corporate aboard the destroyer HMS Antrim where his experience in surveying the area was critical in the retaking of South Georgia as he personally led the SBS in by boat through the ice floes by night. He then re-joined HMS Endurance. Returning to the UK in late August 1982 he at once proposed to Rosemary (who had joined him) and they were married in St Paul's Cathedral (where he once sang as a choir boy). He worked as a surveyor then rose to become Director of Legal Services for Cable & Wireless Marine. He now writes naval action-adventure stories of which his first book *Maelstrom* was published in 2011 followed by *The Cyclops Ransom, In the shade of a Willow* and several others, all to great acclaim.

Bill Muir returned to the Falklands as part of J Company 42 Commando, fighting in the battles of Goose Green, Mount Kent and Mount Harriet and into Stanley where he witnessed the final Argentine surrender. As a reward from Major General Jeremy Moore, he was accorded the honour of raising the Union Jack back over Government House, just 74 days after the first shot had been fired. He held several directorate positions in social care and housing upon leaving the Royal Marines and spoke to the press only in 2014 upon the 350th anniversary of the forming of the Royal Marines. He is now retired and lives in Letham, in his native Scotland. He is considered as one of the great heroes of the action – although he is still most fondly remembered for his contemptuous reply to Diego Quiroga's calls to surrender which were immortalised in the film 'An Ungentlemanly Act'. The Royal Marines remember him as an excellent leader and a model soldier.

THE ARGENTINES

Carlos Busser was appointed Chairman of the Joint Chiefs of Staff after the War, a position he held until his retirement in December 1983. Throughout the mid-late 1980's he published two notable works on the Falklands conflict and enjoyed his retirement until 2009 when he was placed under house arrest for human rights abuses committed in Bahia Blanca during the 'Dirty war' of the 1970's. It was a sad postscript to the career of a man universally liked and admired including by his erstwhile enemies. He died of a heart attack in September 2012 aged 84. He is still remembered as courteous, humorous, considerate and an excellent leader of his men.

Alfredo Weinstabl returned to Argentina with the BIM2 on April 3rd where his battalion went into standby in Tierra del Fuego to deter any potential military involvement from Chile and to coordinate the defence of the Rio Grande Naval Air Base. The BIM2 were on constant alert and patrol and spent the duration of the Falklands War on 4-hour notice to depart once again for the Falklands. The opportunity never came. Weinstabl retired from active service at the end of 1989 as a Marine Captain (Colonel) and was immediately hired by Hoeschst Argentina (a German multinational company) as a security advisor for two years. Later he created a private security firm in which he held the position of partner manager for ten years. In the meantime, he was a member of the Argentine Security and Investigation Chamber, working as President for Institutional Affairs, Arbitral and Ethics Tribunal and head of Training Courses. For several years Weinstabl was a member of the Directorial Board of the 'Unity for Argentines Association' (AUNAR), an association formed with the purpose of pacifying and achieving the unity of all Argentinians and to heal the wounds produced by the revolutionary war of the decade of the 1970's. He remains as popular with his men today, still attending BIM2 reunions and, despite advancing years, has lost little of his 'movie-star' image.

Hugo Jorge Santillan recovered quickly from his foot injury and returned home to his wife Ana María, his childhood sweetheart. He and his 2nd Marine Battalion were deployed in Tierra del Fuego for the duration of the conflict. In 1983 he graduated from the Argentine Naval War College. The following year he was appointed to command a Security Marine Battalion stationed at the Argentine Navy Headquarters. In 1985 he was selected as Aide de Camp to the Chief of the Argentine Navy. Two years later he graduated from the Command and Staff College, United States Marine Corps. Later, with the rank of Commander, he lectured on Landing Force Operations at the Argentine Naval War College. In 1990 he was the Commanding Officer of the 3rd Marine Battalion and, after serving at the Argentine Navy HQ and in joint activities in Buenos Aires, he was promoted to Captain in 1992. During 1994 he held the position of Chief of Staff, Argentine Marine Corps Command. In 1995 he was placed in command of the Landing Force, Argentine Fleet and in 1996 he became the Commanding Officer of the Argentine Marine Corps Base. For two years, he held the office of the Argentine Naval, Military and Air Attaché to the Embassy of Argentina in Pretoria, Republic of South Africa (meeting Royal Navy Commander Andrew Auld, the Commanding Officer of a Sea Harrier squadron during the Falklands conflict). His last active duty post was as Executive Director of the Central Naval Hospital at Buenos Aires. He retired on 1st September 2000. The same day he was appointed as Director of Liceo Naval Militar 'Almirante Guillermo Brown', the Argentine Navy's famous secondary school and reserve naval officers' academy. In 2008 he was under contract to a private engineering and technology company until the end of 2015. Now retired he is very handy on the golf course and, as a keen historian, is researching and writing about the Paraguayan War. In the UK, as a result of "The First Casualty" he is considered something of a celebrity and remains a close friend of the author.

Guillermo Sanchez Sabarots retired from active duty on September 1996 as a full Navy Captain, settling in Buenos Aires to work in electronic security. Some years later he held the position of Security Director, Argentine Post Office (with the British Post Office as a partner). In 2004 he worked in security management of the

Santander Bank Group of Argentina. Later he took a part-time job as bank security advisor for Banco Industrial and at 73, is still working.

Mohamed Ali Seineldin stayed in the Falklands with the 25th Infantry Regiment, leading them to capture Goose Green and Darwin and later serving with great bravery in the opening battles of the war where he fought to impede the British landings, being noted for always leading from the front. Repatriated to Argentina after the final surrender, he was promoted to full Colonel in 1984 and served as Military Attaché to Panama throughout 1985-1986 where he helped reorganise the Panamanian armed forces of General Noriega, staying on at the end of his appointment. During his absence, Seineldin became frustrated at the witch-hunt of army personnel involved in the 'Dirty War' as well as the Argentine government's leanings towards the USA - which he considered something of a 'New World Order' - and slipping back into Argentina in 1988, became involved in several armed uprisings, for which he was arrested but later discharged. In 1990 Seineldin led a major uprising, seizing an army barracks and enduring a bloody 60-day siege until forced to surrender. Accepting full responsibility for the uprising and resulting deaths, Seineldin was tried and convicted by a military court and sentenced to life imprisonment. In 2003 after massed protests from the 'Free Seineldin' movement, which included many thousands of veterans, President Duhalde granted him pardon and he lived a more politically quiet existence, becoming a supervisor for a private security company and becoming a partner in a small agricultural business. He died of a heart attack in Buenos Aires in September 2009 aged 75. He is considered a national hero.

Alfredo Raul Cufre escorted the Royal Marines to Montevideo and then returned to his base at Mar del Plata. He was to have his left leg in plaster twice more; once shortly after the war in an accident which left him requiring an amputation. Luckily, he recovered after extensive surgery in the United States, only to break it again in 2007 after falling from a ladder pruning a branch in his garden. After his military service, cut short by his injury, he became a factory manager. He is outspoken upon the dead of the Falklands (in particular April 2nd) being remembered for their service, and often quotes the ruin of ancient Carthage as a case that such sacrifice should not be forgotten.

Bernardo Schweizer accompanied the body of Pedro Giachino back to Argentina immediately after operation Rosario. He rose through the ranks to full Captain and in 2006-2007 was in Haiti as part of the UN Peacekeeping Force there. Upon his return to Buenos Aires in January 2007 he was arrested and imprisoned for ninety days after an email he had sent was intercepted. In it, he had denigrated President Nestor Kirchner and criticised the official policy of the Argentine armed forces. Rightly, this reaction to his email caused a national outrage, particularly amongst Argentine veterans of the war who considered his treatment disgraceful.

He was still, however, forcibly retired aged forty-eight, left Argentina and is now head of his own International Coaching Consultancy in Mexico City. He is still honoured by the veterans and people of Argentina as the first man to have set foot on the Falkland Islands.

Carlos Cequiera returned to Argentina after April 2nd and went back to his former post, the Marine Corps Non-Commissioned School. In the first half of 1983, as a Marine junior NCO, Cequeira attended a course to get a promotion to become a senior NCO and between 1984-1985 he trained to become a Marine officer where he graduated as a Lieutenant. Marine Lieutenant Cequeira was posted at the Agrupación de Commandos Anfibios during 1988-1989; in 1990-1991 he was Delta Company Commander at the Puerto Belgrano Naval Base Security Battalion. After two years of training he became a Military Photo Interpreter and the following year, graduated as a Naval Intelligence Officer and was transferred as N-2 to Agrupación de Commandos Anfibios. In 1999, he joined the United Nations Task Force XIII at Cyprus as Camp Roca's executive officer, being promoted in 2001 to Lieutenant Commander and transferred as N-2 for four years to Área Naval Austral in Ushuaia, Tierra del Fuego. In 2005, he was the N-2 at the Marine Force Command in Río Grande, Tierra del Fuego. From 2006 to 2009 he went to the Marine Corps Non-Commissioned School. In 2009, he returned to Ushuaia as Special Affairs Officer and his family is currently settled in Ushuaia where, as a serving officer, he is currently attending the Special Staff Course.

Daniel Tosolini returned to Argentina with the BIM2 and on July 7th 1982, after hoisting the national flag on the 2nd Marine Battalion parade ground, Marine Rifleman Daniel Tosolini ended his military service. When he arrived in his home in Ramos Mejía (Province of Buenos Aires) he was greeted as a hero. The following week he started to work with his father, driving a small freight delivery truck and in April 1984 he opened his own store; he still runs it today. Daniel is a very active member of the Malvinas Veteran Association, beginning with an invitation to a radio program 'Malvinas: it's time to come back home' and he has since participated in several radio programs dealing with the subject of the Islands. He currently participates in various media and social nets sharing some of his writings and pictures regarding his involvement in the war. Thirty-four years after the feat, Tosolini proudly took part in the military parade that was held at Buenos Aires to celebrate Argentina's bicentennial as an independent nation. In 2016 Tosolini, together with movie maker Sandro Rojas Filártiga, began shooting a film based on the events of April 2nd 1982.

Horacio Tello left the BIM2 in 1982 after the war but as a veteran, found it hard to reintegrate into society and mainstream employment; a challenge faced by so many VGM's in the period which followed the Argentine defeat. Applying for numerous roles, as soon as he stated that he was a veteran, he was told 'We will call you'. They never did. Today, he has a large family and works in a group of families as surrogate parents and support for children at risk, visiting community centres and providing for children who do not have the basic essentials. Disinterested in 'living off of his medals', Horacio Tello dedicates himself to good causes and believes that he was saved from a worse fate on April 2nd to serve a higher purpose. He is still remembered – be it correct or not - as the first man on either side to be wounded in the Falklands War.

Ernesto Urbina was taken back to Argentina where he recovered in hospital for two months. Upon discharge, he resumed his duties and left the navy in 1984. He worked as a nurse in Punta Alta for many years and now owns a taxi company. Thirty-three years after the war, he met Elsa Rhodes: a fellow nurse whom he had worked alongside in Puerto Belgrano Naval Hospital before the war. When they parted, she had given him a lucky charm – an owl feather which, per Aboriginal legend, gave the bearer good luck, health and protection. Upon meeting her, Urbina at once produced the feather from his wallet where he had kept it for more than three decades and announced that it was more important to him than all his medals. They are now married. Urbina is still a great supporter of veterans' rights in Argentina and is considered a national hero even though he insists that he is not; he was just doing his job, he says, and the bullets of the English did not let him finish. He still proudly shows the scars of the three bullets which struck him.

Diego Garcia Quiroga survived his appalling wounds after three consecutive operations. It took him many months to recover completely, especially from the bullet which had torn into his liver, by which time the war was over. During his recovery, Diego was hailed and decorated as a national hero – to this day, he believes, humbly, that it is undeserved in light of braver people who were to die later in the Falklands War. Upon returning to his unit in November 1982 he made a few parachute jumps to leave his comrades in no doubt about his recovery, but his active military career was effectively ended by the damage to his arm. He and Alejandra divorced but in 2007 he met his current wife Beate', a Norwegian diplomat who was posted to Buenos Aires, by which time he had risen to the rank of Commander in the Navy. He retired in 1999 and moved with his wife's job, first to Switzerland, then Oslo and most recently Santiago in Chile. He is a great campaigner for veterans with PTSD. Upon his travels, he met Rex and Mavis Hunt (whom he apologised to for crushing her roses), is on very good terms with Mike Norman and even met Baroness Thatcher in the Imperial War Museum, London; where they talked for some time, laughed together and on parting, she put her hand on his arm, lent towards him and said; *"Diego, I am so very, very glad we didn't kill you."* - It is a sentiment I have shared with this wonderful man many times.

Pedro Giachino died as a result of several wounds, the most serious – and fatal - being the bullet which cut his femoral artery. He died of blood loss. He was returned to Argentina for burial with honours in the Pantheon of Puerto Belgrano where he was posthumously promoted to Commander and awarded the Cross of Heroic Valour in Combat: Argentina's highest military decoration. His citation read; *"As Head of a small force of troops during recovery actions in the Falkland Islands, he led the final assault facing an enemy group and despite being seriously wounded continued giving orders and avoided being taken prisoner making, despite his life, his subordinates operate decisively in the conquest of the assigned target, fulfilling the order not to produce casualties on the enemy, even at the cost of his own life."* Later his remains were transferred to Cemetery Hill in Mar del Plata where his wife Cristina and his family lived. On April 3rd 1998 he was proclaimed a National Hero of the Argentine Republic by an act of law. His final words – a matter of record in Argentina – were sadly an invention on behalf of one of the nurses of KEMH to whom his mother had written, hoping that he had died well. In truth, with blood loss, he had already passed out and went quietly in his sleep, despite the best efforts of the KEMH staff to keep him alive. In 2011 Giachino's reputation was brought into some disrepute with numerous charges of torture and execution during the 'Dirty War'. It was a sad final epitaph to a man who was undoubtedly a fine Marine, a skilled tactician, an excellent combat officer and a leader of men, who surely would have risen much further. Today he is remembered not only as a National Hero but as the first casualty of the Falklands War.

Notes by Chapter

Chapter 1 - "Guilt, Complicity and shame"

    1 – The Arana-Southern Treaty or Convention of Settlement was signed on November 24th 1849 and ratified on May 5th 1850. The overriding clause governing the treaty was that; *'the treaty of peace leaves everything in the state in which it found it unless there is some express stipulation to the contrary. The existing state of possession is maintained except so far as altered by the terms of the treaty. If nothing is said about the conquered country or places, they remain with the conqueror and is title cannot afterwards be called into question.'* Although the treaty was significant political victory for Argentina, it is evident that, knowingly or not, the Argentine claim to the Falklands had indeed been signed away and indeed, with Argentine President Rosas having already offered to abandon his claim in return for the abolishment of certain debts to Baring's bank (which was not agreed to, since it was considered in Britain that his claim was baseless) it was considered that the matter was certainly in his mind, and that he did not simply forget it. When Rosas questioned afterwards if he had indeed just signed away the Argentine claim, Lord Palmerston replied that; *"I understand the matter to be exactly as described to me in your letters"* – in short, that Rosas had freely given it up, by his own admission. It is interesting to note, however, that the matter of the Falklands' sovereignty was not to be raised again in the Argentine Congress until 1941, nor was there a single official protest from Argentina from this time until 1946. Small wonder that the UK had considered the matter settled throughout that time.

    2 - This is an incredibly truncated version of Falkland Islands history and indeed almost every point of note (or even term of phrase) is contested in one form or another. In this sense, I have attempted to restrict the outline history to key dates and by a general rule of what is known, without any attempt to resolve the larger issues, upon which there is an abundance of material although, as ever, most sources disagree upon most points. The moves to counter the first Argentine incursions into the South Atlantic and Antarctic dependencies came as part of 'Operation Tabarin' which is worth looking up, and which saw the first exchange of fire in the region. It was due to this that the UK invited Argentina to attend the International Court of Justice to arbitrate on the Falkland Islands Dependencies, and which ultimately led to the signing of the Antarctic Treaty. As to Peron, it is worthy of note that he took what was at best an old and largely forgotten gripe and fanned the flames to create a national cause. When asked by British diplomat

Bill Hunter-Christie why he was now stirring up a question almost a hundred years after it was considered settled, Peron laughed and told him that it was useful to unite the people. For a fuller account of the entire Falklands sovereignty dispute, the reader could do no better than to consult the Falklands Timeline by the peerless Falklands historian Roger Lorton.

3 – Again without dwelling too deeply into the 'political question', this bone of contention still rages today. In 1961, the Falklands might very well, of course, have been termed a 'colony'. Decolonisation was seen by many (including the UK) as a good thing but many smaller states simply did not have the wish, the interest or the means to become independent countries and did not like the insistence that they had to. This stance is mirrored by many British, American, French and New Zealand former colonies and dependencies even today. The matter of decolonisation itself is today, somewhat outmoded, for the UN itself states that; *"There are no more colonies"* however, despite an outdated name, the commission seeks to provide a roadmap to independence or any other political future as desired by the peoples of these territories. In 2013 the Falkland Islands voted by 99.8% to remain a self-governing British Overseas Territory. The result, however, is not recognised in Argentina.

4 – In giving this history from all sides evenly, it is only correct that the viewpoint of the Falkland Islanders be represented as they saw it, and to remind the reader that the Falklands were not just land being fought over, but these people's homes and their country. Hopefully this will also provide an objective and balanced reader with a better insight into the Islanders' perspective, again without an attempt to resolve any of the deeper cultural or political issues, although anyone would agree that the position they had been placed in by both the UK and Argentina was a desperate one which simply should never have occurred.

5 – 'Operation Condor' was led by journalist and activist Dardo Cabo (who had come equipped to write the story of the 'recovery' of the Islands) and a gang of scrap metal trade unionists. Although the plan seemed (and indeed was) farcical, yet it almost achieved Cabo's aims as, when news of the operation reached Argentina, large crowds gathered and urged the junta to follow up with an armed invasion to support them which, given the limited timescales, was naturally impossible, whatever the intent. The 'condom-toting blonde' was Cabo's lover, 27-year-old Maria Cristina Verrier, a journalist and playwright who was also Cabo's second in command. Only three of the hijackers received sentences for the incident and Cabo and Verrier married whilst Cabo was still in prison. Dardo Cabo was murdered in January 1977 as a subversive whilst Maria Cristina Verrier was honoured as a national hero in 2006 by Argentine President Cristina Fernandez de Kirchner. The condom story, although widespread, may of course be apocryphal.

6 - Hugh Bicheno served in British Intelligence in Buenos Aires throughout the Falklands War. He is married to an Argentine, is bilingual and refers to Argentina as his 'second home.' His book *'The Razor's Edge'* is an excellent read in which he is (rightfully) damning to both the British Government and Foreign and Commonwealth Office and also the Argentine Government.

7 – It is fair to say that the 'Communications Agreement' of 1971 was one of the most heinous and cowardly sell-outs of a people by its mother country ever witnessed. Argentina can hardly be blamed at this stage for taking advantage of such weak-kneed diplomacy.

8 – Operation 'Journeyman' – Callaghan's mission to send Royal Navy warships to the South Sandwich Islands – has been given far more credit (especially by his former Foreign Secretary, Lord Owen) than it deserved. Indeed, it was only launched when the Argentine base was accidentally discovered and made known publicly. Callaghan's government had been aware of it but had tried to keep it a secret, thinking that any diplomatic response would damage the process of dialogue over the Falkland Islands. In the end, it achieved nothing, and the files on it were only released in 2005. Additionally, Admiral Anaya's report referred to the British as 'Maricones' which, in the sense in which he used it, could translate as 'unmanly' or 'lacking in moral fortitude' and one can hardly help but agree with his observation on many points, including those just made above.

9 – The Falkland Islanders had actually been intrigued as to the leaseback proposal provided that, following the set period, they would be granted the same rights of self-determination as they were entitled to under the UN Charter – in short, a referendum on their nationality after the specified time frame – Argentina refused this point-blank and therefore the freeze option was voted for.

10 – It is almost impossible to think that the British Government did not know that an invasion was – or at least could be – coming. It seems that the Falkland Islanders were as good as told outright in New York that the Islands would be invaded in March or April. Robert Fox's book *'Eyewitness Falklands'* deals with some of these points in more depth. Certainly, this is something to which someone should have been aware and there are many (including the Royal Marines of NP8901) who believe firmly that the British Government did know that they were coming. Rex Hunt, it seems, did not.

Chapter 2 - "Azul"

1 – It should be understood that, unlike most of the world's armed forces, those of Argentina under the junta were largely independent of each other and each served its own 'master'. This would later cause some issues during the planning and execution of the operation. Anecdotally, there were, in fact, Argentine invasion plans dating back to the early 1940's which had considered the use of a number of heavy warships for the task, but these had been scrapped as impractical and the plans from 1976 were at least based upon a more modern mode of warfare.

2 – Amongst other nations on his cleverly contrived 'charm offensive', Galtieri had made overtures to almost all of the South American states barring Chile, to Cuba, Libya, Lebanon, Israel, Russia, France, Spain and was convinced through his agents that the American Department of Defense, most of whom were Latino, would be in his corner. His last act in this securing of international support was when he managed to secure Uruguayan neutrality in early March 1982. As to planned dates for the invasion, there is room for conjecture. Lombardo's orders on December 22nd stated that preparations must be completed by June 1st 1982. The following day, these changed and stated March 31st although it seems this was kept a secret and most authorities stuck with the idea of September 15th, for whatever reasons. Ultimately, the sudden change to March 1982 from the original date of September was to be one of the most critical of the war and, ultimately, was to seal Argentina's fate. If the UK had sold both *Hermes* and *Invincible* and had scrapped HMS *Endurance* too, as it planned, it could have mounted no effective response to the Argentine invasion. By any stretch of the imagination, such a change of so critical a date was almost criminally inept and could only reflect the dire straits of the junta, who needed a victory to galvanise the people as soon as possible. In fact, Galtieri barely managed to survive an attempt to overthrow him on March 29th just one day after he finally launched the task force to capture the Falklands, when 50,000 people marched against him. There were scenes of brutal street fighting and over 1,000 arrests were made, with the violence not stopping until the following day. It was evident that he did not have long left in power and would have to find some common cause to appease the people, and there are suggestions that the junta had known about a popular uprising being planned for at least 45 days before it happened. Small wonder that the invasion date was suddenly brought forward as it was.

3 – Alfredo Weinstabl, known in the Argentine navy as *'El Aleman'* – 'The German' - was new to the battalion and it is interesting to record the respective thoughts, opinions and impressions of the two senior officers upon his appointment. Weinstabl had served under Hugo Santillan's father, Hugo Norberto Santillan, Commander of the BIM2 as a fresh Midshipman and had found him a severe task-master but a friendly man of great humour. He had also had two other Santillan brothers, Haroldo and Hector serve under his command and, although he had met Hugo briefly a couple of times and had heard excellent reports of him, was afraid (in his own words) of Hugo being *'the black sheep of the family'* an impression which he later happily found out not to be the case. For his part, Hugo Santillan was very confident in Weinstabl's appointment and considered him by

reputation as *'an able and dedicated Marine, a sound staff officer and an aggressive Commando Anfibio'* although it is fair to say that he had a reputation to match. Part John Wayne and part Steve McQueen, Weinstabl was tall, broad-shouldered, confident and something of a celebrity. Certainly, this did not affect what was by all accounts an excellent and highly successful career and he did not disappoint when on exercise. Hugo Santillan also recounts that upon meeting, and when Weinstabl first told him of the mission, the pair toasted the venture with a glass of whisky at nine o'clock in the morning! As to the training, there is an accepted piece of war footage and official photographs of the BIM2 landing in the Falklands, however these were actually taken during exercise in Patagonia as confirmed by Hugo Santillan. There was no room, he assures me, for any film cameras during the invasion. This footage is still, however, accepted as 'real time' invasion film, which it was not.

4 – This may again have been Admiral Jorge Fraga, although several sources state that it was repeated by several men and on several occasions. Doubtless it was repeated by someone and became a popular running-joke.

5 – Busser's actual words were; *"If we invite the army, they will have to be given an honourable part to play, so let's give them the chance to seize Government House and take the Governor's surrender."* To which he added; *"The air force is going to fly in behind...they also need representing."* The Argentine navy was thus forced to compromise on what was effectively their operation.

6 – As per the initial plan, Cufre was supposed to be the first although this did not transpire to be the case in the final execution of the plan.

7 – Giachino's original mission had been to seize the Governor, Rex Hunt. This now being (at least for the time) a task allotted to the army, his role had changed to the seizure of the power station, cable & wireless, police station, radio station and other important government buildings. For convenience, I have kept the narrative simple, as ultimately it was to be Giachino's party who did attack Government House.

8 – This was said to British writer and historian Martin Middlebrook. Middlebrook was the first British historian allowed to interview the Argentine veterans and his mission and his results have been invaluable. However, it should be noted that the Argentines interviewed were all still serving and that the interviews were – as has been told to me by several people - very organised and orchestrated by the Argentine Navy. There was certainly a strong element of 'get it right' I am told, and many of the interviewees felt a little unnatural, constrained and without any latitude to expand upon points. Middlebrook did a fabulous job, however it is evident that more accurate and descriptive intelligence can be gained now that these men, once serving officers, are retired.

9 – In his memoirs of the operation, Admiral Busser records that it was he who first stated this. It is evident that he did not. His words were; *"Our intelligence on patterns of the conduct of British troops indicated that they surrender only if on the return to Britain they can prove they have fought valiantly, and evidenced by recounting casualties suffered by the enemy before they surrendered."* The words of Hugo Santillan and Busser's own surprise that the Royal Marines did indeed fight against such odds show that he pretty much 'borrowed' Hugo Santillan's words for his memoir and quoted them verbatim.

10 – In fact, according to Diego Quiroga, all that Giachino's squad was left with was a photograph of the inside of one of the rooms at Government House taken during a cocktail reception which was almost completely useless to the men. Despite all of the gathered intelligence, they actually went in almost completely blind.

Chapter 3 - "Three Little Birds"

1 – Royal Marine 'nick-names' are a Corps tradition dating back hundreds of years in many cases which, to the outsider, might cause some confusion. Typically, each man's surname was tied to an automatic 'Royal Marine name' such as 'Chalky' White or 'Bungy' Williams. There were, in fact two 'Bungy' Williams' in the force which defended the Falklands – Gary and Nick, and at least two named 'Scouse' – those being Dave Morris and Dave Carr.

2 – Major Gareth Noott, an old friend of Mike Norman's might well have added a good word here as he played hockey with York and knew him quite well. Incidentally, regarding Lou Armour, nobody seemed to know where he acquired the name 'Lou' from – a name he still goes by today – until I asked him myself. A platoon weapons instructor, Lou was famed for volunteering for everything and anything, including parachute jumps, so that his mates all thought he was a bit crazy. The term 'Loopy Lou' was coined for him and eventually became just 'Lou.'

3 – *'Booties'* was short for *'Bootnecks'* – an age-old term used by the Royal Marines to refer to themselves. The term *'Hobbits'* was in use for Falkland Islanders prior to the war but evolved after the conflict into the much less popular *'Benny'* – given by the mass of newly-arrived soldiers, after the TV character Benny Hawkins from the series 'Crossroads' due to their style of dress. After a number of complaints, the British military banned the use of the term *'Bennies'* and the name evolved quickly into *'Stills'* – when this was questioned it was explained that although the term was banned, the Islanders were *'still Benny'* - at the time it was considered very rude and somewhat ignorant, although most Falkland Islanders tend to laugh at the joke which, thankfully, has died out now and is not encouraged in a more politically correct age. Incidentally, those who have read former editions of this book will notice the word *'Marines'* changed for what it should properly be - *'Royals'* - a *faux pas* which I am only too happy to correct.

4 - The new NP8901 detachment certainly found the outgoing detachment as 'native' as had been feared. Mike Norman and Bill Muir were overheard 'grumbling' as I am told, about the condition they found them in, with long hair, moustaches and earrings in particular. Royal Marine Dick Overall recalls meeting Geordie Gill after a few years and thinking, *"That's not the Geordie Gill I know!"*

5 – The 22-man South Georgia detachment reached the 800-mile distant island three days later on March 24th and immediately deployed for a full combat operation to arrest or otherwise take out the Argentine landing force that night. They reported back the presence of Argentine Marines and were prepared to move in under darkness when messages from London halted the operation, fearing to provoke an incident. It is often repeated that the UK made an excuse of the episode at South Georgia to somehow force Argentina into a war. The telegrams from London to HMS Endurance and then on to Lt. Keith Mills show that the UK still hoped for a peaceful solution and was desperate to avoid a conflict even at this late stage. Had the UK wanted to start a war, allowing the attack to commence would certainly have provided the excuse. The fact that it was not optioned, and the insistence of the UK to not provoke Argentina in any way, shows this assertion that the UK somehow provoked the war with Argentina to be false.

6 - Noott was not being paranoid and neither were the Falkland Islanders. The incidents here mentioned cover just a few strange happenings over this time which increased in regularity between December 1981 and April 1982. In a small community where everybody knew everybody there were strange happenings, strange faces in town, strange lights, noises, sightings and evidence of people coming and going. Much of this – although not perhaps all - can be attributed to the Argentine campaign now known as *'la Mentira de las Malvinas'* – the Lie of the Falklands - which gradually ramped up its intelligence gathering and covert activities as the date of the invasion grew nearer. The Argentine intelligence-gathering campaign prior to the invasion was an exceptional piece of work by any standard, and Falkland Islanders were afterwards treated to full files on themselves from the information provided through LADE and their identification documents of anything from their trips overseas to the names, addresses and occupations of family members in the UK and elsewhere. One new issue which should be raised is as to exactly how much Mike Norman knew about the impending invasion. Gary Williams, who had served on NP8901 previously, thought it incredibly odd that Norman was called to headquarters on an almost daily basis prior to departure, which never normally happened, and Royal Marine Mark Gibbs recorded in 2017 in an interview for the BBC that Norman absolutely told the detachment that an invasion was imminent and asked if any man wanted to drop

out now. Of course, none did. Whilst Mike Norman maintains to me that he did not know about the incredibly high risk of an invasion, yet perhaps there are things he could not say which may – or may not – be revealed in his own memoir which at present is in the process of being published.

7 – In fact, Stephen 'George' Brown distinctly remembers the incident. The men of the new detachment were kept busy 'chipping and repainting' the ship to keep them occupied (for technical reasons, they had had to enlist as crew of the ship, so this was a way to make them useful whilst on board) when the Argentine aircraft flew overhead. On its last pass, the Royal Marines – taking their lead from Lou Armour who began the movement - lined up, dropped their trousers and 'mooned' their behinds at it, after which, it seems, the pilots got the message.

8 – Andy Macdonald is often described as 'the odd man out' in the 81/82 NP8901 detachment and perhaps for good reasons. When he had first signed up for NP8901 duty, he had done so to covertly investigate the disappearance of a fellow Royal Marine, Alan Addis, who had disappeared in the Falklands under suspicious circumstances. The detachment was full with Corporals, and so he had taken a demotion to regular Marine, just to get there, putting his trade as administrator, which he was not. He often lived amongst the Falkland Islanders as opposed to in Moody Brook, to pick up local gossip, and didn't always mix with the other Royals, although he was always close with Colin 'Tiny' Jones amongst a select few others. Tiny still calls him by his nickname of 'Highlander' although Andy is actually from Dundee. Andy calls Tiny far worse.

Chapter 4 - "April Fools"

1 – Many from the British military still consider the SLR to be the best weapon they had, even up to modern times. The Argentine forces were mostly armed with the almost-identical FAL which differed in a lighter construction, a folding stock in some versions and a full-auto option. The heavy recoil of the weapon made automatic fire incredibly inaccurate, however, and gave the rifle a tendency to 'kick up' and fire high as well as being prone to jamming and quickly expending the 20-round magazine in just a few seconds. There was, I am assured 'the old matchstick trick' which could make an SLR fire of fully-auto, although it was not in common practice, and the SLR was by far a more effective weapon.

2 – Curiously, Royal Marine Corporal Steve Black, based on watch on Sapper Hill did indeed see what he firmly believed to be a nuclear submarine surface to the south just as it was getting dark and it was also seen by several Falkland Islanders in the same location. He radioed the contact in to GH but it seems he was either ignored or nothing was done about it.

3 – April 1st 1982 was ironically also Andy Timms' 20th birthday.

4 - Wilcox and Milne were part of Neil 'Figgy' Duff's Section Five and designated as '5A' and it was Figgy who chose them to be on the beach as they could ride motorbikes. He remembers it as one of the hardest decisions he has ever had to make as he felt, as did many, that it was effectively a suicide mission.

5 – There is some conjecture as to whether Wilcox and Milne had one GPMG between them or one each. Today it is still the matter of friendly debate between several of the Marines, especially Nick Williams and Ray Bloye. Considering that a GPMG was effectively a 'two-man-job' I believe it to have been one between them and have narrated it as such.

6 – Andy Macdonald had previously escorted the diplomatic bag to Buenos Aires and had been arrested on two consecutive nights by junta officials. On the second occasion, he was taken to a room and shown a man, tied to a chair and being repeatedly punched, evidently as some kind of threat or warning. Claiming to be an officer, he was released.

7 – Harold Bennett, a relative of Neville and Valerie, had just retired and was the Falklands' leading legal expert. Following the invasion, he was drafted by the Argentine military to draw up the legal documentation to officially change the name of the Islands to 'Malvinas' and the capital to 'Puerto Argentino'. He dragged his feet over the process intentionally and the war was finished before the paperwork was completed. Despite the terms being in common use in Argentina and Latin America today, they hold no legal title only thanks to Harold Bennett's deliberate stalling.

8 – Whether they were in fact soldiers or not, these men were certainly seen later as part of the occupying force alongside the Argentine army. It was no coincidence and their official reasons for being there were certainly spurious.

Chapter 5 - "No Need for Medals"

1 – The men of the FIDF, even today, have a largely untold story. It is fair to say that many were skilled hunters and excellent shots and, had they been given a greater role, might well have given the Argentine special forces quite a shock, although doubtless at some cost to themselves. Taff Davies' inventory of the FIDF armoury is excellent and to this should be added three GPMG's (there had been six in total, three of which appropriated by the Royal Marines.) There is a rumour that the old Vickers gun was made to work that day but no, Gerald Cheek states that it was taken from the armoury. It is now in a museum in Argentina. Finally, there has remained great conjecture as to exactly how many of the FIDF were actually on duty that night (estimates range from 23-40) and this can be put to bed. The number was 32 men deployed as follows: Drill Hall – 8 men, racecourse and football field – 9 men, wireless transmitting station – 4 men, Cable & Wireless – 1 man, YPF Depot – 2 men, power station – 4 men, telephone exchange – 4 men. The three GPMG's were with the sections on the racecourse and the football field.

2 – Mike Norman's exact words are not remembered. He didn't script them and 'just went for it' as he said. The words from the film 'An ungentlemanly act' upon which Norman was an advisor cannot be too far from the reality and certainly conveys exactly what he said on the night. It should be added that, although the film in 1992 was, effectively, the only coverage given to the men of NP8901 and their defence of the Falklands, the veterans themselves (British and Argentine) feel it did them no justice whatsoever and simply cemented the opinions of a tale of a 'token defence.' It is still, in my own opinion, very watchable for an idea of the fighting and lay of the land, although *'I know what happened, I've seen the film'* is still heard all too often. Major Mike Norman himself has stated that his role was as an advisor on specifics of military correctness and authenticity, but that it was, in essence, a *'faction'* and that *"Once a researcher had been told 'a fact' no matter what I said, the producer would not be advised otherwise. Somebody gave each incident portrayed to a researcher, and it was not me."*

3 – It is a common belief, particularly in Argentina, that the Royal Marines lacked the motivation of the Argentines and were 'just doing their job' – I find this to be universally untrue. Whilst to the Argentine forces, the 'recovery of the Malvinas' was for them a national cause worth fighting and dying for, yet it should be understood (as is apparent from the narrative) that the men of the Royal Marines were not simply defending a flag or an outpost of British rule, but homes, friends, families, girlfriends, wives and even children. There was certainly no lack of motivation whatsoever, nor was the motivation of one force any greater than the other.

4 - Don Bonner appears to have recited this line more than once, including to Jim Fairfield who recounts the incident almost word for word, as said to him. Rex Hunt himself had been trained in the use of pistols by Colonel Grant-Taylor, a legendary figure who was Britain's leading small-arms expert, after which, Hunt recalled that he could fire a Colt .45 from each hand and empty all twelve bullets into a sandbag from twenty paces.

5 – The man in question was Steve Smart of HMS Endurance. Andy and Steve met again in April 2018 and recounted the incident between them which Steve has also recounted to me verbatim.

6 – Andy Macdonald recalls that it was Spaghetti Bolognese.

7 – Simon Winchester's own fascinating book *'Outposts'* gives an excellent account of his visit to the Falklands before, during and after the invasion, including what he was doing in Don Bonner's cottage as the battle raged just outside.

8 – It can still be seen written to this day that the Argentine forces came by helicopter, though it seems they did not, and the noise heard was the sound of muffled outboard motors. The first Argentine helicopter to land in the Falklands did so at 07.34 exactly – long after the invasion had commenced. I should add that the Royal Marines still state absolutely that they well knew the difference and maintain that helicopters were indeed heard. My own answer is that they may well have been but that I cannot find evidence to support it. As with a great deal of this story, however, I should state that their own experience should not be discounted and it could well be the case.

Chapter 6 - "Strangers in the Night"

1 – The communications on the *Santa Fe* had been faulty and Cufre could receive radio traffic but not transmit, therefore he was aware of the delay caused by the storm but was powerless to coordinate his efforts other than through what he could hear on the radio and respond accordingly.

2 - This person was seen at Eliza Cove. This is the first in a series of curious sightings of people by the Argentines during the night and following day. Certainly, there were no Royal Marines nor FIDF men there and the identity of the person seen through the night-scope remains a mystery.

3 – Again, a curious anomaly. Evidently these four men with a GPMG and what Batista termed a 'Jeep' – obviously a Land Rover - were not the men of Carr's Section Six who were hidden several miles away on the Murray Heights, yet they were seen by several including Schweizer, Cequiera and Batista who asked permission to attack them. No Royal Marines were in the Mullet Creek position however, nor were any FIDF men: again more 'mystery men' which will be dealt with in a separate Appendix. It is noteworthy to say that, with all of the conjecture, the Argentine landing force was made up mostly of *Commandos Anfibios* with some *Buzos Tacticos* intermixed. The Buzos were skilled men with technical training whose role was anticipated as being repair, control and operation or shut-down of the power station, radio station, cable & wireless etc.

4 – There is a story, perhaps apocryphal, that Figgy Duff was seen in the garden of Claudette Moseley who knew him well from working with the FIBS. Seeing a figure, she called out; *"Is that you, Figgy? Would you like some coffee?"* and was answered with; *"Get on the bloody floor, you silly bitch, there's an invasion on!"* It is hard to place Figgy here at the end of Davis Street as Section Five drove from Canopus Hill to GH and he himself does not remember the incident. Lou Armour is reasonably sure that the incident occurred with his own section between leaving Section 6 and getting to GH.

5 – See the full list of Amtracks and their occupants at the back of the book. Records show that Daniel Tosolini was in Vehicle #13.

6 – It appears that the plan was officially changed – or at least that the change in plans was announced – only after the fleet had set sail and that the army platoon's role was going to change from the post of honour to a mere guarding role of an airport which was, as it transpired, undefended. Undoubtedly, Hugo Santillan's advice not to send the conscripts against GH was correct as they would have been slaughtered against professional Royal Marines and to have done so would have bordered on the criminally negligent.

7– See Appendix for details of the LCVP Landing Craft.

8 – It is unclear who could have fired at Section Three. Certainly, there were no Argentine forces in this area (or so every report tells us) so either the 'sniper' was someone we don't know about (and there were a few of those) or else it could potentially have been a Falkland Islander (all good shots and most had rifles) assuming that the Royal Marines were Argentine troops. In his section report, Steve Johnson states that Section Three came under fire from the direction of Lookout Rocks about 1,800m away, from two assailants (he says from a machine gun), and then from the rocky ridge above GH which caught the section in a cross-fire and forced their withdrawal south-west. Again, whatever went 'thud' into the ground nearby is another mystery, although Johnson reported it as a mortar round. This incident is covered in more depth in the Appendix on 'Mystery men'.

9 – See Appendix for the Battle on the Airport Road.

10 – A curious anomaly here; Bill Trollope states that Mark Gibbs fired the '66 as repeated by Gibbs himself, yet Burt Reynolds states that it was in fact he who had fired both shots at the Amtrack as mentioned in the original section report. It transpires from the testimony of all, that both Gibbs and Reynolds fired almost simultaneously and that they both claimed the same 'kill'.

11 – By a curious twist, the BIM2 recovered the Carl Gustav and Hugo Santillan found it again in the Marine Corps Museum at the Baterias Marine Corps Base just outside of Puerto Belgrano. He was kind enough to send a picture of it for Brown and Betts to see and by return, their photographs and a short description (written by myself) now hang alongside it.

12 – Burt Reynolds was amazed as, whilst watching Danny Betts take hold of his coffee, he saw three Argentine soldiers hoisting a flag alongside a building just a few houses away. Hanging half-in and half-out of a hedge, he pretended to be dead as they looked over, although there is a chance they simply did not see him.

13 - The building which had received fire from Hugo Santillan's 75mm recoilless rifle was the Ionosphere and a photograph exists, taken by John Smith and shown in his book '74 Days' showing the damage. The large 'warehouse' was actually known as the 'balloon shed' near to the government's atmospheric and scientific stations, from where they launched weather balloons. Hugo Santillan and others were convinced that there was a GPMG firing from here. There was not, as we understand it, however curiously, the location does tally with the 'barn in the direction of Lookout Rocks' from which Section Three took fire shortly before from an unknown assailant, and the broken communications equipment described by Daniel Tosolini was certainly not from the men of the Royal Marines.

14 – The group now in the garden at the end of Davis Street comprised ten men; formed of the six men of Section Two, Troop HQ of Trollope, Shepherd and Gibbs and the medic, LMA Bradford. Bradford had actually still been sat in the Land Rover as the battle at White City unfolded, with the Marines waving frantically at him to run for cover. As smoke was deployed and Egan and Reynolds gave covering fire, Mark Gibbs had dragged him after the retreating section. When the men of the BIM2 searched the Land Rover, they found only several belts of link abandoned in the front.

Chapter 7 - "The Battle for Stanley"

1 – The occupant of this Land Rover has remained a mystery to the Argentine and British forces alike, however it appears to have been Royal Marine John Tyler who was sent to collect spare radio parts from Moody Brook and bring them back. From the timing of the event, it would appear that he barely missed Sanchez Sabarots' men by minutes.

2 – It is unclear who was firing from behind Giachino's position between GH and Stanley. There is some evidence to state that it was the men of Section Six actually engaging the men on the rocky hill to the south of GH. Rod Wilcox claims to have heard Diego Quiroga calling for Rex Hunt to surrender, so it may well be that the fire was simply coming from behind and over their heads if it were indeed the men of Section Six, although the timing seems slightly off. It could, conceivably, have been the FIDF section who were put in place on the football pitch and later retired towards the power station, although the FIDF are claimed as having fired no shots as per orders. More recent testimony from Ernesto Urbina adds detail to this incident. Having arrived around Government House, he was then ordered to undertake his pre-assigned task, to mark out a helicopter landing strip on the football pitch. He had come equipped with stakes and – of all things - long-johns, which were to be staled into a letter 'H' to be seen from the air. Alegre's group formed a security cordon around him as he performed this task and then returned and at this point: *"From behind us, we began to receive fire from a heavy machine gun about 350 metres away,"* Urbina recalls, *"luckily, the shots passed about 25 metres to our right. Giachino then determined to take the house by assault, because they kept firing."* Incidentally, nobody from the Royal Marines then present claims to have heard anyone state that Rex Hunt was going to come out. It is an indelicacy on my own part to suggest that what Diego Quiroga heard might

indeed have sounded like 'Hunt' but was in fact a profanity yelled back by one of the Royal Marines.

3 – A strange anomaly here when we count the characters involved from the Argentine side and contrast against the official story. Giachino's group from here is stated as having himself, Quiroga, Cardillo, Flores, Ledesma, Lopez, Alegre and Urbina, eight men in all and all in the same place which would bear out what Murray Paterson saw. This was fully half of Giachino's force and curiously (see the list of Giachino's snatch squad at the back of the book) they seemed to have come from all three groups; Assault, Support and Security, who all had different missions. One member of Giachino's group, however, remains unmentioned. If the total force used were sixteen men – as is claimed – we must question who was firing from the ridge and from other places during the assault. The man who scrambled back for the ridge must have been Lopez, as per his later testimony, although the chronology of the tale, either from his side or Paterson's, must be off, or else it was another person. It would appear, if the numbers be believed, that Paterson did not hit his target or 'the seventh man.'

4 - There are many various accounts of who precisely shot Giachino, Quiroga and Urbina and the names which can be seen include Andy Timms, Geordie Gill, Murray Paterson, Harry Dorey, Gordon Fleet (who had already left with the advance party for the UK and wasn't present), Frank Sugden and even Gary Noott. Records and their own testimony show that Mick Sellen, Colin Jones, Andy Macdonald and Murray Paterson were in fact here and engaged Giachino, Quiroga and others. The exact chronology would seem to be that Jones issued a challenge or warning and that Giachino fired first, aiming at Andy Macdonald who he saw standing up in the glow of the oil drum, with his rounds going high. Jones – or perhaps Paterson – both of whom were crouched and not silhouetted, fired the first shots which hit Giachino full in the chest, joined a fraction of a second later by the others. Despite the short nature of the action as described, it would appear that the four Royal Marines and five Argentine Commandos / Buzos engaged in quite a gunfight, after which Cardillo, Flores and Ledesma ran for cover back to the maid's quarters. In many Argentine accounts (and some British) it is stated that Giachino, Quiroga and Urbina were shot with a GPMG. There was no GPMG used, however, in this position. They were shot with three SLR's and one SMG (Mick Sellen). Had a GPMG been used at this range it would have cut them all in half. The extreme rate of fire, however, might have given the impression of a GPMG.

5 – Diego Quiroga was, like many of the men in Giachino's team, wearing a bullet proof vest. He believes that the bullet which hit him passed through the seam of the vest, which it may have done, however no vest would have been protection against a 7.62 SLR bullet at such close range. It smashed four ribs and

tore half of his liver away. The other bullet (again a 7.62) passed through his right elbow severing the radial nerve and puncturing the radial artery. In drawing his injured arm up close to himself, Diego actually stemmed the blood loss, or else he would have died then and there. Pedro Giachino likewise received at least one shot through the body (although it could well have been as many as three) which passed through his bullet proof vest and another shot to the leg which severed his femoral artery. It can be read in many Argentine accounts, in particular, that Diego Quiroga was trying to rescue Giachino when he was shot. By Diego's own testimony, that story is untrue, as he was shot a second or two after Giachino. An added note to Urbina's tale should be that, medic as he may have been, he was definitely firing his weapon, as he himself admits. Murray Paterson remembers him firing from behind a mound of earth - not the wall as described by Urbina – and had asked Mick Sellen to put a burst his way to get him moving. Paterson shot Urbina at least once. The other two shots may have been from Mick Sellen. Urbina is often described as having been hit by a grenade. The testimony of himself, the Royal Marines and the obvious lack of a grenade (which Andy Macdonald had asked for and nobody had) puts paid to this idea. Of other rumours (particularly from Argentine accounts) which can be put to bed are the idea that Giachino and Quiroga were shot inside the house, when in fact they were shot in the chicken-run of the back garden, and the oft-repeated story that they were shot by what is described as a rather frightened and youthful 'conscript' who was 'standing guard' and fired in panic, or that Giachino's screams somehow so terrified the Royal Marines that they gave themselves up almost immediately. These stories, like so many others surrounding the events of this day are a matter of pure fantasy, although widely published in Argentina today.

6 – This hopefully ends some ideas that Diego Quiroga's knife was in his top pocket. He has been very clear that it saved him from having his pelvis smashed by a bullet and that it was hanging just left of his belt buckle. A groin injury could have been fatal. This bullet was a 9mm SMG bullet which can only mean it came from Mick Sellen. Diego Quiroga still has the bullet. Curiously, two separate museums in Argentina display a smashed Swiss Army Knife both claiming to be Quiroga's original. An anecdote to add to Urbina's testimony: it can be read that he was struck by three shots, however, further testimony from himself and Murray Paterson recount the exact same incident. It would appear that the 'ripple of shots' came from Mick Sellen with the SMG which made Urbina change direction; something which Murray Paterson had called out to do. Paterson then shot Urbina once with his SLR in the lower abdomen, which lifted him clean into the air and threw him back: such was the power of the SLR. The testimony of Paterson and Urbina match so exactly as to be beyond dispute.

7 – This story was told by Marcus Bennett to Murray Paterson almost verbatim when the detachment reached Montevideo, which certainly verifies its authenticity amongst other evidence which, as will become apparent later in the book, proves the incident certainly occurred.

8 - The chronology here may be wrong although the accounts of the fighting are accurate as described. The fighting in Stanley itself went first uphill then down and it is a touch confusing as to the exact run of events. I have kept the narrative as told by the men themselves, however there are a few anomalies. Ray Bloye remembers the hole in the fence being in the playground but residents who lived opposite stated that the gap in the fence was actually on the other side of the road into the Malvina Paddock – the children used to toboggan down King Street in the winter and aim for the gap in the fence. Likewise, Neville Bennett's graphic account of the fighting on the corner of the road may well have been on the fight downhill as he is confident that he saw the Marines disappear into Malvina Paddock thereafter. This is mirrored by John Smith's book *'74 Days'*. The Marines themselves don't mention it although I believe that it must be true.

9 – This is actually an amalgamation of Lou Armour's official report and his later personal account; however, it sums the action up better and neither account counters or objects the other. Geordie Gill recalls a humorous anecdote when Armour came up to Terry Pares and himself, who had both put down fire to cover them; *"When Lou made it back to Government House, I asked him why he had 'four-by-two' (the rifle-cleaning cloth used to pull the barrel through after firing, so-called because it's four inches wide and marked off in two-inch strips) hanging out of his ears: a common makeshift ear-defender. He gave me a typical P.W. (Platoon Weapons Instructor) look and said it was because he didn't want to get high-tone deafness from all the firing! I pointed out there was no need to worry as he would most likely be dead by dinner! – The look I got back was priceless!"*

10 - One thing upon which Nick Williams, Ray Bloye, Lou Armour and others who witnessed the action attest is to the actual number of Argentine personnel in Stanley itself. This is curious as in the Argentine accounts, there are none and indeed scarcely enough to make a fight of it until the men of Delta and Echo companies BIM2 arrived much later. There is a natural anomaly here as the Argentine personnel are described fighting from gardens, hedgerows, houses and almost on every street from the very start of the battle. Lou Armour reported 5-6 men being engaged as he made his way back to GH, Andy Timms and Terry Pares saw at least a dozen from the start all through the town and Dave Carr's and Nick Williams' section report shows 4-5 assailants at St Mary's Walk, 3-4 more at Allardyce Street and several more on Moody Street. Their identification is difficult, although they have been stated as 'men in black, not the ones in green who arrived later' so they were, it seems, either Commandos or Buzos. Certainly, they were there but are not admitted to and it is interesting to speculate upon who they were and how they got there. The damage described to houses, windows, vehicles, garden sheds and more within Stanley suggest heavy street fighting (much of the damage is still there, including the bullet holes in the corrugated iron fence described by Ray Bloye and indeed, Monsignor Daniel Spraggon of the local Catholic church was almost killed on the toilet when a bust of Argentine fire hit the wall where his head would have been had he not bent over to fetch the toilet roll) and it appears that Argentine numbers overall were far larger than claimed.

11 – Section Six's epic fight certainly raises many questions, some of which already touched upon. In the section report drawn up by Dave Carr and Nick Williams, complete with a sketch map, the section reported no less than seven individual fire contacts with multiple opponents after their initial exchange of fire with the group on the ridge above GH. Of these, six are reported as 'possible hits, no return fire' and only one as 'no hits, no return' from the ends of St. Mary's Walk, Allardyce Street and Moody Street: indeed, they were even opened up on from a house at the end of Moody Street. Again, this begs the question as to who these assailants were, as there should have been no Argentine forces in the town and at the edge of the football field. In short, it is – if we take the 'accepted version' of events - impossible that they should have received any contact whatsoever from the Argentine forces, as the Argentine histories tell us of no fighting in the town at all and indeed, nobody present there. The description of the action strongly suggests otherwise. Ray Bloye's credit given to Marcus Bennett for his ceaseless fire and to Nick Williams for keeping him constantly fed with ammunition is well stated: Section Six reported no less than 3,000 rounds of GPMG ammunition and 450 rounds of 7.62 SLR ammunition expended (more than all other sections combined) to the point whereby Marcus Bennett was shaking so much that he could not even light a cigarette at the end of the battle. The section report ends humorously with the words; 'Number of rounds taken: A lot.'

Chapter 8 - "The Battle for Government House"

1 – Royal Marine Andy Macdonald was the first man to state that this 'SWAT style' tactic was in use, but it has been confirmed by Diego Garcia Quiroga and several others. It actually made for some very easy targets and most of the Royal Marines were bemused as to its use, although it may well be ascribed to more common tactics used against insurgents in Argentina. Andy Macdonald credibly claims to have successfully engaged several men during this time at very close range, one of which was retrieved – still head-down - from Mavis Hunt's raspberry bush as witnessed by Rex Hunt and by nursing staff who came to help

with the killed and wounded. Others also have similar stories which likewise stand up to scrutiny.

2 – See Appendix regarding 'Shooting to Kill'.

3 – There seems to be some confusion over the assistance offered to Pedro Giachino at this time and there are (as there seems to be on many occasions) two running stories. In the first, Argentine sources state that the Royal Marines called upon Giachino to make the grenade safe or throw it away so that they could give him medical attention, that he made it safe and that the British refused and left him there anyway. The second states that he was shouting aggressively and brandishing his grenade and so he was left. The story as we have seen, is slightly different from both versions. Diego Quiroga plainly states that Giachino was unable to make the grenade safe and that the British were trying to help but that there were language barriers: Giachino spoke no English and Quiroga was semi-conscious and in too much pain. Geordie Gill, who came to try to help Giachino likewise states his reasoning that the Argentines were 'improving their position' and 'pepper-potting forward' at this time, so he withdrew, as did Lou Armour who also tried to reach them. It seems, therefore, to be more a culmination of events rather than Gill's negligence or Giachino's threatening. As a curious aside to this story, new testimony from Murray Paterson suggests that Giachino might not have had a grenade at all but in fact a pair of binoculars. When Mick Sellen went to check on him after the action, it seemed that Giachino had been attempting to wrestle his binoculars free, as he was laying on them and they were causing him discomfort. Either he had made the grenade safe by this time or, conceivably, he was bluffing.

4 – An amalgamation of Geordie Gill's official post-action report and several anecdotes given to me by him and his fellow Royal Marines, the detail involved here is both graphic and compelling and it should be added that Geordie Gill was an excellent sniper – many say the second best in Royal Marine Corps history at this time - who had taken on human targets many times before and had at least thirteen confirmed kills prior to this. Terry Pares and Andy Timms had actually been in Stanley with a Land Rover when the battle opened and had abandoned the vehicle and fought their way back to GH on foot from where they took up position. The exact chronology of this event is hard to pinpoint, however.

5 – One of the most scrutinised statements of the entire battle, Rex Hunt suggested (doubtless from reports from Majors Noott and Norman) that the Argentine forces numbered around 200 men. Sixteen men under Pedro Giachino were known to have attacked Government House and of those, three were wounded in the garden, three were upstairs and one more, Pedro Lopez, had run to fetch reinforcements. This left only nine men to engage GH, of which the British reports tell of several more killed or wounded. It seems evident that nine men could not appear as 200 to experienced Royal Marines and indicates that there were evidently more men around Government House than the current histories account for. In speaking with the Royal Marines, more conservative figures arise, although still far more than the stated sixteen even at the most. Gary Noott stated that it sounded more like about thirty although he saw very little, whilst the general-consensus seems to be an initial 50-100 men which grew over time. Their identity remains a mystery.

6 - Sanchez's platoon (2nd platoon Echo Company), along with their LVTP-7 were in the vicinity of St. Mary's Church. They moved towards GH from the east, stopped and deployed not far from the house but did not see any combat as the ceasefire was in effect by the time they reached the scene. Delta Company also arrived, moving through Stanley along Davis Street. Alpha Company BIM1 was the landing force reserve and was meanwhile landing at the airport by helicopter.

7 - In fact, this timely act certainly saved Government House from destruction as Pedro Lopez recalled; *"A 'Michi' (Midshipman) was with me and now aimed his rocket launcher at the Governor's house. I managed to yell at him not to. We could not cause casualties. I said, pointing, 'It's better to hit the truck near the gate. That's going to scare them...' fortunately before we fired, we saw a small white handkerchief...the truck that I had chosen was loaded with anti-tank rockets. If we had hit it, the damage would have been incredible."* - A lucky escape indeed! A quick note on Gilobert is also timely as, although he seemed genuinely distressed about the invasion and professed to know nothing about it, yet in a later recorded interview, he admitted that he had known about it and been preparing for it since the Tuesday before the invasion.

8 – Again this settles another old rumour as the weapon is, in various publications, referred to as either a Carl Gustav or a GPMG and the grenades described as either fragmentation or phosphorous and in various combinations. It was the Carl Gustav which they booby-trapped with two phosphorous grenades. Author Graham Bound states that one Argentine was later killed or wounded by this, although I cannot find further information and he himself seemed either unwilling or unable to provide it. The closest intelligence I can find which might match this, would be on one of two dates; on Friday April 16th in which an Argentine conscript was said to have had an accident with a grenade which killed two of his comrades and left him needing a foot amputated at KEMH, or on May 3rd – a month and a day after the invasion - when another soldier triggered a booby-trap and lost both of his feet. The Argentine forces on the Island stated that both had been booby-traps laid by the Royal Marines prior to the invasion, although the story later circulated around Stanley that the first was merely an accident and the latter had been an inexperienced conscript, laying mines, who

had accidentally walked backwards over his own mine. Certainly, the weapons left by York's Section Four were not quickly discovered, including the Carl Gustav, as Dowling was still asking after its whereabouts 48 hours after the invasion. Had someone picked up the Carl Gustav, the phosphorous grenades would have rolled out, hit the floor and ignited. At some point, someone must have found it, so either of these cases might be a result of that and I believe that it must be the incident on April 16th. The truth will doubtless never be known.

9 – In a curious twist to the tale, it appears that it might not have been the Argentines firing at Busser at all. The Royal Marines in Government House were told not to fire at the party of men and so, more for devilment, they were bouncing rounds off the road in defiance, as confirmed by Lou Armour, until they were ordered to stop by Mike Norman. The fact that Busser's order seems to have worked might suggest that it was both sides who were firing on the white flag party. Certainly, Busser's coolness under fire was admirable, whatever the circumstances.

10 – Murray Paterson, who witnessed the event, states that Geordie Gill actually swung the SMG and smashed it into the face of the Argentine who reached for it, knocking him to the floor, then pointed the weapon down at him, actually shoving the barrel of his SMG into the man's mouth. For a second, it was considered that the situation might become a blood-bath.

11 - In a 2011 interview with the Plymouth Herald, Rex Hunt refuted the use of the word 'surrender' in this statement, stating that; *"I didn't use the word 'surrender' because I knew it wasn't in the Marines' vocabulary."* It is a very sore point – and rightfully so with the Marines of NP8901 – that the word 'surrender' is so commonly used today when in fact there was a negotiated ceasefire.

Chapter 9 - "Counting the Cost

1 – The Argentine Commando was Jacinto Batista and the photograph of him and Lou Armour (which Lou still calls "that bloody photo") is perhaps the most famous image of the day, although Batista claims he did not notice the shot being taken at the time. Batista's own testimony of April 2nd is, in my personal opinion, so suspect as to be virtually unusable (apart from spotting the four men with the heavy machine gun at Mullet Creek, which is verified by several others) and he claims to have dragged one Royal Marine through an open window and forced him to surrender as the battle still raged, and then circled around the house and surprised another two who also surrendered. No British prisoners were taken during the battle and the window incident simply has no evidence or testimony to support it. The second incident relates somewhat to Royal Marine Brian Hobbs and one other man from Endurance, who actually came up behind him after the

ceasefire to offer up their weapons and surprised him. He also claims to have been the first man present with Giachino and to have addressed him; *"Oh Pedrito, what have they done to you?"* It is almost certain that Batista was never there – Diego Quiroga never saw him and was right next to Giachino – and the first Argentines to him were Lieutenant Commander Monnereau, a close friend of Giachino's since primary school who was naval intelligence attached to the landing force, and Lieutenant Tarnoski – known as "el Ruso" or "the Russian" - who actually lifted him from the floor to the stretcher as Diego recalls. Secondly, it is doubtful whether Batista even knew Giachino and certainly not enough to call him "Pedrito" (the English equivalent might be "Petey") considering that one was a Corporal of the Commandos Anfibios and the other a Lieutenant Commander of the BIM1 whom even junior officers were afraid to address by anything less than 'Sir.' The story seems to have sufficiently 'grown legs' over the years and the best that can be said is that the famous photograph made Batista something of a celebrity in Argentina, where he was even reproduced as a child's action figure. The photographs taken by the photographer Rafael Wollmann can still be found today and are amongst the best and most famous of this brief conflict on April 2nd. Wollmann was actually a photographer and journalist and had been in Stanley for several days prior to the invasion. He was not the only 'tourist' to have become 'military property' immediately after the invasion (another, Naval Captain Gaffoglio was recognised as the former 'tourist' who had obtained the plans of GH, and was oddly remembered most for his wife flooding the bathroom of the Upland Goose Hotel on their visit), however, his photographs went around the world and the next day and the following, were in every national newspaper in every country, showing the men of the Royal Marines face down on the road with black-clad Argentine special forces personnel standing over them. These pictures actually did for the Royal Marines and people of Stanley what NP8901's gallant stand did not; they made it impossible for the UK not to respond as it did. Perhaps Rex Hunt summed this up best in a 2011 interview with the Plymouth Herald; *"That was really the best thing they could have done to arouse the people in Britain. They weren't going to let the Argentines get away with that."* In this sense, Wollmann's photographs actually did more to lose the Falklands War for Argentina than anything else and, it is speculated, without them, the UK might not have reacted as it did. For legal reasons, I shall state these as my opinions, based solely upon the evidence.

2 – Nick Williams described the Argentine medical evacuation helicopters as; *"A constant stream. Literally an endless ferry of them."* It seems curious that with the claim of one man killed and but three wounded (only two of which around Government House) there should have been a stream of helicopters, a field hospital and even photographs surviving showing many Argentine servicemen being evacuated on the day with very obvious bandaged wounds, seemingly

proving Nick Williams' statement. Again, this calls into question the claim of a handful of casualties.

3 – Gerald Cheek shared the same sentiments as Taff Davies in being ordered to offer no resistance; *"All the FIDF units received orders from the Governor, that we were not to engage in any way whatsoever with any of the Argentine forces and when we were apprehended to surrender,"* he said later, *"We never really heard why he had made this decision, perhaps he had realised that it would have been futile to do so together with the likelihood that we may have either been killed or injured and he wasn`t prepared to be responsible for that...I should add here that perhaps unfortunately no helicopters came anywhere near to the racecourse. It would have been interesting to have had at least a pot shot at them."*

4 - Alfredo Raul Cufre states that the three prisoners, Cardillo, Flores and Ledesma did not come down until after the final ceasefire and indeed, in an interview in 2007 he described nothing short of a three-hour gun-battle with the Royal Marines which simply did not happen. This must have been told to him by the men themselves, perhaps to save embarrassment. Certainly, this is not the case and it is said, as quoted to me by Diego Quiroga and others, that only Cufre seems to still believe that this was so. The men themselves claim to have had Giachino, Quiroga and Urbina 'covered' from the windows the whole time – they may have done so - and it seems that following the gunfight in the back garden, they found their way upstairs via the spiral staircase which Giachino ignored. Again, they were a mixture of Commandos Anfibios and Buzo Tactico which puts paid to ideas of other units being involved in this attack.

5 – It can be seen in several Argentine accounts that there was some fighting at the airport between the platoon of the 25th Infantry Regiment and Royal Marines and even a report of 'several casualties'. This rumour seems to be somewhere between apocryphal and hyperbole, as there was no fighting at the airport whatsoever. Roberto Reyes, now a Brigadier General, confirms this.

6 – There is a story that the British secretly cut this halyard in order to cause embarrassment. This is plainly untrue. The Union Jack had flown from the flag-pole all through April 1st and all through the night and was in place until taken down by the Argentine forces on the morning of April 2nd. The Argentine flag was simply too big and the Falklands winds too strong. However, they managed to raise it on the second attempt. A photograph exists of an Argentine Marine, Victor Manuel Paz, shinning up the pole to repair the broken halyard. Rex Hunt recalls that it was seen as a very bad omen at the time. An additional note is here required at the behest of Patrick Watts in regard to the Argentine anthem being played. He states that it was not scratchy nor played at the wrong speed, as he was there, although it can be found in Sir Rex Hunt's memoirs and in Neville Bennet's diary that it was.

Initially, earlier copies of this work stated that Dave the overnight presenter was there also. This was an error, given from a Stanley resident to myself, and Patrick Watts states that it was only himself in the studio at the time as he would not have put another broadcaster in that position. Watts, a BBC trained journalist and professional broadcaster, certainly went 'over and above' in reporting the invasion evenly and is fondly remembered for his staunch refusal to broadcast with a gun in his back. Continuing to broadcast throughout the war, whilst under occupation, Patrick Watts was created an MBE for his services after the Falkland Islands were liberated.

    7 - Many Argentine sources state (and the same has been quoted directly to me) that there were two Royal Marines 'slightly wounded' by Argentine fire or shrapnel. Certainly, none were hit at all. The only injury I can find is this one, by accident in scaling a metal fence and, although Valerie Bennett's testimony is, I would say, unquestionable, yet the Royal Marines cannot even think who it was or could have been who was stitched up in the hospital. The closest I can come to this story is from Burt Reynolds who slightly twisted his knee and when seen limping, was sent to the hospital. He described it as full of Argentine soldiers - wounded and unwounded - and recounts almost verbatim the same story as Valerie Bennett with the exception of the stitches, after which he was rather roughly thrown out by the Argentines. It may have suited Valerie Bennett's humour (as I understand it to have been) to concoct the tale as an excuse to inject some of the wounded Argentines and cause some discomfort. Horacio Tello likewise states that he afterwards saw a Royal Marine in the hospital with a bad head wound, having been hit in the head with a rifle butt after the ceasefire, although again, nobody seems to know who this could be and Hugo Santillan, who arrived shortly afterwards, claims no knowledge of it, although Tello claims to know the Marine who inflicted the wound personally.

    8 – This has been cited by several other sources. Records and further interviews from the time before the call went out for additional staff show that two men (one of which was Giachino) received emergency surgery but died and were taken away and that another two were taken away in a critical condition (one of which would be Diego Quiroga) along with several more seriously wounded – this before Diane Stewart arrived and saw three more dead men in the mortuary and around eleven more wounded in the ward – and obviously the testimony of Dr Alison Bleaney who saw at least six more dead in the back of an Amtrack behind the hospital (although she thought many more) and some 30-50 wounded in her area alone, of which she operated on at last ten. Other nurses on duty on the day equally stated 'loads' of killed and wounded being carried in and shipped out again, and many were still there on April 3rd with the nursing staff being run off of their feet for 48 hours solid in what is still considered the busiest day KEMH had ever

seen. The testimony of Dr Haines has, I should add, come in for a great deal of conjecture and questioning and so I have limited myself only to what can be absolutely verified by other sources, all of which have stated that it was actually far worse than Haines described. Certainly, Dr Alison Bleaney confirms the story as described in Haines' memoirs, as do several other nurses. The two men by the fence along St. Mary's walk whom he describes, were evidently the ones shot by Marcus Bennett as described by Nick Williams. They saw one man although evidently there were two, of which one died and the other had little, if any chance. Matron Valerie Bennett recounted several more operations performed overnight by Argentine doctors 'without success' and the hospital staff all independently agree that after April 3rd when the invasion forces left, taking the dead and badly wounded with them, there were still twelve Argentine servicemen left in the hospital receiving treatment for wounds inflicted during the battle of Stanley. If we add in only those seen and counted; one certainly dead and three critically injured by Dr Haines, eleven seen wounded (and drunk) in the beds and another three in the morgue by Diane Stewart, two more seen taken away before Diane reached there (assuming that one was Giachino) and at least six dead and thirty-plus wounded seen by Dr Bleaney, the twelve men still there by morning and add to these Quiroga, Urbina and Tello, the figure climbs to easily twelve or more killed and anywhere from 40-60 wounded physically seen in KEMH alone, and this is just from memory although there were, everyone assures me 'lots and lots more.' This, of course, does not account for many more operations performed by their own surgeons in the hospital (of which I am told there were many) nor their wounded from the field hospital from which no records exist, but which was certainly very busy, nor those simply seen taken away from the streets and surrounding gardens. Certainly, the hundred old stretchers left there from the first world war had all been used and were found, dumped and bloodied, by the airport. The claims of but one man killed and three wounded are, as Dr Alison Bleaney states, simply incomprehensible.

9 – Yet again we have a 'mystery man' – the sixth seen by the Argentine forces on this day. Every Royal Marine was accounted for and it was not one of York's men. His appearance – and then subsequent disappearance - remain a mystery although one of Hugo's men has suggested to him that the shots might have come from an accidental discharge from one of the Amtracks' cannon instead of from the mystery man. Again these 'mystery men' are dealt with in the Appendix. It may also be interesting to note that the claim of 'last casualty' might yet be in dispute. There were, by all records, three accidental Argentine casualties on April 2nd, these being Lieutenant Bardi with a fractured ankle, Hugo Santillan with an acute sprain of the ankle and finally Navy Chaplain, Commander Angel B.

Maffezini who – as recounted to me by Hugo Santillan - when travelling to KEMH in the back of an LARC, stood on top of an ammunition crate to find his bearings and was struck in the face by a low-hanging telegraph wire, for which he received treatment in KEMH to the tune of two stitches to the lower eyelid and a large bandage across the eye. He can be seen in several photographs of the day and presumably he is the 'annoying priest' described by Dr Alison Bleaney. Curiously, some sources erroneously state that both Hugo Santillan and Angel Maffezini were wounded in the skirmishes around Stanley whereas both, as we can see, were accidental injuries sustained after the ceasefire. Going by the chronology, therefore, I believe that Hugo Santillan was indeed the last casualty of April 2nd albeit by means of accident, not combat.

10 – Dave Gerrard tells this story differently and states that he handed the Argentine guard *both* the lever and the phos grenade. Somehow the lever had unscrewed during the battle and by all rights, Dave Gerrard should have been engulfed by the explosion. He afterwards asked an armourer if it were possible and the answer was that it was feasible but a million-to-one chance unless the grenade was a dud. A lucky escape indeed, but one which caused a major panic and much laughter at the result. It is said that, to pay them back for the joke, an Argentine Commando threw a stun grenade near to where the captives were sitting, which was followed by rowdy shouts and swearing from both sides.

11 – Again, see Appendix on 'Shooting to kill".

12 – In fact, Paterson was to see it a second time as, when he reached the airport, he was forced at gunpoint to return and take some newly-arrived Argentine soldiers to their positions. On the way back, he got a good look in the back, to where a number of men were trying to clean it out and take away the charred and bloodied remains of what he stated could only have been the occupants.

13 – This story and many others similar to it seem to be very common. Although many Argentine veterans have stated that it simply could not be the case, yet it seems that, from both verbal and written testimony in scores of accounts, Falkland Islanders state that many of the conscripts who arrived later in the day on April 2nd had little or no idea where they actually were. Most, it seems, believed that they were in Chile or along the Chilean border, whilst many seemed confused to find that the Falkland Islanders were British, and not Argentine people under British occupation as they had believed. The story, even if apocryphal, is widespread and many similar accounts exist.

Chapter 10 - "Dawns and Departures"

1 – It was here in the hotel in Montevideo that the men were reunited with their wives and children and Dave Morris who had been sent to Buenos Aires with

the diplomatic bag and so had missed the battle. He was probably better off out of it but certainly does not feel that way, which is understandable. Whilst at the hotel, it seems that almost every man of the Royal Marines had at least one call to his hotel room asking for a 'scoop'. The Marines were told to talk to nobody and followed that order although they now feel that, had they done so, their story might have been told properly, not 35 years later. The hotel also had no windows, just old shutters and microphones were regularly poked through the opened shutters on poles although the men took care to avoid them. Rex and Mavis Hunt and several others stayed at the consulate.

   2 – The men never did receive their bill, which was paid for by the UK Government. The day they left the hotel, the story goes that a diplomat from London arrived and handed over a briefcase containing £100,000 assuring the staff that it would cover everything. It may, of course, be apocryphal.

   3 – The story of the battle of Grytviken (or King Edward Point, as several of the men prefer) was applauded – rightfully – as a heroic last-stand and served to salve the 'shame' felt by the British public at the supposed 'surrender' of the Falklands. This episode, however, rightly deserves some more attention, as it would appear, from speaking with the men of Keith Mills' detachment, that this action has also been deliberately played down. The 'official' records show an action lasting an hour and ten minutes – everyone involved says it was more like three - and several even made accurate time checks. The number of rounds fired at the *Guerrico* is stated at 200 and again the men quote from their ammo count 1,200 as the ship passed by them once, turned and then made a pass back to head out of the harbour. It would seem that someone, somewhere, applied a touch of Tipp-Ex to the number '1' when the report came in, perhaps thinking that it was in error. Colour Sergeant Pete Leach stated that it was easily over a thousand and this would seem to bear out. A book about the defence of Grytviken, *'Too few, too far'* gained some notoriety some years back, although the Royal Marines who served there have largely distanced themselves from it and Pete Leach is in the process of writing a more balanced history of the day. A few interesting anecdotes; it seems that the Royal Marines were originally taken back to Argentina to bear witness against in a Court Martial against the commander of the troops of the BIM1 who had landed behind them, as the men there had actually found a safe place and sat to eat some lunch as the battle raged! Also, Nigel Peters who was taken aboard the *Bahia Paraiso* and treated in the sick bay reported far more casualties on the ship alone – at least double - than stated for the whole battle, which is certainly intriguing, and I have heard it stated by several authorities that Argentine casualties at Grytviken were also deliberately downplayed as they had been at Stanley. Finally, it appears that the Carl Gustav rocket launcher suffered a number of misfires due to damp getting into the electrics, and only managed two shots after numerous attempts, otherwise the damage to the *Guerrico* might have been even more severe, however this still remains the only instance in history of a warship being taken out by infantry on land.

4 – Mike Norman's report actually listed five 84mm rounds expended and seven 66mm rounds, although it is hard, from speaking with the men and looking through the section reports, to find more than those stated of three 84mm and four 66mm. As to casualties, it is curious that between the British and Argentine reports, only the latter – of 1 man killed and 3 wounded - is seemingly quoted anywhere. The Royal Marines' section reports, which were conservative in the extreme, stated 5 killed and 17 wounded, although these were, as Geordie Gill, Nick Williams and Bill Muir all recounted later, only the men they saw drop down dead or wounded right in front of them and about which there was no mistake. As early as April 12th 1982, Rex Hunt told Time Magazine reporters Briton Hadden and Henry Robinson Luce that he supported the Royal Marines' tally around Government House of 5 killed and 17 wounded although he placed the Argentine dead seen as closer to 15 that he saw. Even allowing for this minimum figure of 22 men all-in as per Major Norman's report, however, we should add in Horacio Tello whom the Royals did not count, to bring the tally to 23 and should factor in that a great many of the Royal Marines weren't even asked about their ammunition expenditure or claimed hits as they were fast asleep on the plane back. Andy Macdonald recalls that he and a number of others were never asked, and neither was Jim Fairfield, of course, both of whom credibly claim several kills. In light of all evidence, and including other casualties seen by Royal Marines and multiple Falkland Islanders, the accounts from the hospital, the LCVP and allowing for the Amtrack on the airport road, the bare minimum Argentine casualty count cannot have been less than 70-80 men and quite easily as high as 100 and indeed perhaps more if all of the accounts given by the Royal Marines, Falkland Islanders and hospital staff are accurate. From reviewing all of the evidence from claimed hits through to killed or injured men found and testimony from the hospital staff, it would appear that somewhere around 110-120 might be the most accurate figure, with 70-80 killed and at least 40-50 wounded. Conceivably, it still could have been more than this. Major Mike Norman's report was only released from secret files in 2012 and has never even been quoted except for here in this work.

5 - This is a point upon which all of the Royal Marines and Rex Hunt have been absolutely firm; the Royal Marines did not 'surrender' – the order was to 'stop fighting' - and many felt that this was the correct thing to do. At the time, it was thought that the Argentines were deliberately shelling and mortaring the houses of Stanley as a threat to the people. This was certainly not the case. Hugo Santillan is a humane man who would not have targeted houses other than those

from which he thought he was being fired upon. However, the Royal Marines felt that this was the case and so 'stopped fighting' to save the people of Stanley. There were also thinly-veiled threats that this would be done. Some years after the action, Ray Bloye remembered Rex Hunt with his hands around the throat of a journalist who had asked him what it was like when he ordered the Marines to surrender. Hunt was enraged and yelling at the man; *"The Royal Marines did NOT surrender! I told them to stop fighting!"* - It should also be noted that at the press conference held after the return to the UK, Rex Hunt called upon the Daily Mail reporter to ask his editor David English to retract the story. Rex Hunt notes in his own book that David English did indeed publish a retraction of what he termed *'the offending article'* a few days later, however by this time, the damage was done.

6 – Several Falkland Islanders and Royal Marines attest to the brutality of Dowling and I have only used words given to me by those people. It is curious that, being as well remembered as he is, not one photograph seems to exist of him nor can a single Argentine veteran be found who claims to have known him. Certainly, he was a brutal and fanatical man whom it seems even the Argentines could not stand, and he was removed by them shortly after his infamous 'Final solution' incident. Rex Hunt gives an excellent account of him in his own book *'My Falklands Days'* as do John Smith, Graham Bound and Neville Bennett in their own accounts of the invasion and early occupation. None of them are favourable. An attempt to track down Dowling led me to an email address in the Republic of Ireland, where he moved some time after the war. I am told, however, that he has since passed away, although I cannot confirm this absolutely.

7 – It was actually reported in the UK press that the 'Magnificent Seven' had been captured after several 'hit and run' attacks and a covert resistance, having been betrayed to the Argentine military by a pro-Argentine traitor. The testimony of the Watson family and of the Royal Marines themselves shows this to be erroneous, although it can sometimes still be heard repeated today. Section Four consisted of six men – not seven – and their capture at Long Island Farm after handing themselves in is well documented. An educated guess might well be that Dowling himself started the rumour, which fed its way back to the press, as he was convinced there were seven men, that they were responsible for a number of small-scale attacks and booby traps being laid and would doubtless benefit from rumours of pro-Argentine traitors in the Falklands. Section Four certainly never fired a shot after escaping across Port William and fought no covert war of resistance, however, and the source for these rumours – if it exists – now seems to be lost. A curious anecdote also exists about the men of Section Four whilst in captivity. Edgardo (not 'Eduardo' although he admits it sounds the same in English) Blaguerman recounts how the prisoners were held at the General Roca Military

Lyceum and tells some good stories about their captivity and how the men liked him, however, Argentine records show not six, but seven prisoners here, and with some different names too, which is a touch confusing and quite unexplainable. Section Four consisted of Stefan York, James McKay, Jeff Urand, Gary Moor, Dick Overall and Wilf Smith (see the full list of NP8901 and Endurance at the back of the book) however, the Argentine list of prisoners from Section 4 includes York, McKay, Moor, Overall and Smith, yet it omits Jeff Urand (who was definitely there, indeed, due to his age, his wardens nicknamed him 'the General') and adds in two other names, listed as 'Martin Thomas Smith' and 'Stefan Dale'. Martin Smith was a Royal Navy man picked up later and who joined Section 4 in their cell, so Dick Overall tells me, although the identity of 'Stefan Dale' is something which remains a mystery, if he existed at all. This, however, does not end the curious tale, as rumours started to circulate that the British were planning a special forces raid to break them out. One night, during their captivity, Edgardo recalls how all of the lights suddenly went out and he could hear the Royals banging things and calling *"Eduardooooo!... Eduardooooo!"* to get his attention. Suddenly, there was 'quite intense shooting' outside, although the Argentines have no idea to this day who was shooting at them. Eventually it was decided to repatriate them via Montevideo, as the 'happenings' around the Lyceum were becoming a bit disturbing. The Royals handed Edgardo and his comrades several cartoons they had made of them, amongst other small keepsakes, which were appreciated, and they left, promising that they would be back to the Falklands but that if they met their guards there, they would look after them as friends. The identity of the remaining man, 'Stefan Dale' and who might have been shooting outside of the Lyceum remain one more mystery to add to the growing collection.

Notes to Epilogue

1 – The story of Mr. Edmund Carlisle is one which has 'done the rounds' for some time. Having questioned this idea that the Argentine forces were firing 'blanks', the Argentine veterans of that day have laughed at the suggestion as much as the British veterans. What is worse is that his story to the local press was given in 2012 some ten years after Major Gareth Noott had already corrected him upon it – proof that some people will remain convinced of certain things despite all of the evidence and even facts to the contrary. Here are Major Noott's words upon the incident which are, I believe, worthy of note; *"I met Mr Carlisle many years later (at his request) when I was living in Solva, Pembs. I cannot recall the exact year, but it was towards the end of our time there, late 1990s, early 2000. Carlisle knew a good friend of my parents and I, who live in the village and it was through him that Carlisle came to our house to talk. Prior to his arrival, I had no real idea why he wanted to see me, but anyway he arrived and was made welcome and we talked about the FI's in general terms. He told me that he had (before 1982) bought a share in one of the settlements, but there was some problem and he had come to the Islands in March '82 to sort it out. On the night of 1/2 April, he was staying at the Upland Goose and was, therefore, in the 'thick of the action' on the fateful morning! The crux of his visit was to ascertain from me, first hand, an acknowledgement that the Argentines had only been firing blanks, which is why we took no casualties. To back up his assertion, he told me he had been assured of this subsequently by the Argentines billeted in the Upland Goose; he had been taken to GH and shown the holes 'The Marines had fired inside the house to make it look as if the Argentines had not used blanks.' I assured him that the Argentines were firing real bullets. Somehow the conversation previously had got around to his WW2 service in India and on the Burmese border, so I said to him something like 'Well you'll know what it's like being fired at, I certainly do from my experiences in Borneo and Aden and I can assure you that the Argentines were using real bullets.' At this juncture, he went very quiet and, after a short pause, he admitted that he had never experienced being under fire. He left shortly afterwards, and I felt rather sorry for him because I felt responsible for shattering an illusion he had held firmly for many years."* - It did not stop him from repeating that 'illusion' to the press and in print to the Plymouth Herald in January 2012 which had Mike Norman and Nick Williams writing back publicly to refute him. In Nick Williams' own letter, he actually referred to the severe Argentine losses, stating that; *"We captured three, destroyed an armoured personnel carrier carrying 27 troops, hit a landing craft and inflicted several casualties. When we were ordered to lay down our weapons, 6,000*

Argentinian troops were by then ashore – we were outnumbered by nearly 100 to one." Mike Norman, who knew Carlisle from his time on the Falklands also said much the same, ending with the blistering rebuke; *"You are as wrong now, Edmund, as you were in 1982."*

Hopefully this assertion will now be laid to rest although it is reassuring to know that all these years after April 2nd the men of NP8901 are still standing up for each other as they did on that fateful day. To further bury this ludicrous claim, I have asked Hugo Santillan for his own thoughts and he has given the following; *"Regarding the use of blanks on D-Day: absolutely no blanks were fired by the Argentine Landing Force on April the 2nd, 1982. Honestly how did that version come up? Who on earth would fire blanks 'in anger'? Why would an Argentine force fire blanks when we were 'in harm's way' for the first time since 1870? No, we did not fire blanks. I even stated in my after-action report that my task unit consumed less than 5% of our ammo prescribed load, which did not include any type of blank ammunition. Perhaps someone thought that some Commandos Anfibios fired blanks at Moody Brook or at Government House: the truth is that they actually opened fire with Sten submachine guns... fitted with muzzle silencers! I must emphasise they used 9mm ball ammo with a given percentage of tracer rounds, but definitely no blanks at all."* - One assumes that between Gary Noott, Mike Norman, Nick Williams and Hugo Santillan we may now bury this rumour for good.

Appendix

Appendix 1 – The LCVP Landing Craft in the Narrows

The existence of this landing craft is something which has caused major conjecture for the last thirty-six years and hopefully this issue can now be put to rest. It is something which has been vehemently denied in Argentina almost since the moment it sank and immediately after the invasion, a report quickly circulated that York's section claimed to have hit the *Drummond* with their Carl Gustav, which was then proven to have been intact and that York's men (I assume whilst still in captivity) withdrew the statement. This entire episode simply did not happen and, I believe, it was a deliberate attempt to confuse this story with that of the *Guerrico* at South Georgia. It is a case in the Falkland Islands that 'everybody knows that 'something' went down in the narrows' and, I must admit, I had thought it to be a rumour until certain evidence, first circumstantial and then physical proof came to light which not only proves that it did so, but which indicates that something deeper was covered up by this being the case. The first of these was Neville Bennett's own diary – he saw it blow up - and, when quizzed further, he stated it to be an LCVP Landing Craft 'Like they used on Iwo Jima'. In most publications, this rumour of a lost vehicle is cited as an Amtrack of Hugo Santillan's command, which it certainly was not. Neville Bennett – whose wonderful diary has been gifted to me for this project - is very clear on the matter. I have been fortunate in meeting Alistair Wilkinson and through him, Paul Ellis, both Falkland Islanders, the latter of whom has been searching for this mystery vehicle for some time in his tug *'Lively'* equipped with a side-scanning sonar. On his investigations, many things have caused excitement and then disappointment, to include a part of a military bridge which seems to have fallen from a ship some time just after the war, a shipping container and even a forklift truck, however soon Paul, through some investigation, discovered the actual vessel and it was an LCVP Landing Craft exactly as Neville Bennett had described.

The story here becomes quite interesting; as ever with the Falkland Islands it is a case of asking the right questions of the right people! The vessel being looked for was actually already on land, on its back as per the photographs, exactly as it was found. It was removed some time just after the war by the Royal Navy who considered it a danger to shipping, however it was stuck fast and navy divers had to use charges to blow it free and, upon doing so, a number of bodies and Argentine kit were seen to float to the surface. The vessel had a large hole in one side near the front and was later repaired with a view to making it serviceable for transporting livestock between the Islands but the project fell through and it still sits in a field, denied for 35 years, where Paul Ellis took pictures of it dated (as can be seen) in early 2016 and my good friend, Falklands MLA Gavin Short has even crawled around inside it for me with his camera, as did Andy Macdonald shortly afterwards. It is almost incredible that this vessel has been ignored (perhaps 'denied' is a better word) considering that there were certainly dead men in it when it came free and that Rex Hunt mentioned it twice on the radio as coming through the narrows towards GH then it simply 'disappears' from the story. Now we know why. One thing is certain; it is an American-made LCVP with a standard capacity of forty men including crew and it seems nobody got out of it alive. As to whether there could have been survivors; the currents in the narrows are well known to be able to suck down even strong swimmers, let alone men laden down with ammunition, heavy equipment and who have been struck with an anti-tank rocket and thrown upside down into the freezing water, in the dark and alongside forty others. It is almost certain that nobody escaped of the forty men on the vessel.

One thing which struck me, however, was that the Argentine plans (which Hugo Santillan and I have gone through in some depth both in person and remotely) did not mention any landing craft and so I asked him. After thinking, he came back to say that the mention of an LCVP Landing Craft was indeed curious as, on the day the Argentine task force set sail, he had noticed several of them strapped to the side of the *Cabo San Antonio* on specially-constructed davits and thought it odd as there were no such craft to be used in the invasion plan which he had worked upon extensively. An investigation into this through photographs has shown clearly that the *Cabo San Antonio* did indeed carry several LCVP's when she left Argentina, Hugo Santillan's photos clearly show two from above and a side picture shows several stacked, one inside the other in four lots of two per side, fore and aft. In all, it appears that the *Cabo San Antonio* could carry up to eight in this manner and did so on April 2nd 1982. However, upon returning on April 3rd, the day after the invasion, she clearly had only one visible on the starboard fore-side, identified as vessel #2 with those aft, unseen. This proves that certainly at least two of the LCVP's were deployed from the port side and one from the starboard which did not return. Since the initial publication of the first edition of "The First Casualty" I have managed to speak with an Argentine veteran from the DNPL or Naval Beach Landing Detachment (of whom there were 30 on board) who confirms that LCVP's were indeed used on April 2nd and that eight were indeed taken. He was an 18-year-old conscript who had only received his orders the day before and he served from April 2nd until June 12th when wounded at Wireless Ridge.

There were definitely some other LCVP's used which brought supplies up to Stanley following the end of the battle, and at least three more can be accounted for. Two were found still afloat by the Royal Navy and confiscated whilst the third vessel, after some investigation, has also been found. After the war, it was found on the coast by Moody Brook amidst a pile of other scrap metal and was sold off along with much of the other equipment. It was bought, I am told, by two brothers for the purpose (again) of ferrying livestock between the Islands and this vessel Paul Ellis has also seen, after making a trip to see it with the idea of making it seaworthy again and using it himself. In the end, he did not. I am told that it is still being used today for transporting sheep and is on Saunders Island and indeed I have also seen recent photographs of it in use. It would seem, therefore, that at least four of the LCVP's were deployed and one of those was definitely destroyed and sunk. It is curious by omission that not one of these craft is mentioned anywhere in a single account from the Argentine side, even for just bringing up supplies after the invasion; they have been blotted out entirely. One is bound to ask why.

Since the first publication of The First Casualty, however, certain documents have come to light which prove absolutely that the British Government and military knew about the LCVP which was sunk on April 2nd but said nothing and indeed shows that the Government or the MOD deliberately acted to play down the rumours almost immediately after they began to circulate, which shows that all is not as it was told to us. Having been informed about the LCVP and also about bodies being seen in the harbour after it sank, the MOD acted quickly to stop the story in its tracks, stating that; *"There is no corroboration of the Reuter's report that Royal Marines sank an Argentinian Landing Craft during the invasion of the F.I. resulting in bodies of Argentinian soldiers being washed ashore in the Port Stanley area. The report originates from the British editor of the F.I monthly newspaper who was flown out aboard an Argentine air force aircraft on 22 Apr."* This, despite it being reported by Rex Hunt and seen by many in Stanley over this time. Later, the MOD would come to acknowledge that it did, indeed, exist and had been sunk, although the explosion is ascribed to 'a premature detonation' of munitions. This seems like a ludicrous suggestion. Nobody would have sent in a vessel loaded with munitions into a combat zone first. To do so would be suicide and besides, there was little reason to expect a prolonged defence by the Royal Marines and certainly not one which would require a boat-load of extra munitions right from the start. If this were the case, it hardly seems worthwhile to hide it in the first place. Had it been loaded with such munitions, the resulting explosion would have torn the vessel apart, not left a neat hole as there is now. It seems that counter-theories – of which there are already many and without a shred of evidence to support them – simply cannot add up to the obvious, although it would appear that General Julian Thompson knows about it, as he too has expounded the 'premature detonation' theory when I enquired. One thing is obvious; it certainly existed and was absolutely lost on April 2nd 1982 as described. The question remains as to why the MOD would deliberately play down the story and one final point of note here, becomes even more interesting. It is stated in at least one (and perhaps two) books that I can find that it was Dick Overall (whom historian Martin Middlebrook mistakenly calls 'Rick') who hit the LCVP with his Carl Gustav. I would like to put this right. Having spoken to Dick, he not only denies shooting the craft but also – despite being listed as such in Mike Norman's official report - he did not even have the Carl Gustav; he had an SLR and cannot remember which pair were allotted the role of rocket team. He confirms that they did not fire upon anything, despite what the books say. The question remains, of course, as to who did; and this – the very reason for which it was denied - we shall discuss in the following Appendices.

Appendix 2 – The Battle on the Airport Road

No single incident of the entire action has caused me more consternation than the battle on the Airport Road between the men of Section Two and the advance guard of the BIM2 led by Hugo Santillan – in short, the two accounts of the action sound completely different from each other and it is seemingly impossible to reconcile the two even allowing for 'fog of war' and other points upon which various sources could easily disagree. I have spoken extensively with Hugo Santillan, with Danny Betts, Stephen Brown, Mark Gibbs and Burt Reynolds about this and all are very clear. I will say again that I not only consider no man I have spoken to, to be a liar, and (considering my own nationality and any accusations of bias) that I absolutely *know* that Hugo Santillan is not. Indeed, I consider him a great friend and must add that this has been a very hard part of the battle to write. We must believe one side or the other and someone's account must therefore be called into question but certainly not by me unless some other story or explanation can be found. Ultimately, we are left with two irreconcilable accounts and, having spoken with the men on both sides, all have suggested that both stories should be told as they are here.

There are a few issues which we can clear up very quickly; firstly, Trollope's report was given several days after the action (April 5-6) on the flight back to the UK and based upon the section report which was written in the Hotel Carrasco, and Santillan's was written ten days after. In the time between the action and writing the reports there is a time gap into which memories can certainly alter or project impressions or – conceivably – in which governments could have 'spun' the story they wished to present. As to some aspects which the two reports disagree upon, a good few can be cleared up quickly – for instance the number of rockets fired - Hugo only saw two rockets fired and was not aware of the rest of the section to Brown and Betts' right. However, having pieced together all of the evidence, I can confirm that there were a total of seven rockets fired as per the narrative; three 84mm and four 66mm. Of the buildings struck, again Hugo Santillan is clear that he saw nobody the whole time except when Brown and Betts stood up to run. He was advised that there was fire coming in from the buildings around and in particular the Ionosphere and balloon shed which had a hole in the gabled roof from which it was believed that a GPMG was firing. The Royal Marines confirm that nobody was there in the buildings and this makes sense; a large white wooden building would have made a very large and easy target to hit, although the abandoned communications equipment in there suggests that someone may well have been.

The obvious anomaly which can also be quickly cleared up is the issue of the colour of the smoke; Trollope says white, Santillan says purple. Brown and Betts also saw white, Gibbs and Reynolds confirm it and, to make this final, there was no purple smoke in the Islands. I addressed this directly to Hugo Santillan and he at least managed to put this issue to bed: *"As a matter of fact, all my subordinates are still asking me 'where in hell have you seen purple smoke sir?'"* he told me, *"I must admit I'm 99.99% probably wrong: I believed I had seen purple smoke, but I can concede with elegance I'm certainly wrong. How can I be wrong with something so evident as colour? Or was I so excited (scared, worried) in the fire fight that I unnoticeably altered my perceptions? Well, human nature, perhaps...I don't want to look evasive: everybody said, 'white smoke' so white smoke it was and I (I wonder why?) wrote purple; I can't explain the reason for saying so, except that I described 'what I honestly believed I remembered I saw' (I wrote my after-action report some 10 days later)."* - Perhaps to further prove how 'fog of war' can change perceptions, Hugo recently met most of his old command at a party and addressed the question to them. Red, Orange and Yellow smoke were also mentioned! Hugo and I came to joke about this incident as 'green smoke' – the only colour nobody mentioned - until I spoke to PJ Berry who watched the action from Sapper Hill. To clear up the matter, I asked him what colour smoke he had seen deployed at White City. He said it was green.

However, such things cannot so easily reconcile the battle on the Airport Road and we must deal with all of the evidence evenly which I feel is the best way to keep my own integrity amongst friends. Firstly, Hugo Santillan states that he engaged at approximately 500 metres and that there were only three vehicles including his own. Bill Trollope's account states that there were six vehicles (Brown and Betts have both stated four or five, Reynolds says four) and that the leading vehicle was engaged at no more than 200-250 metres whilst the others stopped and returned fire at 600-700 metres distant. This is quite a big anomaly. I checked this myself with Danny Betts and asked if the leading Amtracks had all come in at once. He replied that no, one had come on seemingly alone and presented an obvious target, with the others quite far back in support. Looking at the evidence alone, one is driven to ask then, which vehicle was this? The Royal Marines had sighted rifles and even a sniper rifle with good sights, which would lend weight at least to Trollope's account and then we have the fact that the 66 LAW was only effective at 200 metres and indeed Sergeant Shepherd gave orders to the effect. Therefore, we are left with an obvious point: if the other vehicles were engaged at 500 metres or indeed at 700 metres as stated, then this 'lone vehicle' was evidently much closer, yet does not make it into any Argentine accounts, which state clearly that the damaged vehicle was #07 under Sergeant Quiroga. For the record, Vehicle #07 was definitely struck by small arms fire. There are photographs of the vehicle and Hugo personally counted 97 bullet marks (correcting press reports of 103). The vehicle was mildly damaged but was not out of action and continued on into Stanley. It is hard to see, from the maps, how vehicle #07 was struck when so far out to the right. The answer again was provided by Hugo Santillan who stated that the Amtracks left the road and veered left across the undulating ground, placing Hugo No.05 almost in front of No.19 and leaving No.07 out on the right closest to the Royal Marines as he states; *"We were not running on the road all the time, so in some instances Quiroga was closer to White City than my Amtrack: that might be the reason that he got hit instead of me. When the fire-fight began, I recall that the Ionosphere was to my left (let's say to my 10 o'clock) and White City to my right (2 o'clock). As you can see, those were 'instant bearings', because we were not moving in a straight line but taking advantage of the lay of the ground, using the cover it provided and looking for fields of fire...and the enemy. In one of those 'course alterations', Quiroga became for a moment a juicy target for our RM friends, while I was surely a bit farther because of relative positions, speed and angle. Lucky me!"*

As to hitting this vehicle with 84mm and 66mm rockets, there is the idea that the Royal Marines saw the rounds explode near to Vehicle #07 as it went into hull-defilade on the rough ground and thought that they had hit it. Certainly, Lieutenant Trollope, Corporal Bryan, Lance Corporal Reynolds and Marines Brown, Betts and Gibbs all stated that they saw it hit, and all from different angles and points of view. Can they all be wrong? Steve Brown says he knows exactly where he hit it and is quite clear, as are Mark Gibbs and Burt Reynolds. They are all three of them clear that the vehicle they hit was not #07 but another one, on the main road itself and *ahead* of vehicle #05 (Santillan's own) and that the other vehicles then passed it, that #07 was a little way ahead and now closer and that this was then struck with small arms fire, after which the rest of the Amtracks opened up with their cannon. They all accept that #07 was hit but state that this was *after* the previous vehicle was successfully engaged with anti-tank rockets just as it slewed *right* of the road, not left as vehicles #05, #07 and #19 did. A sketch map and description provided by Burt Reynolds also backs this up; that there was another vehicle – the *first* vehicle – out to the far left (as the Marines saw it) which had been hit, and not #07 which then came across their front. A further sketch by Murray Paterson (included in the pictures) also indicates a vehicle which had turned right, not left.

A few things strike me as odd here; firstly, Hugo Santillan was in command and, knowing him well enough, he would not have let anyone take the lead over him, except for one brief period in taking the airport when five Amtracks of Echo Company did so. Secondly, he has promised me faithfully that he did not lose any of his men in that engagement. I believe him. All of his men are still alive. Even without this, he is honest. He did not lose any of his men and he has been kind enough to provide a full list of every vehicle number and even the men inside. If anyone was, therefore, lost on the Airport Road then they were not Hugo Santillan's men. Of this, we can be quite sure. This would seem to favour the idea that the Royal Marines simply missed, that they thought they hit the vehicle (#07) and simply did not. The Royal Marines are adamant; they did hit it and it was a different vehicle. The story that they 'thought' they hit Amtrack #07 but simply didn't does not ring right here; in each account it is a different vehicle altogether, alone and unsupported. Did someone, for reasons unknown, make a dash along the airport road against orders? There was a small window of opportunity to do it, certainly, as Echo Company took the lead at the airport. Did someone take the opportunity to make a dash up the Canache towards Stanley? Could this also tie up with an LCVP being sent to get at GH from the north? Again, this seems to have been against orders or the plan, so was someone trying to approach from the south as well? It is, of course, an open theory and there is no way to reconcile the accounts between the men actually engaged in the combat. However, I remind myself that when the only other option is to call one man or another a liar, all other evidence is worth exploring – and there is more evidence.

Firstly, in two separate accounts, it is recounted how members of the Stanley fire brigade were asked to hose out the inside of the destroyed vehicle as it was covered in blast damage, blood and what we might best describe as 'human gore' (indeed the term *'like the inside of an Auschwitz oven'* was used) this is quite a vivid memory and certainly not one which someone would have invented. If anyone had wished the vehicle to be covered up or at least evidence of casualties (and the Amtracks were packed full – it would have been carnage) then this would have been a way to hide some evidence. Secondly, several people claim to have seen the vehicle afterwards exactly where Brown and Betts claim: just off the road, slewed slightly to the right. Evidently this was not vehicle #07 which continued on into town. Then we must consider the testimony of several other Falkland Islanders of which there are several who saw the vehicle shortly afterwards. In 2012 Gary 'Bungy' Williams received a letter from a Falkland Islander who insisted that his father had been told about the destroyed Amtrack on April 3rd or 4th by an Argentine officer, that he later saw it and that; *"it was a right mess inside; only a few got out."*

There are several more accounts including a father and son who saw the vehicle together, from several others who, as children, knew it was there and were terrified of it, and also Islander Les Harris who wrote to tell me that; *"I was taken by three Argentine marines to the Power Station where I worked and there waiting was a senior Argentine Commander with three rings on his shoulders. He spoke excellent English. After a lecture to toe the line or face the consequences ('You will just vanish like we do in the Argentine.') He said; 'Your Marines are very good shots, they blew up one of our armoured vehicles and not many came out of the twenty-plus people inside.'"* – This man, from enquiries, is believed to have been Lieutenant Commander John Ronald Gough, an Argentine of English descent who spoke perfect English - even with an accent - and was in charge of communications. Les Harris recalls that, following the incident, the officer gathered up a bag of soil and explained that he had a similar bag for each country he had visited and kept them on his mantelpiece. Such small details may help identify him further.

Finally, perhaps the most compelling evidence for the destruction of the Amtrack is from Jim Fairfield who stated the following to me: *"I can positively confirm that one Amtrack was hit and destroyed near to the Ionosphere Station on Davis Street, as I saw it several times. At the time of the invasion, I worked for Cable & Wireless at the Transmitter Station just a few hundred yards farther down from the Ion Station on the Airport Road; I looked after the big HF aerial arrays amongst other things. We were told to report to work as normal a couple of days after the invasion, so I used to pass it on my way to and from work. It was facing into town, slewed to its right, half in the drainage ditch and, despite a few poncho's that were draped over it, it was clear to me that it had taken hits from what looked like a 'Charlie-G' and a 66mm. The Ion Station had also been damaged at its east end; again, the damage was from a large calibre round. After three days, I was told that I was not to report to work anymore. I confess to 'tampering' with the transmitters and shorting out the mains power supply, so I know why I was sent home. The Amtrack was still there the last time I passed on my way home; the wind had taken the poncho's away, the back doors were bent open and large amounts of bloodstains, shrapnel and blast damage could still be seen inside the cabin – from the sheer amount of damage and bloodstains, I doubt if anyone in the back got out in one piece. I went to inspect the Ionosphere Station to see if the equipment there could be recovered. Inside the station were several more poncho's and sleeping bags, more blood and used and bloodied medical supplies. I guess it was a dressing station for the troops from the Amtrack if any got out."* - There are several other accounts which could add to this but none, the reader will agree, which are as compelling as someone who saw it six times in three days and even looked inside it. Jim's testimony also mirrors exactly the same scene reported by Murray Paterson, right down to the angles and Murray (who hasn't spoken to his comrades in over 30 years) yet managed to draw a sketch of the vehicle he saw twice, with the angles and elevation exactly as described by everyone else who saw it. Could everyone be wrong?

I spoke to Hugo Santillan about this and asked plainly how neither he nor Jim Fairfield or any of the men involved could be a liar. Again, he has wisely told me to tell both stories and present all of the evidence from which I and others may draw our own conclusions. Certainly, there are photographs from April 2nd showing a wounded or deceased man in the back of an LARC by Hudson Villas, right by the scene of the White City action with a military chaplain alongside and comrades with ready bandages (curiously, though only the BIM2 should have been here, nobody from there seems to recognise any of the Marines in the vehicle), and another of the KEMH ambulance parked next to the Ion station where, I am told, it would never have had a cause to be. It seems to confirm, at least partially, what Jim Fairfield saw when he went inside.

The investigation into this vehicle has been one of the most arduous, in depth and fascinating of this lengthy study and always clouded by my having friends – good friends – on both sides of the engagement. Unlike the case of the LCVP (now proven fact) there had seemed to be no physical evidence for this vehicle, however some started to appear. In 1984 a mine clearance team was working in the vicinity of White City when, just off the main road at the exact point of contact with the debated Amtrack, one of the soldiers picked up an interesting piece of debris; the rear left light cluster of an LVTP-7 Amtrack. This might have gone unnoticed amongst a mountain of other debris however, it had been pierced by a 66mm round which punched straight through. It now sits on a collector's desk in the UK, proudly bearing the legend of being from the Amtrack hit by Marine Gibbs with a 66mm rocket, indeed I have held it myself. The light cluster, from size, shape, location and even mountings, is clearly that of an Amtrack (and has been independently confirmed) and photographs clearly show that vehicle #07 had both of its rear lights intact after the action. So, the question remains as to which vehicle it belongs to. The blast would not have been enough to disable the vehicle but certainly enough to severely damage the rear door: something which Jim

Fairfield saw after. This confirms, if nothing else, that an Amtrack was hit by rocket fire and that that vehicle cannot have been vehicle #07 as has always been stated. Additional to this, the smashed scope in an Argentine museum, purportedly the gunner's scope of Vehicle #07 is actually a driver's scope, which is very different and it is noteworthy that #07 had an intact driver's scope when she returned on April 3rd. So again, which vehicle was it?

The answer is – and can only be - Amtrack #17 and curiously, it is the only vehicle not on the Argentine lists for that day. According to record (either omitted or altered) it never went to the Falklands and yet it sits today in a municipal park in Quequen, Buenos Aires Province, with a vast welded patch over the centre-right of the nose and an exit-hole patched over on the right-hand side, exactly where Trollope and Gibbs state it was hit and where Jim Fairfield remembers seeing the damage; indeed, he has confirmed that it is the very same vehicle. Additionally, it has another hole – smaller – just behind the driver's cupola, is riddled with bullet scars down the left side and even shows damage and 'pitting' on the bodywork to the rear, around the now-replaced light-cluster. The driver's scope is also missing from the mounting.

No Amtracks were ever before or since in combat other than on April 2nd and Argentine sources have told of one which had returned but which proved, despite attempts, to be unserviceable and was put on display and stripped for parts. As plain as day, Amtrack #17 now sits there and images are found easily on the internet. The damage matches to certainty; George Brown thought he had hit it just behind the driver's cupola – he didn't – from his angle, he hit it straight on the nose (as Trollope and Gibbs saw) and the damage went through the body of the vehicle. What Brown thought he saw was actually either Gibbs' or Reynolds' round, which was fired simultaneously from farther out on the right and which plunged down and caught the vehicle almost from the top, again entering the crew compartment. The final 66mm round, fired from out on the right, plunged down and took out the rear light cluster and the rear door, possibly with those trying to escape. The Amtrack was seen halfway up the bank of the road, the right side slightly down in the ditch and at something around a 30-degree angle. The damage fits perfectly as do the angles and indeed, it can only be exactly what the Royal Marines described.

The Argentine reports and lists provided by Hugo Santillan state that #17 was not in his command and he is correct, as Argentine military historian and vehicle specialist Ricardo Sigal Fogliani found out and stated in his own book; *"On Saturday 27, at 8 o'clock in the morning, the march to Puerto Belgrano began, with two complete sections of LVTP-7 of 8 vehicles each, plus the command group formed by the VAOC (vehicle command) and the Support Vehicle. In the unit two LVTP-7 remained. These were #14, and the #17, who lacked a spare part and could not be* with the main group. At dusk, all the VAOs (including the two delayed in the unit) were boarded onto the ARA Cabo San Antonio, and prepared for the crossing." - And later, describing the Amtracks about to come off the Cabo that; "the huge fans went into operation so that the environment did not become unbreathable when the engines of the 21 amphibious vehicles started..." - In short, both #14 and #17 were delayed and caught up later - so there were 21 Amtracks, not 20. In checking the Argentine official history, "No Vencidos" written by Admiral Horacio Mayorga and commissioned by the head of the Argentine Navy, he also confirms all 21 vehicles being used, which should seem to settle the matter, and finally, after enquiring from the engineering officer in charge of those Amtracks, he too confirms the story, that #14 and #17 were indeed held back for repair, that both were sent on board and both went to the Falklands . In his own report, Major Norman stated that Michael 'PJ' Berry radioed in eighteen Amtracks moving down the road towards White City. Three are known to have been left at the airport which gives a total of 21 which would fit the case. So, Amtrack #17 was certainly there, although seemingly outside of Hugo's command as it never appeared in his list of forces under his or Weinstabl's orders. Someone sent it, and very possibly it joined #14 in Echo company and was evidently not noticed in the darkness amongst the others. Having spoken with one of the Amtrack drivers involved at length, he has stated that each driver knew nothing of their mission until the Marine commander informed him of it when they landed. Therefore, it is plausible that anyone could have ordered the driver anywhere and he would have simply never questioned it. In any event, it went and was hit, and evidently hidden.

Like the LCVP before it, we can now say with certainty that the only case can be that this Amtrack was, as everyone else confirms, destroyed, although the mystery surrounding its use and the identity of the occupants is wide open to conjecture. One other aspect I should like to correct, which stands out, is where George Brown hit the vehicle and who was responsible for what. In his own words, Brown saw the missile impact the commander's cupola, yet this strike, from angle and position, I would probably accord to Mark Gibbs. Brown certainly saw it hit there and may have assumed it was his own round, but Gibbs (backed up by Trollope's and Bryan's reports) stated that; "Danny and George hit it almost at the same time, in the front-left of the nose as we were looking at it. After we hit it, it rocked visibly on its suspension, blew a huge great cloud of black smoke and then just died." Danny Betts also recalled hitting it in the nose. I assume, from the angles and who was where, that Reynolds actually hit it in the rear-left corner, as he and Egan were farthest out on the right. The damage to Amtrack #17 means that it can only be the one which was hit. Finally, if the reader asks (as they may) what happened to this vehicle, being as the Cabo San Antonio loaded up its

Amtracks on April 3rd and sailed for home, there is an account which tells of it being partially dismantled, airlifted and flown out to the *Veinticinco de Mayo* from where it was taken away, although this has proven hard to confirm. It is interesting to note, however, that the rear light cluster mentioned above was not sheared off by a blast, but had been quite obviously cut off with a cutting torch which would lend weight to this theory. The evidence for this vehicle is compelling and, I would say, overwhelming and clears up one of the most fascinating and unexplained aspect of the battle of Stanley.

As a final, additional note to this appendix, I should state that, six months after the publication of The First Casualty, all images of this vehicle had been taken down from Argentine sites. The reader may make of that what they will.

Appendix 3 – Shooting to Kill

Something which I feel needs to be addressed is the idea or suggestion that the Argentines were not shooting to kill on April 2nd 1982. None of the men of the Royal Marines believes this to be the case and indeed many believe that Busser's orders for a bloodless contest were 'cooked up' after the event to save face. Here I feel that my judgement rests in the Argentine case of events.

It is clear from Busser's instructions and general order given whilst on board the *Cabo San Antonio* that this was indeed the idea and also from Hugo Santillan's own information, from Diego Quiroga and indeed every Argentine whom I have spoken to or quoted in this work that the idea was for a bloodless victory. Quite how Busser was going to orchestrate this is, however, another question, although he seems to have felt, as discussed, that once the Royal Marines had seen the size of the force he was coming with, and if he could present a set of military circumstances in overwhelming force, that they would not fight. There are a couple of obvious questions on this, however, which should be addressed. The first is that in the darkness, the Royal Marines would not have seen this force (although Quiroga's message to the Governor stated that they were there in strength) and the second and most obvious is the damage done to Moody Brook. Every single person who went back to Moody Brook states that not a man would have come out alive if they had been in their bunks as they would normally have been. There were holes through everything from, the Royals say, bullets and shrapnel and not just stun grenades but fragmentation grenades also. Again, unless we take the line of 'everybody is lying' then the Marines' testimony must carry a great deal of weight and must be true. Sadly, attempts to contact and clarify this with Commander Sanchez Sabarots have been unfruitful, so we really only have his own report to go by, and the accounts of several others who were there. There is an Argentine source which stated privately that yes, automatic fire was put into

Moody Brook, but that I was not at liberty to quote the source. One other issue is that this damage was later accepted by the junta – but it came complete with its own cover story: it was strafed by a British Harrier on June 12th in an attack which killed one Argentine officer and wounded others. It seems that this must have been a cover story.

Moody Brook aside, I believe that the intention was always to fire high and create what might be termed 'shock and awe' against the Royal Marines. Dick Baker's statement that; *"Either they were trying to put the wind up us or were bloody bad shots"* rings in my mind. Certainly, it seems to have been an order which some and perhaps most of the Argentine servicemen attempted to stick with, as evinced by the testimony of men such as Diego Quiroga and Midshipman Lopez, however the testimony of the Royal Marines shows there to have been some alarming near-misses. A look at the bullet-ridden corrugated iron fence described by Ray Bloye as he hugged the road (it still exists and still with the bullet holes) will show just how close the bullets came and indeed it is a miracle that he was not killed or seriously injured. Whilst Lopez stopped a rocket being fired at a truck loaded with munitions, yet Bill Muir later discovered several grenades in the back of the same truck with bullets actually lodged in them, any one of which could have caused a fatal explosion, and Mike Norman and Jim Fairfield alike both came to within – quite literally – an inch or two of death at the hands of a very near miss. It seems entirely plausible in most cases that it would have been impossible to 'aim to miss' in the darkness and sometimes at range. My own opinion, which seems to strike a chord with several of the Marines is that most of the Argentines did attempt to fire high – at least initially - however that it was simply a nearly-impossible order to follow against Royal Marines who were cornered and fighting for their lives. The intention may well have been there and been a good one. In actuality, no man would shoot to miss against a man facing him and shooting to kill. Typically, the answer is somewhere in the middle and I believe that, whilst the general intention of most of the Argentines was to cause no casualties, that it was simply an impossible task to pull off – at least on purpose - for which a strong measure of good fortune certainly came into effect. Again, the accounts of Ray Bloye, Jim Fairfield, Mike Norman and others show just how close they came to death, although the Argentine accounts also show a constant reminder and diligence not to inflict losses, which I fully believe was in effect wherever possible. Moody Brook remains the exception to this, which I simply cannot answer to and certainly without more evidence from the Argentine side.

Since the publication of the first edition of The First Casualty, Geordie Gill was kind enough to give his thoughts as perhaps the most combat-experienced amongst the men of NP8901; *"The main fact of their inability to hit anyone was not, in my opinion, because they were ordered to shoot to miss and obeyed that order. No soldier – no matter how professional – is going to aim to miss when the enemy are shooting to kill. The most likely reason is that, in the initial stages when it was still dark, most troops tend to fire high – I'm sure a lot of our return fire went high too – and when daylight arrived, our lads were in good cover and were employing good fire-and-movement. Plus, of course, the best-friend a soldier can have – next to his rifle – is good luck."*

Appendix 4 – Mystery Men

One of the most curious aspects of this whole episode is the appearance of a number of 'mystery men' as reported by the Argentine forces. One man was seen along the coast before Bernardo Schweizer landed, then another four with a GPMG were seen in position at Mullet Creek and then there was the curious figure whose apparent appearance – and disappearance - caused Hugo Santillan to nearly break his ankle over on the Camber by the naval station. So far that is six. I believe that there were more. It was during my own investigations into the LCVP Landing Craft that the story took yet another twist. If nobody in Section Four had blown up the vessel, then who had? Through some additional information, it was strongly suggested that there was a covert team on the Islands of SBS. This suddenly changed the face of the entire story.

In asking the men of the Royal Marines, it was Andy Macdonald who then gave the second breakthrough; some years after, he had spoken to a fellow 'naval type' who, in conversation, stated himself to be ex-SBS and that he had watched the Marines at the fall of Government House and even saw them laid down on Ross Road afterwards. At the time, he thought that the man was joking although he noted that his information and detail seemed to be very good. Since then, through other sources, it has been confirmed that there were definitely SBS men in the bushes to the north and west of GH along Ross Road. Although these gorse bushes (which can be seen in many photos) appeared as a thick canopy, the local children used to play beneath them for hours in hiding and, as has been confirmed to me, anyone could have easily hidden there without fear of being discovered. I can only assume that this was where Andy Macdonald's SBS man was watching from and indeed it is a story I have heard from several very credible sources that one of these SBS men even had his hand run over by one of the Amtracks and several accounts tell of severed fingers, of an operation in KEMH (indeed, I know the nurse who stitched them back on) and of the man being hidden and made up as a local, then sneaked out in some borrowed plain clothes. This man, perhaps seen, along with Burt Reynolds' short visit might just account for the Argentine story of seeing two slightly wounded men in the hospital. My own investigations then hit 'jackpot' with one man stating that yes, he was part of the SBS team who were there and then through a military contact, having a confirmation from the officer who led them. He confirmed that yes, the SBS were there that night, unbeknownst to the Royal Marines, that yes, they took out the LCVP with a Carl Gustav and that they were not in the Falklands to repel an invasion but for 'other reasons' – one can only speculate what that might mean. After confirming that no names would be mentioned, the message was clear; 'That's all you get, don't ask any more' – I have not. The evidence for the SBS men is not 'concrete' of course – anyone can possibly say anything - but the sheer amount of evidence is telling and of course we come back to the fact of, if not the men of Section Four, then who blew up the LCVP? Who were the men seen by Schweizer, Cequiera, Batista and others in Mullet Creek whom they even considered attacking from behind? Who fired 2-3 shots at Hugo Santillan's command? Who did Hugo's men see in the balloon shed who also fired at Steve Johnson's section? I believe that the 'shadowy figures' seen in the days and weeks before the invasion (and another group seen running along the Camber towards the naval station on the evening of April 1st), the strange ships, reports of submarines, lights at sea and a dozen more strange happenings from people who 'should not have been there' seem to confirm absolutely that the Royal Marines had perhaps a little bit of 'extra help' which they did not know about. It would certainly lend credibility to why the British were so eager to not publicise the story and to let the Argentine 'walk over' tale run its course.

As to the rumours of submarines seen in the area, I believe that, looking over the information, I may have found the answer. There were stories at the time in the press of one or two nuclear submarines having left Gibraltar just before the invasion, bound for the Falklands; a story which the British government let run for convenience but later retracted. Journalist Simon Winchester had definitely seen HMS *Spartan* on March 30th which rules this out as a possibility, however another, HMS *Superb*, had actually been seen leaving Gibraltar a week or so before the invasion, although the Argentine navy had reason to believe that she – or another – was already operating along their coastline. Then came a curious report announced by the MOD on April 22nd of HMS *Superb* still being in Scottish waters for the last five days, stated for no apparent reason and at a time when the Argentine navy strongly believed her to be in the vicinity of the Falklands; a report which could easily have been there to cover the fact that she may well have been there all along. Again, this is theory and – as I say – it could well have been another. It does at least stand out as curious.

As to how the submarines and the SBS fit together, it is believed that these 'mystery men' came and went via HMS *Onyx*, the UK's last diesel submarine which also had a five-man diving chamber from which such special forces could be deployed. This, I am assured, is how our SBS men came and went and later, I am told, she struck a rock and damaged a torpedo tube whilst carrying the men away or possibly – it has been suggested - even towards Argentina for another mission. It is possible that the intercepted and badly garbled piece of US Intelligence which came through from signit was in fact one of a British covert landing which would correspond to Steve Black's own sighting of a submarine in the area (corroborated by several Falkland Islanders) and we must allow that, although Mike Norman seemingly ignored Black's report, he later mentioned the suggestion in the briefing to the men. It is thought that HMS *Onyx* and a second nuclear submarine – possibly *Superb* - were indeed Mike Norman's *'two grey funnel lines'* in the area and most of the men of NP8901 believe that he knew more at the time than he was allowed to say, as has already been alluded to. Finally, the Marines also tell of a conversation at dinner with some submariners, one of whom, on talking of the invasion, blurted out *"We were there!"* and was quickly silenced. The evidence, although circumstantial, comes with astonishing weight. Curiously, the SBS men who stated that they were indeed there and that they came via *Onyx* also described the impact with the torpedo tube, without prompting, although I should add that *Onyx*'s log doesn't record any mission to land special forces.

Certainly, the evidence gathered so far (including an outright admission) corresponds to extra men being on the Islands who were not accounted for; the four-man team spotted in position at Mullet Creek, the man seen at Camber House and others. The lone man seen by Schweizer and Cequiera in the vicinity of Eliza Cove seems to correspond to a 'man in black' with a backpack seen walking down Eliza Cove Road on the evening of April 1st who was not recognised as a local, indeed some local children even followed him for a short distance. The people who saw him wondered if indeed he was an Argentine gone to signal in the invasion and as he was later seen with a light of some sort. This is of course also possible, although his identity remains a mystery. Of the last man whom Hugo Santillan's platoon chased but could not find, an escape either into the surrounding rocks, into the old coal bunkers or through a network of secret tunnels which were dug during the second world war is entirely plausible, and men were even seen in Camber House on the night of April 1st/2nd whilst the occupants were known to be away. With so many ways to escape, this man and doubtless others could have avoided detection easily. A Carl Gustav – no doubt the one used against the LCVP - was later found in a small boat, wired up with explosives and floating in the harbour. There is no proof of what happened to this although it is believed that an Argentine soldier did try to remove it and was injured or possibly killed, and a very similar Argentine story tells of three men killed in an almost identical incident around this time. It was certainly not Section 4's weapon, which was left on land.

Curiously, Mark Gibbs had seen a vessel with a small red light moving at speed along the harbour on the night of the 1st/2nd and we might conclude with some accuracy that this was the same Gemini boat used by these SBS men. One Argentine report also states that shots were fired at the *Cabo San Antonio* which fell short – this was not Wilcox or Milne - and indeed, if it did happen, then whoever fired those shots remains a mystery. In all, the evidence from all sides is quite compelling and points to the fact that there were indeed British Special Forces on the Islands at the time of the invasion. It is known that the SBS were the first people in to the Falklands and that several of them hid out for a few weeks in the hulks of one of the old ships which had partially sunk in the shallow Falklands waters. It is entirely conceivable that some of them simply never left instead. Since the publication of the first edition of "The First Casualty" several of the Royal Marines of NP8901 have taken this evidence to the right people – the people who were there – and they have also confirmed that the SBS were indeed on the Falklands during the invasion (they claim 8 men in total) and that they did indeed blow up an LCVP Landing Craft in the narrows. History should now record this as fact.

Argentina seems to have had its own fair share of 'mystery men' too, as mentioned in the text and notes. Certainly, the men of Section Six and Section One, as well as Andy Timms who, with Terry Pares, was in the town when the fighting started, all state the same thing; that within moments there were Argentine special forces actually in the town, firing from gardens, houses, alleyways and other cover. These 'mystery men' are not mentioned in any Argentine account, nor can their identity be certain, but Section One, Section Six and Timms and Pares certainly successfully engaged a number of targets at very close range almost immediately after the firing started. It can only be assumed that they were brought there before the invasion, perhaps by way of one of the container ships which arrived in the days before. Then we come to Rex Hunt's '200 men' which, according to the history, should have been just nine men. With three casualties in the garden, three men upstairs and Chief Petty Officer Pedro Lopez away, the figures become impossibly small. Considering the experience of the Royal Marines as well as their own claimed 'kills' this figure seems impossible to reconcile. Just as with the British, it seems that the Argentine side had additional help which the men on the ground did not know about. I should add that during or just after the attack on Moody Brook, some residents also saw what they believed to be Argentine special forces coming down from the Murrell in the north towards the old barracks - where the reports state that there were none - although feasibly, these could in fact have been British SBS. Sanchez Sabarots has stated to Hugo Santillan, when quizzed, that he knows nothing about these people, although Andy

Macdonald claimed to have seen two military looking figures silhouetted against the sky on the high ground towards the Murrell as he left Moody Brook on the night of April 1st which he put down to FIDF or his mind playing tricks on him. Curiously, at least two Argentine publications claim that several men of the *Buzo Tactico* entered the harbour by night and landed somewhere near to GH. This would also potentially fit with the dim red light seen by Mark Gibbs and perhaps there is some truth in this which requires further investigation.

A best guess for the additional men might come from the fact that something around or just over 200 members of the BIM1 (Giachino's own battalion) were seen on board the *Cabo San Antonio* by several members of the beach landing detachment who were to operate the LCVP's. Alpha Company BIM1 had flown in by helicopter from the *Almirante Irizar* and there is no record of these additional 200 men being deployed, although the Marines photographed in the LARC by Hudson villas would suggest that they were. It is impossible to say, but is an open guess that these men might well have been utilised on the LCVP Landing Craft, perhaps even on the 'first' Amtrack and might additionally have come in by some other means. This would make the figure about right, if so, whilst allowing for the fact that it is at best an interesting theory which, if true, might even implicate Giachino as the man who ordered them there. Doubtless the truth of this will never be known. In Argentina, there are rumours about the BIM1's participation in the battle of Stanley (they were certainly at Grytviken) and one Argentine historian was given to write that; *"About the truth behind this battalion there is very little information. It is not known how many men of the BIM1 participated in this group, but some data shows that their Alpha Company landed between 04.00 and 06.00 in the morning and operated in the vicinity of the Governor's House with some evidence of losses in their ranks."* – With their records left oddly incomplete and now amalgamated with those of the BIM2, anything could be possible. Perhaps one day, we shall know more.

Since the publication of the first edition of this work there has been confirmation of a further story in which both British and Argentine 'mystery men' were seen together. Residents of Barrack Street had seen three military men around the 'Tab' or Tabernacle Church whom they recognised as not Royal Marines – they had different weapons and kit although they spoke English – and these men engaged four Argentines at close quarters. A curious statement, repeated by three different sources, is that their rifles made a flash, but no sound. The Argentines were seen to run back towards GH along St. Mary's Walk with one being shot at the corner of the playground on the junction of King Street (also confirmed by one other yet-to-be-published contemporary source) and another two slightly farther on. The fourth carried on running and was seen by a Stanley resident in a quote used previously in the first edition; *"Early in the morning of 2nd*

April I woke to the sound of loud shooting. It was still half-light and I was in the upstairs bedroom. My dad came creaking up the stairs into my bedroom. He stood looking out of my window. What is he doing here? Very noisy outside, loads of shooting. He stood for a while then said something about it was time for me to head downstairs. He left. I peeped out of the window to see what had been so interesting to Dad. I saw dark clothed men, they had guns, they were creeping in the shadows along the corrugated iron fence at the side of Allardyce Street. Somewhere there were guns shooting. I looked farther on, to the football field. More men creeping near the gorse hedge on the right. Much shooting. Ricochet squeals. Suddenly there was a man running across middle of the field, coming from the direction of the big bridge, going towards GH. Seemed like he was being chased. More shots. He swayed and fell. He was laying still. I looked away. I went downstairs. Mum and Dad were in the kitchen. I told them I'd seen a man fall on the field. They told me 'Shhhh, we're trying to listen to the radio'. I kept my story to myself."*

This testimony certainly shows a number of men in Stanley and captures the final moment of this gun-battle in the streets. The man was said (by several who corroborate the story) to be running in blind panic when he pitched forward as if shot from behind, perhaps by a head shot. Several Royal Marines saw him also, but did not claim him as a 'kill' because – simply – nobody had shot at him. A heavy machine gun was later found next to the post box (from where Neville Bennett had earlier seen Marcus Bennett exchanging fire shortly before) and it certainly was not British, although a number of people saw it. As to the timing of this incident, it is recalled that the radio was broadcasting Ally Grieves' experience at White City, which would place the incident at approximately 07.20. With SBS teams usually operating in four-man sections, this brings sightings of British 'mystery men' to nine and with others on Ross Road, although allowing for different men being seen at different times, we might consider that a figure of at least eight-to-twelve is accurate.

One other interesting new aspect comes from Daniel Tosolini whose official account states that, whilst at his guard post after the battle, a comrade told him that some dogs had been found dead who, having been sent after the Royal Marines, had been shot so they could not detect any fugitives. Although neither Hugo Santillan or Alfredo Weinstabl have been able to account for the presence of any dogs during the invasion, yet PJ Berry certainly heard them. Perhaps, if they did exist, they ran into the four-man section first seen at Mullet Creek? Finally, the identity of the sniper who fired at Section Three (and whatever went 'thud' into the ground near them, described in Section Three's report as a mortar round) remains a mystery, although oddly, from Steve Johnson's section report, it seems possible that this fire came from the direction of the balloon shed around White City, from where Hugo Santillan's men also later reported incoming fire. Oddly, Section Three's final position actually masked the SBS patrol at Mullet Creek. Having gone to search for the men seen earlier with the GPMG, the Argentine special forces found Section Three and naturally assumed that they had found their men. In all, it points to a lot more going on than all of the participants in the battle knew about, and which I may only guess at whist presenting the evidence which is, if not concrete in some cases, both overwhelming and compelling.

Appendix 5 - "Erics"

Immediately after the invasion, news started to spread about a great number of dead Argentine servicemen being found and soon they, wherever they cropped up, had been begun to be known by the people of Stanley by the given name of 'Eric'. People would say to each other; *"I saw another Eric last night"* and so forth and, from the accounts given, there were quite a few seen immediately after the invasion by the Stanley residents; on the football field, around Government House and in the town, including one found on the east end of Davis Street in the garden of the Newman family, a very accurate account of one man found lying dead with his legs protruding from under a small bridge linking a peat shed in a garden to the road on Pioneer Row, the two men seen shot at the back of the hospital, one more in the hospital's vegetable garden, another (previously mentioned) head-down in a raspberry bush, two more on the junction of King Street and St. Mary's Walk (now confirmed by three verbal sources and one written), three around the back of the Paddocks, seen by Geordie Gill's ex-wife as she came to check on the men immediately after the ceasefire and another outside Number 5 Ross Road East on the Harbour front. More seem to appear daily as Falklands residents remember back with great reluctance and Neville Bennett – the Stanley fireman – even found two more in the hedge of an abandoned house he was checking, just a week or two after the invasion, who were dressed like the invaders – not the conscripts who came later – and were already in some considerable state of decomposition. Although he didn't mention it in his book, it has appeared on a recording where he describes being alerted by the smell, after which the Argentine authorities were called to take them away. Doubtless there are more stories which will be uncovered over time.

Say the name 'Eric' in Stanley and everybody will know who you mean; the name is normally met with sad, downward looks and a desire to move the conversation on. The Falkland Islanders don't much care to talk about those horrible days, understandably. However, the need to get this story straight for the first time has forced me to ask and jog some memories and, although it is a subject most will absolutely avoid, yet it seems that the vast majority of these *'Erics'* came from the sunken LCVP of which there are innumerate accounts.

One Falkland Islander, writing to me, has stated that; *"We took to calling dead Argentines 'Erics', not sure why, it was a name that someone thought up early on during the war. There were plenty of Erics around, after a few days the smell from them was terrible. A couple of days after the invasion, a school child – a friend of mine, was on the Government jetty with her father. This child looked over the side of the jetty and saw 2 or 3 bodies floating just below the surface of the water. They were dressed in Argentine uniform, one of them had his hands in his pockets."* Over twenty people interviewed have stated to have seen *'Erics'* for the most part floating in the harbour or washed up on the beach. Again, an Argentine officer admitted this to one Falkland Islander, another who understood Spanish heard several of them talking about it and the same person who sent Gary Williams the letter about the Amtrack also finished his letter with; *"It seems the Argentines took quite a pasting from you guys, also losing a landing craft in the narrows with huge loss of life. Grandad said he saw them a few days after, dragging bodies off the harbour front that had washed ashore."* Jim Fairfield was another who had seen the *'Erics'* claiming that bodies being washed up was *"a nightly occurrence"* and most people in Stanley can tell you about the infamous 'Green truck' which went to the harbour each time a new body was washed up in the days after the invasion, and which returned with its macabre cargo.

In his own account of the invasion and subsequent occupation, John Smith mentions specifically Tuesday 13th April as a day upon which he witnessed a party of Argentine troops searching the beach down past the FIC offices; *"For bodies from one of their landing craft which was sunk during the invasion. Some have already been washed up."* Again, this is repeated numerous times by others. One final tale, provided by a young (at the time) Falkland Islander should suffice; *"One fairly calm morning, only a couple of weeks into April '82, there was a flock of many seabirds not far from The Narrows. They were clearly feeding on something. It was common for a few birds to be seen feeding somewhere in the harbour, but this was a surprisingly large group. Later, I went to the Co-op, shopping with Mum. In one corner, the dairyman, Malcolm Ashworth, would put a basket of heat sealed bags of fresh milk for sale. Beside this was 'the cupboard', in here were an assortment of women's' supplies. So, this was a natural place for the women to congregate for news sharing and general gossip. On this particular day one of the topics of conversation was that flock of birds. The general and rather gruesome consensus was that they were feeding on 'those poor buggers who went down on the landing craft.'*

Indeed, it seems that every story tallies almost exactly with the others and that the bodies in the water, which were washed up and sometimes dragged up onto the beach were from the LCVP which blew up in the narrows. The detail is graphic and compelling. It is natural to ask how something like that could have been covered up? Families would know, surely? That said, with the rule of the junta in which thousands of people were made to 'disappear' without a trace, it could be feasible that people were simply threatened not to say anything or that these deaths were simply 'inserted' into the losses for other actions. Can people just disappear? Certainly, General Galtieri thought so when he stated that; *"In any war there are people who 'disappear'."*

And what of the bodies? Well this much is easy enough. The bodies were stored, swaddled, in a red shipping container (several people managed a curious look in and the local children often dared each other to) and then moved by stages. Several Falkland Islanders reported piles of bodies seen on the Darwin Road into town over a few days before April 15th in what John Smith referred to as *'Several heaps of dead soldiers - the total varies been thirty and fifty – stacked up on the side of the road up near Sapper Hill'* along with a large number of wounded men on stretchers, which he put down to exposure. Given the barely two weeks since the invasion, this seems quite extreme and again, the Argentine forces record only three or four men dying of exposure in the whole war, yet Neville Bennett also records the same dates and figures in his own diary. These men were shipped, it appears, to the Beaver Hangar on the western side of the harbour. The smell, many said, was already pretty bad. Then on April 15th something happened. Again, I will refer to Neville Bennett's diary; *"While waiting for supper to be cooked, I whiled away the time by looking at the world go by from the front porch windows. 'Something going on here' I thought. Half a dozen HU1 helicopters flying down the harbour at 6-8 feet above the water. They had the cargo doors open and it was possible to see through the body of the machines. I discretely got a pair of binoculars and looked at the 'Hueys'. There was what appeared to be a heap of large grey plastic bags in each machine. They went out through the narrows and back again in a few minutes, empty. I suppose they had time to fly to the Islands in Port William. They made the journey perhaps three times each that evening. They had come from the direction of the Beaver Hangar but that was out of sight behind Sullivan House so I couldn't see exactly where they had lifted off from."* Six helicopters three times each - eighteen loads of 'grey sacks' which seemed to match the Argentine body-bags Valerie was so impressed with and now they were out on the Tussock or 'Tussac' Islands in Port William from where, over the next couple of days, the smell of decay was truly repugnant.

On April 17th the clear-up operation began, with Pucaras bombing the Tussac Islands with napalm, and smoke and flames rising hundreds of feet into the air.

These unfortunates - whomever they may have been - were added to by twenty more men seen again on the Darwin Road by Sapper Hill on Monday 19th - again put down to exposure - and anything up to ten more found the following day, all wholly denied as losses either from the invasion or the war in entirety. The piles of men would appear and then disappear, to be replaced, it would seem, by another. Then on April 21st a new diary entry from Neville Bennett; *"We heard some loud bangs and some thumps. Wondering what it was all about, we had a look outside and to the north-east we could see some aircraft flying around Port William and diving towards Yorke Bay probably at the Tussac Islands. A large, black, oily cloud billows well up into the sky before it was flattened by the breeze. It must have been quite hot stuff. No doubt 'they' wouldn't tell us the truth if asked. Anyway, I'm sure someone is going to ask 'them'."* John Smith, in his own book, was more forthright stating of the incident that; *"It is being said that the Argentine dead still being recovered from the invasion are being put on the islands, so that no trace remains of their losses, which during the invasion period were far heavier than admitted."*

The people in Stanley were under no illusion; the bodies of the Argentine soldiers killed on April 2nd had been bombed with napalm and indeed a photograph even exists of both incidents, that from April 21st displayed in the images inside this book, as well as of the same Huey helicopters at the airport alongside a great number of napalm bombs. A best guess would be that as more men washed up or were found, they were taken out to the Darwin Road, although there were certainly a number of other accidents, including one man fried to death on power lines on April 3rg, those already mentioned in other accidents and some Argentines being blown up by their own weapons – perhaps a mine or heavy round - in the Dairy Paddocks on the 15th whom doubtless the junta officials might have added to the tally, which is listed as anything from 53 men to 80 seen over several days. Nobody – I am told by many – will ever forget that day of April 21st in Stanley. Bloomer-Reeve later (some think weakly) admitted that napalm had been 'tested' on the Tussac Islands and insisted that the air force had to have somewhere to practice. A telling remark from one Falkland Islander was that she thought it was awful, doing such a thing on the Queen's birthday, whilst several more have also stated seeing bodies being taken out and burned and one chilling comment was that; *"I thought it was common knowledge that the Argies used the Tussac Islands as a human dumping ground."* Interestingly enough, Galtieri came to the Falklands only the next day. Was someone eager to hide something?

A short time after the war, several people went out to the Tussac Islands to take a look. The island was still scorched and barren apart from a few scraps of uniforms and a very large collection of human 'almond' or *Luz* bones – the bone in the spine which survives even cremation – in short, as seems evident, the men who were lost in the LCVP and perhaps others whose deaths remain unaccounted for were napalmed into complete and almost utter denial, apart from a few traces of evidence. I believe that this evidence presented (and a great deal more which could be said and has been said to me) is enough that people should begin to ask some very serious questions. It is a sobering thought that just after the war, the Argentine newspapers reported, from official sources, up to 1,000 men killed and another 2,500 missing, and even a year after the war, many Argentine families were still appealing for the return of over 500 men whom - they believed and had been told - were still being held prisoner by the British forces and were on Ascension Island. The incident was reported in The New York Times on April 8th 1983 under the title, *"No Clues on Lost Troops, British Tell Argentines"* and reported anything up to 1,000 dead or missing about whom there were no records, prompting the Argentine families to demand their release from Ascension. Of course, there were none. To this day, these 500-1,000 men remain unaccounted for and, seemingly, forgotten.

Appendix 6 – Theories & Conclusions

In war - as in most aspects of life - theories are useful but also dangerous things, especially when, as may well be the case here, they can be preceded by the word 'conspiracy' and yet we must admit that, whilst we may never know the answers fully, the ones we have been given for 36 years (as I write) simply do not add up to any kind of scrutiny. In short, the truth must therefore be something else. The term 'cover up' of course, is nothing really new, however much some might deride it, and I would point the reader back to the quote from Sir Rex Hunt at the opening of this book where even he alluded to the idea that there were some who would rather the story stayed buried: Rex Hunt was no fool.

It is a natural trap, when one starts down the road of what we might term a 'conspiracy theory', that it is relatively easy to shoot down the 'official version' of events until one inserts their own version which, typically, seems more ludicrous than the original. In this sense, I am only giving my own idea of what *might* have been the case whist allowing that I could ultimately be in error on some points. All I know is that, whatever we have been told about the 'official history' of April 2nd 1982 it is most definitely a fabrication. I can set out the 'what' but not the 'why' and do not intend that my own theories as to this battle be taken as fact, but as an educated guess which might in future lead us to more answers upon this fascinating subject.

One of the most important questions which must doubtless be asked is why the battle of Stanley was covered up in the first place and, from a review of the evidence, I believe I may have an answer. After the war, with the FCO humbled and

Thatcher triumphant, two letters were found in the Foreign Office files, both written before the April 2nd invasion. The first stated that *'that woman'* as she had become known, had allowed the Falkland Islands to be invaded and had feebly done nothing and should resign immediately. The second stated that she had rashly responded to the invasion with an act of war, been beaten and caused a national disaster and must therefore resign immediately. It would seem that Margaret Thatcher was deliberately placed in a bind from which she could not escape except by some very clever gambling and it was evident that she was not blind to her situation. In what has been dubbed, 'The Whitehall War' by Max Hastings and Simon Jenkins, the build-up to the Falklands War should be seen less as the UK vs. Argentina and more as the UK Government vs. the Foreign & Commonwealth Office. The Falklands were to be the lever which saw one or the other come tumbling down.

It was known – almost definitely – that an invasion was coming although probably not exactly when it would come and that a set of circumstances would need to occur if Thatcher was to keep her place and the Falklands were to remain as a British territory. Firstly, Britain could under no circumstances act pre-emptively or appear as the aggressor. Had a submarine been in the area and torpedoed the *Cabo San Antonio* or *Veinticinco de Mayo* without warning, Britain's standing in the world would have taken a significant plunge. The signits and flash telegrams prior to the Davidoff incident and right up to the invasion itself on April 2nd bury the myth that Britain was trying to provoke a war. Each one mentions – with a growing concern - the need to not provoke any hostility or invasion and cautions against any rash moves. This would seem consistent with the theory. Secondly, the invasion – if and when it came – would have to look like a complete surprise if the world and the country was going to get on Britain's and Thatcher's side, and there would have to be sacrifices. In reality, this meant dead Royal Marines under a commanding officer (Norman) known for a 'hit first ask questions later' style which would ensure a fight to the finish, a shocked and horrified international community and the UK able to use the slaughter to enact article 51 of the UN Charter on self-defence.

It is a personal theory that, unable to pre-empt and unwilling to provoke, Margaret Thatcher instead 'managed' the invasion which she knew must come, and ensured an outcome which would be politically suited to respond with a UN mandate and the support of the world powers and from there, to gamble on victory in the Falklands. It would, however, require a detachment of Royal Marines to be sacrificed. You have to hand it to the Argentine planners; with not a single British casualty, they very nearly pulled it off. Only the photos of the Marines laid out on Ross Road and a cover-story of a national embarrassment saved the situation for the UK – who seized gratefully upon the Argentine story, their own being in tatters - and the Royal Marines would have to sacrifice their tale and their honour instead and be content with not being slaughtered to a man. As Rear Admiral Chris Parry himself said; they should be grateful for their lives and should ask for nothing more than that.

As for Argentina, of course, the reasons for this story to have been buried by the junta are more plain common sense. Galtieri had barely survived a civil uprising. Could he really announce the 'recovery of the Malvinas' whilst adding in that sixty Royal Marines had walked out without a scratch but chalked up over a hundred casualties? He would have looked like a fool and indeed, this would have worked to destroy any elation the public might have had. Politically, of course, a bloodless victory was required: the idea that the Royal Marines gave up without a fight and obviously knew their cause to be wrong was something which Galtieri wanted to promote as much as the martial superiority of his own side, and he wanted to show something like a British acceptance of the reality of the situation. A 'Rorke's Drift' battle around Stanley was never going to make that a reality. Pedro Giachino, the one man whom the junta admitted did die, was the perfect martyr to set the seal on the cause, and a man whose death could hardly be ignored. A theory which I have alluded to earlier in regard to Giachino might also fit the case, and I am led to think – or at least to wonder - if a great deal of the things now brought to light were not of his own doing. At the time at which the task force sailed, the men of the IR25 were going to be sent to GH and Giachino was certainly smart enough to know that they would have been massacred against experienced Royal Marines. I am led to wonder that it was he who ordered his own men of the BIM1 to take an LCVP from the *Cabo San Antonio* and to jump into Amtrack #17 – would anyone with a quick glance have noticed that the Marines were not BIM2 but BIM1? If he could have both units rushed to GH – one from the north and another to the south – he could quickly put over 60 Marines in place which would tip the balance, but with the pride of the Army at stake, he could certainly not tell them. On the voyage the orders changed: Giachino would lead the attack upon GH and of course, he had no way of communicating this to the men on the *Cabo*, so that it went ahead anyway, with disastrous consequences. Now, with Giachino a martyr and national hero, that mistake would have to be covered up. This, at least, is my personal theory. Who else had the authority and knew the plan well enough to know what was going on and who would be where? Who else could have used BIM1 Marines and got them there? How comes none of the BIM2 Marines recognise a lot of Marines in the photographs, supposedly from their own unit? Why are the BIM1 records incomplete? Finally, how else could it have happened if not by him? Dead men tell no lies, as they say, and if there is a better theory, I haven't heard it.

Herein, I believe, is the true story of April 2nd and why it has remained buried for 36 years until this publication. For the junta it was a political necessity, to announce a bloodless victory, a convenient martyr and to clear away anything which might alter the tale of either, and for the UK, the Argentine invasion was to be carefully stage-managed, the Royal Marines sacrificed, the world in shock, the world powers behind the United Kingdom and Margaret Thatcher, and then a gamble on a military and / or political victory which the top military specialists from the UK, USA and the Soviet Union considered impossible. Had the world known that the UK had one and possibly two submarines in the area and special forces troops, it doubtless would not have gained much sympathy in the international community and hence, despite the power to halt or at least seriously retard the invasion, the British government allowed it to happen and gambled upon a result which would settle the matter with the world firmly in its court. When this failed to happen, and all the Royals came out without a scratch, the British Government instead borrowed the Argentine story and even made it worse and more humiliating, which actually created the desired effect. It is an interesting theory, however right or wrong, although it answers to every point almost perfectly.

There is, of course, one final twist which shows complicity and this would lay with the Prime Minister's husband, Dennis Thatcher. Having made his money in the oil industry (and ironically enough, from Gordon's Gin), Dennis Thatcher was a director and major share-holder in 'Coalite' which pretty much owned half of the Falkland Islands - and the mineral rights – and another quarter of them through various subsidiaries, including the Falkland Islands Company. Despite his later assertion that he had no idea where the Falkland Islands were and had to look them up in an atlas, it would seem that Dennis Thatcher had a lot of money tied up in the Falklands which, along with Margaret Thatcher's own position at the time, would lead one to suspect that both of them had much to lose – and gain – from a successfully-managed Argentine invasion of the islands. Theories can indeed be dangerous things.

We must, however, accept a few absolute truths from this book and from the accounts within it which can only be true, these being the sinking of the LCVP, the destruction of Amtrack #17 on the Airport Road at White City, the presence of British submarines and special forces, the significantly greater amount of Argentine forces and also of casualties and of course, the heroic stand of the outnumbered Royal Marines of Naval Party 8901 which should now over-write this threadbare tale of a 'token defence'. It is an important and not obvious point that not one of the men involved in this, British or Argentine, has an idea of most of this beyond what they actually saw with their own eyes and in the immediate vicinity and many on both sides have greeted new information and evidence with a growing sense of amazement. There was indeed more – much more - going on than any one person knew about and a whole battle surrounding that which they themselves fought.

Of course, there are and will be questions thrown up by this new evidence. I do not intend to answer all of them (even if I could) as it is evident that a renewed study of this period and this battle – a battle which history tells us was not a battle at all and at best a light skirmish – is required in greater depth. Indeed, from the merest glimpses it should be said that the story of the Falklands War – at least as we know it – is one of the most shrouded in myth, mystery, conjecture and political cover-up as can be found and perhaps deserves an entirely fresh look: and it starts here, on day one.

If elements of the story seem fanciful at times, particularly the concept of a whole battle denied and covered up for 36 years, then I should like to remind the reader that a very similar action, the siege of Jadotville, was entirely denied from 1961 until being recognised in 2004 before which time it had been a point of shame and even ridicule pointed at the brave men from Ireland who were termed 'Jadotville Jacks' by those who sneered at their actions – again there, just as with the Royal Marines of Naval Party 8901 - not a single one of the recommendations for bravery were accepted. Finally, the brave men of Jadotville have been recognised and their story told. Proof that history, as we know it, can and does change.

I hope that in the UK, in Argentina and around the world, this history will be viewed with the diligence, respect and credibility deserving of all of the men who fought in the Falkland Islands on April 2nd 1982 and, whilst there is always more glory to be found in the arms of the outnumbered defender, we should credit too, the arms of Argentina which launched an impressive armada probably not equalled since Normandy, carried out a plan which was ultimately successful and who pulled it off with the almost-impossible orders to cause no casualties against a determined and skilful opponent. The glory of one only adds to that of the other – whichever way you look at it.

1. Pedro Giachino – BIM1

2. Diego Garcia Quiroga
– Buzo Tactico.

3. Hugo Santillan – BIM2.

4. Alfredo Weinstabl – BIM2.

5. LVTP-7 Amtracks of the 1st Marine Amphibious Vehicles Battalion with rifle companies of the BIM2 during training in Patagonia prior to the invasion, March 21-23 1982.

6. LVTP-7 Amtracks boarding the ARA Cabo San Antonio in Punta Buenos Aires after exercise, March 21-23 1982.

7. BIM2 training for the mission – L-R: Lieutenant di Paola (Commander, Delta Co.), Commander Weinstabl, Marine Midshipman Ciaglia (Heavy Mortar Platoon Commander) – March 21-23 1982.

8. BIM2 Machine gun and mortar platoon preparing for embarkation, March 28 1982.

9. Communications equipment being lifted onto the deck of the ARA Cabo San Antonio, March 28 1982. In the foreground the platoon of the 25th Infantry under Colonel Seineldin and in the distance, the Almirante Irizar and aircraft carrier, ARA Veinticinco de Mayo.

10. LARC amphibious vehicle nearly lost overboard in the storm. At bottom-right also an LCVP Landing Craft: one of eight which the Cabo San Antonio was modified to carry for the mission.

11. The three senior men involved in Operation Rosario – L-R: Admiral Carlos Busser, General Osvaldo Garcia and Admiral Gualter Allara.

12. Amtracks on board the Cabo San Antonio. The vehicle on the left is #05 commanded by Hugo Santillan, who was to spearhead the amphibious assault.

13. Admiral Busser announces the mission to the task force and reveals their final destination.

14. Alfredo Weinstabl (centre), Marine Captain Pita, Landing Force Chief of Staff (left) and Hugo Santillan (right) discussing plans in the war room aboard the Cabo San Antonio.

15. Nick Williams – up close with the wildlife.

16. Geordie Gill with his daughter Tanya.

17. Dave 'Ginge' Gerrard, 8901's mechanic and resident comedian.

18. Ray Bloye by the entrance to Moody Brook.

19. Men of the 81/82 NP8901 detachment – Back L-R: Nick Williams, Steve Porter, Mick Sellen. Front L-R: Figgy Duff, Steve Holding.

20. Men of the 82/83 NP8901 detachment – Back L-R: Chris Bryan, Terry Pares, Mark Coombs, Burt Reynolds. Front L-R: Sean Egan, Gary Williams, Stephen 'George' Brown, Danny Betts.

21. On board HMS Endurance – L-R: Figgy Duff, Ray Bloye, Dave Gerrard –
in the engine room.

22. On board HMS Endurance – Back row L-R: Mick Sellen, Nick Williams,
John Tyler, Figgy Duff, Tel George, Cas Clay, Ray Bloye, Les Milne. Front:
LMA Alex Pickthall.

23. Aerial shot of the isthmus, clearly showing the invasion beaches up which the Argentine forces would attack and also the long, white strip of the runway. To the extreme right, the Canache winds its way to Stanley, whilst on the left, the tip of Navy Point can be seen, where Section Four guarded the entrance to the narrows.

24. Stanley Airport with the runway blocked by an assortment of vehicles and other obstacles – 07.00hrs approximately – April 2 1982.

25. Government House, Stanley; "A ridiculous place to try to defend....
Not exactly the Alamo."

26. Moody Brook Barracks taken from the air. A condemned collection
of ramshackle huts on the outskirts of Stanley.

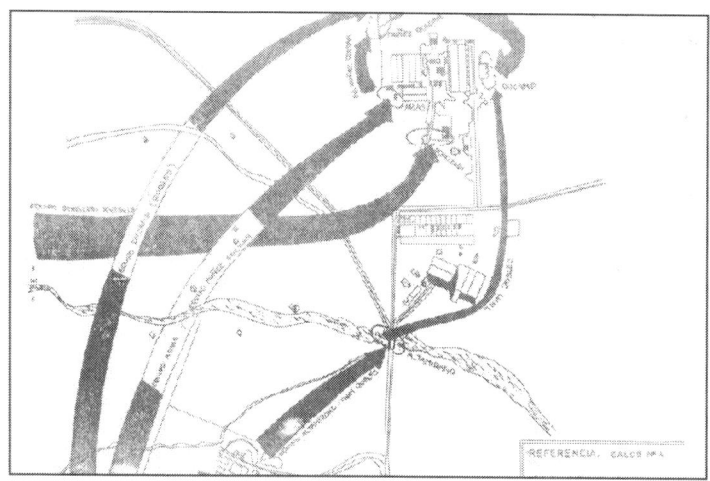

27. Post-invasion Argentine map of the assault on Moody Brook Barracks.

28. Commandos Anfibios assembling outside of Moody Brook after the assault. Having waited for first light, they were now ready to advance upon GH.

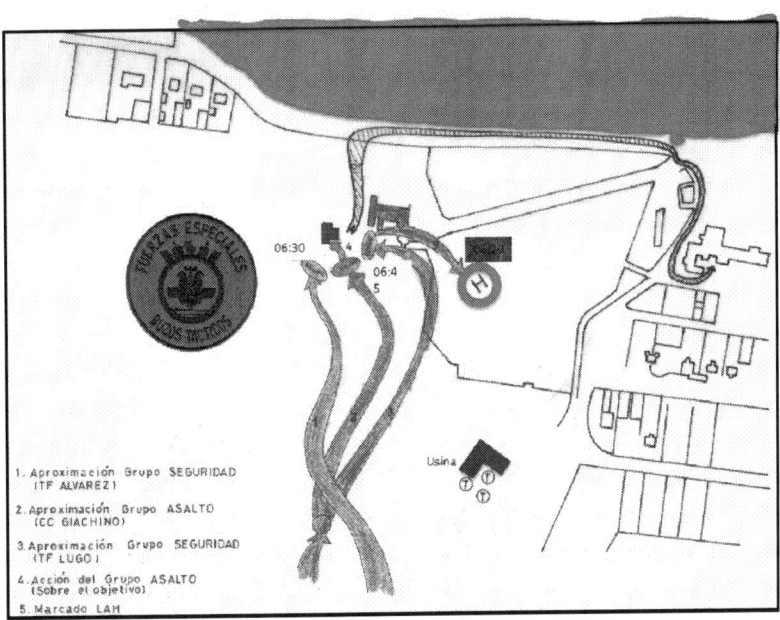

29. The assault upon Government House, showing the positions of the
respective groups as they advanced. From a presentation as
hand-drawn by Diego Quiroga.

30. The back garden of GH where Giachino, Quiroga and Urbina were shot, as the Royal Marines would have seen it on the night. The Argentine Commandos rounded the corner to the left, running straight into Mick Sellen, Tiny Jones, Andy Macdonald and Murray Paterson.

31. Amtracks of Echo Company advancing along the road to White City just past the LADE beacon. At 29 tonnes apiece, they were the heaviest vehicles ever seen in the Falklands.

32. Marines of the BIM2 deploying for action during or just after the action at White City.

33. The Ionospheric Station at White City, clearly showing the impact damage from the round which struck it. The Royal Marines ran across the ground to the bottom of the picture and crossed Davis Street beyond, into the gardens of Hudson Villas.

34. Marines of the BIM2 on guard at White City just after the action. Note the road repair machine in the centre of the picture and Tom Davies' house on the extreme right, hit on the corner by a mortar round. Between the houses of White City and the Amtrack parked on the road (extreme left) is the Ionospheric Station. The Royal Marines were emplaced on the far side of the road to the extreme left of the picture and slightly beyond it.

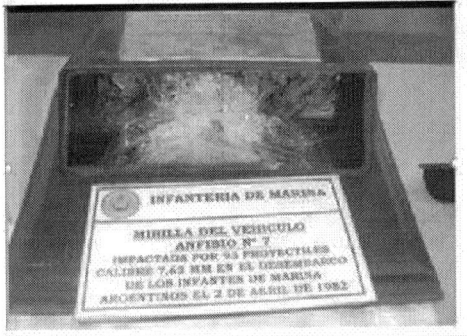

35. Montage showing the gunner's scope of Amtrack #07 now held in an Argentine museum. The right-hand and lower images show, however, that this smashed scope is clearly a driver's scope and not the gunner's scope as has always been maintained. As can be seen, the vehicle's driver scope on Amtrack #07 is intact and so the question remains as to which Amtrack this item could have belonged to. Clearly, they are not the same ones, nor is the damage in any way similar. Could a second Amtrack have been hit – and possibly destroyed – at White City?

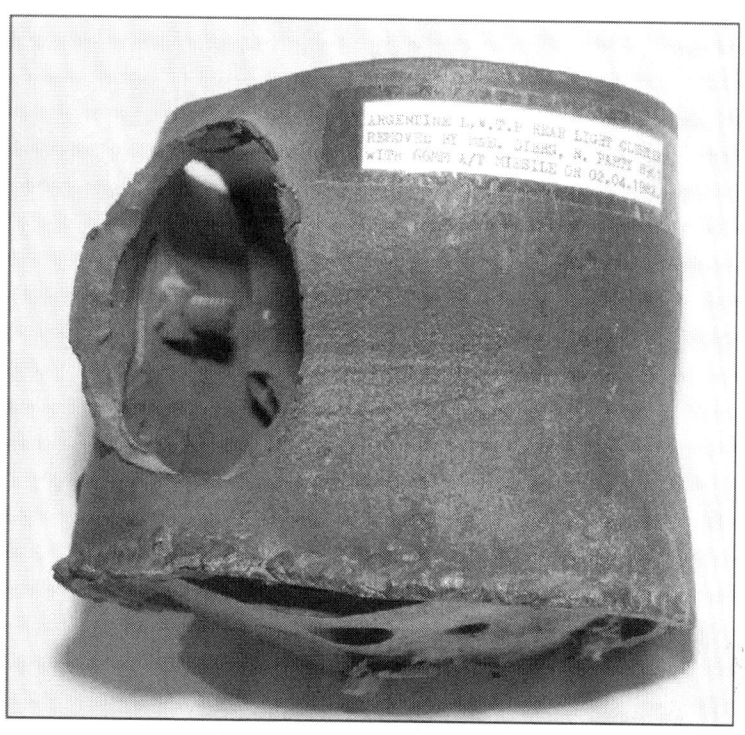

36. Rear left light cluster from an LVTP-7 Amtrack, found at White City in 1984 and clearly showing the impact of a 66mm HEAT rocket. The legend attached to the unit credits the strike as being from Marine Mark Gibbs. It is interesting to note that Amtrack #07 – the only one claimed by Argentina as having been hit – had both rear light clusters intact after the action and also that, in accordance with some local testimony, it appears to have been cut off with a cutting-torch after impact. The cluster – which has been professionally verified as belonging to an Amtrack – formed the centrepiece attraction at the launch of The First Casualty at the Royal Marines Museum, Portsmouth, in 2017 and the mystery of the Amtrack at White City remains one of the most compelling puzzles of the entire history of Operation Rosario.

37. Amtrack #07 showing some of the 97 bullet scores across its front and right and the smashed gunner's scope. Hugo Santillan was later to recall the bullets as they ricocheted from the hull as like the effect of spraying water from a hose at a car radiator.

38. Amtrack #17 showing patching obviously from a large-calibre impact which entered the nose and caused a severe 'blast-scab' on the opposite side. The damage corresponds exactly to where Mark Gibbs, Chris Bryan and Bill Trollope saw it hit, indicating that the vehicle was slewed to its right at an angle, as the Royal Marines always maintained.

39. Close-up side view of Amtrack #17 from the left, with numerous bullet scores and a hole behind the commander's cupola (extreme right) exactly where the Royal Marines remember hitting it, now circled around with local graffiti.

40. The rear of Amtrack #17 showing heavy 'pitting' around the left-hand-side rear light cluster (now replaced) from the 66mm round which struck it.

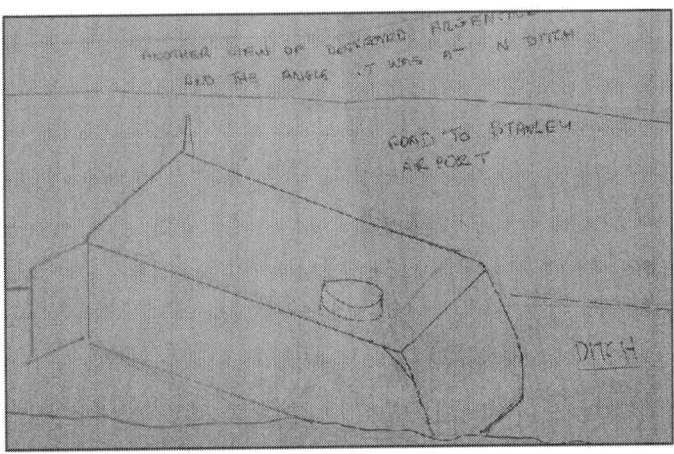

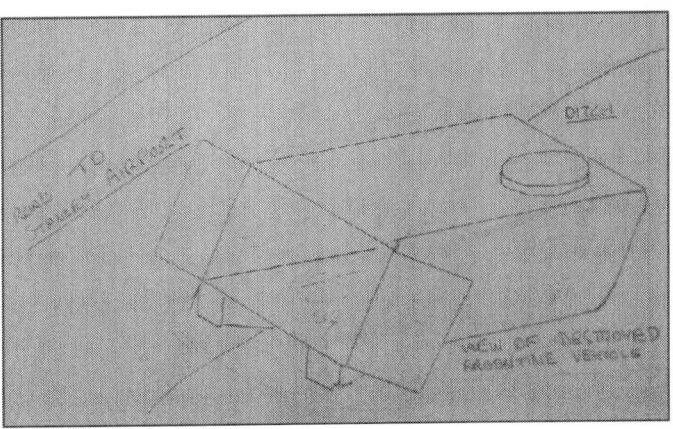

41 & 42. Original sketches made by Murray Paterson of the damaged Amtrack he saw twice on the Airport Road. Though the rear doors should actually be a ramp, yet the angle, elevation and position on the right of the road match exactly with descriptions of everyone who saw it both during and after the action. In the official version of the history, this vehicle never existed.

43. After the ceasefire, Major Gary Noott (centre) turns and addresses Mike Norman as meanwhile, Argentine Commandos and Buzos gather the Royal Marines' weapons.

44. Major Mike Norman talking with Lt. Commander Roscoe the Argentine liaison officer as meanwhile, Major Noott gives a disdainful glare to the cameraman.

45. The men of Section Four after giving themselves up at Long Island Farm on April 4. Dick Overall is the second man from the left of the picture.

46. George Brown and Danny Betts' Carl Gustav rocket launcher, recovered after the action at White City and which Hugo Santillan tracked down to the Marine Corps Museum, Puerto Belgrano.

47. Happy to be alive, the Royal Marines and Royal Navy men drink the Hotel Carrasco dry. Clockwise from centre-rear: Nick Williams, Tel George, Ray Bloye, Rod 'Jock' Wilcox, Bill McGrath (Endurance), Marcus 'Benny Bennett, Alex 'Doc' Pickthall, Steve Brooks (Endurance), George Carr, Michael 'PJ' Berry, Dave 'Scouse' Carr, Mick Sellen. The hotel was drunk dry three times in as many days with a bill, according to rumour, of £100,000 paid for by the British Government.

48. Old Comrades, L-R: Hugo Santillan, Alfredo Weinstabl, Daniel Tosolini and Hector Marcos of the BIM2 at a reunion in 2011.

49. Old Comrades, L-R: Dave Gerrard, Figgy Duff, Nick Williams, Mike Norman, Ray Bloye, Sir Rex Hunt and Tel George at a reunion in 2002.

50 & 51. 'The offending articles' which circulated after the invasion. The Daily Mail led in with 'Shamed!' and reported that 'with hardly a shot fired' Argentina took complete control. The Sun headed with 'Surrender!' and called it 'A moment of humiliating defeat'. These images and similar headlines went around the world and fuelled the myth of a 'token defence' which persists to this day. The Daily Mail later issued a retraction of this statement and reported the full story on July 22 2017 under the double page spread, 'Falklands Final Secret' and the Sun followed with 'Hidden Battle of War Heroes' the next day as a result of the publication of The First Casualty.

52. Dated picture of the LCVP Landing Craft sunk on April 2 1982 and later pulled from the narrows. It has undergone extensive repair but remains unserviceable. Its existence is still denied to this day.

c.   M66 x 7 rounds

23. <u>Casualties.</u> The following u

 a.   Killed   - 5

 b.   Wounded - 17

 c.   Prisoners - 3

 d.   Amtrac   - 1

No casualties were sustained by

POST ASSAULT

53. Major Mike Norman's official casualty report, stating 5 killed, 17 wounded, 3 prisoners and 1 'Amtrac' (sic.) destroyed.

54. The Tussac Islands aflame April 21 1982, bombed with napalm.

Photography Credits

1. Pedro Giachino from credit-free sources.
2. Kind permission of Diego Garcia Quiroga.
3. Kind permission of Hugo J Santillan.
4. Provided by Hugo J Santillan, credit to Cofradia 2 de Abril Galeria.
5. Provided by Hugo J Santillan, credit to Cofradia 2 de Abril Galeria.
6. Provided by Hugo J Santillan, credit to Cofradia 2 de Abril Galeria.
7. Provided by Hugo J Santillan, credit to Cofradia 2 de Abril Galeria.
8. Provided by Hugo J Santillan, credit to Cofradia 2 de Abril Galeria.
9. Kind permission of Hugo J Santillan.
10. Kind permission of Hugo J Santillan.
11. Provided by Hugo J Santillan, credit to Cofradia 2 de Abril Galeria.
12. Provided by Hugo J Santillan, credit to Cofradia 2 de Abril Galeria.
13. Provided by Hugo J Santillan, credit to Cofradia 2 de Abril Galeria.
14. Provided by Hugo J Santillan, credit to Cofradia 2 de Abril Galeria.
15. Kind permission of Nick Williams.
16. Kind permission of Barry Gill & Tanya Argue.
17. Kind permission of David Gerrard.
18. Kind permission of Ray Bloye.
19. Kind permission of Neil Duff.
20. Kind permission of RM Association.
21. Kind permission of Ray Bloye.
22. Kind permission of David Gerrard.
23. Kind permission of Terry Mooney.
24. Provided by Hugo J Santillan, credit to Cofradia 2 de Abril Galeria.
25. Credit to John5199 via Flickr.
26. Kind permission of Ray Bloye.
27. Artist unknown, source Taringa.
28. Credit to Cofradia 2 de Abril Galeria.
29. Kind permission of Diego Garcia Quiroga.
30. Kind permission of Andy Macdonald.
31. Kind permission of Hugo J Santillan.
32. Credit to Cofradia 2 de Abril Galeria.
33. To the owner.
34. Kind permission of Hugo J Santillan.

35. Originals credit Cofradia 2 de Abril Galeria, montage courtesy of Rachel Simons.
36. Kind permission of Paul Hannon.
37. Provided by Hugo J Santillan, credit to Cofradia 2 de Abril Galeria.
38. From Tripadvisor.
39. From Tripadvisor.
40. From Tripadvisor.
41. Original sketch by Murray Paterson, photograph by the author.
42. Original sketch by Murray Paterson, photograph by the author.
43. Provided by Hugo J Santillan, credit to Cofradia 2 de Abril Galeria.
44. Provided by Hugo J Santillan, credit to Cofradia 2 de Abril Galeria.
45. Credit to Cofradia 2 de Abril Galeria.
46. Provided by Hugo J Santillan by kind permission of Mrs P. Noriega.
47. Kind permission of Ray Bloye.
48. Kind permission of Daniel Tosolini.
49. Kind permission of David Gerrard.
50. Original artwork by The Daily Mail, photograph by the author.
51. Original artwork by The Sun, photograph by the author.
52. Kind permission of Paul Ellis.
53. Original report by Major M.J. Norman RM, photograph by the author.
54. To the owner.

NP8901 Tactical Organisation Chart

TAC HQ – OC's ROVER GROUP

Maj M J Norman – OCRM

Mne R A Farnworth – S3

Mne M G Paterson – Dvr (L/Rover)

DET HQ

Csgt W W Muir – DSM

Mne J A Tyler – Dvr (L/Rover)

Mne J A Turner – C3

Mne A B Timms – Dvr

ADMIN SECTION

WO2 W L Aspinall – DQMS

Cpl T D Pares – K2

Cpl P N Van Heerden – VM2

Mne G Duncan – K2

Mne G P Williams – K3

Mne S Tighe – Storeman

Mne G C Evans – Dvr

Mne D F Adey – Dvr

OPERATIONS ROOM

Maj G R H Noott – RM

Sgt A N Short – S1 Ops Operator

Cpl P Rounding – Carp Ops Log

RN SECTION AT GOVERNMENT HOUSE

Lt Ball – RN HMS Endurance

Lt Todhunter – RN HMS Endurance

Csgt J Noone - RM

GPO (SR) Woodhouse – HMS Endurance
PO (Wtr) Vind A – HMS Endurance
PO (MEM) Smart – HMS Endurance
LS (SR) Ward – HMS Endurance
LS (SR) Lawson – HMS Endurance
LMEM (R) Almond – HMS Endurance
AB (SR) McGrath – HMS Endurance
AB (R) McMeekin – HMS Endurance

MEDICAL COVER
LMA T H C Bradford
LMA A G Pickthall

GOVERNMENT HOUSE SECTION
Cpl M D Sellen – RM
Mne H W W Dorey – Personal Guard to HE
Mne C Jones – RM
Mne P J Fairclough – RM
Cpl B M Gill – RM (Acting Tp Sgt)
Mne A Macdonald – RM
Mr J Fairfield – Ex Cpl RM NP8901 80/81

TROOP HQ
Lt C W Trollope RM – Tp Cdr
Sgt R G R Shepherd – Tp Sgt
Mne M Gibbs – Arm

1 SECTION
Cpl D J Armour – RM
LCpl G Clifton – RM
Mne J Alden – RM
Mne A C Brindley – RM
Mne R E Parker – RM

Mne B L Eccles – RM

2 SECTION
Cpl C F Bryan – RM

Lcpl M Reynolds – GPMG No 2

Mne D J Betts – 84 No 2

Mne S Egan – GPMG No 1

Mne S Brown – 84 No 1

Mne M E Coombs - RM

3 SECTION
Cpl S C Johnson – RM

Lcpl S M Black - RM

Mne M A Branch – GPMG No 2

Mne R A N Butcher

Mne S Dronfield – GPMG No 1

Mne M D Macleod – RM

4 SECTION
Cpl S C York – RM

Lcpl J N McKay – GPMG No 2

Mne J N Urand - RM

Mne G Moor – RM

Mne R W F Overall – RM

Mne M T Smith – GPMG No 1

5 SECTION
Cpl N S Duff – RM

Cpl D Gerrard – RM

Mne B J Hobbs – RM

Mne S M McCalhan – RM

Mne F M Sugden – RM

Mne B M Clay – Dvr (L/Rover)

6 SECTION

Cpl D L Carr – RM
Cpl N J N Williams – GPMG No 2
Mne R D Bloye – RM
Mne T M George – RM
Mne M E M Bennett – GPMG No 1
Mne M Carr – RM

BEACH OP – MOTORCYCLES (5A SECTION)

Mne L Milne – GPMG No 1
Mne R P Wilcox – GPMG No 2

SAPPER HILL OP – MOTORCYCLE

Mne M J Berry – RM

Operation Rosario Tactical Organisation Chart

Commanders:

Task Force Commander (TG40): VLNA Walter O. Allara
Landing Force Commander (TG40.1) CLIM Carlos Busser
Landing Force Deputy Commander: CLIM Miguel Pita

Units:

TU40.1.1 – 2nd Marine Battalion – CFIM Alfredo Weinstabl

TU40.1.2 – 2nd Marine Battalion – Section CCIM Hugo J. Santillan

TU40.1.3 – Amphibious Commando (APCA) – CCIM Guillermo Sanchez-Sabarots

TU 40.1.4 Combat Divers (APBT) – CCNA Alfredo R. Cufre

TU40.1.5 – APCA/APBT Combined Section – CCIM Pedro E. Giachino

TU40.1.6 – "A" Battery, Field Artillery Battalion – TNIM Mario F. Perez

TU40.1.7 – 1st Marine Battalion – Reinforced Section - TNIM Oscar Oulton

TU40.1.8 – Combat Support Section – CFIM Victor H. Theaux

TU40.1.9 – Civilian Affairs – CCIM Martin Arillaga

TU40.1.10 – Army Section – TCNL Mohamed A. Seineldin

BIM2 Tactical Organisation Chart

1. First Wave, Advance Party and Link-up Force (Marine Lt Cdr Hugo Jorge Santillán):

   a. LVTP7 #05 (Marine Lt Cdr Hugo Jorge Santillán):
      i. Command Group Leader: Marine Petty Officer Third Class Agüero.
      ii. Radio Operator and runner: Marine Conscript Class 1992 Ángel Tello.
      iii. Two stretcher-bearers.
      iv. Rocket Launcher Team.
      v. Rifle Squad.
      vi. Light Machine Gun Team.
      vii. Total: 24 men.

   b. LVTP7 #19 (Marine Lt Schweizer):
      i. Rifle Squad.
      ii. 81 mm Mortar Team.
      iii. 75 mm Recoilless Rifle Team.
      iv. Light Machine Gun Team.
      v. Total: 25 men.

   c. LVTP7 #07 (Marine Chief Petty Officer Quiroga):
      i. Rifle Squad.
      ii. 81 mm Mortar Team.
      iii. 75 mm Recoilless Rifle Team.
      iv. Rocket Launcher Team.
      v. Total: 25 men.

   d. LVTP7 #10 (Army Lt Col M. A. Seineldín):
      i. Army 2nd Lt Reyes.
      ii. Twenty three (23) Army Infantry Soldiers from 25th Infantry Regiment.
      iii. Total: 25 men.

2. Battalion Landing Team Commander (Marine Cdr Alfredo Weinstabl): LVTP7 #03 (25 men)

3. Delta Rifle Company, 2nd Marines Battalion (Marine Capt Jr Gde Di Paola): LVTP7 #01, 02, 13, 16 and 18 (125 men).

4. Echo Rifle Company, 2nd Marines Battalion (Marine Capt Jr Gde Arruani): LVTP7 #04, 08, 09, 11 and 15 (125 men).

5. 106.6 mm Heavy Mortar Platoon (Marine Midshipman Ciaglia): LVTP7 #06 and 14 (40 men)

6. Landing Force Commander (Marine Rear Adm Büsser): LVTPC #01 (command post model; 10 men) and LVTP7 #12 (25 men).

7. LVTP's Recovery and Maintenance Team (Marine Lt. Lacalle): LVTPR #01 (recovery model; 6 men).

Pedro Giachino's Snatch Squad

Ship to Shore:

Boat #18 – Giachino / Flores / Salas / Gomez

Boat #19 – Garcia Quiroga / Cardillo / Ledesma / Urbina

Boat #20 – Lugo / Lopes / Ortiz / Alegra

Boat #21 – Alvarez / Gutierrez / Mansilla / Vargas

Attack on GH:

Assault Group (Blue)
Lt. Cmdr. Giachino
Ens. Garcia Quiroga
Cpl. Flores
Scpo. Salas
Scpo. Lopez

Support Group (Red)
Lt. Lugo
Cpl. Ledesma
Cpl. Ortiz
Cpl. Alegre
Po1 Med. Urbina

Security Group (Green)
Lt. Alvarez
Scpo. Mansilla
Scpo. Cardillo
Scpo. Gutierrez
Cpl. Vargas
Cpl. Gomez

References

All first-hand accounts are given directly from source as from the original. Additional references provided from stated sources. References in quotation from 'Operacion Rosario' by Carlos Busser, 'The Falklands War from the end of our street' by Neville K Bennett and from 'Invasion 1982' by Graham Bound and 'Argentine fight for the Falklands' by Martin Middlebrook both courtesy of Pen & Sword Books as per Pen & Sword guidelines as advised by Navy Books in representation of The First Casualty. All additional sources and references provided by sources previously stated wherever possible. The author also acknowledges a number of secondary sources provided from personal accounts, interviews, translations and other anecdotes given him, the ownership of which, in some instances may be uncertain, the credits to the owners of those statements, likewise with several photographs, the ownership of which has been sought and where not defined or claimed, to the owner with kind regards.

Praise for "The First Casualty"

"As a boy, I remember well the Task Force setting off for the Falklands, all focus was on the coming battles such as Mount Tumbledown and later documentaries such as 'The Raid on Top Malo'. Later, when a developing young soldier and as an officer-cadet in the Irish Defence Forces I recall studying books such as 'No Picnic', Major General Julian Thompson's account of the Falklands War. But nowhere did I read of the gallant defence of Stanley by the Royal Marines of NP8901. The only story I knew of their plight was that of being outgunned and quickly overwhelmed by a superior force of Argentine troops, including Special Forces. The only image that sprang to mind was of men in the famous green berets being forced to their knees after being disarmed. The fact that these men put up a heroic and highly proficient defence of the territory they were tasked to defend and were then promptly forgotten about and written out of history is gut-wrenching in its unfairness! Their story is so strikingly similar to the book I wrote about the small Irish garrison holding out at the siege of Jadotville in the Congo in 1961 that the story is compelling; the men of NP8901 fought and behaved in the highest traditions of the Royal Marines. In fact, against better soldiers with better 'over the horizon' support ranged against the bootnecks, I think maybe the men at Stanley had it worse than the Irish in 1961. They did their duty, but were to be ignored by the powers-that-be; much like their brothers-in-arms before them, the Irish at Jadotville.

However, we also look forward to the record being set straight as it was for the men of Jadotville and as this book will undoubtedly do. No matter how long it takes, every serviceman who has seen action or risked himself in the service of his nation is at the very least deserving of their actions being recorded accurately and in this, I can say that the author has done a great job of contextualising this history and bringing it to life. I daresay that The First Casualty is one of the very few to also give a very accessible history of the Falklands and their relevance to both the UK and Argentina as well as a fantastic insight on the Falkland Islanders themselves. Ricky D Phillips has kept the faith with the Royal Marines of NP8901 and given them a voice. Let us hope that the British people and indeed all people of goodwill will now value the efforts made by this band of brothers in 1982 to defend the democratic rights of Falkland Islanders in the face of overwhelming force, without any guidance or military support whatsoever. In all, a gripping story of action and heroism, denied for political convenience and which, I hope, shall change the face and the history of this fascinating conflict for good."

Declan Power – Author of 'Siege at Jadotville'

*   *   *   *   *

"I find Ricky D Phillips´ book both innovative and engaging. It is written with respect and sympathy for the men who fought on 2nd April and shows once again how difficult it is to ascertain the events that take place in the complex landscape of the frontline. I read his effort to throw light into them after over thirty years not only as the keenness of a true historian but also as his personal tribute to the expense and tribulations of men serving under arms."

Diego Garcia Quiroga – VGM, Buzo Tactico

*   *   *   *   *

"The First Casualty succeeds in being an important work of military history that rips along like a compelling adventure novel, as it tells for the first time the full story of the fight to defend the Falkland Islands against the Argentine invasion. There are numerous books on the Falklands War, but most of them reduce this vital episode to a few paragraphs before moving on to the better-known battles which followed the landing of the British Task Force. Not before time, The First Casualty gives this crucial episode the attention it deserves and has the rare distinction of including both sides of the story, with both British and Argentine veterans recalling their experiences. This is military history from the sharp end – visceral and compelling - written in an engaging style but with enough detail to keep even historians of the conflict satisfied. I teach the history of the Falklands War to students and the University of Glasgow and will be very happy to add The First Casualty to my course reading list."

Professor Tony Pollard - Professor of Conflict History and Archaeology / Director, Centre for Battlefield Archaeology, Glasgow University and co-presenter of 'Two men in a Trench' and 'Nazi Megastructures'.

*   *   *   *   *

"Narrative History at its best. Ricky D. Phillips has successfully weaved the accounts of the men who fought at ort Stanley into a riveting and fast aced narrative which reads like a novel rather than the meticulously researched history which it is. This is a story which has waited for more than three decades to be told, but the result is a testimony both to the courage of those who fought and the skill of the author as a gifted military historian."

Andgus Konstam – Author & Historian

Key to Maps

Map 1: Operation Rosario: March 28 - April 3, 1982.

Map 2: Stanley and its Environs.

Map 3: Royal Marines Deployment by Sections.
Key: All sections denoted by number. PJ = PJ Berry.

Map 4: Assault on Moody Brook and Government House.
Key: All sections denoted by number. MN = Mike Norman. HQ = Headquarters section. X = Mystery men seen at these points.

Map 5: Assault on the Isthmus / Airport.
Key: All sections denoted by number. A = Cufre & Buzo Tactico. B = Hugo Santillan & Vanguard. C = LCVP Landing Craft sunk. D = Runway cleared.

Map 6: Phase 1: Situation 06.00-07.30 (Approx.)
Key: All sections denoted by number. PG = Pedro Giachino. SS = Sanchez-Sabarots. HS = Hugo Santillan. AC = Alfredo Cufre. 25 = 25IR platoon (Seineldin).

Map 7: The Action at White City.
Key: Amtracks denoted by number. A = Section 2 in ditches. B = Brown & Betts. C = Yellow digger. D = Tom Davies' house. E = Alistair Grieves' house.

Map 8: Phase 2: Situation 07.30-09.30 (Approx.)
Key: All sections denoted by number. PG = Pedro Giachino. SS = Sanchez-Sabarots. HS = Hugo Santillan. AC = Alfredo Cufre. 25 = 25IR platoon (Seineldin).

Map 9: Street Map of Stanley.

Maps

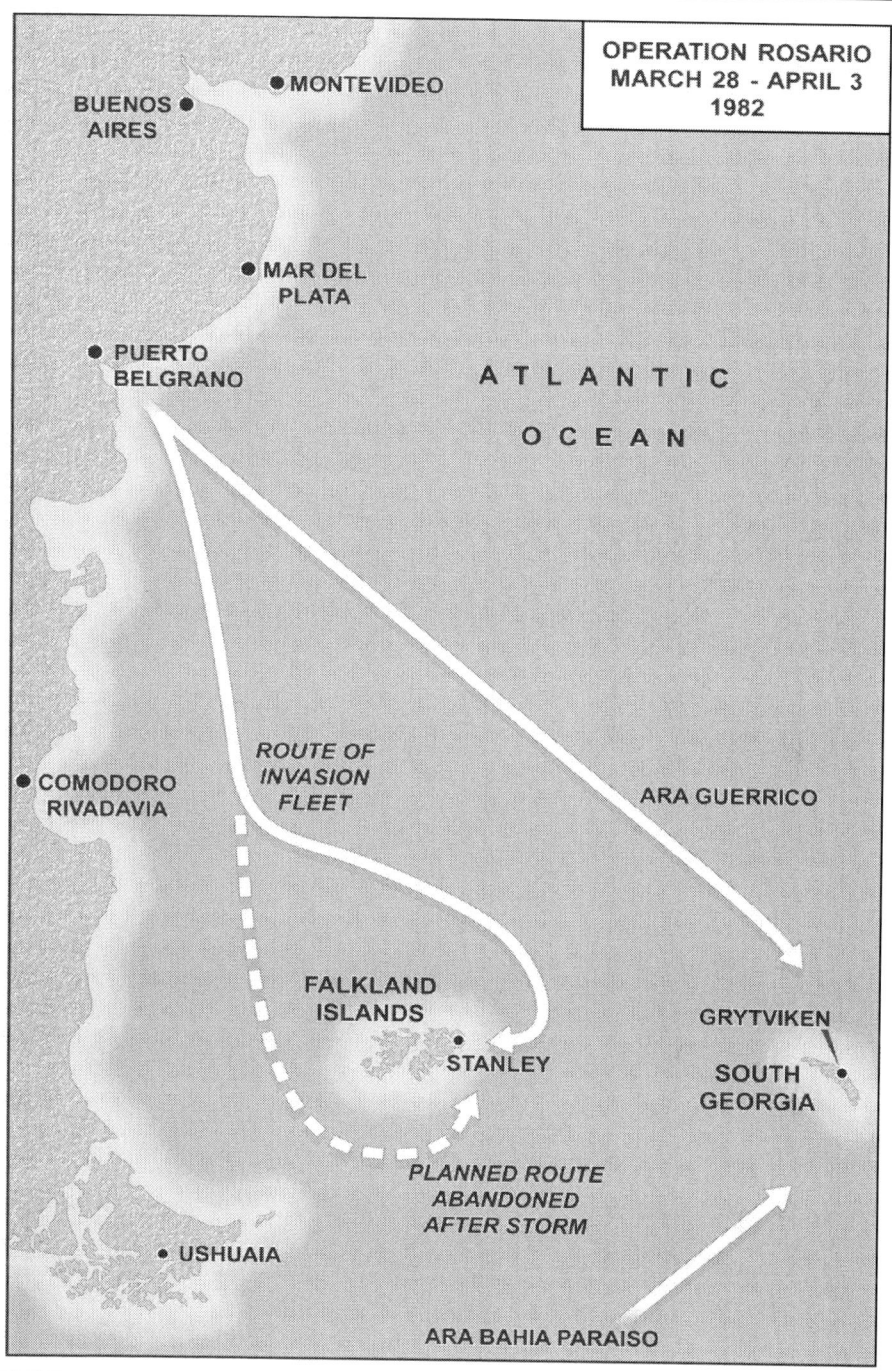

OPERATION ROSARIO
MARCH 28 - APRIL 3
1982

MONTEVIDEO

BUENOS
AIRES

MAR DEL
PLATA

PUERTO
BELGRANO

ATLANTIC

OCEAN

ROUTE OF
INVASION
FLEET

COMODORO
RIVADAVIA

ARA GUERRICO

FALKLAND
ISLANDS

GRYTVIKEN

STANLEY

SOUTH
GEORGIA

PLANNED ROUTE
ABANDONED
AFTER STORM

USHUAIA

ARA BAHIA PARAISO

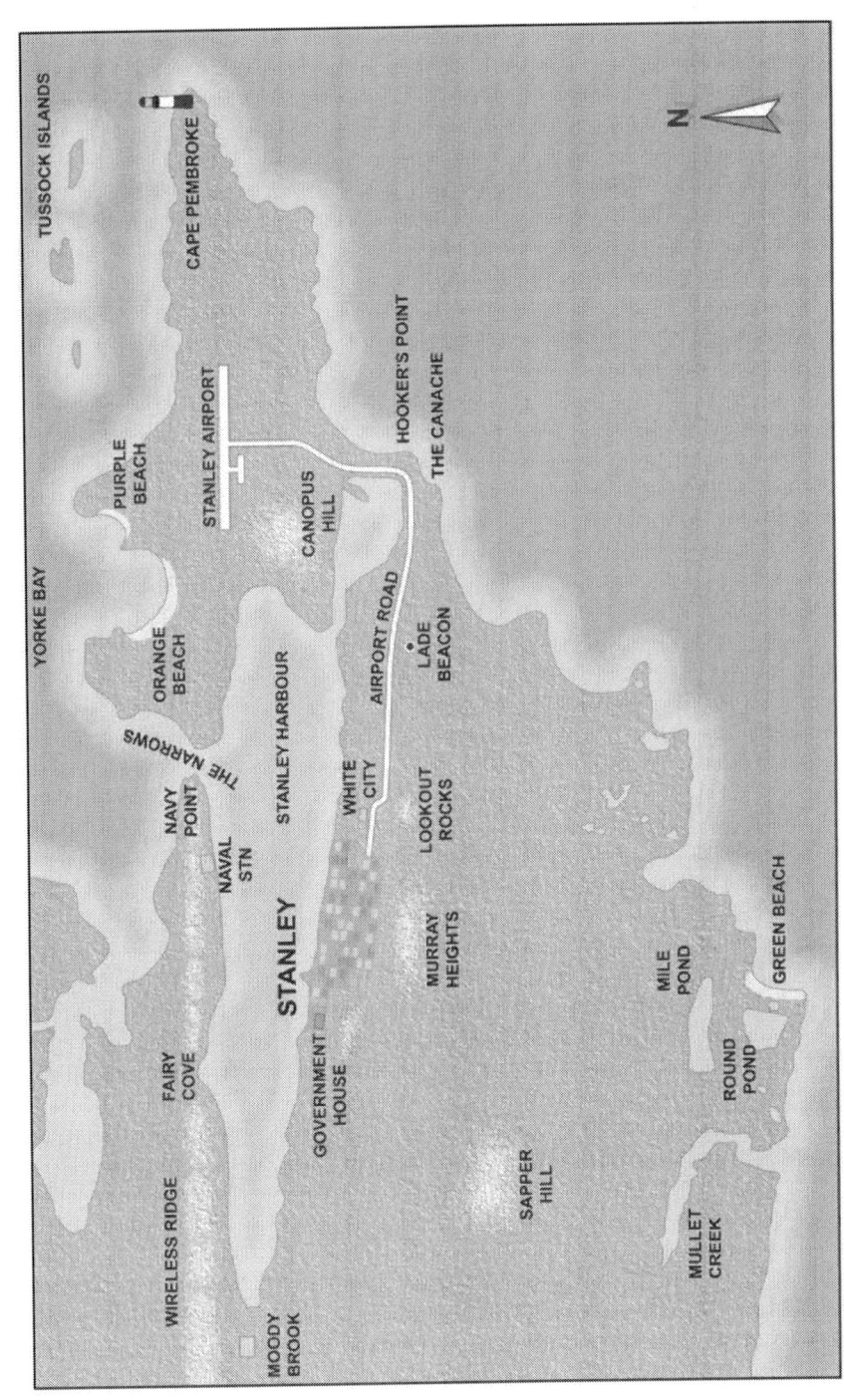

TUSSOCK ISLANDS

CAPE PEMBROKE

N

YORKE BAY

PURPLE BEACH

STANLEY AIRPORT

HOOKER'S POINT

CANOPUS HILL

THE CANACHE

ORANGE BEACH

THE NARROWS

STANLEY HARBOUR

AIRPORT ROAD

LADE BEACON

NAVY POINT

NAVAL STN

WHITE CITY

LOOKOUT ROCKS

WIRELESS RIDGE

FAIRY COVE

STANLEY

GOVERNMENT HOUSE

MURRAY HEIGHTS

MILE POND

GREEN BEACH

MOODY BROOK

SAPPER HILL

ROUND POND

MULLET CREEK

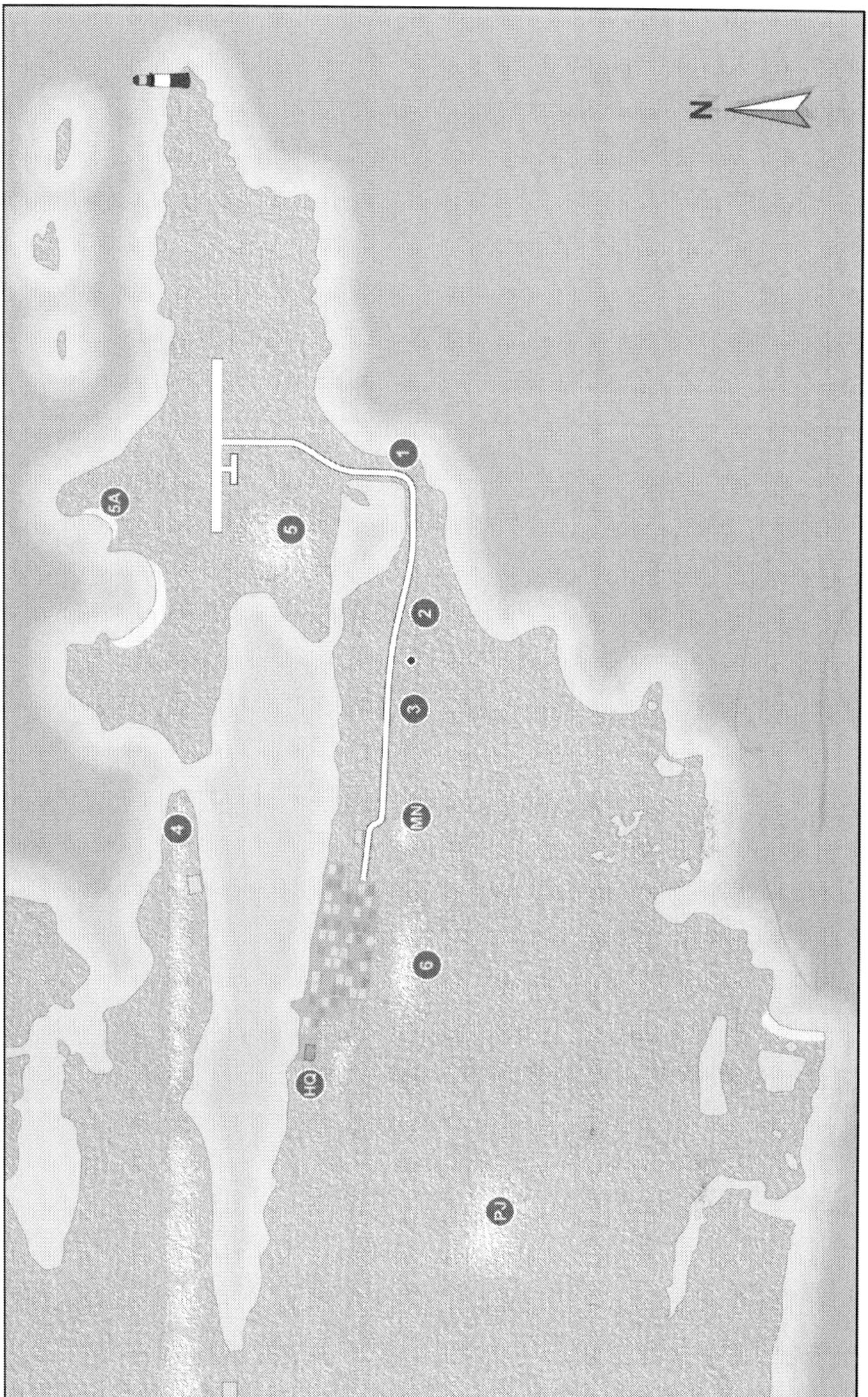
N
1
2
3
4
5
5A
6
MN
HQ
PJ

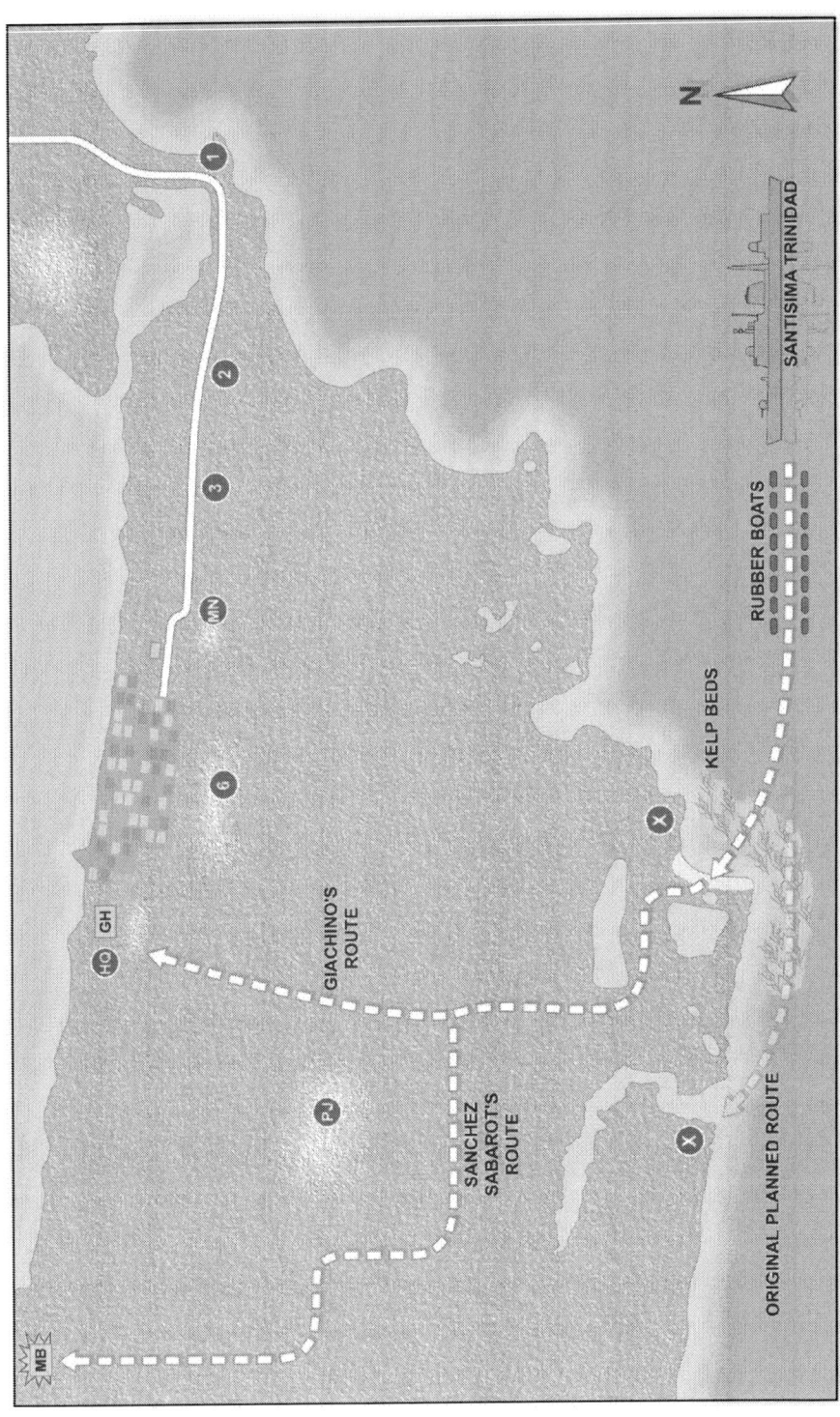

SANTISIMA TRINIDAD

RUBBER BOATS

KELP BEDS

GIACHINO'S ROUTE

SANCHEZ SABAROT'S ROUTE

ORIGINAL PLANNED ROUTE

GH

MB

N

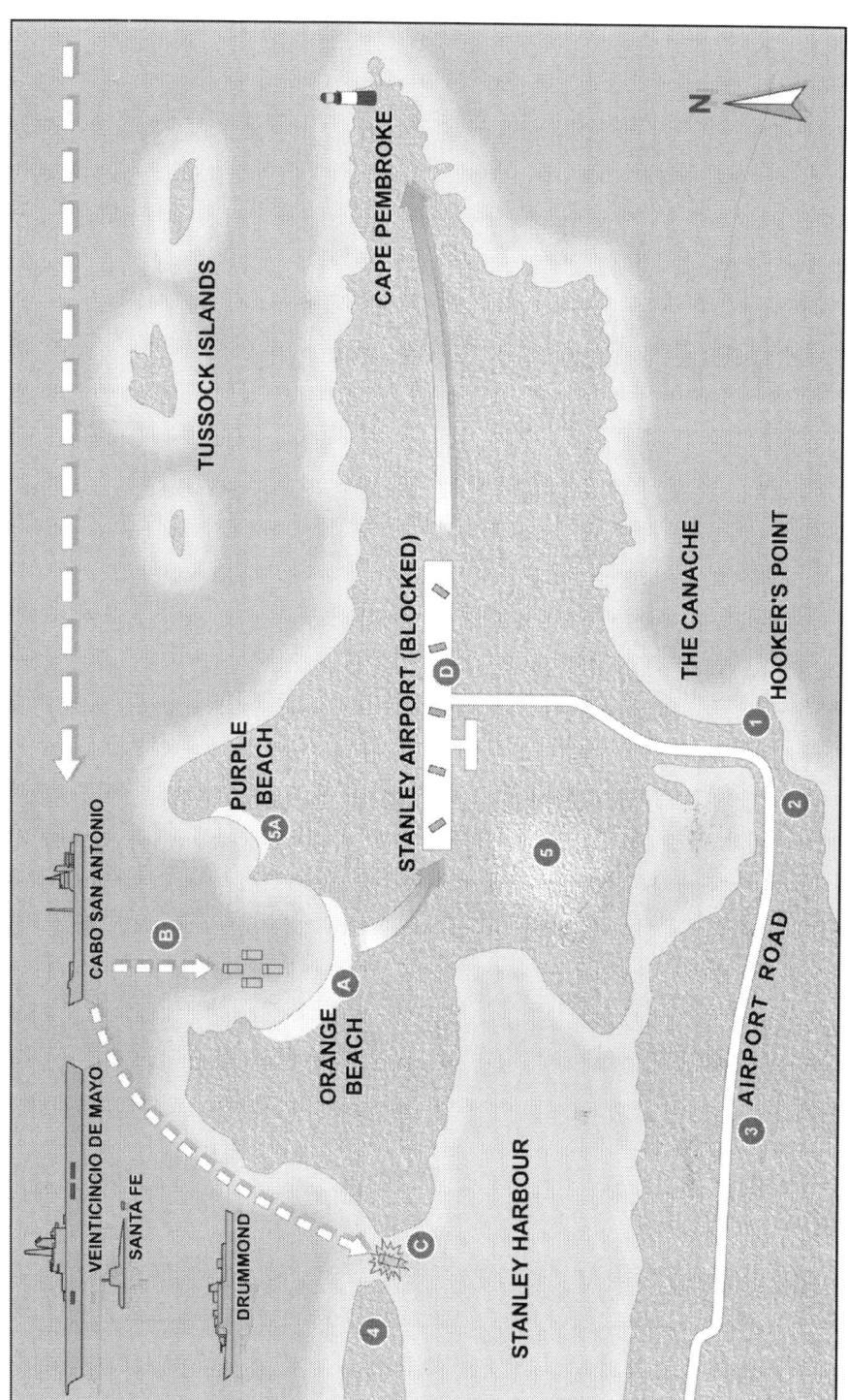

N

TUSSOCK ISLANDS

CAPE PEMBROKE

PURPLE BEACH

STANLEY AIRPORT (BLOCKED)

D

3A

THE CANACHE

HOOKER'S POINT

1

2

AIRPORT ROAD

3

5

CABO SAN ANTONIO

B

ORANGE BEACH

A

VEINTICINCIO DE MAYO

SANTÀ FE

DRUMMOND

C

4

STANLEY HARBOUR

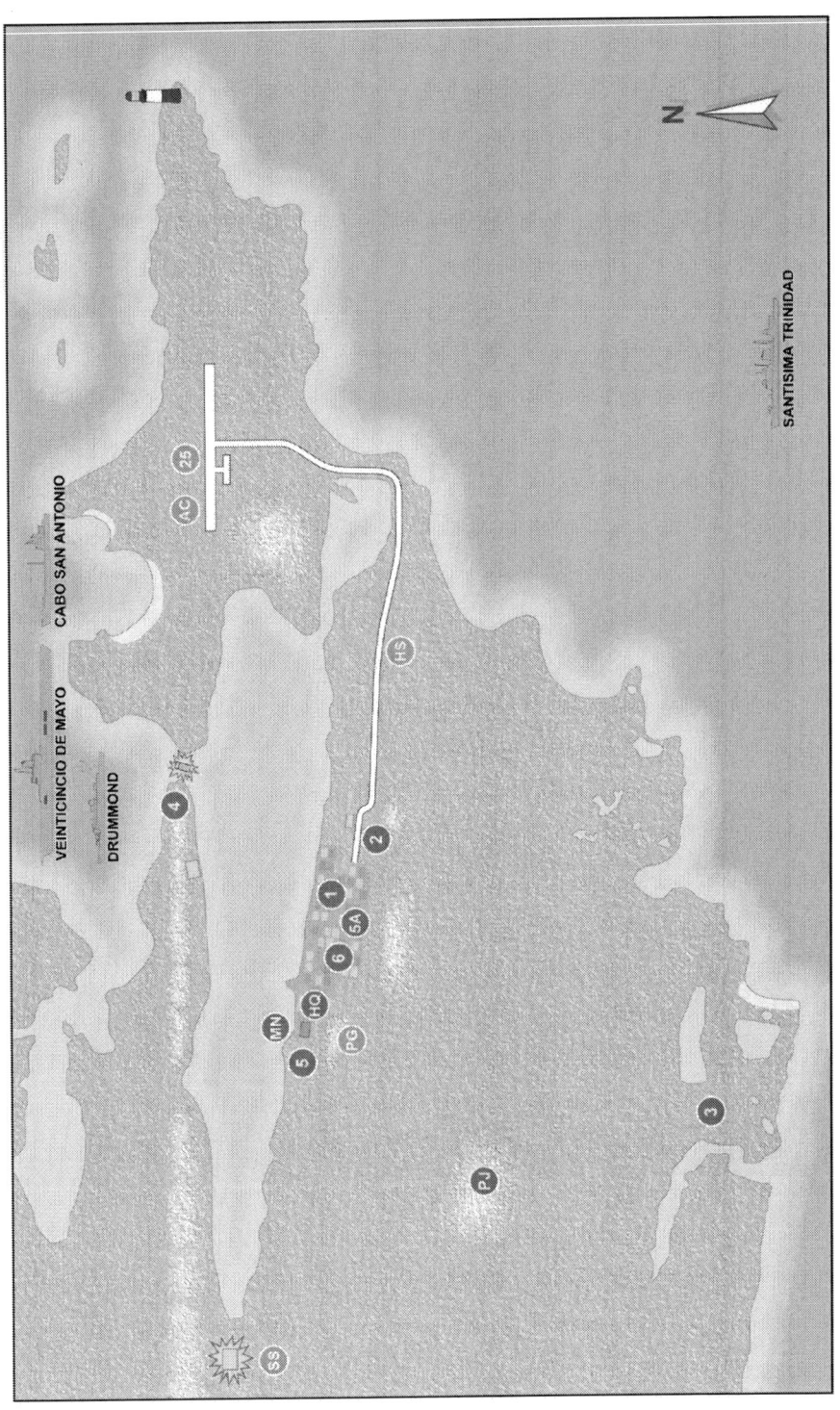

VEINTICINCIO DE MAYO   CABO SAN ANTONIO

DRUMMOND

SANTISIMA TRINIDAD

N

The First Casualty

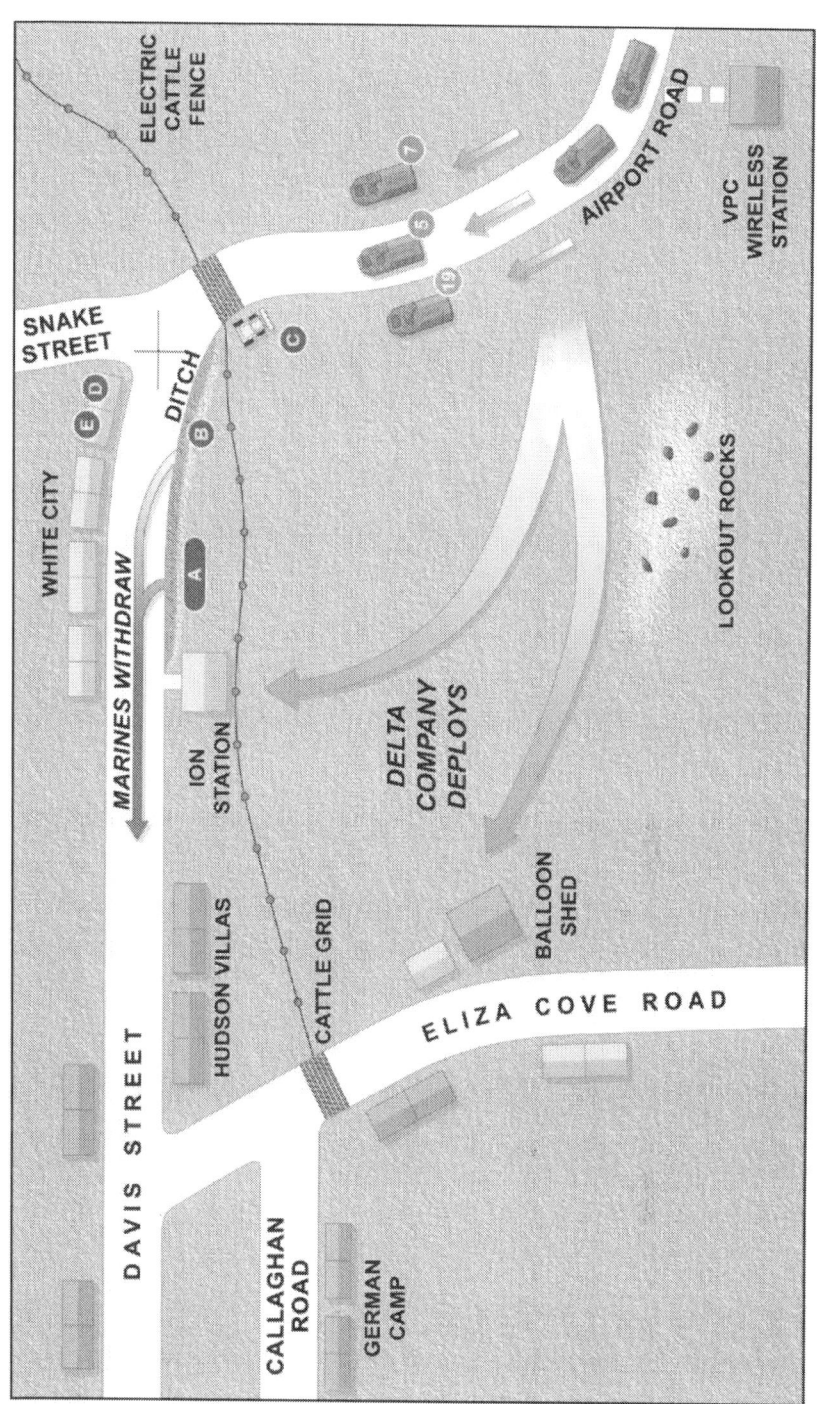

ELECTRIC CATTLE FENCE

AIRPORT ROAD

7

6

19

VPC WIRELESS STATION

SNAKE STREET

DITCH

C

E D

B

WHITE CITY

MARINES WITHDRAW

A

ION STATION

DELTA COMPANY DEPLOYS

LOOKOUT ROCKS

HUDSON VILLAS

BALLOON SHED

CATTLE GRID

DAVIS STREET

ELIZA COVE ROAD

CALLAGHAN ROAD

GERMAN CAMP

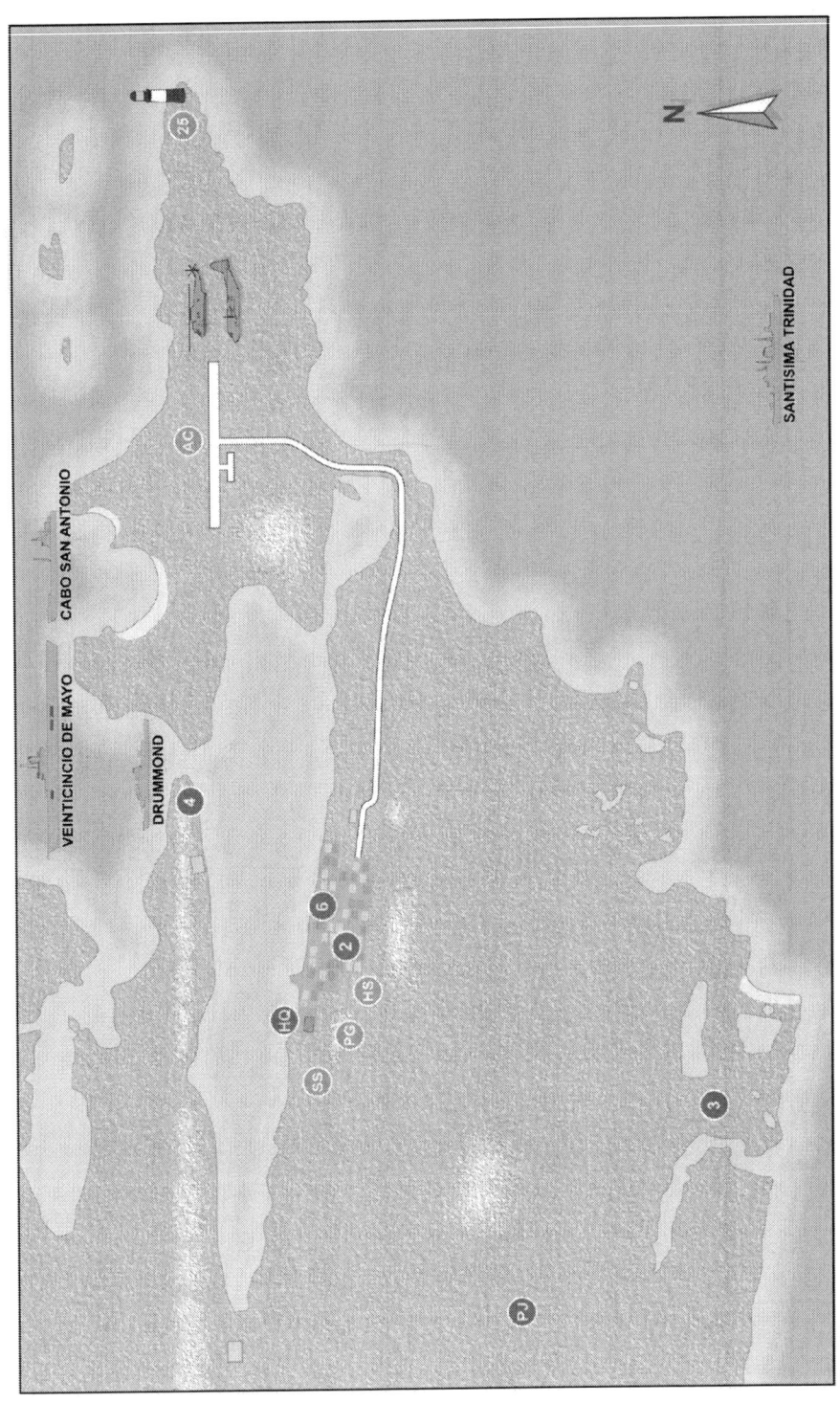

N

SANTÍSIMA TRINIDAD

CABO SAN ANTONIO

VEINTICINCIO DE MAYO

DRUMMOND

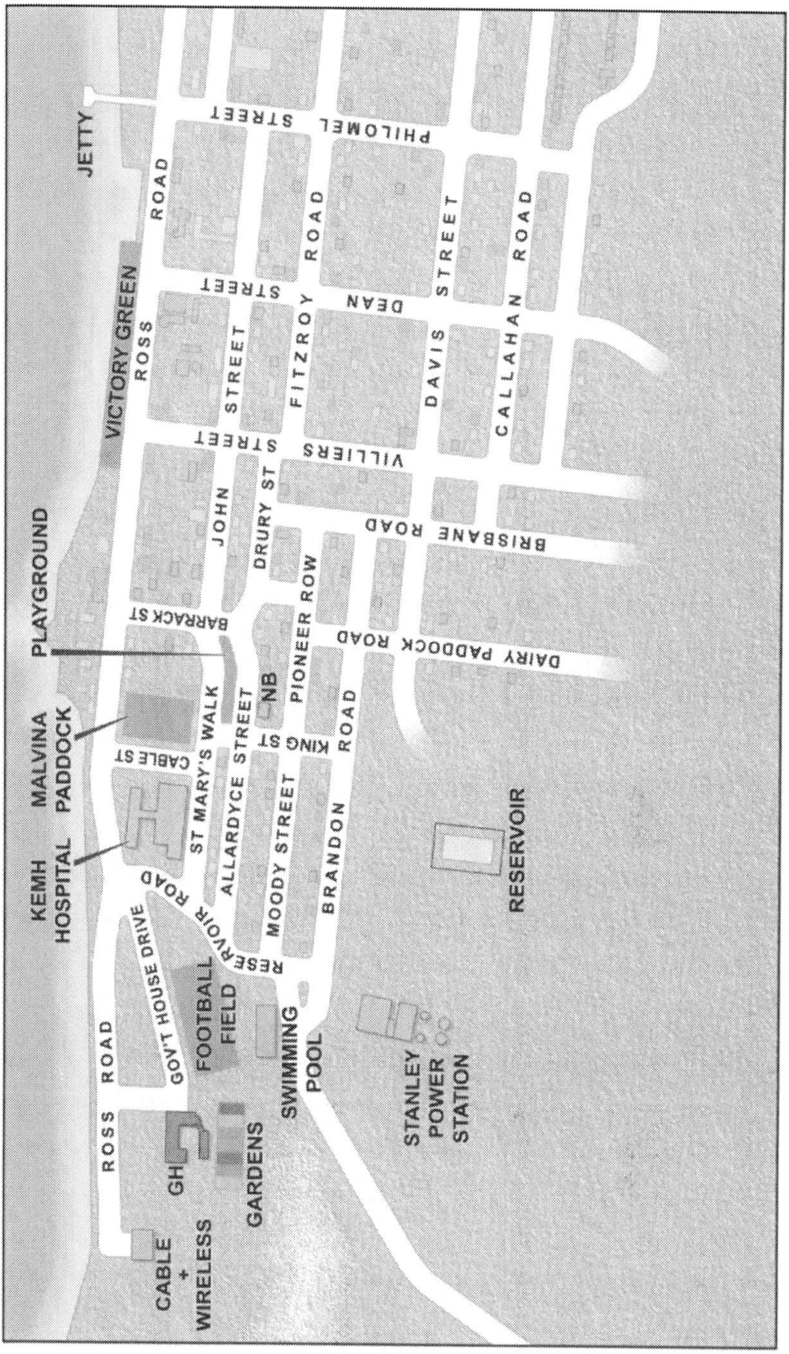
JETTY
VICTORY GREEN
PLAYGROUND
MALVINA PADDOCK
KEMH HOSPITAL
CABLE + WIRELESS
GH
GARDENS
FOOTBALL FIELD
SWIMMING POOL
STANLEY POWER STATION
RESERVOIR
ROSS ROAD
GOV'T HOUSE DRIVE
RESERVOIR ROAD
ST MARY'S WALK
ALLARDYCE STREET
MOODY STREET
BRANDON ROAD
CABLE ST
KING ST
NB
PIONEER ROW
BARRACK ST
JOHN STREET
DRURY ST
DAIRY PADDOCK ROAD
BRISBANE ROAD
VILLIERS STREET
FITZROY ROAD
DAVIS STREET
CALLAHAN ROAD
DEAN STREET
PHILOMEL STREET

Printed in Great Britain
by Amazon

Managing
IBD

A balanced guide to
inflammatory bowel disease

This book is dedicated to the best family a girl could ask for – to my husband Matt, who held my hand on our first date at 17 and has never stopped taking care of me since then; to my Mom and Dad, whose support has been constant and unwavering; to Jonathan, Jack, Leanne and Kate and my beautiful niece Ophelia who can brag that she already has her name in print at a few months old. None of this would be possible without each of you and I love you all.

Jenna xx

A huge thank you to all of my readers who made this possible and the IBD community who so willingly shared their feedback and stories (especially Bexie and all the other lovely folks in the *Healthy Living with IBD* Facebook group).

Managing IBD

A balanced guide to
inflammatory bowel disease

JENNA FARMER

With contributions from

KAY GREVESON
– award-winning IBD nurse and creator of IBD Passport
&
SALLY BAKER
– award-winning therapist and author of
How to Feel Differently About Food

Hammersmith Health Books
London, UK

First published in 2017 by Hammersmith Health Books – an imprint of
Hammersmith Books Limited
4/4A Bloomsbury Square, London WC1A 2RP, UK
www.hammersmithbooks.co.uk

Disclaimer: The information in this book is of a general nature and is
meant for educational purposes only. It is not intended as medical advice.
The contents may not be used to treat, or diagnose, any particular disease
or any particular person. Applying elements from this publication does
not constitute a professional relationship or professional advice or
services. No endorsement or warranty is explicitly given or implied by
any entity connected to this content.

As always, if you are have pre-existing health issues and especially if you
are taking any medications, you are advised first to consult your health
practitioner before making any changes to your lifestyle and diet.

British Library Cataloguing in Publication Data: a CIP record of this
book is available from the British Library.

Print ISBN: 978-1-78161-098-5
Ebook ISBN: 978-1-78161-099-2

Editor: Georgina Bentliff
Cover design: Sylvia Kwan
Text designed and typeset by: Sylvia Kwan
Index: Dr Laurence Errington
Production: Helen Whitehorn of Path Projects Ltd
Printed and bound by: TJ International Ltd, Cornwall, UK

Contents

Foreword

Jenna has written an honest and very personal account of her journey with Crohn's disease from well before diagnosis and through many of her most difficult and painful moments. She also describes her personal battles and the difficult decisions she has taken. Her nutrition background helps this book stand apart from many other personal accounts of living with Crohn's disease, with a great deal of detail on diet and dietary therapies, and the section written by Kay Grevson, a specialist IBD nurse, adds clinical detail which the reader will find helpful.

Many patients with Crohn's and ulcerative colitis will find Jenna's words resonate with them and this book will provide support and comfort to them, especially the experiences of other IBD sufferers and the broad range of topics covered which deal with many of the less commonly discussed aspects of IBD. There are tips on dealing with investigations, advice about taking care of oneself and discussion of several controversial and important topics in IBD such as diet, anxiety and complementary therapies.

At times funny (the description of inpatient care in China is almost unbelievable!), always engaging, this book is a mixture of advice, information and a warm hug, which IBD sufferers will enjoy reading and which does exactly what Jenna promises: 'Help you take a balanced and holistic approach to managing your life with inflammatory bowel disease'.

forCrohns, 2017

About the author

Jenna Farmer was first diagnosed with Crohn's disease in 2012 and has been passionate about raising awareness of what it is like to live with the condition ever since. Her love for healthy eating led to her studying for several Nutritional Therapy qualifications and she began to chronicle her attempts at living a balanced, healthy lifestyle with IBD on her blog www.abalancedbelly.co.uk in 2013. The website covers everything from travelling with the disease to easy-to-digest recipes and medication tips. Over the years, her site has grown significantly and Jenna has written for a variety of other health and nutrition websites also.

About the contributors

Kay Greveson has worked as an Inflammatory Bowel Disease nurse specialist since 2005 and now works as Lead IBD nurse specialist at the Royal Free Hospital Centre for Gastroenterology, London, UK, where in 2014 she founded IBDpassport, an evidence-based resource containing useful information regarding travel and IBD (www.ibdpassport.com). She also has personal experience of IBD, having been diagnosed with Crohn's disease aged 13. Following university, she embarked on a year-long solo round-the-world trip that gave her personal insight into and empathy with the challenges faced in balancing life and travel with a chronic illness.

Sally Baker is a therapist, speaker and writer who has been working in London for more than a decade. She specialises in helping clients to resolve self-sabotaging behaviour in whatever form it shows up and to resolve and release limiting beliefs that inhibit them from living to their full potential. As well as being a hypnotherapist, she is a Master Practitioner of PSTEC (percussive suggestion technique) and an Advanced Practitioner of EFT (emotional freedom technique).

Introduction

Most books about chronic conditions begin with the facts, perhaps the percentage of people who suffer from the disease, a clinical definition or a checklist of symptoms you mght be experiencing. Yet if you are reading this, then I am sure inflammatory bowel disease needs no introduction. I am certain that, like me, you are all too familiar with the symptoms: the classic ones the textbooks list (diarrhoea, pain, mouth ulcers) and the extra intestinal manifestations that nobody seems to really understand but are just as big a part of the disease (anxiety, skin rashes, nutritional deficiencies – I'm looking at you!). When we are first diagnosed with this (at times, extremely debilitating) disease, a doctor thrusts a leaflet into our hands and sends us on our way. This book does not aim to be one of these leaflets.

I know that facts certainly have their place and there are plenty of websites that will tell you the average age of diagnosis or the percentage of people who require surgery if that's what you are looking for. Instead, *this* book aims to do everything else. It aims to provide a practical and balanced approach to help you live with your Crohn's disease or ulcerative colitis, to provide all the information on things you'd like to ask your doctor but can't, from figuring out the foods that work for you, to making the most of your appointments to balancing your medication with the appropriate supplement routine.

So what makes me the expert? Well, this book is the culmination of my struggles and triumphs. From the 12 years I lived with stomach pain, anaemia, diarrhoea and abscesses only to be told I had 'IBS' and 'stress'. It's the story of the moment of diagnosis and beyond, as I learnt to live with and accept my disease.

My diagnosis could be a book in itself, for it took a move to the exotic land of China to finally figure out what was wrong with me. I had always felt unwell but since I had been labelled as suffering from 'IBS', managing my symptoms seemed almost part of my daily routine. Yet around a year after I moved abroad, I started to deteriorate and suffered from vomiting and weight loss; within days of seeing a doctor I was finally given a proper colonoscopy and diagnosed with Crohn's disease. Being alone in a foreign country (the language of which I could not speak – not a word!) forced me to become my own doctor, nutritionist and health advocate all rolled into one. As Crohn's is extremely rare in China, I could not rely completely on the expertise of the medical professionals and thus began researching everything to do with the disease, treatment and ways to manage it. I navigated my way through hospital visits, Infliximab treatments, blood tests and colonoscopies, all while trying to master the basics of the language and adjust to the reality that my body had been trying to fight itself for the past 10 years.

Alongside my desire to find out everything about the disease was my growing interest in nutrition, which later led me to study for a Nutritional Therapy Diploma. I felt my travelling days were not yet over and was determined to try everything possible to give my body the best support to stay as healthy as it could. I decided to chronicle my efforts at leading a healthy, balanced lifestyle online (www.abalancedbelly.co.uk) and was overwhelmed by the number of people who too needed guidance in managing this condition.

Whilst diet is an important part of my IBD management (alongside many other aspects) this book certainly doesn't aim to offer a cure or any kind of prescriptive meal plan for sufferers. My experiences have taught me that all the correct food choices (and I use this term very loosely, as we'll explore later why this is such a hugely personal issue) in the world won't work if you are stressed out and neglecting your body in other ways. In turn, we also need to recognise that our body sometimes needs more help than we can offer it and know when to turn to the professionals. Like many IBD patients, I've had periods of being med-free and periods when I've had no choice but to medicate to give my body the best chance possible to recover. Both of these choices are OK. Yet whether we are being treated with medication, awaiting surgery or enjoying remission, it is so important to consider the many aspects of self-care that can help IBD patients, such as food, sleep, exercise, support networks and stress relief. Of course, these self-care methods may, for some, be enough to maintain remission, while for others they will simply work alongside their treatment plan. This book is not designed to tell you what to do but instead how to help you take a balanced and holistic approach to managing your life with inflammatory bowel disease. Throughout the book, you'll see case studies from other sufferers alongside my own experiences, which I hope will reassure you that, however you are feeling, there's someone else out there feeling exactly the same. You will also find contributions from Kay Greveson – an award-winning IBD nurse and creator of the IBD Passport (see page 38) – who gives a brief overview of the types of investigations and medical treatments there are for those sufferers who are newly diagnosed.

I hope this book will provide you with the support and guidance you need when tackling this disease. Let me end on a note that many other IBD books don't acknowledge: I know how difficult it is to live with this disease day in day out, yet the very fact you've bought this book shows you are trying your best to fight it. Be kind to yourself, work with your body and use this book to help you live the best life you can despite having IBD.

ADJUSTING TO LIFE WITH IBD

Chapter 1

Being diagnosed

Going back to the beginning

Let's go back to the start for a second and think about the moment you were diagnosed. Perhaps this happened to you just recently, or perhaps it seems like a distant memory. Either way, post-diagnosis can be a scary place: a mixture of emotions, from initial relief to bafflement at the array of conflicting information available online. Doctors often send us packing shortly after a colonoscopy and the shock combined with the side effects of possible sedation or anaesthesia mean we can barely take it in. So first of all, let's clear up some confusion and try to offer an overview to answer any burning questions you may have.

How did I get this? Did I do something wrong? Or was it in my genes?

There is no real way, with present medical and scientific knowledge, of finding a cause for IBD and it's important to stress that even though there are some triggers, there is nothing that you have done wrong. As we know, IBD is a disease that causes the immune system to react, turning on the digestive system and attacking it.

Lots of times we hear the phrase 'genetic', but we need to make a distinction: inflammatory bowel disease isn't genetic in the sense that we can yet isolate one 'specific' gene that causes it (in the same way there's the BRCA cancer gene for example). Yet there is definitely evidence that genetics play a part in the condition (for example, in the case of Crohn's disease, about three in 20 patients have a close relative with the condition (NHS Choices, 2016) [1] and it's likely that a combination of genetic susceptibility and another trigger kick the disease process off. Sometimes it can be helpful to try to understand these triggers, yet much of the time news reports are inaccurate and can make us feel as though we've done something wrong. The most important thing to stress is that the cause or trigger of IBD is almost always completely out of your control.

Is it to do with my gut bacteria?

At the moment, gut bacteria are a popular discussion topic. (Probiotics are explored in Chapter 5, page 61). The gut 'microbiome' is being widely explored in relation to IBD, with Crohn's and Colitis UK announcing a study with Norwich Medical School on the role of bacteria in IBD. There are some suggestions that bacterial disruption can occur from birth – for example, some suggest that children who are born by caesarean and not breastfed are disadvantaged, often ending up depleted in essential good bacteria (Neu and Rushing, 2011). [2] Therefore, in the past, studies have gone so far as to suggest that being born by caesarean or not being breast-fed may actually put you more at risk of IBD, yet a more recent study analysing population data for 2015 concluded this is not a risk factor in developing the disease. [3] However, there may be more of a link later in life: patients may sometimes develop IBD after food poisoning or contracting a parasite abroad; such infections can interfere with the gut flora and essentially cause disruption. Therefore, while it is certainly a fascinating topic (and likely one we'll learn more about in the future, with faecal transplants now being used as a potential treatment in America), there is no conclusive evidence of causation at this point in time. I'll explore the role of gut bacteria in more detail later in the book (page 62), and explain how probiotics may help in Chapter 5 (page 61).

Did I bring it on through stress?

Stress can also be a huge influence; the theory here is that stress affects the immune system and while this is sustainable in a 'fight or flight' situation, longer periods of stress could cause the immune system to become overactive (and thus lead to autoimmune disease). Many patients with IBD can recall a stressful period in which the disease first began. While it's impossible to eradicate stress altogether, the tips in Chapter 4 (see page 53) may help if you find this is a big trigger for your body.

Is it due to a junk food diet?

'Diet and IBD' is one of the most controversial topics in the inflammatory bowel disease community. News reports in the past have linked IBD with anything from sugar, preservatives, junk food and dairy – worrying patients who feel they may be to blame. As explained in the Introduction, this book will explore the many dietary approaches to IBD but, from a management perspective, there is still no concrete evidence to support the claim that IBD is caused solely by poor diet choices.

Why does it often begin in puberty?

Scientists don't know the exact mechanism, but for women in particular there is a strong link between hormones and IBD. Many sufferers are diagnosed during their teenage years, suggesting the surge of hormones at that time could play a part. This link could also explain why many women's symptoms are much worse when they are menstruating. It may be useful to consider whether your menstrual cycle is linked to any past flares. While it isn't easy to stop these from happening, it can be useful to understand what it causing them.

What about MAP?

Since there is growing awareness of the MAP bacterium, it seems only right we consider this in brief too, especially as you may have seen the many news reports that suggest that this is the best chance of an IBD cure. MAP (short for *Mycobacterium avium* subspecies *paratuberculosis* – which is why we need the acronym!) is a type of bacterium that causes Johne's disease in cows; this is a disease where the symptoms mimic those of inflammatory bowel disease.

MAP cells hide inside the body's cells so until a new test was developed at St George's University, London, they were impossible to detect. Interestingly, that test has shown that when compared with the rest of the population, a much higher percentage of Crohn's disease patients (but not those with ulcerative colitis) appear to be carrying this bacterium, suggesting a clear link between Johne's disease and Crohn's disease (Hermon-Taylor, 2016). [4]

MAP bacteria are found in cow's milk; this links also with the finding that Crohn's exists in more westernised populations, which have a greater tendency to drink pasteurised milk. It may also explain why some IBD patients find milk difficult to digest. This is a theory that is still being studied and research trials are currently in progress for a vaccine that 'un-blinds' the immune system to MAP, 'reversing immune dysregulation and programming the body's own T-cells to seek and destroy cells containing MAP'.

There are still many scientists who remain sceptical about MAP yet it may still offer promise for the future. As always, I would urge you to do your own research and you can head over to www.

crohnsmapvaccine.com for more information.

Understanding the many symptoms of IBD

As I mentioned in the Introduction, this book does not aim to be a textbook for those with IBD. I don't intend to dedicate much time to explaining the obvious and most commonly discussed symptoms of the condition – you will very likely have already experienced them! But it is essential to acknowledge that inflammatory bowel disease is about very much more than your toilet habits. Here are some other possible symptoms that can affect your daily life if you have inflammatory bowel disease, existing as they do alongside the more common symptoms of diarrhoea, weight loss, bleeding and cramping.

- **Tiredness:** More and more awareness is emerging of a relationship between fatigue and IBD, with the fatigue-in-IBD scale (www.fatigueinibd.co.uk/) being launched in 2014 as a way for patients to measure their fatigue as part of their symptoms. Fatigue can arise for many reasons, including anaemia, nutritional deficiencies, IBD symptoms disturbing sleep or stress.

- **Joint pain:** Inflammation of the joints – usually the arms and legs – is another symptom of inflammatory bowel disease. Since both are inflammatory in nature, it is no surprise many people experience this complication of IBD, yet it is also a side effect of some medications, such as biologics (Infliximab, Humira).

- **Mouth ulcers:** Oral manifestations of IBD are common, one of the most common being mouth ulcers.

- **Eye inflammation:** The most common eye condition affecting people with IBD is 'episcleritis'. This affects the layer of tissue covering the sclera – the white outer coating of the eye – making it red, sore and inflamed (Crohn's and Colitis UK). [5]

- **Erythema nodosum:** This is a skin condition that causes red, painful lumps, usually on the legs or arms. While this is not regarded as a symptom of IBD, it has been found that IBD patients are more likely to develop it.

- **Anal complications:** Skin tags, fissures and fistulas are all a part of inflammatory bowel disease.

- **Loss of normal menstrual cycle in women:** This can be due to weight loss, hormonal disturbance, nutritional deficiency or disease activity.

- **Night sweats:** These can be symptoms in their own right (if a fever is present) or side effects of many medications.

- **Growth delays in younger children as a result of malnutrition and disease activity.**

- **Constipation:** This is not often thought of as an IBD symptom but it can happen with an inflamed or obstructed bowel.

- **Nutritional deficiencies:** As well an iron deficiency, IBD patients are more prone to deficiencies in vitamin B12, vitamin D and calcium.

Your personal glossary

Sometimes when you are first diagnosed, it can feel like the doctors are speaking a whole other language altogether. I've asked Kay Greveson – IBD nurse and founder of www.ibdpassport.com (a fantastic support for those with IBD travelling abroad) – to provide a key to the medical terms used when explaining investigations, medication and surgical options. This is not a comprehensive list and is simply intended to give an overview of the main terms used in IBD. A more detailed explanation of these topics can be found on the Crohn's and Colitis UK website; a list of free factsheets are provided here: www.crohnsandcolitis.org.uk/about-inflammatory-bowel-disease/quick-list

What tests are involved?

Colonoscopy

A colonoscopy is an investigation that looks at the colon (large bowel) and first part of the small bowel (terminal ileum). This is usually done to investigate people who are suspected to have Crohn's disease or ulcerative colitis and also to assess the disease in people who already have a diagnosis. Shortly before the test you will be required to drink a solution that clears the bowel out so that things can be seen clearly during the procedure. You will be offered sedation prior to the test and so it is important that you have someone to collect you afterwards as you will feel drowsy.

Ten top tips for surviving a colonoscopy

Nothing evokes more fear for IBD patients than a colonoscopy. The procedure can feel invasive, degrading and extremely embarrassing, yet unfortunately remains a key part of IBD testing; despite being uncomfortable it is extremely important for helping understand disease activity and any changes in the colon. Here are my 10 top tips to surviving a colonoscopy:

1. Mix the prep (the drink to clear the bowels) with coconut water. As you'll learn later in the book, I'm not a huge fan of soft drinks but coconut water is a healthier option to make bowel prep more palatable. It's also packed with potassium too, which helps replace electrolytes when dehydrated.

2. Use a drinking straw to help the prep go down more easily.

3. Drink the whole amount, even if your bowel movements are running clear. There's nothing worse than having to reschedule the colonoscopy because the doctors can't get a clear image. It may make you feel poorly but try to keep as much prep down as possible.

4. Be creative with fluids: herbal teas (no milk), clear broth, fruity water (with no actual fruit pieces) are all good drinks. Using jelly (not red or black) can also satisfy a sweet tooth.

5. Keep a ton of magazines and books nearby.

6. Coat your bum cheeks with Vaseline to prevent any chaffing and burning.

7. Avoid over-wiping with toilet roll to prevent irritation. Try wet wipes (check they're not fragranced first) or water spray or using the shower hose to clean off.

8. If you are not having anaesthetic, practise deep breathing beforehand to help control the pain. This can also help take your minds off things in the room.

9. Be mindful it might take a couple of days to recover – colonoscopies are invasive and can also cause the gut flora to be disturbed. While you may want to indulge straightaway (see tip 10), you may also find you still have diarrhoea and cramping, even though it seems there's nothing left in your stomach! Some patients find it helpful to use a probiotic for a few days afterwards, or introduce food slowly.

10. Plan a treat afterwards. It's okay to wallow and feel sorry for yourself, when you start daydreaming about solid food and you still have two hours to go. Plan something amazing as a reward for being so brave afterwards, whether it's a pampering weekend or a giant burger.

Flexible sigmoidoscopy

A flexible sigmoidoscopy is very similar to the colonoscopy in that it examines the large bowel (colon). The main difference is that it doesn't look as far around the large bowel and is usually done in people who have colonic Crohn's or ulcerative colitis that is limited to the left side and/or bottom part of the colon. Since it does not

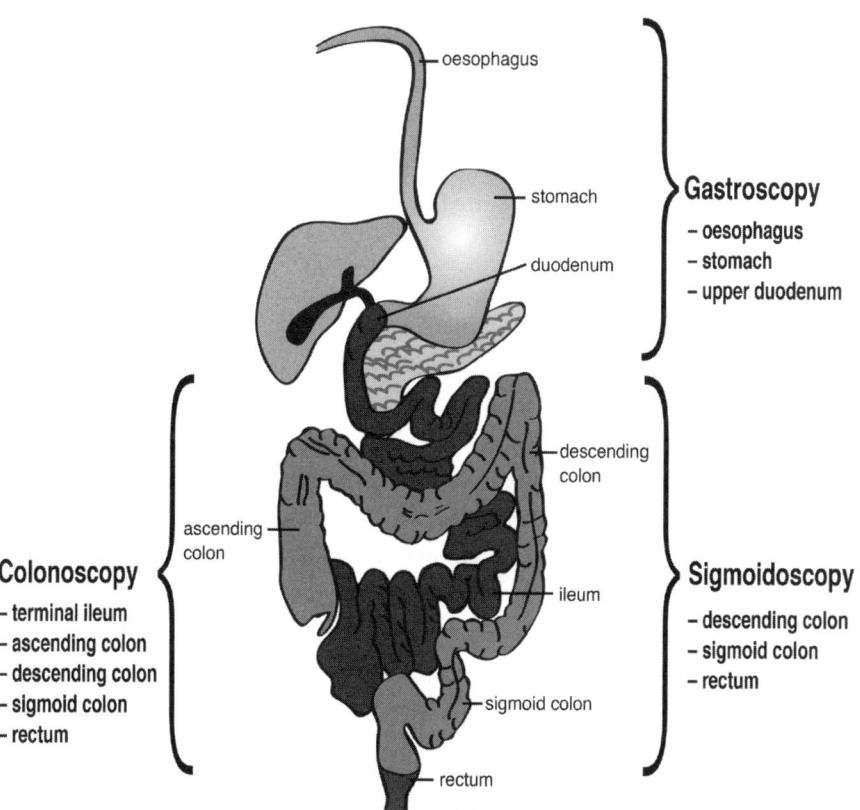

Figure 1 The gut – Schematic diagram of the gut showing which sections can be accessed by endoscopy

look at the whole colon, you do not need to take the usual bowel preparation drink prior to the test and instead you have an enema to clear the bowel, which is usually administered by the nurses in the endoscopy department on the day of the test. You will be offered sedation prior to the procedure.

Gastroscopy

This test involves a small tube that passes through the mouth to examine the oesophagus (food pipe), stomach and first part of the small bowel (duodenum). The test is usually very quick and only requires a local anaesthetic with a 'numbing' throat spray, although sedation can be given if required.

Capsule endoscopy

Capsule endoscopy is an alternative way of looking at the stomach, entire small bowel and, more recently, colon (large bowel). It can see many parts of the small bowel that tests such as gastroscopy and colonoscopy cannot reach. The test involves swallowing a small plastic pill (the size of a large vitamin pill) that contains a tiny camera. You usually swallow the capsule in the morning and then wear a discreet belt that contains a recording device that captures all the video footage as the capsule travels through your intestines. You then pass the capsule into the toilet and flush it away and return the belt to the hospital for the results to be analysed. Sometimes you may need a 'dummy capsule' made of sugar before you have the real thing to ensure there are no contraindications in your having the actual test (narrowings in the bowel sometimes caused by Crohn's may mean you can't have the capsule test).

MRI scan

Magnetic resonance imaging (MRI) scans avoid the use of X-rays and instead use strong magnetic fields and radio waves to create images of the inside of the body. The scanner looks like a small tunnel, with a bed that you will lie on that moves slowly in and out during the test. It can be quite noisy so you will be given ear phones during the test through which you will be able to hear and communicate with the radiology team undertaking the test.

MRI scans are used mainly in Crohn's disease to assess the small bowel or pelvic area (for people with a fistula – see page 19). Prior to the test, you may be asked to drink a special liquid containing a contrast agent or you may be given a contrast (dye) through a drip in your arm that helps identify any inflammation.

CT (computerised tomography) scan

The CT scanner looks like a ring doughnut with a bed that moves in and out during the test. Similar to the MRI scan, this is used mainly for people with Crohn's disease to assess the small bowel. You may be asked to drink a special liquid containing a contrast agent or you may be given a contrast (dye) through a drip in your arm that helps identify any inflammation.

Sometimes a CT scan can be used to look at the colon (called a virtual colonoscopy). This can look for inflammation in the bowel, but a disadvantage is that tissue samples (biopsies) cannot be taken and so a colonoscopy or flexible sigmoidoscopy may still be needed.

Blood tests for IBD

Blood tests are regularly used to assess your disease or response to treatment and also as screening tools prior to starting new medications. We will not go into details here but you can find more information on the Crohn's and Colitis UK website, www. crohnsandcolitis.org.uk

Faecal calprotectin

This is a simple test that looks for inflammation in the bowel. It involves collecting a small sample of faeces into a pot that is then analysed in the hospital laboratory. Some hospitals send the sample away to be analysed but there are also newer tests available that allow you to test and see the results from your home.

What medications might be prescribed?

Aminosalicylates (5-ASAs)

Aminosalicylates can also be called 'mesalazine' and are usually prescribed for people with mild to moderate ulcerative colitis. They may also help to control mild Crohn's in the ileum and colon. However, there is little evidence that 5-ASAs are effective in maintaining remission in Crohn's disease. They include drugs such as Pentasa, Asacaol, Octasa and Salofalk and come in different forms such as tablets, granule sachets, enemas and suppositories, which can be used depending on the location of your disease within your bowel. They are used to treat a flare-up of the condition but are commonly taken every day, even when you are symptom free, to prevent symptoms.

Anti-TNFα drugs

Anti-TNFα drugs (also called 'biologics') work by blocking the action of a protein called 'tumour necrosis factor alpha' (TNFα). This protein is found in everyone's blood as part of the body's response to infection. However, in people with IBD, too much TNFα is produced, and this causes excessive inflammation. Biological drugs block the action of TNFα and reduce inflammation. Common anti-TNFα drugs include Infliximab, Adalimumab and Golimumab. Some are given as a drip into your arm in a hospital day unit whereas others you can be trained by a nurse to give yourself via an injection at home. The choice of which treatment is right for you will be made after discussion with your IBD team.

Vedolizumab

Vedolizumab is also classed as a biologic but it works in a different way from the anti-TNFα drugs mentioned above. Vedolizumab is a 'gut-selective integrin blocker' that works by stopping the white blood cells from entering the lining of the gut. [6] White blood cells are made by the immune system to fight against infection. However, in Crohn's disease and ulcerative colitis, overproduction of white blood cells leads to inflammation.

Biosimilars

Biosimilars are drugs which are similar to, but not identical to, the original biological drug. Infliximab is the first biologic drug in the UK to have biosimilars. The original is Remicade and the biosimilar versions are called inflectra, Remsima and Flixabi. In order for a biosimilar to gain approval to be used, it has to meet strict standards to show it is as safe and effective as the original biologic drug. Biosimilar Humira will be launching in the next few years.

Steroids

Steroids are often used in people who have severe Crohn's or colitis symptoms. They help to reduce inflammation in the bowel and can be given as a tablet, or in cases where someone is in hospital they are given via a drip. The most common steroids used are prednisolone and budesonide (brand name, Pulmicort). Budesonide is used mostly for people with Crohn's disease affecting the last part of the small bowel (terminal ileum) as it is specifically designed to target this area, but it can be used for people with colonic Crohn's.

Azathioprine and mercaptopurine

Azathioprine and mercaptopurine belong to the group of drugs known as 'immunosuppressants'. They work by reducing inflammation and damping down over-activity of the cells of the immune system. They are mainly used when other medication, such as mesalazine or steroids, has not worked to control symptoms.

Methotrexate

Methotrexate is an immunosuppressant medication that works by reducing inflammation in the bowel by dampening down the activity of the immune system. It is commonly given via a weekly injection that you will be trained to administer yourself. It is also available in tablet form but this can have more side effects such as nausea so is not used as often.

My personal experience with medication

When I was first diagnosed, I will be honest and say I didn't want to take medication. However, I went from thinking I had nothing wrong with me to being given my first dose of infliximab in a very short space of time. This was because I was living abroad with private healthcare and had been undiagnosed for 12 years. I imagine that if I had been diagnosed earlier in England, then perhaps I'd have been given the obligatory dose of steroids that would have eased me into medication. Perhaps the 'moonface' (a side effect of steriods, which is almost an initiation for IBD patients) would have left me in a hurry to sign the infliximab consent form in a bid to feel better. But instead, an American doctor handed me a very scary medication leaflet that had the headline: 'Warning: may cause death'. (I'm not exaggerating; since the US is known for its litigious culture and private healthcare they have very clear warnings to avoid being sued.) So I went straight to the serious stuff. This is known as 'top down' medical care, designed to prevent future complications even if symptoms aren't actually severe.

I did not like taking infliximab. The physical side effects (a bit of fatigue and neck pains) paled into significance compared with the mental aspect: a fear of becoming seriously ill from it. Looking back, it was not the infliximab itself that caused this but the fact I hadn't really dealt with my diagnosis yet. I was really anxious about my health constantly and found, although my symptoms and inflammatory markers were much better, I still didn't feel 100 per cent. As I had never had terrible IBD symptoms pre-diagnosis (I never had bleeding or severe pain), I found this treatment hard to get my head around.

After going gluten-free when on holiday in Bali, I felt amazing and I began to be convinced this was the missing piece of the puzzle and wanted to come off infliximab. I started to spread my treatments out slightly – first every 10 weeks, then every 12. Stretching these out didn't worsen my inflammation or symptoms so after an almost clear colonoscopy I decided I would stop it after being on it a year.

During the year that followed, I was off all medication. I felt great during this time and because my new doctor in the UK wanted to run all my tests again, I had another colonoscopy. This and biopsies showed very mild Crohn's in one area and the rest was normal. I was screaming from the rooftops and then three days later… bam: I had an abscess and needed surgery. A few months later MRI showed I now had Crohn's in two areas and my doctor suggested trying azathioprine. I was understandably frustrated: the fact that biopsies had come back normal meant I knew the pressure of the colonoscopy had most likely inadvertently caused the abscess. It was too much of a coincidence. The stress of everything had then caused me to flare and I felt helpless because I'd believed everything I had been doing was enough. Yet it also taught me a valuable lesson – that sometimes we can just be unlucky and things are out of our control. I could juice five times a day but it would be pointless if I didn't find better ways to deal with stress and, more importantly, some kind of acceptance.

That brings me up to the present. I am working on dealing with stress, sticking to my diet and on Azathioprine too. In a way, this whole episode taught me to be a little more balanced (hence the title of this book). After all, a holistic approach to living sometimes has to include medication too. I would like to think I'm now in a position where I can be more of a realist: my doctor knows that I don't want to be on medication forever. I don't feel my symptoms warrant it and given I am my own biggest health advocate he knows I will keep up with regular blood tests even when off medications and march myself straight down to hospital if there is the start of a problem.

Yet at the same time, I respect my doctor's opinion and if he tells me I need medication then I will take it. Even on medication, I feel unwell if I veer off my diet, which simply reinforces my belief that the response to this disease has to be more than one-dimensional.

I used to feel a bit of a fraud being a nutritional therapist and health writer who takes medication every day, but I am actually proud that my blog and this book don't push one way of life to my readers. The best advice I have read about medication is that you should ask yourself whether the risk of being unwell from a flare-up outweighs the risk of the drug side effects. This is what I always keep in mind and I know that at different times in my life the answer will change. Approaches to IBD and chronic illness are changing all the time and hopefully eventually will evolve to show that diet, lifestyle and medication can all co-exist alongside each other and ultimately give the patient more choice on deciding the best medical and non-medical approaches for themselves.

Will I have to have surgery?

This can be one of the most frightening thoughts when first diagnosed with inflammatory bowel disease. With more medical treatments available, surgery is no longer inevitable. Yet for many sufferers, it is still part of their IBD journey. Crohn's and Colitis UK estimate that seven out of 10 Crohn's disease patients, and one in four of those with ulcerative colitis, will end up having surgery. [7]

What types of surgery are there?

- **Strictureplasty:** This is done to open up a narrow section of the intestines to treat blockages or strictures (a narrowing that can slow the movement of food) that result from inflammation.

- **Resection:** The removal of a damaged part of the gut altogether, if an area is severely scarred or there is a long stricture.

- **Pouch:** This surgery is done when someone has severe ulcerative colitis. It is generally done in two stages; the first to remove the inflamed large bowel and create a temporary ileostomy; then the second stage a few months later to create an 'internal pouch' made from the lower part of the intestine (ileum) which is attached to the anus. This allows stools to pass out through the anus in the usual way. This is also sometimes called a 'J pouch'.

- **Colostomy:** This is a surgical operation in which part of the colon is removed and the cut end is brought through the abdominal wall to create an opening called a stoma. Digestive waste is then collected in a bag which is fitted over this opening and attached to the skin. It may be temporary or permanent.

- **Ileostomy:** This is similar to a colostomy but with an ileostomy, the entire colon is removed and the small bowel is brought through the abdominal wall to create an opening called a stoma. Digestive waste is then collected in a bag which is fitted over this opening and attached to the skin. It may be temporary or permanent. (Be aware that the part of your bowel where vitamin B12 is absorbed is the ileum; if you are without an ileum you may need B12 injections for life.)

- **Fistulotomy:** This is done when a fistula (an abnormal tract between two organs or parts of organs that forms as a result of chronic inflammation) is opened up to prevent further abscesses from forming. The nature of the procedure varies depending on the complexity of the fistula and whether it is connected to other internal organs or the skin.

My experience of a fistulotomy

One of the most frustrating parts of my IBD journey has been perianal disease. I have had several abscesses in the past, which were treated by incision and drainage. I then had a fistulotomy in December 2015 after complaining of pain at the site of previous abscesses. The doctor identified a simple, low-lying fistula on an MRI scan and this was laid out flat via a fistulotomy to prevent the abscess from recurring. I was deemed one of the lucky ones for not needing a 'seton' (special stitching) but although my surgery was deemed 'simple' the recovery was far from it. After the fistulotomy, I had to have a nurse visit me each day to pack the wound. The thing I found the hardest was having to control when I needed the loo – sometimes I would have the nurse come out in the morning and then need the loo 20 minutes after and have to take the whole dressing off again! I personally do not think there is enough guidance for fistulotomy aftercare – keeping the wound clean became a bit of an obsession and I never went anywhere without my cleaning fluid. This led to all kinds of anxiety about socialising, my body and any kind of exercise. I also found it difficult to know what to wear, since tight-fitting clothing irritated my wound. After about three months, the nurse was happy to let me manage the wound myself and the surgeon declared it had pretty much healed after six months. I personally still find the area sensitive after lots of walking, but I'm not sure if that is psychological rather than physical. I know how lucky I am to not need any further, more complex surgery at the moment of writing but I still think a fistulotomy is one of the most difficult aspects of my IBD and has had a big impact on my body image and confidence. It is something I am working on and hope to get more confident with in time.

PATIENT EXPERIENCE: Tig, diagnosed 1996

'My experience with a J-Pouch.'

I've had my large intestine removed. It was full of holes and I was being slowly poisoned so there was no other option. I now have an internal pouch, called a J-pouch. This cannot be seen. So few people have one that many healthcare professionals know little to nothing about them. I've had all the nurses on a ward come to my bedside after handover to ask me to explain, a radiographer look on his screen and ask me what he's looking at, doctors ask me about my stoma (I don't have one) etc. A fellow J-poucher even had a doctor ask her to show him her pouch. Remember, it's on the inside!

Since I got my J-pouch I've found I can have an almost normal life, I do have to be careful what I eat and the list of triggers is surprising but I can work full time and spend time with the grandchildren without absolute exhaustion and constant toilet trips. It's helped to make me feel 'normal' – by that I mean that I didn't cope with the stoma and colostomy bag, I hated them – having an internal pouch has helped my body image and mental health enormously.

However, the procedure is still relatively uncommon so I have to explain to GPs, radiographers, general nursing staff and basically anyone who isn't experienced in matters GI, what it is and how it works. This has left me fearful of travelling to any country where I don't speak the language. Still, it's a small price to pay for being out of hospital, out of bed, and out and about again.

Understanding potential triggers

We have already talked about possible triggers that you may have noticed when your IBD first started. Later in the book (page 72), we'll look at food, which for many plays a big part in causing symptoms or worsening a flare. Yet, there can also be many other things that affect your IBD. Here are some things to be mindful of.

Antibiotics

Antibiotics have a close relationship with inflammatory bowel disease: in mild cases (and for those with perianal disease) they are suggested as a line of treatment – indeed, some patients find their symptoms greatly improved when routinely prescribed antibiotics for non-IBD-related health issues. Yet others find antibiotics greatly exacerbate symptoms; this can be because of antibiotic-associated diarrhoea, c-diff (that is, *Clostridium difficile* – always make sure you are checked for this if symptoms are persistent as prolonged use of some antibiotics can increase the risk of this greatly) or simply changed bacteria, since antibiotics 'kill off' all types of gut bacteria – including the good kind. It is definitely worth increasing your intake of probiotic foods when taking antibiotics; just make sure any supplements/foods are taken at least two hours after each dose.

Menstrual cycle

Doctors have acknowledged there is a link between hormones and IBD in the case of female patients; this is most commonly cited due to many people experiencing remission during pregnancy, but many patients also feel symptoms worsen when they are on their period. (I have asked many doctors about why this is and they are yet to have a definitive answer other than that it is something they have noticed in their patients.)

A study by Lim et al (2013) examining this noted that the number of stools during a patient's period did increase yet other symptoms specifically related to IBD did not, suggesting that this may be due to hormonal changes rather than inflammation.[8] In turn, many women do experience loose stools, cramping and nausea during their periods, regardless of IBD. Lim et al also noted symptoms of PMT were worse in IBD patients than in regular 'controls' (women without IBD).

Weather

Although there is little scientific evidence for this, many patients find changing weather can affect their disease. For example, symptoms may worsen during periods of humidity.

Colds/'flu

Catching a cold or 'flu is highly likely during the winter, even more so if you are on immunosuppressants. However, many patients find that along with the usual symptoms, having a cold can cause their IBD to be more problematic too. This can be for many reasons. When fighting a cold, the body's white blood cells and inflammatory markers are often raised, just like when a patient is in a flare. As the immune system is fighting a cold, it can often divert resources away from the rest of the body to do so, leaving your body more vulnerable to the impact of IBD. In turn, a common symptom of colds can be loose stools and cramps. Finally, many cold remedies contain ingredients like ibuprofen (which should not be taken by IBD patients), glycoren (which can cause loose stools) or caffeine (see the section on foods to understand why this is a problem).

What makes my disease flare?

To demonstrate how wide is the range of different things that trigger IBD flares or worsen symptoms, I asked a group of patients to share their experiences of what makes their diseases flare up. Please note that for some of these there is no scientific evidence (and your doctors may disagree), but these examples show how IBD is sometimes beyond the rules of the standard medical literature; you can see just how much variety there is, which demonstrates how important it is for us to connect with our body and understand how it works beyond textbooks. After you've read the examples, there's space below to make notes on your own personal triggers.

Lorna, diagnosed 2012: My main trigger is stress. I don't have periods any more due to the coil but I found the pain immense and could affect my bowel habits when on my period – to the extent that I felt crippled some days and was hardly able to move.

Catherine, diagnosed 2014: I always flare a couple of weeks after something has stressed me out or upset me.

Shirley, diagnosed 2010: For me, I find symptoms flare when I least expect it and have done something daft, like eating a whole pack of peanuts because I think I can!

Kirsty, diagnosed 1992: I find my symptoms flare when I ignore the signs from my body that I need sleep or certain foods. If I am addicted to cheese, it's because I need calcium; fruit because I need vitamin C. The only problem is I feel like I stock up on what my body needs and then it changes my mind!

Kay, diagnosed 2008: I had my colon removed in 2010 but even now I find my periods make my flares much worse and cause watery output.

Clare, diagnosed 2012: If not in complete remission, my trigger is exercise. If I am having a mild flare and do any exercise, it makes the flare much worse. Obviously being very active doesn't seem to agree with me!

Helen, diagnosed 2010: I find my flares are much worse when I drink coffee. (Author's note: I'll explain why this might be in Chapter 5.)

Vicky, diagnosed 2007: For me, my symptoms flare when I have strong emotions. So if I'm overly excited, angry, happy, sad or stressed, I will flare. It's extremely annoying!

Marie, diagnosed 2013: I experience symptoms when I overdo it, like if I have a long busy day followed by a gig or night out. I generally feel awful the next day!

Samantha, diagnosed 2012: I know that a week before my period my Crohn's flares hugely, without fail. A day after I begin my period, it rapidly calms down.

Richard, diagnosed 2016: I was only diagnosed this year but I think the hot weather has something to do with my flares. I'm having my first flare up since diagnosis/treatment and it all started when the hot weather began.

Notes on your personal triggers

_____

_____

_____

_____

_____

_____

_____

_____

_____

_____

_____

Notes on your personal triggers (cont'd)

_____

_____

_____

_____

_____

_____

_____

_____

_____

_____

_____

_____

_____

_____

_____

Chapter 2

Dealing with your diagnosis

Understanding your condition

The first step to understanding your disease is to make sure you have all the facts. As we know under the British NHS, appointments with a gastroenterologist (doctors who specialise in conditions of the digestive system) are hard to obtain, so it's really important that you make the most of them. For you to really understand your condition, no question is too stupid to ask. In fact, most consultants will appreciate you taking such an active interest in your health. It is surprising (but understandable) how little people know about their condition after many years of suffering. While it is your choice as to how much you research the condition, it is essential that you chat to your doctor and not rely on forums or other people's experiences – inflammatory bowel disease varies widely in its disease activity and symptoms. The section on pages 28-30 gives you space to record information on your condition, should you wish to use it. Use the questions below to help frame the conversation with your medical team and remember, 'Don't ask, don't get' is key here. Don't leave until you feel you've had your questions answered and you feel more equipped to understand exactly what you are dealing with.

Ten questions to ask your doctor

1. What is my long-term treatment plan?_____

_____

_____

2. What medication are you prescribing for me and how long will I stay on it?

_____

_____

_____

3. How often do I need to get my blood tested?

_____

_____

_____

4. How often do I need colonoscopies or other types of testing?

_____

_____

_____

5. Do I need to take any supplements for nutritional deficiencies?

_____

_____

_____

6. When should I expect to feel better? _____

_____

_____

7. What if my medication doesn't work?

_____

_____

_____

8. Are there any side effects I should be aware of?

_____

_____

_____

9. When will I see you next?

_____

_____

_____

10. Who do I contact if my symptoms worsen?

_____

_____

_____

Other notes/questions

_____

_____

_____

_____

_____

_____

_____

_____

_____

_____

_____

_____

_____

_____

_____

_____

_____

_____

My experience: Dealing with diagnosis

My diagnosis of Crohn's disease finally came in 2012, after suffering with gut symptoms for at least 10 years. At first, I was strangely excited – I felt like nobody had taken me seriously for such a long time that I was really happy to have something tangible. I also naively assumed that I would get better quickly and all the dietary restrictions I had attempted to make in the past would no longer be needed. Ultimately, it took about five months to get on medication and I don't think it really hit me until then. I remember crying on the way home as it finally hit me how serious the condition was. Over the years, I have tried to get the balance right: between being knowledgeable, and not researching for hours on end. I am honest enough to admit it's not always a balance I get right. I like to be in control of things and therefore I spend lots of time trying to pinpoint exactly what has caused symptoms. In many ways I still dread doctors' appointments but taking a notebook with a list of questions makes me feel a bit more empowered; I'm really glad that I have a doctor who takes my opinions seriously and does his best to make me feel no question is too silly! In a way, I feel I have more control of the disease if I get the most out of my appointments.

PATIENT EXPERIENCE: Kelly, diagnosed 2010

After almost a year of pain, suffering and what felt like endless tests I was finally diagnosed with Crohn's disease in October 2010. It was a relief to finally know what was wrong; I had suspected the other C word, but at the same time it was not what I wanted to hear. I was totally ignorant about the disease but remembered that the only other person I'd known who had it had gained lots of weight due to steroids, so my initial question to the consultant was, 'Am I going to get fat?'

Five and a bit years later I feel I am one of the lucky ones – my disease only affects my large intestine, not the small bowel which I'm assured is a good situation to be in. Most of the time I am fit and well in relation to other sufferers; I can live a 'normal' life. Occasionally a flare knocks me for six but steroids always get things back under control. My job of In-Flight Supervisor is a challenge as it takes me away for days at a time; I have to take all my own food in order to avoid stomach issues. This means I have to be super organised and often have to eat things I don't fancy at the time as they are all I have with me. I do find that due to the pressurisation, eating anything in the air affects my stomach massively, with bloating and pain; most of my food is eaten on the ground for this reason but this is not always possible due to short turnarounds. Days often involve four flights, which plays havoc with my insides!

Chapter 3

Finding support

Talking to family and friends

As I'm sure you are aware, IBD can have a huge impact on your life and therefore it is extremely important to build a good support network around you, to help with everything from childcare and taking you to appointments to simply letting you have a good rant! This can seem really difficult to begin with, so I'd like to outline my experiences and tips here on talking to others about my condition (see below). Now I am proud to say that as someone who freely writes about her condition, I feel confident explaining it to new people I meet. However, it wasn't always this way. As I have said, I was diagnosed when living abroad, making it even more difficult to explain to friends I had only recently met without the support network of my family back in England. Yet I was very lucky that the friends I had made abroad were incredibly supportive, which led me to being much more open with others I have met since. I have found everyone to be understanding about my condition, but it is not always easy to talk about things like dietary requirements or worse... when you feel symptoms starting and you are away from home! I've outlined some of my suggestions below to help make talking to others a little bit easier.

1. **It's embarrassing**. I think the first thing here is to acknowledge that IBD is an embarrassing topic for you – and that's okay. There's lots of things you may feel embarrassed about: the physical symptoms; the impact they have on socialising; explaining absences from work. None of this embarrassment will go away overnight and while there are plenty of people who do choose to share their experiences freely (and do an amazing job to raise awareness), yet there are plenty who prefer to keep things much more private. Although there remains a huge stigma around digestive issues, we can sometimes feel as if we have to speak out to break this. Like any illness, it is always up to you as to how much about the condition you share; don't force yourself out of your comfort zone immediately.

2. **Start with the facts.** Like almost all topics in the world today, ignorance often comes from misunderstanding. There are lots of ignorant assumptions about IBD and I bet, like me, you've heard them all: everything from 'Well, at least you'll lose weight' to 'I have a bit of IBS'. While it can be easy to fly off the handle, ask yourself how much you knew about IBD before diagnosis? I bet, like me, it was very little. That's why it's only fair we give our loved ones the opportunity to learn about our condition; feel free to show them this book or the many relevant, informative publications available on the Crohn's and Colitis UK website.

3. **Write it down.** There's a reason why so many of us are choosing to start writing about our health: it can be a great way to get all of your feelings out and spark conversations with others. I'm not suggesting you grab your laptop and build a website – a simple journal which you eventually share with family and friends could be a starting place. Who knows? You may end up loving it so much, you'll find a new hobby!

4. **Be patient.** Being diagnosed with IBD can be life-altering and one aspect of this is that it can change our relationships. This

can be simple changes like the activities you do together or more drastic, if health problems prevent you from working or you are in hospital for long periods of time. Although it is easy to feel resentful when loved ones appear to not be supportive, it can be a huge change for them too initially, especially when they have to sit back and watch you suffer and can't help. There are now specialist Facebook groups for parents and partners of those with IBD; it might be worth your getting your other half or family members to join one of these groups so they can chat to others in a similar situation.

5. **Be realistic.** Like any major life change, there will always be people who are supportive and people who are not. IBD often makes it clear to us who our real confidantes are; although this can be difficult to deal with initially it is often for the better in the long run.

Support networks outside friends/family

While many of us are really lucky to have family and friends around us, it might be that they are not particularly understanding or cannot comprehend what we are going through. Therefore, outside support networks can be extremely invaluable in helping you through your life with IBD. Sometimes it is just enough to know that we are not alone in what we are going through and other people throughout the country (and in fact all over the globe) are going through a similar thing.

These support networks range from online forums, to meet-up groups, to buddying systems where you can find a partner to discuss your issues via email. So, let's go over a few support networks that could really help you.

Crohn's and Colitis UK

Website: www.crohnsandcolitis.org.uk
Phone: +44 (0)121 737 9931

This is the biggest and most well-known charity for those with Crohn's disease and ulcerative colitis. It can offer you a range of services to help you deal with your IBD. Firstly, it runs a 'listening service': Crohn's and Colitis support (call +44 (0)121 737 9931, Mon-Fri 1.30-3.30 pm and 6.00-9.00 pm). The main idea behind this support line is to provide a friendly understanding ear for you to call and talk about your issues. The idea is not to offer medical advice but just to let people know there is somebody at the end of a phone who can understand what they are going through. Crohn's & Colitis UK also offers a dedicated Facebook forum which has thousands of users and gives you the chance to interact with others and ask questions about your symptoms. Finally, they can also offer you financial support. They run a bursary scheme and can support those in financial hardship. They can support you with lots of different things, such as providing you with funding for a specific item that you need to manage your condition.

If you choose to join Crohn's and Colitis UK, you will be issued with a 'Can't Wait' card. This can be really useful to carry around with you should you need to use the loo urgently in the event of your Crohn's symptoms flaring.

Finally, Crohn's and Colitis UK also offers smaller regional support groups. For example, I live in Birmingham so I would come under the West Midlands region. These regional groups are great to help you find local sufferers and offer the chance to meet with other patients in person. Many of these support groups also offer medical talks and advice events where you are able to meet professionals and other sufferers at the same time. This is a great service for those who don't want to share all their information online but benefit by meeting up with people face to face.

forCrohns

Website: www.forcrohns.org

Another charity offering a lot of support for dealing with Crohn's disease is forCrohns. It is a smaller charity whose mission is to fund research that helps those with the condition today and contributes to finding a cure for Crohn's disease in the future whilst making more people in the UK aware of the disease and its symptoms. One great feature of its support is its Buddy System which pairs sufferers together, and you can also specify things like gender and location should you have any preference about your buddy. Once paired up with another patient you will be able to communicate with him or her via email. This is a great way to contact people if you are not confident with social media and do not feel comfortable discussing your problems with everybody online. The buddy system is really effective and gives people the chance to share their issues. Another unique thing about the charity is that it is run entirely by volunteers, which means virtually all of the money raised goes directly to fund research into Crohn's disease.

Facebook groups

As well as charities there are many other groups 'out there' dedicated to helping people. Some of the most popular Facebook groups are *Get Your Belly Out*, which is an organisation that raises money for Crohn's and Colitis UK but also holds lots of meetings throughout the year such as a Get Your Belly Out Ball and different regional meetings to allow people to meet up in person and chat about their lives with IBD. Finally, I run a Facebook group called *Healthy Living with IBD* which I set up as a way for me to find and connect with other people who were interested in living a healthy lifestyle with

IBD. We chat about things such as diet, stress relief and generally coping with IBD whilst trying to lead a busy life. Both groups (and many more) can easily be found by searching your Facebook toolbar.

IBD Passport

Website: www.ibdpassport.com

I will address travel in more detail later on in this book, but if you are looking for detailed information and support with travelling while dealing with IBD this resource is the best place to go. It is a one-stop website for everything to do with travel, from the vaccinations you will need, to coping with the food abroad. I find it a really great resource to show people that it is perfectly possible to travel and live a full and balanced life while living with IBD.

My Crohn's and Colitis Team

Website: www.mycrohnsandcolitisteam.com

You may also wish to sign up for My Crohn's and Colitis Team, a social media site exclusively for those with IBD. This organisation also offers an app to download, allowing you to chat with other users on the go.

PATIENT EXPERIENCE: Brandon, diagnosed 2014

Finding support

I was diagnosed with Crohn's disease after I was rushed into hospital with a kidney stone that had become blocked. We had not long had our first child, and all I remember was being in hospital and everything being rushed, going for my first ever MRI, CT scan and then a colonoscopy. Everything was so rushed, I just didn't understand what was happening – only that one minute the doctor suspected I had Crohn's disease, then the next minute yes I definitely had it. I was sent to a recovery ward for a night and then given pain relief and the consultant in charge just sent me away with a leaflet about Crohn's disease and a prescription. I'd never heard of Crohn's disease before. I had no idea. The first question that kept circling in my head was, 'Am I dying?' Luckily I had a friend on my Facebook who has ulcerative colitis, and she directed me to some of the groups on there. For the first few days I just browsed and followed nearly every post to try and learn more and more, because searching the web just scared me even further. Being part of the groups has really helped me understand and accept this disease. I was only diagnosed two years ago, so I'm still learning. But without social media and the groups I'm part of I really don't know how I'd have learnt anything. It was hard enough being told I had Crohn's and not knowing what it was, but even harder trying to tell the people around me, so even my partner made herself a member. It sounds clichéd, but these groups really helped improve my life after being diagnosed.

Understanding your medical team

After your diagnosis you will notice the many people are involved in helping you with your condition. It is important to get the most out of your treatment and services and that you know the different people who play a part in helping you deal with IBD.

GP

Your GP will be your first port of call if there is anything you need to discuss so it is important that you keep your practice regularly informed about your health. However, do not expect your GP to be an expert and there are certain medications (such as azathioprine and other immunosuppressants) that they are unable to prescribe because such rigorous monitoring is needed. It is essential for your GP practice to be advised of your condition as they will be able to prescribe medication, check your blood tests and keep an overview of your health. Make sure you remind your GP of your IBD before he or she prescribes you any medication. A big thing many GPs fail to realise is that many people with IBD cannot take drugs like ibuprofen as they create an inflammatory response in the body and therefore it is essential to keep track of the medications you are on so you do not get unknowingly prescribed a drug that could make your condition worse.

IBD nurse

An IBD nurse is often the most valuable person in your treatment plan. Many hospitals offer IBD nurses as support; there are currently around 300 such nurses in the UK, and Crohn's and Colitis UK are campaigning to recruit more to support patients. If you are offered this type of support I would urge you to take it and make sure that you contact your IBD nurse regularly. IBD nurses are trained and experienced in understanding blood test results and symptoms and in ensuring you get to see a doctor/consultant promptly when your symptoms warrant it. Hospitals with IBD nurses attached often offer an IBD Helpline where you can leave a message and they will call you back in a couple of hours; this can be really reassuring if you are unsure about the symptoms you are experiencing and need advice before going to your GP or A&E.

For more information about the specific role of the IBD nurse, you can visit: http://ecco-jcc.oxfordjournals.org/content/7/9/744

To join the Crohn's and Colitis UK campaign for more IBD

nurses (More IBD Nurses – Better Care) visit here: http://action. crohnsandcolitis.org.uk/ea-action/action?ea.client.id=1995&ea. campaign.id=51097&ea.tracking.id=web

Consultant

As you have probably recognised by now, it can be difficult to get an appointment with a consultant and therefore it is really important that when you do, you make the most of it. If you are in touch with your IBD nurse, s/he should be in a position to arrange for you to see your IBD consultant on a regular basis – usually every three months until you are in remission for a sustained length of time. Your IBD nurse can also arrange for you to see a consultant sooner if she feels your condition warrants it. Many gastro doctors run clinics with a certain amount of appointments allocated to patients that the IBD nurses refer.

As I have said already and must emphasise, it is of the utmost importance to make the most of your consultation. Remember consultants see lots of different patients and therefore they need to be updated accurately and quickly as to your symptoms so you are able to spend most of your time seeking advice from them and making sure that you are happy with your treatment plan. The most important thing that you have to do is to ask them any questions that you need answers to; I suggest taking a notebook in with you with all your questions written down. Also, make sure that you write down their advice at the same time.

Dietician

Another service that may be offered to you is the use of a dietician. This depends on the area that you live, whether your hospital has that resource available and whether you think diet is playing a big part in your symptoms. We will talk about diet more later (page 71) as it is an area that is important in managing your IBD and a dietician can be really helpful. Many dieticians prescribe rigorous diets, such as elementary diets and low-residue diets, which I will talk about on page 72. It is therefore important that you explain to the dietician exactly what you are eating and what foods you feel are causing your problems, and get the best possible advice from them.

Other practitioners

Many people seek further professional help when dealing with IBD; this can include acupuncture, reflexology, nutritional therapy and other disciplines – I will give further information on this in Chapter 14 (page 135).

Chapter 4

IBD and mental health

Understanding the impact of IBD on your mental health

Why did I choose to include this chapter – essentially on anxiety – straight after the diagnosis section? Well, the answer is obvious: I hear so much from fellow sufferers about the fatigue, the pain, the ulcers and all the horrendous physical ailments we have to suffer, yet there is very little open discussion about the rest of it: anxiety, worry, guilt, loneliness and despair – all of the emotions that IBD causes us on a regular basis.

It is important to emphasise that I cannot offer medical advice on the area (and you must always talk to a doctor if this is something you are suffering from), but I do believe that the psychological impact of IBD is just as important as the physical one and something that we must start discussing and focusing on more. Therefore, this chapter explores my own and other patients' struggles with mental health issues and IBD with the aim of demonstrating that this is something that should be given adequate attention when managing your life with IBD.

Anxiety and IBD: The key facts

- People with Crohn's disease were found to be twice as likely to suffer from anxiety as people without the condition in a recent study.[10]

- Anxiety and depression have been linked to possible IBD flare ups.[11]

- Some animal studies have found anxious behaviour in rats linked to gut inflammation and bacteria – although more human studies are needed, this suggests a possible link between gut health and anxiety.[12]

- Vitamin B12 deficiency is common in IBD patients and is also linked to anxiety.

Let's look at the studies there have been regarding this. Recently, a study by Rubin et al (2009),[9] showed that while almost 40 per cent of physicians thought ulcerative colitis made it difficult to lead a normal life, over 60 per cent of UC patients did – showing a disproportion between how we see our lives with IBD when compared with how the medical profession sees them. Anxiety, worry and stress all play a big part in this perception.

Anxiety

First up, let's talk about anxiety and the link with inflammatory bowel disease. A recent study found that people with Crohn's were twice as likely to suffer from anxiety as people without the condition (Fuller-Thomson, Lateef, and Sulman, 2015).[10] At first this might not make surprise reading since it's natural to be anxious about your health problems and especially living with a digestive disease. Yet, the link may go deeper than this, with studies emerging connecting anxiety and depression to recurrences of flare-ups (Mikocka-Walus et al, 2016). [11] There could be several reasons for this: as I mentioned earlier, there is more discussion now centring around the link between inflammatory bowel disease and altered gut bacteria, and this is also the case for mental health. For example, a review of recent findings (Foster and Neufield, 2013) found that both increased gut inflammation and different doses of probiotics altered the amount of anxiety-like behaviour in rats.[12]

Alongside this, certain vitamins and minerals may play a part too. For example, the gut is responsible for the production of vitamin B12. Many patients with IBD may find they are deficient in this since their gut is unable to absorb it in the ileum effectively. Perhaps you've guessed what's coming next. What are among the classic symptoms of B12 deficiency? Anxiety and depression.

Although checking your levels of B vitamins is a good idea, it's certainly not the complete answer. We've discussed anxiety but what about worrying in general? Worry may also play a massive part in patients' lives. Patients may worry when they're ill and also when they're actually healthy and happy. IBD is an ever-changing disease; even when we're in remission we can't help but wonder: 'What next?' Perhaps if I share my experiences of worry with you, it may help you understand yours a little better.

My journey with anxiety

Before I go on to offer advice about dealing with this issue, I'd like to explain anxiety on a personal level, because, as I mentioned at the beginning of this chapter, this is not something I believe the IBD community are talking about enough.

I have always been a 'worrier'; growing up I would fret about everything from whether I'd turned the hair-straighteners off to the consequences of failing a test. I'd thought this was 'just me', and this was why I easily accepted my initial diagnosis of irritable bowel syndrome, caused by – you've guessed it – stress.

Once diagnosed with IBD, I found anxiety hard to deal with, specifically health anxiety. After 10 years of being wrongly diagnosed, I had almost convinced myself the next diagnosis was around the corner. What else had the doctor missed? Should I seek a second opinion on that seemingly innocent mole/rash/skin tag?

In turn, the side effects of medication didn't help. What some doctors don't realise is that the side effects need to be put into context and patients need real reassurance. Unfortunately, I never received this so I was plagued with worry that I was putting myself in harm's way and regularly checking my body for signs of another illness or side effects from medication.

Another major blow to this was in July 2015; this was the period I described earlier when I went from having an almost perfect colonoscopy to an abscess requiring an emergency operation within the space of four days. I'd barely had time to finish my post-colonoscopy meal when I was back on 'nil by mouth' for surgery. This experience led to more major anxiety when receiving positive news as I would also be questioning whether the next health problem was just around the corner.

Indeed, the erratic nature of immune disease itself means the logical and rational amongst us (like me!) search desperately for patterns, threads, links; anything to find a reason for this often baffling disease. At times, I am still prone to this and questions simply circle my mind: What has caused it? Why now? What did I do differently? What didn't I do? Was it the medicine/stress/food I ate? Can I prevent this? I must admit that lack of control is something I find particularly hard. If you work hard you can control many things: your exam results, your success in life, your future plans. Yet I can't control this disease and it's scary. I have no idea what's happening in my inside or what's around the corner. Sure, I do my absolute best with diet and even if I'm flaring, I know I'm still doing what I can to help my body recover. But it's difficult not to turn inwards and start to feel guilt.

I have tried many things to help me deal with my anxiety and I do feel it's something I will keep having to fight (much like IBD). Since beginning cognitive behaviour therapy (CBT – see page 53), I feel I am more able to understand where the anxious thoughts are coming from and also to rationalise a bit quicker when my brain goes off at tangents. For me it is still a work in progress but I hope by sharing this with you all, you'll realise just how normal it is to feel this way with IBD.

PATIENT EXPERIENCE: Jennifer, diagnosed 2002

I never really understood perianal Crohn's as it was never fully explained to me. When I developed fistulas in 2002, I soon realised I wasn't normal 'down there'. When surgical treatments, such as 'laying open' the fistula and 'setons' were suggested, I never fully grasped what this meant until I had the operations. I felt totally unprepared emotionally and due to the embarrassment, I didn't know who to talk to about it. My anxieties manifested themselves in several ways.

My first anxiety was around how the surgery left me feeling. I was in immense pain and also felt I had been disfigured down there. It meant that I avoided intimacy with my partner and engaging in affection in order to prevent things leading to intimacy. These fears then meant I developed further anxieties about my relationship as I wondered how long my partner would stay with me if I couldn't satisfy him. My second anxiety was around cleanliness. I was never advised how to manage the constant drainage of fluids from the fistula or told that the leaking would be a long-term thing. I had to feel 'clean' and was paranoid that others could smell me. It changed how confident I felt in my clothes, as my underwear became 'practical' to accommodate the extra padding and dressings I needed to wear. I also rarely wore light colours or skirts for fear of leaking or in case the extra padding I wore in my underwear became visible or fell out. The thought of leaking forever left me feeling determined that I would 'heal' myself from these fistulas and I began searching on the internet for how others had done this. Looking back now, I became obsessive about healing and partook in some extreme regimes and diets in order to prove the doctors wrong.

My anxieties changed to obsession as I became quite ritualistic in my approach to healing myself – if I didn't soak three times a day, or follow my clean eating regime, then I felt was preventing my own healing. At this point, I had set myself a high expectation that was difficult and expensive to meet, but I had to feel in control of what was happening to me.

Much of my anxiety left me when I had to face having a colostomy stoma in 2015. Prior to my stoma, I was determined to heal myself and I had spent the previous 12 years either fighting IBD myself or in denial that I even had it (when in remission). But when faced with an emergency situation, I recognised that I could no longer fight IBD by myself and actually, though working with my medical team could be frustrating at times, it does halve the burden. I have found great comfort in discovering that others have similar issues and am much more open and comfortable knowing I'm not suffering alone.

How can we deal with anxiety and IBD? (With input from therapist Sally Baker)

Since many patients feel stress can trigger their symptoms, it is vital to try to get a handle on anxiety. It has been suggested that support for this should be part of IBD patients' care plans, yet currently only 12 per cent of IBD clinics offer this. Therefore, it is clearly an area where more medical services need to be directed. As I discussed in Chapter 1, initial consultations after being diagnosed can lead to the patient being overwhelmed with information and having a variety of leaflets thrust into their hands about the disease that they can only take in later. But where's the leaflet that tells us how to cope with the associated emotions? The leaflet that gives us ways of not breaking down, and staying strong? The leaflet that offers support groups and websites?

Hopefully the studies I have cited have highlighted the growing link between mental health and IBD. Of course, if you feel you are struggling with anxiety and depression it is vital you speak to your GP urgently. If you have done this and are looking for some self-help suggestions to deal with times of worry and help manage your anxiety, then the guidance below from Sally Baker – a therapist who works specifically with the mind-body connection – may be beneficial. (It is important to be aware at the same time that these tips offer general guidance which cannot replace the individual advice of a medical professional and if you are feeling any new symptoms of anxiety and depression, then it is very important to see your GP.)

Advice from Sally

When Sally works with clients living with chronic ill-health she recognises how having little or no confidence in how one will physically feel from day to day encourages self-doubt and frustration. As you are probably aware, feeling negative about yourself can create a vicious circle of frustration, disappointment and anger, all of which are often directed inward. One of the first therapeutic approaches she suggests to break this cycle of negative self-thinking is to encourage patients to gain an enhanced level of self-awareness to highlight the impact those uncomfortable emotions have on them.

She has found one of the most beneficial ways of discovering if a person is prone to negative thoughts about themselves is to explore the kind of things their inner voice says to them. If on reading this your response is, 'What inner voice? – I don't have one!' then that is your inner voice.

Your inner voice runs an almost continuous internal dialogue commenting on everything you do and often makes judgements on how well you do it too. Happening as it does just below conscious awareness, one's inner voice goes unchecked, and unchallenged, for most of the time.

For many people, especially those living with chronic illness, their inner voice is rarely a source of uplifting encouragement. It is more likely to give an unremitting flow of self-criticism, and negative self-judgements (everything from 'I hate my body' to 'What am I doing wrong?'). Taking the time to become aware of how your inner voice speaks to you can accurately demonstrate to you your own level of self-judgement and self-condemnation.

Tuning in, and clearly hearing your inner voice, is the crucial first step to silencing the draining and dispiriting stream of negativity that can hinder moving forward and making positive changes. Sally suggests spending a little quiet time – just a few moments – every day for about a week tuning in to your inner voice, and simply listening and noting down the negative statements. A therapy tool she then uses to resolve those negative, limiting beliefs is called Emotional Freedom Technique (EFT or 'Tapping'). EFT is an energy therapy that has proved highly effective for revealing true feelings, in this case prompted by one's negative self-talk.

Once you have a greater awareness of your own negative self-talk you can then apply another of her core therapy tools – called Percussive Suggestion Technique (PSTEC) – to turn-down, or dispel, the emotions attached to the negative beliefs you have about yourself. Turning off negative self-talk is the beginning of a powerful journey which can transform a former inner-critic into your greatest advocate – someone cheering for you instead of undermining you.

Understanding specific therapies

Emotional Freedom Technique

Originating in the US, Emotional Freedom Technique (EFT) has been around now for over 25 years. It is easy to learn as a self-help tool, and can be applied to alleviate a myriad of negative emotions. The technique involves tapping with two fingers on various points, mainly on the face and upper body. It works on the same energy lines, or Chi meridians, as acupuncture, the traditional technique of ancient Chinese medicine. Whereas acupuncture is used to relieve physical conditions, EFT works on dispelling uncomfortable emotions.

It is measurable in its effect by setting a 'SUD rating' at the beginning of your work, and checking back in again after performing a few rounds of EFT. SUD stands for 'Subjective Unit of Discomfort'. It uses a scale from zero to 10 to assess the degree of negative feelings you experience around your health, for instance. Zero is none at all and 10 represents the highest level of discomfort. (Be aware, it is recommended you begin learning and practising the use of EFT with specific aspects of your illness that are not too distressing.)

Working with EFT begins with a set-up phrase that helps to focus the mind on the issue you are working with. After repeating the set-up phrase three times, a short reminder phrase is spoken as you follow the tapping guide. Sally says, think of EFT as peeling back the layers of an onion. This is merely the outer layer but as you tap more, becoming more practised with the technique, you will reveal to yourself your real blocks to letting go of stress, many of which will centre around negative limiting beliefs you have, such as 'Nothing works for me', or 'I've been ill for too long now' or 'Too many things are stacked against me'.

After a few rounds of EFT, especially if you customise the words to suit your own unique experience of your health challenges, you may notice a change in how you feel or think about the prospect of trusting your body to repair and heal itself. You can check this by re-assessing your SUD rating.

You can access a free pdf guide to how to learn EFT for yourself from Sally's website www.your7simplesteps.com (see Therapy Tools).

Percussive Suggestion Technique

As mentioned, another positive tool recommended by Sally is Percussive Suggestion Technique (PSTEC) created by Tim Phizackerley in the UK well over a decade ago. It involves listening and interacting to an audio click track. The listener taps with the fingers of both hands to a complex sequences of three rhythms that Tim devised. As an expert in artificial intelligence, Tim has used his knowledge of how the brain processes information, and in particular memory, to effectively turn down, or break, the connection between negative emotions attached to memories, or events from the past, either real or imagined.

PSTEC for you to try

There are no reminder phrases with PSTEC. It works very differently from EFT. Remember a time when you had a really bad flare-up, for instance. Focus once again on those feelings of anxiety about your medical condition. For many people who live with chronic disease, health anxiety can often unhelpfully contribute towards a negative self-image. Focus on a specific anxiety, and then set a SUD rating. Listen and interact with one of the PSTEC click tracks (available for free on www.your7simplesteps.com) and you should very quickly begin to feel less overwhelmed and anxious. You can decide how much more positive or empowered you feel by re-assessing your SUD rating.

Hypnotherapy

NICE, the National Institute from Health and Care Excellence, has recognised the role stress plays in IBD and cited hypnotherapy as a possible treatment for those who have not responded well to other treatments. The Cochrane Library, [14] a global independent network of health researchers and professionals, includes studies that provide some evidence that suggests that hypnotherapy might be effective in treating symptoms, including abdominal pain and the parts of the brain that influence the movement of the bowel.

In her work, Sally has found that resolving limiting beliefs with EFT and breaking the connection between anxiety and events or memories with PSTEC, together with hypnosis for stress reduction, is a powerful therapeutic approach to bringing about lasting change in how clients think and feel about themselves and their health.

I'd like to thank Sally for sharing her invaluable tips. You can find more information on all the advice above (along with free downloads of PSTEC click track MP3s and EFT PDF) from her website: www. your7simplesteps.com (See Therapy Tools).

Five useful coping strategies for anxiety

1. Ask your GP to refer you to a mental health service. Cognitive Behaviour Therapy (CBT), in particular, can help hugely – especially when dealing with the impact of diagnosis. It is a type of therapy that helps you understand where negative and

harmful thoughts come from and reframe them into more positive ones. You might also ask to be referred to some of the services talked about above, such as EFT and PSTEC, which are becoming more readily available.

2. If you can't immediately access a therapist, there are many good CBT guides. Try *Overcoming Health Anxiety* by David Veale.[15]

3. Meditation is becoming more common as a possible treatment for anxiety and GPs are now exploring mindfulness as a route instead of antidepressants. There are many useful apps to download to help with meditation. Calm (ITunes/Android, free) and Headspace (ITunes/Android, free) are two apps that teach you the art of mindfulness through your phone. A real block to developing a meditation or mindfulness technique can be the challenge of turning off that inner voice which often is carping and negative. Sally Baker says: 'Meditation and mindfulness advice often underestimates how over-powering our negative self-talk can be and the challenge it can be to silence that voice so that meditation/mindfulness can even become a viable route to stress management.' For this reason, addressing self-talk issues as outlined above may be essential before successfully using meditation and mindfulness.

4. Share your experiences of dealing with IBD. This could take the form of a journal, chatting to others online or even (as I did, many years ago) starting your own blog.

5. Visit Anxiety UK for information on regular anxiety support groups as well as online chat services.

It is important to say again that these tips cannot replace the advice of a medical professional and if you are feeling any new symptoms of anxiety and depression, then it is very important to see your GP.

Changing your thought patterns

The worksheet on page 56 reflects CBT principles but as a standalone cannot hope to replace or measure up to the advice and support of a qualified therapist. However, if you are looking to record your thoughts, it might be beneficial to use it as an introduction. The idea is to record negative thoughts about your illness that arise, consider their validity and replace them with more realistic thoughts.

Understanding self-esteem and body image

Alongside anxiety go self-esteem and body image. Any chronic illness can hugely affect your confidence and how you see yourself, but with something as personal as IBD (where unfortunately the symptoms are largely seen as taboo), it is hard for it not to have any impact on how you see yourself. What about style? It turns out that goes out the window when you swap heels for comfy slippers. If you are recovering from surgery, comfort is key and it is often impossible to wear tight-fitting garments.

Often, it may seem that it's been a while since you thought about what your body actually looks like since you've been too preoccupied with what's going on on the inside. Healthy people never think about their colon but once you've been diagnosed you become hyper-aware of your insides (and, as a result, less concerned about the outside). In some ways, it's refreshing and reminds us about what's really important. Yet in other ways it's sad: when it seems like our bodies are struggling, we forget all the things we like about ourselves and our body can easily become something to despise rather than love.

A big part of this defining ourselves can be the feeling that we can't trust our bodies. It can feel like our bodies have betrayed us and thus we start to question symptoms we had never thought about before. This can also be exacerbated by the baffling array of side effects

NEGATIVE THOUGHT	EVIDENCE Is there really any true factual evidence for this? (Would it stand up in court?) How much do you believe it is true? (On a scale of 1-10)	ALTERNATIVE POSITIVE THOUGHT	EVIDENCE
I am always unwell and I'm never going to get better.	I have had three flare-ups this year but I have also had some periods of feeling well. Score: 5/10	I am struggling to cope with my illness right now but that doesn't mean it will always be this way.	Last year I was in remission and felt very well. My average flare-up lasts two weeks which means I will start to feel better soon.

caused by the cocktail of medications we're prescribed that make our body do all the kinds of freaky things. Why is my face suddenly puffy and round? Why is my tongue so furry? Why can't I stop itching? These are just some of the questions we might ask ourselves on a daily basis.

Being happy with your body in this day and age is pretty damn hard for all of us, let alone those of us who are battling health problems. Women in particular are bombarded with images of the likes of Victoria's Secret models and Kylie Jenner trying to make wheelchairs fashion accessories. These unrealistic expectations can have a bad effect on the best of us; but when we are suffering from IBD it feels even more difficult to keep up.

What can we do? Well, managing our expectations is important. Many people with IBD report stronger relationships post-diagnosis and we realise what our loved ones care more about is us being healthy than our appearance.

Opposite is a space to record some positive thoughts about your body image. This might seem a little bit far-fetched, but if you're reading this chapter you're probably used to feeling a little bit angry at your body for not doing what it should. IBD can make us feel less confident, less pretty/handsome, less sexy, less healthy and sometimes less of a person. But there are lots of amazing IBD advocates raising awareness of loving your body with the condition (such as the Get Your Belly Out's campaign). I can't ask you to take a photo of your belly but instead encourage you to use the space opposite to record some things you are proud of.

PATIENT EXPERIENCE: Suzanne, diagnosed 2011

Body image

It's funny as most people would think a negative body image would be due to being overweight. I've never had a huge problem with negative body image but I guess the main issues would be looking pale and tired (due to anaemia) and I'd always be a bit sensitive about my stomach area (thanks to years of bloating). It's hard not to compare yourself with other people who are more toned, strong, healthy looking. I practise gratitude every day and when I do yoga I'm grateful for my flexibility. Now that I can wear tighter jeans I'm grateful my stomach isn't inflamed any more. I see how far I've come and I'm grateful to myself.

FOOD AND SUPPLEMENTS

Chapter 5

Nutritional supplements and IBD

The list below is not intended to be a supplement shopping list or a prescribed regime. Supplementation is a hugely personal decision and will depend on lots of different factors including your disease activity, the medication you are on, any surgery you have had and your current diet. However, since the supplement market is huge this guide explains possible supplements you may find useful. After this you will find a section on monitoring your supplements since it is vital you introduce these slowly to avoid unwanted side effects. Finally, as with all advice in this book, please talk to your doctor about any supplements you plan on taking.

A guide to probiotics

Whenever we read about gut health or supporting our immune system, probiotics are the first item to be mentioned so it's a good place to start. Hugely beneficial to our health, we often read about probiotics for IBS but now more people are turning to these for a possible solution to IBD as more research begins to focus on the bacterial balance in IBD (as was discussed in Chapter 1).There are more brands on the market than ever before and probiotics are no longer confined to health food stores; you can buy them in the form of tablets, yoghurt drinks, chocolate and even chewing gum! Yet while more of us than ever are buying them, we're not as clued up on them as we might think, meaning lots of people often waste their money on pointless products.

The first thing that is important to emphasise is that supermarket yoghurt drinks – such as Actimel and Activia – are not an adequate source of probiotic for IBD patients and are not actually scientifically proven to significantly alter your health.[16] They can also contain dairy and lots of sugar, both of which may potentially exacerbate symptoms.

The second is to consider that probiotics are not yet proven to have any benefit for people with IBD and this is likely to be due to the huge amount of strains available and the fact that gut bacteria balance varies widely between patients. However, it is clearly an area worth exploring – with Crohn's and Colitis UK announcing a research study to focus on a specific bacteria strain (Hall, 2015)[17]. If you decide you would like to try a probiotic supplement, be aware that not all probiotics are the same. There are very few supplements that have been proven to improve gut bacteria: the most notable being Symprove (a liquid probiotic by Biocare, which showed some recent success in a trial with ulcerative colitis patients – see below). Therefore, it is best to stick to probiotic foods or invest in a good quality supplement as listed below. One size doesn't fit all. For example, *Lactobacillus salivarius* is particularly beneficial for bloating and gas in IBS. *Steptococcus thermophilus* helps us break down lactose and *Bifidobacterium lactis* can protect cells from damage caused by gluten. Do your research before buying to check the strains are beneficial to you.

There are many good quality strains on the market but the only supplements that have had some proven benefit for digestion in general are:

- Biokult

- VSL3, and

- Symprove – its manufacturer recently published a study suggesting some success with ulcerative colitis (Sisson et al, 2015)[18], but larger-scale studies are needed.

When trying any probiotic supplement, it is really important to try only one type at a go and consider beginning at half doses to avoid bloating and cramping.

An alternative to probiotics can be to introduce probiotic-rich foods, such as miso, tempeh, kefir or sauerkraut. Again, it is very important these too are introduced slowly to avoid disrupting your digestive system and may not be suitable if you are suffering from severe diarrhoea. On page 68, I outline my personal experiences of using sauerkraut as a probiotic food. It is important to note that introducing probiotics or probiotic foods can cause 'die-off symptoms', where diarrhoea initially feels worse due to change in gut bacteria – that is, ridding the body of bad bacteria (this is similar to antibiotic-associated diarrhoea). While this is normal, if symptoms do not improve or noticeably worsen, it is always wise to stop the probiotic source and consult a doctor.

Other possible supplements to introduce

As a nutritional therapist, I always emphasise the importance of getting your nutrition from your food but sometimes this is not possible, especially when your immune system is under pressure or your body is not absorbing nutrients correctly, which is often the case when you are in a flare. Of course, if you are not digesting your food correctly and having symptoms such as diarrhoea or loose stools, then it can be essential to turn to supplementation. This will ensure that it does not lead to more complications – most commonly, anaemia, vitamin B12 deficiency, vitamin D deficiency and fatigue. Below are some of the key supplements that can help support you in managing your life with IBD. As with all the advice in this book, it is important to decide what it is applicable to you and it is always advisable to ask your doctor to test you for key nutritional deficiencies before deciding what exactly you need to supplement your body with. (Be aware some blood tests are controversial because of differences in parameters between laboratories; symptoms should always be taken into account too.)

1. Vitamin B12

Vitamin B12 is probably one of the key supplements for patients with IBD. This is because extraction of vitamin B12 from our food (starting in the stomach, which we need to be highly acid) and its absorption in the terminal ileum (but only in the presence of 'intrinsic factor' produced by the parietal cells in the stomach lining) are highly vulnerable to issues with the gastrointestinal tract. If you are suffering with any kind of gut problem it is going to be difficult for your body to get the amount of vitamin B12 it needs. In turn, one of the most well-known side effects of vitamin B12 deficiency is fatigue which, as mentioned in Chapter 1, is one of the key symptoms of IBD. Many people believe that fatigue is caused by Crohn's itself when it could equally be caused by a vitamin B12 deficiency. Vitamin B12 is massively linked to anxiety and depression, therefore many patients who believe that Crohn's is causing their anxiety can often find their symptoms improve with vitamin B12 supplementation. Vitamin B12 is readily available in sources such as eggs, good quality meat and nutritional yeast (many brands fortify this with vitamin B12) – but only if you have the capacity to digest it. Many sufferers find they need to take a supplement. If your doctor says you are severely deficient, you may be given an infusion or injection. Otherwise, under the tongue drops or spray – thereby avoiding the digestive system – may be worth investing in; see if this has any impact on your energy levels and mental health.

2. Magnesium

Magnesium is another key nutrient that is linked to our ability to deal with stress, get a good night's rest and deal with anxiety. Although magnesium is commonly touted as easing constipation (it is a muscle relaxant), it is still an important nutrient in managing IBD. The best way to use this supplement is by way of a magnesium spray on the skin. When this supplement is used just before bedtime, it can help with relaxation of muscles and also assist you in a good night's sleep.

3. Turmeric

For many, turmeric is a really important natural supplement in managing their IBD. Turmeric is a natural anti-inflammatory which has been linked to helping with everything where inflammation is a problem, including rheumatoid arthritis and cancer. There have been very small scale studies which suggest turmeric can have an impact on inflammatory bowel disease. A review of human studies in 2011 suggested these studies showed promise but there is a need for larger scale research (Taylor and Leonard, 2011).[19] It can also provide general health benefits, such as increased antioxidant levels and improving joint pain, which makes it an all-round nutritional supplement to take. It is important that you invest in the right turmeric supplement to maximise the benefit. Many supplements now come combined with bioperine, which is another word for black pepper. This combination is very important as it helps the body absorb turmeric efficiently. If you are not willing to invest in a supplement you could start small by using turmeric in your cooking or even grating ginger and turmeric with hot water to make a delicious anti-inflammatory tea.

4. Digestive enzymes

When your gut is under strain it can often lack the enzymes it needs to fully digest food. This can lead to things like temporary lactose intolerance, indigestion, bloating and just generally poor 'gut' health. Digestive enzymes can therefore help support your body with this process. There are plenty of digestive supplements out there and it would be best to use these when you feel you are eating a heavy meal or having a night out. If you are looking to bring this into your everyday routine you could also try peppermint tea or peppermint oil, which is a great digestive aid and helps to relax the gut. (However, be mindful it can cause reflux as it relaxes the oesophageal sphincter.)

5. Vitamin D

Vitamin D is crucial for boosting the immune system and supporting it, which as you know is essential in IBD which puts such strain on the immune system. It is also crucial for allowing your body to absorb calcium, which many patients are prescribed after being given many doses of steroids, which are a risk factor for osteoporosis. Therefore, unless you are getting regular access to sunshine and eating lots of wild oily fish, I would strongly recommend you include a vitamin D3 supplement in your regime. Vitamin D deficiency is becoming much more common in the general population and more GPs are willing to test patients via a simple blood test. Over-supplementation can lead to vitamin D toxicity and hypercalcaemia so it is worth being tested for this before you supplement.

6. Fish oil

If you are already eating the recommended two portions of oily fish a week (such as mackerel, tuna or salmon) then this supplement is probably not essential for you. However, otherwise it is worth investing in an omega-3 fish oil supplement as these are known to have an anti-inflammatory effect on the body and more studies are on the way to isolate this issue in terms of inflammatory bowel disease (Barbalho et al, 2016).[20] For example, a number of studies have found that cells from bodies that have regular omega-3 supplementation have much lower levels of inflammation. You can buy a regular omega-3 supplement or invest in foods like flax seeds and chia seeds which also have a high omega-3 value. These can be particularly useful for vegetarians and vegans, but require more digestion to break them down to the active ingredient – EPA – which may be an issue when your gut is not working correctly/you don't have the right enzymes.

7. Iron

Iron-deficiency anaemia is extremely common in Crohn's disease and ulcerative colitis patients. Both iron stores and the level of red blood cells are regularly tested as markers for anaemia (the former being an indicator of whether anaemia is likely to occur). Anaemia is common because IBD often leads to bleeding in the digestive system and this loss of red blood cells leads to a high iron requirement to replace them. Yet even if bleeding is not a symptom, the body may struggle to absorb the iron it needs from food sources. Therefore, an iron supplement is often recommended by doctors but it can be difficult to find one that does not upset your digestive system and thus exacerbate your symptoms. Choose your iron supplement carefully – many doctors now prescribe liquid iron instead of tablets to avoid this. If your iron deficiency is severe you will probably be given an iron infusion or injection to ensure that you are not losing out on this vital nutrient. If, however, your deficiency is mild I would recommend something like Spa-tone which is a water-based iron supplement. If you are taking a traditional iron supplement, please be aware this may cause black stools (which can be alarming and mistaken for blood) as well as digestive discomfort. Talk to your doctor if you have any problems.

8. Calcium

Calcium is often supplemented in patients who take steroids, as being on this type of medication can damage bone density. Yet, as many patients can struggle to absorb nutrients and may also have to limit milk in their diet (more on page 78) calcium can be a useful supplement. Calcium as a supplement is slightly constipating so can sometimes also help with diarrhoea. Be aware too that it should be taken with vitamin D3 and you also need plenty of vitamin K2 to ensure it goes into your bones rather than your arteries.

Summary

This list may have overwhelmed you with supplements. Read it again and decide which are right for you, in collaboration with your doctor. Introduce them one at a time to monitor their effects. Use the chart (page 69) to track what you take and how it affects you.

My experiences with supplementation

When I was first diagnosed, I was overwhelmed by the sheer number of supplements on the market offering to improve gut health. Although I had studied nutrition, at this point I think logic goes out the window when you want to get better and I snapped up lots of supplements. I soon found this made my symptoms worse – I had overloaded my body with too many things for it to deal with. I also assumed that I was deficient in lots of things and was pleasantly surprised when my doctor told me that my vitamin D and vitamin B12 levels were normal – I had been supplementing these based on what I'd read. I then realised that everybody is different and I needed to explore what supplements worked for me. My two top supplements are probiotics and turmeric. Turmeric has been my biggest success – I take two 500 mg capsules a day with food (make sure you pick a brand with bioperine) and I've found they help me bounce back from gut disturbances much more quickly. While they can't do much when I'm in a full-on flare, if I have a bad day I feel much better quickly. I add turmeric and black pepper to everything – even smoothies.

SUPPLEMENT	DAY OF INTRODUCTION	DOSAGE + INSTRUCTIONS	ANY SIDE EFFECTS
Turmeric	Monday	1 tablet once a day. After one week move to 2 tablets twice a day	

I have tried lots of probiotic supplements but found that my gut bacteria were very delicate; I constantly suffered from the 'die off' of bacteria which frustrated me. Instead, I decided to introduce naturally probiotic food and I have found that sauerkraut is particularly beneficial in helping when I have stomach ache, wind or loose stools.

Chapter 6

The role of food in managing IBD

The role of diet in inflammatory bowel disease is widely debated by doctors and patients. Many publications tell sufferers to 'monitor their diet' or 'keep a food diary' without wanting to give specific advice since IBD is such a personal experience. Yet this advice is often near to useless since patients don't know what to monitor or to keep a diary of! Therefore, I regarded it as really important to devote a significant section of my book to this issue. I'd like to make it clear that as a nutritional therapist, I am passionate about people understanding food: what it consists of, how it can help and how it might harm. Yet the following pages do not in any way attempt to suggest that diet is a cause or a cure of IBD, nor do they offer you a prescriptive plan. Although I am a big fan of creating healthy, easy-to-digest recipes on my blog (www.abalancedbelly.co.uk) I have decided not to share these with you in this book (other than a few simple drink recipes in Chapter 15: 24-Hour Flare-Up Plan, page 139) since this book is about your IBD journey and there are no quick-fix recipes for this disease. Instead, the first thing to do is to understand food and begin to monitor your diet carefully so that you can figure out what may work for you. I aim to share with you what I've learnt about food and hopefully help you feel empowered to understand what are the best choices for you. Once you understand food and its components, you may then feel it's time to introduce new recipes into your diet. As well as my blog, I have included a list of possible resources at the end of this book to help you in exploring new recipes when you feel you have gained a greater understanding of the role of food in your life with inflammatory bowel disease. Here I outline specific foods and food groups and consider what impact they may have on your gut and your symptoms.

Dietary approaches to IBD

First of all I will provide an overview of common diets that you may discover when searching for advice on food and IBD.

DIET 1: Low residue

Low residue is one of the diets often discussed by doctors specifically for IBD patients. Its aim is to reduce the amount of fibre (which is discussed later in the chapter) and fat. (It is not a long-term diet so is not designed in terms of optimal nutrition.)

Does it work?

The thought behind this diet is that when a patient is flaring, reducing fibre and fat will stop further gut irritation. The diet can often help reduce the number of bowel movements and ease symptoms. Yet the foods recommended often have little nutritional value, making it difficult to sustain in the long run. In turn, a reliance of white bread, white pasta and other low-fibre carbs can alter the gut bacteria and cause IBS-type symptoms. If advised to follow this, it may be better to try to adapt the suggested foods to make them as nutritious as possible, e.g. mashed bananas, cooked apples and rice.

DIET 2: LOFFLEX

Designed by Professor John Hunter, LOFFLEX is a low-residue diet that also includes other potential allergens. These are then monitored through an elimination diet and reintroduced slowly.

Does it work?

Professor John Hunter has shared many testimonials of patients whose IBD has been successfully controlled by the LOFFLEX approach as it helps sufferers to isolate potential triggers as well as eliminate fibre; it helps them understand more about their diet in general and is a much more rigorous approach. It almost certainly has to be undertaken with the support of a qualified dietician to ensure the elimination process is done accurately and the patient receives adequate nutrition. For more information go to: http://www.crohns.org.uk/crohns_disease/nutritional_therapy/the-lofflex-diet

DIET 3: Paleo

Paleo, or as it's often billed 'the caveman's diet', centres around eating purely natural foods, largely meat, fish, nuts, fruit and veg. There's also 'Autoimmune Paleo' (AIP), designed specifically for those with autoimmune disease (this is more restrictive and cuts out nuts altogether as well as pulses, such as beans and lentils).

Does it work?

Paleo can definitely help anyone cut all the rubbish out of their diet. Many of the banned foods, such as sugary snacks, gluten and most types of dairy, can be pro-inflammatory, so avoiding these might make a real difference to overall wellbeing. However, you may also need to adapt it to your own needs, especially if you find fibre a problem – for example, swapping raw nuts for nut-butters (to minimise fibre) and high-fibre raw green veg for more tummy-friendly cooked pumpkin. (More on fibre later in this chapter, page 87.) You may find you can tolerate more fibre as your gut improves. As for AIP, it's great to see dietary advice that is specifically focusing on autoimmune disease, but this diet is even more restrictive, so you'd need to plan meals carefully and work in conjunction with a dietician or nutritional therapist. In summary, paleo is a useful philosophy but difficult to implement without support.

DIET 4: Fasting/5:2 diets

Traditionally in places like India, fasting has been seen as hugely beneficial from a spiritual point of view; the focus now in the West has shifted from spiritual wellbeing to weight loss! Nevertheless, many still promote the idea of fasting as a way to 'detox' and give the body a break: this ranges from water fasts to juice fasts to a 5:2 diet (where fasting is undertaken two days out of seven).

Does it work?

It's no secret that liquid diets (like elemental shakes) have a good success record with IBD and many patients are offered this to rest the bowels and allow healing. As for undertaking a fast yourself, very careful guidance is needed. I will discuss juicing in more detail later (page 93) as I have found it can be helpful for the body since the nutrition uptake can be higher without the need to break down fibre. Yet I strongly recommend you do not undergo a juice fast without proper support, since it's important the body has protein to repair itself; this is especially true if you are underweight or anaemic. If you are experiencing lots of diarrhoea and looking to rest your bowel, it may be better drinking the water of cooked vegetables or bone broth (since some say cold juice can be too irritating on the colon).

The best advice I was ever given related to the term 'detox' (which I use very loosely here). It can be individual to the user and should be done one step at a time. By doing this (detoxing one step at a time instead of drastically starving), the body isn't tricked into anything too severe; this avoids 'die off' symptoms such as headaches and upset stomach (which often make people feel as if it's not working). The 5:2 approach in theory can be a good way to introduce gentle fast but many people swing from poor choices on normal days to starvation mode on fast days, creating havoc in the gut and with their metabolism. Rather than following such a drastic diet, it may be useful to introduce small steps to give the bowel a chance to rest, such as replacing breakfast with a smoothie on days you feel it necessary.

DIET 5: Low FODMAPs

FODMAPs stands for Fermentable Oligosaccharides, Disaccharides, Monosaccharides and Polyols. These are types of carbohydrates (short-chain carbs and sugar alcohols) that are difficult for the body to digest, which can lead to them quickly fermenting in the gut (causing bloating). They also attract water into the large bowel, which can affect gut function. They include fructans (found in wheat, rye, barley and the onion family), lactose (milk sugar) and the 'polyols' (sugar alcohols found in many fruits). Foods to avoid are therefore numerous and include wheat, dairy products, high-fructose corn syrup and many fruits. Patients on the low FODMAPs diet aim to limit high FODMAPs foods. This diet has been around for a while but is beginning to gain approval in the IBS community and now many are trying it with IBD. Some doctors recommend FODMAPs if a patient is still suffering from symptoms despite being in clinical remission.

Does it work?

If you are suffering from IBS, research shows it is definitely worth a try but you'll need to do it with the support of a dietician (or, at the very least, one of the many FODMAPs apps you can buy). The list of YES/NO foods can seem a bit baffling but it's not hugely hard to eat naturally if you use your common sense.

DIET 6: SCD

SCD stands for the 'specific carbohydrate diet'. This diet is broadly similar to Paleo but focuses more on the role of the bacteria balance in the gut (which, as we know from Chapter 1 (page 4), is hugely important). Whether foods are allowed or not, is all to do with whether they contain single-sugar molecules or complex ones. Probiotics is a big part of the diet, with users making homemade natural yoghurt daily

Does it work?

For some, the answer is yes. If you are looking for a diet with many success stories, this is the one. In fact, Stanford University has started a study on whether this induces remission in Crohn's patients so the medical profession is starting to take it seriously (www.med. stanford.edu).[21] There are many patients who find it is extremely beneficial and since more is being discovered about the link between bacteria and IBD it makes some sense. However, it can be difficult to follow in the UK since many ingredients (eg pure gelatine, dry cottage cheese) are difficult to find. It is a diet you need to follow for the long haul since many find it takes months to work. As dairy is a problem for some, you'll need to introduce the probiotic yoghurt slowly or substitute kefir that is not dairy based.

DIET 7: GAPS

GAPS ('gut and psychology syndrome') is often billed as the British version of SCD and has many similarities. It also focuses on eliminating many foods and on probiotics – although it does allow supplementation rather than the yoghurt. I'd suggest trying this over SCD purely because you will be able to find a registered GAPS dietician here in the UK and will also find it easier to get everything needed on your shopping list.

DIET 8: Weight-loss diets (Slimming World, Weightwatchers, etc)

I've decided to group these types of diet together since many people comment on a change of gut symptoms when trying Weightwatchers/ Slimming World. I do think these diets can be a useful starting point if you are making poor food choices and need encouragement but I don't really agree with them as a way to approach food (many foods they class as 'free' or 'unlimited' are actually pretty bad for us, such as unlimited sweeteners).

Does it work?

Many people find their gut symptoms improve on these kinds of diet and proclaim them as a miracle. It's more likely that the secret is that cutting down on things like alcohol and junk food gives your gut an easier time. Others say it actually makes symptoms worse, and that's probably because they may increasingly eat things like salad for lunch which are just too raw and irritating for a sensitive and inflamed colon. Ready meals marketed by these companies are usually full of sugar so I would definitely not recommend them. So in answer, these diets won't really help your gut health alone, but using them as a way to introduce healthier alternatives might help your overall wellbeing.

Summary

I hope this overview has helped you somewhat with making a diet decision. It can definitely be a tricky area to navigate and it may take some time to find the right diet for you. What the majority of the diets have in common is the focus on fresh foods, avoidance of gluten and dairy and the rejection of lots of preservatives, chemicals and sugar. I will explain specifically in the next section why gluten and dairy in particular are commonly excluded. It is also common sense that less sugar and more fresh foods might be a good place to start for any person looking to improve their health – not just those with IBD!

Understanding food

We've begun by looking at specific diets but I think it is far more important to actually understand how food works. As mentioned previously, there is no one IBD diet; it is far more important to understand nutrition and then use this to find ways to monitor your diet and find your own path. In the rest of this chapter, I'll look at the common foods that may cause issues for IBD patients, as well as those than can be beneficial. There will be space at the end to record your own food intake, as an initial first step on your food-monitoring journey.

The role of dairy

Dairy consumption is one topic that is often linked to Crohn's disease so it is a good place to start. There is no suggestion that dairy products cause Crohn's disease, although the MAP bacteria theory which I mentioned in Chapter 1 suggests specifically that the bacteria in cow's milk can be a cause of Crohn's (and this is why the MAP vaccine is being developed). While most doctors do not necessarily support this theory, there are studies to suggest that people with Crohn's disease and ulcerative colitis do find it difficult to digest dairy. This does not mean that giving up dairy can cure or prevent flare-ups but rather it is an item of food to consider when logging your food diary and looking at possible triggers for you. As with anything, before we give up or cut down on an item of food it is important to understand the science behind it and why dairy could be a problem for you.

There are actually many different levels of dairy intolerance so it is essential to understand what you may or may not be suffering from. Firstly, let's talk about lactose intolerance. This is the inability to digest milk sugar properly because you are not producing enough of the enzyme lactase that breaks lactose down to glucose (which you use for energy) and another simple sugar, galactose. Lactose intolerance can easily be diagnosed by your GP and there are some suggestions in studies that people with IBD have an increased level of this problem. However, there are also many people who feel they are intolerant of lactose despite receiving a negative test; it may be that they are producing some lactase but not always enough. Lack of lactase can be something that you are born with or something that happens over a short period of time – for example, after a bout of gastroenteritis or even a bad flare-up. This is because when the gut is under stress it can fail to produce the enzymes that it needs.

If you are lactose intolerant you should find that you can tolerate things like yoghurt, and even some types of cheese as they have low to no levels of lactose. However, you will need to switch from regular milk to lactose-free alternatives or even to dairy-free alternatives, such as coconut yoghurt. You might also find a lactose supplement useful since these replace the enzymes your body needs to digest the milk.

Symptoms of lactose intolerance include abdominal pain and loose watery stools, which of course are difficult to distinguish from the symptoms of IBD.

Some people are not intolerant of lactose but nevertheless find it difficult to digest milk altogether. These people may find that even though they replace their usual dairy with a lactose-free alternative they still have a reaction when drinking milk. This could be because they find the milk protein (whey, casein) and/or fats difficult to digest. If you find that you are regularly having symptoms when consuming foods that contain whey and/or casein, then it may be better that you initially avoid all forms of dairy.

When keeping a food diary you can start to experiment with other such forms of 'dairy', such as goats' milk, sheeps' milk, almond milk or soya milk. (Be aware that many people who have a problem with casein also have a problem with soya.) There is another type of milk called 'A2 milk' which has recently been launched on the market and many people believe this is a healthier option. This is an alternative if you are allergic to 'A1 milk protein', but unfortunately there is no real way of knowing if you have this specific problem unless you experiment with the product. You can probably see that, after reading this chapter, experimentation (and patience) will be key.

Finally, you may feel that your milk intolerance is fine one day but not the next. This is because there are many factors at play here. You may, for example, find you are sensitive to milk when it is in a fatty product, such as ice cream or cheese. It could be during your flares you become more sensitive but during remission you are fine. All of this is due to the change in your gut bacteria. Therefore, if you feel that you are intolerant of milk now you may find that after three or four weeks you can reintroduce it slowly to see if your symptoms recur.

In terms of scientific evidence for a connection between IBD and milk consumption, studies vary. One (by Judaki et al) that reported in 2014 concluded that there was a significant relationship between ulcerative colitis, cows' milk and casein specifically since the number of ulcerative colitis patients who demonstrated a mild to severe reaction to cows' milk and casein was much higher than was found in people in a control group.[22] However, a similar study (by Jones et al) back in 1981 had concluded there was no difference in allergy bodies between ulcerative colitis patients and controls when presented with a range of allergens, including egg, celery, fish and milk.[23] There are other studies, ongoing at the time of going to press, but it is clear that cows' milk may have some link to symptoms in at least a proportion of IBD patients. This may be because inflammation makes it much harder to break down the milk fats and proteins or due to lower enzyme levels or different gut bacteria. For example, a study in rats found that milk fats were associated with a change in the level of different types of bacteria in their guts. Similarly, as IBD is a disease linked to the immune system, it seems logical that allergic reactions or intolerances (also caused by the immune system) would be higher in patients when compared with the average member of the population. Despite these mixed research findings, it is of course very important to know that dairy products are a nutritious source of calcium so if you do feel that dairy is exacerbating your symptoms it is very important to seek help from a dietician or nutritional therapist to support you in eliminating milk.

PATIENT EXPERIENCE: Karen, diagnosed 2010

'Giving up milk helped me'

My name is Karen. I am 46 years old and was diagnosed after a long period of pain and symptoms about six years ago. It was great to get a diagnosis after so long. I have been married to Howard for 16 years this year and we have been together nearly 30 years. He is also my best friend and is a great carer of me when I'm poorly. I took a while to come to terms with all the tablets that I was going to have to take and what my diet was going to have to consist of. It has taken a while for my family to understand my condition. Some of them still don't really understand but I go with them. Life has totally changed for me through my diet. I have cut out all brassicas as they are really gasy and make me bloat very easily. Also, I have cut out as much dairy as possible. I have now introduced soya and 'lacto-free' products into my diet. I use them for most of my cooking and the family can't tell the difference. I had a noticeable improvement: I don't feel nauseous anymore and my stomach doesn't make the horrible churning noises before having the urge to go to the bathroom.

I bake and cook a lot and the family can't tell the difference. I make cheesecakes, lots of different desserts and cakes and in cooking I make creamy sauces, soups etc, all with soya and lacto-free milk and cream (which can be whipped), and different assortments of lacto-free cheeses too.

My father is Austrian and when he returns home for a visit or holiday he does a bit of shopping for me and mum (she is dairy-free too). In their local supermarket 'Spar' they have a whole selection of lacto-free cheeses from smoked and Danish blue through to Camembert and Brie. The manufacturers make the cheese like anyone else but add an enzyme to take the lactose out of the cheese. It is the exactly the same as normal cheese; you wouldn't know the difference. Cheese on toast or melted stilton on a steak never tasted so good...

I think I should write a cookery book to incorporate all my recipes!

Understanding the role of gluten

Like milk, gluten has been linked to autoimmune conditions, specifically those that are gut-based, like Crohn's disease and ulcerative colitis. There are many reasons for this and it is important not to instantly give up gluten just to see if you are intolerant; especially if you have not been tested for coeliac disease.

First of all, I will explain the different types of reaction the body may have against gluten. Coeliac disease is an autoimmune condition: when someone with coeliac eats gluten they form antibodies to gluten that attack the intestinal lining. It has a wide range of symptoms including diarrhoea, abdominal pain, fatigue, brain fog and anaemia. Coeliac disease is linked to Crohn's disease and ulcerative colitis in that they all fall into the autoimmune category. Therefore, if one person has an autoimmune disease they are automatically more likely to be at risk of coeliac disease. If you do feel that you are susceptible to gluten products, it is very important that you do not stop eating gluten until coeliac disease has been ruled out. This can usually be done with a blood test via your GP. However, this type of blood test, which aims to look at the immunoglobulins and antibodies in your blood, is not always 100 per cent accurate, so if you are still suffering after receiving a negative result, it may be worth asking your doctor to take a biopsy when you have your next endoscopy (or scheduling one). However, if you are sure that coeliac disease is not a possibility and you are still suffering from gluten issues, you may well be suffering from what is called 'non-coeliac gluten sensitivity' (NCGS). Although there has been some debate over the existence of NCGS, there are many people who feel that gluten causes symptoms such as diarrhoea, upset stomach, tiredness and brain fog (this is when you feel it is difficult to remember things, concentrate or figure things out) and therefore they decide to give up gluten. Again, there is no accurate test for this once coeliac disease has been ruled out, and although some companies claim to offer to test for gluten intolerance via hair, skin or blood, none of these methods is completely scientifically accurate. The only way therefore to see if gluten is a real trigger in causing your symptoms is, with the cooperation of a dietician or nutritional therapist, to go through a careful elimination diet to see if gluten-free could be an option for you. This is not a decision to be undertaken lightly since gluten is in a wide range of foods and if this is not done with careful supervision, it can lead to nutritional deficiencies. (For example, whole grains are an important source of some of the B vitamins.) In turn, individuals who give up gluten and then try to return to it may find that their body becomes more sensitive to the protein because they are not used to digesting it.

Some studies are now suggesting a link between gluten and IBD where coeliac disease is not a factor; one recent study, by Herfarth et al (2014), suggested that 42.6 per cent of IBD patients had an improvement in diarrhoea on a gluten-free diet.[24] This is clearly an area that requires more study but it could be because gluten, like dairy, is a difficult protein to digest. Many people believe that if their body and/or gut is inflamed, the gut may essentially become more permeable; this is called 'leaky gut syndrome', and when the gut is in this state, particles such as gluten and dairy may pass into the bloodstream before being fully broken down in the small intestine; when the gut lining is healthy only the end products would be able to get through. This can cause an inflammatory response and worsen the symptoms of IBD. Again, it is important to note that there is some debate over whether leaky gut syndrome actually exists. However, removing gluten will not cure the disease but it may help prevent further inflammation and symptoms.

Alternatively, another type of reaction is an allergy to wheat itself. Wheat allergy will usually cause skin symptoms such as rashes, irritation etc. It can also cause wheezing problems and difficulty breathing. These symptoms are very easy to spot and are quite rare, yet it is important to note the difference between a reaction to gluten and a reaction to wheat. Wheat products include pasta, bread, biscuits and many sauces. Even when gluten has been removed ('gluten-free') they can still contain wheat (and vice versa: non-wheat products can still contain gluten) so it is essential that you understand exactly what is triggering your issue.

Finally, many people who feel that they cannot digest gluten may find that it is not the gluten itself but the FODMAPs that the gluten contains. I explained FODMAPs earlier in this chapter (page 75) as one possible diet that could help ease your symptoms and help you manage your IBD excludes all FODMAPs-containing foods.

Although eliminating any major food group is best done with the support of a trained dietician, here are a few naturally gluten-free foods that may give you some ideas. (It is best to start with these as some 'free-from' products can contain preservatives, added sugar, soya and other things that may be problematic)

Naturally gluten-free foods

- Rice

- Gluten-free oats (oats contain avidins, not gluten, but have often been contaminated by being milled where wheat is also processed; hence the need to be specifically 'gluten-free')

- Rice noodles

- Potatoes

- Sweet potatoes/butternut squash

- Corn

- Quinoa

- Beans and lentils

PATIENT EXPERIENCE: Seb, diagnosed 2008

'Going gluten-free helped me'

I didn't really start thinking about the link between my ulcerative colitis symptoms and the food I was eating until 3.5 years after my diagnosis. I always noticed a few trends between certain foods I ate and the frequency of my toilet visits – tomatoes, salad leaves, most fruit and veg always made it worse. I tended to live on a diet of white potatoes, bread, cakes and sweets.

But, in 2012 it was suggested to me by an acupuncturist that gluten could be contributing to my symptoms. I decided to give him the benefit of the doubt and gave it a go.

I started by going through a transition period where I used gluten-free products as a substitute for those containing gluten that I had previously eaten. After several weeks I started to feel a lot better – fewer toilet trips and I was able to drop some of the strong medication I hated taking (prednisolone and 6-mercaptopurine). I studied chemical engineering at university and I have a very scientific mind so I wanted to know why this was working. Before I gave up my beloved bread and cakes for good I needed to understand if there was any science behind the suggestion. And, after doing some reading, I decided the evidence stacked up and I haven't looked back since.

I soon realised that gluten-free products are no healthier than their gluten counterparts (they are still packed with just as many bad, processed ingredients and sugars) so once I'd got mentally used to my new gluten-free status I started transitioning away from them. I now eat an incredibly nutrient-dense diet – lots of meat, fish, fruit and veg (I've been able to introduce almost all the ones I previously avoided).

Along with giving up gluten I also cut out dairy and nightshades [that's tomatoes, peppers, chilies, potatoes etc] (as well as making some other lifestyle changes) and the difference I've seen has been huge. I was able to come off steroid medication (something I'd found impossible for two years) and now just manage really well on a maintenance dose of mesalazine. A colonoscopy in January 2016 showed that my previous severely inflamed colon (pancolitis) is now only showing mild to moderate inflammation and I have been re-diagnosed with proctosigmoiditis.

The fibre story

The final thing to understand about food is the amount of fibre different foods contain. Many people find following a diet for inflammatory bowel disease very difficult because many fruits and vegetables (which of course we consider to be the healthy foods) can be extremely hard to digest and make symptoms such as stomach pain and diarrhoea worsen. This can lead people to believe they cannot tolerate fruit and vegetables and leave them out of their diet altogether. Of course, this can be potentially dangerous because of the nutrients that we need from fruit and vegetables – as well as fibre which is important for helping the digestive system. It is therefore extremely important that we understand the types of fibre involved and how we can best utilise fibre to help our gut (see page 90).

There are two types of fibre – soluble fibre and insoluble fibre. Most foods are a mix of both so it's important to get the right balance of these two types of fibres rather than just the amount of overall fibre.

Soluble fibre is likely to be the most beneficial for those who have a sensitive gut and are dealing with inflammatory bowel disease. Examples of foods higher in soluble fibre are carrots, butternut squash, sweet potatoes, bananas and apples. Soluble fibre is much gentler on the system than insoluble fibre. It sweeps through the colon and provides bulk. It is often given as a supplement for both constipation and diarrhoea because it works gently, unlike laxatives which are irritants. Soluble fibre also helps lower cholesterol so it is a very important fibre that we need in our diet. Some people might find a soluble-fibre supplement such as psyllium husk beneficial, but it is always more beneficial to find soluble fibre through food. You may find that these types of vegetables are easier to digest, especially if they are well cooked. However, if you find that you can't cope with them you can experiment with boiling them, mashing them, pureeing them, blending them or even juicing them to make sure you get the nutrients from them (though this will remove the fibre).

Insoluble fibre is what we traditionally think of as fibre. Foods such as bran, raw vegetables and whole grains contain these. There is no doubt that insoluble fibre is beneficial to our health: it has a cleansing effect on our bowel, keeps bowel movements regular and is often part of very nutritious foods. However, it does tend to have a harsher, 'abrasive' effect on an already sensitive or inflamed gut, in particular if one is suffering from strictures or has had surgery.

Insoluble fibre in its original form is cellulose which the human gut cannot break down. This does not mean that foods that contain it are unhealthy or that they should be avoided totally, just that they should be eaten with caution until the body is able to fully digest them.

Foods with a high proportion of insoluble fibre include bran, whole wheat, salad items such as cucumber and celery, leafy greens, broccoli and cauliflower.

A useful test to identify if a fibre is soluble or insoluble is to look at its consistency. Bananas and apples quickly soften when cooked or mashed and that is because they contain soluble fibre which breaks down and becomes very mushy. On the other hand, it is almost impossible to break down broccoli and celery unless it is very well cooked; this is because they contain much more insoluble fibre which makes them very much tougher. Therefore, when you look at a fruit or vegetable item, consider how quickly the body can break it down. You may not need to do this forever and once the gut becomes more used to insoluble fibre you may find that you can tolerate a much wider range of fruit and/or veg. In the beginning it is suggested that you stick to soluble fibre sources and gradually introduce insoluble over time. Try to think of the fibre as something that needs to be broken down by the gut.

There are many ways you can help break fibre down: by using the juicing method (which we will talk more about later, page 93); by using a blender which will break the tough fibre down; by boiling it; or by mashing it. All of these methods will help make the fibre easier to digest.

It is therefore exceedingly important to include natural fibre in your diet; the trick is working out the best way to do it for you.

Other possibly problematic foods

As with any of the advice in my book, it is always vital to figure out what works best for you. However, below I have listed other foods that may also be problematic for digestion.

Carrageenan:
This is an additive that is added to many free-from products like dairy-free ice cream and drinks. Although often deemed more natural than many additives (it's derived from seaweed), it has been linked to digestive issues. For example, in an attempt to investigate a possible link with inflammatory bowel disease, an animal study by Randhawa et al (2014) found that carrageenan caused gut ulceration in rats that was morphologically similar to that found in ulcerative colitis.[25] Again, this is clearly an area that requires more research but

INSOLUBLE FIBRE	SOLUBLE FIBRE
Bran	White bread and pasta
Wholegrains – brown pasta, brown bread, rye, seeds	Oats
Salad – Raw celery, cucumber, tomato (better when cooked), lettuce	Beans and lentils (although these can present separate issues)
Some vegetables – broccoli, spinach, kale	Some vegetables – pumpkin, squash, sweet potato, courgette, carrot (when cooked)
Some fruits – seeded fruits (strawberries, blueberries, kiwis, grapes, blackberries), grapefruit, pineapple	Some fruits – bananas, apples, mango
Nuts – when blended into nut butters/nut milk they are much more tolerable	White rice (although brown rice is often well tolerated)

it may be worth considering when keeping a food diary.

Sweeteners:
Many sweeteners have a laxative effect, which whilst it may not cause a flare-up can make diarrhoea worse. Xylitol (often found in natural health food products), aspartame (used in low calorie drinks) and mannitol (which is also used for small bowel X-rays!) are the worst culprits for this, so it is often best to avoid any foods advertised as 'sugar free' or 'low calorie' as these sweeteners are often used as a replacement.

Nightshades:
Although many people with IBD report issues with nightshades, many others can eat them just fine. It is worth keeping track of common nightshades (such as potatoes, tomatoes and peppers) when keeping a food diary.

High-fructose corn syrup:
Derived from corn, high-fructose corn syrup has been linked to a whole host of health problems. While there is little evidence specifically linking it to IBD, it is definitely worth being aware of, given that many gluten/dairy-free products use this to flavour their products.

Other allergens:
Since IBD involves the immune system, IBD patients may find themselves temporarily or permanently intolerant of some of the most common allergen foods. I have already talked about dairy and gluten but others include: soy, peanuts, egg, celery and yeast. Keep a note of these in your food diary.

Chapter 7

Beneficial foods to add to your diet

As I mentioned earlier, this book will not give specific recipes but given that this chapter is all about understanding and monitoring your food intake, this section aims to provide an overview of foods you may find beneficial to introduce into your diet.

Juicing

There are often reports of 'juice cleanses' in the media; these conjure up images of fad approaches that are designed to clean you out (which is the last thing that many of us want with IBD). However, juicing can be a useful part of your IBD regime, especially if you are finding it difficult to digest whole foods. First of all, let's make sure we make a clear distinction: I am not talking about shop-bought juices or smoothies here. There is a huge difference between these and freshly produced juice. Shop-bought juices are quite acidic and may contain preservatives and sugar, all of which can irritate those with IBD. Smoothies are also certainly a good source of nutrition, but blending keeps all of the fibre of fruit/veg (which can be difficult for you to digest, as explored in the previous section) and they may contain dairy too. Therefore, in its purest form, juicing is very different. It should get rid of all the fibre from a fruit or vegetable, leaving you with just the nutrients in pure liquid form.

How to begin juicing with IBD

As with any dietary or lifestyle changes in IBD, it is important to introduce juicing slowly to your diet. Rather than embark on long cleanses (which can be quite dangerous) you can instead try adding one juice into your morning routine. It is important to note that you may think there are some fruits or vegetables that you can't have due to a bad experience in the past (mine was with spinach and asparagus). However, if you juice these 'no-nos' in small quantities you may find you do just fine with them. Stick to a combination of two or three fruits/vegs to begin with to allow you to quickly determine if any exacerbate your symptoms. Good choices might be:

½ apple (using a full apple may significantly increase the sugar content of your juice)

1 kiwi

1-2 sticks of celery

1 courgette

2 carrots

1 slice of ginger.

As you grow more confident you can start to bring in more varied choices, such as: leafy greens, beetroot, cabbage, turmeric and pineapple. It is important to introduce these in small quantities (particularly cabbage and pineapple, which can both cause diarhoea).

The type of juicer you buy may depend on your finances and your situation. You will see two basic models: centrifugal and cold-pressed. A centrifugal juicer is much the cheaper, but is often all you need when you are first starting out. These types of juicer apply more heat, which means the nutrient content can be lower (and thus the drinks need to be consumed immediately). A cold-pressed juicer extracts nutrients much more slowly, so it is worth investing in one of these once you know juicing is for you. Cold-pressed juicers can be used to make batches of juices since nutrients are retained for longer. In both cases, it is worth buying a strainer: this will ensure no fibre remains in your drink and make it very easy to digest.

A final point to note is that many people start juicing with a Nutribullet. While a Nutribullet is a fantastic gadget, it does not extract fibre in the way a juicer does – instead it blends it extremely finely. Therefore, many people with IBD find Nutribullet-made smoothies difficult to digest in some cases. If you find that you are sensitive to fibre, it is worth investing in a juicer to ensure your drinks are fibre-free to begin with.

My experience with juicing

I first began juicing in 2013, shortly after being diagnosed with IBD. I was living in China and would walk my dog to the local vegetable stall each morning and then juice my finds in a very old and basic juicer. I found within days that it just made me feel better: my eyes were whiter, my skin was clearer and I had way more energy. The most exciting thing was being able to have things like spinach and celery – foods I'd previously considered 'no-nos' due to their high-fibre content. It was reassuring to start each day with a juice, as I knew that my body would be getting some good nutrition in as absorbable a form as possible; this became especially important to me during IBD flares as I'd lose weight and worry about absorbing nutrients from foods. The best thing for me is that the juice is digested almost instantly, meaning the gut has to do very little work; I never suffered any diarrhoea or IBD effects from juicing but would advise anyone to start slowly, using my suggested ingredients list (page 94) and see this as a useful way to top up their nutrients rather than any kind of fad diet.

PATIENT EXPERIENCE: Jennifer, diagnosed 2003

'How juicing helped me'

I have fond, positive experiences of juicing. For me, it gave me no undesirable effects and I relied on it heavily when suffering flares, as a substitute for not eating. For me, perianal Crohn's did not affect what I could eat but more affected how I got food out of my system. At times, I would suffer from constipation and not go to the toilet for days; I'd also have some bloating, cramps and inflammation through straining. I then developed abscesses which led to fistulas; these created much pain, mucus and soreness and it would affect my mobility and energy levels.

Juicing for me gave me the opportunity to get nutrients without having to go through the pain and trouble of going to the toilet. It also allowed my bowels to have a break. I found that with no food going through my system, it allowed the inflammation to die down quite quickly and I was always amazed that within a few days, I would go from not being able to walk or sit without wincing to skipping, running and rejoining my gym activities. It certainly enabled me to function as it increased my energy levels and I always found that abscesses would disappear and my mucus and leaking from fistulas would decrease drastically.

I must finish by saying that while juicing definitely helped me, I knew it wasn't a long-term fix. However, in my times of need, it is something that I still rely on now to help me through.

Probiotic foods

In Chapter 4 (page 43), we touched on the probiotic nature of some foods. Probiotics are live bacteria that can be beneficial to your gut health (while prebiotics support the growth of these probiotics). It is often worth slowly introducing these foods into your diet to see if they help with symptoms. Be aware that diarrhoea can be worsened at first (especially if juices are introduced at high doses) since the gut bacteria change and this includes 'die off', when bad bacteria are 'killed off' and release toxins. Of probiotic foods, I have personally found the most useful to be sauerkraut as it is non-dairy-based and very easy to introduce in small quantities.

A guide to introducing sauerkraut as a probiotic food

Cabbage itself is great for the gut, since as well as being rich in a whole host of vitamins and minerals, it is an amazing source of L-glutamine. Most often discussed in terms of body building (for building muscle), this amino acid (building block of protein) also has an amazing impact on the lining of the gut. This is why cabbage has long been recommended for the treatment of stomach ulcers: it heals ulceration in the digestive track. Cabbages, and L-glutamine in particular, can help repair permeable areas of the gut, making it stronger and able to digest food more effectively; on the other hand, being quite fibrous unfortunately if we eat it in large amount it can cause stomach upsets. The best way to eat cabbage is when we ferment it: sauerkraut is one of many powerful probiotic foods, teeming with rich gut bacteria. You can purchase *raw, unpasteurised* sauerkraut from health food shops or read my guide below to making your own.

Method for introducing sauerkraut

Days 1-2: 1 teaspoon of the brine from the jar (no actual cabbage; just brine juice). Just scoop a teaspoon out to begin with before you get on to the actual cabbage.

Days 3-4: 1 teaspoon of sauerkraut (cabbage and brine).

Day 5 and beyond: 1 tablespoon of sauerkraut, gradually increasing if needed.

Bone broth

You may have heard of this, since it's a recent healthy food trend, yet, like cabbage, bone broth (or thin soup made from the bones of cows or chickens) contains amino acids and thus can be highly beneficial to improving gut health. It is also very nutrient dense, containing a good mixture of fats and amino acids if you are trying a temporary liquid diet to rest your bowel. Bone broth is easily made in a slow cooker by using chicken or beef bones, carrots and a slug of apple cider vinegar. Alternatively, you can also purchase it ready-made; there is a list of stockists in the 'helpful info' section (page 151).

As always, be mindful of introducing this too fast – start with small quantities at first.

Chapter 8

Staying hydrated with IBD

Although I have spent lots of time discussing food, hydration in patients with IBD is equally important. Good hydration helps with the movement of food through the digestion system, improves fatigue and crucially prevents dehydration. Yet, hydration needs to be done properly, so here are some good source of hydration (and some that you may wish to avoid!).

Good sources of hydration

Water:
The obvious choice, of course, but with IBD patients it is particularly important to get adequate amounts of water, since dehydration is much more likely during a flare.

Coconut water:
This helps replenish levels of potassium in the body so it can act as a natural rehydration drink (much healthier than Lucozade). As with any food or drink, some patients report a mild laxative effect with some coconut products, although usually not with coconut water; it is worth starting slowly and seeing how you go.

Herbal tea:
Herbal teas can be extremely beneficial for IBD patients: ginger and peppermint teas are extremely soothing after a larger meal, while chamomile is great for anxiety. Although all herbal teas are healthy, be cautious of nettle, spearmint, senna and green tea as they can all have an undesired laxative effect!

Drinks that may affect symptoms

Fizzy drinks:
Carbonated drinks such as cola and lemonade can be problematic for a number of reasons. Many IBD patients find they are difficult to digest. These drinks often contain sweeteners or high-fructose corn syrup which again can have a laxative effect on the body.

Coffee:
Coffee is known to be a laxative since it increases gut peristalsis – the muscular action of the digestive tract walls that pushes food through the gut. Studies of inflammatory bowel disease and coffee specifically are however limited. A review of research into the topic showed that some studies had proven the inflammatory nature of coffee while others had suggested it might have an almost protective quality in the gut ((Barthel et al., 2015).[26]

Alcohol:
Many patients find they have to curb their alcohol intake significantly once diagnosed. This can be for many reasons including the side effects of medication and increased symptoms due to wheat (from beer) or sulphur dioxide (from wine). Alcohol in general is not conducive to a healthy gut environment. IBD patients may be able to do better with certain types of alcohol; however, large quantities are often problematic whatever the type.

Tea:
Many patients do fine with tea, but the tannins in tea can make it a

diuretic and it is therefore not ideal if you are already suffering from dehydration. In turn, if you like milk in your tea the dairy may be problematic. As ever, it depends on the individual.

Aloe vera:

I debated whether to put this in, as aloe vera can be a naturally soothing drink for those with gut issues. However, it is generally problematic in IBD as it is suggested it can heighten the immune response – to quote Crohn's & Colitis Foundation of America (www. ccfa.org): 'When taken orally, aloe vera has a laxative effect; in addition, it has qualities of an "immune booster"… that can boost an already overactive immune system.' There are also many products on the market (such as Forever Living) that promise miraculous results, making it difficult to differentiate good from bad. After researching this, it is evident from IBD patient testimonials that responses to aloe vera are very mixed and therefore I would urge caution before trying it.

Energy drinks:

It is natural to think these types of drink are necessary, since fatigue is a huge part of the condition. However much you feel the need, however, I would strongly advise against them. Usually the combination of sugar, sweeteners, artificial colourants and caffeine can irritate the gut. (They are not good for your health in general either, never mind your digestion!)

'Teatoxes':

A final note goes to the many slimming teas or detox drinks that are currently on the market. As many as 99 per cent of these work by using laxative herbs (such as senna) which trigger diarrhoea and thus lead to weight loss. Therefore it is strongly recommended you avoid these packages.

Going foward: Understanding the role of food and drink in your management of IBD

The previous chapters featured a lot of information about food. What is evident is that food has the power to affect your symptoms greatly, but to an extent that is individual to you. You should now be aware of some possible foods to introduce to your diet to help support your gut and also which foods to monitor carefully when looking at your diet. Ideally, IBD sufferers should undergo a proper elimination diet under the expert direction of a dietician or nutritional therapist, who can guide them carefully through reintroducing each food and monitoring the response. The table below is intended merely to start you on your food journey and record your choices and responses to them. It is not recommended that you give up more than one possible trigger at the same time in order to monitor accurately which may be causing you problems. In turn, introducing lots of new foods at the same time can initially worsen symptoms despite these being beneficial foods in themselves. On page 103 you can record your food choices; you can either photocopy the page or use a notebook to record what you eat and how it affects you. Most dieticians and nutritionists will need to see at least seven days' worth of food logging as foods may not cause immediate symptoms. In turn, there is a space to note down other possible triggers, the significance of which I explained in Chapter 1 (see page 23).

My shopping list

Below is what I hope you will find a handy checklist of all the beneficial foods and drinks featured in the previous chapters.

Bone broth
Sauerkraut
Coconut water
Herbal teas – peppermint, ginger, turmeric and fennel
Vegetables for juicing
Fresh turmeric.

TIME OF DAY	FOODS EATEN (Be as clear as possible, e.g. 'two slices of wholegrain bread' instead of simply 'bread')	SYMPTOMS	POSSIBLE OTHER TRIGGERS (e.g. stress, dosage of antibiotics, menstrual cycle)
MORNING			
AFTERNOON			
NIGHT			

SECTION III

LIVING LIFE TO THE FULL WITH IBD

Chapter 9

Travelling with IBD

When I was first diagnosed, the biggest question I wanted answered was whether it was still possible to enjoy travelling with Crohn's disease and enjoy all the wonderful trips I had planned for the summer. I'm lucky that I managed to spend several more years in China and travelled all over South East Asia during that time: Macau, Hong Kong, Bali, Thailand and more. It wasn't always easy but I wanted to show it was possible to see the world while battling a disobedient immune system.

Although the prospect of even a short trip can be overwhelming with inflammatory bowel disease, it is important to try to lead as full a life as possible. Here are some tips you may find useful when travelling with IBD.

Take your own food

Although a pain to organise, it can help to take some of your own foods if travelling to somewhere that is less westernised. This is always helpful if your flight is delayed or you need time to get your bearings when arriving at your hotel. Of course, everyone is different, but possible easy-to-travel-with items could be:

Mini cartons of soy or rice milk: If you are intolerant to dairy, carrying these cartons around can make life easier. You might also want to carry mini-porridge sachets for a quick and easy breakfast on the go.

Quick snacks: Possible choices may be granola bars, bananas, dried fruit or peanut butter sachets. These are all great if you are at somewhere like a train station/airport which only stocks fast-foods. All of these items will give you an energy boost without being too high in fibre or fat. It isn't perfect but it tides you over until you can find somewhere healthier to eat.

A juicer: If like me, you can't live without juicing, there are plenty of mini juicers (or bullets for smoothies) available, allowing you to just buy local ingredients and get whizzing. If staying in an apartment for a long period of time, try to negotiate with the owner to install one.

Allergy cards: Finally, if you are following a particular diet – such as gluten-free – invest in translated allergy cards. These cards are printed in the language of your choice and are perfect to present to your waiter before dining.

Speak to your airline

Flying with IBD can be a traumatic experience, not least the prospect of having to queue for ages to use the loos or navigate the nightmare that is inflight meals. A recent campaign #flywithIBD aimed to raise awareness of airlines offering more adaptations for IBD sufferers. It's also interesting to note that Thompson's Airways have partnered with forcrohns.org to raise money for Crohn's research. This means, more airlines have a greater understanding of the condition. Possible adaptations that can be made are seats near toilets, special in-flight meals and express check-in.

Email the hotel in advance

Hotels can be very helpful if you put yourself out there and explain your requirements. Possible questions you might want to ask are:

Is there a fridge? (Useful for storing medication and whatever food you are bringing)

Is there a bath or just a shower? If you suffer from complications of Crohn's like abscesses or fistulas, then you'll need a bath, but then again even if not, who doesn't like a good soak in the tub?

What are the breakfast options? Is it possible to have things made to order like a poached egg white for breakfast? Or soya milk? If places don't provide these things they are usually very helpful and offer to source it for you or to store the stuff for you if you bring it with you. I always find breakfast the hardest thing on holiday so getting it sorted out in advance can help.

Where is the nearest medical facility? It is always a good idea to research this in advance, just in case there any issues while you are abroad.

Get medication savvy

Before leaving, make sure you've checked the side effects of medication carefully. Some (primarily azathioprine) can cause you to be more sensitive to the sun so make sure you bring things to cover up and plenty of sunscreen.

Many destinations require vaccinations in advance and you'll need to discuss this with your doctor since you are not allowed live vaccines while on immunosupressants such as infliximab and azathioprine. It can also be helpful to get your doctor to write a summary of your condition and the medication you are on, just in case you need it when abroad. A handy tip is to store half your medication in your travel bag and the other half in your suitcase - just in case there's a problem with your luggage.

The insurance issue

The most vital thing to consider is medical insurance. It is so important to ensure you are fully covered before your travel. You must check that you are covered for IBD as a pre-existing condition and the amount for which you are covered. If symptoms change before flying, make sure you keep the insurance company informed, as the slightest change in your condition could cause your policy to be invalid. Insurance with inflammatory bowel disease can be expensive, especially if you've had surgery, but there are insurance companies that cater for those with chronic illnesses so just shop around.

My experience of travelling abroad with IBD

When I was first diagnosed with IBD, I was living in South Asia and had some terrible travelling adventures. I remember being stuck in Beijing and not able to go to see the Great Wall because my stomach was so bad and the heat was making my symptoms 1000 times worse!

After spending most of my time in Hong Kong in the toilet, I decided I needed to make more of a conscious effort to prepare in advance. Firstly, I picked parts of South Asia with low humidity, since the heat made me feel much worse. (I finally realised this was a real thing after chatting with many other IBD patients; I thought I was imagining it.)

Then, I made more of an effort to find hotels with fridges and safe breakfast choices – so I didn't abandon the diet that helped my symptoms. I filled my suitcase with safe foods (such as dairy-free milk, gluten-free snacks and travel-sized nut butters) and did lots of research about possible restaurants before I left. Although not many places advertised themselves as 'gluten- and dairy-free', I looked for restaurants that focused on clean and organic foods, hoping they would be more sympathetic to my plight.

I emailed my hotel to make sure I had a room near the pool with a bath and fridge; all of this made me feel so much more in control of my illness. I had two fantastic trips to Bali and Chiang Mai – my family actually loved the restaurants I'd selected and I wasn't ill at all during my trip!

PATIENT STORY: Brenda, diagnosed 2012
Travelling around the UK

What comes to mind initially with regards to travelling with IBD is cost. Although I don't travel abroad, which means I don't have to worry about travel insurance, I do have to book all trips away at the dearer flexible rate as I have to be able to cancel at short notice. This is even if I'm only going overnight. In the first year after diagnosis I paid for concert tickets at the O2 and a hotel for the night but ended up in hospital. My daughter bought tickets for six months later for another concert and hotel to make up for it and yet again I was in hospital. Since two lots of surgery I'm much better but still won't take a chance on paying in advance for anything.

Eating out while travelling is a bit of a problem as I'm on the low-residue diet [page 72] which means there's usually little on the menu that I can order without having to adapt what I'm choosing. A lot of hotels seem to have 'all you can eat' breakfasts, which are no good to me as not only can I not eat most of what's in a cooked breakfast; I also have quite a small appetite now. We usually check out the area where we're staying and find a cafe where I can have just some toast.

Toilets were a problem before my surgery as leakage and urgency were a big issue. Now I have a stoma I still need to know where toilets are but the urgency isn't the same.

One little thing I do whenever we go anywhere in the UK, I would also have to be sure there were plenty of benches for me to have a rest and usually parked myself on one of those benches while my partner went off exploring the area. With a little planning, I've found it perfectly possible to take trips all around the country.

Checklist: Travelling with IBD

Have you:

✓ Packed safe foods in hand luggage and case?

✓ Packed extra supplies of medication in hand luggage and case?

✓ Checked storage information for medicine, e.g. if it needs to be refrigerated?

✓ Asked doctor to provide an overview of condition and medication?

✓ Spoken to insurance company to check condition is covered?

✓ Kept a copy of emergency insurance company number?

✓ Emailed hotel to request a fridge and for information on nearest hospital?

✓ Packed extra supplies of IBD essentials – e.g. Immodium, hand sanitiser, fresh cleaning fluid, wipes?

✓ Packed translation cards for key phrases, such as, 'I am gluten free' or 'Where is the nearest toilet?' ?

✓ Spoken to the airline about any extra requirements?

Chapter 10

Working with IBD

Sometimes it seems that living with IBD is a full-time job (albeit one with zero pay or benefits!). Time spent at the hospital, recovering from flares and trying to live a healthy life can all add up. Unfortunately, most of us are not millionaires and work is a necessity, and for lots of us a fulfilling part our lives. Working with IBD isn't always easy but for the vast majority of us it is possible. However, you may need to talk to your employer and have adaptations made.

Be honest

It is very important that you are honest with your employer about your condition and what it involves. IBD, like any chronic illness, is covered under the 2010 Equality Act since it is a physical and long-term impairment (definition of disability under the Equality Act 2010, 2015).[27] This means employers must make necessary adaptations to help you in your role. This could include flexible working hours, access to a disabled toilet or a fridge to store your medicine in. Most employers are accommodating if you talk to them and explain what your condition actually entails (and if this is disclosed at interview, employers cannot discriminate against you in the recruitment process).

Be realistic

Many people with inflammatory bowel disease have really high expectations of themselves, which is also reflected in their careers. However, it is important to reflect on your career path and whether it is adaptable to life with IBD. Does it involve lots of travel? Is it stressful? Are you often on the go? Having IBD doesn't mean giving up on your career dreams but just making sure the job is right for you.

Be informed

Reading the paperwork and the terms and condition that comes with a job is more important than ever with IBD. Here are some things you need to find out:

- What is the sick pay entitlement?
- What is the policy for long-term periods of sickness?
- How flexible are the working hours?
- If you are working abroad, is medical insurance included and does this include pre-existing conditions?
- Will you get regular breaks? (This can be easy for office workers; not so easy for those in retail.)
- Is there a refrigerator on the premises to store your food?
- Is there the possibility of reduced hours or going part-time further down the line?

Keep records

It may be worth having a notebook to keep a list of any time you have had to take off work for IBD and the corresponding symptoms and hospital trips.

My experience of working with IBD

I am a teacher by trade and have taught both in the UK and abroad. In every job, I've been honest about my condition from day one and luckily all my employers have been great. When I was on infliximab, my employers were great at giving me time off to go to hospital appointments and in my previous role I had surgery and the school arranged for me to come back on a phased return. It can be really hard teaching with IBD – I have had days where I felt like I wanted to faint in front of a class – but luckily most of the time I'm fine. In some ways doing a demanding job means I often forget about my symptoms, but I have had to dash out of class on a few occasions. I think this is why talking with colleagues about your condition is so important – it has meant they have been able to quickly step in if needed. Yet over the years, I think I've also become more realistic about my teaching career and this year I've reduced my workload to three days a week, aiming to spend more time on my health and my writing. I don't see this as a step down but a necessary adaptation to help me live as balanced a life as possible; hopefully I can combine the security of a teaching job with my other passions in life – writing and nutrition.

PATIENT EXPERIENCE: Chris, diagnosed 2006

Working with IBD

I was 20 when I was diagnosed with Crohn's colitis in 2006. This was while I was at University. When I graduated I was working for a temp agency and this was very difficult as I had no paid sick leave or leave for medical appointments. To attend my appointments I had to take time out as holiday.

In 2009 I was taken on as permanent staff at the company

I had been temping for. At the beginning, I had difficulties getting my line manager to understand my condition. I found that I needed to be open with my manager about the way I had been feeling on any particular day and also accept support from my employer.

I found that an Occupational Health referral to a third party helped my company to understand the need to have flexible working and to give me time to go to appointments.

I am on infliximab infusions and these are given every six weeks. I go to work in the morning, then get paid leave for the afternoon. I also find that at times of flare-ups of my Crohn's if I notify my managers that my health is poor they can put me on lighter duties which are less pressurised; this has not affected my chance to develop, although I have found it very difficult to progress.

Overall I feel that my employers have offered me sufficient support and I am not discriminated against or given special treatment because I have a chronic illness. To help my company understand IBD I gave them the *NACC Employer's Guide*,[28] which they have followed to provide reasonable adjustments, such as providing me with a fan and seating me not too far from the nearest disabled toilet.

I always thought my illness would stop me from getting a job but I have been lucky to find such an understanding employer.

Chapter 11

Exercising and IBD

Exercise is a huge part of keeping well: it does everything from regulating our bowel movements and helping us to deal with stress to keeping our bones and joints healthy. Yet IBD patients can have a bit of a love-hate relationship with exercise: for some it can ease symptoms while for others it makes them much worse.

How can exercise help my IBD?

There is little research evaluating the impact of exercise on the gastrointestinal symptoms of IBD but there is no doubt it can help with the many extra-intestinal manifestations we discussed in Chapter 1 (page 7). The first thing that exercise can undoubtedly help with is fatigue. Fatigue is a common complication of inflammatory bowel disease, and while many patients may not feel like it, regular exercise can help improve fatigue symptoms – even if it is only done in short bursts. Another aspect is mental health: it is well established that regular exercise can help you with anxiety and depression – which, as we learnt in Chapter 3, is another complication of IBD. Another specific complication is osteoporosis, largely caused by the medication given to many patients, plus nutrient deficiency. An overview of studies into osteoporosis (by Narula and Fedorak in

2008) recommended that, 'Crohn's disease patients should engage in regular exercise to achieve and maintain maximal bone density'.[29]

How does exercise affect the gut?

Exercise can affect the gut in many ways. The most notable difference is when patients increase the intensity of exercise rapidly, such as when training for a long-distance event. Long periods of intense exercise can quickly speed up the movement of food through the bowel; while this can reduce the impact of diseases like colon cancer, it also makes IBD sufferers more susceptible to diarrhoea. However, gentler forms of exercise can support the gut, helping ease digestion (such as a slow walk after dinner) and reduce stress. Therefore, it is important to adapt the exercise you do to how you're feeling.

Tips for exercising with IBD

Avoid intense exercise during flares:
This will cause increased risk of diarrhoea and dehydration.

Stay hydrated:
It is worth noting that many sports drinks can actually contain potential gut irritants, such as sweeteners, and many protein shakes contain whey and sugar. (All of these irritants are discussed in more detail in Chapter 6, page 71.) Therefore, choose your hydrating drinks carefully: if you are planning short bursts of exercise (such as a 30-minute gym session or a long walk) these drinks are not necessary. If planning longer periods of exercise, think carefully about your choice of refuelling. There are many recipes online for natural rehydration drinks, and vegan protein powders may be an option for building muscle without the impact of dairy-based products.

Wash after exercise:
I know this sounds like an obvious point, but sweat rash can quickly occur in folds of skin and since IBD patients are likely to have more sensitive areas (from stomas, fistulotomies etc), then a painful sweat rash may occur. It is also better to wear breathable fabrics to help the skin breathe during exercise.

Find exercise that works for you:
Yoga, pilates and walking are all good choices if you are suffering from a flare. They will help support your joints and digestion without putting too much pressure on your gut. Once in remission, many sufferers are able to commit to varied exercise programmes, although if training for a long-distance event, it is always best to seek professional advice on how to refuel the body. You can also explore home-based options (via online exercise videos) or pay-as-you-go gym deals, if you don't want to commit to monthly gym fees when your symptoms change often.

Monitor your heart rate:
This will help you monitor the intensity of the exercise and allow you to keep your workout under control. There are many gadgets that help you to do this.

PATIENT EXPERIENCE: Josh, diagnosed 2013

Exercising with IBD

When I was finally diagnosed with Crohn's disease I did wonder if I would ever get back to exercising again. I had always been very active and really enjoyed regular exercise but in the period leading up to diagnosis my health had declined to the point where just leaving the bed or house was a real struggle. Following diagnosis I had my worst ever flare and ended up having emergency surgery. After recovering from surgery, I was put on different medications and my health started to improve.

Regaining some physical fitness was my next goal. I had always loved cycling but still didn't feel up to going out on my bike so I got an indoor training bike; this was amazing as I was cycling again but I was still in the comfort of my house so I didn't have to battle with traffic or the weather – plus I was only a few metres from the bathroom!

After spending a few weeks using the indoor training bike, I had built a bit of fitness and confidence. I really wanted to get back outside and feel the wind in my face again but I was still anxious about being too far from home so I mapped out a short 5 km loop that circled my house; that way I was always just a few minutes away if I needed to get back quickly. Taking this next step and getting back outside was massive progress for me and really lifted my mood.

After sticking to short rides on that 5 km loop for a few weeks and not having any real issues, my confidence grew even more and I progressed onto longer rides, gradually getting further from home. Now I'm at the point where I can go out for relatively long unplanned rides and am really enjoying exploring new places again.

The greatest improvements I've noticed since starting exercising again are my mental health and my fatigue level; these are two areas of IBD that are very hard to treat and often get overlooked so the progress I've made has dramatically helped me in my day-to-day life. I would recommend exercise to anyone struggling with these issues. Find something you enjoy and if possible find someone who you can enjoy it with; some of my rides flew by because I was catching up with good friends – before I knew it I'd been out for two hours! Remember to start slowly and build up gradually, and if you need a few days or a week off that's fine.

PATIENT EXPERIENCE: Annabel, diagnosed 1998

'Why I love yoga'

I started yoga about three years ago when I was unfortunately diagnosed with ME alongside my Crohn's disease. I firstly find yoga very relaxing; it lifts my mood and helps me feel calm. I also have strictures due to my Crohn's so it helps with the pain that I currently struggle with and allows me to think a lot more clearly. Yoga is perfect for IBD and is a gentle form of exercise, meaning anyone can do it even when they're not feeling so great. In turn, it is great for the body in general, helping to strengthen and tone it. I'd highly recommend trying yoga to anyone as it's helped me no end.

Chapter 12

Hospital visits and IDB

My experience with hospital visits

I like to share my experiences of IBD in the hope it will help others who are going through exactly the same thing. In this case, however, I can't imagine any of my readers will have been in my shoes. This is because most of my hospital trips (touch wood!) were actually in China, where I was diagnosed in 2012. And, let me tell you now, if you haven't ever been in a Chinese hospital then you will probably think everything I've written below is made up. (I promise, it isn't!) So, why I am telling this story? Because, (a) it'll probably make you laugh, and God knows we all need a good laugh with IBD and (b) it'll make you think, as I do on a daily basis, thank goodness for the NHS!

My first trip to a Chinese hospital began a few months after I had arrived in China, during what I fondly refer to as the 'honeymoon period' of my time living there – the time when I wore rose-tinted glasses and ignored the smell of unrefrigerated meat and the sight of people spitting on the street. I made my way to a local doctor and told him that I had had 'IBS' for 11 years but couldn't stop feeling nauseous and being sick. I can still remember that doctor now. He was lovely, and to be fair, the hospital was very clean. As he left, he told me, 'You need to have a colonoscopy; what you've described is not IBS.' Considering I'd spent a grand total of 80 pence on his services, and there was no anaesthetist attached to the hospital, I wasn't keen on his suggestion of 'being really brave' and letting him investigate my colon. So I dismissed him and went on my way.

Two months (and £26,000 – thank goodness for my work's health insurance) later I was diagnosed with Crohn's disease. The private hospital where I was diagnosed was a glitzy foreign hospital, five minutes from the Shanghai bund, yet its diagnosis was the same: I didn't have IBS after all.

Unfortunately, my local hospital was not quite as glitzy as that short trip to Shanghai. In fact, it had no rules whatsoever. The doctors were amazing. They'd add me on WeChat (China's version of What'sApp) and send me dancing cat animations when my blood tests were good and reassuring emoticons when I was worried they were not. If I needed to see them, they'd cancel their afternoon nap (yes, they had afternoon naps, and I had to wake some of them up from them on several on occasions) if I texted to say I needed to see them and nothing was ever too much trouble. Okay, patient confidentiality didn't exist – I'd see doctors giving results out to a patient while 20 other people overheard, trying to get through the door to be diagnosed next. But they were honest – they didn't know if I'd get the terrible side effects my medications can cause; they didn't know if my blood tests would come down and whether I could stop the drugs, but they'd do everything they could to help either way (dancing cat included).

Everyone wanted to help me, including doctors who weren't actually treating me. Crohn's disease is growing rapidly in Asia but is still much rarer than in the western world. As I wasn't living in a particularly international part of China, the doctors treating me weren't used to many IBD patients and one in particular asked to chat to me one day as he'd never met somebody with Crohn's disease before. I say chat – it actually consisted of him poking me in various parts of my digestive system and asking, 'Does that hurt?' over and over again. He was fascinated that I wasn't in pain as his textbook had told him this was a symptom. After asking me for the tenth time: 'How does it feel?' I replied, 'Like someone keeps poking me in the stomach!'

My first proper hospital stay in China came in the summer of 2014. I was convinced it was a terrible flare-up, but looking back it was so humid it was no wonder my stomach wasn't happy. I had been checked into a private room (the nurse had explained it would be an extra £20 a night and had nervously enquired whether my insurance could afford it): it was spotless. I had my own TV, a beautiful view of the river and a cleaner who knew no boundaries and kept coming in to the room to tut loudly if something was on the floor and feed me something that looked like cement. Needless to say, I did not eat said cement, but that only made me more endearing to her – I was the crazy, ill foreigner who didn't know what she was missing out on! One day my doctor was going over my blood test results when a man wandered into the room and stood by his side, staring at me. 'Is he with you?' I asked when the doctor didn't bat an eyelid. 'Oh no, nothing to do with me,' he replied. 'He's probably come to look at the foreigner,' he laughed. As you can tell, patient security was paramount!

I stayed in the hospital for four days – there was no such thing as a bed shortage, and after taking three-hour naps each day, the doctors didn't actually have much time to do tests on me. It was funny how accustomed I became to Chinese hospital life during that time. There was no such thing as 'visiting hours' – in fact, I was the one who seemed so odd for being by myself at any moment; everyone else was surrounded by family. (As the nurse put it so kindly one day, 'Why you so lonely?') No one worried about paperwork or liability; in fact one nurse caused me bad nerve pain after a steroid injection and the doctor joked, 'She's terrible for doing that!' There was a juice bar with wi-fi and no one batted an eyelid at me walking around at my leisure. Then on day 3, the doctors decided they actually needed to do some more investigations and arranged the camera test; unfortunately, there was no anaesthetic as the person who provided that wouldn't 'be back for a month' (this sounded perfectly legit) so for the second time I was told to be very brave. Having that colonoscopy is still one of the proudest achievements of my life; no one said encouraging words or held my hand. In fact, I was convinced the news was terrible until my doctor shrugged and said, 'Oh, it looks fine actually!'

I don't ever remember seeing a file with my name on it – in fact, when I left China to come back to England, I was handed a giant X-ray of my colon, screenshots of blood test results and some coloured photographs of my insides. I kept that X-ray for about two years until I realised that no doctor was going to suddenly ask me, 'So, what was your colon like in 2014?' When I came back to the UK, I was initially really excited to go to see a doctor who could understand what I was saying and wouldn't resort to constant poking. Yet I must admit, I couldn't help but miss the craziness of the Chinese hospital system. No doctor here would even tell me my blood results (let alone take a screenshot of the computer and text it to me with a thumbs-up sign); it took weeks to hear back from anybody and I felt nobody truly listened to me like those doctors back then had. While I am very grateful for the wonder that is anaesthesia, nothing says I care like a dancing cat gif!

Dealing with hospital visits

Although my tale may have made you smile, hospital visits are one of the most stressful parts of IBD. Not only is being in hospital scary for anybody, but is made additionally difficult by the added worry of managing all the other aspects of life with IBD – stress, food choices, medication. I asked the *Crohn's and Colitis Facebook Group* to share their top tips on how they manage hospital stays. This is their invaluable advice:

Jackie, diagnosed 2015:
My advice from when I was in hospital after surgery for a week is to take an eye mask as they turn the lights off very late and turn them on very early. Earplugs are also a must as you never know what other patients are going to be dealing with. I was on a ward with a few dementia patients and was kept up all night every night from their tremors, but ear plugs at least allow you to get some sleep. Finally, take a goody-bag of treats because the food is so hit and miss and if you have dietary requirements, the majority of the time (in my experience) they won't be catered for. Colouring books, puzzle books and music help pass the time.

Dawn, diagnosed 2010:
Get your family to bring in food that you can tolerate as in my experience there was very little on the menu I could eat following surgery. Take each day as it comes because there is always one bad day following surgery. Write it off and start again the next day. Don't try to run before you can walk as well. Listen to your body and nap when you need to and do little things that you can manage.

Sharon (son diagnosed 2015):
Buy the cleaner a box of chocolates as well as the nurse. As the cleaner makes sure your room is nice and clean.

Emma, diagnosed 2013:
I always pack my fleece blanket and teddy (yes, I'm 32 but they smell of home) and a goody-bag of treats. I'm a heavy sleeper so never bother with an eye mask or ear plugs (I've slept through the nurses giving me my IV meds and changing fluid bags in the night!) but make sure I take my fully charged kindle plus a few well-read books

and magazines for those days when I don't feel too great and can't concentrate. I also take my iPad with movies downloaded and get my partner to take it home each week and download my favourite programmes so I'm not missing out too much. When I was 'nil by mouth', I used to time my shower for breakfast time as the shower was empty and I didn't have to deal with the smells of breakfast while feeling hungry. I took a walk at lunch and always planned for my visitors to arrive at tea time. I also couldn't have survived without my family and friends' visits and calls/texts just to check if I was okay or needed anything

Tig, diagnosed 1996:
I used my iPad to note the things I wished I'd said to the consultant. They often rush their rounds and some don't seem inclined to listen to patients. The first time I handed the big chief doctor my iPad notes to read, I explained that I was tired and emotional and struggling to communicate verbally. He was a bit nonplussed at first but once he had read what I had to say regarding my symptoms and my need to be involved and properly consulted regarding any proposed treatment, he understood that I'm not unintelligent. He started to speak to me like I'm a person, sent his juniors back to me several times to communicate action plans and discussed medication with me. I always do it now!

Martina, diagnosed 2009:
A little battery-operated fan was a lifesaver for me when I was last in hospital; they're always roasting hot.

Chapter 13

Socialising with IBD

I often think ruined social life should be added to the official symptom list of inflammatory bowel disease. It is one of those things that has a massive impact on your life but is rarely mentioned in books. If you are like me, your socialising pre-IBD probably centred around food and drink: a cheeky post-work glass of wine; a romantic meal out; a family buffet; a Sunday carvery. All of a sudden, it can seem that all of those events become associated with being ill, having to dash home or just a general feeling of awkwardness. I'm not going to lie and tell you to just be confident, IBD is at times an awkward and frustrating disease: it's awkward when you feel ill halfway through the night; it's awkward when there's nothing on the menu you can eat and everyone thinks you are on a diet; it's awkward when you are at a friend's house and you feel that stomach twinge that means you need the toilet right now! Yet, it is also so important to lead as full a social life as possible with this disease.

Eating out can be difficult with IBD, but not impossible. Before you do so, do your research. Look up the menu online and if it's not clear, give the restaurant a call. It is a bit of a spontaneity-killer, but it can help ease any worries about eating out. I've found that most places don't bat an eyelid if I call, tell them what trigger foods I have to avoid or diet I'm following and ask if they can recommend something. Another option is to offer to organise the get-together yourself. If you feel super-awkward chatting about diet, then offer to find the venue; then you can sneakily direct people to places with suitable options that are also close to home (should you need to dash home when symptoms strike). Good places to try are usually seafood/fish restaurants and Indian restaurants (since they are less likely to contain allergens) or big chains that are used to dealing with allergens such as Pizza Express, Zizzi's, Bella Italian, Ask and Las Iguanas (all these chains offer a detailed allergen menu with good awareness of gluten-/dairy-free). Selecting a restaurant that has suitable choices and is near to home can greatly help when beginning to socialise with IBD – after all, if you are feeling nervous then there's every chance the stress of socialising may trigger symptoms whatever you eat!

Another important thing when socialising is to know your 'deal breakers'. There might be foods or drinks that you feel you can tolerate in small doses – such as the odd glass of champagne or a small bar of chocolate – and others that are your deal breakers: things that you know are going to wreak havoc with your digestive system. Understanding and accepting what these things are will mean you are less likely to indulge and then beat yourself up about it.

Meals when eating out are so much bigger than you might eat at home, you may feel unwell even if you stick to what you can eat. Being portion-savvy is important here.

Although all of this may sound terribly awkward and uncomfortable, there are always going to be those people who roll their eyes when you ask for the allergen menu or snigger when you're speaking to the waiter. When I first started keeping track of my diet, I'd get so embarrassed I just wouldn't ask or would cave in (cue kicking myself a few hours later when in agony!). I then realised that I needed to be more confident. Now I either make a joke of it or just shrug it off. If nothing else, these things teach you who your friends really are.

Drinking and IBD

As mentioned in Chapter 7, alcohol is a big gut irritant and many patients feel they can no longer tolerate it post-diagnosis. Of course, we live in a big drinking culture and for young people in particular it can be difficult to adapt. The best thing is to make adaptations that work for you, whether it is to cut alcohol out of your life altogether or cut down to special occasions only (and be prepared for the possible consequences the next day). At first it may seem impossible to imagine life without drink, but many people find that they can have a more varied social life because of it.

PATIENT EXPERIENCE: Carol, diagnosed 1980

'My tips for socialising with IBD'

Socialising is something I've found really hard. When you've planned a big night/day out you are always hoping you're going to be well enough to enjoy it. No one wants urgent trips to the loo, or even a bloated tummy ruining the line of a new outfit or close-fitting trousers.

Anyone with chronic inflammatory bowel disease will know what it's like to have a social event when it all goes wrong – an accident with no spare underwear, let alone the embarrassment of a possible audience; disappearing to the bathroom for so long that someone sends out a search party to see if you're still alive! And, of course, possible stoma-related incidents. I'm sure we have all had them at some point – yet with time and experience, I've realised it can get easier and it helps if you can learn to accept whatever happens.

Despite this, when socialising there are still questions going through my mind: Will I be up to it, with enough energy to enjoy it? What about the food and drink? Will there be decent toilets and enough of them? (There never seem to be enough women's cubicles, and don't even go there about the state of men's toilets!) How can I explain about my health issues without droning on obsessively or underplaying my (relevant!) problems/situation?

As someone who has had Crohn's disease for over 30 years, including a temporary stoma and multiple surgical resections and complications, I've now got my own three-step plan:

1. I always plan ahead if I can – especially about dietary restrictions and toilet facilities.

2. I'm realistic about what I can do if I'm having a bad day – for example, a nap beforehand and pacing myself whilst I'm out.

3. I always aim to relax, have fun and try to live with the life/health I have.

Failing that, I've also learnt a box of matches works wonders on unpleasant smells!

SECTION IV

OTHER POSSIBLE APPROACHES

Chapter 14

Alternative therapies and IDB

Complementary medicine may be another aspect of your IBD treatment plan. To be clear, complementary medicine cannot cure IBD but can help sufferers with things like stress, relaxation, pain management and extra-intestinal manifestations. Alternative therapies include:

Reflexology
This practice is based on the concept that our organs are linked to certain pressure points on the foot, which, when stimulated can improve health.

Reiki
This is a healing technique which is said to unblock 'channels' around your body.

Acupuncture
Inserting needles into pressure points around the body to strengthen the body's organs.

Evidence to support using alternative therapies in IBD

The alternative therapy that has been most researched in relation to IBD is acupuncture. A 2014 study, by Bao et al, found that acupuncture with moxibustion (a Chinese medicine therapy) significantly reduced patients' Crohn's disease 'index score'.[30] Therefore, acupuncture is probably the most well supported scientifically, but as in that study improvements were also noted in the control group (who did not receive acupuncture), though to a lesser extent, it looks as though anticipating positive results and relaxation may generally have an effect. In the resources section, I have included a link that provides an overview of beginning a complementary therapy with IBD, including whether to talk to your doctor and how it might help.

My experience with alternative therapies

I am a natural worrier so I've found that alternative therapies can certainly help me deal with stress. I have tried reflexology in the past; I had expected the therapists to be able to predict my IBD based on the digestive pressure point on the foot, but they never managed to. Yet, I did have this daily while abroad in Thailand and found it helped digestive symptoms such as cramping and bloating. (On the other hand, I imagine lying down and being massaged played a part in this.)

Earlier this year, I embarked on a course of reiki. I was originally sceptical yet found that as soon as the treatment began, my stomach started making the strangest twisted, gurgling sounds that proceeded to last for most of the session. While it didn't seem to make much difference to my overall symptoms, I did find it relaxing and the strange twisting feeling I had each time did suggest my stomach was responding in some way.

Both of these treatments have proved that alternative therapies can be great in helping me to relax and take time for myself but I am yet to see whether they have a sustained impact on my health. Either way, anything that allows me to have complete peace and quiet for an hour has to be a good thing.

PATIENT EXPERIENCE: Nicky, diagnosed 2005
'Reflexology helped me'

I was at home following an obstruction and had a huge amount of colicky pain in spasms which kept me in bed. My friend practises reflexology and offered to come over. At this point, I was desperate as I was only allowed paracetamol as directed by the stoma nurse. As she massaged my feet, I leapt in pain when she reached the instep, which in refloxogy signifies the small bowel.

My therapist-friend explained that she could feel a gristly nobble. She massaged and the pain from my foot continued to be really strong. However, she gradually massaged it away and then I realised that the pain in my bowel had pretty much gone! She did this on the other foot with the same result (she, again, found a spot which was gristly to her touch and painful to me by my ankle; this she told me is linked to the area of the knee. My knees were damaged from running, so she worked on that too). The pain was reduced each time for a good three hours and she came every day.

Unfortunately, I was readmitted as there were complications from my obstruction (hence the pain I was experiencing). I know reflexology didn't cure my Crohn's but it definitely helped me manage my pain and I'd massively recommend it.

Chapter 15

Dealing with a flare-up – a 24-hour self-care plan

The purpose of this chapter is to provide a stand-alone section that you can reach for if you are having a bad day. It can absolutely not replace medical advice but instead offers guidance on how to deal with your symptoms if you've already spoken to a doctor. If you are experiencing any of the following, you should seek urgent medical assistance before following this self-care plan:

- Severe or unusual bleeding
- Significant change in bowel movements
- Pain that does not seem to ease
- Significant weight loss
- Any symptoms that seem new or unusual.

Symptoms log

Use the table on page 140 to keep track of your symptoms. (It is also available online at www.abalancedbelly.co.uk) You can print this as many times as you like to help with accurate tracking and give feedback to your doctor.

TIME	NO. OF BOWEL MOVEMENTS	CONSISTENCY (USE BRISTOL STOOL CHART)	PAIN ON A SCALE OF 1-10	FATIGUE ON A SCALE OF 1-10	EXTRA-INTESTINAL MANIFESTA-TIONS

Bristol Stool Chart

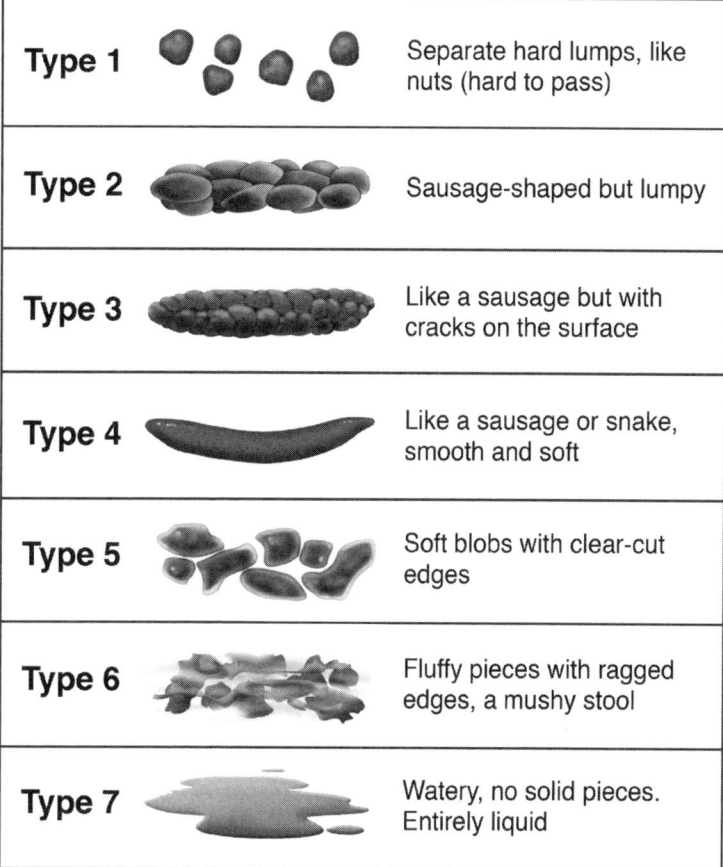

Type 1		Separate hard lumps, like nuts (hard to pass)
Type 2		Sausage-shaped but lumpy
Type 3		Like a sausage but with cracks on the surface
Type 4		Like a sausage or snake, smooth and soft
Type 5		Soft blobs with clear-cut edges
Type 6		Fluffy pieces with ragged edges, a mushy stool
Type 7		Watery, no solid pieces. Entirely liquid

Figure 3 The Bristol stool chart (1997): This is widely recognised as a way to monitor the consistency of stools and can be used to report back to your doctor. Copyright © 2006, Rome Foundation. All rights reserved.

You can also use the following measures to determine the severity of your symptoms. After calculating your score, you can then take appropriate action as the suggestions in this chapter on page 144 are for mild disease activity only; moderate to severe cases will instead require medical intervention.

Harvey Bradshaw scale for Crohn's disease (1980)[31, 32]

This is a simplified version of the 'Crohn's Disease Activity Index'.

1. Score general wellbeing (0 = very well, 1 = slightly below average, 2 = poor, 3 = very poor, 4 = terrible)

2. Score abdominal pain (0 = none, 1 = mild, 2 = moderate, 3 = severe)

3. Add number of liquid stools per day

4. Add one point for each complication: joint pain, uveitis (inflammation of the middle layer of the eye), erythema nodosum, aphthous mouth ulcers, pyoderma gangrenosum, anal fissure, a new fistula and an abscess.

A score of less than 5 is generally considered to represent clinical remission while 5-7 suggests mild symptoms. A score of 8 and above suggests moderate-severe disease and therefore medical intervention is required.

Simple Clinical Colitis Activity Index

The Simple Clinical Colitis Activity Index is likewise designed for patients to get a good understanding of their ulcerative colitis symptoms (Crohn's disease patients may also find it useful) and is recognised by lots of doctors. A score of less than '5' is generally associated with clinical remission. You can find an easy to follow version of the Simple Colitis Index here http://cdn-flightdec.userfirst. co.nz/uploads/sites/crohns/files/files/SCCAI_Patient_Education_ Leaflet_v_3.2.pdf

How it works

The index asks you to consider your symptoms over the previous three days and rate them. It of course asks you about your bowel movements (including frequency, urgency and presence of blood), but it also asks you to rate a whole host of other issues, such as:

overall wellbeing,

possible joint pain,

eye problems,

mouth problems,

skin issues and

any possible perianal issues.

This can provide a more holistic picture of what is going on in your body, making it beneficial for both the doctor and patient.

The scoring system

Each answer is given a point value. For example, passing more than three bowel movements a day is given 1 point whilst those having more than nine movements are awarded 3 points. Any extra-intestinal issues, such as mouth ulcers or eye problems, are then given an extra point. A patient who receives fewer than 5 points in total is generally considered to be in remission.

The 24-hour self-care plan

8 am: Breakfast

It may be the most important meal of the day, but if you are in a flare-up the last thing you'll probably feel like doing is tucking in. It's called 'breakfast' for a reason: our bodies break the fast from our sleep the night before, so it's important to have something. Yet because of this, it's often the time your digestive system is the most awake and therefore many people with IBD find their symptoms the most problematic at this time. Because of that, you're going to start with some soothing and easy to digest liquid breakfast options. These should give your gut a bit of a break while it wakes up. However, if you really can't stomach anything, try a simple anti-inflammatory tea.

Anti-inflammatory tea recipe

1 tablespoon of turmeric powder (bought in health food shops or the 'world food' aisle of supermarkets)

1 thumb-sized piece of ginger chopped into small pieces

Add the ingredients to boiling water and leave simmering for five minutes. Once cooled, add one tablespoon of manuka honey to sweeten. (If you do this when the water is boiling, you'll lose the health benefits.)

Soluble-fibre smoothie

You may think you need to avoid all types of fibre but you'd be wrong. In fact, soluble fibre has a soothing effect on the bowel (as discussed in Chapter 6, page 87). This smoothie is nutrient dense and shouldn't irritate a touchy colon. Liquidise together:

1 peeled banana
½ tin of tinned pumpkin (found in supermarkets, usually in US section)
1 cup of almond milk

Rice congee

Rice congee may be plain but it's a staple in Asia, where it's a must-have remedy for food poisoning. It's very gentle and can be customised depending on how you are feeling:

Add ½ cup of rice to 3-4 cups of water in a saucepan. Bring to the boil.

Turn down the heat and leave on the stove until the rice is soft and all the water has been absorbed.

You can add lots of things to congee, such as: chicken, tofu, fruit, jam etc.

11 am: Time to de-stress

By this time, you have probably had a few hours of work, school or simply life. It's easy to get stressed, especially on days when you just want to feel better. Take five minutes out of your day and try these de-stress techniques:

1. Download the Headspace app or run it off your computer (www.headspace.com). Aim to stick to their free 10-day programme.

2. Find a mantra to repeat when you're feeling stressed, such as, 'I'm doing the best I can to help my body'. Or, 'This too shall pass.'

3. Abdominal breathing: Spend a few minutes each morning focusing on this. When you breathe in, relax your abdominal muscles and allow your chest cavity to expand downwards as well as outwards (see Figure 5); hold for five seconds. Then breathe out.

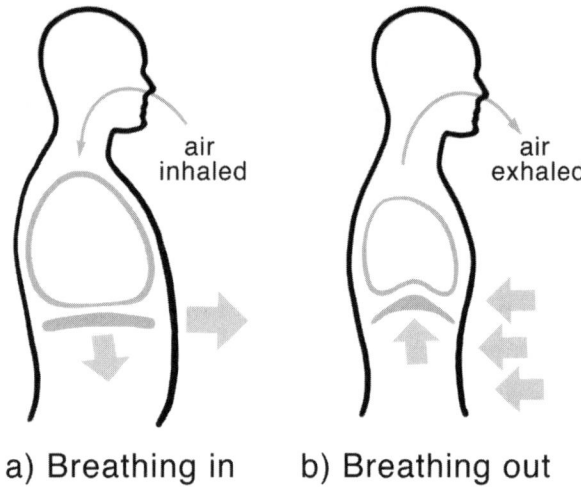

a) Breathing in   b) Breathing out

Figure 5 When breathing using your diaphragm, rather than your chest, your stomach will lift as you inhale and dip as you exhale

Noon: Lunchtime

It's likely you are starting to feel peckish. Our bowels are more active in the morning which is why getting some liquid nutrition is a safer bet. If you are feeling a little better, here are some 'Dos' and 'Don'ts':

Dos

- DO eat naturally – potatoes, sweet potatoes or rice are all good bets.
- DO try some easier-to-digest protein options – such as white fish, tinned tuna, chicken (no deli meats) or tofu.
- DO start with small portions and leave 30 minutes to see how you feel.

Dont's

- DON'T eat anything deep fried.

- DON'T eat any gluten or dairy (they're hard to digest).
- DON'T eat any fruit or veg, unless they are well cooked or juiced.

3 pm: Keeping hydrated

It's essential to keep hydrated during a flare. Many people turn to energy replacement drinks or Lucozade. These contain way too much added sugar, sweeteners and preservatives to be helpful. Stay super-hydrated with these tips:

Coconut water:
This is an excellent source of potassium and electrolytes, which we often lose too quickly with an upset stomach.

Herbal tea:
Peppermint and ginger are the best bet as they're very soothing, or of course there is the anti-inflammatory tea on page 144.

Fruit-infused water:
Sometimes simple H_2O is best. Add a squeeze of lemon or some grated ginger to make it more refreshing. (You can also buy fancy fruit-infused water bottles which are great for making fruity water.) Do not drink shop-bought fruit water which is usually jam-packed with sweeteners.

6 pm: Dinner time

If you are starting to feel better, you might be in the mood for some dinner. Follow the Dos and Don'ts on page 146 to make sure you're still safe. Some super-quick suppers include:

- Boiling potatoes in chicken stock cubes. (Try to buy organic, gluten-free ones if possible, or better yet, use actual chicken stock.) Serve with cooked chicken or tofu.

- Steaming white fish and serving with boiled rice and lemon juice.

- Another serving of rice congee (page 145).

10 pm: Bedtime supplements

Well done for surviving the day. Whether you have found yourself feeling a lot better or have noticed only a little change, you've done your best to look after yourself and give your body what you need. Supplements can be a tricky business as many well-intentioned sufferers take a lot of supplements which can naturally worsen symptoms. My rule is one supplement at a time and introduce it at half doses. If you are looking to give your body a little extra help as you sleep, you might try:

Slippery elm powder: Add 1 teaspoon and stir with hot water – super-soothing.

L-glutamine: This helps the gut repair its cells. Add half a teaspoon to a glass of water on an empty stomach. Drink it slowly.

Turmeric: Try a supplement with added pipperine to help digestion.

SECTION V

APPENDIX, REFERENCES AND INDEX

Appendix

Useful resources

Support networks and useful information sources

For Crohn's: www.forcrohns.org

Crohns and Colitis UK: www.crohnsandcolitis.org.uk

IBD Passport: www.ibdpassport.com

My Crohn's and Colitis Team: www.mycrohnsandcolitisteam.com

Anxiety UK: www.anxietyuk.org

Radar Key Toilet Finder: www.crohnsupport.com/toilet-finder/

IBD Relief: www.ibdrelief.com

A guide to MAP vaccine: www.mapvaccine.com

Complementary therapies
and IBD: www.ccfa.org/resources/
                            complementary-alternative.
                            html?referrer=https://www.google.
                            co.uk/

Girls with Guts: www.girlswithguts.org
                            www.iasupport.org/

Blogs about living with Crohn's disease

www.abalancedbelly.co.uk

www.sobadass.me

www.inflamed-and-untamed.com

www.crohnologicalorder.blogspot.co.uk

www.ktmy.co.uk

www.veganostomy.ca

www.semicolonmovie.com

www.tummywoes.wordpress.com

www.crohnsnomore.org

Resources for dietary changes

My own blog, www.abalancedbelly.co.uk, is a good starting point for exploring the role of food and IBD. Below are some sites that may be beneficial for researching different dietary approaches. I am in no way involved with them or endorse them beyond their being sites I have personally found useful.

Stockist of Bone Broth: www.ossa.com

Advice on juicing: www.juicing4crohns.com

Guides/Recipes for Paleo diet: www.paleowithmrsp.com

Diet and Personal Experiences with IBD: http://www.sarahkayhoffman.com/category/ibs-ibd/

Find a Nutritional Therapist: www.nutritionist-resource.org.uk

Sally Baker's therapy tools are at: www.feeldifferently.co.uk'

References

Chapter 1: Being diagnosed

1. NHS Choices (2016) Crohn's disease – causes. www.nhs.uk/Conditions/Crohns-disease/Pages/Causes.aspx (Accessed: 25 July 2016)

2. Neu J, Rushing J. Cesarean versus vaginal delivery: Long term infant outcomes and the hygiene hypothesis. *Clinics in Perinatology* 2011; 38 (2): 321-331.

3. Bernstein CN et al. Cesarean Section Delivery Is Not a Risk Factor for Development of Inflammatory Bowel Disease: A Population-based Analysis. *Clinical Gastroenterology and Hepatology* 2016; 14 (1): 50-7. DOI: 10.1016/j.cgh.2015.08.005. (Epub 2015 Aug 8.)

4. Hermon-Taylor J. Could a vaccine be the cure for Crohn's disease? Crohn's MAP vaccine. http://crohnsmapvaccine.com/ (Accessed: 25 July 2016).

5. Crohn's & Colitis UK. Crohn's – What are the symptoms? Crohn's & Colitis UK. www.crohnsandcolitis.org.uk/about-inflammatory-bowel-disease/what-are-the-symptoms#sthash.3PpMfvZV.dpuf (Accessed: 25 July 2016).

6. Crohn's & Colitis UK. Biological Drugs (1a 2015, amended March 2016) http://s3-eu-west-1.amazonaws.com/files.crohnsandcolitis.org.uk/Publications/biological-drugs.pdf (accessed 31 October 2016)

7. Crohn's & Colitis. Surgery for Crohn's Disease. (Edition 3, 2014) http://s3-eu-west-1.amazonaws.com/files.crohnsandcolitis.org.uk/Publications/surgery-for-crohns-disease.pdf (accessed 31 October 2016) and Surgery for Ulcerative Colitis (edition 3, 2014) http://s3-eu-west-1.amazonaws.com/files.crohnsandcolitis.org.uk/Publications/surgery-for-ulcerative-colitis.pdf (accessed 31 October 2016)

8. Lim SM, Nam CM, Kim YN, Lee SA, Kim EH, Hong SP, Kim TI, Kim WH, Cheon JH. (2013) The effect of the menstrual cycle on inflammatory bowel disease: A prospective study. *Gut Liver* 2013; 7(1): 51-57.

Chapter 4: IBD and mental health

9. Rubin DT, Siegel CA, Kane SV, et al. Impact of ulcerative colitis from patients' and physicians' perspectives: results from the UC: NORMAL Survey. *Inflammatory Bowel Disease* 2009; 15(4): 581-588.

10. Fuller-Thomson E, Lateef R, Sulman J. Robust association between inflammatory bowel disease and Generalised Anxiety Disorder. *Inflammatory Bowel Diseases* 2015; 21(10): 2341-2348. DOI: 10.1097/MIB.0000000000000518.

11. Mikocka-Walus A, Pittet V, Rossel J, Känel von S. Symptoms of depression and anxiety are independently associated with clinical recurrence of inflammatory bowel disease. *Clinical Gastroenterology and Hepatology* 2016; 14(6): 829–835.

12. Foster AJ, McVey KA. Gut–brain axis: How the microbiome influences anxiety and depression. *Trends in Neurosciences* 2013; 36(5): 305-312

13. McMaster University. Link between intestinal bacteria and depression found. *Science Daily* 28 July 2015. https://www.sciencedaily.com/releases/2015/07/150728110734.htm (Accessed 28 Sept 2016)

14. Webb AN, Kukuruzovic RH, Catto-Smith AG, Sawyer S. Hypnotherapy for treatment of irritable bowel syndrome. *Cochrane Database of Systematic Reviews* 17 October 2007. DOI: 10.1002/14651858.CD005110.pub2

15. Veale D, Wilson R. *Overcoming Health Anxiety*. Robinson, 2009.

Chapter 5: Nutritional supplements and IBD

16. Thomas P. Behind the label: Actimel. *The Ecologist* 1 October 2006. www.theecologist.org/green_green_living/behind_the_label/269115/behind_the_label_actimel.html (Accessed: 31 October 2016)

17. Hall LJ. A new super protective probiotic for IBD. Crohn's & Colitis UK, 2015. www.crohnsandcolitis.org.uk/research/projects/a-new-super-protective-probiotic-for-ibd (Accessed: 25 July 2016).

18. Sisson G, Haye B, Bjarnason I. Assessment of a Multi Strain Probiotic (Symprove) in IBD. *Gastroenterology* 2015; 148(4): S-531.

19. Taylor R, Leonard M. Curcumin for inflammatory bowel disease: A review of human studies *Alternative Medicine Review* 2011; 16(2): 152–156.

20. Barbalho SM, de Alvares Goulart R, Quesada K, Bechara MD, Antonely de Cássio Alves de Carvalho. Inflammatory bowel disease: Can omega-3 fatty acids really help? *Annals of Gastrentology* 2016; 29(1): 37-41.

Chapter 6: The role of food in managing IBD

21. Burgis J. Specific carbohydrate diet as maintenance therapy in Crohn's disease. *Stanford Medicine Clinical Trials Directory* http://med.stanford.edu/clinicaltrials/trials/NCT01749813 (Accessed: 31 October 2016)

22. Judaki A, Hafeziahmadi M, Yousefi A, Havasian MR, Panahi J, Sayehmiri K, Alizadeh S. Evaluation of dairy allergy among ulcerative colitis patients. *Bioinformation* 2014; 10(11): 693-696

23. Jones DB, Parker JH, Kerr GD, Wilson RSE. Dietary allergy and specific IgE in ulcerative colitis. *Journal of The Royal Society of Medicine* 1981; 74(4): 292-293.

24. Herfarth H, Martin C, Sandler R, Kappelman M, Long M. Prevalence of a gluten-free diet and improvement of clinical symptoms in patients with inflammatory bowel diseases. *Inflammatory Bowel Diseases* 2014; 20(7): 1194–1197.

25. Randhawa PK, Singh K, Singh N, Jaggi AS. A review on chemical-induced inflammatory bowel disease models in rodents. *Korean Journal of Physiology and Pharmacology* 2014; 18(4): 279-288.

Chapter 8: Staying hydrated with IBD

26. Barthel C, Wiegand S, Scharl S, Scharl M, Frei P, Vavricka SR, Fried M, Sulz MC, Wiegand N, Rogler G, Biedermann L. Patients' perceptions on the impact of coffee consumption in inflammatory bowel disease: Friend or foe? – a patient survey. *Nutrition Journal* 2015; 14: 78.

Chapter 10: Working with IBD

27. Gov.UK. Definition of disability under the Equality Act 2010. Gov.UK, October 2016) www.gov.uk/definition-of-disability-under-equality-act-2010 (Accessed: 31 October 2016).

28. Crohn's & Colitis UK. Employment & IBD: A Guide for Employers. Crohn's & Colitis UK, 2014. https://www.crohnsandcolitis.org.uk/about-inflammatory-bowel-disease/publications/employment-ibd-a-guide-for-employers (Accessed 31 December 2016)

Chapter 11: Exercising and IBD

29. Narula N, Fedorak RN. Exercise and inflammatory bowel disease. *Canadian Journal of Gastrentology* 2008; 22(5): 497-504.

Chapter 14: Alternative therapies and IBD

30. Bao CH, Zhao JM, Liu HR, Lu Y, et al. Randomized controlled trial: Moxibustion and acupuncture for the treatment of Crohn's disease. *World Journal of Gastrentology* 2014; 20(31): 11000-11011.

Chapter 15: Dealing with a flare-up

31. Harvey RF, Bradshaw JM. A simple index of Crohn's-disease activity. *Lancet* 1980; 315 (8167): 514.

32. British Columbia Ministry of Health Services. Worksheet based on the Harvey-Bradshaw Index. British Columbia Ministry of Health Services website. www.health.gov.bc.ca/exforms/pharmacare/5374fil.pdf. (Accessed 23 September 2010.)

33. Evertsz FB, Nieuwkerk PT, Stokkers PCF, Ponsioen CY, Bockting CLH, Sanderman R, Sprangers MAG. The Patient Simple Clinical Colitis Activity Index (P-SCCAI) can detect ulcerative colitis (UC) disease activity in remission: a comparison of the P-SCCAI with clinician-based SCCAI and biological markers. *Journal of Crohn's and Colitis* 2013; 890-900. DOI: http://dx.doi.org/10.1016/j.crohns.2012.11.007

Useful websites accessed

www.med.stanford.edu/clinicaltrials/trials/NCTO1749813

www.ccfa.org

www.crohnsandcolitis.org.uk/about-inflammatory-bowel-disease/treatments

http://ecco-jcc.oxfordjournals.org/content/6/10/991

http://ecco-jcc.oxfordjournals.org/content/4/1/28

http://s3-eu-west-1.amazonaws.com/files.crohnsandcolitis.org.uk/Publications/biological-drugs.pdf

www.york.ac.uk/news-and-events/news/2016/research/ibd-anxiety-depression/

www.theecologist.org/green_green_living/behind_the_label/269115/behind_the_label_actimel.html

www.gov.uk/definition-of-disability-under-equality-act-2010

www.nhs.uk/Conditions/Crohns-disease/Pages/Causes.aspx

http://crohnsmapvaccine.com

Index

Notes

How to Feel Differently About Food
– liberation and recovery from emotional eating

By Sally Baker and Liz Hogon

Sally Baker and Liz Hogon, informed by helping thousands of clients achieve a sustained healthy approach to eating, have researched and written *How To Feel Differently About Food* to break the painful cycle of yo-yo dieting and emotional eating. The book cuts a clear path through the conflicting nutritional information that fills the popular media to reveal the best way to eat for improved health and enhanced mood, boost energy without triggering feelings of hunger and stop wildly fluctuating blood-sugar levels that lead to cravings. They explain how to make informed and appetising food choices and how to implement small but empowering new eating habits from breakfast onwards.

Learning new ways of thinking and feeling about food will naturally enable readers to approach food differently. These positive changes are designed to be effortlessly integrated into a busy life with minimum planning and preparation, including how to eat for nourishment, become healthier, lose excess weight if appropriate, and boost mood as well as help to combat anxiety and depression.

www.hammersmithbooks.co.uk/product/feel-differently-about-food/

Irritable Bowel Syndrome and GIARDIA
– the parasite within

By Susan Koten
With Karen Evennett, Health Writer

Many people are diagnosed with IBS – a catch-all for chronic gut problems for which no cause can be found – but what if a parasite named Giardia lamblia were the cause? Medical herbalist Susan Koten explains in detail in a step-by-step approach how to detect and treat this common but under-recognised parasite using natural herbal medicine. Based on many years of helping tackle digestive disorders, she explains the signs, symptoms and treatments for both lay persons and professional naturopathic therapists. Understanding what Giardia is – and its connection with the malaria parasite – is key to overcoming it. Throughout she includes case studies to explain and illustrate her approach. Anyone with unexplained digestive problems should read this and investigate.

www.hammersmithbooks.co.uk/product/IBS-and-giardia/

Irritable Bowel Syndrome
Navigating Your Way to Recovery

By Dr Megan Arroll and Professor Christine Dancey

Based on their experience as both patients and health specialists, Dr Arroll and Professor Dancey (co-founder of the IBS Network) provide the latest guidance on the causes, diagnosis and treatments of IBS, including the hugely significant part played by the 'brain-gut axis' and by the micro-organisms within our large intestines, which are ultimately responsible for many aspects of our health.

In their book you can find a route to understanding and mitigating the consequences of IBS through:

- Causes and consequences – living with IBS
- How IBS is diagnosed – what to expect
- Medical treatments
- Nutrition, diet and probiotics
- Psychological and behavioural approaches
- Self-help strategies
- How IBS is understood and what new research offers
- A guide to IBS for family and friends

www.hammersmithbooks.co.uk/product/irritable-bowel-syndrome/

What's Up With Your Gut?
Why you bloat after eating bread and pasta...
and other gut problems

By Jo Waters and Professor Julian Walters

Do you get bloating when you eat pasta? Is your social life restricted by uncertainty about your bowels? Is your ability to work affected? This book will help you find out what your underlying gut problem is and understand how to make things better. With 80% of our immune system in our gut, sorting out digestive problems is essential for good health.

What's Up With Your Gut? takes a practical look at the full range of gut problems, using a symptom-led approach so that sufferers can recognise what may have been troubling them for years and find solutions. It then describes the range of solutions, both standard and alternative, emphasising the importance of what is eaten/food intolerances and the impact of poor digestion on overall health. Whether you suffer cramping diarrhoea when you are stressed out, get constipated when you're on holiday or just feel fatigued by your grumbling guts, they show what the options are for diagnosis, symptom improvement and tackling the underlying causes.

www.hammersmithbooks.co.uk/product/your-gut/